Theology, Explained and Defended in a Series of Sermons
by Timothy Dwight

Address:
HardPress
8345 NW 66TH ST #2561
MIAMI FL 33166-2626
USA
Email: info@hardpress.net

THEOLOGY,

EXPLAINED AND DEFENDED,

IN

A SERIES OF SERMONS,

BY

TIMOTHY DWIGHT, S. T. D. LL. D.

LATE PRESIDENT OF YALE COLLEGE.

WITH

A Memoir

OF

THE LIFE OF THE AUTHOR.

IN FIVE VOLUMES.
VOL. II.

LONDON:

STEREOTYPED AND PRINTED BY J. HADDON,

Tabernacle Walk, Finsbury Square

FOR WILLIAM BAYNES AND SON, PATERNOSTER ROW; AND THOMAS TEGG, CHEAPSIDE;

SOLD BY H. S. BAYNES AND CO. EDINBURGH; M. KEENE, AND

R. M. TIMS, DUBLIN; AND ALL OTHER BOOKSELLERS.

1824.

CONTENTS

OF

THE SECOND VOLUME.

DWIGHT'S

SYSTEM OF DIVINITY

SERMON XXXII.

HUMAN DEPRAVITY,

DERIVED FROM ADAM.

WHEREFORE, AS BY ONE MAN SIN ENTERED INTO THE WORLD, AND DEATH BY SIN, AND SO DEATH HATH PASSED UPON ALL MEN, FOR THAT ALL HAVE SINNED.

ROMANS v. 20.

FROM these words I proposed, in a former Discourse, to discuss the following doctrine :

That in consequence of the apostasy of Adam all men have sinned.

In the three last Discourses, I have considered the universality and the degree of human corruption. The next subject of our inquiry is *the source whence this corruption is derived.* In the text, as well as in the doctrine, it is exhibited as existing in consequence of the *apostasy of Adam.*

Before I proceed to a direct examination of this branch of the doctrine, it will be advantageous to make a few preliminary observations.

(1) *It will, I presume, be admitted that there is a cause of this depravity.*

The depravity of man is either caused or casual. If it be casual, every thing else may, for aught that appears, be casual also. A denial of this position, therefore, becomes a direct establishment of the atheistical scheme of casual existence.

B 2

Besides, uniformity is in all cases a complete refutation of the supposition of casualty. That mere accident should be the parent of the same moral character in all the progeny of Adam, or of uniformity of any kind, in so many thousand millions of cases, is contradictory to plain mathematical certainty.

(2) *This cause, whatever it is, is commensurate with its effects.* As therefore the effects extend to all men, it follows that the cause also is universal.

(3) *The cause of this depravity is undoubtedly one and the same.* This is argued irresistibly from the nature of the effects, which is everywhere the same.

(4) *This cause did not always exist.* Before their apostasy, our first parents were undepraved. As the effect did not then exist, the cause plainly did not exist.

These observations must, I think, be admitted without a controversy. It follows therefore that in searching for the source of human corruption we must, if we act wisely, be guided by them : since nothing can be this source of which all these things cannot be truly predicated.

(5) *In inquiring after the source of human corruption we inquire only after a fact.*

This subject, sufficiently difficult in itself, has been almost always embarrassed by uniting with it foreign considerations. A fact, it ought ever to be remembered, is what it is, independently of every thing else. If it be true that the corruption of mankind exists in consequence of the apostasy of Adam, this truth cannot be affected by any reluctance in us to admit it ; by any opinions which we may form of the propriety or impropriety of the dispensation ; nor by any inexplicableness, arising from the efficient cause, the moral nature, or the consequences of the fact. These things may be the foundation of other inquiries, and of perplexities and difficulties ever so great ; still they cannot even remotely affect the subject of the present investigation.

(6) *When I assert, that in consequence of the apostasy of Adam all men have sinned, I do not intend that the posterity of Adam are guilty of his transgression.*

Moral actions are not, so far as I can see, transferable from one being to another. The personal act of any agent is in its very nature the act of that agent solely, and incapable

of being participated by any other agent.   Of course, the
guilt of such a personal act is equally incapable of being
transferred or participated.   The guilt is inherent in the action, and is attributable therefore to the agent only.

So clear is this doctrine, that I presume no evidence was
ever supposed to be derived originally from reason to the contrary doctrine.   If therefore any evidence can be found to support this doctrine, it must be found in Revelation.   But in
Revelation, it is presumed, it cannot be found.   Unquestionably it is nowhere directly asserted in the Scriptures.   If it be
contained in them, it must be by implication.   Let me ask,
Where is this implication?   Certainly not in any use of the
term ' impute,' commonly appealed to by the supporters of this
scheme.   I have examined with care every passage in which
this word and its connections are used in the Scriptures, and
feel completely assured that it is used in a totally different
sense, in every instance without an exception.   The Verb
λογιζομαι, which is the original word, rendered by the English
word ' impute,' denotes originally and always, *to reckon, to
account, to reckon to the account of a man, to charge to his
account ;* but never to transfer moral action, guilt, or desert,
from one being to another.   Thus it is said by Shimei, ' Let
not my lord impute this sin unto his servant :' that is, Let
not my lord charge my sin of cursing David against me, or to
my account.   Thus also it is said, ' Abraham believed God ;
and it was counted to him for righteousness ;' that is, his faith
was reckoned to him in the stead of that perfect legal righteousness, in the possession of which he would have been accepted before God.

The passage which seems the nearest to the purpose of those
against whom I am contending is 1 Cor. xv. 22, ' As in Adam
all die, even so in Christ shall all be made alive.'   The words
in the original are ἐν τῳ Ἀδαμ and ἐν τῳ Χριστῳ.   The Greek
preposition Ἐν signifies very often, as any person acquainted
with the language must have observed, exactly the same thing
with the English phrase *by means of.*   The passage would,
therefore, have been explicitly and correctly translated, As by
means of Adam all die, even so by means of Christ shall all
be made alive.   Adam is therefore only asserted here to be
an instrumental cause of the death specified.   A parallel passage will, I think, make the justice of these remarks evident

beyond any reasonable debate. In 1 Cor. vii. 14, it is said, ' the unbelieving husband is sanctified by the believing wife, and the unbelieving wife is sanctified by the husband.' No person will pretend that in this passage the apostle declares the sanctification of the believing wife to be transferred to the husband, so as to become the personal state or character of the husband. This is evidently not the fact, because he is still an unbeliever. The meaning plainly is, that by means of his wife he is in such a sense considered as sanctified, as to prevent his children from being unclean ; or, in more explicit terms, from being incapable of being offered to God in baptism.

7. *Neither do I intend that the descendants of Adam are punished for his transgression.*

This doctrine is completely set aside by God himself, in Ezek. xviii. 20, ' The soul that sinneth it shall die. The son shall not bear the iniquity of the father ; neither shall the father bear the iniquity of the son ; the righteousness of the righteous shall be upon him ; and the wickedness of the wicked shall be upon him.' In this passage it is, I think, as explicitly as language will admit, declared that no man shall be punished for the sin of another ; particularly that the son shall not be punished for the sin of his father ; and, by obvious and, I think, irresistible implication, that the sons of Adam shall not be punished for the sins of this their common parent.

Having thus prepared the way, as I conceive, for the direct discussion of the doctrine, I shall now proceed to adduce in support of its truth the following proofs :——

1. *The Text.*

Here it is asserted, that ' by one man sin entered into the world :' δι ἑνος ἀνθρωπου ; ' through, or by means of, one man.' I will not take upon me to say that the apostle declares the sin of Adam to be the only supposable or possible cause of the entrance of sin into the world ; but he plainly declares it to be the actual cause. The sin which thus entered he declares also to be universal, even as universal as the death which entered by sin. In the 18th verse, which is separated from the text by a parenthesis only, the apostle teaches us in the most direct terms that this universal sin is a consequence of the transgres-

sion of Adam.   His words are, ' Therefore, as by the offence
of one ' (or as in the original, δι ενος ωαραωτωματος, ' by one offence) judgment came upon all to condemnation ;' and in the
19th verse, ' By one man's disobedience many' (in the original
οι ωολλοι, *the many*) ' were made,' (in the Greek, κατεσταθησαν,
were constituted) ' *sinners.*' The meaning of these passages is,
I think, plainly the following : that by means of the offence,
or transgression of Adam, the judgment or sentence of God,
came upon all men unto condemnation ; because, and solely
because, all men, in that state of things which was constituted
in consequence of the transgression of Adam, became sinners.

I have heretofore declared that the manner in which the
state of things became such, is not at all involved in the present discussion.   I now observe further, that I am unable to
explain this part of the subject.   Many attempts have been
made to explain it ; but I freely confess myself to have seen
none which was satisfactory to me ; or which did not leave the
difficulties as great and, for aught I know, as numerous as
they were before.   I shall not add to these difficulties by any
imperfect explanations of my own.   At the same time I repeat, that the fact in question is not at all affected by these
difficulties ; and that a denial of this fact is perplexed with
difficulties which are greater both in number and degree.

II. *The doctrine is evident also from the sentence pronounced on our first parents.*

In this sentence God declared, that ' the ground was cursed
for the sake ' of Adam, or because of his transgression ; ' that
it should bring forth thorns and thistles ; that he should eat
bread in the sweat of his brow ; and that both he and his wife
should lead lives of toil, suffering, and sorrow, until they
should finally return to the dust, from which they were taken.'
In a former Discourse it was shown that all the parts of this
sentence have been regularly fulfilled from the beginning to
the present day.   All of them therefore constituted a sentence
actually pronounced on all the progeny of Adam, and proved
to be so, because it is executed on them all.   The cursing of
the ground, particularly, by which it was deprived of its former
spontaneous fruitfulness, and condemned to perpetual sterility ;
by which thorns and briars were substituted for the fruits of

paradise; and by which ease, happiness and immortality were exchanged for labour, suffering and death, inwrought into the very constitution now given to the earth; was a fact which involved of course the punishment of all men, because all men suffer distress by means of this fact, and because no rational beings, beside sinners, are in the providence of God subjected to any suffering. Every descendant of Adam must of course be an inhabitant of the world which was thus cursed, and must of necessity be a partaker of the very evils denounced in this curse. When the sentence was declared, therefore, it was certainly foreseen that all those who would afterwards share in the sufferings which it disclosed, that is all the children of Adam, would be sinners. As all the progeny of Adam must inhabit the world thus cursed, all must necessarily partake of these evils, because they were inseparably united to the world, in which they dwelt. If then it was not foreseen that they would be sinners, the curse must have been denounced against them, either when obedient and virtuous, or while their future moral character was uncertain. The former will not be admitted by any man; the latter will no more be admitted by any man, if he reflect at all on the subject; for God can no more be supposed to condemn and punish those who are not known by him to be sinful, than those who are known to be virtuous. It follows therefore that, as the world was thus changed in consequence of the transgression of Adam, and of a paradise became a wilderness of thorns and briars, so, in consequence of the same transgression, the character of man was also changed; and instead of being immortal, virtuous and happy, he became the subject of sin, suffering and death. With respect to one of these considerations, viz. the mortality of mankind, the apostle Paul expressly asserts the doctrine in a passage already quoted for another purpose. ' In,' or by means of, ' Adam, all die.' As neither death nor any other suffering befals virtuous beings, this passage may be fairly considered as a full confirmation of the doctrine at large.

III. *The doctrine is directly declared by Moses, when he informs us that Adam begat a son in his own likeness.*

The meaning of the word ' likeness,' that is, the meaning intentionally attached to it by Moses, cannot, I think, be mistaken.   In the first chapter of the same history he introduces God as saying, ' Let us make man in our own image, after our likeness ;' and subjoins, ' so God created man in his own image ; in the image of God created he him.'   In a former Discourse I have shown that the likeness, or image, here mentioned, is the moral image of God ; consisting, especially, in knowledge, righteousness and true holiness,' as we are informed by St. Paul.   After dwelling so particularly on the image of God in which man was created, and on the fact, that man was created in this image, it cannot, I think, be questioned that Moses intended to inform us, that Seth was begotten in the moral likeness of Adam after his apostasy ; and sustained from his birth a moral character similar to that which his two brothers, Cain and Abel, also sustained.   This view of the subject appears plainly to have been adopted by Job, when he asks, ' Who can bring a clean thing out of an unclean ? not one,' (Job xiv. 4 :) by Bildad, when he asks, ' How then can man be justified with God ; or how can he be clean that is born of a woman ,' (xxv. 4 :) by David, when he says (Psalm li. 5.) ' Behold I was shapen in iniquity, and in sin did my mother conceive me ;' and by St. Paul, when he says, ' As we have borne the image of the earthly (Adam,) so we shall bear the image of the heavenly' (Adam,) (1 Cor. xv. 49.)   But if Seth, Cain and Abel derived their corruption from the apostasy of their parents, then it is true, not only that their corruption, but that of all mankind, exists in consequence of that apostasy.

Accordingly, our Saviour declares universally, that ' that which is born of the flesh, is flesh ;' and that ' that' only ' which is born of the Spirit,' or ' born again, is spirit.'   In this declaration he certainly teaches us, that the fleshly character is inseparably connected with the birth of man, it being an invariable attendant of that birth.   In other words, every parent, as truly as Adam, begets children in his own moral likeness.   It hardly needs to be observed, that the moral character, denoted in this observation of our Saviour by the term ' flesh,' is a corrupt character.   ' *The carnal*,' or fleshly, ' mind,' says St. Paul, ' is enmity against God ; not subject to his law, neither indeed can be :' and again, ' To be carnally, or fleshly, minded is death.'   In the original, the words in both passages are φρονημα της σαρκος ; *the minding of the flesh :*

the exercise of our thoughts and affections in that manner which accords with the fleshly or native character.

IV. *In exact accordance with this scriptural representation, the doctrine is strongly evinced by the conduct of children as soon as they become capable of moral action.*

Children in the morning of life are, as was remarked in the preceding Discourse, unquestionably amiable ; more so in many respects than at any future period ; that is, whenever they do not at some future period become the subjects of sanctification. Some children also, as we are taught in the Scriptures, are sanctified from the womb. Still even these in some degree, and all others in a greater degree, exhibit, from the dawn of moral action, evil affections and evil conduct. They are rebellious, disobedient, unkind, wrathful and revengeful. All of them are proud, ambitious, vain, and universally selfish. All of them, particularly, are destitute of piety to God, the first, and far the most important exercise of virtue. They neither love, fear, nor obey him ; neither admire his divine excellence, nor are thankful for his unceasing lovingkindness. Immense multitudes of them are taught these duties from the commencement of their childhood, yet they can be persuaded to perform them by no species of instruction hitherto devised. A virtuous mind would, of course, from the mere knowledge of God, without any known law, without any other motive except what is found in his greatness, excellency and goodness to us, admire and love, reverence and glorify him with all the heart. But no instance of this nature can be produced. I have been employed in the education of children and youth more than thirty years, and have watched their conduct with no small attention and anxiety. Yet, among the thousands of children committed to my care, I cannot say with truth, that I have seen *one* whose native character I had any reason to believe to be virtuous, or whom I could conscientiously pronounce to be free from the evil attributes mentioned above. In addition to this it ought to be observed, that no child unspotted with sin is mentioned in the records of history. This, I think, could not be, had the fact ever existed. Mankind therefore, according to the language of the Psalmist, ' are estranged from the womb, and go astray as soon as they be born.'

The opposers of the doctrine undertake to avoid the force of this argument, *by attributing the corruption of children to example, and the propensity of human nature to imitation.*

The power of example I readily acknowledge to be great, and the propensity to imitation strong.   I acknowledge also, that from these sources we may derive a satisfactory explanation of many things, both good and evil, which are done in the world.   Still, I apprehend, the objection is a very insufficient answer to the argument in question.   For,

1. *On beings who were virtuously inclined, a good example ought certainly to have more power than an evil one.*

On beings neither virtuously nor viciously inclined, virtuous and vicious examples must, of course, be equally influential ; as on beings sinfully inclined, it is acknowledged, sinful examples have an influence entirely preponderating.   All this is evident, because virtuous beings must love virtuous conduct, and follow it, as much as vicious beings love and follow vicious conduct, and because neutral beings, if such are supposed to exist, can have no bias to either.   If then mankind were virtuously inclined, they would follow, with a clear and universal proponderation, virtuous examples.   If neither virtuously nor sinfully inclined, they would follow virtuous and sinful examples alike, and with an equal propensity to imitation.   But neither of these facts is found in human experience.   Virtuous examples it is acknowledged have some degree of influence, but all men know this influence to be exceedingly and distressingly small.   This truth is seen every day, in every place, and in every person.   Whence arises the superior influence of vicious example, but from the fact that it is more pleasing to the human heart?   In heaven such example could have no influence.

2. *If the first men were virtuous, as the objection supposes all men to be by nature, and as, according to the objection, these must have been, there could have been no evil examples, and upon this plan, no sin in the world.*

Virtuous men, that is, men wholly virtuous, cannot exhibit an evil example.   If then the first men were virtuous, their immediate successors had no vicious example to follow, and must therefore have been themselves virtuous.   Of course, the example which they set also was only virtuous. Hence those who followed them must have been virtuous, and in like manner all their successors. Upon this plan, sin could never have entered the world. But sin is in the world, and is, and ever has been, the universally prevailing character of the human race. The objectors, therefore, are reduced by their scheme to this dilemma: Either virtuous men set sinful examples, which is a plain contradiction; or men became sinful without sinful examples.

Should it be said that after Adam and Eve apostatized, they corrupted their children by their own sinful example, who again corrupted theirs, and thus every generation became the means of corrupting those who followed them; and that in this manner the existence of a sinful character in mankind may be explained; I answer, that I readily admit the premises to a certain extent, but wholly deny the conclusion. Adam and Eve, speedily after their apostasy, that is, before they had children, became penitents. The example therefore which they exhibited to their children was such as penitents exhibit, expressive of their abhorrence of sin, and of their humble obedience to God. Such an example penitents now exhibit, and such a one, without a question, they have always exhibited. But this example, preponderating greatly in favour of virtue, must have had substantially the same influence with one perfectly virtuous. Of course, the perfectly virtuous minds of Adam's children must by this example have been strongly biassed to virtue, and according to this scheme, could not have failed of retaining their virtuous character. But this is plainly contrary to the fact. The descendants of Adam, of the first and of every succeeding generation, were evidently sinful beings, and in the course of ten generations became so universally and absolutely sinful, that, except Noah and his family, God destroyed them all by the deluge. God himself declares concerning them, that ' every imagination of the thoughts of their hearts was only evil continually; that it repented the Lord that he had made man upon the earth, and grieved him at his heart.' In vain therefore do we look for the proper influence of virtuous example, on children born virtuous among the early descendants of Adam.

If mankind are born with neutral characters, not inclined either to good or to evil, the difficulty will not be seriously

lessened. In this case, men ought now to be as generally
virtuous as sinful : because this character furnishes exactly the
same probability of the prevalence of virtue as of sin.   But no
such equality has at any period of time existed.   On the contrary, men are now and ever have been without an exception,
sinners.

Uniform sin proves uniform tendency to sin ; for nothing
more is meant by tendency, in any case, but an aptitude in the
nature of a thing to produce effects of a given kind.   With
this meaning only in view, we say, that it is the nature or tendency of an apple tree to produce apples, and of a fig tree to
produce figs.   In the same manner we must, I think, say, if
we would say the truth, that it is the tendency or nature of the
human heart to sin.

It is further objected, that the uniformity of sin in children,
and therefore in all the human race, may be fairly explained
by the nature of moral agency.

It is to be observed, that such as make this objection suppose the freedom of the will to lie in self-determination, the
liberty of indifference, and the liberty of contingency.   By
persons who hold this scheme, a more unfortunate objection to
the doctrine could not, I apprehend, have been easily devised.

If the freedom of the will is the freedom of contingency,
then plainly its volitions are all accidents, and certainly the
chances, arithmetically considered, are as numerous in favour
of virtuous volitions as of sinful ones.   There ought therefore
on this plan to be, and ever to have been, as many absolutely
virtuous persons in the world as sinful.   Plainly, *all* ought not
to be sinful.

If the freedom of the will is the freedom of indifference,
the same consequence ought to follow ; for, if there be no
bias in the mind towards either virtue or sin at the time immediately preceding each of its volitions, and the freedom of each
volition arises out of this fact, then, certainly, there being no
bias either way, the number of virtuous and that of sinful volitions must naturally be equal, and no cause can be assigned
why every man, independently of his renovation by the Spirit
of God, should be sinful only.

If the liberty of the will consists in self-determination,
and the mind, without the influence of any motive, first wills
that it will form a second volition, and this volition depends for

its freedom on the existence of such a preceding one, then it is plain, that from these preceding volitions as many virtuous as sinful ones ought to be derived; because the preceding or self-determining volitions are, by the supposition, under no influence or bias from any cause whatever.

Thus it is evident that, according to all these suppositions, there could be no preponderancy, much less a universality, of sin in the world. The state of facts is therefore contradictory to the objection, as supported by them all.

Further: the freedom of will, and consequently moral agency, in man in this world is the same with that of ' the spirits of just men made perfect' in heaven; the same with that of angels; the same with that of the man Christ Jesus. Whence then does it come to pass, that the same moral agency leads or influences these beings universally to virtue, and men in this world universally to sin? This question the objectors are bound to answer.

V. *The last proof of the doctrine which I shall adduce at the present time is the death of infants.*

A great part of mankind die in infancy, before they are or can be capable of moral action, in the usual meaning of the phrase. Their death is attended with all the apparent suffering usually experienced by persons of riper age, and with such suffering, at least, as plainly is often intense. Their death is also an ordinance of God; a dispensation of his immediate government. The language of this dispensation cannot, I think, be mistaken; and its meaning cannot be that of approbation. It is also the language literally of the curse denounced against our first parents, and the execution of that sentence, so far as this world is concerned. So St. Paul has directly declared, ' death has passed upon all men, for that all have sinned.' ' The wages of sin is death.' Death then, the fruit or wages of sin, the punishment denounced against it in the original sentence, must, I think, be acknowledged to be indubitable evidence of the existence of depravity in every moral being, that is, every being capable of depravity, who is the subject of death.

It ought here to be remembered, that death arrests infants in every form of distress and terror in which it befals persons of riper years. They together with others are swept away by the immediate hand of God, in those various judgments with which he awfully punishes mankind. They are swept away by the silent, awful hand of the pestilence; are consumed by the conflagration, overwhelmed by the volcano, swallowed up by the earthquake, and wasted by the lingering agonies of famine. At the same time, they suffer *from mankind*, all the deplorable violence of war, and the unnatural cruelties of persecution.

With these facts in view, we are compelled to one of these conclusions: either that infants are contaminated in their moral nature, and born in the likeness of apostate Adam, a fact irresistibly proved, so far as the most unexceptionable analogy can prove any thing, by the depraved moral conduct of every infant who lives so long as to be capable of moral action; or that God inflicts these sufferings on moral beings who are perfectly innocent. I leave the alternative to the choice of those who object against this doctrine.

There are but two objections to this argument within my knowledge. The first is, *that beyond the grave infants may be compensated for their sufferings by receiving superior degrees of happiness.* This objection will be easily seen to be of no validity. It is certainly unnecessary for God to make infants unhappy here, in order to make them happy in any manner whatever hereafter. Angels are made completely happy in heaven, without having suffered any preceding unhappiness. Plainly, infants might be made happy to any degree in the same manner. But, if the sufferings of infants are unnecessary, then they are causeless, on the scheme of this objection; and God is supposed to create so much misery, merely to compensate it by so much future enjoyment. I think this conduct will not soberly be attributed to the Creator, since it would plainly be disgraceful to any of his intelligent creatures.

The second objection is, *that God governs the universe by general laws, and that in their operation, inequalities and evils ought to be expected.* There are two answers to this objection. The first is, that God cannot be supposed to establish any general law which produces injustice, such as the suffering of virtuous beings must be acknowledged to be. The second is, that this is itself a general law, extending probably to one third or one fourth of the human race. The dispensation therefore, and not the exceptions, is unequal and evil according to this scheme. Surely the difficulty is not lessened by such a supposition.

It will probably be farther said, *that so many difficulties attend this part of the doctrine, as to perplex and distress the mind no less than the suppositions already refuted.* The difficulties attending the existence of moral evil are, I readily acknowledge, very great, and they easily become very distressing, whatever scheme of thought we may adopt concerning this subject ; that is, if we pursue it to any extent. But, I apprehend, the chief of those difficulties which necessarily attend us will be found to lie in the fact, that moral evil *exists*. To these we may or may not as we please, add others found in the particular scheme of doctrine which we choose to adopt. The doctrine asserted in this Discourse is, I think, unanswerably supported by Revelation, and by facts. Of course, it adds to the original difficulties inherent in the existence of moral evil no new ones of its own. The schemes which I am opposing contain, on the contrary, a new series of embarrassments, beside those which are common to them and to the doctrine of this Discourse. The truth is, the subject of moral evil is too extensive and too mysterious to be comprehended by our understanding. Some things the Scriptures teach us concerning it, and these are usually furnished with important evidence from facts. Many other things pertaining to this subject lie wholly beyond our reach. What we can know, it is our duty and our interest to know. Where knowledge is unattainable, it is both our duty and interest to trust humbly and submissively to the instructions of him, who is THE ONLY WISE.

But in this so difficult and perplexing dispensation, there is nothing more absolutely inexplicable than in many others which, because we are less interested in them, we generally consider as scarcely mysterious at all. I will mention one, out of very many. The state of the animal world, generally, is such as to baffle all human investigation. Why most animals exist at all, and why any of them are unhappy, are subjects which defy and silence the most ingenious inquiries of man. Nor is it originally strange, that the dispensations of a

Being whose ways are above ours, ' as the heavens are higher than the earth,' should be incomprehensible and inexplicable by us.

It ought to be here remembered, that that which is true, is not affected by any difficulty whatever, so far as its truth merely is concerned ; and that that which is known, is not rendered less certain by that which is unknown, whatever connection may exist between them, or whatever embarrassments may arise concerning that which is unknown.

It was with these views that I chose to state the doctrine of this Discourse in the words in which it was expressed.   I observed, that ' in consequence of the apostasy of Adam all men have sinned.'   The universality of sin was, I trust, proved sufficiently in two preceding Discourses.   In this, if I mistake not, it has been proved, that the sin of mankind has existed in consequence of that apostasy.   By this language I presume my audience understand me to intend, *that if Adam had not fallen, sin would not have entered this world.*   To this single fact I have confined all my observations, because this is the simple account given in the Scriptures ; and because I supposed it capable of being easily comprehended, and satisfactorily proved.

I shall only add, that a cause of human depravity is here alleged, of which all the characteristics mentioned in the commencement of this Discourse may be truly predicated : viz. the corruption of that energy of the mind whence volitions flow, and which I have heretofore asserted to be the seat of moral character in rational beings.   This cause must be acknowledged to be universal, to be everywhere the same, and not to have always existed.   It must also be conceded that it began to exist, according to the Scriptures, as early as the effects, which have given birth to all our inquiries concerning the corruption of mankind.

SERMON XXXIII.

DEPRAVITY OF MAN:

REMARKS.

WHEREFORE, AS BY ONE MAN SIN ENTERED INTO THE WORLD, AND DEATH BY SIN; AND SO DEATH HATH PASSED UPON ALL MEN, FOR THAT ALL HAVE SINNED.

ROMANS VI. 12.

IN the four preceding Discourses I have endeavoured to show the universality and extent of human corruption, and its existence in consequence of the apostasy of Adam. It is now my design to subjoin to the observations made in these Discourses several REMARKS, naturally arising from the consideration of this subject, and of no inconsiderable importance. The end of all doctrinal preaching is to persuade men cordially to receive truth, that they may be governed by it in their conduct; and of preaching, in any particular instance, to persuade them thus to receive one truth, in order to their reception of others.

From doctrines so important and so absolutely fundamental as those which have occupied these Discourses, very numerous inferences of great moment cannot fail to be drawn by a mind addicted to solemn contemplation. A small number of them only can, however, be mentioned with advantage in a single sermon. For the present occasion I have selected the following :——

I. *It is evident, from the last of these discourses, that the corruption of man is not the result of any given form of government, nor of any given character in rulers.*

At this subject I have glanced in a former discourse, but have reserved the more extensive discussion which it merits, for the present occasion.

It has been frequently and triumphantly said, particularly in modern times, that the corruption of mankind is wholly artificial, and owes its existence to civilized society ; particularly to the form and administration of government, and to the civil and ecclesiastical rulers of mankind.

The method in which these orders of men are supposed to have corrupted their fellow-men is that of *oppression ;* at least this is considered as the chief instrument of the corruption, and is supposed to operate principally in two ways ; viz. keeping them *poor,* and keeping them *ignorant.*

It ought, undoubtedly, to be acknowledged that the rulers of mankind have extensively corrupted them ; that they have also greatly oppressed them ; and that by keeping them poor and ignorant, they have contributed in a very great and guilty degree to the increase of their corruption. It ought to be further acknowledged, that rulers, and other men of wealth and influence, have much more effectually and extensively corrupted their fellow-men by example, art and seduction ; by exhibiting to them powerful temptations, placing within their reach the means of sin, making the path to perpetration smooth, easy and safe, and presenting to them arguments, ingeniously and laboriously contrived to justify them in the commission, than they have ever done by both the methods alleged above. The philosophers with whom I am contending have probably insisted less on this source of human corruption, partly because they wished to render the men in question odious, and thought this an efficacious mean of accomplishing their purpose ; and partly because they were sensible that themselves were deeply implicated in the charge of corrupting mankind in the manner last mentioned. So far as argument and influence have increased the turpitude of the human character, few men are chargeable with so great a share of the guilt. Their arguments concerning moral subjects have been commonly mere means of seduction, and their example has only seconded their arguments. A host of ancient philosophers were banished from Rome as a public nuisance. Had a large proportion of modern ones lived in the same city at the same time, there is little reason to doubt that they would have shared the same fate, for the same reason.

The form of government also, in some cases, and the peculiar administration of it in others, have undoubtedly contributed in a distinguished degree to the depravation of mankind. Monarchies have produced this effect by immense patronage ; by the operations of despotic power, demanding and effectuating a slavish dependence and a base sacrifice of principle in their subjects ; by splendour, luxury, war, and a general dissoluteness of manners. Republican governments, although in certain circumstances more favourable to virtue, have yet at times been equally pernicious, by furnishing opportunities and strong temptations for the sacrifice of integrity at elections, for caballing, bribery, faction, private ambition, bold contentions for place and power, and that civil discord which is naturally accompanied by the prostration of morality and religion. Thus Rome, in the time of Marius and Sylla, degenerated with inconceivable rapidity. This example many other republics have been but too willing to follow. The heathen priests and princes also, although generally believing in the most serious manner the miserable, demoralizing idolatry which they professed, found a deep interest in the establishment of their religious systems, and the deplorable corruption by which they were of course attended.

The Romish hierarchy, uniting in itself all authority both secular and ecclesiastical, presented immense inducements to the love of wealth, power, splendour and sensuality, and vast means of gratifying these corrupt propensities of the human heart. At the same time, it held out the most efficacious motives to the perpetuation of these enjoyments by keeping mankind in a state of abject ignorance, slavery and corruption. In this manner it contributed more to this dreadful purpose than any other political system which the world has ever seen. Like the mountains piled up by the Giants, it seemed, for a time, to menace heaven itself with the loss of its dominion over the earth, and, like the deluge, swept from this world almost every thing which had life.

It must further be conceded, that among Protestant ministers, although plainly the most unblameable and exemplary class of men who in equal numbers have ever appeared in this world, there have not been wanting those who, by means of their latitudinarian doctrines and loose lives, have exercised a malignant influence over their fellow-men, and contributed in a serious degree to the depravation of the human character.

Finally: Infidel philosophers of modern times have surpassed, in the wonderful rapidity and success with which they have dissolved the human character, and destroyed the very remembrance of principle, even the portentous mischiefs of the Romish hierarchy. Were it not that such nuisances to the world are in their very nature incapable of operating with such efficacy for any long continuance, they would change the earth into a desert, where no principle would spring, and no happiness grow. Like the Genü, fabled in Arabian tales, they would enchant the towns and cities of this world with a more than magic wand, and where rational and immortal beings once lived and acted, where morals flourished, religion scattered her blessings, and the worship of God ascended to heaven as the odour of sweet incense, leave nothing but the forms of men, without motion, without life, without souls; imprisoned beyond the hope of escape within their encompassing walls, and surrounded by nothing but silence, solitude and death.

These concessions will, it is presumed, be thought sufficiently liberal and ample. Still the doctrine against which they have been pleaded is not even remotely affected by them, but stands in full force, and on the basis of conclusive evidence. For,

1. *The subjects of virtuous rulers have been deeply depraved.*

Rulers, although in a great majority of instances corrupt, and in many wonderfully corrupt, have yet in many others been virtuous, and in some eminently virtuous. It will not, as with truth it plainly cannot, be denied, that virtuous rulers have had a real and happy influence in reforming those whom they governed. The example and efforts of all men in high authority have ever been efficacious; if good, to encourage virtue; if evil, to promote vice. The good which virtuous rulers have done has not been here merely negative; that is, they have not merely ceased to corrupt their fellow-men, but with a positive efficacy they have directly contributed to make them better. This is so evident from uniform experience, that an attempt to prove it would be only a waste of time. Example and influence are proverbially powerful even in private life, and no man needs to be informed that they are more effectual in the chair of authority than in the cottage. Nor will any man acquainted with history deny, that David, Hezekiah, and Josiah ; the Maccabees, Alfred the Great, Edward vi , or the two elder Gustavuses , reformed in a serious degree the nations over whom they presided.

Still it is equally well known to all persons of information, that no ruler and no succession of rulers ever changed the native character of man in any such manner as to make the nations whom they governed generally virtuous, or at all to lessen the evidence which supports the doctrine of universal depravity. What they have done we style with metaphysical exactness, *reformation* ; that is, forming anew the moral character which they actually found, and which only was everywhere the subject of their efforts. In our very language we thus testify, unwillingly perhaps, that the moral character of our race is such as needs to be formed anew ; or, in other words, is depraved. Even this reformation, good rulers have accomplished with great labour and difficulty ; and it was confined to a number of instances in a melancholy degree moderate. Of this truth flagrant proof has been furnished in the sudden and deplorable revival of all kinds of iniquity, at the moment when the restraining influence of a good ruler has been taken away by death, and new license has been given to the free indulgence of the native human propensities, by the succession of a wicked prince to the sceptre. Such a prince has had more influence to corrupt a nation in a year, than a virtuous one to amend them during his whole reign. Manasseh pulled down in a day what Hezekiah had been building up through his life. Or perhaps, in more exact language, what virtuous princes accomplish with such vast labour, dissolves of itself, under the malignant influence of corruption universally experienced and universally operating, whenever that corruption is freed from the restraints imposed on it by virtue seated upon the throne. Were the mind of man originally inclined to virtue, this would be impossible.

2. *Those subjects who have been raised above the oppression*

and ignorance contended for, have not been more free than others from this depravity.

If the oppression and ignorance specified were indeed the causes of this corruption, then the corruption ought not to be extended to those subjects who were neither ignorant nor oppressed.   But we do not find these men, in fact, any better than their fellow-subjects.

On the contrary, the more that men have possessed the means of pleasure and sin, the more wealth, independence, and self-controul they have enjoyed, the more corrupt they have usually been.   How often do we see a youth, or a poor man, by coming suddenly to opulence and high personal independence, lose his former sober, decent character, and become at once grossly immoral.   So common is this fact as to be proverbially remarked, and to be the foundation of important prudential maxims concerning the management of our children.   All observing men, even of the most ordinary education, hold it as a fundamental doctrine of experience, that *it is harder to bear prosperity than adversity.*

Men of science, learning and extensive information have, in the mean time, been to a great extent exceedingly corrupt and wicked; incomparably more so, in degree, than the ignorant; and proportionally as much so in the number of instances.   The ancient philosophers, the most learned and intelligent men of the heathen world, were very generally gross examples of sin.   Infidel philosophers in modern times have, in this respect, certainly not fallen behind them.   Of the former of these assertions Cicero, Plutarch, Lucian, Seneca, and Diogenes Laertius, themselves philosophers, are ample and unimpeachable witnesses; of the latter, the writings and lives of the philosophers themselves.   The truth is, as any man who knows any thing of the subject readily discerns, knowledge is a thing entirely distinct from virtue, not necessarily connected with it, and without virtue, is but too often the means of ingenious, powerful, and dreadful iniquity.   There is not a reason furnished by experience to induce a belief, that the increase of knowledge is of course the increase of virtue.

8. *In those states of society where rulers have the least influence which is possible in the present world, men are not less vicious in proportion to their power of being vici-*

ous, than they are where rulers have the greatest influence.

For complete proof of this assertion I appeal to the state of the aboriginal Americans. In the state of society existing among these people, men are as independent, and as little influenced by power, authority and governmental example, as men living together can be. Here neither kings, nor nobles, nor priests, have any other weight or controul than that which springs of course from the mere gathering together of human beings. Yet no man who knows any thing of the morals of these people, can hesitate to acknowledge them corrupt in a degree enormous and dreadful. Fraud, falsehood, lewdness, drunkenness, treachery, malice, cruelty and murder, acted out in the most deplorable manner, are strong and dreadful features of the whole savage character. Here then the vice exists anterior to artificial society, and in the state nearest to that which is called ' the state of nature.' What is true of the American savages is true of all others ; and universally furnishes undeniable proof of fearful depravity, originally inherent in man, and wholly independent of the causes alleged in this objection.

4. *Republics have been equally corrupt with monarchies.*

In republics the influence and the oppression of kings are unknown. If then republics have been no less corrupt than monarchies, regal oppression and influence are falsely alleged as the proper and original causes of human depravity ; since here they do not exist. In the most absolute freedom ever found in republics, wickedness has been as truly the character of men as in kingdoms. This character also has been equally depraved, not in all instances I readily grant, but in more than enough to establish the doctrine. Carthage, Rome, Athens, Sparta, Venice, the Grison states, and republican France, are undeniable examples. It ought particularly to be remarked, that republics have usually oppressed their provinces with more unfeeling cruelty than monarchies. Their own freedom, therefore, has not made them at all more friendly, but less so, to the freedom and happiness of their fellow-men. The deplorable vassalage, existing in our own country to an enormous extent, is a flagrant and melancholy, although it may be thought an invidious proof of this assertion. If then some republics have been distinguished by a higher degree of virtue, as has undoubtedly been the fact, the cause was not their freedom, for that has universally existed and operated, but something peculiar to themselves.

5. *In the republics which have been most distinguished for virtue, ministers of the gospel have had the greatest influence.*

Switzerland, Holland, Massachusetts, and Connecticut have long by general acknowledgment, been placed among the most virtuous republics. But in all these, clergymen have had more influence than in any other. On the contrary, where clergymen have had little influence, there has been comparatively but very little virtue. Of this truth instances are numerous and at hand. They are also too clear to admit of a doubt. The general voice of mankind has decided this point, and from this voice there can be no appeal.

Hence it is evident, that the influence of clergymen is so far from contributing to the corruption of mankind, upon the whole, that it has meliorated their character most where it has most prevailed, and rendered them materially better than they have been elsewhere. I speak here, it will be observed, only of Protestant ministers of the Gospel. I know it has been the custom of infidels to groupe them together with Romish priests, to whom of all men they have been most opposed, and whom they more than any other men have contributed to overthrow; and with heathen priests, with whom they have nothing in common, except the essential characteristics of men, and a title at times applied to both; a mere generic name, formed by the same letters indeed, but meaning in the different applications things as unlike as folly and wisdom, holiness and sin. As well might Newton, Locke, Butler, and Boyle be united in a monstrous assemblage with Spinosa, Voltaire, Diderot, and Condorcet, because they have all been styled philosophers; Alfred twinned with Kouli Khan, because they have both been called Kings; and Sydenham be coupled with an Indian Powwaw, because they have both been named physicians.

It ought further to be observed as an universal truth, that in all Protestant countries, the countries where virtue has flourished more than in any other, the existence of virtue has been exactly proportioned to the influence of ministers of the gospel. All real virtue is the effect of the gospel crowned with the divine blessing. But wherever the gospel has the greatest effects, its ministers are the most respected and influential; for the principal efficacy of the gospel is conveyed through their preaching, candidly and kindly received. Scotland may be mentioned as a strong instance of this general truth. In that country, under a regal government and amid the influence of a powerful body of nobles, supposed by my antagonists to be so hostile to the existence of virtue, there has perhaps long been less vice and more virtue, than in any European country of equal extent. Yet there the influence of clergymen has, in all probability, been greater than in any other protestant country.

6. *In a state of anarchy, virtue is uniformly at the lowest ebb, and vice most prevalent and dreadful.*

In a state of anarchy all lawful authority and regular influence, both civil and ecclesiastical, are extinguished, and lose therefore whatever efficacy they may be supposed to possess towards the corruption of mankind. Yet of all situations in which society can be placed, anarchy is the most pernicious to the morals of men. Of this truth we have proverbial evidence in the great practical maxim, that ' no people can exist for any length of time in a state of anarchy.' Of the soundness of this important doctrine our own country, during the late revolution, gave sufficient proof. When the restraints of government and religion were only partially taken off, men became vicious in a moment, to a degree here unexampled. I myself have seen a number of men, commonly sober, decent, moral and orderly in their deportment, lose upon joining a mob even the appearance of these characteristics, and exhibit more and grosser vice in a few hours than in many preceding years.

The restraints of government and religion are, therefore, so far from making men worse upon the whole, that without them, men become so profligate as to render it impossible for them even to live together. All this is indeed very easily understood. Government, in the great body of cases, restrains men only from vice; and religion, that is, the religion of the gospel, in every case. The sanctions of government are protection to those who obey, and punishment to those who disobey. The sanctions of religion are endless rewards to virtue, and endless punishments to sin. That these sanctions promote vice is a paradox which I leave to be solved by others. He who can solve it will prove in his solution, that men are disposed to be virtuous and vicious without motives to either; and to be virtuous only under the influence of the strongest motives to vice, and vicious only under the influence of the strongest motives to virtue. The honour of this discovery I shall not dispute with any man who is willing to claim it as his own.

The truth plainly is, and ever has been, mankind as a body are uniformly more or less wicked in proportion to the means which they possess of vicious indulgence, and to the temptations by which they are surrounded. Kings, nobles, and all others possessed of wealth, power, talents and influence, although having the same nature with other men, are usually more vicious, because these things furnish them with ampler means of sin, and stronger temptations. Mediocrity of life, on the contrary, has ever been believed by wise men among heathens, as well as Christians, to be the state most favourable to virtue, and has, therefore, proverbially been styled the golden mean. Agur has taught this doctrine from the mouth of God. Experience and common-sense have given it their fullest attestation.

Even poverty and persecution have in many instances proved favourable to morals and religion. The poverty of Sparta was a prime source of whatever was honourable in its character, and Christianity flourished amid the sufferings of its martyrs.

From these observations it is evident, that the depravity of man exists independently of every state of society, and is found in every situation in which man is found; that it exists wherever oppression is, and wherever it is not; with and without the authority or influence of privileged men; in the independent savage, and the abject slave of Asiatic despotism; in the wild Arabian and the silken courtier; in the prince who is above all law, and the peasant who is subjected to every law. The scheme which I am opposing is, therefore, a mere plaything of doubting Philosophy, making for herself worlds as children make soap-bubbles, amusing herself less rationally, and hoping for their permanency with more egregious credulity.

II. *It is evident from these Discourses that the scheme of human perfectibility is without any foundation.*

There are two methods, in which this truth may be satisfactorily evinced.

1. *From Fact.*

Mankind have in every age laboured with great earnestness to perfect the human character. The immense toils of education have been intentionally directed to this end. Schools and colleges without number have been erected, multitudes of wise and industrious men have laboured through life, books have been written, laws have been enacted, and magistrates have been employed, in an almost endless multitude, for the same great purpose. Nay, God has himself revealed his own will ; requiring with infinite authority, instructing with infinite wisdom, and urging with infinite motives, that men should become virtuous. The Redeemer of mankind was born, lived, and died ; the Spirit of grace has descended, influenced, and blessed ; the worship of God has regularly been celebrated through a great part of the world ; and a vast succession of wise and faithful ministers have spent life, to accomplish this glorious design. Yet how little has been done. How few have been seriously amended ! What one has been raised to perfection ? Trace the history, search the race of man, and tell me where he is to be found.

Shall we then believe that the schemes of modern philosophy will accomplish what all preceding philosophers, and men much wiser than philosophers, what the word of God, the redemption of his Son, and the communications of his Spirit have never yet accomplished ? Can human perfection be the result of a benevolence which, indeed, utters good words, but is a total stranger to good actions ; which is occupied in lamenting while it should relieve ; which says to the poor, the hungry, and the naked, ' Depart in peace ; be ye warmed, and be ye filled ;' which is exhaled in sighs, and emptied out in tears ; which shrinks from the cottage of poverty, and withdraws its icy hand from the supplications of distress ; which agonizes over imagined sufferers in Japan, but can neither see nor hear real ones at its own door ; which deplores the disastrous fate of profligates and villains, and arraigns the justice, which consigns them to the gaol or the gibbet ; but exults in the ruin of worth, the destruction of human peace, and the contemplated devastation of a world ? Can the perfection of man be the result of intelligence which dictates, as the happiest state of society, a community of labours, in which the idle would literally do nothing, and the industrious nothing more than to supply their own absolute wants ; a community of property, in which little would be earned, and much of that little wasted on mere lust, and the remainder lost, because none would preserve what none expected to enjoy ; a community of wives, in which affection would cease, principle vanish, furious animosity distract, and fierce revenge assassinate ; and in which children would grow up, when they did not perish in infancy, without a known father, without comfortable subsistence, without education, without worth, without a name ? When men become immortal by medicine and moral energy, according to the dreams of the same philosophy, they may perhaps become perfect by the proposed schemes of its discipline.

To such persons as insist that the melioration suggested has failed, because the means used were imperfectly fitted to accomplish the end, I answer : If the end were possible, it is reasonable to believe that amid so great a variety, extent, and continuance of these means, directed to this end by the highest human wisdom, some one system would have succeeded. As these have all failed, it cannot be rationally doubted that all others will fail. Those, particularly, which are now offered as substitutes, promise not even the remotest degree of success ; and are, on the other hand, fraught with the most portentous threatenings of absolute ruin. To these things I will add, that the authors of them, on whom their efficacy ought first to be proved, are farther removed from virtue than mankind in general. Until their own character, therefore, is materially changed for the better, they may be unanswerably addressed with the forcible Jewish proverb, ' Physician, heal thyself.'

2. *It is also clearly evinced by the nature of the case.*

The depravity of man is a part of his constitution, of his nature, of himself. To perfect his character, it would be necessary to change him into a new creature ; and separate a part of that which makes him what he is ; viz. his moral character. It would be equally rational to say, that man in the present world can become a flying creature, as that he can become a perfect creature. If he can be turned into a bird, he may also, perhaps, be changed into an angel. All that has been hitherto done, and therefore all that will hereafter be done, is to confine one class of his desires, viz. those which are sinful by their excess, within juster bounds; and to prevent in some measure the risings of the other, viz. those which are sinful in their nature. Until more than this shall be effected, the world will be equally and justly astonished at the folly which could persuade Godwin that a plough could be made to move through a field of itself, and that man could be rendered perfect by his scheme of discipline.

III. *From these Discourses it is evident, that the fundamental principle of moral and political science, so far as man is concerned, is his depravity.*

It will not be questioned, that virtuous and depraved beings differ from each other radically, nor that the science of the one must of course differ in its fundamental principles from the science of the other. A philosopher might, if possessed of competent knowledge, describe exactly the character of an angel, and yet scarcely say any thing except what pertains to a moral being as such, which would be at all applicable to the character of man. A book, displaying the whole nature and conduct of our first parents in paradise, would contain scarcely any thing descriptive of their apostate decendants. But all science of this nature is founded in facts, and is formed of facts, and the relations which spring from them. The first great fact in the science of man is, that he is a depraved being. This is the first and fundamental fact, because out of it arise, and by it are characterized, all his volitions, and all his conduct. Hence every thing pertaining to man is coloured and qualified by this part of his moral nature, and no description of him can be true, and no doctrine sound or defensive, into which this consideration does not essentially enter; equally true is it, that no system of regulations can be practically suited to him, or fitted to controul his conduct with success or efficacy, which is not founded on the same principle.

From these observations it is evident, that much of what is published and received as moral and political science, is only ' science falsely so called.' It considers man as originally a virtuous being, accidentally and in some small degrees warped from the path of rectitude, and always ready to return to it again ; deceived and abused by insidious and peculiarly corrupted individuals, but, left to himself, designing nothing beside what is good, and uttering nothing but what is true. This indeed is a character ' devoutly to be wished :' but the picture is without an original ; in the language of painters, a mere fancy-piece : and it would be as easy to find the human character in a gryphon of Ariosto, or the sylphs, gnomes, and nymphs of Rosicrucius, as in a library filled with this species of philosophy.

Were these systems to terminate in speculation only, their authors might be permitted to dream on without disturbance. But unhappily, their doctrines are made the foundation and directory of personal conduct, and public administration. Rules of private life, municipal laws, and other governmental regulations, are drawn from these pleasing but merely hypothetical doctrines ; and are intended and expected actually to controul men and their affairs, so as to effectuate good order, peace, and prosperity. Here the influence of systems, which proceed according to this scheme, becomes eminently dangerous, malignant, and fatal. All the measures founded on them are fitted for the inhabitants of some other planet, or the natives of fairy land, or the forms which haunt the dreams of a distempered fancy, with an incomparably better adaptation than for men. Of course they can never become practical or useful to such beings as really exist in this world, impatient even of necessary restraints ; selfish, covetous, proud, envious, wrathful, revengeful, lewd, forgetful of God, and hostile to each other. Open your eyes on the beings around you ; cast them back on the annals of history ; turn them inward upon yourselves, and you will find ample and overwhelming proof of the truth of these observations.

On this fundamental folly was founded all those vain, empty, miserable systems of policy which, in a portentous succession, deluded republican France into misery and ruin. In the treatises, laws, and measures brought into being in that nation, during its late wonderful struggle to become free, the people were uniformly declared to be good, honest, virtuous, influenced only by the purest motives, and aiming only at the best ends. These very people at the same time were employed in little else except unceasing plunder, uniform treachery, the violation of all laws, the utterance of all falsehood, the murder of their king, nobles, and clergy, and all the boundless butchery of each other. In a state of immorality, in a prostration of all principle, at which even this sinful world stood aghast, this despicable flattery was continually reiterated, and the miserable objects of it very naturally concluded that, as they were praised while they were doing these things, they were praised for doing them. Of course they were fixed in this conduct beyond recal. Every malignant passion was let loose, the reins were thrown upon the neck of every sordid appetite, the people became a collection of wild beasts, and the country a den of ravage and slaughter. In this situation nothing could restrain them but force. The wretches who by their songs and incantations had called up the fiends of mischief, could not lay them; but became, in an enormous and horrid succession, victims of their own spells, and were offered up by hundreds to the sanguinary Moloch which they had so absurdly and wickedly idolized.

Sound and true policy will always consider man as he is, and treat him accordingly. Its measures will be universally calculated for depraved beings, and it will, therefore, never hesitate to establish every necessary restraint. Whatever is good in man it will regard as the result of wise, careful, efficacious discipline, realized and blessed by God. Such discipline, therefore, it will regularly establish, protect, and encourage. Honest, well disposed and orderly citizens, it will protect; the violation of private rights, and the disturbers of public peace, it will punish. Nor will its restraints and punishments stop, until they have gained in some good measure their end.

IV. *From these Discourses it is evident, that the redemption of Christ was absolutely necessary to mankind.*

If man is a depraved creature, it is plainly impossible that he should be justified by the law of God. When he comes before his Maker, to 'be judged according to his works,' he must be declared to have done evil, because he has in fact done it. The law has declared, that ' the soul which sinneth shall die:' by the law therefore he must die, because he has sinned. Of course God cannot pronounce him just, or acquit him of guilt, because he is guilty. Under mere law, the only situation in which he can be, independently of the redemption of Christ, he can never be justified nor rewarded, but must be condemned and punished. In this situation, an atonement for his sins, such as God with propriety can and will accept, is just as necessary for man as his salvation. No being in the universe could, so far as we are able to discern, render this atonement except Christ. All other beings are, in the nature of things, under every possible obligation to render to God all the services in their power, as their own proper obedience, an obedience indispensably necessary for their own justification. A supererogatory service does not appear to be possible for any created being, as there is no service which he can render to God which is not his indispensable duty. Thus, so far as we are able to discern, the atonement of Christ is absolutely necessary for the human race, and without it we can conceive of no possible way of salvation.

V. *The same doctrine equally teaches the absolute necessity of regeneration to mankind.*

That ' without holiness no man shall see the Lord,' is a doctrine so evidently rational and just, that it cannot but be believed by every sober man, even independently of the express declaration of the Scriptures. But without regeneration man is only unholy, and can therefore never ' see the Lord.' The first great effect of the redemption of Christ is to render it possible for man to become holy, in order to his justification and acceptance. Had the dispensation stopped here, man would still have been lost. The next step in this wonderful procedure is the renovation of man, or that implantation of holiness in his heart, styled in the Scriptures, regeneration or the new birth. From the commencement of this great change in his character, he becomes the subject of evangelical holiness; of real piety, real benevolence, real self-government, or, generally, of real obedience to God. All his obedience however is imperfect, and could not be accepted but for the sake of Christ. His mediation, his righteousness, is ' the sweet incense' which perfumes every offering and act of man, and renders it acceptable before that pure and awful Being, ' in whose sight the heavens themselves are not clean.' But, though imperfectly holy, man when renewed is really holy. 'There is some good thing found in him towards the Lord God of Israel.' This, as a seed of inestimable worth, is seen by the all-searching eye to promise a future and eternal production of fruits, invaluable in their nature, and endless in their multitude.

VI. *With equal evidence we are here taught the necessity of the mission of the Holy Spirit.*

The Holy Spirit is the only author of the regeneration of man. 'That which is born of the flesh is flesh: that which is born of the Spirit is spirit.' 'Except a man be born of the Spirit, he cannot see the kingdom of God.' 'Not by works of righteousness which we have done, but according to his own mercy he saved us, by the washing of regeneration, and the renewing of the Holy Ghost.' As therefore, regeneration is absolutely necessary to man, and as man is renewed only by the Holy Spirit, so the mission of the Spirit is as necessary to man as his regeneration, and both are no less necessary than his eternal life.

On these three great evangelical doctrines I have here descanted very briefly, because they will hereafter be primary subjects of investigation. They have been now mentioned chiefly to show their connection with the doctrine of human depravity, and the manner in which they necessarily arise out of this part of the scriptural scheme.

VII. *The same considerations also teach us the manner in which a preacher ought to address mankind.*

Every congregation will be regarded by a minister of Christ, who discerns this doctrine to be what it plainly is, a leading doctrine of the Scriptures, as a collection of depraved, guilty beings, exposed to endless punishment for their sins. On this basis will all his sermons be founded; and to this point will they all refer. He will exhort them to repent; because they are sinners, and therefore need repentance. He will exhort them to believe in Christ; because they cannot save themselves, and because He can, and if they believe in him, will save them. He will teach them to seek for pardon of God; because they are sinners, and must either be pardoned or lost; to rely on the grace of God for their justification, because they have no merit of their own ; and if they depend on their own righteousness, cannot be saved ; and to feel the necessity of sanctification, because ' without holiness no man shall see the Lord ;' and because without the sanctification of the Spirit of grace, no man can become holy.

The ' terrors of the law' he will set before his hearers in their own awful light, because by these, and by nothing but these, such beings can ordinarily ' be persuaded.' The gospel he will declare to be ' glad tidings of great joy ;' because it is the news of forgiveness, justification and everlasting life, to sinners who would otherwise perish. Mercy he will unfold as the peculiar ' glory of God in the highest,' and as eminently displayed when ' peace and good-will' are published to mankind. The distinguishing excellence of the Redeemer he will explain to be his willingness ' to seek, and save that which was lost.' The duty of Christians, now become peculiarly their duty, he will teach to consist ' in denying all ungodliness and worldly lusts, and living soberly, righteously, and godly in the world.' Thus, whether God or man, the law or the gospel, heaven or hell, morality or piety, are the themes of his preaching, he will make the corruption of the human heart the foundation on which all will be built, the great point to which all will be continually referred.

These are subjects of preaching which cannot fail to interest the preacher who really believes them, or the hearers who listen to them with serious attention. They state to man, they bring to full view, they carry home to the heart, his real condition and only hope. He sees, if not prevented by sottish sloth or criminal prejudice, that the whole is the truth of God, truth infinitely important to himself, ' commending' itself ' to his conscience,' explaining his danger, disclosing the only way of escape, unfolding deliverance from hell, and pointing out the path to heaven. The preacher who utters these things is readily believed to have a real meaning, when he speaks of the solemnity and importance of religion, and presses upon his hearers the necessity of embracing it. They clearly discern that there is something, which they easily comprehend, to be done by them, and a momentous reason why it should be done ; that a change real, great and indispensable, is to be accomplished in their character, and that, unless it is accom-

plished, they must perish. Christianity hence assumes a solemnity which can be derived from no other considerations,
and accords with no other scheme.

The preacher who regards man as originally virtuous, can
neither explain to him his guilt nor his danger, show him the
necessity of Christ's mediation, or the importance of an interest in it, explain to him the value of faith or the use of repentance, nor exhort him to fly to the mercy of God for forgiveness or sanctification. He urges, therefore, a religion in
in which both his hearers and himself find little interest. His
addresses to them are naturally made up of cold, common-
place morality, such as Plato taught long since, and taught
much better, or at least with greater force. They of course
become dull and lifeless, unfrequent visitors to the house of
God ; and when there, are rarely of that number ' who have
ears to hear.'

VIII. *In the same manner are all men taught how they
ought to regard themselves in their religious concerns.*

The question, What will become of me hereafter ? is of
infinite moment to every child of Adam, and is to be always
determined by the true answer to another, Am I virtuous
or sinful ?

The man who commences his moral course with a full conviction of his guilt, his exposure to the wrath of God, and his
danger of final condemnation, will, if he goes on, direct his feet
into a path widely distant from that which is pursued by men
directed by the contrary doctrines. To such a man, all the
accounts given in the Scriptures, and in religious discourses
built on the Scriptures, concerning human guilt and danger,
will be true and important. The tidings of redemption will be
to him ' tidings of great joy,' because they are directed to such
a creature as himself. Christ to him will be infinitely precious, because he is the Saviour of sinners. The renewing power
and goodness of the Spirit of grace will appear to him un-
speakably necessary and desirable, because, without this divine energy exerted on his heart, he will be a sinner for ever.
To the atonement of Christ he will fly for refuge, because he
cannot make an atonement for himself. To the purifying influence of the Divine Spirit he will look for his preservation

in holiness, and his safe arrival in the kingdom of life, because he will know that he cannot preserve nor conduct himself to that kingdom.

As a sinner he will feel himself guilty, condemned and ruined ; but, as an object of the divine mercy he will see glorious hopes dawning upon him from heaven. Separated from Christ, he will feel that he ' can do nothing ' effectual toward his salvation ; but as a candidate for heaven by faith, repentance and holiness, he will discern that ' all things ' may be done for him by the Spirit of God. Left to himself he will perceive that he must die for ever, but that in Christ he may for ever live.

With these views, all his self-examination, prayers, praises, hopes, resolutions and efforts will take their peculiar character from the great truth, that he is a depraved, ruined creature. His whole life, therefore, will be the life of a believing, penitent, and returning sinner, owing infinite blessings to the mere grace of God ; and he will find more to animate his love, faithfulness, and gratitude than an angel with the same powers could feel, because he is a forgiven and restored creature ; forgiven an immense debt, and restored to holiness and endless life.

But if a sinner feel himself to be originally virtuous, he will feebly realize his guilt, his danger, or his need of a Saviour. The necessity of being born again, of being sanctified, guided, and quickened by the Spirit of God, he cannot know. Justification he will regard as due to him, as the proper reward of his merit, and holiness, as his original character, the native growth of his mind. He may, indeed, admit it to be imperfect, and to require some additions ; yet even these he will esteem rather as advantageous than necessary. Christ he will consider rather as a convenience, as an auxiliary to him, than as his Saviour. His ultimate reliance will be on himself, not on the Redeemer. The Gospel, instead of being the only and most joyful news of salvation to sinners, will be considered by him merely as a valuable book, somewhat better than any volume of philosophy, in which some interesting instructions may be found, and some useful precepts are given ; but which is not indispensable to his eternal life. In a word, according to his predominant feeling, both he and others like him might have done very well without the gospel here, and, with little danger of failure, might have obtained salvation beyond the grave.

SERMON XXXIV.

APOSTATE MAN

CANNOT BE JUSTIFIED BY WORKS OF LAW.

THEREFORE, BY THE DEEDS OF THE LAW THERE SHALL
NO FLESH BE JUSTIFIED IN HIS SIGHT.

ROMANS III. 20.

In several preceding Discourses I have considered the universality and Degree of human corruption, and its existence in consequence of the apostasy of Adam; and have also derived from the observations made in them concerning these subjects, several inferences, which I supposed to be of serious importance to mankind. The next object of inquiry in a System of Theology is *the situation in which mankind are by means of their corruption.* It is impossible for a rational being to know that he has offended God, and is now the object of his displeasure, without being, if he is not absolutely stupid, deeply alarmed by a sense of his danger at least, if not of his guilt.

All creatures are absolutely in the hands of God, and must be disposed of according to his pleasure. If he wills it, they are happy; if he wills it, they are miserable. He speaks, and it is done; he commands, and it stands fast. From his eye there is no concealment; from his hand there is no escape; from his anger there is no refuge. What, then, will become of those, who are found guilty at the final trial; who can plead no excuse for their sins, and offer no expiation for their souls ? ' He is not a man,' as we are, ' that we should answer him ; ' and that we ' should come together in judgment. Neither is there any day's man (any mediator) betwixt us, who might lay his hand upon us both,' and make reconciliation between us. When I say that there is no day's man between us and him, you will undoubtedly understand that I intend this as our situation while under law, and independently of the redemption of Christ. Of this situation it is immensely important for us to form clear and just views. False opinions here may easily be fatal to any man. If he feels safe while he is really in danger, as his danger, if it exists, must be immensely great, and threaten his whole well-being, his sense of safety must of course be ruinous. Whatever is to be done for his future good must be done in this world, since he is to be ' judged' and rewarded ' according to the deeds done in the body.'

The text is the close of a long discourse concerning the depravity of both Jews and Gentiles, or, in other words, of all mankind ; and contains the great and affecting inference, drawn by St. Paul himself, or rather given by the Spirit of God, from this humiliating doctrine : ' Therefore by the deeds of the law shall no flesh be justified in his sight.'

In order to understand the import of this interesting declaration, it is necessary to form distinct and correct views of the meaning of the term *justify*. This word is a term of law, in the judicial proceedings of which it denotes *a sentence of acquittal* passed upon a person who has been tried, concerning his obedience or disobedience. The person tried, being found to have obeyed the law in the manner required, is declared by the judge to be guiltless of any disobedience. In the language of the text, he is ' justified ; ' that is, declared to be just, or blameless, in the sight of the law. With exactly this meaning the word is here used by St. Paul.

There have been frequent disputes concerning the *law* here specified. Some commentators have insisted that the *moral,* some that *the ceremonial,* and some that the *whole law* given by Moses, is here intended. That neither the ceremonial nor political law of the Jews is here designed by the Apostle is, I think, completely evident from a bare consideration of the passage itself ; the language is, that ' NO FLESH shall be jus-

tified' by means of the law intended.   It can hardly be supposed that St. Paul meant to say this with reference to the
ceremonial or political law of the Jews ; because, except the
Jews themselves, none of the human race can be either acquitted or condemned, or even tried, by those laws ; since the
rest of mankind not only have never known them, but have in
almost all instances been absolutely unable to come to any
knowledge of them.

The truth, I apprehend, is, that this difference of opinion
has arisen only from the translation of the text.   The words
in the original are Διοτι, εξ εργων νομε ε δικαιωθησεται πασα σαρξ
ενωπιον αυτε.   ' Wherefore, by works of law no flesh,' that
is, no man, ' shall be justified in his sight,' that is, in the
sight of God.   By works of law in the absolute sense : that
is, no man shall be justified by any works whatever of any law,
whether natural or revealed.

The doctrine contained in the text is, therefore, *That no
man can be justified on the ground of his obedience to the Law
of God.*

This doctrine is so absolutely asserted in the text, that a plain
man in the exercise of sober common sense, would naturally
conclude all attempts to prove it to be misplaced and superfluous.   " Whom," he would instinctively say, " shall we believe, if we do not believe God ; and what declaration of God
can be believed, if this, so plain, so unambiguous, is not to be
believed ?   The efforts of reason to make it more certain or
more evident are merely holding a rushlight to the sun."   So
much has, however, been written and said to explain away
even this declaration, and to avoid the truth which it contains,
and the same truth as expressed in all other similar passages
of the Scriptures, that, notwithstanding these decisions of common sense, it has become really necessary to examine this doctrine, as well as others.   Nor is it only necessary to examine
this doctrine as contained in the Scriptures.   It is also of importance to consider the manner in which it is regarded by reason ; and to show that here as well as elsewhere, notwithstanding several objections suggested against the doctrine,
reason still entirely harmonizes with Revelation.

In pursuance of the scheme which I have thus proposed,
I observe,

I. *That the Law of God demands perfect obedience to all its requisitions.*

This is indeed true of every law ; for it is no more than saying that the law demands what it demands.   Yet it is true, in a peculiar sense, of the divine law.   The requisitions of this law are two : 'Thou shalt love the Lord thy God with all thy heart, and with all thy soul, and with all thy strength, and with all thine understanding ; and thou shalt love thy neighbour as thyself:' that is, Thou shalt devote, with supreme affection, all thy powers to the service of the Lord thy God, throughout the continuance of thy being ; and thou shalt do unto others, who are included under the word ' neighbour,' that is, all intelligent creatures, whatsoever thou wouldest that they in the like circumstances should do unto thee ; and this also thou shalt do throughout the continuance of thy being.   The peculiar perfection of the obedience here required is the *universality* of it.   No other law requires the absolute consecration of all our powers to the obedience of its precepts, or extends its demands to every moment of our existence.

That, which is commonly called the law of *nature, viz.* that part of the law, which is discoverable by unbiassed reason, without the aid of Revelation, requires that we render continual reverence and gratitude to God, and that we invariably do justice, speak truth, and show kindness to our fellow-men.   All these things are required by the law of nature, because all men either do or may see them to be certainly their duty.

Without inquiring at this time, whether any man in a state of nature ever did any one of these duties in the manner commanded, I shall consider it as sufficient for the present purpose to observe, that no man ever performed them universally, as they are here enjoined.   No man, to whom the law of God was revealed, ever loved God, uniformly, with all the heart : or rendered, uniformly, to his neighbour what he would that his neighbour in the like circumstances should render to him : neither did any man in a state of nature ever uninterruptedly render to God the reverence and gratitude, or to his neighbour the truth, justice, and kindness, which it required.   Of this obedience every man has plainly fallen short ; and very few can be found who will not in this view of the subject, confess themselves to be sinners.

II. *The only condition of justification known by law is complete obedience to its precepts.*

The language of the divine law, generally resembling that of every other, is, ' Do these things, and thou shalt live ;' and ' Cursed is every one that continueth not in all things written in the book of the law, to do them. The soul that sinneth shall die : for not the hearers of the law are just before God, but the doers of the law shall be justified.

This condition of justification is inherent in the very nature of law. The law of God, for example, requires certain things of mankind, and promises that those who do them shall be rewarded. But the reward is promised to no others. On the contrary, those who do them not it declares shall be punished. The former it pronounces just, or guiltless, the latter it pronounces guilty. Obedience and disobedience are plainly the only conditions by which creatures subject to this law can be justified, condemned, or even tried. The same things, substantially, are true of every other law. It is presumed no law was ever promulged by any authority whatever, which specified any other condition.

III. *It is impossible for mankind, or any other rational beings, to do more than the law of God requires.*

This law requires that we love him with all the heart, and soul, and mind, and strength. Higher love than this cannot possibly be rendered by any creature. It requires that we love him thus at all times. There is no time, therefore, in which such love is not our duty. Supererogatory love or obedience of course cannot possibly be rendered by man. Hence, if man ever fails of obeying, he cannot atone for the sin by any future obedience, because all his future obedience is demanded for the time being. If, then, he is ever guilty of disobedience, his future obedience, however perfect, cannot contribute at all to his justification.

But all men have disobeyed ; nay, all are disobedient every day and every hour ; and never render complete obedience, even in a single instance. No man, therefore, is justified even for the time being.

IV. *The authority of the law is great in proportion to its importance to the universe, and to the greatness and dignity of the lawgiver.*

The law of God is the foundation of his government, and of the happiness which it confers on his intelligent creatures ; a happiness partly attendant on the obedience, in its very nature, and partly its reward from the lawgiver. The importance of the law, therefore, cannot be measured.

The greatness and dignity of the lawgiver are infinite.

That the guilt of disobedience bears, at least, a general proportion to these things will not be denied. Of course, it must be very great, much greater than we can comprehend. Particularly, it is incalculably greater than if committed merely against human laws, so inferior in their importance, and their capacity of producing happiness ; or against mere human lawgivers, infinitely inferior in dignity and excellence.

The worth of our services, at the same time, is proportioned to the worth of ourselves who render them. The law of God requires the obedience of archangels as well as that of men. The law is the same, but the difference between the subjects and the services in this case is inestimable by us. The services of the archangel are plainly of very great worth, in a comparative view, those of man of very little. The difference evidently arises from the difference of worth in those who render them.

But the lowest created being, as truly as the highest, can sin against any law and any ruler. His crimes, therefore, can be very great, while his services must of necessity be very small in their importance.

Hence it is plain, that, if we could do works of supererogation, or services not required, we still could make no atonement for our sins. Our sins are enormous evils, and our services in a sense nothing.

V. *The law of God threatens punishment to the first transgression, and also to every succeeding transgression.*

' Cursed is every one that continueth not in all things written in the book of the law, to do them.' He, therefore, ' who continues in all things written in the book of the law,' except one, ' and does them ' as required, yet for the omission of that one ' is cursed.' ' The soul that sinneth shall die.' The soul that sinneth once, that sinneth at all ; not that sinneth in a long course and to a given degree of transgression.

' In the day that thou eatest thereof,' said God to Adam,

' thou shalt surely die.'   Adam ate the forbidden fruit once, and lost his immortality.

Human laws also are always formed in the same manner. The thief, the burglar, the murderer, are all punished by human laws for the first theft, burglary, or murder. This is indeed the very nature of law. It forbids whatever it forbids, and requires whatever it requires, under a penalty for every transgression. The plea, that this is the first transgression, though often alleged as a reason for tenderness and clemency, was, it is presumed, never proposed to a tribunal of justice as a cause of exempting the criminal from punishment, or, perhaps more properly, as a proof that he did not merit punishment.

These considerations plainly cut off all hope as well as all ground of the justification of transgressors in the sight of God on the score of justice ; and prove the absolute impossibility of justification by works of law. Still multitudes of mankind, and among them no small number of divines, have thought proper, notwithstanding this peremptory and decisive language of the law of God, to annex to it a condition upon which, in their view, the hope of acceptance may be rationally formed. I say *a condition,* because I know of *but one,* viz. *repentance,* As this has been abundantly insisted on, it demands a particular consideration.

The scheme of those who urge this condition is, so far as my information extends, the following ; *that, although the law of God does indeed demand perfect obedience, yet from the benevolence of God it may be fairly expected that, even under this law, every sincere penitent will be accepted.*

On this scheme I observe,

1. *The law itself makes no mention of any such condition.*

Hence the evidence of this scheme, if it exist at all, must be extraneous to the law itself. It cannot but be seen that a case of this nature must demand evidence clearly decisive, both because it is a case infinitely interesting to every child of Adam, and because the law is perfectly silent on this subject. This circumstance renders the scheme originally suspected ; for wo cannot easily conceive of a reason why, if acceptance was intended to be granted according to this scheme, God in publishing his law should observe an absolute silence concerning this condition, and should couch the law in such language as, for aught we can see, is directly contradictory to this scheme.

2. *Revelation is everywhere silent concerning this condition of acceptance.*

That Revelation nowhere expressly annexes the final acceptance of mankind to repentance alone will, I suppose, be granted. I have been able to find no passage of this nature myself, and, so far as I know, such a passage has not hitherto been pointed out by any one of those who adopt the scheme. Whatever importance is annexed to repentance, it certainly cannot be said with truth, that faith in the Redeemer is not considered in the Gospel as absolutely necessary to the justification of the penitent. It is nowhere said, that ' God may be just, and yet the justifier of him who' repenteth. Until something equivalent to this can be pointed out, as expressly declared in the Gospel, all the evidence in favour of this scheme must be found in inference and argument.

3. *Revelation declares the contrary doctrine.*

In Galatians iii. 21, St. Paul says, ' If there had been a law which could have given life, verily righteousness had been by the law.' In this passage it is evident beyond denial, that no law exists, or has ever existed, which could give life, or furnish acceptance and consequent salvation, to men. It is further evident also, that righteousness is not to man by the law, or, more properly, as in the Original, *by law*; that is, by any law whatever. But how those who are not the subjects of righteousness, that is of moral excellence, or holiness, can ' see the Lord,' or be justified and saved, the Scriptures have nowhere explained.

In Galatians ii. 21, the same Apostle says, ' If righteousness come by the law, then Christ is dead in vain ;' or, more accurately according to the Greek, ' if Righteousness exist by means of law, Christ certainly hath died in vain.' If righteousness do not exist by means of law in any sense whatever, then man as a mere subject of law can never be accepted. If righteousness do exist by means of law, then, as God himself has declared, ' Christ died in vain.' A serious man must find an insurmountable difficulty in receiving any doctrine which involves this consequence.

In Romans iii. 25, 26, the Apostle says, ' Whom God hath set forth to be a propitiation, through faith in his blood, to declare his righteousness for the remission of sins that are past, through the forbearance of God ;   To declare, I say, at this time his righteousness, that he might be just, and the justifier of him that believeth in Jesus.' In this passage of Scripture it is declared, that God set forth Jesus Christ to be a propitiation, to declare his righteousness in the remission of sins, that he might be just, while justifying him that believeth in Jesus.   It is therefore certain, that, if he had not set forth Christ to be a propitiation, he either would not have justified any of mankind ; or if he had done it, would not have been just.   Of course, all men who are justified are justified only in consequence of this propitiation, and not by means of law in any sense whatever.

It is also evident, that Christ becomes a propitiation to us through faith in his blood ; and that those only are justified who believe in Jesus.   In the same manner, in Romans v. 9, the Apostle says, ' Being justified through,' or by means of, ' his blood.'   It is therefore certain, that those who do not believe will not be justified, and that none are justified without the blood of Christ.

In Romans iii. 30, it is said, ' One God who shall justify the circumcision by faith, and the uncircumcision through faith.'   Therefore, God will justify neither circumcision nor uncircumcision through or by repentance.   The prophet Habbakkuk, chapter ii. verse 4th, repeatedly quoted by St. Paul, says, ' The just shall live by his faith ;' more exactly, ' The just by faith shall live ;' that is, he who by faith is just, shall live.   Therefore no other will live.

All these and the like considerations have, however, been unsatisfactory to the abettors of this scheme ; not, as it appears to me, from any want of explicitness in the declarations themselves, but from their want of accordance with a pre-conceived system ; a system derived, I am apprehensive, more from philosophy than from the Scriptures.   Let us, therefore, examine the dictates of reason concerning this subject ; and see whether they do not plainly and exactly harmonize with Revelation.

What then must be the nature and language of a law prescribing repentance as the condition of acceptance and justification? Plainly it must be this: He, who disobeys the law, shall be punished with death; but if he repents of his disobedience he shall not be punished. What would be the consequences of such a law?

1. *All men who hoped to repent would disobey.*

But from universal experience we are assured beyond a doubt, that every man would hope that he should at some time or other repent, because every man would consider repentance as in his power. The consequence therefore is irresistible, that every man would disobey.

It is equally evident also, that from the love and the habit of disobedience every man would continue to disobey so long as be thought repentance was in his power. But disobedience protracted to so late a period, would become a habit so strong that none would repent. Nothing is more self-deceiving than a spirit of procrastination. We see it in every thing, and always see it the same. Such a law, therefore, would frustrate itself, and prove a mere encouragement to disobedience.

2. *The thing punished by such a law would not be disobedience, but impenitence.*

It is undoubtedly true, that every law designs to punish that which it considers as the transgression, and that only. The thing punished, whatever it is, is in the view of the law the crime; and in that view nothing is a crime except that which is punished. But here the law does not threaten the punishment to disobedience, but to impenitence. Impenitence, therefore, is in the view of such a law the only crime. Disobedience, according to the very language of the law, is no crime. But nothing can be a crime except that which is constituted a crime by the law. It may be said, that disobedience, being forbidden by the law, is for that reason the crime. This opinion, however, is wholly a mistake. The law, without a penalty, or with respect to whatever it does not threaten with a penalty, ceases to be *a law;* and becomes *mere advice.* Disobedience to what it thus prohibits may indeed be imprudence, or impropriety; but cannot be a crime in the eye of such a law. Undoubtedly, if the law regarded disobedience as a crime it would punish it, as every law has done. As, therefore, the divine law according to this scheme punishes impenitence only, it regards impenitence as the only crime.

But if disobedience be not a crime, it cannot be repented of; for repentance is a sorrow for crimes, and for them only. Repentance, therefore, would by such a law be rendered impossible.

3. *In the present case, that of man with respect to his Maker, what degree of repentance will excuse the transgressor from punishment?*

Must it be a *perfect* repentance? that is, entire, and followed by no future sin. On this condition who could be saved? No man ever has repented, no man ever will repent, in this manner. Shall the repentance be imperfect; a sorrow for sin inferior in degree or continuance to that which the nature of the case actually demands; a sorrow extending only to a part of the sins actually committed; a confession sincerely and cheerfully made with respect to some sins, and reluctantly concerning the rest; a renunciation of sin, partial in degree, partial as to the number and kinds of transgressions, and never aiming at, as well as never accomplishing, a thorough reformation of character?

The first difficulty which attends this scheme is, that it is nowhere found in the Scriptures. Few men who believe the Scriptures to be the Word of God will question the fact, that they contain all the terms of salvation. It can hardly be supposed that when God unfolded his will to mankind concerning this great subject, and declared that he had taught them ' all things pertaining to life and to godliness,' he omitted this, which is altogether the principal thing, the point, which they were infinitely concerned to know. But there is not a declaration of this nature in the Scriptures; at least 1 have never been able to find one; nor have I ever seen one alleged. Can it be believed that this should be the main term, nay the only one, of our salvation, and yet that it should be nowhere expressed in a revelation from God, professedly declaring all the terms of salvation?

This, however, is far from being all. The Scriptures teach us in a thousand forms, both expressly and implicitly, that ' we have redemption through the blood of Christ, even the forgiveness of our sins.' As this is the doctrine of the Scriptures, so it is plainly their only doctrine. Indeed, nothing is more evident in the nature of the case, than that if we have redemption through his blood, we have it not without his blood; and therefore not by a repentance of our own.

Nor does reason furnish us any additional light in favour of this scheme. Reason, indeed, finds itself at a loss to conceive in what manner even a perfect repentance can cancel former iniquities, or how an absolute penitent can be accepted of God. His sorrow for his sins can in no respect alter their nature or lessen their demerit, and his future reformation cannot at all obliterate the guilt of his past life. Sorrow for sin is itself the most unequivocal acknowledgment of guilt. If, then, the penitent sees and knows himself to be guilty, God must see it also. What then should prevent him from expressing his views of it in the punishment of the sinner?

If this repentance is *imperfect*, these difficulties are multiplied and enhanced. The penitent in this case is still a sinner, and does not even perform the duty of repenting in the manner in which he is bound to perform it. He also still loves sin in some degree, and still, occasionally at least, practises it. After he becomes a penitent, therefore, he goes on through life accumulating guilt and meriting punishment. Can any man in these circumstances rationally expect acceptance with God? Yet these are the best circumstances in which man is ever found.

It is to no purpose to allege, that such a man obeys the law in part. The law knows of no such condition as partial obedience. Adam obeyed in part; and, what no one of his progeny has ever done, obeyed for a time perfectly. But for the first transgression he was condemned to death, just as if he had never obeyed at all. So far as law is concerned, God deals with his descendants exactly in the same manner. Accordingly, in Ezekiel xviii. 24, he says, ' But when the righteous turneth away from his righteousness, and committeth iniquity, all his righteousness that he hath done shall not be mentioned. In his trespass that he hath trespassed, and in his sin that he hath sinned, in them he shall die.' He, therefore, ' who hath continued in all things written in the book of the law to do them,' except one, would still be incapable, according to law, of being justified. Should he have repented of his first transgression, and should we, contrary to both reason and Revelation, allow repentance to be a real ground of justification, generally considered, yet if he should die in the commission of sin, or without repentance of the sins which he had last committed, be must, according to this passage, die without justification, and be finally condemned.

Thus, if I mistake not, it has been rendered clearly certain, that ' by deeds of law no flesh shall be justified in the sight of God.'

REMARKS.

1. *From these observations it is evident, that the atonement of Christ was absolutely necessary in order to the salvation of Mankind.*

Man was originally placed under a dispensation of law ; and in consequence of perfect obedience was promised immortal life ; while to his disobedience was threatened eternal death. Obedience, therefore, was the only condition of his justification, and the only source of hope to him beyond the grave. This law was perfect, and therefore immutable. No part of its demands or threatenings could be changed. It was more proper ' that the heavens and the earth should pass away, than that one jot or one tittle of the law should pass ' without an exact fulfilment. The truth plainly is, that the law is a direct exhibition of the perfect character of God, and to change it, would be to manifest that his character was changed from its absolute perfection. Such an event is evidently impossible.

This perfect law, however, man has disobeyed. By his disobedience be has lost the possibility of justification, and the hope of reward ; and exposed himself, without any means of escape or safety, to the punishment denounced against his transgression. Had he been left in this situation he must have finally perished. In this situation Christ found him, when ' he came to seek and to save that which was lost.' In this situation he assumed the character of a mediator between God and man, and ' made his soul an offering for sin ; a sacrifice of a sweet savour,' accepted of God as a satisfactory expiation of human guilt. In this manner he rendered it possible, for before it was impossible, that man should be restored to the favour of God.   The honour of the divine law was maintained, and even enhanced.   The immutability of the love of God to holiness, and of the hatred of God to sin, and the perfect harmony of the divine government in the condemnation of sin and the forgiveness of sinners, were all illustriously displayed to the view of the universe.   To forgive such as should repent and return to their duty, became now a dispensation divested of all inconsistency and impropriety.   But independently of this interference of the Redeemer, no method appears to the human eye, in which the justification of mankind could have been accomplished without a serious and inadmissible change of the law and government of God.   Accordingly, we are informed in the Scriptures, that ' by his stripes only we are healed.'   ' Neither is there,' nor, so far as we can understand, can there be, ' salvation in any other : for there is no name given under heaven among men, whereby we must be saved, but the name of Jesus Christ.'

2. *Speculative unbelief prevents every hope of salvation.*
By speculative unbelief I intend, First, *the disbelief of divine Revelation*, or *what is commonly called infidelity*.   Every infidel not only feels, but glories in feeling, a privileged exemption from what he calls the superstition of the Gospel ; by which he primarily intends the great evangelical requisitions of ' repentance towards God, and faith towards our Lord Jesus Christ.'   It is superfluous for me to insist, that he who believes not speculatively in Christ, cannot believe in him cordially ; for nothing is plainer, than that without the assent of the understanding there can be no yielding of the heart.   The infidel will very cheerfully take this labour off my hands, and boast that he yields neither his understanding nor his heart to the Redeemer.   Of course, he places himself under mere law ; and must therefore find justification and consequent acceptance to him impossible.   When I say impossible to him, you will undoubtedly understand me to mean that it is impossible for him to be justified or accepted in his *present character*, or on his *avowed principles*.   I do not mean that his understanding or his heart cannot be changed ; for, though I regard an infidel as a very dangerous and alarming character, yet I do not believe every infidel to be of course a final reprobate.   Infidels have undoubtedly been changed into Christians, and in

some instances have become exemplary ministers of the Gospel. Infidels voluntarily place themselves under mere law, and reject with scorn, as well as obstinacy, an interest in the blessings of redemption. Under that law, however, even after it is narrowed by all his own indefensible limitations, the infidel has still committed innumerable sins, sins for which he himself cannot atone, and for which he will not ask nor even accept the atonement made by the Redeemer. By the law he chooses to be tried, and by the law he cannot fail to be condemned. The God of truth in that day will declare that he has sinned, and, according with his own choice, must consign him to perdition. Such is the situation to which he voluntarily reduces himself, and which he prefers to Christ, with all his infinite blessings.

Secondly: Speculative unbelief is the proper character of multitudes who admit the reality of divine Revelation. Those who in modern language are called Unitarians, deny the Deity, and therefore deny, either explicitly or implicitly, the atonement of the Saviour. Dr. Priestley and, I presume, all his followers deny the atonement expressly: some of the Socinians and Arians have admitted it, but I think inconsistently with their commanding doctrines. The disbelief of the atonement of Christ has the same practical influence with that of the disbelief of his mediation at large. If he is only a prophet, and a pattern of righteousness, I see not that he can be any more a saviour to mankind than Moses, Isaiah, and Paul. He was indeed a wiser and better man. But it will not be denied, that all these men were saved; nor that, therefore, their righteousness was such as, if we faithfully imitate it, would secure our salvation; that is, according to this Unitarian scheme. Nor will it be denied by any man, that the instructions of Moses and Isaiah are such as, if faithfully obeyed, will insure salvation. Nor can it be doubted that Paul has taught mankind more of the Gospel than Christ himself personally taught. To believe in Christ, therefore, is substantially the same thing as to believe in Paul, Isaiah, or Moses. Yet, although we are required to believe all these men, and all other Prophets and Apostles, as being inspired by God, we are nowhere required to believe in them, or on them. They are nowhere styled the saviours or redeemers of mankind. On the contrary, we are expressly told, that there is no other Saviour of

men but Jesus Christ ; and that ' there is salvation in no other.'
There is, therefore, something in Christ wholly different from
any thing in these men ; and that something constitutes his
peculiar and essential character as *the Saviour of mankind.*
As Christ is expressly declared to have been ' the propitiation
for the sins of men ;' ' to have made his soul an offering for
sin,' and ' to have redeemed us with his blood ;' and as we are
said to ' have redemption, even the forgiveness of our sins,
through faith in his blood ;' it is unanswerably evident, that in
this wonderful particular he differs totally from all other persons of whom we have any knowledge.   To disbelieve his
atonement, therefore, is to refuse belief in his peculiar, distinguishing, and essential character, as the Saviour of mankind.
Of course, this scheme shuts out all the benefits of Christ's
redemption, and places mankind again under law.   But ' by
works of law no flesh can be justified ;' and, therefore, by this
scheme no flesh can be saved.

There are, indeed, Unitarians of both these classes who acknowledge the atonement of Christ, but who yet in effect deny
it by the necessary consequences of their leading principles.
Concerning these men I have no more to say at present, than
that the hearts of some persons are sounder than their heads ;
and that, although their leading principles by their proper influence destroy the hopes of salvation, yet, as all errors which
are imbibed are not obeyed, and, as among such errors the
leading principles of men may, for aught I know, be sometimes
included, I am disposed to entertain better hopes concerning
them than I should feel myself authorized by these principles,
considered by themselves, to indulge.

3. *Practical unbelief also equally cuts off the hope of salvation.*

We become partakers of the benefits of Christ's redemption
only by exercising evangelical or cordial faith in him, as the
Redeemer.   It is to no purpose that we believe the several
records given us in the Scriptures concerning his incarnation,
life, preaching, miracles, death, resurrection, and exaltation.
It is to no purpose that we believe him to be a divine person,
the real and all-sufficient Saviour ; ' able,' willing, and faithful, ' to save unto the uttermost all that will come unto God
by him.' This and all other speculative faith is to no purpose,
if we stop here.   It is indeed a step toward salvation, and a

necessary step, but it is one step only; and, if no more be taken, we shall never arrive at the end of the Christian progress.   In addition to this, we must with the heart confide in Christ, and his righteousness, and cheerfully trust our souls in his hands.   This the practical unbeliever does not; and, so long as he continues to be of this character, cannot do.

Let every practical as well as every speculative unbeliever, then, remember that by his own choice, by his voluntary refusal to receive Christ as his Saviour, he cuts himself off from justification, and consequently from immortal life.   Every one of these men has broken the law of God, and sinned against him in innumerable instances of great and dreadful iniquity. Every one infinitely needs forgiveness and salvation.   At the bar of God how terrible will be the remembrance of this voluntary perdition, this suicide of the soul?

' Repent, therefore, every one of you, and believe on the name of the the Lord Jesus Christ, for the remission of your sins.'   Repent *now*.   ' Behold, now is the accepted time : behold, now is the day of salvation .' If repentance, if faith, be not now your duty, they can never be.   Now, therefore, if you intend ever to ' hear his voice, even while it is called to-day, harden not your hearts.'   ' Boast not yourselves of to-morrow, for you know not what' evils another ' day may bring forth.'   Now you are called to repentance, faith, and holiness, and invited to eternal life.   To-morrow you may be summoned to the grave, and to the judgment.   To-day you are before the mercy-seat, surrounded with blessings, in the presence of a forgiving God, and at the feet of a crucified Saviour.   To-morrow, nay, this very night ' your souls may be required of you ;' your probation ended, your account given, the final sentence pronounced against you, and your souls consigned to suffering and sorrow which shall know no end !

SERMON XXXV.

THE CHRISTIAN SYSTEM

GROUNDED ON THE RELIGION OF NATURE, AND INTRODUCED BY CHRIST.

DIVINITY OF CHRIST.

PROOF FROM THE NAMES GIVEN TO HIM.

FOR WHAT THE LAW COULD NOT DO, IN THAT IT WAS WEAK THROUGH THE FLESH, GOD SENDING HIS OWN SON IN THE LIKENESS OF SINFUL FLESH, AND FOR SIN, CONDEMNED SIN IN THE FLESH: THAT THE RIGHTEOUSNESS OF THE LAW MIGHT BE FULFILLED IN US, WHO WALK NOT AFTER THE FLESH, BUT AFTER THE SPIRIT.

ROMANS VIII. 3, 4.

FOR GOD, SENDING HIS OWN SON IN THE LIKENESS OF SINFUL FLESH, AND OF A SIN-OFFERING, HATH CONDEMNED SIN IN THE FLESH (THE THING IMPOSSIBLE TO THE LAW, BECAUSE IT WAS WEAK THROUGH THE FLESH:) THAT THE RIGHTEOUSNESS OF THE LAW MAY BE FULFILLED BY US, WHO WALK NOT ACCORDING TO THE FLESH, BUT ACCORDING TO THE SPIRIT.

DR. MACKNIGHT'S TRANSLATION.

IN my last Discourse I endeavoured to show, 'that man could not be justified, and of course could not be saved, by works of law.' The plain and necessary result of the establishment of this doctrine is, either that he cannot be saved *at all*, that is, he cannot be happy in a future existence; or that he must be saved by *some 'other* than the legal dispensation. The Scriptures inform us, that the latter part of this alternative is the true one ; and declare, *that salvation, or future happiness, is attainable by man.* This subject then, infinitely interesting to every child of Adam, this subject, boundlessly great, sublime, and glorious ; immensely honourable to God, and inestimably beneficial to man, becomes the next object of our inquiry.

It ought, perhaps, to be observed here, and certainly ought to be remembered, that our preceding investigation has been confined chiefly to what is commonly called *the religion of Nature.* By this I intend the same with that which was *the religion of Adam in Paradise ;* or, generally, the religion of beings placed under law only. The truths to be believed and the duties to be done by beings, placed under the law of God, constitute the system, which we call *natural religion.* This religion is found nowhere clearly explained and solemnly sanctioned except in the Scriptures. In them it is presented to us in its perfect form, and with its proper lustre. In all the exhibitions of philosophy it is defective, mutilated, and deformed, with superadded features, created only by the imperfect reasonings, and wild imagination, of man. In the Scriptures it is disclosed in its native beauty, freed from every defect and every mixture.

On this system *Christianity,* properly so called, is erected. By Christianity I intend The religion of fallen beings ; a religion furnishing effectual means of redemption from their apostasy, guilt, and punishment, and of. their restoration to the favour of God, to virtue, and to future happiness. The means provided for this end, the truths to be believed and the duties to be done by. such beings, in order to their escape from sin, condemnation, and misery, and their attainment of justification, holiness, and happiness, constitute the sum and substance of the Christian Religion.

To such beings as we are, fallen from the favour of God, polluted with immoveable guilt, and destined to die for ever, under the law which we have broken, such a religion is plainly of infinite importance. From the bare contemplation of the subject one would think, that the tidings communicated by such a religion must be welcome to mankind beyond degree. Every thing which they need, every thing which they can reasonably wish, every thing which can purify, adorn, or bless them, which can make them useful and comfortable here, or happy and glorious hereafter, it announces from the mouth of God.   By such beings it ought certainly to be received as ' tidings of great joy unto all people.'

In the text the great and commanding doctrines of this religion are briefly declared ; and these are the following :

I. *That it was impossible for the law to condemn, or, in other words, destroy sin in men, while in the state of nature, or under the legal dispensation.*

II. *That God has accomplished this great work by sending his own Son in the likeness of sinful flesh, as an offering for sin.*

III. *That this was done in order that the righteousness of the law might be fulfilled by those who, under the influence of the Gospel, live lives of new obedience.*

It will be easily seen, that these three great propositions contain the substance of Christianity ; that they teach *our ruined condition under the law ; our recovery by Christ ;* and *our duty and obedience in the Christian character.*

The first of these propositions, *that it was impossible for the law to destroy sin in man while in the flesh, or to furnish redemption to apostate beings,* has been already considered at length in the preceding Discourses.   This is the state in which Christianity found man, and took the charge of his concerns. On this state Christianity is erected, as on its proper foundation ; and but for this state appears, in my view at least, to have neither use, explanation, nor meaning.

The second proposition is now to become the subject of discussion.   As it is a proposition of vast extent, and contains a great many particulars of vast importance, demanding seve- rally a minute examination, it will furnish an ample field for many Discourses.

In this proposition it is asserted, *that God has accomplished the great work of destroying sin in man by sending his own Son in the likeness of sinful flesh, as an offering for sin.*

The inquiries excited by this assertion are :

I. What is the Character of the Person thus sent ?

II. What has he done ?

III. How has he destroyed sin in man ?

In this order I propose to consider these highly interesting subjects.

I. I will proceed to investigate *the character of the Person who was thus sent.*

The character given of him in the text is plainly a singular one.   He is called ' God's own Son,' and is yet said to have been ' *sent in the likeness of sinful flesh.*'   These two great particulars, so unlike, so contrasted, form a character differing altogether from every other, and demand a very diligent consideration.   The first of them shall be the immediate object of our attention.

At our entrance upon the investigation of this subject, the first thing which strikes the mind is, that it is a subject of *mere Revelation.*   Without the criptures there is no knowledge in this world that such a person exists.   The philosopher, therefore, has no other concern with this subject, except either to believe or disbelieve the testimony which the Scriptures give.   By his own reason he can add nothing to what is revealed, and without impiety he can alter nothing.

Secondly : As Revelation communicates to us our original knowledge of this subject, so it communicates to us *all which we now know.*   The things, which it testifies were not designed to be, neither can they become, the materials of future philosophical investigation and improvement.   The knowledge which at this day exists concerning this subject is all found in the Bible.

Thirdly : The things communicated concerning it, being communicated, ' not in the words which man's wisdom teacheth, but in those which the Holy Ghost teacheth,' are communicated *in the best and wisest manner possible ;* the manner which was approved by infinite Wisdom.   There is no error, no oversight; nothing superfluous, nothing defective.   That, and that only, is taught, which God thought it proper to teach, in the manner which God thought it proper to adopt.

Fourthly : As the doctrines concerning this singular Person are of the highest moment to plain, uneducated men, as well as to men of learning, it is certain, *that the things really revealed, are so revealed that such men, acting with integrity, can understand them sufficiently to make them proper and useful objects of their faith.*   Of course, the terms in which they are revealed are used in such a manner as these men can understand. They are therefore used *according to their plain, customary, obvious meaning ;* the meaning which they have in the usual intercourse of mankind. Of course, also, they have no technical, philosophical, or peculiar signification; because, if thus used, they could never be understood by such men; or, in other words, by almost the whole body of mankind.

Fifthly: Just so much is revealed concerning this extraordinary Person, *as it is useful for us to know.* This truth is derived with absolute certainty from the wisdom and goodness of God. Whatever is revealed is revealed by this wisdom and goodness, and whatever is withheld is by the same wisdom and goodness withheld. That which is revealed, therefore, we are required by the authority of God to believe; and are bound to have no reference in our faith to that which is withheld. Whatever mysteries may be inferred, or may seem to be inferred, from the things actually revealed, can in no manner affect them, and ought in no manner to affect our faith in them. All that is taught is exactly true, and to be faithfully believed, although all that is true is not taught, nor capable of being divined by such minds as ours.

Sixthly: Whatever is contained in the Scriptures concerning this subject, as concerning every other, that is, in the Scriptures as they now are, *is to be regarded as unquestionably the Word of God,* unless proved not to be genuine by manuscript authority. Nothing is to be admitted with respect to this subject which would not be justifiably admitted with respect to any other scriptural subject. Particularly, all conjectural emendations of the text are to be rejected with scorn, as miserable attempts to mend the word of God according to the dictates of human philosophy. The reasonableness of this rule is too obvious to need illustration.

With these observations premised, I proceed to examine the *Character of this singular Person,* denoted by the phrase, ' God's own Son.'

The Scriptures are undoubtedly the best commentators on themselves, wherever they professedly undertake to explain their own language. Christ has in many instances called himself the Son of God; and in many more (which is exactly equivalent) has declared God to be his Father. In one of these instances the Jews attempted to kill him for challenging this character. The words which he used were ' My Father worketh hitherto, and I work. Therefore,' says the Evangelist, in the following verse, ' the Jews sought the more to kill him, because he not only had broken the Sabbath, but said also, that God was his Father, making himself equal with God.' John v. 17, 18.　We have here the comment of the Evangelist on Christ's meaning in adopting this language; and it is no other than this, That in declaring God to be his Father, he made himself equal with God.'　No comment can be plainer, or more decisive.　But we have, farther, the comment of Christ himself, for such it ought undoubtedly to be esteemed. He had healed the impotent man at the pool of Siloam on the Sabbath day.　The Jews ' sought to kill him ' for this action. He justified himself by this remarkable declaration, ' My Father worketh hitherto, and I work:' that is, My Father worketh hitherto on the sabbath day in his providence; I, who am his Son, work also in the same manner and with the same authority, being ' Lord of the sabbath,' even as he is. In the following part of the context, to cut off all room for misconception concerning the import of this phraseology and the character claimed in it, he informs the Jews, in the verses immediately following, that ' he does all things which the Father does;' that ' the Father shows him all things, which himself does;' that ' he has life in himself, even as the Father has life in himself;' that, ' as the Father gives life to whom he pleases, so does the Son;' that ' it is the will of the Father, that all men should honour the Son even as they honour himself;' that ' those who do not thus honour the Son do not honour the Father;' that ' the Son is constituted the only Judge of the quick and the dead;' and that ' all who are in the graves shall hear, and obey his voice, and come forth to the resurrection, either of life or damnation.'　Such is the comment of the Evangelist on this phrase; such are the proofs that it is uttered in its simple and obvious meaning.　Who would imagine that this meaning could be differently understood by different readers, or be mistaken by any reader?

　　In John x. 30, Christ said to the Jews assembled around him, ' I and my Father are one.'　The unity here challenged, seems not to have offended them (see verse 36;) but they attempted to stone him because he said, ' I am the Son of God;' as he informs us in the verse last mentioned.　Upon being asked by him, for what good work they stoned him; they replied, ' for a good work we stone thee not, but for blasphemy, because thou, being a man, makest thyself God.' It will be admitted by all men, who believe the Bible, that Christ was a person of irreproachable benevolence and integrity. The Jews declared to him, as the reason why they were about to stone him, that in saying, ' he was the Son of God, he, being a man, made himself God.' If, then, they had misapprehended his meaning, a very moderate share of benevolence and integrity must have compelled him to undeceive them; much more must the perfect integrity and benevolence of Christ have produced this effect. It is impossible that he should be justified in voluntarily suffering this imputed blasphemy to rest upon his good name; and to prevent, as it could not fail to prevent, their reception of his doctrines, precepts, and mission. This would have been voluntarily to lay a fatal stumbling block, or offence, before them : but he himself has said, ' Woe to that man by whom the offence cometh.' It would, also, have been voluntarily to leave *the full impression of a falsehood, uttered by himself, on their minds;* which would be the same, in a moral view, as to utter intentionally the same falsehood. Finally, under this mistake they were about to murder him; a crime which he certainly could not fail of preventing, if they were influenced to commit it merely by mistaking his meaning: a thing so easily rectified by his own explanation. It is certain, then, that they did not mistake his meaning.

But, to put the matter beyond all doubt, he himself has settled the point. ' If,' said he, ' I do not the works of my Father, believe me not ; but if I do, though ye believe not me, believe the works, that ye may know and believe, that the Father is in me, and I in him.' *

The same subject of controversy arose again when Christ stood as a prisoner before the Sanhedrim. After attempting in vain to prove him guilty of any crime by various means, Caiaphas put him upon oath, to tell the Sanhedrim ' whether he was the Christ, the Son of God.' Christ immediately replied in the affirmative. The high priest then rent his clothes ; and declared, that he had spoken blasphemy ; *viz.* the very blasphemy, of which the Jews had before accused him, for the very same declaration ; and the Sanhedrim pronounced

---

* That the Jews understood Christ to confirm *their* construction of his words is certain : for St. John says, that they now sought again to take him.

·him guilty of death.   Here, as in the former case, Christ went on to challenge, unequivocally, the character denoted by this phrase ; and said, ' Hereafter shall ye see the Son of Man sitting on the right hand of power, and coming in the clouds of heaven.   Thus we have the comment of St. John on this phrase, declaring, that Christ in using it ' made himself equal with God ;' the comment of the Jewish people and Sanhedrim ; declaring, that Christ in using it ' was guilty of blasphemy, because, that, being a man, he thus made himself God ;' and Christ himself, according directly with this interpretation of it, justifying his own use of it with this meaning, and bringing irresistible proofs that he applied it, thus understood, to himself, with the most absolute truth and propriety. If we allow the language here used, to be used in the customary and obvious manner, the only manner in which it could be understood by those to whom it was addressed, and in which it can be understood by ninety-nine hundredths of those who read it ; nay, farther, if we do not assign it a meaning which each man must laboriously contrive for himself, because the obvious meaning does not suit his own system, or must receive from another, who has for the same reason contrived it in this manner, we must admit all this to be clearly and unquestionably said, and to determine the meaning of this phrase in the text beyond any rational debate.

   If I have satisfactorily settled the meaning of this phrase, the text contains, among other things, the following inportant Doctrine :

THAT JESUS CHRIST IS TRULY AND PERFECTLY GOD.

   This Doctrine I shall attempt to maintain by a variety of considerations, arranged in the following manner :

   I. *I shall attempt to show, that Christ is spoken of in the Scriptures as the true and perfect God :*

   II. *That the Deity of Christ is the only ground of consistency in the scheme of redemption :*

   III. *That the Jews, according to the opposite doctrine, are unjustly charged with guilt in putting Christ to death :*

   IV. *That the Prophets and Apostles, according to the same doctrine, cannot be vindicated from the sin of leading mankind into idolatry :*

V. *To these arguments from the Scriptures I propose, in another place, to subjoin several testimonies to the same doctrine from Jews, Christians, and Heathens.*

I. *I shall attempt to show, that Christ is spoken of in the Scriptures as the true and perfect God.*

This argument may be advantageously exhibited by showing,

1. *That the names of God ;*
2. *That the attributes of God ;*
3. *That the actions of God ;* and,
4. *That the relations, which God sustains to his creatures, are in the Scriptures ascribed to Christ ;* and,
5. *That divine worship is in the Scriptures required to be rendered, and by persons inspired was actually rendered, to Christ.*

1. *The names of God are in the Scriptures ascribed to Christ.*

(1.) *He is directly called God.*

John i. 1. ' In the beginning was the Word, and the Word was with God, and the Word was God.' In this passage St. John not only declares Christ to be God, but to be eternal. ' In the beginning was the Word.' And in the following verse he declares that he is co-eternal with God : ' The same was in the beginning with God :' Words exactly equivalent to those in Proverbs viii. 23, 24. where the same truth is also asserted : ' The Lord possessed me in the beginning of his way ; before his works of old. I was set up from everlasting ; from the beginning, or ever the earth was.' In the following verse the Evangelist farther declares, that Christ was the Creator of the universe, and that ' without him was not even one thing made, which has been made. * In this passage of Scripture St. John has not only declared, that Christ is God ; but to prevent any possible mistake concerning what he meant by the word *God,* has told us, that he is co-eternal with God the Father ; and that he is the Creator of every thing which exists. Were the Scriptures allowed to speak their own language, this single passage would decide the controversy ; for it is impossible to declare in stronger language, or more explicit, that Christ is God in the highest sense, originally, and without derivation.

* See the Original.

Romans ix. 5. ' Of whom, as concerning the flesh, Christ came, who is over all, God blessed for ever. Amen.' This passage cannot be avoided by any means, except a resolute denial.

1 Timothy iii. 16. * ' Without controversy great is the mystery of godliness. God was manifest in the flesh, justified in the Spirit, seen of angels, preached unto the gentiles, believed on in the world, and received up into glory.' Nothing is more evident than that these things are said of Christ, and that they can be said of no other. No other person, and no attribute can be said to be ' God, manifested in the flesh, justified in the Spirit, seen of angels, preached unto the gentiles, believed on in the world, and received up into glory.' Let any person make the experiment, and he will find it impossible to make the application of all these things to any other than the Redeemer.

Matthew i. 23. and Isaiah vii. 14. ' Behold, a virgin shall conceive, and shall bring forth a son ; and thou shalt call his name Emmanuel ;' that is, ' God with us.' Christ, therefore, is ' God with us.'

2 Peter i. 1. ' To them that have obtained like precious faith with us, through the righteousness of God and our Saviour Jesus Christ.' According to the Original, *of our God and Saviour, Jesus Christ :* τυ Θευ ημων, και Σωτηρος, Ιησυ Χρισυ. The common translation is a violation of the Greek : and, besides, it is ' through the righteousness of Christ ' only that ' the precious faith ' of the Apostles and other good men is ' obtained.' Jesus Christ is, therefore, ' our God and Saviour.'

Psalm xlv. 6, 7. quoted in Hebrews i. 8, 9. ' Unto the Son he saith, Thy throne, O God, is for ever and ever : a sceptre of righteousness is the sceptre of thy kingdom. Thou hast loved righteousness, and hated iniquity : therefore God, even thy God, hath anointed thee with the oil of gladness above thy fellows.' This is addressed by God the Father to the Son. The Father, therefore, has thought proper to call the Son, *God.* Who can question the propriety of the application ?

---

* These Sermons were written before the results of Griesbach and others were extensively known in this country. The author was satisfied, from an examination of these results, that the common is the genuine reading of the text.

That we may be assured, that he is called God, in the full and perfect sense, he declares, that ' the throne of the Son is for ever and ever.' To whom, but God in the absolute sense, can an everlasting throne, or dominion, be attributed?

Revelation xxi. 5—7. ' And he that sat upon the throne said, Behold, I make all things new ; and he said unto me, I am Alpha and Omega, the beginning and the end, the first and the last. He that overcometh shall inherit all things, and I will be his God, and he shall be my son.' That it is Christ, who is spoken of in this passage, is evident by a comparison of Rev. i. 11. and Rev. iii. 21. In the former of these passages Christ says, ' I am Alpha and Omega, the first and the last.' In the latter he says, ' To him that overcometh, I will give to sit on my throne ; even as I overcame, and am set down with my Father in his throne.' In Rev. xx. 11, 12. we are informed, that John ' saw a great white throne, and him that sat on it, from whose face the heavens and the earth fled away, and there was found no place for them ;' and that he ' saw the dead, small and great, stand before God.' He that sat upon the throne, in Rev. xxi. 5. is plainly the same person who, in chap. xx. 11. is exhibited as sitting on the great white throne ; and this person we certainly know to be Christ ; because ' the Father judgeth no man, but hath committed all judgment unto the Son ;' and because the throne here spoken of, is the throne of final judgment. In the second and third of these passages Christ declares himself to be ' the Alpha and Omega, the first and the last,' or the beginning and the end ; and to be ' set down upon the throne of his Father.' In the first passage *he* declares, that ' he will be a God to him that overcometh.' In the last he is declared by the Evangelist to be *God*.

There are many other passages, in which Christ is directly called *God*. But these are sufficient to establish the point.

(2.) Christ is called the *Great God*.

Titus ii. 13. ' Looking for the blessed hope and glorious appearing of the great God and our Saviour, Jesus Christ.' In the Greek it is *the great God, even our Saviour Jesus Christ*, or *our great God and Saviour Jesus Christ*. God the Father will not appear at the judgment. If then Christ is not ' the great God ;' God will not appear at the judgment at all. Και, the conjunction here used, is rendered exactly, in many cases, by the English word *even ;* particularly in the phrase *God and our Father*, found Gal. i. 4. 1 Thess. i. 3. 2 Thess. ii. 16, &c. In the last of these places the Translators have rendered it *even*, as they plainly ought to have done in both the others ; since the present rendering makes the Apostle speak nonsense.

(3.) *Christ is called the True God.*

1 John v. 20. ' In his Son Jesus Christ.' This, in the Original, *This Person* ' is the true God and eternal life.' If this passage admits any comment, it must be that of Christ himself ; who says, ' I am the life ;' and that of the Evangelist ; who in the first chapter of this Epistle, and second verse, says, ' For the life was manifested ; and we have seen it, and bear witness, and show unto you that Eternal Life, which was with the Father, and was manifested unto us.'

(4.) *Christ is called the Mighty God.*

Psalm l. 1—3. ' The mighty God, even the Lord, hath spoken, and called the earth from the rising of the sun unto the going down thereof. Out of Zion, the perfection of beauty, God hath shined. Our God shall come, and shall not keep silence : a fire shall devour before him, and it shall be very tempestuous round about him.' This Psalm is a prediction of the last judgment. In the first verse, the Person, who comes to judge the world, and who speaks the things recorded in this Psalm, is called AL, ALEIM, JEHOVAH ; and is exhibited as calling mankind before him, ' from the rising of the sun to his going down.' In the second, he is represented as ' shining,' or displaying his glory, ' out of Zion ;' that is, by his dispensations to his church. In the third, is described the awful splendour, with which he will appear, the fire which shall consume, and the convulsion which shall rend asunder, the world, at that great and terrible day. But Christ alone will appear on that day ; and at his presence ' the heavens shall pass away with a great noise ;' and by ' the flaming fire, with which he will be surrounded, ' the elements will melt with fervent heat, and the earth and the works that are therein will be burnt up.' *Christ*, therefore, is *the God, the Mighty God*, the Jehovah, who is here mentioned.

Isaiah ix. 6. ' For unto us a Child is born ; unto us a Son is given ; and the government shall be upon his shoulders : and his name shall be called Wonderful, Counsellor, the

Mighty God, the Father of the everlasting age, the Prince of Peace.' This *Child*, this *Son*, is ' the Mighty God; the Father of the 'everlasting age, and the Prince of Peace.' He who admits, that ' *a Child, a Son,*' is ' the Mighty God,' will certainly admit that this can be no other than Christ. He who does not, will charge Isaiah with uttering falsehood.

The same name, ' Wonderful,' is also given to him by himself, when appearing as an angel; or rather as ' the Angel,' to Manoah and his Wife, Judges xiii. 18. ' And the Angel of the Lord said unto him, Why askest thou thus after my name; seeing it is secret?' in the Hebrew, *seeing it is Wonderful;* the same word being used in both these passages. The Hebrew words which are translated ' the Angel of the Lord,' may be literally rendered, *the Angel-Jehovah,* or *Jehovah-Angel:* that is, He who, though Jehovah, is yet a Messenger.* For this view of the subject the Scriptures themselves furnish the most ample authority.

In Isaiah xlviii. 12, and onward, we have these words: ' Hearken unto me, O Jacob, and Israel my called. I am he; I am the first, I also am the last. Mine hand also hath laid the foundation of the earth, and my right hand hath spanned the heavens. I call unto them; they stand up together. Come ye near unto me; hear ye this: I have not spoken in secret from the beginning: from the time that it was, there am I. And now the Lord God and his Spirit hath sent me. Thus saith the Lord, thy Redeemer, the Holy One of Israel: I am the Lord thy God. ' Here the Person speaking informs us, that ' he is the first and the last; that he has founded the earth, and spanned the heavens: that he is Jehovah-God, the Redeemer, and the Holy One of Israel;' and yet he says, ' that the Lord Jehovah and his Spirit hath sent him; or, as Origen and Lowth translate it, ' The Lord Jehovah hath sent me and his Spirit.' The Person sending, therefore, is Jehovah; and *the Person sent* is also *Jehovah.*

The same Person, under the appearance and by the name of a man, wrestled with Jacob at Peniel, and there gave him the name Israel, or a Prince of God: assigning for it this remarkable reason; ' For as a prince hast thou power with God,

---

* See *Horsley's* New Translation of Hosea. Appendix.

and with men, and hast prevailod.' After asking his name, and receiving a blessing from him (upon which he departed,) ' Jacob called the name of the place Peniel ; for, said he, I have seen God face to face, and my life is preserved.'

This Person is called by Hosea, *God, the Angel, and Jehovah.* ' He had power with God ; yea, he had power over the Angel, and prevailed. He wept, and made supplication unto him. He found him in Bethel ; and there he spake with us, even Jehovah, God of Hosts.' Horsley, whose biblical opinions will rarely be disputed with success, has the following observations on this subject : " This *Man,* therefore, of the book of Genesis, this *Angel* of Hosea, who wrestled with Jacob, could be no other than the Jehovah-Angel, of whom we so often read in the English Bible, under the name of the *Angel of the Lord.*" A phrase of an unfortunate structure, and so ill conformed to the Original, that, it is to be feared, it has led many into the error of conceiving of ' the Lord ' as one person, and of ' the Angel ' as another. The word of the Hebrew, ill rendered ' the Lord,' is not, like the English word, an appellative, expressing rank or condition ; but it is the proper name Jehovah. And this proper name Jehovah is not in the Hebrew a genitive after 'the noun substantive ' Angel,' as the English represent it ; but the words יהוה and מלאר ' Jehovah,' and ' Angel,' are two substantive nouns, in apposition ; both speaking of the same person, the one by the appropriate name of the *essence ;* the other by a title of *office. Jehovah-Angel* would be a better rendering. The Jehovah-Angel of the Old Testament is no other than He who, in the fulness of time, ' was incarnate by the Holy Ghost of the virgin Mary.'

According to the scheme of these observations, Manoah understood the character of ' the Angel who appeared unto him :' for he said unto his wife, verse 22, ' We shall surely die, because we have seen God.' In the same manner is the same person presented to us, Mal. iii. 1. ' Behold, I will send my Messenger, and he shall prepare the way before me ; and the Lord, whom ye seek, shall suddenly come to his temple ; even the Angel of the covenant, whom ye delight in : behold, he shall come, saith the Lord of Hosts.' In Luke vii. 27. Christ, speaking of John the Baptist, says, ' This is he, of whom it is written, Behold I send my Messenger before thy face, who shall prepare thy way before thee.' John the Baptist was, therefore, ' the Messenger, who was to prepare the way ;' and ' the Lord, even the Angel of the covenant,' was Christ. The person also speaking, who is here called ' Jehovah of Hosts,' and who says, this Messenger shall prepare the way before himself, is also Christ.

(5) *Christ is called the God of Israel.*

Exodus xxiv. 9, 10. ' Then went up Moses and Aaron, Nadab and Abihu, and seventy of the elders of Israel. And they saw the God of Israel.' Psalm lxviii. 17, 18. ' The chariots of God are twenty thousand, even thousands of angels. The Lord is among them, as in Sinai, in the holy place. Thou hast ascended on high, thou hast led captivity captive, thou hast received gifts for men.' Ephesians iv. 8. ' Wherefore he saith, When he ascended on high, he led captivity captive, and gave gifts unto men. Now that he ascended, what is it, but that he descended first into the lower parts of the earth. He that descended is the same also that ascended up far above all heavens, that he might fill all things : and he gave some apostles, and some prophets,' &c. Here the apostle informs us, that the Person who ' ascended on high, and led captivity captive,' is Christ. The Psalmist informs us, that the Person who ' ascended on high, and led captivity captive,' is the Lord, ' who appeared in Sinai.' And Moses informs us, that ' the Lord who appeared in Sinai,' was ' the God of Israel.' We also know, ' that no man hath seen God,' the Father, ' at any time.' Christ therefore is ' the God of Israel.' Of course, ' the God of Israel,' so often mentioned in the Old Testament, is everywhere, peculiarly, Christ.

(6) *Christ is called Jehovah.*

On this subject Horsley observes, " The word Jehovah, being descriptive of the Divine Essence, is equally the name of every one of the Three Persons in that Essence. The compound Jehovah-Sabaoth belongs properly to the second Person, being his appropriate demiurgic title ; describing, not merely the Lord of such armies as military leaders bring into the field, but the unmade, self-existent Maker and Sustainer of the whole array and order of the universe."

Isaiah vi. 1, and 3, ' In the year that king Uzziah died, I

saw Jehovah* sitting on his throne, high and lifted up, and his train filled the temple ; and one of the seraphim cried to another, and said, Holy, Holy, Holy, is Jehovah of Hosts ;' and again, in the 5th, 8th, 11th, and 12th verses of the same chapter. St. John, quoting the 9th and 10th verses of this chapter, in his Gospel, chapter xii. 40, says, ' These things said Esaias, when he saw his (that is, Christ's) glory, and spake of him.' To prove beyond controversy, that Christ is the Jehovah of Hosts here mentioned, I observe, that no person is spoken of in the chapter, except Uzziah, Jehovah of Hosts, the seraphim, the prophet Isaiah, and the people of Israel. The seraphim and the people of Israel being mentioned only in the aggregate, must be laid out of the question. Christ, therefore, being, by the decision of the Evangelist, spoken of in this chapter, must be either the prophet himself, king Uzziah, or Jehovah of Hosts. It happens also, unfortunately for Unitarians, that the prophet saw the glory of no other person but Jehovah of Hosts ; yet St. John assures us, he saw the glory of Christ. St. John's opinion on this subject we cannot mistake, if we remember, that he commences his Gospel in this manner : ' In the beginning was the Word, and the Word was with God, and the Word was God.

Isaiah xl. 3. ' The voice of him that crieth in the wilderness, Prepare ye the way of Jehovah, make straight in the desert a highway for our God.' John the Baptist, when asked by the messengers of the Sanhedrim. ' Who art thou ?' answered, John i. 23, ' I am the voice of one crying in the wilderness, Make straight the way of the Lord, as saith the prophet Esaias.' St. Matthew, speaking of John the Baptist, chapter iii. 3, says, ' This is he that was spoken of by Esaias the prophet, saying, The voice of one crying in the wilderness, Prepare ye the way of the Lord, make his paths straight.' From these passages compared, it is evident that Christ, before whom John cried, was ' the Lord' whose way he directed thus to be prepared in the wilderness ; ' the Jehovah,' spoken of by the prophet : ' the Jehovah of Hosts,' who said, Malachi iii. 1, ' Behold, I will send my messenger before MY face, and he shall prepare the way before ME.'

Exodus iii. 2—6. ' And the Angel-Jehovah appeared unto

---

* Lowth's Notes on this Verse.

him, in a flame of fire, out of the midst of a bush: and he looked, and behold the bush burned with fire, and the bush was not consumed. And Moses said, I will now turn aside, and see this great sight, why the bush is not burned. And when Jehovah saw that he turned aside to see, God called unto him, out of the midst of the bush, and said, Moses, Moses! And he said, Here am I. And he said, Draw not nigh hither; put off thy shoes from off thy feet; for the place whereon thou standest is holy ground. Moreover he said, I am the God of thy Father, the God of Abraham, the God of Isaac, and the God of Jacob. And Moses hid his face, for he was afraid to look upon God.' In this passage we are informed, that the Angel-Jehovah appeared ' to Moses in the burning bush,' and said to him, ' I am the God of Abraham, the God of Isaac, and the God of Jacob.' The word *Angel*, as you well know, denotes *a person sent*; and, of course, implies a person sending. The Person here sent is called Jehovah, and styles himself ' the God of Abraham.' It needs no words to show, that the Person *sent* cannot be God the Father; or that he must be the Angel of the Covenant, God the Son. Christ therefore is the Jehovah mentioned in this passage as ' the God of Abraham, the God of Isaac, and the God of Jacob.'

The application of these peculiar names of the Godhead to our Saviour furnishes, in my view, an unanswerable argument to prove his divinity: for,

1. In Isaiah xlii. 8, God says, ' I am Jehovah, that is my name, and my glory I will not give to another.'

In this passage, God declares, that ' he will not give his name,' or glory. both terms meaning here the same thing, ' to another.' Yet, in the word of this same God, his several peculiar and distinguishing names are given to Jesus Christ; not indeed communicated to him, but applied to him, as his own original, proper appellations. This we are taught at large, Exodus xxiii. 20, 21. ' Behold I send an Angel before thee, to keep thee in the way, and to bring thee into the place which I have prepared. Beware of him, and obey his voice; provoke him not; for he will not pardon your transgressions, for my name is in him.' Here we are informed, that the ' Angel,' sent before the Israelites, would not ' pardon their transgressions, if they provoked him;' and are thus certainly taught, that he possessed the right and the power of pardoning sin. ' But who can forgive sins, except God?' We are farther informed, that the ' name' of God is ' in ' this Angel; not that it is *given* or *communicated* to him, but that it *existed in him,* and *belongs to him, originally.* What' this name is, the passage last quoted from Isaiah, declares to us: ' I am Jehovah, that is my name.' It is also declared in the same manner to Moses, when asking of God, Exodus iii. 13, what was his *name,* that he might declare it to the children of Israel: ' And God said unto Moses, I am that I am. Thus shall ye say unto the children of Israel, I am hath sent me unto you.' It is hardly necessary to remark, that the name, *I am,* has the same import with Jehovah. All this is rendered perfectly consistent and obvious by the scriptural accounts of Christ. ' I and my Father are one,' said our Saviour to the Jews.

For God, therefore, in his own word to give or apply his *name,* or *glory,* to Christ, is not to give it to another; but to apply to Christ names which are his own proper appellations. But, according to the Unitarian doctrine, this assertion on the part of God cannot be true. The doctrine therefore is false; for ' Let God be true, but every man a liar;' that is, every man who opposes God.

2. In Deuteronomy xxxii. 39; in Isaiah xliii. 10; xliv. 6, 8; xlv. 5, 14, 21; and in various other places, God says, *that there is no God beside him; that there is none else; and that he knows not any.* Yet Christ is called God, and announced by other names of the Deity, in the several passages above mentioned, and in many others; and this by the same God who made this declaration. That he is not so called in a subordinate, delegated, or derived sense, is unquestionably evident. First, from the *titles* given to him, viz. *The True God; The Mighty God; the Great God; The God of Israel; Jehovah;* and *I am;* all of them names never given in the Scriptures to any being but the Deity. Secondly, from the *things ascribed to Christ* in the same passages, many of which, as you must have observed, cannot be predicated of any being, except the one living and true God.

If it be admitted, then, that the Scriptures speak language which is to be understood in its customary sense, the only sense

in which it can be intelligible to those to whom it was addressed, and to ninety-nine hundredths of those for whom the
Scriptures were written ; if it be admitted, that God has chosen
the most proper terms to communicate true ideas of himself to
mankind ; it cannot be denied, that Jesus Christ is truly and
perfectly God.

SERMON XXXVI.

DIVINITY OF CHRIST.

PROOFS FROM THE ATTRIBUTES AND ACTIONS ASCRIBED TO HIM.

FOR WHAT THE LAW COULD NOT DO, IN THAT IT WAS WEAK THROUGH THE FLESH, GOD SENDING HIS OWN SON IN THE LIKENESS OF SINFUL FLESH, AND FOR SIN, CONDEMNED SIN IN THE FLESH: THAT THE RIGHTEOUSNESS OF THE LAW MIGHT BE FULFILLED IN US, WHO WALK NOT AFTER THE FLESH, BUT AFTER THE SPIRIT.

ROMANS VIII. 3, 4.

FOR GOD, SENDING HIS OWN SON IN THE LIKENESS OF SINFUL FLESH, AND OF A SIN-OFFERING, HATH CONDEMNED SIN IN THE FLESH (THE THING IMPOSSIBLE FOR THE LAW, BECAUSE IT WAS WEAK THROUGH THE FLESH:) THAT THE RIGHTEOUSNESS OF THE LAW MAY BE FULFILLED BY US, WHO WALK NOT ACCORDING TO THE FLESH, BUT ACCORDING TO THE SPIRIT.

DR. MACKNIGHT'S TRANSLATION.

IN the preceding Discourse I observed, that the great and commanding doctrines of Christianity are briefly declared in this passage of Scripture, and, as such, recited the following;

I. That the law could not destroy sin in Man:

II. That God has accomplished this work by sending his own Son into the world:

II. That this was done in order that the righteousness of the Law might be fulfilled by Christians.

As the *first* of these propositions had been sufficiently discussed, I proposed, in a series of Sermons, to examine the *second*; and to commence the examination by inquiring into the character of him who is here called ' *God's own Son.*' After reciting several scriptural comments on this phrase, I asserted, that it contains the following important Doctrine:

THAT JESUS CHRIST IS TRULY AND PERFECTLY GOD.

This doctrine I proposed to illustrate under several heads of Discourse, then specified; the first of which was—
That Christ is spoken of, in the Scriptures, as the true and perfect God.

The argument, contained in this proposition, I proposed to exhibit by showing, that the *names, attributes,* and *actions of God* , together with the *relations which he sustains to his creatures, are in the Scriptures ascribed to Christ ;* and, *that divine worship is in the Scriptures required to be rendered, and by persons inspired was actually rendered, to him.*

The first of these subjects, viz. *the names of God,* I then showed, at sufficient length for my design, to be abundantly applied to Christ in the Scriptures. I now propose to exhibit this truth concerning *the attributes.*

I. *The peculiar attributes of God are ascribed to Christ in the Scriptures.*
1. *Eternity.*
Revelation i. 10, 11, &c. ' I was in the Spirit on the Lord's Day, and heard 'behind me a great voice as of a trumpet, saying, I am Alpha and Omega, the first and the last : and I turned to see the voice that spake with me; and being turned I saw seven golden candlesticks; and, in the midst of the seven candlesticks, one like unto the Son of Man : and when I saw him I fell at his feet as dead : and he laid his right hand upon me, saying unto me, Fear not, I am the first and the last; I am he that liveth and was dead, and behold, I am alive for evermore.   Amen.'
Revelation ii. 8. ' These things saith the First and the Last, who was dead and is alive.'
Isaiah xliv. 6. ' THUS SAITH JEHOVAH, King of Israel,

and his Redeemer, JEHOVAH OF HOSTS, I am the first, and
I am the last, and beside me there is no God.'

Isaiah xlviii. 12. ' Hearken unto me, O Jacob, and Israel
my called ; I am he ; I am the first ; I 'also am the last.
Mine hand, also, hath laid the foundation of the earth,' &c.

In the two first of these passages it will not, for it plainly
cannot, be disputed, that the person spoken of by St. John,
and afterwards speaking of himself, ' who was like unto the
Son of Man, who was dead, is alive, and liveth for evermore,'
was Christ ; and this person in four instances declares himself
to be ' the First and the Last ;' the strongest assertion, that
Eternity past and to come belongs to himself.   If he is the
First, none can have been before him : if he is the *Last*, none
can be after him.

In the two last passages, from the prophet Isaiah (the latter
of which has in the preceding Discourse been clearly proved
to be written concerning Christ,) JEHOVAH OF HOSTS, who
declares, that ' beside himself there is no God,' declares also,
that ' he is the first, and that he is the last.'   This language,
with mathematical certainty, is attributable to but one being,
and that being is the only living and true God.

Proverbs viii. 22, 23. ' The Lord possessed me in the beginning of his way, before his works of old.   I was set up
from everlasting, from the beginning, or ever the earth was.'

That the person here spoken of under the name of Wisdom,
is Christ, cannot be rationally questioned by any man who
reads this chapter with attention ; especially if he compares
it with the account given by the same Person of himself, in
the first chapter of the same book ; where he exhibits himself as the judge, and rewarder, of mankind.   To place the
matter out of doubt, St. Paul informs us, that ' Christ is the
wisdom of God.'   But this person says, ' he was set up from
everlasting.'

Micah v. 2. ' And thou Bethlehem Ephrata, though thou
be little among the thousands of Judah, yet out of thee shall
he come forth unto me, that is to be ruler in Israel ; whose
goings forth have been from of old, from everlasting :' in the
Hebrew, *from the days of eternity.*   This passage was, in a
sense proverbially. acknowledged by the Jewish nation to be a
prophecy of Christ.   See Matt. ii. 6, where it is quoted as
such by the Pharisees, in answer to Herod's inquiry concern-

ing the birth place of the Messiah.   Besides, God, speaking in the passage itself, says, ' yet out of thee shall he come forth unto me,' &c.   Here ' he, whose goings forth have been from the days of eternity,' is said by another Person to ' come forth unto' the Person speaking ; that is, unto God the Father.

John i. 1, 2.   ' In the beginning was the Word, and the Word was with God, and the Word was God.   The same was in the beginning with God.'

1 John v. 20.   ' This is the true God, and,' or even, ' the eternal life.'

The names *Jehovah, I am,* and *I am that I am,* already proved to belong to Christ, are also the strongest expressions of original and eternal existence.   The phrase, ' I am,' Christ in a peculiar manner applies to himself.   John viii. 58.   ' And Jesus said unto them, Verily, verily, I say unto you, before Abraham was I am.'   John viii. 24.   ' If ye believe not that I am, ye shall die in your sins.'   Matthew xxviii. 20.   ' Lo I am with you alway.' &c.   Here Christ does not say, Before Abraham was, I was ; or I will be with you alway ; but *I am,* teaching us explicitly, that past and future are perfectly present to himself, and that his own existence is one present time.

2. *Both by these names, and by other ascriptions of eternity to Christ, he is declared to be underived, or self-existent.*

He who is *the first,* he whose existence is one present time, necessarily exists only of himself.

3. *Omnipotence is directly ascribed to Christ.*

Rev. i. 8.   ' I am Alpha and Omega, the beginning and the ending, saith the Lord, who is, and who was, and who is to come, the Almighty.'   In the 11th verse of this chapter Christ utters these words of himself.   Either, then, there are two persons who truly say these things, each of himself ; or Christ declares them of himself in both these verses.   The choice in this alternative I willingly leave to the Unitarians ; for, either way, the great question in debate is determined with equal certainty.   If Christ speak the words in the 8th verse, he is the Almighty ; if not, there are two Persons who are ' the Alpha and the Omega, the first and the last.'   Origen comments on these words in the following manner :— " And that thou mayest know the omnipotence of the Father and the Son to be one and the same, hear John speaking in the Revelation in this manner, ' These things, saith the Lord God, who is, and who was, and who is to come, the Almighty ;' for who is the Almighty to come, except Christ ?" Origen supposed ὁ ἐρχόμενος to indicate the coming of Christ at the day of Judgment. Psalm xlv. 3. ' Gird thy sword upon thy thigh, O most mighty.' He, who is *most mighty*, is plainly all mighty. Matthew xxviii. 18. ' And Jesus came and spake unto them, saying, All power is given unto me in heaven and in earth.' The Greek word here is ἐξουσια ; the most proper meaning of which is *authority, controul,* or *dominion*. But he who has the authority, controul, or dominion over all things, unquestionably possesses all power, in the original or absolute sense.

This controul was manifested by Christ in the obedience of diseases, life, and death, the elements of this world, and angels both good and evil, to his command. The manner in which he exercised his controul over all these things was, it should be remembered, the same which he used at the creation. In both cases ' he spake and it was done.' The bread, with which he fed the two companies of four thousand and five thousand men, came into existence, just as the heavens and the earth had before done, in obedience to his mere pleasure. To the leper he said, ' I will, be thou clean :' to the deaf ears, ' Be opened :' to the blind, ' Receive thy sight :' to the demons, ' Come out of the man :' and to the winds and waves, ' Peace, be still :' as he had before said, ' Let there be light ;' and was in the same manner obeyed. The most proper mode, however, of exhibiting the omnipotence of Christ is to appeal to those acts by which it is peculiarly displayed. When we read John i. 3, ' All things were made by him, and without him was not any thing made which was made ;' and Hebrews i. 2, ' Upholding all things by the word of his power ;' we are presented with the strongest possible proof that his power is unlimited. He who created and who upholds the universe, plainly can do every thing which in its nature is possible ; and is, in the absolute sense, omnipotent.

4. *Omniscience is also ascribed to Christ.*

John xxi. 17. ' Peter saith unto him, Lord, thou knowest all things.' To this ascription of omniscience, Christ makes no reply, and therefore admits it in its full latitude. If it had not been true, it is impossible that he should have permitted Peter to continue in so dangerous an error.

Matthew xi. 27. ' All things are delivered unto me of my Father, and no one knoweth the Son but the Father ; neither knoweth any one the Father, save the Son ; and he to whomsoever the Son will reveal him.' In this passage both the omniscience and incomprehensibility of Christ are declared by himself. He who knows the Father, is omniscient. He who is known only by the Father, is *incomprehensible.*

No exercise of omniscience is more peculiarly declaratory of this perfection than ' searching the heart,' and none more peculiarly challenged by God as his sole prerogative. Accordingly, 1 Kings viii. 39, Solomon, addressing himself to God in his prayer at the dedication of the temple, says, ' For thou, even thou only, knowest the hearts of all the children of men.' Yet, Revelation ii. 23, Christ says, ' And all the churches shall know, that I am he, who searcheth the reins and the hearts :' and St John, chapter ii. 23, 24, says, ' Now when he was in Jerusalem, at the passover, on the feast day, many believed in his name, when they saw the miracles which he did. But Jesus did not commit himself unto them, because he knew all men.' Accordingly, in Matthew ix. 4, it is said, ' And Jesus, knowing their thoughts :' in Matthew xii. 25, ' And Jesus knew their thoughts :' in Luke v. 22, ' When Jesus perceived their thoughts :' in Luke vi. 8, ' But he knew their thoughts :' in Luke ix. 47, And Jesus perceiving the thought of their heart :' and in Luke ix. 17, But he, knowing their thoughts.' In all these passages we have the most absolute proof that it is the prerogative of Christ to search the heart ; and that, therefore, he is the God to whom Solomon prayed. The same truth is also declared in the fullest manner by Christ, in each of his messages to the Seven Churches, in the verses beginning with, ' I know thy works, &c.' See Rev. ii. iii.

5. *Omnipresence is ascribed to Christ.*

Matthew xviii. 20. ' Where two or three are gathered together in my name, there am I in the midst of them.' This fact, the gathering together of persons in the name of Christ, has, from the times of the apostles, yearly existed in many thousands of places. Yet Christ, according to his own declaration, is in the midst of all these assemblies.

Matthew xxviii. 20. ' Lo, I am with you alway, even unto the end of the world.' Here Christ declares, that he is with the apostles and succeeding ministers alway, unto the end of the world. But Ministers are in a sense scattered throughout the world. With all these Christ has promised alway to be present.

Unitarians object against the interpretation of this passage, that ἕως τῆς συντελείας τοῦ αἰῶνος ought to be rendered 'unto the end of the age.' To this I answer, First, that this phrase is used three times in the Gospel of St. Matthew by Christ himself: Matthew xiii. 39, 40, and 49, 'The harvest is the end of the world; as therefore the tares are gathered and burned in the fire, so shall it be in the end of this world:' and again, 'So shall it be at the end of the world: the angel shall come forth, and sever the wicked from among the just.' These, if I mistake not, are the only instances in which the phrase is used at all; and in all these, except the passage now in dispute, it certainly signifies *the end of the world* at the general Judgment. There is no warrant for supposing that Christ, who used it in this sense in three instances out of four, totally varied his meaning in the fourth instance, without giving any notice of such variation.

Secondly: If the interpretation contended for be admitted, the passage will still equally declare the truth alleged from it. For, if Christ was present alway with the Apostles, only to the end of the Jewish age, he is omnipresent. They preached throughout a great part of the world. But no being could be present with them 'alway,' in these separate and distant regions, but he 'who filleth all things.' Ephesians iv. 10.

To avoid the difficulty, which is presented to the Unitarians by this passage, Mr. Belsham, one of the most considerable Socinian writers at the present time, informs us, that Christ was with St. Paul, (and, I presume, therefore, with the other Apostles, since the promise was made personally to them,) by his bodily presence, which yet was invisible. Accordingly, Christ must be supposed to have been constantly and most rapidly flying throughout that age, from place to place, and from apostle to apostle. I cannot but blush for human nature, to see such wretched subterfuges resorted. to by a man, styled a minister of the Gospel, as serious comments on the Word of God, for the sake of escaping from the plain meaning of his direct declarations, and for the sake of retaining a system palpably contradictory to those declarations. What mind does not revolt at such a debasing representation of the Redeemer? Surely this gentleman might have recollected, that St. Peter said, that ' the heavens must receive Christ until the times of the restitution of all things:' that St. Paul said, ' When he had purged away our sins, by himself on the cross, he sat down at the right hand of the Majesty on high:' that Christ himself said to his disciples, ' And now I go my way to him that sent me:' and to the Father, in his intercessory prayer, ' And now I am no more in the world; but these are in the world; and I come to thee.'

But this interpretation will not help the Unitarians over the difficulty. He could not, on this plan, be with them *alway*; and therefore his promise could not be fulfilled. Besides, this promise, thus understood, would be scarcely at all applicable to the purpose for which it was given; viz. *the support and consolation of those who should disciple and baptize all nations: for these, existing in every age, as well as in many countries, unto the real end of the world, need alike the blessing which is promised.*

This is one of the instances in which a meaning, laboriously contrived to make the Scriptures accord with a pre-conceived system, is substituted for 'the obvious and true one; and may serve as a representative of the rest.

6. Immutability is ascribed to Christ

Hebrews xiii. 8. ' Jesus Christ, the same yesterday, to-day, and for ever.'

Psalm cii. 27, &c. quoted Hebrews i. 10, &c., ' And thou, Lord, in the beginning hast laid the foundations of the earth, and the heavens are the works of thy hands. They shall perish, but thou remainest: yea, all of them shall wax old as doth a garment, and as a vesture shalt thou change them, and they shall be changed; but thou art the same, and thy years shall have no end.' This passage is declared by St. Paul to be spoken of Christ, as I shall have occasion to show more particularly hereafter: and in *both* passages he is declared to possess absolute immutability. On this subject I argue in the following manner:——

If Christ is unchangeable, he is so, either because his faculties are so immensely great, and his character is so perfectly good, as to be incapable of change, either by increase or diminution: or, if the supposition be possible, because he possesses a mind which having originally received all its ideas, is unable, by means of its singular constitution, either to lose any of those which it has received, or to receive any more; and which, having originally possessed a certain degree of energy and moral worth, is, by its singular nature, also made incapable in both these respects of any alteration. No words are necessary to show, that every new idea makes a real change in the recipient; and that, therefore, every intelligent creature changes of necessity every day, in the manner which we actually behold.

That Christ is not unchangeable, according to the latter of these suppositions, will I suppose be admitted without a debate. For though I have made the supposition, it is, I think, clearly inconsistent with the essential nature of an intelligent being. No such being, turning his mind to the objects by which thought is excited, can possibly fail of receiving new ideas. Besides, that Christ is not in this manner unchangeable is certain, from Luke ii. 52. ' And Jesus increased in wisdom and stature, and in favour with God and man.' Here it is asserted, not only that he changed when twelve years of age, but so perceptibly, as to have the change distinctly marked by those around him.

Therefore, by necessary consequence, *he*, concerning whom this attribute is asserted, is infinitely different in nature from the *infant*, which was born of the Virgin Mary; and was united to that infant by a mysterious union, so as to become one person, denominated with strict propriety by the one name Jesus Christ, or the *Anointed Saviour*.

II. *The peculiar actions of God are ascribed to Christ in the Scriptures.*

On this subject I observe,

1. *That the creation of all things is ascribed to Christ.*

John i. 3. ' By him all things were made: and without him was not even one thing made, which hath been made.'

Colossians i. 16. ' For by him were all things created, that are in heaven, and that are in earth, visible and invisible, whether they be thrones, or dominions, or principalities, or powers, all things were created by him and for him.'

Hebrews i. 10. quoted from Psalm cii. 25. ' Thou, Lord,

in the beginning hast laid the foundations of the earth; and the heavens are the work of thy hands.'

It has been denied, that this last passage is applied by the apostle to Christ; but the denial cannot, I think, have proceeded even from prejudice. It must have resulted from absolute inattention. In the 7th verse the apostle says, ' And of the angels he saith, Who maketh his angels spirits, and his ministers a flame of fire. But unto the Son he saith What? Two things, which follow: the first, quoted from the xlvth Psalm, beginning, ' thy throne, O God, is for ever and ever;' the second, quoted from Psalm cii. and beginning with, ' Thou Lord in the beginning hast laid the foundation of the earth:' and these two are coupled by the conjunction Καί, or ' and.'* In this manner the passage has meaning and syntax; but without it, has neither. If the passage be not applied to Christ by the apostle, he departs entirely from his discourse begun before and continued after this passage; that is, carried through the whole chapter; and inserts these three verses, containing, according to. this scheme, not even a parenthetical reference to any thing in the chapter, nor indeed to any thing in the whole book. In the mean time, the ' and,' by which it is connected with the former quotation, and which determines it, beyond debate, to be a part of the speech of the Father to the Son, makes it, according to this scheme, to be ungrammatical nonsense. Surely such writing ought not to be attributed to the Apostle Paul, even if we regard only his character as a man of understanding. It ought, however, to be remarked, that for the present purpose the passage may be dispensed with, without any disadvantage: those which remain being abundantly sufficient to establish the point. In the two former of these passages it is asserted, that ' all things in heaven and in earth, visible and invisible:' nay, that ' every thing which has been made,' without the exception even of one, ' were created by Jesus Christ;' in the latter, ' the heavens and the earth,' the Jewish appropriate phrase to denote the universe, are declared to be ' the work of his hands.'

On these passages I observe, that if a person, thoroughly acquainted with language, were to sit down purposely to express the proposition *that Christ created all things,*

* See an example of the same mode of connection, Matt. xxiii. 16—18.

he could not find words to express it more clearly, and decisively, than those, which convey to us each of these scriptural declarations.   St. John, particularly, has gone the utmost
length which human language will permit ; when, after saying,
' And by him all things were made,' he subjoins, ' and without
him was not even one thing made, which has been made.'

2. *The preservation of all things is also ascribed to Christ
in the most explicit manner.*

Colossians i. 17. ' By him,' that is, Christ, ' do all things
consist.'

Hebrews i. 1, 2. God, who at sundry times, and in divers
manners, spake unto our fathers by the prophets hath in these
last days spoken unto us by his Son : whom he hath appointed
heir of all things ; by whom also he made the worlds : who,
being the brightness of his glory, and the express image of
his person, and upholding all things by the word of his
power,' &c.

On these passages it cannot be necessary to dwell.   They
plainly have but one meaning ; and that meaning is too explicit to admit even of an ingenious misconstruction.   The
words make it evident, if words can make it evident, that
Christ is the upholder of all things.

3. *The government of all things is, in the same direct and
distinct manner, applied to Christ.*

Psalm xlv. 6. ' Thy throne, O God, is for ever and ever.'

The second Psalm throughout, is an illustrious exhibition of
the universal dominion of Christ.

The seventy-second Psalm is a still more glorious exhibition
of the same subject.   Here it is said, that ' his dominion shall
extend from sea to sea, and from the river to the ends of the
earth ; that all kings shall bow down to him ; that all nations shall serve him : that they shall fear him as long as
the sun and the moon endure : that his name shall endure,
and be blessed, for ever : and that the whole Earth shall be
filled with his glory.   Amen.'

Psalm cx. 1. The Lord said unto my Lord, Sit thou on my
right hand, until I make thine enemies thy footstool.

Psalm viii. 5. Thou madest him a little (for a little time)
lower than the angels, and hast crowned him with glory and
honour : Thou madest him to have dominion over the works
of thy hands.' See this passage applied to Christ, Heb. ii. 9.

Isaiah ix. 6, 7. ' Unto us a Child is born, unto us a Son is given : and the government shall be upon his shoulder. And his name shall be called Wonderful, Counsellor, the Mighty God, the Father of the everlasting Age, the Prince of Peace. Of the increase of his government and peace there shall be no end.'

Daniel vii. 13, 14. ' And I saw in the night visions, and behold, one like the Son of Man came with the clouds of heaven, and came to THE ANCIENT OF DAYS ; and they brought him near before him. And there was given him dominion, and glory, and a kingdom ; that all people, nations, and languages, should serve him : his dominion is an everlasting dominion, which shall not pass away : and his kingdom that, which shall not be destroyed.

The same doctrine is pursued throughout the New Testament in the same explicit manner. Acts x. 36. ' The Word, which he sent to the children of Israel, proclaiming glad tidings of peace by Jesus Christ. This person is Lord of all things.'

Rom. ix. 5. ' Of whom, as concerning the flesh, Christ came, who is over all things, God blessed for ever and ever. Amen.'

1 Cor. xv. 25. ' For he must reign, until he hath put all enemies under his feet.'

Ephesians i. 20. ' Which he wrought in Christ, when he raised him from the dead, and set him at his own right hand in the heavenly places, far above all principality, and power, and might, and dominion, and every name that is named, not only in this world, but in that which is to come : and hath put all things under his feet ; and given him to be head over all things unto the church.'

Philippians ii. 9—11. ' Wherefore God hath highly exalted him, and given him a name, which is above every name ; that at the name of Jesus every knee should bow, of things in heaven, and things in earth, and things under the earth ; and that every tongue should confess, that he is Lord, to the glory of God the Father.'

These numerous passages are, comparatively, but a few of those in which the Scriptures assert the absolute and universal dominion of Christ. I have recited such a number of them, to show that this doctrine runs through the whole sacred volume.

No words can be conceived which can express absolute and supreme dominion over all beings, and all events, more unequivocally or more forcibly than these. The name of Christ is here declared to be 'above every name that is named, not only in this world, but in that which is to come, in earth and in Heaven,' in time and in eternity. All things in all worlds are required to *bow* to him. Angels of every order, as well as men, it is declared, shall thus 'bow' to him, either voluntarily or involuntarily; and shall 'confess, that he is Lord, to the glory of God the Father.' This dominion also is asserted to be without limits, and without end. I shall only add, from the mouth of Christ himself, 'I am the first, and the last, and the living one.' Also, 'I was dead, and behold, I am the living one for ever and ever: and I have the keys of hades and of death. I shut and no one openeth; I open, and no one shutteth;' Rev. i. 17, 18; and iii. 7: and the equivalent passage, Matthew xxviii. 18. 'And Jesus came, and spake unto them, saying, All authority in heaven and in earth is given unto me.' Here Christ asserts that the rightful exercise of all power in heaven and in earth is in his possession; that he has 'the keys of hades and of death;' or the absolute controul over the world of the dead and the region of departed spirits. From that world, from that region, none of the numberless inhabitants can escape without his permission; but when the gates are unlocked by him, none can hinder them from coming forth; as at his call they will actually do on the great and final day.

4. *The act of giving and restoring life, is also expressly ascribed to Christ in a variety of ways.*

Particularly while he resided in this world, *he raised the dead at his pleasure.* The daughter of Jairus, the son of the Widow of Nain, and his beloved Lazarus, were illustrious examples. All these returned again from the world of departed spirits at his command. 'Damsel, I say unto thee, Arise;' 'Young man, I say unto thee, Arise;' 'Lazarus, Come forth!' were the only means which he employed; and the spirits of these deceased persons instantly obeyed the call. This amazing power he accordingly asserts of himself in terms absolute and universal. John v. 21, 26. 'As the Father raiseth up and quickeneth, even so the Son quickeneth whom he will. As the Father hath life in himself, so hath he given

to the Son to have life in himself.* In the same manner St.
Paul declares, 1 Cor. xv. 45. ' The first Adam was made a
living soul ; the last Adam was a quickening spirit.   In a still
more striking manner did he exemplify this wonderful power
in raising himself from the dead.   That he did this cannot be
doubted, unless we are disposed to doubt the truth of his own
express declaration.   John x. 17, 18. ' Therefore doth my
Father love me, because I lay down my life, that I might take
it up again : no one taketh it from me, but I lay it down of
myself.   I have power to lay it down, and I have power to
take it up again.'

In this passage it is as evident, as words can make it, that
Christ ' laid down his life,' of his own accord only, and of
his own accord ·· took it up again ;' and that ' no one was
able to take it from him.'   Accordingly, St. Peter declares,
Acts ii. 24, that ' it was not possible for him to be holden of
death.'

Another most wonderful exhibition of this astonishing power
will be made by him, as he himself has told us, *in raising up
the dead at the last day.*   ' And this is the will of him that
sent me, that every one who seeth the Son, and believeth on
him, may have everlasting life : and I will raise him up at
the last day.' John vi. 40.   And again, verse 54. ' Whoso
eateth my flesh, and drinketh my blood, hath eternal life, and
I will raise him up at the last day.'   See also verse 39 and
44.——John v. 28. ' Marvel not at this ; for the hour is coming,
in the which all that are in the graves shall hear his voice, and
shall come forth ; they that have done good to the resurrection
of life, and they that have done evil to the resurrection of damnation.'

After Christ had ascended to heaven, the apostles, according to his promise, raised the dead by his power and authority ;
and thus proved the ubiquity of his power, as well as of his
presence.

As there can be no rational doubt concerning these passages, and no misconstruction of them, except by violence , I
do not suppose any explanation of them to be necessary.   They
carry their own meaning perfectly in themselves, and therefore
demand no comment.   The united language of them all is,

* See also Phil. iii. 21, and Col. iii. 4.

that Christ in himself perfectly possesses the power of giving life ; that in this world he exercised it on himself, and many others ; and that he will most wonderfully display the same power at the end of this earthly system, by raising to life the great congregation of the dead.

5. *The forgiveness of sin is expressly ascribed to Christ.* Thus in Exodus xxiii. 20, 21, already quoted for another purpose, it is said, ' Behold, I send an Angel before thee to keep thee in the way, and to bring thee into the place which I have prepared. Beware of him, and obey his voice ; provoke him not ; for he will not pardon your transgressions ; for my name is in him.' In this passage it is evident beyond a doubt, that the *Angel* who was sent before the Israelites, was possessed of the power and right to forgive sins. Otherwise God could not have thus cautioned the Israelites not to provoke him for this reason, since the reason would not have existed ; and would therefore have been alleged insincerely. But this cannot be attributed to God. 2 Corinthians ii. 10. ' For, if I forgave any thing, to whom I forgave it, for your sake forgave I it, in the person of Christ.' The apostle here declares to the Corinthians, that he forgave the offenders referred to in his former epistle, in the person of Christ, or standing as his representative ; but, if Christ could not himself forgive sins, the apostle might with equal propriety have said, that he forgave it in the person of any other : *the person* of Christ, here, being equivalent to the *name* and *authority* of Christ. But, if Christ had not the power to forgive sins, this authority would have been nothing. Colossians iii. 13. ' Forbearing one another, and forgiving one another, if any man have a quarrel against any, even as Christ forgave you.'

The import of this passage will be sufficiently understood, if it can need any explanation, by reciting the parallel passage, Eph. iv. 32. ' Forgiving one another, even as God, for Christ's sake, hath forgiven you.'

Acts vii. 59, 60. ' And they stoned Stephen, invocating, and saying, Lord Jesus, receive my spirit. And he kneeled down, and cried with a loud voice, Lord, lay not this sin to their charge.'

In this affecting passage, Stephen, full of the Holy Ghost, and vouchsafed a vision of the glory of God, and of Jesus standing on the right hand of God, prays to Christ to forgive the sin of his murderers. Words, one would think, cannot be more decisive.

Matthew ix. 2—7. 'And, behold, they brought to him a man sick of the palsy, lying on a bed ; and Jesus seeing their faith, said unto the sick of the palsy, Son, be of good cheer ; thy sins are forgiven thee. And, behold, certain of the scribes said within themselves, this man blasphemeth. And Jesus, knowing their thoughts, said, Wherefore think ye evil in your hearts? For whether is easier to say, Thy sins be forgiven thee ; or to say, Arise and walk? But that ye may know that the Son of Man hath power on earth to forgive sins (then saith he to the sick of the palsy,) Arise, take up thy bed, and go unto thine house. And he arose, and departed unto his house.

In this passage, Christ said to the sick of the palsy, ' Son, thy sins are forgiven thee.' Some of the scribes who were present accused him in their own hearts of blasphemy, and said, as Mark informs us, ' Who can forgive sin, but God only?' In this also they spoke the truth. Christ knew their thoughts, and asked them ; ' Wherefore think ye evil in your hearts ? For whether is easier to say, Thy sins be forgiven thee, or to say, Arise, and walk?' Both these acts belonging to God only, the latter is here, with supreme force, proposed as a test of the former. Christ, therefore, makes it such ; and tells the scribes, that he will prove to them his power to forgive sins by his power to raise up the sick of the palsy, with a command. Accordingly as a proof in form, that he possessed this power, he says to the sick of the palsy, ' Arise, and walk.' The sick man ' immediately arose, and departed to his house.'

Here the power of Christ to forgive sins was denied by the scribes, and expressly asserted by himself. Of this assertion he undertook the proof, on the spot ; and the proof proposed was a miracle. A miracle can be wrought by none but God ; and God cannot work a miracle to prove a falsehood. The miracle was wrought ; the assertion therefore was true.

6. The act of giving eternal life is abundantly ascribed to Christ in the Scriptures.

John x. 27, 28. ' My sheep hear my voice, and I know them, and they follow me ; and I give unto them eternal life ; and they shall never perish.'

Revelation xxi. 6. ' I am Alpha and Omega, the beginning and the end. I will give unto him that is athirst of the fountain of the water of life freely.'

Revelation ii. 7. ' To him that overcometh will I give to eat of the tree of life, which is in the midst of the paradise of God.' See also verses 17 and 28.

Revelation iii. 5. ' He that overcometh, the same shall be clothed in white raiment ; and I will not blot out his name out of the book of life.' See also verses 12 and 21.

These passages need no explanation.

7. *To Christ is ascribed the great and awful act of judging the world, and of acquitting and condemning angels and men.*

John v. 22. ' The Father judgeth no man, but hath committed all judgment unto the Son.' See also, what will preclude any further inquiry, the account of the last judgment, given by Christ himself, in the 25th chapter of Matthew.

All these are confessedly the acts of the infinite God alone ; and involve the absolute *possession of power and perfection without limits.* To create, preserve, and govern the universe ; to give and restore life ; to forgive sin ; to bestow eternal life ; to judge the world of angels and men, and to acquit, or condemn, finally and for ever, all intelligent beings ; is, if any thing is, *to be,* and *to act as being,* the true God ; the only infinite and eternal Jehovah.

In the great act of judging the world, particularly, the absolute exercise and the most wonderful display ever made of omniscience, as well as infinite justice, will be made. To judge righteously in this amazing case plainly requires the most exact and minute, as well as the most comprehensive and perfect, knowledge of all the thoughts, words, and actions of intelligent beings ; together with all the aggravations and palliations of guilt, and all the enhancements and diminutions of virtue, which have existed in the universe. Consequently, whatever circumstances have attended these innumerable beings must be perfectly known, and actually present at once to the view of such a judge. Nor must he be less perfectly acquainted with the precise kinds and distributions of punishment and reward which the respective works and characters of these numberless individuals, in their endlessly various circumstances, justly require.

To these things must be added, what Christ directly challenges to himself, the power of opening and shutting heaven and hell, or hades, at his pleasure, and of conferring the happiness of heaven and inflicting the miseries of hell on whom he pleases.

If, then, Christ be not God, the real God has so ordered things in his providence, that the peculiar displays of divine perfection, the greatest which will ever be made will be made by a creature, and not by himself. The creation, preservation, and government of the universe; the giving of life, and the restoration of it to the dead; the forgiveness of sin; the communication of endless life; and the final judgment of Intelligent beings; are the highest, the most peculiar, and the most perfect displays of the Godhead. Omnipotence and infinite wisdom are pre-eminently manifested in the formation and government of all things; infinite benevolence, in the forgiveness and salvation of sinners; and omniscience and infinite justice, in acquitting, and condemning, rewarding and punishing, the righteous and the wicked.

If then these, the most perfect displays of the Godhead, do not prove Christ to be the real and supreme God, let me ask, In what manner and by what arguments shall we prove that there is such a God? The existence and perfections of this glorious Being have hitherto been always evinced from the creation, preservation, and government of the Universe. But these, if the Scriptures are true, are the acts of Christ. If then, they prove the existence of God at all, they certainly prove Christ to be God. If they do not prove him whose acts they are to be God, they do not prove God to exist at all; for they cannot prove *him* to be God, whose acts they are not. To what proofs, then, of the being of God are we to recur, unless we admit these to be the proofs? and if we admit them, how can we deny or doubt the Deity of Christ?

Let me further ask each member of this assembly to apply this subject to his own case, and say, whether he is not ready fearlessly to commit his all to *him*, who has done, and will do, all these amazing things? who in the Scriptures is called God, and Jehovah; and to whom all the attributes of the infinite mind are ascribed? If he is not, let me ask him, To what being is he willing to trust this mighty deposit—himself—his soul—his all?

SERMON XXXVII.

DIVINITY OF CHRIST.

PROVED FROM DIVINE RELATIONS, SUSTAINED BY HIM; AND FROM DIVINE WORSHIP REQUIRED, AND RENDERED, TO HIM.

FOR WHAT THE LAW COULD NOT DO, IN THAT IT WAS WEAK THROUGH THE FLESH, GOD SENDING HIS OWN SON IN THE LIKENESS OF SINFUL FLESH, AND FOR SIN, CONDEMNED SIN IN THE FLESH : THAT THE RIGHTEOUSNESS OF THE LAW MIGHT BE FULFILLED IN US, WHO WALK NOT AFTER THE FLESH, BUT AFTER THE SPIRIT.

ROMANS VIII. 3, 4.

FOR GOD, SENDING HIS OWN SON IN THE LIKENESS OF SINFUL FLESH, AND OF A SIN-OFFERING, HATH CONDEMNED SIN IN THE FLESH (THE THING IMPOSSIBLE FOR THE LAW, BECAUSE IT WAS WEAK THROUGH THE FLESH :) THAT THE RIGHTEOUSNESS OF THE LAW MAY BE FULFILLED BY US, WHO WALK NOT ACCORDING TO THE FLESH, BUT ACCORDING TO THE SPIRIT.

DR. MACKNIGHT'S TRANSLATION.

HAVING shown, in the two preceding Discourses, that *Christ is spoken of in the Scriptures as the true and perfect God;* because, 1. *the names,* 2. *the attributes,* and, 3. *the actions of God are ascribed to him ;* I shall now proceed to consider the remaining particulars, proposed under this head : *viz.*

IV. *That the relations which God sustains to his creatures are in the Scriptures ascribed to Christ ;* and,

V. *That divine worship is in the Scriptures required to be rendered, and by persons inspired was actually rendered, to Christ.*

In examining *the relations, sustained by God to his creatures, and ascribed in the Scriptures to Christ,* so copious a field is opened for discussion, that it can only be partially surveyed at the present time.   I shall, therefore, confine my attention to the following particulars :—

1. *Christ sustains to the universe the relation of Creator.*

In the passages quoted in the preceding Discourse, to prove that the act of *creating* is ascribed to Christ in the Scriptures, it is asserted, that he is ' the Creator of the heavens and the earth ; of thrones, Dominions, principalities, and powers ; and of every individual thing which hath been made.'   In the relation of Creator he stands, therefore, to every being, great and small, in the heavens and in the earth.   Atoms were called into existence by his word ; Angels owe to him their exalted being.   This is a relation which no being but the infinite Jehovah can sustain ; and is plainly that on which all the other relations of God to his creatures depend.   Accordingly, God challenges this character to himself, as *his* character alone, sustained by himself only.   ' I,' saith he, ' am Jehovah, and none else ; forming light, and creating darkness ; making peace, and creating evil : I Jehovah am the author of all these things.'*   Whatever the Creator makes is in the most absolute sense his own ; and can in no sense belong to any other, unless by his gift.   Whatever connection, therefore, exists between God, as God, and creatures, as such, arises originally and entirely from the act of bringing them into being.   All the rights which the infinite mind claims and holds over the 'universe, and all the duties of intelligent creatures, spring originally from this source only.   It is *his* universe, because he made it.   They are *his* property, because by him they were created.   As their Creator, therefore, they look to him and him alone, to whom they are indebted for every thing, and to whom they owe every thing which they can do, because every thing in which they can be concerned depends upon their existence.   But for this, however excellent, great, and

* Isaiah xlv. 6, 7.   Lowth.

desirable he might be, and however deserving of their love and admiration, still they would not be *his.* This God himself teaches us in direct terms. ' Remember these things, O Jacob ; and Israel, for thou art my servant. I have formed thee ; thou art my servant. But now, saith the Lord, that created thee, O Jacob, and he that formed thee, O Israel, fear not, thou art mine.' Out of this act of giving existence arises, then, his property in all creatures ; and his right to give them laws, to controul their actions, to judge, reward, and punish them, and universally to dispose of them according to his pleasure ; together with all their corresponding duties. To Christ, then, belong all these rights. But who can possess these rights, or sustain the relation out of which they arise, beside the only living and true God ?

In sustaining this relation to the universe, Christ possesses also, of course, all the attributes necessary to it, and displayed in the work of creating ; particularly the power and wisdom manifested in the production of all things. This power and wisdom are plainly infinite.

I know it is said by Emlyn, and other Arians, that we do not see the infinity of these attributes displayed in creating the universe ; and that they may, for aught that appears to us, have existed in a sufficient degree for the production of all things, and yet not have been infinite.

On this subject I observe,

(1) *That of creating power in the abstract, or unexercised, we have no idea at all , and therefore cannot thus discern it to be infinite.*

(2) *We cannot comprehend infinity in any sense.* The mind which can comprehend infinity must itself be infinite. When we speak of infinite power, as evident in the creation of all things, we simply declare the fact, *that this power is infinite.* That infinity exists with respect to duration, expansion, or any thing else which is infinite, we may perceive distinctly, and yet are perfectly unable to comprehend eternity or immensity.

(3) *The power of creating, or giving existence, is evidently a subject to which limits can no more be assigned in our thoughts, than to duration, or space.* Plainly, he who gave existence to one atom, can give existence to atoms, and therefore to worlds, without number. He who gave intelli-

gence, who formed men, and angels, and archangels, can form all kinds and degrees of intelligence which can be formed, and can raise men, and angels, and other rational beings, to any height, to any perfection of intelligence which in the nature of things is possible.   To this power, therefore, no other bound can be set beside possibility.   He who formed all things cannot create contradictions.   This however is no circumscription of his power ; for if it could be done he could do it.   The only difference which would exist, would be in the nature of the things themselves, and not in the power of the Maker.

(4) *If creation and preservation be not a proof of infinite power, there is no proof that such power exists.*   Of this there needs no illustration but one, *viz.* that these are the only sources whence infinite power has been hitherto argued in the present world; for the argument *a priori*, I consider as of no value.

(5) *We plainly cannot see, that creating power is not infinite; nor can we furnish a single argument for the support of such a conclusion.*   The doctrine is, therefore, a mere gratuitous assumption, and merits as little consideration as any other such assumption.

(6) *Creating power is the source of all power that exists, except itself.   If, therefore, creating power is not infinite, there is no infinite power.*   Christ, therefore, as the Creator of all things, possessed originally all existing power, whether we allow it to be infinite or not.

(7) The Scriptures have determined this point, so far as the subject of this Sermon is concerned : for in Hebrews iii. 4. they say, ' Every house is builded by some one ; but he that built all things is God.'

It will easily be discerned, that the remarks made here concerning the *power* displayed in Creation, are with equal force applicable to the *wisdom* exhibited in that work.

2. *Christ sustains also the relation of Preserver.*

' By him all things consist,' Coll. i. 17.   ' Upholding all things by the word of his power.' Heb. i. 3.

That God is the only preserver of the universe, is unquestionably evident to the eye of reason, and has accordingly been acknowledged by all men who have acknowledged a God.   It is also, in the most definite manner, declared in the

Scriptures.   In Nehemiah ix. 6. the Levites, at the head of the congregation assembled for a solemn national fast, blessed God in these terms : ' Thou, even thou, art Jehovah alone ; thou hast made heaven, the heaven of heavens, with all their hosts ; the Earth, and all things that are therein ; the seas, and all that is therein ; and thou preservest them all : and the host of heaven worshippeth thee.   Thou art Jehovah, the God who didst choose Abram, and brought him forth out of Ur of the Chaldees, and gavest him the name of Abraham.'   In this passage it is declared in the most explicit terms, that he who preserves all things, is the Being worshipped by the host of heaven ; ' Jehovah alone ;' ' the Jehovah ;' ' the God ;' according to Parkhurst and Lowth, The Jehovah, the true, eternal, and unchangeable God ; the God who chose Abram, brought him forth out of Ur of the Chaldees, and gave him the name of Abraham.   In the subsequent verses we are farther informed that he is the ' God of Israel ; the great, mighty, and the terrible God ; gracious and merciful :' the Author of all the wonders in Egypt, the Red Sea, and the Wilderness, and of the dispensation of the law at Sinai ; the only object of prayer, supreme love, faith and obedience. Yet ' all things consist by Christ,' and ' he upholds them all by the word of his power.'   He, therefore, is this Jehovah ; this God.

The relation of universal Preserver is plainly a relation incapable of being sustained by any being but Jehovah.   It involves *a knowledge* of all beings, and all their circumstances ; a *power* present in every place, and to every being, at every moment ; sufficient in degree to hold in existence, to keep together, and to continue in order and harmony, the mighty frame of the universe ; to roll the innumerable worlds of which it is composed, unceasingly, through the expansion ; and to controul, with an irresistible sway, all their motions, affections, and inhabitants ; and a *wisdom* sufficient to contrive the proper employments and destinations of this endless multitude of beings, as well as the natures and attributes necessary for them, so as to accomplish those ends, and those only, which are worthy of the incomprehensible workman.   Of this power, knowledge, and wisdom, the Scriptures therefore assert Christ to be possessed, when they declare him to be the Preserver of of all things.   Our ideas of the power exerted in the preservation and also in the creation of the universe, they exceedingly enhance, by informing us, that both these amazing works are accomplished by his word. ' Upholding all things by the word of his power.' ' He spake, and it was done.' Of course, both are performed with perfect ease ; and he who does them ' fainteth not, neither is weary.'

In the character of the Preserver of the universe, all creatures owe to Christ the continuance of their blessings and their hopes. As we should have been nothing, had we not been created, so we should become nothing, were we not preserved. On this relation therefore, next after that of Creator, we depend for every thing, and to him who sustains it we owe every thing. Were it possible that he who sustains it should be any other than God, we should still, originally and continually, owe all things to him, and nothing to God. To such a monstrous absurdity does the opinion, that the Creator, and Preserver is any other than the true and perfect God, ultimately conduct, and, if they would be consistent with themselves, does in fact conduct those who deny Christ to be God.

As the Preserver of the righteous, Christ is appropriately called in the Scriptures by the emphatical name of *the shepherd.* ' I' saith he of himself ' am the good Shepherd. The good shepherd giveth his life for the sheep. I am the good Shepherd and know my sheep,' John x. 11, 14.——' Our Lord Jesus, that great Shepherd of the sheep,' Hebrews xiii. 20.—— ' And when the chief Shepherd shall appear, ye shall receive a crown of glory, which fadeth not away.' 1 Peter v. 4.—— ' There shall be one fold, and one shepherd.' John x. 16.—— ' Awake, O sword, against my Shepherd, against the Man that is my fellow,' &c. Zech. xiii. 7.——' Behold the Lord God will come with strong hand, and his arm shall rule for him : behold, his reward is with him, and his work before him. He shall feed his flock, like a shepherd ; he shall gather the lambs with his arm, and carry them in his bosom, and shall gently lead those that are with young,' Isaiah xl. 10, 11.—— Jehovah is my shepherd ; I shall not want. He maketh me to lie down in green pastures ; he leadeth me beside the still waters. He restoreth my soul ; he leadeth me in the paths of righteousness, for his name's sake.' Psalm xxiii. 1—3. In these passages we are informed, that Christ is ' th good Shepherd,' ' the great Shepherd' ' the chief Shepherd,' and the ' Shepherd of God, the Man that is the fellow,' or *compeer*, of Jehovah of Hosts. We are farther informed, that there is one Shepherd to the flock ; that he is the final Judge of the quick and the dead : that Jehovah is the ' Shepherd' of David, one of the righteous, and therefore, by irresistible consequence, of all the righteous ; that the Lord God will feed his flock ' like a shepherd, will gather the lambs with his arm, and carry them in his bosom.' If therefore Christ be not Jehovah, if he be not the Lord God, then there are *two* Shepherds instead of *one*, of whom Christ is still the ' chief' and the ' great Shepherd ;' and, although the Shepherd of David was Jehovah, yet Christ is the Shepherd of all other righteous persons. This character Christ recognizes, when he informs us that at the great day he will ' separate the sheep from the goats ;' and this character he will for ever sustain in the future world ; for there, we are taught, he will ' feed them, and lead them to living fountains of waters.'

3. *Christ sustains the character of the Possessor of all things.*

At his entrance into this world it is said, ' He came unto his own things, (τα 'ιδια ;) and his own men, or kindred (ὁι ιδιοι,) received him not ;' that is, he came into the world, but mankind, or the Jewish nation, received him not. John i. 11.—— ' All things,' saith Christ, ' which the Father hath, are mine,' or, *my things.* John xvi. 15.——Again, in his intercessory prayer, he says to the Father, ' All things that are mine, are thine, and the things which are thine, are mine.' John xvii. 10. It will be needless to add any farther passages to texts so perfectly explicit and unambiguous as these. It is proper however to remark, that the possession of all things is inseparably connected with the creation and preservation of all things. All things are necessarily the property and possession of Christ, because he made them, and because he upholds them in being, as saith the Psalmist, ' The earth is Jehovah's, and the fulness thereof, the world, and they that dwell therein ; for he hath founded it upon the seas, and established it upon the floods.'

But the possession of the universe involves in the Possessor, to say the least, *an absolute knowledge of every thing that is thus possessed.* No mind can possess any thing, to which its comprehension does not extend. *Entitled* to it, it may be ; in the *actual possession* of it it cannot be.   But no mind except the Omniscient can comprehend, or ever discern, more than a little part of the universe ; and therefore none but the Omniscient Mind can possess any more than this little part.

There is indeed a humbler and totally different sense, in which it may be figuratively said, and in which it is said in the Scriptures, that the *saints* shall inherit all things ; and in which all things are said to be theirs ; *viz.* ' that all things shall work together for good to them.'   In this manner all things cannot with propriety be said to belong to Christ ; because; being ' the same yesterday, to-day, and for ever,' his enjoyment is like himself, unchangeable ; and cannot in any sense be the result of the changes of which created things are the subjects. The happiness of created beings results only and necessarily from his government of all things for their benefit ; but his happiness existed before the things themselves, and can be dependent on nothing but his own mind.

Farther : The possession of all things involves, inseparably, the controul over them, in such a degree as to direct them immediately to the use and purposes of the possessor.   That which we cannot command for our own use, we do not in the proper sense possess.   But the power and the knowledge necessary to the possession of all things are in this view plainly infinite.

4.   *Christ sustains the relation of supreme Ruler to the universe.*

Revelation xix. 11, &c.   ' And I saw Heaven opened ; and behold a white horse, and he that sat on him was called Faithful and True, and his name is called the Word of God.   And he hath on his vesture and on his thigh a name written, King of kings and Lord of lords.'——Rev. xvii. 14.   ' These shall make war with the Lamb, and the Lamb shall overcome them ; for he is Lord of lords, and King of kings.'—— 1 Tim. vi. 15.   ' Which in his times the blessed and only potentate shall show, the King of kings, and Lord of lords.'——Acts x. 36.——' Jesus Christ : this person is Lord of all things.'—— Romans ix. 5.   ' Christ who is over all things, God blessed for ever, Amen.'——Philippians ii. 10, 11.   ' That at the name of Jesus every knee should bow, of things in heaven, and things in earth, and things under the earth : And that every tongue should confess that Jesus Christ is Lord, to the glory of God the Father.' In these passages Christ is directly exhibited as the Lord or Ruler of the universe, in the most absolute sense; the Lord of all things; whom things in heaven, and things in earth, are respectively required to confess as their Lord.

But the government of the universe requires, if any thing requires, the attributes of an infinite mind: goodness to prompt, justice to direct, knowledge to discern, and power to execute, whatever is right, wise and good to be done; and to prevent the existence of whatever is not. It demands also existence everywhere present and eternally enduring throughout the boundless and everlasting kingdom of God. Without these attributes Christ must be the Lord only in name, and rule only in pretence; and such must undoubtedly be the character attributed to him in these and the almost innumerable other passages of Scripture, in which he is styled Lord, and said to hold the dominion over all things, unless he is essentially possessed of these attributes. The Scriptures are not thus deficient in their own scheme; for, when they attribute universal dominion to Christ, they teach us that he is qualified for such dominion, by declaring, that ' in him dwells all the fulness of the Godhead.' We are not, therefore, left at a loss by the Scriptures themselves concerning his perfect qualifications for the exercise of this government; nor can we wonder that he who made and preserves should also govern all things.

In this relation Christ gave the law to the Israelites and to mankind at Mount Sinai; and in this character, as the rightful lawgiver, he directed his own Spirit to inspire the prophets and apostles with the knowledge of his word, as the universal law to mankind. ' But when the Comforter is come, whom I will send unto you from the Father, even the Spirit of truth, He will guide you into all the truth; for he shall not speak of himself; but whatsoever he shall hear, that shall he speak; and he will show you things to come. He shall glorify me: for he shall receive of mine, and shall show it unto you. All things which the Father hath are mine; therefore said I, that he shall take of mine, and show it unto you.' John xv. 26; xvi. 13—15.—' Of which salvation the prophets have inquired, searching what or what manner of time the Spirit

of Christ, which was in them, did signify.' Accordingly the
Scriptures are called *the word of Christ* ; ' Let the word of
Christ dwell in you richly, in all wisdom ;' and *the law of
Christ* ; ' Bear ye one another's burdens, and so fulfil the law
of Christ.' The law here referred to is no other than the
second command of the moral law, ' Thou shalt love thy
neighbour as thyself ;' or that branch of this command which,
respecting Christians peculiarly, is called *the new commandment* ; ' A new commandment give I unto you, that ye love
one another,' John xiii. 34.——In this character Christ, when
he began to preach, expounded, altered, and annulled the law
of Moses, in his own name, and at his own pleasure. All
the prophets who came before him introduced their messages
to mankind under the name and authority by which they
spoke ; prefacing them with ' Thus saith the Lord ;' ' Thus
saith Jehovah ;' and ' Thus saith Jehovah of Hosts.' Christ
on the contrary, when altering and annulling these very things,
uses no name but his own, and speaks directly by his own
authority, introducing his own laws with ' Verily, I say unto
you ;' plainly intended to be equivalent to ' Thus saith the
Lord ;' because the things which were prefaced with this
latter phrase, were openly altered and revoked by him.

In this character also he disposes of the present and future
allotments of all beings, opens and shuts at his pleasure the
world of death, and departed spirits ; consigns whom he
pleases to endless suffering, and bestows on whom he pleases
immortal life. In this character, he is ' the head of all principality and power,' Col. ii. 10.——' Who having gone into
heaven,' saith St. Peter, ' is on the right hand of God ; angels,
authorities, and powers being subjected to him.' In this relation it is obvious that all intelligent beings are bound to
render him their supreme and ultimate homage and obedience ; that the law is the rule of all their conduct, from obeying which nothing can excuse them ; the law by which they
will be tried, and approved or condemned ; that his word is
the only rule of life and salvation to mankind ; that his dominion is the supreme and universal controul, to which, in this
and every other world, intelligent beings are rightfully required to bow, to which every one of them in this and all other
worlds will ultimately bow, and by which all things are, and
will for ever be, regulated at his pleasure ; that he is the

Judge, who will finally acquit or condemn, reward or punish, every intelligent creature. I scarcely need to ask, who can sustain this stupendous relation to the universe, except Jehovah ?

5. *Christ is the last end of all things.*

Collossians i. 16. ' All things were created by him, and for him :' that is, they were all created for his use, that he might destine them to such purposes, and conduct them to such an issue, as were agreeable to his pleasure. In the same manner as it is said, Prov. xvi. 4. ' Jehovah hath made all things for himself.'

It will I suppose be granted, as I do not see how it can be questioned, that *the end* for which any thing exists, under the controul of divine wisdom, is more important than the thing itself ; or, universally, that *the end* is more important than *the means.* I suppose it will also be granted, that the end for which *all things* exist is the most important of all ends. I suppose it will farther be granted, that Jehovah, in making all things *for himself,* regarded himself, and in this design proved that he regarded himself, as more important than all things else ; and his glory or pleasure, for which they were created, as the most important of all the ends, discerned by his omniscience, and perfectly worthy to be preferred to every other. But this plainly could not be, unless he who thus proposed himself as the end of all things, was in the view of his omniscience a more excellent, great, and glorious being than any other. If there were any other being superior to himself, such being ought plainly to be preferred to him ; otherwise that which was of inferior importance and worth, would be preferred to that which was superior ; a preference obviously unfounded, and unjust. Jehovah therefore, in making all things for himself, hath testified in the most solemn and forcible manner possible, that himself is more important, great, and excellent than all other things whatever.

But *all things* are declared in the passage quoted from Collossians, to have been *created by Christ for himself.* Christ, therefore, in this act of making himself the end of the creation of all things, has declared that himself is, in his own view, the most important, great, and excellent of all things. This declaration is either true, or false. If false, it proceeded from ignorance or from sin. It could not be from sin ; for

' Christ knew no sin ;' and is declared to be ' without spot, or blemish :' ' the Holy One and the Just ;' even the ' Holy One of God.'   It could not be from ignorance ; because no intelligent creature who knew Jehovah at all, could possibly suppose himself to be more important, great, and excellent than Jehovah ; and because Christ will not be supposed, even by the Unitarians, to be capable of such ignorance.   It is therefore true.   But if it be true, it is by inevitable consequence also true, either that Christ is greater and more important than Jehovah, or that he is *Jehovah himself.*

Farther: As Christ is the end of all things, if he be not Jehovah, there is nothing of which Jehovah is the end.   As *all things* were made *for Christ* ; if Christ be not Jehovah, there is nothing which is made for Jehovah.   The united tendency and result of all that has been, is, or will be in the universe, is the accomplishment of the pleasure and glory of Christ ; and if Christ be not Jehovah, Jehovah will exist without any glory displayed, without any interest, or concern, in the universe.

It ought also to be added, that he who is the end of all things, for whose glory and pleasure they are to operate, must possess *power* sufficient to direct them to his glory, and *intelligence* to discern that this purpose is accomplished by them all.   When we consider the greatness and multitude of the things themselves, and their everlasting continuance and operation, it will I think be impossible not to conclude, that this power and intelligence must be, in the strictest sense, *unlimited.*

It is with reference to this very subject, as I apprehend, that our Saviour, in his intercessory prayer, utters to the Father these remarkable words:* ' All things which are mine, are thine ; and all things which are thine, are mine : and I am glorified in them,' John xvii. 10.   Here, in two forms of expression, he declares to the Father the co-extension of the property which the Father and the Son have in the universe, and their mutual possession of all things ; and then adds, that ' he is glorified in,' or by means of, ' them all.'   This may be properly styled Christ's own comment on the declaration of St. Paul, that ' all things were made for him ;' that is, for his

* See the original Greek.

use, his glory ; for here Christ declares his glory to be actually accomplished by them all.

This doctrine is plainly and utterly inconsistent with the Arian notion of Christ's being a *subordinate God ;* to whom divine power is supposed to have been delegated, and who in this character of a delegate is supposed to have created the universe, and to be worshipped. On this notion I propose to make some observations hereafter. At present I shall only remark, that he who is the first cause, or Creator, and the last end, of all things, is all that is or can be meant by the SUPREME GOD. All things being made for *his* use, and being the means of *his* glory, there is nothing left to a being higher and greater than himself ; nor does it appear that such being can have any material concern with the universe in any manner whatever.

I shall now consider the fifth, and last particular mentioned under this head : viz. *That divine worship is in the Scriptures required, and by persons inspired was actually rendered, to Christ.*

Divine worship is required to be rendered to Christ, **John v. 22, 23.** ' For the Father judgeth no man, but hath committed all judgment unto the Son : that all men should honour the Son, even as they honour the Father. He that honoureth not the Son honoureth not the Father that sent him.' In this passage of Scripture we are informed, that the infinite prerogative of judging the universe is committed by the Father to the Son for this, as at least one, if not the only great end, ' that all (that is, I apprehend, all intelligent creatures, the word *men* not being in the original) should honour the Son even as (that is, just in the same manner as, and in the same degree as) they honour the Father.' The final judgment, being an act which eminently displays the infinite perfections, is committed to the Son, that he may be perceived with indubitable evidence to possess these perfections, and may therefore receive that peculiar honour which is due to Him only by whom they are possessed. The honour which is due in a peculiar sense to God consists supremely in *religious worship ;* in making him the object of our *supreme affection ;* and rendering to him our *supreme obedience.* All this is here required to Christ in the same manner in which it is required to the Father.

Whether it be supposed that this passage be intended to include angels, or not, they are expressly required to worship him in Psalm xcvii. 7. ' Confounded be all they that serve graven images : worship him, all ye gods.'   St. Paul quotes a part of this verse in the following manner : ' And again, when he bringeth in the first begotten into the world, he saith, Let all the angels of God worship him.'   It is therefore certain, that all the angels of God are required to worship Christ.

The only possible debate which can arise here is concerning the kind of worship which is to be rendered.   On this I observe, first, that the Greek word is προσκυνησατωσαν, and that this word is used twenty-four times in the New Testament to denote the worship of the true God ; that it is used many times more to denote the religious worship of false gods ; and that it is, so far as I have observed, the only word used to denote what is intended by *worship*, when considered as an act *immediately performed*.   The words Θεραπευω, Λατρευω, and Σεβομαι, rendered also *to worship*, appear rather to express either habitual reverence or service, or a general course of worship, considered as a character or course of life.   Προσκυνεω, so far as I have been able to observe, is the only term used to denote religious worship by St. John ; and is certainly the appropriate word for this idea, if there is any such appropriate word in the New Testament.   It is particularly the word used by Christ in his answer to Satan ; ' Thou shalt *worship* the Lord thy God :' and in his discourse with the woman of Samaria concerning the place where, the manner in which, and the persons by whom, God is acceptably worshipped.

Secondly : That religious worship is here intended is certain, because the *Object* of the worship commanded, is *directly opposed*, in the command itself, *to idols* ; and the worship *required* to that which is *forbidden*.   ' Confounded be all they that serve,' that is, religiously worship, ' graven images ; that boast themselves of idols.'   As if God had said, Worship no more graven images, nor idols of any kind ; for all their worshippers shall be confounded : Worship *him*, the Messiah, the Son of God ; and not only you, the sottish men who are guilty of this idolatry, but all ye angels also, to whom this worship is often sottishly rendered.

In the same manner is worship commanded to both men

and angels. Phil. iii. 9—11. ' Wherefore God also hath highly exalted him, and given him a name which is above every name ; that at the name of Jesus every knee should bow, of things in heaven and things in earth, and things under the earth ; and that every tongue should confess that Jesus Christ is Lord, to the glory of God the Father.' In this passage, all things celestial, terrestrial, and subterranean (as it is in the original,) are required to bow the knee to Christ, and to confess him to be Lord. To *bow the knee* is well known appropriate pharasology to denote religious worship. ' I have left me,' says God to Elijah ' seven thousand in Israel, all the knees, that have not bowed unto Baal, and every mouth which hath not kissed him,' 1 Kings xix. 18.* St Paul also says, ' I bow my knees to the Father of all mercies.' But to place it beyond all doubt, we need only refer to Isaiah xlv. 22, 23. whence this passage is quoted : ' Look unto me, and be ye saved, all ye ends of the earth : for I am God, and there is none else. By myself have I sworn, and the truth is gone out of my mouth ; the word, and it shall not be revoked. Surely to me shall *every knee bow*, shall *every tongue swear :* saying, Only to Jehovah belongeth salvation and ·power'†. To ascribe to Jehovah salvation and power (the thing which, the Apostle informs us, is the same with confessing that Christ is Lord), and to bow the knee when making this ascription is undoubtedly religious worship, if any thing is. Accordingly, this ascription is often made by the saints in the Scriptures, and the saints and angels in heaven.

In accordance with these requisitions, we find Christ actually worshipped in great numbers of instances. I shall omit here the numerous instances in which we are directly told that persons worshipped Christ, while here in the world, merely because they would give birth to a critical controversy too minute and too extended for the present occasion. The instances about which such a controversy cannot at least decently arise are sufficiently numerous for my design.

1. In Genesis xviii. we are told that ' Jehovah appeared unto Abraham in the plains of Mamre, as he sat in the door of his tent.' The manner of his appearance was the following. ' As he lifted up his eyes and looked, lo, three

* See Hosea xiii. 2 ; and Psalm ii. 2   † Lowth.

men stood by him, and he ran to meet them, and bowed himself toward the ground.' To one of them he said, ' My Lord, if I have now found favour in thy sight, pass not away, I pray thee, from thy servant,' &c. The person here spoken to is called by Abraham, אדני. This person in the 13th verse is called Jehovah; and in the 14th says, ' Is any thing too hard for Jehovah?' and informs Abraham of the destruction of the cities of the plain, which he had determined to bring upon them for their sins. To this person Abraham *prays* repeatedly for the preservation of these cities. Lot also, to whom he appeared in the following chapter, *prayed to him* for his own preservation, and that of the city Zoar, and was accepted. These persons are in the first place called ' three *men*.' One of them, whom Abraham calls Adonai, or Lord, is afterwards called by himself, by Abraham, and by Moses, Jehovah; and was worshipped by both Abraham and Lot. The other two are afterwards repeatedly called *angels*. Now it will not be pretended that God the Father appeared as a man, or that he ate of the provision furnished by Abraham; for ' no one hath seen God ' the Father, ' at any time.' Yet this person is here styled Jehovah, and was worshipped; and this person was Christ.

2. In Judges xiii. the Angel-Jehovah appeared to Manoah and his wife. When he departed, it is said, that ' Manoah knew that he was the Angel-Jehovah :' and it is added, ' Manoah said unto his wife, We shall surely die, because we have seen God. But his wife said unto him, If Jehovah were pleased to kill us, he would not have received a burnt-offering and a meat-offering at our hands.' In verse 16, the Angel had said to Manoah, ' If thou wilt offer a burnt-offering, thou must offer it unto Jehovah ; for,' it is subjoined, ' Manoah knew not that he was the Angel-Jehovah.' But after he had ascended in the flame of the altar, ' then,' it is declared, ' Manoah knew that he was the Angel-Jehovah.' The burnt-offering and the meat-offering Manoah and his wife then perceived themselves to have offered unwittingly to him who had manifested to them his acceptance of both at their hands.

Here the worship was not only presented to Christ, but, what is of much more importance to my purpose, was accepted by him.

3. *David worships Christ in* Psalms xlv. and lxxii. and cii. *in ascribing to him the praise which is due to God only.* In the two first he declares, that ' the people shall praise him, and fear him, and fall down before him, and serve him for ever and ever.' In the last he makes to him a long continued prayer.

4. In Isaiah vi. the seraphim worshipped him, saying, ' Holy, holy, holy, is Jehovah of Hosts.'

5. Stephen, in Acts vii. 59, 60. prayed to Christ. · And they stoned Stephen, calling upon God ;' or as in the original, ' they stoned Stephen invoking, and saying, Lord Jesus, receive my spirit. And he kneeled down, and cried with a loud voice, Lord, lay not this sin to their charge ; and, having said this, he fell asleep.'

On this prayer of St. Stephen I make the following remarks :—

(1.) Stephen at this time was ' full of the Holy Ghost,' (verse 55.) and therefore perfectly secured from error.

(2.) He was singularly favoured of God on account of the greatness of his faith and obedience ; and, as a peculiar testimony of the divine favour, he was permitted to ' see the heavens opened, and to behold the glory of God, and Jesus standing on the right hand of God.'

(3.) In the full assurance produced by this vision, and the faith with which he beheld it, he presented his final petitions to Christ.

(4.) The first of these petitions respected the highest personal object which can be prayed for, viz. the eternal salvation of his soul ; and attributed to *him* to whom it was made that infinite power, wisdom, and goodness which alone can bestow salvation.

(5.) The second petition was of the same nature, being a prayer, that his enemies might not be finally condemned for the sin of murdering him ; and of course attributed to the person, to whom it was addressed the power of forgiving or condemning these murderers. No higher act of worship was ever rendered than this, nor was any act of worship ever performed on a more solemn occasion, nor by a person better qualified to worship aright, nor with a more illustrious testimony of acceptance. Yet this act of worship was performed to Christ.

(6.) This was the very worship, and these were the very prayers offered to God, a little before, by Christ at his crucifixion. Stephen, therefore, worshipped Christ just as Christ worshipped the Father.

6. *St. Paul often prayed to Christ directly.** Particularly 1 Thess. iii. 11, 12. ' Now God' himself, ' even our Father, and our Lord Jesus Christ, direct our way unto you. And the Lord make you to increase and abound in love one toward another, and toward all men, even as we do toward you.' Here a prayer is offered up by St. Paul, that he may be guided to the Thessalonians; and that they may be made to increase and abound in holiness, and established unto the end. This prayer is offered up to God the Father and to our Lord Jesus Christ, in the same manner and the same terms; both being unitedly addressed in the same petition, without any note of distinction. The second of these petitions is also offered up to Christ alone. The same petition in substance is presented to the Father and Son united, in the same manner: 2 Thess. ii. 16, 17. In the third chapter, verse 5, Paul prays, ' Now may the Lord direct your hearts to the love of God, and to the patience of Christ:' and verse 16, ' Now the Lord of peace himself give you peace by all means. The Lord be with you all.' Again, 2 Cor. xii. 8, ' Concerning this,' that is, the messenger of Satan to buffet him, St. Paul says, ' thrice I besought the Lord, that it might depart from me. But he said unto me, My grace is sufficient for thee: for my power is made perfect in weakness. Most gladly, therefore, will I rather glory in mine infirmities, that the power of Christ may rest upon me.' In this passage St. Paul informs us that he thrice prayed to Christ respecting the particular subject mentioned.

7. St. Paul, in all his epistles except that to the Hebrews, and St. John, in his second epistle, pray to Christ, in that noted request, in which also Silas, Timothy, and Sosthenes united, that ' Grace, mercy, and peace might be multiplied,' or communicated, to those to whom they wrote, ' from God our Father, and from our Lord Jesus Christ.' This is an express prayer to the Father and the Son united, to grant grace, mercy, and peace to men. These are the highest of all

---

* See Bishop Burnet on the Articles, p. 48.

blessings, and such as none but Jehovah can grant. Yet Christ can grant them, because the Spirit of inspiration directed that he should be prayed to for them.

8. *The baptismal service, directed by Christ himself, is an act of religious worship to Christ.*

' Baptizing them in the name of the Father, of the Son, and of the Holy Ghost.' Whether this be interpreted to mean, Baptizing them *into* the name, or *in* the name, it makes no difference. If Christians are baptized *into* the name, they are baptized into the name of God only; for they are the children of God only by adoption; that adoption by which they take his name upon them; and Christ is here declared to be the God whose name they assume. If they are baptized *in* the name, they are baptized in the name, or authority, of God only: but Christ is this God.

9. *The blessing pronounced on Christian assemblies, is an act of religious worship, rendered to Christ.*

' The grace of the Lord Jesus Christ, and the love of God, and the communion of the Holy Ghost, be with you all. Amen.' ' Peace be to the brethren, and love with faith from God the Father, and the Lord Jesus Christ, Eph. vi. 23. Or, as it was more commonly, ' The grace of our Lord Jesus Christ be with you all. Amen.' The first of these is equivalent to the blessing anciently pronounced by the high priest on the children of Israel. ' Jehovah bless thee, and keep thee: Jehovah make his face to shine upon thee, and be gracious to thee: Jehovah lift up his countenance upon thee, and give thee peace.' It is the appropriate office of the Father to bless and preserve, of the Son to give grace and illumination; and of the Spirit to communicate peace.

Finally: So universal was the custom of praying to Christ, that Christians were originally entitled, as their distinguishing appellation, " Those who called on the name of Christ." Thus Ananias says to Christ, Acts ix. 14. ' And he hath authority from the chief priests to bind all those that call on thy name.' The people of Damascus also, when they heard Paul preach, ' were amazed, and said, Is not this he, who destroyed them that called on this name in Jerusalem?' 1 Cor i. 1. ' Paul called to be an apostle of Jesus Christ, and Sosthenes the brother, unto the Church of God which is at Corinth, called to be saints, with all that in every place call

upon the name of Jesus Christ our Lord.'   2. Tim. ii. 22.
' Follow righteousness, faith, charity, peace with them that
call on the Lord out of a pure heart.'   Romans x. 12.
' The same Lord over all is rich unto all that call upon
him.'   That Christ is here meant is evident from the preceding
verse.

In all these instances, and in this universal manner, was
Christ worshipped.   In the greater part of the instances, the
persons who rendered the worship were inspired, and in the
remaining instances were plainly under divine direction, because the worship was approved and accepted.

But religious worship is lawfully rendered to God only.
This we know from the mouth of Christ himself, quoting Deuteronomy x. 20. in Matthew x. 12. ' It is written, thou shalt
worship the Lord thy God, and him only shalt thou serve.'
The angel also forbade John to worship him, saying, ' See thou
do it not ; worship God.'   Isaiah also commands, ' Sanctify
the Lord of Hosts himself: and let him be your fear and
your dread.'   God, also, in Exodus xxxiv. 14. says to the Israelites, ' Thou shalt worship no other God :   for Jehovah,
whose name is Jealous, is a jealous God.'

Yet Christ is here directed to be worshipped, and is actually worshipped, by persons inspired.   If then Christ be not
God, God has commanded another to be worshipped ; and
persons under the immediate direction of his Spirit have worshipped another.

The whole church, the bride, is commanded, in Psalm xlv.
by that God who said unto him, ' Thy Throne, O God, is for
ever and ever,' thus : ' Hearken, O daughter, and consider,
and incline thine ear ; so shall the King greatly desire thy
beauty ; for he is thy Lord, and worship thou him.'   The
church has in all ages obeyed this command, and worshipped
him ; prophets have worshipped him ; apostles have worshipped
him : men, full of faith and of the Holy Ghost, have besought
his guidance, aid, grace, and blessing while they lived, and
when they died have besought him to receive their spirits into
his own eternal kingdom.   If Christ is God, if he is Jehovah,
they have done their duty.   If he is not God, if he is not
Jehovah, they have violated through life and in death the first
of Jehovah's commands in the decalogue ; ' Thou shalt have
no other God before me.'

SERMON XXXVIII.

DIVINITY OF CHRIST.

PROOFS.

THIS THE ONLY GROUND OF CONSISTENCY IN THE SCHEME OF RE-
DEMPTION.
THE JEWS OTHERWISE NOT CHARGEABLE WITH GUILT IN CRUCIFY-
ING CHRIST.
THE APOSTLES OTHERWISE CHARGEABLE WITH LEADING MANKIND
INTO IDOLATRY.

FOR WHAT THE LAW COULD NOT DO, IN THAT IT WAS WEAK
THROUGH THE FLESH, GOD, SENDING HIS OWN SON IN THE LIKE-
NESS OF SINFUL FLESH, AND FOR SIN, CONDEMNED SIN IN THE
FLESH: THAT THE RIGHTEOUSNESS OF THE LAW MIGHT BE FUL-
FILLED IN US, WHO WALK NOT AFTER THE FLESH, BUT AFTER
THE SPIRIT.

ROMANS VIII. 3, 4.

FOR GOD, SENDING HIS OWN SON IN THE LIKENESS OF SINFUL
FLESH, AND OF A SIN-OFFERING, HATH CONDEMNED SIN IN THE
FLESH (THE THING IMPOSSIBLE FOR THE LAW, BECAUSE IT WAS
WEAK THROUGH THE FLESH:) THAT THE RIGHTEOUSNESS OF THE
LAW MAY BE FULFILLED BY US, WHO WALK NOT ACCORDING TO
THE FLESH, BUT ACCORDING TO THE SPIRIT.

DR. MACKNIGHT'S TRANSLATION.

ACCORDING to the plan originally proposed from these words,
I have, in the three preceding Discourses, considered at
length, the proofs of the Deity of Christ, arranged under the
first general head: viz. *That Christ is spoken of in the Scriptures as the true and perfect God.*

I shall now proceed to consider the three following heads of Discourse, originally proposed; *viz.*

II. *That the Deity of Christ is the only ground of consistency in the scheme of redemption.*

III. *That the Jews, according to the opposite doctrine, are unjustly charged with guilt in putting Christ to death.*

IV. *That the prophets and apostles, according to the same doctrine, cannot be vindicated from the sin of leading mankind into idolatry.*

The last argument then proposed, I shall omit to examine, until I have considered the Divinity of the Holy Spirit; and shall now proceed to the consideration of the

II. *That the Deity of Christ is the only ground of consistency in the scheme of redemption.*

The truth of this assertion I shall attempt to evince by showing, that the Deity of Christ is the only ground of consistency in the things spoken of him, as the *light of the world ;* the *Saviour of the world ;* and, the *propitiation for sin.*

1. *As the light of the world.*

Christ is exhibited in the Scriptures *as the light of the world,* in two respects :

(1.) *As revealing the will of God to mankind ; and,*

(2.) *As communicating spiritual or divine light to the soul.*

In both respects the things said of Christ in the Scriptures, as ' the Light of the world,' are consistent only on the supposition that Christ is the true God. That the Scriptures are the word of Jehovah will not be questioned by any man who believes in a Revelation, since they are called by this title, and by others equivalent to it, in hundreds of instances, from Genesis to the Revelation of St. John. But the Scriptures are expressly declared to be the word of Christ : ' Let the word of Christ dwell in you richly in all wisdom, teaching and admonishing one another in psalms, and hymns, and spiritual songs.' In this passage the Old Testament is in so many terms declared to be the word of Christ. The Gospel, every man knows, is appropriately entitled *The Gospel of Christ.*

St. Mark prefaces his account of the Gospel with these words : ' The beginning of the Gospel of Jesus Christ the Son of God.'

St. Paul informs us, that he received the Gospel immediately by revelation from Christ; and accordingly he everywhere styles it the Gospel of Christ. The greatness of the authority which it derived from this source he teaches us in the strongest manner, when he says, 'Though we, or an angel from Heaven, or any one whatever, preach another Gospel, let him be accursed,' Galatians i. 8, 9. This Gospel, he also says, is 'Christ the power and wisdom of God unto salvation.'

St. Peter teaches the same truth, in a manner equally forcible, when he says, 'Of which salvation the prophets have inquired, searching what and what manner of time the Spirit of Christ which was in them did signify.' Here the Spirit which inspired the prophets, is styled 'the Spirit of Christ;' and this Spirit, the same Apostle says, is 'the Holy Ghost.' 'For prophecy,' saith he, 'came not in old time by the will of man;' 'but holy men of God spake as they were moved by the Holy Ghost.' The Old Testament, therefore, *was revealed to the prophets by the Spirit of Christ.*

Concerning the New, Christ himself teaches us the same doctrine, in the same decisive manner. 'Howbeit, when he, the Spirit of truth, is come; he will guide you into all truth; —for he shall not speak of himself; but whatsoever he shall hear, that shall he speak. He shall glorify me; for he shall receive of mine, and shall show it unto you. He shall teach you all things, and shall bring all things to your remembrance, whatsoever I have said unto you.'

All things, therefore, which Christ had said to the apostles, the Spirit of Truth brought to their remembrance. He taught them all things, and guided them into all the Truth. Yet he spake not of himself, but that which he heard, which he received from Christ, and that only, he declared unto them. The Gospel therefore is originally and only derived from Christ. Yet it is repeatedly styled by St. Paul, 'the Gospel of God.'

This Character of the revealer of the will of God, St. John declares repeatedly in the introduction of his Gospel. After having declared, that 'the Word was in the beginning,' or eternal; 'was God;' and 'was co-eternal with God;' and that 'all things were made by him;' he goes on to say, 'In him was life, and the life was the light of men. And the light shineth in darkness; and the darkness comprehended it not.' He then informs us that John the Baptist 'came to bear witness of the light:' that ' he was not that light: but was sent to bear witness of that light:' Then he adds, 'That was the true light, which lighteth every man that cometh into the world.' To all this he adds farther the testimony of John the Baptist, the very witness which he bore concerning Christ as the light. ' No one,' said this harbinger of the Redeemer, who was sent for the very purpose of declaring his true character, ' No one hath seen God at any time ; the only begotten Son of God, who is in the bosom of the Father, he hath declared him.' To declare the character and designs of God is plainly impossible, unless for him who knows these things intuitively, or for him to whom God is pleased to make them known. But no other person beside the Son and the Spirit knows the things of God intuitively. This we know certainly without inspiration; but the Scriptures have determined the point, if it were otherwise uncertain. ' No one,' saith our Saviour, ' knoweth the Father but the Son, and he to whomsoever the Son will reveal him.' ' The things of God,' saith St. Paul, knoweth no one, but the Spirit of God: and the Spirit searcheth all things, even the deep things of God.' From all these passages it is, I apprehend, certain, that Christ is the sole author of Revelation ; and that the Spirit has not, as the Spirit of inspiration, spoken of himself, but has received from Christ his mind, or pleasure, and declared it to the men whom he inspired. Accordingly, St. Paul says, speaking of his own inspiration, and that of the other Apostles, ' We have the mind of Christ.' It is therefore true to this day, that ' no one knoweth the Father but the Son, and those to whom the Son hath revealed him.' This knowledge thus revealed, was not revealed to Christ, but was possessed by him, because he dwells in the bosom of the Father, and has dwelt there from eternity, ' being daily his delight, and rejoicing alway before him.'

Should it be objected, that *mankind know something of God by their reason, independently of Revelation, and therefore possess a knowledge of God which is not derived from Christ :* I answer, that with some qualifications I admit the premises, but deny the consequence. The very reason of man was formed by Christ, as was man himself; as were also all those materials from which reason derives whatever knowledge of this nature it possesses. It has, I trust, been proved beyond reasonable debate, that Christ created, preserves, and governs all things, and therefore is the author of those works of creation and providence whence reason obtains all its knowledge of this subject. Of course in this sense also, Christ is ' the light that lighteth every man that cometh into the world.' Thus all the knowledge which exists of God is derived from Christ; and since he is ' the same yesterday, to-day, and for ever;' and ' dwells in the bosom of the Father:' this knowledge was his originally, intuitively, and eternally. I need not say, that these things cannot be true of any mind but the omniscient.

(2.) *Christ is the author of spiritual light to mankind.*

The communication of spiritual light is spoken of in the Scriptures as a work peculiar to God. 2 Cor. iv. 6. ' For God, who commanded the light to shine out of darkness, hath shined into our hearts, to give us the light of the knowledge of the glory of God in the face (or person) of Jesus Christ.' John vi. 45. ' And they shall all be taught of God.' And thus in many other places. But this office is also ascribed to Christ. Simeon says, Luke ii. 30. ' For mine eyes have seen thy salvation, which thou hast prepared before the face of all people : A light to lighten the Gentiles, and the glory of thy people Israel.' ' In him,' says St. John, ' was life, and the life was the light of men.' ' I,' said our Saviour, John viii. 12. ' am the light of the world ; he that followeth me shall not walk in darkness, but shall have the light of life.' Isaiah xlix. 6. quoted Acts xiii. 47. ' I will also give thee for a light to the Gentiles, that thou mayest be my salvation to the ends of the earth.' In all these passages it is manifest that spiritual or divine light is the light spoken of, and that it resides in Christ, as its source, and is by him communicated to mankind. All this also is completely expressed by the prophet Malachi in a word ; when he calls Christ ' the sun of righteousness ;' the orb, in which righteousness is originally inherent ; in which it dwells, and from which it emanates to mankind. In the same manner it is said by David, ' the Lord God is a sun.'

2. *The things spoken of Christ as the Saviour of the world, are consistent only on the supposition that he is the true God.*

Psalm lx. 16. ' I Jehovah am thy Saviour.' Hosea xiii. 4. ' I am Jehovah thy God; thou shalt know no God but me; for there is no Saviour beside me.' Isaiah xliii. 11. ' I even I am Jehovah; and beside me there is no Saviour;' and thus in various other places in the Old Testament.

The same thing is often declared in the New Testament. 1 Tim. i. 1. ' The commandment of God our Saviour:' and Titus ii. 10. ' adorn the doctrine of God our Saviour.'

Yet in the same absolute sense Christ is declared to be the Saviour of mankind. ' Who is this,' saith the prophet Isaiah, ' that cometh from Edom, with dyed garments from Bozrah; this, that is glorious in his apparel, travelling in the greatness of his strength? I,' saith Christ ' that speak in righteousness; mighty to save.' John iv. 42. ' this is the Christ, the Saviour of the world.' Acts iv. 12. St. Peter, speaking of Christ, saith, ' Neither is there salvation in,' or by means of, ' any other; for there is no other name under heaven given among men, whereby we must be saved.' And thus in very many other places. The importance of the work of saving mankind, and the glory derived from it to the divine character, are strongly exhibited by God in Isaiah lxv. 17 18. ' For behold I create new heavens and a new earth: and the former shall not be remembered nor come into mind; But be ye glad and rejoice for ever in that which I create; for Behold, I create Jerusalem a rejoicing, and her people a joy.' In this passage it is evident, that the new creation is, in the view of God, so much more glorious than the original one, that, compared with it, the original creation shall not be remembered. But the new creation is no other than ' creating Jerusalem a rejoicing, and her people a joy;' that is, renovating the souls of mankind, and thus making them holy, lovely, a rejoicing, or foundation of joy, in the sight of God. This work then is, in the sight of God, a far more glorious work than the formation of the heavens and the earth. Such also it is in the eye of reason. One mind is of more importance than any number of worlds, inanimate and unconscious. The renovation of one mind to righteousness, and its reinstatement in the divine favour, is the production of eternal and by us incomprehensible worth and enjoyment in that mind. This work repeated in ' a multitude' of minds ' which no man can number,' is the work which is styled the new creation. How immensely more glorious a work than the production of ever so many masses of lifeless matter!

When we consider the nature of this work, and the things involved in it, we cannot hesitate to admit the peculiar import-ance attached to it in the Scriptures. In this work are in-volved, the creation of a new heart in man ;——the communica-tion of divine knowledge ;——the adoption of man into the divine family ;——a perpetual presence with the souls of all who are created anew ;——a continual communication of strength, patience, fortitude, peace, consolation, and hope ; the preser-vation of the soul from the fatal influence of temptations, lust, and all other spiritual enemies ; the final justification of the soul at the judgment, and its establishment in the possession of immortal life ; together with, what will be the subject of the next head of discourse, the accomplishment of such a *propi-tiation*, as may be the proper source of all these wonderful consequences. He who admits these things to be included in the work of saving man, must admit also that there can be no Saviour beside Jehovah.

Should it be said, that all these things, except the last, are the work of the Holy Spirit, and that therefore they are here erroneously attributed to Christ; I answer, that they are in-deed the work of the Holy Spirit ; but, notwithstanding this they are truly attributed to Christ, not only as he laid the foun-dation for them all, but as the Spirit acts not of himself, and only executes the pleasure of Christ under *his* com-mission.

This work, then, of saving man is in the Scriptures attribut-ed to Christ in a manner so peculiar, that from it he derives his own appropriate name, Jesus Christ, the Anointed Savi-our ; and is considered by Jehovah as being so much greater and more glorious than the work of creating the Heavens and the Earth, that in comparison with it, that work ' shall not be remembered, nor come into mind.

3. *As the propitiation for sin, the Deity of Christ is the only ground of consistency in the scriptural exhibi-tions.*

As I expect hereafter to discuss *Christ's atonement for sin*, as one of the great parts of the Christian system, I shall here omit every thing concerning this subject which is not necessary to the doctrine just now declared.

That Christ is in some sense ' a propitiation for the sins of the world, ' cannot be denied, unless by a direct denial of the express words as well as the unquestionable doctrines of the Gospel. 1 John ii. 2. ' And he is the propitiation for our sins : and not for ours only, but for the sins of the whole world.' 1 John iv. 10. ' He loved us, and sent his Son to be the propitiation for our sins.' See also Romans iii. 25. ; Isaiah liii. 10, &c. The text also is a direct declaration of this doctrine. ' God sending his own Son in the likeness of sinful flesh, and of a sin-offering, or an offering for sin,' &c.

By Christ being a propitiation for sin, it is here necessary to mean only *that something, which being done for the sinner, the sinner may be forgiven and restored; but which not being done, he must be punished according to the sentence of the law by which he is condemned.* That so much as is here specified is included in Christ's being the propitiation for the sins of mankind, is unquestionably evident.

(1.) From the name by which it is called in the Scriptures in many instances, *viz.* απολυτρωσις, translated *redemption.* When a person was taken captive in war, and condemned to perpetual slavery or to death, a sum of money was not unfrequently paid and accepted for his ransom from these evils ; this sum was called λυτρον ; and the redemption of the captive from death or slavery, was called απολυτρωσις. The redemption of mankind from the slavery of sin, and the everlasting death to which the sinner was exposed by it, is called by the same name. The λυτρον, or *price of redemption,* was paid, not by the captive, but by another person. The price of man's redemption, in like manner, was not paid by himself, but by Christ ; that is, Christ accomplished something, without which man would not have been redeemed from the bondage of death and sin.

(2.) This truth is evident from Isaiah liii. 10. ' Yet it pleased Jehovah to crush him with affliction. If his soul shall make a propitiatory sacrifice, he shall see a seed which shall prolong their days ; and the gracious purpose of Jehovah shall prosper in his hands. Of the travail of his soul he shall see (the fruit) and be satisfied : by the knowledge of him shall my righteous servant justify many ; for the punishment of their iniquities he shall bear. Therefore I will distribute to him the many for his portion ; and the mighty people shall he share for his spoil : because he poured out his soul unto death ;

was numbered with the transgressors ; and he bare the sin of many ; and made intercession for the transgressors.' *

In this passage it is clear, that in the covenant of redemption, here recited, Jehovah promised to Christ, ' the seed which should prolong their days,' or be eternally blessed, a promise here repeated in many forms, on the condition that ' he made his soul a propitiatory sacrifice for sin.' It is therefore certain that if he had not made this sacrifice, he would not have received this reward ; or, in other words, mankind would not have been saved.

(3.) The same truth is evident from Romans iii. 25, 26.—— ' Christ Jesus ; whom God hath set forth to be a propitiation for sin, to declare his righteousness in the remission of sins that are past ; that he might be just, and yet the justifier of him that believeth in Jesus.'

From this passage it is evident, that if God had not set forth Christ as a propitiation, his righteousness in the remission of sins that are past would not have been declared ; and that he would not have been just in the act of justifying believers. In other words, if Christ had not become a propitiation, the sins of mankind could not have been remitted, nor themselves justified.

In a former Discourse it has, I trust, been proved that, in the literal sense, ' by works of law no flesh can be justified before God ;' and that the future obedience and the repentance of the sinner are alike and wholly unavailing to this end. Independently of Christ's redemption, therefore, or independently of his being ' the propitiation for the sins' of men, every sinner is condemned, lost, and without hope. The Scriptures in multiplied instances teach us that Christ became a propitiation for sin especially by his death. Isaiah liii. 5. ' He was wounded for our transgressions ; he was bruised for our iniquities ; the chastisement of our peace was upon him.' Romans v. 6. In due time Christ died for the ungodly.' 1 Cor. xv. 3. ' Christ died for our sins, according to the Scriptures.' 2 Cor. v. 14. ' One died for all.' 1 Thess. v. 10. ' Who died for us, that we should live with him.' Col. i. 20. ' Having made peace through the blood of his cross.' 1 John i. 7. ' The blood of Christ cleanseth from all sin.' 1 Peter i. 18, 19.

* Lowth.

' Ye were not redeemed with corruptible things, but with the precious blood of Christ.'   Rev. v. 9.   ' Thou hast redeemed us to God by thy blood.'   More proofs of this point cannot be necessary.   Let me now ask, if Christ be not in the strictest sense God, how is it possible that he should become in this or any other manner, *a propitiation for the sins of mankind?* If Christ be merely a man, or in any other sense a mere creature, how is it possible that he should be able to perform any act which would not be absolutely necessary for his own justification before God?   The law, by which every creature is governed, requires him to ' love God with all the heart, soul, strength, and understanding ;' or in other words, to consecrate all his powers supremely and absolutely, so long as he exists, to the service of God.   More than this he cannot do ; and if all this be not done he is a sinner, and cannot be justified. How then can it be possible for him to perform any thing which can be accepted on the behalf of another?   It is impossible that any service should be accepted for another which is entirely due for one's self.   It is impossible that the debt due from another should be cancelled by my payment of money due for a debt of my own.   When I have paid my own debts, if I can offer more money, I may then satisfy the creditor for the debt of another.   The obedience which the law requires of me as *my obedience,* will satisfy the demands of the law on me, and prove the means of my justification ; but cannot be transferred from me to *another* subject of the *same* law, so as to answer the demands of the law on *him.*   The law demands all his obedience of him, and all mine of me ; but mine only being rendered, the demands of the law are not and cannot be satisfied.

Supererogatory service, or service not required by law, is absolutely necessary to the very existence of all vicarious interference.   But no creature can possibly perform supererogatory service ; because all that he can do is required of him by the law.   Thus ' exceeding broad,' in the scriptural language, ' is the commandment ;' and thus it is impossible that any creature should become, in any sense, a propitiation for the sins of mankind.

To avoid this immovable difficulty, Dr. Priestley, and other Socinians, have denied wholly the doctrine of Christ's atonement ; and in this denial have, at least in my view, acted in

the only manner consistent with the main part of their scheme,
viz. that Christ is a *mere man.*   But in this denial they have
at the same time contradicted the main doctrine in the Christian system, after that of the existence of God.   According
to the scheme of these men, *Christ came into the world, or
was born, merely to be a prophet and example of righteousness,*
or *a teacher of the will of God to mankind,* and *died only to
bear witness to the truth of his precepts.*   In the same manner,
Moses and all the succeeding prophets came into the world to
be teachers and examples of truth and righteousness ; and, in
the same manner, Peter and Paul, both the Jameses, and
almost all the other apostles, together with Stephen, and a
host of martyrs who followed him, bore witness to the truth
of the precepts which they taught, by voluntarily yielding themselves to death.   All these persons taught the truth of God,
and practised righteousness ; and a multitude of them sealed
their testimony with their blood.   The *only difference,* according to the Socinian scheme, between Christ and them is, that
he was wiser and better than they.   Paul however taught
more of the Gospel than Christ himself, and both Paul and
Peter sealed the truth of their testimony on the cross.   Of
what consequence then was the death of Christ to mankind,
any more than that of Zechariah, Jeremiah, James, Peter, or
Paul?   Each of these men died as a witness to the truth.
Christ, according to Dr. Priestley, appeared in no other character in his death.   All these men also taught the truth ;
according to Dr. Priestley, Christ did no more.   Each of these
men was an eminent example of righteousness ; according to
Dr. Priestley, Christ was only a brighter example.   With
what meaning, then, can it be said, that ' God hath set forth
Christ as a propitiation for the remission of sins ;' that Christ
is said to be ' the propitiation for the sins of the world ;'
that ' his soul' is said to make ' a propitiatory sacrifice for
sin ;' that ' he bare the sin of many ;' that we ' are justified
and redeemed by his blood ; that ' by himself he purged our
sins ;' that ' he made peace through the blood of the cross ;'
that ' he reconciled both Jews and Gentiles unto God in one
body by the cross ;' that ' by his stripes we are healed ;' that
' the chastisement of our peace was laid upon him ;' and that
' we have redemption through his blood, even the forgiveness
of sins ;' together with many other things of the same import,

so many as to constitute no small part of the Scriptures? And why did Christ say, ' he came to give his life a ransom for many?' and why did Paul say, ' Christ gave himself a ransom for all?' Could these things be said of Moses, or Jeremiah, or Peter, or James, or Paul? Are we justified by the grace of God through the redemption which is in Moses? Did Paul make peace by the blood of his cross? Was Peter a propitiation; an *ιλασμος*; the means of appeasing the anger of God, of reconciling him to us, and rendering him propitiatory to sinners?

Farther: In what sense was the death of Christ necessary as *a testimony to the truth of his precepts?* Were not his miracles, and the unspotted excellency of his life, ample proofs of the sincerity of his declarations, and the reality of his mission from God? Are they not now appealed to by Dr. Priestley and most if not all other divines, as the chief proofs? Is not his death rarely appealed to for this purpose? And is it not manifest from this fact, that it is a testimony plainly inferior to his life and miracles?

If, then, this was *the end* and *amount* of Christ's death, is it not evident, on the one hand, that the end was in a great measure useless, and very imperfectly accomplished; and on the other, that the amount of Christ's death was no more than the amount of the death of Paul and Peter; that *they*, as truly as *Christ*, were a propitiation for the sins of the world; and that we are as truly justified by faith in *them*, as in *him*; and by *their* blood, as by *his?*

I shall now proceed to show,

III. *That the Jews, according to the Unitarian doctrine, are unjustly charged with guilt in putting Christ to death.*

The law of God, as given by Moses, required the blasphemer to be stoned. Christ, in his conversation with the Jews, recorded John v., declared himself to bo ' the Son of God.' By this phrase the Jews, as I mentioned in a former Discourse, understood him to declare that himself *was God, or equal with God.* Their own construction they declared to him ' For a good work we stone thee not, but because thou, being a man, makest thyself God.' John x. 33. St. John also, as I then observed, understood the phrase in the same manner. ' Therefore,' he says, ' the Jews sought the more to kill him, because he not only had broken the sabbath, but said also that God was his father, making himself equal with God.' This is the apostle's own construction of Christ's averment, and is plainly alleged by him as being that of the Jews also.

When Christ was brought before the Sanhedrim, after several vain attempts to convict him of any crime, the high priest ' adjured him,' that is, put him upon oath, ' to tell him whether he was the Christ, the Son of the blessed' God. In answer to this question, thus solemnly put, Christ said, ' I am ;' and, as a proof that he said this truly, added, ' and ye shall see the Son of Man sitting on the right hand of power, and coming in the clouds of heaven. In reply to this declaration ' the high priest rent his clothes,' and declaring all farther testimony needless, pronounced him guilty of blasphemy for this saying; in consequence of which, the Evangelists inform us, they all condemned him to death.

Now it is evident, that Christ was understood by the Jews to declare, that he was *equal to God,* and *was God,* by asserting himself to be *the Son of God.* Of this there cannot be a doubt, because it is asserted both by the Jews themselves, and by the Evangelist. If then Christ was a man merely, he was, for aught that I can see, truly a blasphemer. For, when he declared himself to be God, or equal with God, he plainly declared God to be neither greater, wiser, nor better than himself. But to assert in any form of words, that the infinite Jehovah is of the same character with a man, and possessed of no more greatness, excellency, or glory than that which is human, would be acknowledged in any other case to be blasphemy, because it would be a denial of all the perfections of God, and an ascription to him of all the frailties of man. If this be not blasphemy, what can be ?

But if Christ was a blasphemer, he was justly put to death The law, which *he* as well as the Jews acknowledged to have been given by God himself, required the blasphemer to be stoned ; as a blasphemer, therefore, he was, according to the requisitions of a divine and therefore a just law, deservedly condemned to death.

Thus, according to this scheme, the Jews instead of being guilty in putting Christ to death, acted meritoriously, for they only obeyed the divine law.

But it will be said, Christ did not intend by this declaration to assert that he was God, nor that he was equal with God. This indeed is said, and must be said, by the abettors of the Unitarian scheme. I answer, It is clear that the Jews thus understood him, and that he knew them thus to understand him. They had formerly attempted to stone him for using the same language; and had then told him in express terms the manner in which they construed the phrase. The Sanhedrim also sufficiently explained to him their own views of it by pronouncing it blasphemy. In consequence of this mode of understanding the phrase, he saw them now about to imbrue their hands in his blood. If it was a mistake on their part, he was bound to remove it. He was bound not to suffer his own character to be stained in *their* view with the crime of blasphemy. He was bound to use language as he knew it would be understood. He was bound not to lose his own life, nor suffer them to incur the guilt of taking it away, merely through a mistake of theirs. If, then, they are supposed in this case to have sinned at all, they sinned only through a mistake which Christ himself voluntarily created, and voluntarily declined to remove. The sin therefore, so far as I can see, lies, on this supposition, primarily at his door. What then shall we say of the solemn and awful charge brought against the Jews by St. Peter? ' Him ye have taken, and by wicked hands have crucified, and slain? What shall we say of the whole body of Scriptural representations on this subject? What shall we say of the terrible destruction of their nation; of their judicial blindness; and of all the calamities which have befallen them as monuments of the divine indignation for more than seventeen hundred years?

IV. *The prophets and apostles, according to the same doctrine, cannot be vindicated from leading mankind into the sin of idolatry.*

The prophets and apostles have in a great variety of places, called Christ God, The true God, The great God, The mighty God, Jehovah, and I AM. They have declared him to be eternal, self-existent, incomprehensible, almighty, omnipresent, omniscient, and immutable. They have attributed to him the creation, preservation, and government of all things; and the acts of giving life, forgiving sin, judging the world, and rewarding both the righteous and wicked. They have ascribed to him the infinite relations of Creator, Preserver, Possessor, Ruler, and final Cause, of all things. Beyond this, they have on many occasions worshipped him themselves; and have taught us that God requires him to be worshipped; and that he is in fact worshipped by saints and angels in earth and heaven. They have also exhibited Christ, when on earth, as challenging these things to himself, and as receiving them from others without reprobation or censure. They have farther declared him to be the only Saviour of the world, a character evidently demanding infinite attributes, and according to their account, challenged by Jehovah as exclusively his own.

Beyond all this, they have informed us that he was condemned to death for declaring, under the sanction of an oath, that he was the Son of God; a phrase which he knew was understood by them to be no other than a declaration, that he was *God*. Yet, though knowing this, and though directly charged with blasphemy, although on two occasions they attempted to stone him, and on a third pronounced him guilty of death, instead of explaining, softening, or at all modifying the declaration, he proceeded directly in two of the instances to allege proofs that he used this declaration with exact truth and propriety; proofs, which in themselves are a direct arrogation of the divine character. The Scriptures of truth they also declare to be *his word*; and inform us, that the Holy Ghost who inspired them, received them from him; and that Christ himself, when promising them the gift of inspiration, personally told them this wonderful truth. In this account they have taught us, that the Scriptures, which they everywhere style ' the word of God,' are no other than *the law of Christ* himself; partly uttered by his own mouth, and partly taught by the Holy Spirit in conformity to his pleasure; and accordingly in his own name and by his own authority explained, altered, and annulled by him as he thought proper; and that the Holy Spirit, whom, as we shall see hereafter, they pronounce to be a divine person, was commissioned and sent by him into the world to execute his purposes; an act of authority on the part of Christ, to which there is no parallel in the universe, except his own mission from the Father. Finally, in the view which is given us of the heavenly system in the Revelation of St. John, we find the same exalted character completely recognized.   In that world we behold him sitting on the throne of infinite dominion, styled ' the throne of God, and the Lamb;' unfolding, and declared by the heavenly host to be worthy to unfold, the book of God's counsels, which they also declare no being in the universe to be worthy or able to do ; being, together with the Father, the everlasting temple of heaven; controlling all the affairs of this world, of heaven, and of hell ; the light and glory of heaven ; and the bestower of future and everlasting happiness. In all these wonderful characters he is also worshipped in that glorious world with the highest ascriptions which were ever made, or which can be made, to Jehovah. ' Worthy,' they cry, ' is the Lamb that was slain, to receive power, and riches, and wisdom, and strength, and honour, and glory, and blessing.   Every creature,' says St. John, ' which is in heaven, and on the earth, and under the earth, and such as are in the sea, and all that are in them, heard I saying, Blessing, and honour, and glory, and power, be unto Him, that sitteth on the throne, and unto the Lamb, for ever and ever.' Of all these things it is to be remarked, that they are expressed on every occasion which admits them, and in every form of phraseology which language can easily be supposed to allow ; commence with the first chapter in the Bible, and terminate only with the last.

Now let me ask, Whether all these things are not a complete exhibition of Christ, as the proper object of religious worship?   But the apostles have directly and fully declared all these things.   If then Christ is not God, have they not clearly so represented him as to persuade mankind that he is God, and that he is to be worshipped?

How is it possible, that their readers, and especially the plain men who constitute ninety-nine hundredths of them, how is it possible that any men, acknowledging the apostles to have used language as other men use it, and so as to be understood by those for whom they wrote (an admission absolutely necessary to exculpate them from plain fraud,) should distinguish between a person thus described, and the being, who alone is the proper object of worship?   What can their minds, what can any mind, add to this exhibition, to make such a being more great, awful, lovely, glorious, and godlike?

Do not these things include all which we can conceive to be included in infinite perfection? Has any thing superior to these been ever published to mankind? Has any thing been published in any other instance which can be compared with these?

But if Christ be not truly God, he cannot be worshipped without idolatry. He himself says, and recites it as the command of God, ' Thou shalt worship Jehovah thy God, and him only shalt thou serve.' Can inspired men then, writing a Revelation, the great end of which was to inculcate the unity of God, the existence of but one God, and the supreme obligation incumbent on all men to worship him only, can such men have been directed by the Spirit of God so to write as they have actually written? Could they, being Jews with the Old Testament in their hands, have so written even of themselves, as naturally, not to say necessarily, to lead all their followers into the sin of idolatry? That they have so written as naturally to produce this consequence, if Christ be not God, is unquestionable; because the great body of their followers have actually understood them to assert the Deity of Christ, and have actually worshipped him. The Scriptures therefore written for the professed purpose of preventing idolatry, have, according to the scheme of my opponents, been the direct cause of promoting and establishing it among almost all those who have believed them to be the word of God. Mr. Belsham accordingly pronounces the system, of which the worship of Christ is a leading principle, " a pernicious system : a mischievous compound of impiety and idolatry." Lest it should be supposed, however, that those who adopt this worship have really been impious, let it be remarked, that Dr. Priestley himself expressly says, " he considers the principles of Calvinism as generally favourable to that leading virtue, devotion ; even an habitual and animated devotion." Another writer * also, no way favourable to these principles, says in the British Encyclopedia, † " If we consider the character of the Calvinists " (whom he mentions together with several others,) " when compared with that of their antagonists, we shall find that they have excelled in no small degree in the practice of the most rigid and respectable virtues ; and have

* Robert Forsythe, Esq.   † Article Predestination.

been the highest honour of their own ages, and the best model for imitation to every age succeeding." But Calvinists, to a man, have been worshippers of Christ; as have also been almost all other members of the church universal; and to this idolatry, if it be such, the Scriptures have led them. Of course the guilt of leading mankind into that gross sin is, on this scheme, chargeable to the prophets and apostles. But can the prophets and apostles have led mankind into the abominable sin of idolatry? Can the principles which lead to idolatry be favourable to habitual and animated devotion? Can the men who have excelled in the practice of the most rigid and respectable virtues, who have been the highest honour to their own age, and the best models for imitation to succeeding ages, have been regularly guilty of this sin? Can the system which asserts or involves these things, be truth?

Can all or any of the things which I have asserted concerning Christ from the Scriptures, be *true* of *a man :* or of *any created being?* Can a man, can an angel, be the first cause or last end, the Preserver, Proprietor, Possesser, and Ruler of all things? Can a creature be ' the brightness of the Father's glory, and the express image of his person;' ' the Light of the world,' the ' propitiation for sin,' ' the Saviour' of mankind, or the object of religious worship? Can any religious man on a death-bed say, " Gabriel, receive my spirit?" or " Lay not the sin of my murderers to their charge?" Can Gabriel give life, raise the dead, or bestow immortal life? Can he judge the world, reward the righteous and the wicked, or be the glory, light, and temple of heaven? What would be the impression, were a minister of the Gospel to say, " I baptize thee in the name of the Father, and of Gabriel, and of the Holy Ghost?" or " The grace of Gabriel, the love of God the Father, and the communion of the Holy Ghost, be with you all. Amen!" Would not these things beyond measure shock the minds of any Christian assembly, as the most palpable blasphemy? Was there ever a minister, even an Arian or a Socinian who could bring himself thus to speak in such an assembly? Would not this be, not merely comparing or likening one of the angels to Jehovah, but placing him on the same level? Yet these things are said of Christ.

Why are they said of him, if his nature be like that of Gabriel? Why are they *seemingly* said? Was it not perfectly easy. for the omniscient God to have said, if he chose to say it, *that Christ was a mere man, or a mere creature?* and so to have said this, that it would not have been misunderstood even by the plainest man? Did he not understand language sufficiently? Has it not been said in such a manner as to be intelligible to all men, by Arius, Socinus, Zuicker, Price, Priestley, Belsham, and many others? Did any man ever mistrust that they have not said it? Was not Jehovah more interested to say it, if it is true, than they were? and so to say it, as to be easily, generally, and certainly understood? Was he not more able? Did he not foresee all the doubts, difficulties, errors, misconstructions, and consequent sins and idolatries, if they have indeed been misconstructions and idolatries, arising from unhappy language used in the Scriptures? Have not the Prophets, who ' spake as they were moved by the Holy Ghost ;' have not the Apostles, who ' spake the things freely given to them of God, not in the words which man's wisdom taught, but which the Holy Ghost taught,' expressed the mind of God on this subject, and every other, in the very manner chosen by God himself? Has not his infinite faithfulness and mercy then sufficiently guarded every honest mind against this erroneous sin ?

But if Christ be not the true God, the great body of Christians have in every age of the church wholly misunderstood the Scriptures concerning this most important doctrine, and mistaken infinitely the real character of their Saviour. Of course the Scriptures have been so written, as that the natural interpretation of them is a source of total and dreadful error, even of that which they themselves denounce in terms of the highest reprobation, *viz.* idolatry. For the interpretation which has been given them by the great body of Christians in every age and country in which they have existed, is beyond a controversy the natural interpretation. *That men, who first make a philosophical system of religion, and then endeavour to reconcile the Scriptures to it,* should understand them falsely, cannot be wondered at ; but that they should be falsely understood by *the great body of mankind, who for their religion come to them only ; and yet the way of holiness be still a highway, in which wayfaring men, though fools, shall not err,* is a position which is yet to be explained.

SERMON XXXIX.

DIVINITY OF CHRIST.

OBJECTIONS ANSWERED.

LORD KNOWETH THE THOUGHTS OF THE WISE, THAT THEY
[...] VAIN.

1 CORINTHIANS III. 20.

[...] eighteenth verse of this chapter, St. Paul says, ' Let
[...] deceive himself. If any man among you seemeth to
[...] in this world, let him become a fool, that he may be
[...] For the wisdom of this world is foolishness with
[...] for it is written, He taketh the wise in their own
[...]ss.'

[...] words, together with the text, are paraphrased by
[...]ge in the following manner: " I know there are those
[...]ou, whose pride and self-conceit may lead them to
[...]his admonition, especially as coming from me; but
[...]an deceive himself' with vain speculations of his
[...]h and abilities. If any one of you ' seem to be
[...]s world,' if he value himself on what is commonly
[...]dom among Jews or Gentiles; ' let him become a
[...]he may be wise' indeed. Let him humbly acknow-
[...]wn natural ignorance and folly, and embrace that
[...]ich the wisdom of the world proudly and vainly
[...]foolishness, if he desire to approve himself really
[...]tially wise, and to reap at last the honours and
[...]hose who are truly so in the sight of God. ' For'
[...]sted ' wisdom of this world is foolishness with

K 2

God;' who with one glance sees through all its vanity; as it is written (Job v. 13.) 'He entangleth the wise in their own' crafty 'artifice;' often ruining them by those designs which they had formed with the utmost efforts of human policy, and were most intent upon executing.   And again it is said, elsewhere, Psalm xciv. 11, 'The Lord knoweth the thoughts of the wise, that they are vain.'   He sees how they ensnare themselves in their own subtleties; and, when they think themselves most sagacious, are only amused with their own sophistry and deceit."

This paraphrase expresses exactly my own views concerning these declarations of St. Paul; declarations which appear to me to be continually and abundantly verified by experience. No man is in the way to true wisdom who does not first become, in the apostle's sense, 'a fool;' that is, who has not a just and affecting consciousness of his own ignorance and weakness, his utter inability to devise a system of religion, or to amend that which God has taught; and who is not altogether willing to submit his own opinions to the dictates of inspiration.

Concerning the text it will be only necessary to observe, that the word διαλογισμὸς, translated 'thoughts,' is properly rendered *reasonings*; and that the word, translated 'the wise,' is σοφων; denoting *the learned men* of Greece, and ultimately of other countries, most usually called Philosophers.   'The reasonings' of these men, as the apostle proves from the Scriptures of the Old Testament, are in the sight of God 'vain;' or utterly incapable of accomplishing the end to which they were then chiefly directed; viz. the formation and establishment of a sound theological system.

What was true of these men in ancient times is equally true of men of the same sort in every age.   Modern wise men are no more able to perform this work than ancient ones.   Hence, the proposition in the text is written in the absolute or universal form; and extends this character to the reasonings of all men employed either in making systems of theology, or in amending that which is revealed by God.

Of the truth of this declaration experience has furnished the most abundant evidence.   The great body of such systems, including all which have been originally devised by man, and which have existed long enough to be thoroughly examined.

have been successively exploded; and as objects of belief, forgotten. Those which have been devised for the purpose of amending the scriptural system, have been generally of the same frail and perishing character. Some of them, however, under the wing of that divine authority, which by their abettors was supposed to shelter them, and under the garb of sacredness which was lent them by their inventors, have lasted longer, and been more frequently revived. New forms have in the latter case been given to them, new arguments suggested in their behalf, and the splendour of new and respectable names has been employed to recommend them to mankind. After all, their existence and their influence have been generally limited by bounds comparatively narrow.

From the nature of the subject the same truth is completely evident. Theology is *the science of the will of God concerning the duty and destination of man.* What the will of God is concerning these subjects cannot possibly be known, unless he is pleased to disclose it. That it is disclosed by him in the works of Creation and Providence in a very imperfect degree, and that it cannot be discovered by man beyond that degree, must be admitted by every one who would make even a plausible pretension to good sense, or candour. All that remains undiscovered in this way must be unknown, unless revealed by the good pleasure of God. When thus revealed, it can never be safely added to, diminished, nor otherwise in any manner altered, by man. To him whatever God is pleased to withhold must be unknown. By him whatever God is pleased to reveal must be unalterable, either as to form or substance; for no authority less than infinite can change that which infinite authority has been pleased to establish. As, therefore, the scriptural system of theology could not have been invented by man, so neither can it possibly be amended by man. In the strong, but accurately just, language of St. Paul on this subject, ' Let God be' acknowledged to be ' true ;' *but* let ' *every man*,' who denies or opposes what he has revealed, be accounted ' a liar.' Or in the still stronger language of the same apostle, ' though an angel from heaven preach any other Gospel, let him be anathema.'

Among the various denominations of men, denoted in the text by ' the wise,' whose ' reasonings are vain,' are included, so far as I can discern, the Arians and Socinians ; or, as both sometimes choose to term themselves, Unitarians. I feel myself obliged to warn my audience, that this name, however, contains in itself an error, and appears to have been formed with a design to deceive. It was professedly assumed for the purpose of challenging to those who assumed it the exclusive character, among Christians, of believing in the unity of God; and of denying particularly, that Trinitarians entertain this belief; whereas Trinitarians believe in the unity of God as entirely and absolutely as their opposers. That every Trinitarian asserts this of himself, every Unitarian, possessing a very moderate share of information, *knows :* and he knows also, that the charge of admitting more gods than one cannot be fastened upon the Trinitarian, except by consequences professedly derived from his doctrine, which he utterly disclaims. To prove that such consequences do indeed follow from it is, if it can be done, altogether fair and unobjectionable; but to charge him with admitting them, while he utterly disclaims them, is unworthy of a disputant assuming the character of a Christian.

For the assertion which I have made above, concerning the Unitarians generally, I am bound to give my reasons. This I intend to do without disguise, or softening; but at the same time with moderation and candour. My observations I shall distribute under two heads: *Answers to the objections of the Unitarians against the doctrine of the Trinity; and objections to the doctrine of Unitarians, and to their conduct in managing the controversy.* It will not be supposed that under either of these heads very numerous or very minute articles can find a place in such a system of Discourses. All that can be attempted is, to exhibit a summary view of such particulars as are plainly of serious importance.

In the present Discourse, it is my design to *answer the principal objections of Unitarians against the doctrine of the Trinity.* Of these the first, and as I conceive the fundamental one, on which their chief reliance is placed, is, *That the doctrine of the Trinity, or of three Persons in one God, is self-contradictory.*

This objection, therefore, merits a particular answer.

Those who make this objection to the public, express themselves in such language as the following : " The Father, according to the Trinitarian doctrine, is God ; The Son is God ;

and the Holy Ghost is God.   Here are three, each of whom is God.   Three cannot be one, three units cannot be one unit."   Were this objection made professedly, as it is actually, against the inconsistency of tritheism with the unity of God, it would be valid and unanswerable.   Equally valid would it be against the Trinitarians, if they admitted the existence of three Gods, or if their doctrine involved this as a consequence.   But the former of these is not true, and the latter has not been, and, it is presumed, cannot be shown.   Until it shall be shown, every Trinitarian must necessarily feel that this objection is altogether inapplicable to his own case, and although intended against *his* faith, is really aimed against another and very distant object.   Until this be shown, this objection will, I apprehend, be completely avoided in the following manner :

1. *The admission of three infinitely perfect Beings does not at all imply the existence of more Gods than one.*

This proposition may, perhaps, startle such persons on both sides of the question as have not turned their attention to the subject, but can, I apprehend, be nevertheless shown to be true.   It is clearly certain that the nature, the attributes, the views, the volitions, and the agency of three Beings infinitely perfect must be exactly the same.   They would alike be self-existent, eternal, omniscient, omnipotent, and possessed of the same boundless moral excellence.   Of course, they would think exactly the same things, choose the same things, and do the same things.   There would, therefore, be a perfect oneness of character and conduct in the three ; and to the universe of creatures they would sustain but one and the same relation ; and be absolutely but one Creator, Preserver, Benefactor, Ruler, and final Cause.   In other words they would be absolutely One God.   This radical objection therefore is, even in this sense, of no validity.

2. *The doctrine of the Trinity does not involve the existence of three infinite Beings : and therefore this objection does not affect it.*

The scriptural account of Jehovah, as received by every *Trinitarian*, is, *that he is one perfect existence, underived and unlimited ; and that this one perfect existence is in the Scriptures declared to be the Father, the Son, and the Holy Ghost.* These, in the usual language of Trinitarians, are styled *Per-*

sons, because, in the Scriptures, the three personal pronouns, *I, thou*, and *he*, are on every proper occasion applied to them. As this is done by the Father and the Son, speaking *to* each other, and *of* the Holy Ghost, and by the Holy Ghost, speaking of the Father and the Son, we are perfectly assured that this language is in the strictest sense proper. Still, no Trinitarian supposes that the word *person* conveys an adequate idea of the thing here intended; much less that, when it is applied to God, it denotes the same thing as when applied to created beings. As the Father, Son, and Holy Ghost are distinguished, some terms generally expressing this distinction seems necessary to those who would mark it, when speaking of the three together. This term therefore, warranted in the manner above mentioned, has been chosen by Trinitarians, as answering this purpose, so far as it can be answered by human language.

If I am asked, as I probably shall be, what is the exact meaning of the word *person* in this case; I answer, that I do not know. Here the Unitarian usually triumphs over his antagonist. But the triumph is without foundation or reason. If I ask in return, What is the human soul, or the human body? He is obliged to answer, that *he* does not know. If he says, that the soul is organized matter, endowed with the powers of thinking and acting; I ask again, What is that organization, and what is that matter? To these questions he is utterly unable to furnish an answer.

Should he ask again, to what purpose is the admission of the term, if its signification is unknown? I answer, to what purpose is the admission of the word *matter*, if its signification is unknown? I farther answer, that the term in dispute serves to convey briefly and conveniently the things intended by the doctrine, *viz.* that the Father is God, the Son is God, and the Holy Ghost is God: that these are three in one sense, and one in another. The sense in which they are three and yet one, we do not and cannot understand. Still we understand the fact; and on this fact depends the truth and meaning of the whole scriptural system. If Christ be God, he is also a Saviour; if not, there is no intelligible sense in which he can sustain this title, or the character which it denotes.

In addition to this, he is asserted in the Scriptures to be God, in every form of expression and implication, from the beginning to the end, as plainly as language can admit; and so fully and variously that, if we deny these assertions their proper force, by denying that he is God, we must, by the same mode of construction, deny any thing and every thing which the Scriptures contain. If the declarations, ' In the beginning was the Word, and the Word was with God, and the Word was God,' and ' Christ, who is over all things, God blessed for ever,' do not prove Christ to be God, the declaration, ' In the beginning God created the heavens and the earth,' does not prove that there was a creation, or that the Creator is God. The declaration, ' All things were made by him, and without him was not any thing made which is made,' is as full a proof that Christ is the Creator, as *that* just quoted from Genesis is that the Creator is God. An admission or denial of the one ought therefore, if we would treat the several parts of the Bible alike, and preserve any consistency of construction, to be accompanied by a similar admission or denial of the other. Here then is a reason for acknowledging Christ to be God, of the highest kind; viz. *that God has declared this truth in the most explicit manner*.

The *mysteriousness* of the truth thus declared, furnishes not even a shadow of reason for either denial or doubt. That God can be *one* in one sense, and *three* in another, is unquestionable. Whatever that sense is, if the declaration be true, and one which God has thought it proper to make in the Scriptures, and one therefore to which he has required our belief, it is, of course, a declaration incalculably important to mankind, and ' worthy of all acceptation.'

The futility and emptiness of this fundamental objection of Unitarians, as applied to the doctrine of the Trinity, is susceptible of an absolute and easy demonstration, notwithstanding the objection itself claims the character of intuitive certainty. It is intuitively certain, or in other language self-evident, that no proposition can be seen to be either true or false, unless the mind possess the ideas out of which it is formed, so far as to discern whether they agree, or disagree. The proposition asserted by Trinitarians, and denied by Unitarians, is, *that God is tri-personal*. The ideas intended by the words *God*, (here denoting the infinite Existence,) and *tri-personal*, are not, and cannot be, possessed by any man. Neither Trinitarians nor Unitarians therefore can, by any possible effort of the understanding, discern whether this proposition be true or false; or whether the ideas, denoted by the words *God* and *tri-personal*, agree or disagree. Until this can be done, it is perfectly nugatory, either to assert or deny this proposition, as an object of intellectual discernment or philosophical inquiry. Where the mind has not ideas, it cannot compare them; where it cannot compare them, it cannot discern their agreement or disagreement; and of course it can form out of them no proposition, whose truth or falsehood it can at all perceive. Thus this boasted objection is so far from being conclusive, or even formidable, that it is wholly without force or application.

After all that has been said, it may still be asked, Why, if this proposition be thus unintelligible, do Trinitarians adopt it as an essential part of their creed? I answer, Because God has declared it. Should it be asked, Of what use is a proposition, thus unintelligible? I answer, Of inestimable use: and this answer I explain in the following manner. The unintelligibleness of this doctrine lies in the nature of the thing which it declares, and not in the fact declared. The nature of the thing declared is absolutely unintelligible; but the fact is, in a certain degree, understood without difficulty. *What God is*, as one or as three in one, is perfectly undiscernable by us. Of the *existence* thus described we have no conception. But the assertions, that *he is one*, and that *he is three in one*, are easily comprehended. The propositions, that, *the Father is God*, that *the Son is God*, that *the Holy Ghost is God*, and that *these three are one God*, are equally intelligible with the proposition, that *there is one God*. On these propositions, understood as facts, and received on the credit of the divine witness, and not as discerned by mental speculation, is dependent the whole system of Christianity. The importance of the doctrine is therefore supreme.

The utmost amount of all that can be said against the doctrine of the Trinity is, that it is *mysterious*, or *inexplicable*. A mystery, and a mystery as to its nature wholly inexplicable, it is cheerfully acknowledged to be by every Trinitarian; but no Trinitarian will on that account admit that it ought to be less an object of his belief. Were the faith or even the knowledge of man usually conversant about objects which are not mysterious, mysteriousness might, with a better face, be objected against the doctrine of the Trinity. But mystery envelopes almost all the objects of both.   We believe, nay, we know the existence of one God ; and are able to prove him self-existent, omnipresent, omniscient, almighty, unchangeable, and eternal.   But no more absolute mysteries exist than in the being, nature, and attributes of God.   The soul of man, the body of man, a vegetable, an atom, are all subjects filled with mysteries, and about them all a child may ask questions which no Philosopher can answer.   That God, therefore, should *in his existence* involve many mysteries inexplicable by us, is so far from violating or stumbling a rational faith, that it ought to be presumed.   The contrary doctrine would be still more mysterious, and far more shock a rational mind.

   " As to the doctrine of the Trinity,' says a writer* of distinguished abilities and eloquence, " it is even more amazing than that of the incarnation : yet, prodigious and amazing as it is, such is the incomprehensible nature of God, that I belive it will be extremely difficult to prove from thence, that it cannot possibly be true.   The point seems to be above the reach of reason, and too wide for the grasp of human understanding.   However, I have often observed, in thinking of the eternity and immensity of God ; of his remaining from eternity to the production of the first creature, without a world to govern, or a single being to manifest his goodness to ; of the motives that determined him to call his creatures into being ; why they operated when they did, and not before ; of his raising up intelligent beings, whose wickedness and misery he foresaw ; of the state in which his relative attributes, justice, bounty, and mercy remained through an immense space of duration, before he had produced any creatures to exercise them towards ; in thinking, I say, of these unfathomable matters, and of his raising so many myriads of spirits, and such prodigious masses of matter out of nothing ; I am lost and astonished, as much as in the contemplation of the Trinity.   There is but a small distance in the scale of being between a *mite* and *me ;* although that which is food to me is a world to him, we mess, notwithstanding, on the same cheese, breathe the same air, and are generated much in the same manner ; yet how incomprehensible must my nature and actions be to him !   He can take in but a small part of me

* Skelton.   Deism Revealed, Dialogue vi.

with his eye at once ; and it would be the work of his
make the tour of my arm ; I can eat up his world, in
as it seems to him, at a few meals : he, poor reptile !
tell but there may be a thousand distinct beings, or p
such as mites can conceive, in so great a being. By th
parison I find myself vastly capacious and compreh
and begin to swell still bigger with pride and high th
but the moment I lift up my mind to God, between wh
me there is an infinite distance, then I myself become
or something infinitely less ; I shrink almost into noth
can follow him but one or two steps in his lowest
est works, till all becomes mystery and matter of ama
to me. How, then, shall I comprehend himself? Ho
I understand his nature, or account for his actions? I
he plans for a boundless scheme of things, whereas I
but an inch before me. In *that* he contains what is i
more inconceivable than all the wonders of his crea
together ; and I am plunged in astonishment and b
when I attempt to stretch my wretched inch of line
immensity of his nature. Were my body so large that
sweep all the fixed stars visible from this world in
night, and grasp them in the hollow of my hand, and
soul capacious in proportion to so vast a body, I sh
withstanding, be infinitely too narrow minded to co
wisdom when he forms a fly ; and how then should I
conceiving of himself? No, this is the highest of all
bilities. His very lowest work checks and represses
contemplations ; and holds them down at an infinite
from him. When we think of God in this light, we c
conceive it possible, that there may be a trinity of
his nature."

II. *It is asserted by Unitarians, that the doctrine
Trinity is anti-scriptural.*

It has undoubtedly been observed, that in this Dis
have considered objections against *the Deity of Ch
the Trinity*, as being commensurate. The reason is
far as my knowledge extends, those who deny one
doctrines, deny also the other. Although it is not
true therefore, that every objection against the Trinit
of course be an objection against the Deity of Christ ;

this is the ultimate and is most of all concern that
made, I have not thought it necessary or needful
necessary in this Discourse.

As this objection is designed to be obviated, and is some
of being mischievous, reasoned I will be proper to
to take a more critical at the time I mean it and need it to
be my intention however a real one has occurred a
plications of it on which he alludes of the whole and I
have laid the greatest stress.

The general import of his evidence and force is exhibited in the Scriptures is answered in the Father as in
alleged evidence of his nature may be of his own
ranged under two heads. Those that is asserted are those
made by the Prophets and Apostles.

An answer to the principal of these will I trust be
an answer to the rest.

1. Christ, as the Unitarian asserts, calls himself inferior to the Father, and therein of true a unity in
language, that he is not true God, because ... In
declares, that he is not omnipotent.

John v. 19. 'Then Jesus answered and said unto them,
Verily, Verily, I say unto you, the Son can do nothing of himself.' And again in the same verse, I can do nothing of myself
do nothing.' And again, John viii ... 'Then said he
unto them, When ye have lifted up the Son of man, then
shall ye know that I am He, and that I do nothing of myself; but as my Father hath taught me, I speak these things.'

It will not, I presume, be pretended that in either of the
either of the passages are we to understand in the
sense. That Christ could literally do nothing of himself
will not be asserted in the sense, that he had the power at
all, and could not act in any manner whatever. Because
Christ was, he doubtless possessed some degree of natural
power, or power which was no mere act of it is at
least, some such things as are done by men ... in a
then is intended. Undoubtedly either the whole and is
nothing, compared with that the Father can do, or that
Christ could do nothing either by his own power or that
Father, according to the commission given to him by the
Father, to act in the ministerial character.

────

be false, the other,
assumed as the true
be easily evinced

specified.
esses what is true,
nothing of himself;
n from his Father,
, but must do all
commission which
tted by every man.
e, than it is appli-
se things of which
the authority and
received from the
right.   Of course
Jews were without
ense the answer of
only valid answer

evident from John
ove.) 'Then said
p the Son of man,
t I do nothing of
me I speak these
e Jews that, after
hould know that he
of himself: not that
nothing by his own
lo with the subject;

h taught me,' or, as
e instructions which
these things.'   It
speaks of his autho-

the same manner,
In Gen. xix. 22.
rial character, says
f and his family to
er; for I cannot do

with his eye at once ; and it would be the work of his life to make the tour of my arm ; I can eat up his world, immense as it seems to him, at a few meals : he, poor reptile ! cannot tell but there may be a thousand distinct beings, or persons, such as mites can conceive, in so great a being. By this comparison I find myself vastly capacious and comprehensive ; and begin to swell still bigger with pride and high thoughts ; but the moment I lift up my mind to God, between whom and me there is an infinite distance, then I myself become a mite, or something infinitely less ; I shrink almost into nothing. I can follow him but one or two steps in his lowest and plainest works, till all becomes mystery and matter of amazement to me. How, then, shall I comprehend himself? How shall I understand his nature, or account for his actions ? In *these*, he plans for a boundless scheme of things, whereas I can see but an inch before me. In *that* he contains what is infinitely more inconceivable than all the wonders of his creation put together ; and I am plunged in astonishment and blindness, when I attempt to stretch my wretched inch of line along the immensity of his nature. Were my body so large that I could sweep all the fixed stars visible from this world in a clear night, and grasp them in the hollow of my hand, and were my soul capacious in proportion to so vast a body, I should, notwithstanding, be infinitely too narrow minded to conceive his wisdom when he forms a fly ; and how then should I think of conceiving of himself? No, this is the highest of all impossibilities. His very lowest work checks and represses my vain contemplations ; and holds them down at an infinite distance from him. When we think of God in this light, we can easily conceive it possible, that there may be a trinity of persons in his nature."

II. *It is asserted by Unitarians, that the doctrine of the Trinity is anti-scriptural.*

It has undoubtedly been observed, that in this Discourse I have considered objections against *the Deity of Christ* and *the Trinity*, as being commensurate. The reason is that, so far as my knowledge extends, those who deny one of these doctrines, deny also the other. Although it is not strictly true therefore, that every objection against the Trinity must of course be an objection against the Deity of Christ ; yet, us this is the ultimate aim of almost all such objections, actually made, I have not thought any distinction concerning them necessary in this Discourse.

As this objection is designed to be extensive, and is capable of being indefinitely diversified, it will not be possible for me to take notice of all the forms in which it may appear. . It will be my intention, however, to dwell upon those particular applications of it on which the authors of the objection seem to have laid the greatest stress.

The general import of this objection is, that *Christ is exhibited in the Scriptures as inferior to the Father.* All the alleged exhibitions of this nature may be advantageously ranged under two heads; Those made by *himself;* and Those made by *the Prophets and Apostles.*

An answer to the principal of these will, it is believed, be an answer to the rest.

1. *Christ,* as the Unitarians assert, *exhibits himself as inferior to the Father, and therefore declares, in unequivocal language, that he is not truly God.* Particularly (1.) *He declares, that he is not omnipotent.*

John v. 19. ' Then Jesus answered, and said unto them, Verily, Verily, I say unto you, the Son can do nothing of himself.' And again in the 30th verse, ' I can of mine own self do nothing.' And again, John viii. 28. ' Then said Jesus unto them, When ye have lifted up the Son of man, then shall ye know that I am He, and that I do nothing of myself; but as my Father hath taught me, I speak these things.'

It will not, I presume, be pretended that these words, in either of the passages, are used in the strict and absolute sense. That Christ could *literally* ' do nothing of himself,' will not be asserted in the sense, that he had no power at all, and could not act to any purpose whatever. Whoever Christ was, he doubtless possessed some degree of inherent power, or power which was his own; and by it could do, at least, some such things as are done by men generally. What then is intended? Undoubtedly, either that *Christ could do nothing, compared with what the Father can do;* or *that Christ could do nothing, except what was directed by the Father, according to the commission given to him by the Father, to act in the mediatorial character.*

That the latter is the true interpretation is, in my view, unanswerably evident from the following considerations :

[1.] *The subject of a comparison between the power of Christ and that of the Father is not even alluded to in any preceding part of the chapter, either by himself or by the Jews.* The only debate between Christ and the Jews was concerning the *rectitude* or *lawfulness of his conduct.* As the Jews were about to kill him for having acted unlawfully, both in healing a man on the sabbath day, and in saying that God was his Father; it is incredible (because it is imputing to him a gross absurdity,) that Christ should here, instead of replying to the accusation of the Jews, and justifying his conduct as lawful, enter on a comparison between his ability and that of the Father. This would have been a total desertion of the important subject in controversy, and could not have been of the least use either for the purpose of justifying himself, or of repressing the violence of the Jews. On the contrary, it would have been the assumption of a subject totally foreign, totally unconnected with the case in hand, without any thing to lead to it, incapable of being understood by those to whom it was addressed, and a species of conduct which, so far as I can see, would have been irreconcileable with common sense.

[2.] *This interpretation is refuted, so far as the objection is concerned, by the discourse of which it is a part.*

The whole drift of this discourse is to show the extent of that *authority* which Christ possessed as the mediator. In displaying this authority, he also displays, necessarily, the *power* which he possesses. In chapter v. 19. from which the first of the objected declarations is taken, is this remarkable assertion : ' What things soever, he,' that is the Father, ' doeth, these also doeth the Son likewise.' It is presumed that not even a Unitarian will imagine, that in a verse in which this declaration is contained, Christ could intend, by any phraseology whatever, to exhibit a limitation of his own power.

With this complete refutation of the meaning now in question in our hands, it can scarce be necessary to observe, that in many subsequent parts of this discourse of Christ, it is also overthrown in the same complete manner.

This interpretation being thus shown to be false, the other, the only remaining one, might be fairly assumed as the true interpretation.   At the same time, it may be easily evinced to be the true one by other considerations.

[1.] *It is perfectly applicable to the case specified.*

That the proposition containing it expresses what is true, *viz.* that Christ, as the mediator, could do nothing of himself; that is, that while acting under a commission from his Father, he could do nothing of his own authority, but must do all things by the authority and agreeably to the commission which he had received, will, I suppose, be admitted by every man. But this proposition is not more clearly true, than it is applicable to the case in hand.   If Christ, in those things of which he was accused by the Jews, acted by the authority and agreeably to the commission which he had received from the Father, then plainly, that which he did was right.   Of course the objections and the animosities of the Jews were without cause, and wholly reprehensible.   In this sense the answer of Christ was perfectly pertinent, and the only valid answer which could be given.

[2.] That this *is the true meaning* is evident from John viii. 28. (the last of the passages quoted above.)   'Then said Jesus unto them, When ye have lifted up the Son of man, then shall ye know that I am he, and that I do nothing of myself; but as my Father hath taught me I speak these things.'   In this passage Christ informs the Jews that, after they had lifted him up on the cross, they should know that he was the Messiah, and that he did nothing of himself: not that he did nothing by his own power; but nothing by his own authority.   The former having nothing to do with the subject; the latter being perfectly applicable to it.

Therefore he adds, ' As my Father hath taught me,' or, as we say in modern English, According to the instructions which I have received from my Father, ' I speak these things.'   It will hardly be questioned that Christ here speaks of his authority only, and not at all of his power.

[3.] *We find the same language, used in the same manner, in various other passages of Scripture.*   In Gen. xix. 22. Christ himself, acting in the same mediatorial character, says to Lot, beseeching him to permit himself and his family to escape to Zoar, ' Haste thee, escape thither; for I cannot do any thing till thou be come thither.' It will not be pretended that, so far as his power only was concerned, Christ could not as easily have begun the work of destroying the cities of the plain before Lot had escaped, as afterwards. But as it was a part of the divine determination to preserve Lot and his family, so the authority of Christ did not in this case extend to any thing, nor permit him to do any thing, which involved the destruction of Lot.

Numbers xxii. 18. Balaam says, ' If Balak would give me his house full of silver and gold, I cannot go beyond the word of the Lord my God, to do less or more.' This declaration of Balaam, I consider as expressing fully and completely the very thing which in the objected passages Christ expressed elliptically. And again, chapter xxiv. 12, 13. ' And Balaam said unto Balak, Spake I not also to thy messengers which thou sentest unto me, saying, If Balak would give me his house full of silver and gold, I cannot go beyond the commandment of the Lord, to do either good or bad of mine own mind; but what the Lord saith, that will I speak ?'

I shall only add to these observations the obvious one, that persons acting under a commission now use similar language, in similar circumstances.

Should any one question whether Christ acted under a commission, he himself has answered the question in his intercessory prayers, John xvii. 4. ' I have glorified thee on the earth; I have finished the work which thou gavest me to do.'

From these observations it is, if I am not deceived, clear, that the declarations of Christ here objected to, do not in any sense refer to his power, but only to his authority as mediator ; and are therefore utterly irrelevant to the purpose for which they are alleged.

(2.) *The Unitarians object, that Christ exhibits himself as inferior to the Father in knowledge.*

The passage quoted to prove this assertion is especially, Mark iii. 31. ' But of that day and that hour knoweth no man, no, not the angels which are in heaven, neither the Son, but the Father.'

Here it is said, Christ confesses himself to be ignorant of the day and hour specified.

On this objection I observe,

[1.] *That the subject of which Christ is here declared to be ignorant, is a subject which demanded no greater extent of knowledge, or rather, which demanded knowledge in a less extent, than many subjects disclosed by him in the same prophecy.* The subject is the time of the destruction of Jerusalem. In this very prophecy, as well as in various others, he had uttered many things which appear to demand as great a measure of prescience as this can be supposed to have done. Such were, the arising of false Christs and false prophets ; the preaching of the Gospel through the world ; the earthquakes, famines, and pestilences ; the fearful sights and great signs which should precede the destruction of Jerusalem ; the hatred and treachery of parents and others to his disciples, and the protraction of the ruinous state of Jerusalem until the times of the Gentiles should be fulfilled. The foreknowledge of the particular period of its destruction was, certainly, no very material addition to the foreknowledge of these things ; and would imply no very material enlargement of the mind by which they were foreknown. Several of the prophets, it is to be remembered, were furnished with a foreknowledge of dates, not differing from this in their importance : thus Isaiah foreknew the date of the destruction of Ephraim ; Jeremiah, that of the Babylonish captivity ; and Daniel, that of the death of Christ ; and no reason can be imagined why the foreknowledge of this particular date should be withholden from Christ, even if we admit that he was a mere man, when so many other things relating to the same event, of so much more importance, were revealed to him.

There is, therefore, no small reason to believe, that the Greek word, οἶδε, has here the signification of γνωρίζω, according to the comment of Dr. Macknight, and denotes, not *to know*, but *to cause to know* ; a signification which it sometimes has, as he has sufficiently shown : particularly in 1 Cor. ii. 2. ' For I determined to know nothing among you, save Jesus Christ, and him crucified :' that is, I determined to *make known* nothing among you, &c. If this sense of the word be admitted, the meaning of the passage will be, Of that day no one *causeth men to know*, but the Father : that is, when in his providence he shall bring the event to pass. In other words, the time of the destruction of Jerusalem shall not be disclosed by prophecy, but shall be made known only by the providence of God, bringing it to pass. I need not say that was literally the fact.

[2.] *Christ himself informs us, that no one knows the Son but the Father, and that no man knows the Father but the Son, and he to whomsoever the Son shall reveal him.**

In this declaration Christ asserts, that he possesses an exclusive knowledge of the Father, in which no being whatever shares with him; a knowledge totally distinct from that which is acquired by revelation, and therefore immediate and underived.

He also declares, John v. 20. that ' the Father sheweth him all things, that himself doeth;' that he ' searcheth the reins and the heart,' Rev. ii. 23; and that he ' is with his disciples alway, to the end of the world,' Matt. xxviii. 20. and therefore, *omnipresent* ; Peter also says to him, John xxi. 17. ' Lord, thou knowest all things :' an ascription which, if not true, Christ could not have received without the grossest impiety; and which he yet did receive, because he did not reject nor reprove it.

But he, of whom these things are said, certainly foreknew the time of the destruction of Jerusalem. If, then, the objected text denotes that Christ did *not* know that time, the declaration cannot be true, except by being made concerning Christ considered in a totally different character and sense from those in which the same book teaches us that He ' knows the Father,' and ' knows all things.' It is, therefore, not a shift, or fetch, or evasion in the Trinitarians to assert, that this passage, if thus understood, is spoken of Christ in his *human nature only*, and not in the nature exhibited in the passages with which it has been compared. On the contrary, it is a deduction from the Scriptures, irresistibly flowing from what they say, and the only means by which they can be either consistent or true.

(3.) *It is objected by the Unitarians, that Christ has denied himself to be originally and supremely good.*

The passage chosen to support this objection is the answer of Christ to the young ruler, Matt. xix. 17. ' Why callest thou me good ? There is none good but one : that is God.' Here Christ is supposed to disclaim original and supreme

---

* Matthew xi. 27.

goodness, as belonging to himself, and to distinguish between his own goodness and that of God.

What the real reason was for which Christ gave this answer, I shall not here examine. If Christ is not God, then he certainly would disclaim, and ought to disclaim, this character. If he is, then this assertion does not at all declare that he is not possessed of this goodness. The decision of this question will, therefore, determine the true application of this answer.

It has heretofore been proved in these Discourses, that Christ was the person who proclaimed on Mount Sinai his own name to Moses. This name he declared to be, ' the Lord, the Lord God, merciful and gracious, long-suffering, slow to anger, abundant in goodness and truth.' It will not be contested, that the person who made this proclamation was good in the original or absolute sense. Until this person is proved not to have been Christ, the objection founded on this text is a mere begging of the question.

But it is farther to be remembered, that Christ was also a man. According to the doctrines of the Trinitarians, therefore, as entirely as to that of their opposers. Christ used this declaration in the very sense in which they allege it, with the most perfect propriety.

(4.) *Christ, as the Unitarians allege, exhibits his inferiority to the Father, by praying to him.*

How, if it be admitted, as Trinitarians universally admit, that he was a man, could he with propriety do otherwise? He was placed under the same law, and required, generally, to perform the same duties demanded of other men.

(5.) *Christ declares himself to be inferior to the Father in express terms:* ' My Father is greater than I ;' and ' My Father is greater than all.'

These declarations are perfectly consistent with the doctrine of the Trinity, in two ways. First, *As Christ was a man ;* Secondly, *As in the character of mediator he acted under a commission from the Father.* He who acts under a commission from another is, while thus acting, inferior to him from whom he received the commission.

But it is further objected, that Christ is exhibited as inferior to the Father by the Prophets and Apostles.

L 2

It will be unnecessary, under this head, to mention more than a single instance. I shall select that instance, which seems to be the favourite one among the Unitarians. It is contained in the following words, taken from the 24th and 28th verses of 1 Cor. xv. ' Then cometh the end, when he shall have delivered up the kingdom to God, even the Father,' and ' When all things shall be subdued unto him, then shall the Son also himself be subjected unto him that put all things under him, that God may be all in all.'

To comprehend the apostle's meaning in these declarations it is necessary to remember, that Christ, as sustaining the office of mediator, received from the Father *a kingdom*, according to the Scriptures ; and that when his mediatorial office ceases, because the purposes of it are accomplished, *that* kingdom, as we should naturally expect, is exhibited in the Scriptures as ceasing also ; there being no end for which it should be any longer retained. Christ will, therefore, deliver it up to the Father when, at the consummation of all things, he ' presents' to him ' the church, as a glorious church, without spot, or wrinkle, or any such thing ;' and makes his final triumphant entry into the heavens.

Concerning the latter article, here objected, that ' the Son shall then be subject to the Father,' it can scarcely be proper that I should attempt to determine the exact import. It is perfectly evident, however, that this must be true of the human nature of Christ. It is also evident, that the act of rendering up the kingdom which he had received, is an act of subjection to the Father : nor does the passage demand any other interpretation.

That these declarations do not intend what the objectors allege, we certainly know. ' For unto the Son' the *Father* ' *saith* (Heb. i. 8.) Thy throne, O God ! is for ever and ever.' ' His dominion (says Daniel) is an everlasting dominion, which shall not pass away ; and his kingdom that which shall not be destroyed.' ' He shall reign (said Gabriel to Mary) over the house of Jacob for ever, and of his kingdom there shall be no end.' ' The throne of God and the Lamb' is, as we are informed by St. John, the throne of eternal dominion in the heavens ; out of which ' proceeds the river of the water of life,' or the endless felicity and glory of all the happy inhabitants. To God and the Lamb also are equally addressed those sublime ascriptions of praise which constitute the peculiar and everlasting worship of saints and angels.   In this superior sense, therefore, the kingdom of Christ will literally endure for ever.

It ought here to be added, that the same Apostle, who here says, that the Father put all things under Christ, informs us in the same paragraph, that Christ *himself* ' put all things under his feet :' and elsewhere, that *Christ* ' is able to subdue all things unto himself,' and that ' he is head over all things.' Phil. iii. 21 ; Eph. i. How plain is it that he, ' who is able to subdue all things unto himself, is able to do any thing ? that he, ' who puts all things under his own feet,' does it by his own agency ; and that he, who is now ' head over all things,' is of course qualified to be ' head over all things ' for ever ?

SERMON XL.

DIVINITY OF CHRIST.

OBJECTIONS TO THE DOCTRINE OF UNITARIANS.

THE LORD KNOWETH THE THOUGHTS OF THE WISE, THAT THEY
ARE VAIN.

1 CORINTHIANS III. 20.

IN the preceding Discourse from these words, after observing that *the reasonings of mankind,* when employed in devising and establishing a scheme of theology, or attempting to amend that which is taught by God, *are vain ;* I mentioned that, in my own view, the Arians and Socinians were fairly included within this declaration of Scripture. For this assertion I considered myself bound to give my reasons, and proposed to do it under two heads :

I. *Answers to their objections against the doctrine of the Trinity ;* and,

II. *Objections to the doctrines which they hold concerning Christ, and their conduct in the management of the controversy.* The former of these was the subject of the preceding Discourse ; the first part of the latter shall furnish the materials of the present.

To the Doctrines of the Unitarians I make the following objections :—

I. *The Arians hold, that Christ is a super-angelic being, so much greater than all other creatures, as to be styled a*

God ; *and to perform the various divine offices ascribed to him in the Scriptures, by delegated power and authority.*

To my own mind, this doctrine is utterly inconsistent both with the Scriptures and reason.

The only argument which, so far as I know, is derived directly from the Scriptures to support this opinion, is, *that angels are sometimes called Aleim, and that magistrates have once this name given to them.* That neither of these facts will warrant the doctrine in question, will I trust, be evident from the following reasons :

1. *Angels and magistrates are called by this name only in the aggregate, Gods ; no angel or magistrate being ever called, God.* It is well known to my audience, that the same name is also given to the idols of the heathen ; to animals, vegetables, the souls of departed men, or demons, and to all the other objects of heathen worship. The term *Gods*, is here evidently used in a figurative sense ; natural and obvious, because the beings to whom it is applied, sustained, or were supposed to sustain, some attribute or character resembling those which belong to the true God. Thus God says to Moses (Exodus vii. 1,) ' See, I have made thee a God to Pharaoh :' that is, I have given thee authority over him, and armed thee with power to controul and punish him. In the same manner magistrates are called lords, and kings, because they rule with subordinate power and authority.

But the term God, in the absolute, is never given to any created being, unless Christ can be proved to be a creature : a thing which, it is apprehended, cannot be done. To him, however, it is applied in many instances, without any qualification, or any notice whatever that it is not applied in the highest sense. At the same time it is, when applied to him, connected with other objects attributable only to the Deity.

Thus in Romans ix. 5, when Christ is said by the Apostle to be *God*, He is also said to be ' over all things,' and ' blessed for ever.' Thus, when St. John informs us, that ' the Word was God, he informs us also, that the ' Word was in the beginning,' or eternal ; ' was in the beginning with God,' or co-eternal with God ; and that ' all things were made by him,' or that he was the Creator of all things. The attribution, therefore, of these things to Christ, when he is called God, *viz.* that he exists from eternity; is co-eternal with God, or the Father; and is the Creator and Ruler of all things; marks in the most definite as well as decisive manner, the meaning of the word *God*, when applied to him; and proves that it *is* applied in the highest sense. Nothing parallel to this, or distantly resembling it, is found in any application of this term, to any other being, except God.

2. *Christ is called by all the other names of God, except one,* viz. *the Father.*

It has been shown in a former Discourse, that Christ is called ' the true God,' ' the great God,' ' the mighty God,' ' Jehovah,' &c. The application of these names to Christ, is clear evidence that, when he is called God, this appellation is given to him in the same sense in which it is given to the Father; to whom and the Holy Spirit, exclusively, these other names are also given.

3. *The attributes and actions, universally, of God are ascribed to Christ.* It is plain then, that the Scriptures, which give this name to Christ, connect with it all the other appellations, together with all the attributes and actions which make up the Scriptural character of God.

In all these respects, the application of the term *Gods* to angels and magistrates differs totally and, I apprehend, infinitely from that of God to Christ. The application of the term *Gods* to angels and magistrates, therefore, furnishes not the least reason to believe that Christ is called God in the sense alleged, or that Christ is a delegated God.

Having removed the only scriptural argument on which I suppose any serious reliance to be placed, as a proof that Christ is a delegated God, I proceed to observe, that this scheme is utterly inconsistent with the things which are said of him in the Scriptures. It is utterly inconsistent with the ascription to him of the names, attributes, and actions which have been just now mentioned. Particularly it is inconsistent with the declarations, that he ' made all things,' and that ' he upholds all things, by the word of his power.' In the account given us by St. John and St. Paul of the creation of all things by Christ, both apostles use phraseology which, with an exactness scarcely paralleled, denotes an absolute universality. ' By him,' says St. Paul, ' were all things created that are in heaven and that are in earth, visible and invisible, whether they be thrones, or dominions, or principalities, or powers: all things were created by him, and for him.'   ' All things,' says St. John, ' were made by him ; and without him was not one thing made, which hath been made.'   If these two passages do not denote an absolute universality, language cannot express it.   Every possible as well as actual thing is either visible or invisible.   Every actual thing which is either visible or invisible, it is here expressly said, Christ created. ' Without him,' it is expressly said, ' was not one thing made, which hath been made.'   Unless therefore something has been created that is neither ' visible nor invisible ;' unless there is something existing in the creation, ' which has' not ' been made ;' there is nothing which was not created by Christ.

The interpretation of these passages by the Unitarians, which makes them mean no more than *that Christ published the Gospel and constituted the church*, is a violation of common sense and common decency.   Let us try the same mode of construction with another passage, to which it must be acknowledged to be equally applicable.   In the passage quoted from St. Paul, it is said that ' Christ created all things that are in heaven, and that are in earth.'   This the Unitarians say, means no more than that Christ published the Gospel, and constituted the church.   In the first verse in Genesis it is said, ' In the beginning God created the heavens and the earth.'   This, I say, and upon their plan of construction am certainly warranted to say it, means no more than that in the *beginning God published the Gospel and constituted the church.*   Ought not any man to be deeply ashamed of the prejudice, and strongly to censure the confidence, which has led him to use such licentious freedom with language in any case ; especially with ' words which were taught, not by man's wisdom, but by the Holy Ghost ?'

Dr. Price, and other Arians, attempt to evade the force of these and the like passages, by introducing *a distinction between formation and creation.*   In this, however, they must be acknowledged to be unhappy.   The words, used by St. John are εγενετο, and γεγονεν ; the proper English of which is *existed.*   Γινομαι, of which they are derivatives, signifies also *to be born, to spring up, to be brought into being and to be caused to exist.*   No word, therefore, more comprehensive or more appropriate to the object in view can be found, either in the Greek or, so far as I can see, in any other language. The word used by St. Paul is κτισθη, from κτιζω; the appropriate meaning of which, as you well know, is *to create*. As, therefore, the act of creating all things in the most absolute sense is, in the most express and unequivocal language, ascribed to Christ by these apostles, by what authority or with what decency can it be denied by any man?

The work of *creating all things* Christ performed by *his command*. All things, also, he *upholds* by the same *word of his power*. If these acts, and this manner of performing them, are not proofs of infinite power, such proofs have never existed. It is to be remarked, that the Apostle asserts directly, that Christ ‘ upholds all things by the word of his *own* power ;’ τω ρηματι της δυναμεως αυτο. This act, therefore, is not performed by delegated power ; and neither of these acts could possibly be performed by any being, except *one*, whose power is without limitation.

Among the numerous other things ascribed to Christ, which are utterly inconsistent with the supposition of his being a delegated God, I shall mention only *two;* as the mention of more would demand a longer time than can now be devoted to this part of the subject. The first is, that divine *worship was rendered to him by inspired persons on earth, and is also rendered to him in heaven.* This, it is presumed, has been proved beyond controversy. Stephen prayed to him. Paul prayed to him : and the whole Christian church was, at its commencement, distinguished by the appellation of *those who invoked the name of Christ in prayer.* The anthems of praise in the heavens, sung by saints and angels, ascribe to him, both separately and jointly with the Father, that peculiar glory and honour which is expressive of the highest worship of the heavenly inhabitants. But Christ himself says, quoting Deut. vi. 13; and x. 20, ‘ Thou shalt worship the Lord thy God, and him only shalt thou serve.’ No *creature*, therefore, can be lawfully worshipped ; but Christ *is* lawfully worshipped ; for he is worshipped by apostles, angels, and glorified saints.

The second and last thing of this nature is, *that Christ is immutable.* ‘ Jesus Christ, the same yesterday, to-day, and for ever.’ If Christ were only the exalted creature, the super-angelic being, the delegated God, whom the Arians declared him to be, he would of all virtuous beings be the most changeable ; because, with his superior faculties and advantages, he would advance more rapidly in knowledge, and virtue, and in power also ; for the increase of knowledge is in itself the increase of power. Such a being cannot possibly, therefore' be ' the Jesus Christ, who is the same, yesterday, to-day, and for ever.' At the same time it is farther to be remarked, that a wonderful instance of change is asserted of Christ, if he be this super-angelic being, in the Scriptures themselves. St. Luke declares, that when he was twelve years old, ' he increased in wisdom and stature, and in favour with God and man.'. According to the Arians, this super-angelic being, the greatest of all created minds, brought into existence antecedently to every other creature, was united to the body of an infant, and born of the virgin Mary, and thus constituted the person named Jesus Christ in the Scriptures. This infant differed so little from other infants as to intelligence, that the first time he was regarded as extraordinary, appears plainly to have been the time when he conversed with the Jewish doctors in the temple, as recorded in the second chapter of St. Luke. At this time he was observed to increase in wisdom, so as to increase in favour with mankind. He also actually increased in wisdom, and actually increased in favour with God. He therefore changed, not only really but obviously. If, then, we admit that Christ was this super-angelic being, we must also admit that he was not the Christ, who was ' the same yesterday, to-day, and for ever.' But we cannot admit Christ to be this being. From infancy to twelve years of age he had unceasingly changed also. What, then, was his mind when he was born ; or when he had arrived at one, or two years of age ? Doubtless, as much inferior to what it was at twelve years of age, as other infants are to what they become at the same period. But how evident is it, that such an infantine mind could not be a super-angelic mind. The change, it is to be remembered, is declared by the evangelist to be real, and not merely apparent. And it is presumed no Arian will admit that his infantine character was merely assumed and hypocritical. Arians will undoubtedly agree, that he was then equally sincere, as ever afterwards. But a super angelic mind must have lost all its peculiar powers and characteristics, to have become such a mind as that of Christ in his infancy, or his childhood. Such a mind, originally formed with these sublime faculties, existing in a singular proximity to Jehovah, and expanded and exalted by his peculiar advantages for improving in knowledge and virtue, throughout four thousand years, must have risen to so transcendent a height of intellectual and moral attainments as, if it were not entirely changed in its whole character, must have excited the attention, the amazement, and probably, if it had not forbidden it, the worship of every spectator. At the same time, such powers and attainments must have been so utterly incomprehensible by mankind, that, however rapidly they had increased, the change could never have been perceptible by such eyes as theirs. It is therefore certain that, if the Christ born in Bethlehem, was this super-angelic being, he ceased to be super-angelic, when united to the body of an infant; and differed in no other respect from the minds of other infants, except that he was perfectly holy, and possessed a superior susceptibility of wisdom. In other words, he was changed into a human being, perfect indeed, as such, but still a human being; and shorn wholly of his super-angelic greatness. If Arians will put these things together, it is believed, that themselves will acknowledge *mysteries*, of an inexplicable kind, to be contained in this part of their system.

Nor is this idea of a delegated God a whit more consistent with reason. Nothing is more repugnant to reason, than that a finite being should have made the universe; should uphold it; should possess it; should govern it; should judge and reward its intelligent inhabitants; should forgive their sins; should be the source of life; should communicate endless life; and should be the ultimate end for which they and all things else were created. Every one of these things is not only utterly aside from the dictates of reason on this subject, a mystery utterly inexplicable; but is directly repugnant to common sense. Nothing is more strongly realized by reason, than that ' He who built all things is ' very ' God;' that he who made the universe can alone uphold, possess, or govern it; or be the ultimate end for which it was created; or do all or any of the things just now recited. If this being be not God, in the absolute sense, reason has no knowledge and no evidence that there is a God.

Accordingly Dr. Priestley has, if I mistake not, observed, and justly, that no doctrine is more preposterous than the doctrine that Christ created the world, and that yet he is not God.   Still the Scriptures assert in terms as comprehensive, as precise, as appropriate, and as unambiguous as human language can furnish, that Christ ' created every ' individual ' thing that hath been made.'   Yet, in spite of this language, chosen by God himself to express his views on the subject, Dr. Priestley asserts, that Christ is not God!   The manner in which he satisfies himself concerning this declaration will be examined hereafter.

II. If these things are preposterously and irreconcileably asserted concerning a super-angelic being——a delegated God, what shall we say concerning *their compatibility with the Socinian doctrine, that Christ is a mere man ?*   If the fact had not already taken place, would it not be absolutely incredible, that any sober man living should believe such assertions as these?   Let me however, before I make them, instead of the name of a man substitute that of Gabriel ; a being, in holiness, wisdom, and power originally superior to any man ; and in a still higher degree superior by the improvements made in them all through the four thousand years which preceded the work of redemption.   This I do, that the repetition of the name of a man may not shock the ears of my audience, while I am making a simple and perfectly equitable statement, in that very form in which it must be made by every conscientious man, before he can feel himself warranted to receive it.   ' In the beginning was ' *Gabriel* ; ' and ' *Gabriel* ' was with God ; and ' *Gabriel* ' was God.   The same was in the beginning with God.   By him were all things made ; and without him was not one thing made, which hath been made. And ' *Gabriel* ' became flesh, and dwelt among us (and we beheld his glory, the glory as of the only begotten of the Father,) full of grace and truth.'*   ' For by ' *Gabriel* ' were all things created, that are in heaven and that are in earth ; visible and invisible.   All things were created by him, and for him.   And by him all things consist ;' †   ' and he is head over all things unto his church,'   ' Of whom, as concerning the

* John i. 1—3, 14.   † Col. i. 16, 17.   ‡ Eph. i. 22.

flesh,' *Gabriel* ' came, who is over all things, God blessed for
ever.'* *Gabriel* ; ' who being in the form of God, thought
it no robbery to be equal with God ; but made himself of no
reputation, and took upon him the form of a servant, and was
made in the likeness of men. And, being found in fashion
as a man, he became obedient unto death, even the death of
the cross. Wherefore God hath highly exalted him, and given
him a name, which is above every name ; that at the name of'
Gabriel ' every knee should bow, of things in heaven, and
things in earth, and things under the earth ; and that every
tongue should confess, that he is Lord, to the glory of
God the Father.'† ' Hearken unto me, O Jacob my servant ;
and Israel whom I have called. I am he : I am the first ;
and I am the last. Mine hand also hath laid the foundation
of the earth ; and my right hand hath spanned the heavens ;
I call unto them ; they stand up together. Come ye near
unto me ; hear ye this : I have not spoken in secret from the
beginning. From the time that it was, there I am. And now
the Lord, Jehovah and his Spirit hath sent me.'‡ ' God, who
at sundry times, and in divers manners, spake unto the
fathers by the prophets, hath in these last days spoken unto
us by' *Gabriel* ; ' who, being the brightness of his glory, and
the express image of his person, and upholding all things by
the word of his power.'§ ' The throne of God and' *Gabriel*.||
' And' *Gabriel* ' hath on his vesture and on his thigh a name
written, King of kings, and Lord of lords.'¶ ' Every creature
which is in heaven, and in earth, and under the earth, and in
the sea, heard I saying, Blessing, and honour, and glory, and
power, be unto him that sitteth on the throne, and unto'
Gabriel, ' for ever and ever.'**

Is there a person present who is not shocked with these
declarations ? Would not the insertion of them in the sacred
canon stumble, irrecoverably, every sober man who now believes it to be the word of God ? Is it possible for the mind
to ascribe the things declared in them to any being less than
infinite ? Is not this favoured angel infinitely too humble in
his nature and station to claim or receive them ? Who could

---

* Rom. ix. 5.   † Phil. ii. 6.
‡ Isaiah xlviii. 12, 13, 16.   § Heb. i. 1, 3.
|| Rev. xxii 1, 3   ¶ Rev xix. 16.   ** Rev. v. 13.

bring himself to pray to Gabriel for the forgiveness of his enemies; for the acceptance of his soul, when expiring;[*] or for the removal of his distresses; or for any thing? Who could be baptized in his name;[†] or receive a blessing from him united with the Father and the Holy Ghost?[‡] But if these things are monstrous when applied to Gabriel, one of the highest created intelligences, how must they appear when applied to *a man,* one of the lowest? How would they appear, for example, were we to substitute the name of Moses, or the name of Paul, for that of Gabriel? Is it not plain that the incongruity would be so excessive as to appear to have been written, not in serious earnest, but in blasphemous sport, with a direct design to entail impiety and contempt upon the book in which they were found? and would they not, instead of being read with sobriety and reverence, fill a light mind with ludicrous emotions, and a serious mind with horror? Yet such, so far as I can see, is substantially the very alteration which must be made, according to the Socinian doctrine, concerning Christ. It is true, that Socinians regard Christ as a wiser and better man than Moses or Paul, but in no other respect do they suppose him to differ from either.

III. *I object to the doctrine of the Unitarians, that it has compelled them to renounce, successively, many other important doctrines of the Gospel, beside that of the Trinity.*

The Deity of Christ must be acknowledged by all men, if it be real, to affect materially every thing which is said of him in the scriptures. The difference between his character, according to this scheme, and according to the scheme which makes him a creature, is infinite. Every thing, therefore, which is recorded of him, and consequently every view which is formed of him, must be exceedingly diverse in the mind of a Trinitarian and the mind of an Unitarian. In the view of a Trinitarian, he is Jehovah, the Alpha and Omega, the first cause and the last end of all things. In that of an Arian, he is a being infinitely different; a creature somewhat higher than the angels, brought into being somewhat before them: and in that of a Socinian still different from this: a man, born about

---

* Acts vii. 59. 60.   † Matt. xxviii. 19.   ‡ 2 Cor. xiii. 14.

eighteen hundred years since in Judea; somewhat better than Moses, Isaiah, or Paul. Now nothing is more evident than that every thing belonging to the first of these beings, his existence, actions, and attributes, together with the relations which he sustains to creatures, must be infinitely different from those which belong to either of the others. Those who adopt one of these opinions, naturally and necessarily fall into very different systems of thought concerning Christ; concerning the station which he holds in the universe, and the part which he acts in the work of redemption; and concerning many highly important doctrines of the Christian faith. Accordingly, the whole scheme of Christianity adopted by Trinitarians is widely different from those adopted by Arians and Socinians. That this is true is well known to all who are conversant with the schemes of doctrine embraced, severally by these classes of men, and is abundantly confessed and boasted by the Unitarians themselves. Some very important doctrines, constituting and illustrating this difference, I shall now mention. If the doctrines of the Trinitarians are really contained in the Scriptures, if they are clearly and abundantly declared, and if they are accordant only with the Divinity of Christ, then it will follow by unavoidable consequence, that the Unitarians have been compelled to renounce them in consequence of having renounced the Divinity of Christ.

If, at the same time, the doctrines thus renounced are of high importance to the Christian system, and those which distinguish it from all philosophical systems of theology, then it will appear, that the renunciation of these doctrines is an error of dangerous influence, and deeply to be regretted; and, as it grows necessarily out of the renunciation of the Divinity of Christ, that that is an error also, of the same unhappy nature. Of these doctrines,

The first which I shall mention is the doctrine of human depravity.

This doctrine, it is believed, has been fully evinced in these Discourses to be a doctrine of the Scriptures. If it has not, it must have arisen either from the weakness or the inattention of the Preacher; for no truth is more clearly declared in any book, than this doctrine in the Scriptures; and none is more amply supported by the evidence of fact. In the Scriptures we are taught, in the most unequivocal language, that ' all

men have sinned, and come short of the glory of God ;' that
' all are concluded under sin ;' that ' all are by nature children of wrath,' being ' children of disobedience ;' that ' all are
shapen in iniquity, and conceived in sin.'   These declarations,
to which the whole history of man gives the fullest attestation ;
and to which there is not even one solitary contradiction in
fact, certainly stand with the Unitarians for nothing, or for
nothing like what the words themselves customarily mean.   In
their view, we are *not* by nature the children of wrath, as *not*
being children of disobedience ; we are *not* shapen in iniquity,
nor conceived in sin ; we are *not* concluded, or shut up together, under sin ; and every imagination of our hearts, as
they believe, is *not* evil from our youth.

   2. *The impossibility of justification by our own righteousness, is another of these doctrines.*

   To *justify* is to declare a being, placed under a law, to be
just or *righteous ;* or, in other words, *to have done that which
the law required.*   Mankind are placed as subjects under the
law of God.   They have not done what the law required, and
therefore cannot, with truth, be declared to have done it ; or,
in other words, they cannot be justified.   Accordingly, St.
Paul, after having proved at length that all men, both Jews
and Gentiles, are sinners, says, ' Therefore by deeds of law,
there shall no flesh be justified in his sight.'   And again, ' If
there had been a law, which could have given life, verily, righteousness should have come by law ; but, if righteousness come
by law, then Christ died in vain.'   But the Unitarians, in a
vast multitude of instances (for it is not true of them all,)
utterly deny this doctrine, and hold that we are justified by
our own repentance and obedience, both of which, they teach,
are accepted for their own sake.   God therefore, is exhibited
by them, as justifying us in direct opposition to the express
language of his law : ' Cursed is every one that continueth not
in all things written in the book of the law to do them.'   ' He
that doeth these things shall live by them ; but the soul, that
sinneth, shall die.'   In direct contradiction to these declarations
of God himself, they hold that the soul which sinneth shall *not*
die ; and that *he* is *not* cursed who does not continue in all
things written in the law, to do them : while he who doeth *not*
these things shall yet, according to their scheme, live.   Thus,
although God has declared, ' that heaven and earth shall

pass away, sooner than one jot or tittle of the law shall fail;' their doctrine teaches us, that the whole law, so far as its penalty is concerned, shall fail with respect to every person who repents. Not even an entire, unmingled repentance is demanded; nor a pure, uncontaminated future obedience. Both are professedly left imperfect. All the former sins are imperfectly repented of; and all the future obedience is mixed with sin. On the ground of this repentance and this obedience, God is expected to justify man, still placed under a legal dispensation.

3. *Another doctrine of the same nature is the doctrine of Christ's atonement.*

The Unitarians, to whom I referred under the last head, as not holding the doctrines opposed to it, are those who admit the doctrine of Christ's atonement. This I suppose to be true of some of the Socinians, and some of the Arians. Some of the Socinians hold, that ' the fulness of the Godhead dwells,' and will through eternity dwell, ' in Christ, bodily.' What is supposed by them to be the proper import of this declaration I know not that they have explained, and therefore may probably be unable to divine. So far as I can conjecture their intention, I should believe, with Dr. Price, that they really make Christ God, and therefore may not unnaturally suppose that he accomplished an expiation for the sins of men. If this conjecture be just, they harmonize substantially with Praxeas, because, as they deny a distinction of persons in the Godhead, they must suppose the Father, by a mysterious union, to have dwelt in the man Christ Jesus; and thus influencing and directing all his conduct, to have accomplished, through him, an atonement for himself: a doctrine on account of which Praxeas and his followers were called Patripassians; as believing that the Father himself suffered. Some of the Arians also have acknowledged that Christ made atonement for the sins of men. In what manner this was done, or can be done by a creature, a subject of law and government, all whose obedience is due to the utmost extent of his powers and circumstances, and through every moment of his existence, for himself, for his own justification, I know not that they have attempted to explain. I rather suppose that, though professed enemies to mystery, they choose to leave this as a mystery which allows of no investigation. How an atonement can be made by such a being, and how it can be accepted by God, in accordance with the doctrines taught in the Scriptures, I confess myself unable to discern.   Still it is but just to observe, that an atonement is believed by a number of both Socinians and Arians to have been made by Christ.   Dr. Priestley, and most if not all the modern Socinians, and many of the Arians, though I am not able to say how many, utterly deny, so far as my knowledge extends, any atonement at all; and thus take away from the Christian system what the great body of the Church has in every age esteemed the capital doctrine in the scheme of redemption, and from mankind every rational hope of escape from future punishment. The only encouraging declaration to sinners, exclusive of those which are founded on it, which I can find in the Gospel, is this; that ' Christ has redeemed us from under the curse of the law by being made a curse for us.'   Accordingly, this *declaration*, repeated in very numerous forms, is everywhere insisted on in the Gospel, as the commanding theme, and as the only consolation to apostate men.   If the doctrine contained in this declaration be taken out of the Gospel, mankind are left wholly under the dominion of law, and must necessarily suffer its penalty.

In my own view, Dr. Priestley, and those who accord with him in denying an atonement, are more consistent with themselves, or with the other parts of their system, than the rest of the Unitarians.   He who denies the Deity of Christ, appears to me to cut off the possibility of any vicarious interference in the behalf of sinners.   At the same time, the atonement of Christ is so plainly, so frequently, and so unequivocally asserted in the Scriptures, and the whole system of divine dispensations is made to depend upon it so extensively and essentially, that to deny it appears to me to be the same thing as to deny the Scriptures themselves.   So necessary also, and so consolatory is the doctrine of an atonement for sin to such beings as we are, as well as so abundantly asserted in the Scriptures, that I can scarcely suppose any man *willingly* to deny it, unless compelled by something entirely different from the Scriptures themselves, and from the nature of the doctrine. One error infers another.   The error of denying the Deity of Christ has, I apprehend, compelled those who have adopted

it, to deny also all the doctrines which have been here mentioned, and particularly the atonement, notwithstanding they
were opposed in this denial by so many express declarations
of the sacred volume.

4. *The doctrine of justification by faith in Christ, is also
of the same nature.*

As mankind cannot be justified by their own righteousness, it is absolutely necessary, if they are justified at all,
that they should be justified by the righteousness of another.
Accordingly, the Scriptures assert in the most direct and abundant manner, that we are ' justified by' mere ' grace,' or favour, on account of the righteousness of Christ, through that
faith in him, in the exercise of which we give up ourselves to
him, to be his here and for ever. As this doctrine is not only
asserted in very many instances, and in the most express
manner, but is also repeatedly proved in form, especially in the
Epistles to the Romans and the Galatians ; it would seem
incredible that it should be denied by any man, who believed
in divine Revelation. Still it is abundantly denied by Unitarians. Nor do they only deny the doctrine generally, but all
the particulars also of which it is made up. Beside rejecting
the atonement of Christ, and the justification supposed to be
accomplished by means of it, and the influence which faith is
supposed to have in securing such justification to us, they deny
also, the very nature of the faith to which this influence is
ascribed. The faith of the Gospel is an affection of the heart,
being no other than *trust*, or *confidence*. ' With the heart,'
says St. Paul, ' man believeth unto righteousness.' In direct
opposition to this and many other passages of the Scriptures,
the Unitarians, generally at least, consider faith as *a mere
assent of the understanding to probable evidence :* the same
which is called a speculative or historical faith. By this opinion
they strip faith of the moral nature everywhere attributed
to it in the Gospel. ' Abraham believed God, and it was
counted to him for righteousness.' But surely no exercise of
the understanding was ever counted for righteousness to any
man, or can possess any moral nature whatever. ' Thou believest, that there is one God ;' says St. James ; ' thou doest
well. The devils also believe, and tremble.' Certainly that
affection of the mind of which devils are the subjects, cannot

possess moral excellence. ' Without faith it is impossible to please God.' But surely the faith which pleases God must be essentially different from the faith of devils.

5. *Another doctrine of the same nature is the regeneration of the human soul by the Spirit of God.*

That ' without holiness,' or moral excellence, ' no man shall see the Lord,' is, I think, the irresistible dictate of reason, as well as the express declaration of the Scriptures; for it cannot be supposed, that the infinitely holy God can be pleased with creatures who are wholly destitute of such excellence, and who, being wholly sinful, have nothing in them which he can approve, or with which he can be pleased. That ' in us, that is, in our flesh,' or original nature, ' dwelleth no good thing ;' no holiness, no moral excellence, is, as you well know, a declaration contained in the Scriptures. From these two doctrines thus declared, arises indispensably the necessity of such a change in our character as will make us the subjects of holiness. This change is in the Scriptures termed *regeneration, being born again, being created anew ; becoming new creatures, being renewed ;* and is expressed by other similar phraseology, and declared to be indispensable to our entrance into the divine kingdom. ' Except a man be born again,' said our Saviour to Nicodemus, ' he cannot see the kingdom of God.' The production of this change is in the Scriptures ascribed, as his peculiar work, to the Spirit of God. ' Except a man,' says our Saviour again, ' Except a man be born of water, and of the Spirit, he cannot enter into the kingdom of God :' that is, except a man have his mind purified by the Spirit of God, as the body is purified by water, he cannot enter into the kingdom of God. ' Not by works of righteousness which we have done,' says St. Paul, ' but according to his mercy he saved us, by the washing of regeneration, and renewing of the Holy Ghost.' Accordingly, those persons who experience this change of character, are said to be ' born, not of blood. nor of the will of the flesh, nor of the will of man, but of God ;' that is, they derived this change of character not from their parents, nor from their own efforts, nor from the efforts of any man, but from God.

But this change the Unitarians deny, and the agency of the Holy Spirit in effectuating it in the mind of man. Nay, they deny the existence of the Holy Spirit as a person, or agent

As a substitute for regeneration they declare mankind to become better in a gradual manner, by their own will or efforts, and the efforts or will of their fellow-men, to such a degree, that God will accept them. In this manner they make the immense splendour of apparatus for our redemption and sanctification, and all the magnificient exhibitions of Christ and the Holy Spirit, terminate in this; that Christ came to declare divine truth to mankind, and to prove it to be divine truth; and that men, assenting to it with the understanding, change themselves by the ordinary efforts of a sinful mind, into such a character as is denoted in the Scriptures by being born again, and created anew. Such, it would seem, was not however the opinion of St. Paul, when he said, ' The natural man receiveth not the things of the Spirit; for they are foolishness unto him; neither can he know them; for they are spiritually discerned.'

The present occasion will not permit me particularly to follow this subject any farther. It will be sufficient to mention, summarily, several other doctrines which have been denied by Dr. Priestley and his followers.

Our Saviour says, ' A spirit hath not flesh and bones, as ye see me have.' Dr. Priestley, on the contrary, informs us, that the human spirit is constituted only of organized matter; that is, of flesh and bones. St. Paul tells us, that when he is ' absent from the body,' he shall be ' present with the Lord.' Dr. Priestley holds, that Paul was nothing but body; and therefore could not be absent from the body, unless the body could be absent from itself. When the body dies, the soul, according to Dr. Priestley, terminates both its operations and its being, until the resurrection, then to be created again; and therefore is not, and cannot be, present with the Lord until after that period. The Scriptures assert the existence of angels of various orders, both good and evil; and delineate their characters, stations, actions, and enjoyments. Dr. Priestley utterly denies, and even ridicules, the doctrine, that evil angels exist; and labours very hard to disprove the existence of good angels. I do not remember that he expressly denies it, and am not in possession of the volume in which his opinions on this subject are expressed, but he says all that is short of such an explicit denial, and plainly indicates that he does not believe them to exist.

Beyond all this, he denies the plenary inspiration of the apostles; and declares, that we are to acknowledge them inspired only when they say they are inspired; and this, he says, we are to do because the apostles were honest men, and are to be believed in this, and all their other declarations. Dr. Priestley says expressly, that he does not consider the books of Scripture as inspired, but as authentic records of the dispensations of God to mankind, with every particular of which we cannot be too well acquainted. The writers of the books of Scripture he says, were men, and therefore fallible. But all, that we have to do with them is in the character of historians, and witnesses of what they heard and saw: like all other historians, they were liable to mistakes. "Neither I," says he to Dr. Price, "nor, I presume, yourself, believe implicitly every thing which is advanced by any writer in the Old or New Testament. I believe them," that is, the writers, "to have been men, and therefore fallible." And again: "That the books of Scripture were written by particular divine inspiration, is a thing to which the writers themselves make no pretensions. It is a notion destitute of all proof, and that has done great injury to the evidence of Christianity." The reasonings of the divine writers, he declares, we are fully at liberty to judge of, as we are those of other men. Accordingly, he asserts St. Paul in a particular instance to have reasoned fallaciously; and maintains, that Christ was both fallible and peccable. Other English Socinians unite with Dr. Priestley in these sentiments; while Socinians of other nations proceed so far as to treat the writers themselves, and their books, with marked contempt. In these several things there is plainly an utter denial that the Scriptures are a revelation from God. To all these opinions Dr. Priestley was once directly opposed, for he was once a Trinitarian and a Calvinist. The inference seems, therefore, to be necessary, that he was led to them all by his denial of the Deity of Christ. A similar transformation appears to have been undergone by many other Socinians, and something very like it by no small number of Arians. The observation of Mr. Wilberforce, therefore, seems to be but too well founded, when he says; "In the course which we lately traced from nominal orthodoxy to absolute infidelity, Unitarianism is, indeed, a sort of half-way house, if the expression may be pardoned; a stage on the journey, where sometimes a person, indeed, finally stops; but where, not unfrequently, he only pauses for a while, and then pursues his progress."

IV. *The last objection which I shall make at the present time against the doctrine of the Unitarians, is its immoral influence.*

Mr. Belsham says, " Rational Christians are often represented as indifferent to practical religion." Dr. Priestley says, " A great number of the Unitarians of the present age are only men of good sense, and without much practical religion; and there is a greater apparent conformity to the world in them than is observable in others." He also says, that he hopes they have more of a real principle of Religion than they seem to have. He farther allows, that Unitarians are peculiarly wanting in zeal for religion.

At the same time, Dr. Priestley acknowledges that Calvinists have less apparent conformity to the world; and that they seem to have more of a real principle of religion than Socinians. He also acknowledges, that those who, from a principle of religion, ascribe more to God and less to man than other persons, are men of the greatest elevation of piety. Mr. Wilberforce declares it to be an unquestionable fact, that Unitarians are not, in general, distinguished for superior purity of life; and that Unitarianism seems to be resorted to by those who seek a refuge from the strictness of the practical precepts contained in the Bible.

That these representations are just, I consider as completely proved by the Rev. A. Fuller in his Letters; and no less completely the immoral tendency of the Socinian system.

It is also a well known truth, that Unitarian churches are in general moderately frequented on the sabbath, that the sermons of their preachers are generally cold, especially on the peculiar duties of religion, that they have never formed nor united with others in forming missions for the propagation of the Gospel among the heathens and Mohammedans, nor distinguished themselves by any discernable earnestness in the cause of practical Christianity. On the contrary, their own declarations, too numerous to be here recited, teach us abundantly that, in the view of a great part of them, almost all the seriousness, fervour and self-denial, that deep sense of sin, and that prayerful, watchful, and strenuous opposition to temptation, which their opponents esteem indispensable to salvation, are mere enthusiasm, superstition, or melancholy. Christianity with them seems to be an easy, pleasant kind of religion, unincumbered by any peculiar restraints, admitting without difficulty of what are usually called the pleasures and amusements of the world, and only confining them within the bounds of delicacy and politeness. Can this, let me ask, be taking up the cross, denying ourselves, and following after Christ?

DIVINITY OF CHRIST.

OBJECTIONS TO THE MODE IN WHICH THE UNITA-RIANS CONDUCT THE CONTROVERSY.

THE LORD KNOWETH THE THOUGHTS OF THE WISE, THAT THEY ARE VAIN.

1 CORINTHIANS III. 20.

IN my last Discourse I proposed several objections against the *doctrine* of the *Unitarians.* I shall now allege *some objections against their conduct in the management of the controversy.*

Before I proceed to the execution of this design, I shall premise the following general doctrines concerning the Scriptures :——

That the Old and New Testaments were revealed to the several writers of them by the Spirit of God.

That, although the several writers were left to use their own characteristical style, or manner of writing, yet they have always written such ' words as the Holy Ghost taught,' and ' not such as are taught by the wisdom of man.'

That these Scriptures contain ' all things pertaining to life and to godliness.'

That they were written for the use of mankind, the learned and unlearned alike ; and therefore were written in the usual language of men, with the usual signification of that language, as being that only which such men can understand.

That, therefore they express true ideas of God, of Christ,

of human nature, of human duty, and of the way of salvation, in such a manner that unlearned men, as are ninety-nine hundredths of those for whom they were written, can and, if sincerely disposed, will understand them, so far as is necessary to enable them to perform their duty, and obtain their salvation.

Every one of these doctrines I believe not only to be strictly true, but capable of the most satisfactory proof, and proof of which I feel myself satisfactorily possessed. Ocasional remarks I shall make on this subject in the present Discourse; but a fuller discussion of it must be left to a future time. I have mentioned these doctrines *here*, because they are in my view just, important, and necessary to enable those who hear me to understand the real import of the following observations.

1. *The Unitarians, to a great extent, have interpreted the Scriptures according to preconceived opinions of their own, and not according to the obvious meaning of the passages themselves.*

That I may not be thought to charge this upon the Unitarians without ground, I will recite some of the opinions which they themselves have expressed concerning the Scriptures. You may remember that in my last Discourse I mentioned that Dr. Priestley pronounces Christ to be fallible, the Scriptures not to be written by particular inspiration, and the writers to make no pretensions to such inspiration. The contrary notion, also, he asserts to be destitute of all proof and to have done great injury to the evidence of Christianity. He declares the writers of the New Testament to have improperly quoted some texts from the Old, and to have been sometimes misled by Jewish prejudices. Another Unitarian writer says, " It is not the nature and design of the Scriptures to decide upon speculative, controverted questions, even in religion and morality; not to solve the doubts, but rather to make us obey the dictates of our consciences." Mr. Belsham says, " The Bereans are commended for not taking the word even of an apostle;" and pleads this as an example for us. Steinbart, a foreign Unitarian, speaking of the narrations in the New Testament, says, " These narrations, true or false, are only suited to ignorant, uncultivated minds." Semler, another,

says, that " Peter speaks according to the conception of the
Jews, when he says, ' Prophecy came not in old time by the
will of man ; but holy men of God spake as they were moved
by the Holy Ghost;'" and adds, that " the prophets may
have delivered the offspring of their own brains as divine revelation." Concerning the reasoning of the apostles, Dr.
Priestley says, " We are to judge of it, as of that of other
men, by a due consideration of the propositions they advance,
and the arguments they allege." That men who entertain
such views concerning the Scriptures will not, and, according
to their own opinions, ought not to receive the declarations of
the Scriptures in any other manner than that in which they
receive the declarations contained in every other book, is
obvious to the least consideration. If the Scriptures were not
written, and the writers do not pretend that they wrote, by
particular divine inspiration, then they certainly stand on the
same footing with all other books ; and the writers are undoubtedly to be regarded, as Dr. Priestley says, merely in the
character of historians and witnesses.

If Christ and the apostles were fallible men, and St. Paul
has actually reasoned fallaciously, then undoubtedly their reasonings and all their doctrines are to be examined in the same
manner as those of other men. If the Scriptures were not
designed to settle speculative opinions or doctrines even in
morality and religion, then it is plain, that they must be
settled, if settled at all, by some other tribunal ; and there is
no other tribunal, but our own reason. If the doubts of conscience were not intended to be solved by the Scriptures,
then, certainly, the mind must solve them, so far as it can,
for itself. These gentlemen have, therefore, prescribed a rule
for themselves which every man may certainly know beforehand, even without reading their works, they could not fail to
follow : for no man ever believed the Scriptures not to be an
infallible rule of direction in these things, who did not also
make his own reason his directory ; unless he, indeed, implicitly submitted to the dictates of his fellow-men. In truth it
would be difficult to find a man who does not distinctly perceive that there is no other directory.

Accordingly, every reader of Unitarian books must have
observed, that the writers evidently refer the interpretation of
the Scriptures to their own pre-conceived opinions, or the

previous decisions of their own reason.   That is, they form their system of theology, and then make use of the Scriptures to support or countenance it.   Wherever they find passages whose obvious meaning will countenance their own opinions, they make the most of them, by admitting this meaning. Wherever the obvious meaning, that is, the meaning derived from the language, according to customary use, or according to the tenour of the discourse of which it is a part, will not countenance their opinions, they contrive for it some other meaning which will better suit those opinions.

That the Unitarians have actually conducted the controversy in this manner, can be made abundantly evident by an appeal to their writings.   One strong proof of this conduct is found in the Arian notion, *that Christ is a delegated God.* The present occasion will permit me to exhibit but one, out of several modes, in which the truth of this declaration may be evinced.   Christ is undeniably many times asserted in the Scriptures to be God.   These assertions are as unqualified and absolute as those in which the Father is declared to be God. . They are also accompanied with a great variety of declarations, in which are ascribed to him, without any qualification, all the attributes, actions, and relations attributable to God, exclusively of those which belong to the Father as such; and are also followed by the very same worship, unconditionally required, and actually rendered to him by inspired men, and by the host of Heaven.   Now from all these assertions I will withdraw the name of Christ, and substitute that of the Father.   Let me ask, Would any of the Arians have ever thought of denying that the name God, in any one of these passages, did not mean the true and real God, but only a God by delegation?   To this question there can be no answer but a negative.   Whence, then, do they refuse to acknowledge the same passages to mean the same thing, as they now stand? Plainly for this undeniable reason, that they have beforehand determined that God is not, and cannot be *tri-personal,* or *triune.*   In this determination, however, they are unhappy, as being unwarranted, not only by the Scriptures, but also by that very *reason* to which they make so confident an appeal; for nothing is more opposed to both, than that a finite, dependent being can have these things ascribed to him with truth.

On the same grounds do the Socinians declare *Christ to be a mere man;* not because he is not abundantly declared to be God in the Scriptures, but because they pre-determine by their reason, that a person cannot exist by the union of God with man; and that God cannot be triune. Let any man read their comments on the Scriptures relative to Christ, and he will see this to be abundantly shown by the nature of the comments, and the words in which they are uttered.

I have observed, that the Arians are unhappy in choosing this position as the basis of their distinguishing doctrine; because it is unwarranted either by reason, or Revelation. Both *they,* and the Socinians, are unhappy on other accounts. They know not, and cannot know by any dictates of reason, that God is not triune. The nature and manner of his existence, so far as this subject is concerned, lie wholly beyond their reach, and beyond that of all other men. We cannot even begin to form ideas concerning them. It is, therefore, idle and fruitless to form propositions about them; still more idle to reason and conclude; and still more idle to make such conclusions the basis of our faith in a case of such magnitude. All that we know, or can know, is just that, and that *only,* which God has been pleased immediately to reveal.

The same observations are, with the same force, applicable to the doctrine of *the union of the divine and human nature in the person of Christ.* Of this subject we literally know nothing, beside what is revealed.

That a mere man, also, can have these names, attributes, actions, and relations, and this worship ascribed to him *with truth,* is not only unaccordant with reason, but common sobriety, or decency. A few more instances of this nature: which, because I have not the means of multiplying examples, nor time for such a purpose, I shall select wholly from Dr. Priestley's *Notes on the Books of Scripture.*

In his notes on the first chapter of John, Dr. Priestley informs us that *the word* Λογος, which, you know, is translated ' the Word,' *is nothing more than the power of God, by which all things were made; and therefore,* he says, *it was no distinct, inferior principle, but God himself.* On this explanation I shall make but one general remark; *viz.* that this is the only known instance in which an attribute of God, either in sacred or profane writings, has been asserted to be God. If

St. John, therefore, had this meaning, he has used language to express it which was probably never used by any other human being.* Having premised this remark, I shall proceed to examine the soundness of the explanation by the most unobjectionable of all methods ; viz. *the substitution of the explanation for the thing explained; Power* and *God,* for *the Word,* or Λογος; as being the two things, which the term Λογος is, successively, declared to denote. This experiment, to which no Socinian can object, shall be first made with *power.* ' In the beginning was the *power of God,* and *this power* was with God, and *this power* was God. The same was in the beginning with God. All things were made by *it,* and without *it* was not any thing made, that was made. In *it* was life, and the life was the light of men. And the light shineth in darkness, and the darkness comprehended *it* not. *It* was in the world, and the world was made by *it,* and the world knew *it* not. *It* came unto *its* own, and *its* own received *it* not. But as many as received *it,* to them gave *it* power to become the sons of God ; even to them that believe on *its* name. And the *power* was made flesh and dwelt among us (and we beheld *its* glory, the glory as of the only begotten of the Father) full of grace and truth. John bare witness of *it,* and cried, saying, This was *it* of which I spake : *It* that cometh after me is preferred before me, for *it* was before me. And of *its* fulness have we all received, and grace for grace. For the law was given by Moses, but grace and truth came by Jesus Christ.'

Dr. Priestley says, *the power was God;* St. John says, it ' was made flesh and dwelt among us, full of grace and truth.' According to his comment, therefore, God became flesh, and dwelt among us. According to his comment, also, this power was Christ ; for he says, *it* ' dwelt among us, full of grace and *truth :*' but St. John immediately subjoins, ' Grace and truth came' (that is, into this world) ' by Jesus Christ.' Therefore, Jesus Christ is God.

This passage, formed in the very manner prescribed by Dr. Priestley himself in his explanation, certainly can need no comment from me. I shall only say, that if there is a Socinian in the world who can make the parts of it, taken together,

---

* 1 John iv. 16, to be hereafter explained.

mean any intelligible thing, I think I may safely yield him the point in controversy.

Let us now make the trial with the other term, *God.* ' In the beginning was *God*, and *God* was with God, and *God* was God.' Two verses more will suffice. And *God* was made flesh, and dwelt among us, and we beheld his glory (the glory as of the only begotten of the Father,) full of grace and truth. No one hath seen God at any time, but the only begotten Son, who is in the bosom of the Father, he hath declared him.'

Once more, let us try the same experiment with *the super-angelic being* of the Arians. ' In the beginning was ' *a super-angelic creature*, named *the Word*, ' and ' *this super-angelic creature* ' was with God, and ' *this super-angelic creature* ' was God. The same was in the beginning with God. All things were made by ' *this super-angelic creature*, ' and without him was not any thing made that was made.' I presume, I need proceed no farther. That interpretation of a passage can need nothing added to it, which makes God himself say, that *a creature was in the beginning with God, and was God ; and that, although he was himself created, or made, yet he made every thing that was made ; and of course made himself.* I had designed to subjoin two or three more specimens, but the time will not permit me to recite them. That which I have recited, will serve to show to what lengths the interpretation of the Scriptures, according to our preconceived opinions, will lead men of superior learning and abilities. At the reading of this only, how can we avoid exclaiming, ' Who is this, that darkeneth counsel by words without knowledge ?'

On this plan of interpretation at large I ask, Can it in any respect consist with what the Scriptures say of themselves ? The prophet Isaiah (chapter viii. 29.) says, ' To the law, and to the testimony : if they speak not according to this word, it is because there is no light in them.'

' All Scripture,' says St. Paul, ' is given by inspiration of God ; and is profitable for doctrine, for reproof, for correction, and for instruction in righteousness ; that the man of God may be perfect, thoroughly furnished unto every good work.' ' No prophecy,' says St. Peter, ' is of private interpretation : for never at any time was prophecy brought by the will of man ; but the holy men of God spake, being moved by the

Holy Ghost.' *   ' We,' says St. Paul, speaking of himself, and his fellow-apostles, ' have the mind of Christ.'   And again, ' For God, who commanded the light to shine out of darkness, hath shined in our hearts, to give us the light of the knowledge of the glory of God in the face of Jesus Christ.'   And again, ' I certify you, brethren, that the Gospel, which was preached of me, was not after man ; for I neither received it of man, neither was I taught it, but by the revelation of Jesus Christ.'

In perfect harmony with these and the like declarations, Moses, the first of the inspired writers, says, ' Ye shall not add unto the word which I command you ; neither shall ye diminish aught from it.'   ' St. John,' the last of them, says at the close of his writings, ' For I testify unto every man that heareth the words of the prophecy of this book, if any man shall add unto these things, God shall add unto him the plagues that are written in this book.   And, if any man shall take away from the words of this prophecy, God shall take away his part out of the book of life.'   From these passages it is evident, that the character which the Scriptures attribute to themselves is altogether opposite to that which has been mentioned in the former part of this Discourse, as given to them by Unitarian writers : That they are in fact ' revealed by God, by the inspiration of the Holy Ghost :' That no man, therefore, can ' add to them, or diminish aught from them,' without exposing himself to the ' plagues' which they denounce, and to the loss of ' his part of the book of life.'   ' If we speak not according to them,' it is declared that ' there is no light in us.' In our interpretation of them we are directed in the most solemn manner to receive the things which they declare.   ' Let God be true,' says the Apostle, ' but every man a liar.'   ' See,' says Agur, ' that thou add not to his words, lest he reprove thee, and thou be found a liar.'   ' If we,' says St. Paul, ' or an angel from heaven, preach any other Gospel, than that which we have preached, let him be accursed.'   Who, with these solemn commands and awful denunciations before him, can think for a moment of rejecting the obvious meaning of the Scriptures, and substituting a meaning not contained in the words, but contrived by himself?

Nor are these gentlemen less unfortunate in another impor-

* Macknight

tant particular. The Scriptures were written for mankind at large. Of these, ninety-nine hundredths, to say the least, are plain, uninformed men, incapable of understanding language in any other manner than the known, customary one. If, then, the obvious meaning is not the true one, *they* are absolutely unable ever to find the true one ; and so far the Scriptures were written in vain. But it cannot be supposed that God would do any thing in vain ; and still less that he would disregard the salvation and the souls of ninety-nine hundredths of his creatures, when publishing his word ; and cause it to be so written that this great number could not, if ever so sincerely disposed, possibly find out its meaning, nor of course the way to eternal life ; while, at the same time, he made provision for the remaining *one* hundredth. It will not, I suppose, be pretended that the soul of a learned man is of more value in the sight of God than that of an unlearned man. But if the meaning of the Scriptures is to be discovered, not by the words, but by a contrived accordance with preconceived philosophical opinions, no unlearned man can find out this meaning at all.

But the Scriptures themselves have decided this point. In Prov. viii. 8, 9, Christ says, ' All the words of my mouth are in righteousness ; there is nothing froward or perverse in them. They are all plain to him that understandeth' (that is, to him that hath understanding ; or, in other words, to him that departeth from evil ;) ' and right to them that find knowledge.' In John vii. 16, 17, the same glorious Person says, ' My doctrine' (that is, the scheme of doctrine which I teach) ' is not mine, but his that sent me. If any man will do his will, ho shall know of the doctrine, whether it be of God.' Now it will not be pretended, that plain men do not depart from evil as truly and as often, in proportion to their number, as learned men. Of course, it must be confessed that plain men find a plain meaning in the words of Christ, or of the Scriptures. It will be acknowledged, that unlearned men, in many instances at least, ' do the will of God ;' and therefore, unless Christ has erred in this point, ' know of his doctrine, whether it is of God.'

One more passage will be amply sufficient to cut off even *cavilling* on this point. The prophet Isaiah (chapter xxxv. 8,) says, ' An highway shall be there, and it shall be called the way of holiness; and the way-faring men, though fools, shall not err therein.' It will hardly be necessary to observe, that this ' highway,' this ' way of holiness,' is no other than the Gospel. But it is evidently impossible that plain men should ever find the meaning attached by Unitarians to the numerous passages which speak of Christ as God. No such man would ever mistrust that a super-angelic creature was ' called Wonderful, Counsellor, the mighty God, the Father of the everlasting age, the Prince of Peace :' that ' of the increase of his government and peace there should be no end,' Isaiah ix. 6 : that ' his goings forth were from of old, from everlasting :' or, as in the Original, ' from the days of eternity :' or that this creature ' was in the beginning with God, and was God :' that ' all things were made by him, and that without him was not any thing made that was made :' or that ' he was over all things, God blessed for evermore.' No such man would ever have thought of reading, " In the beginning was divine power, and this power was with God, and this power was God. That it was in the world; that the world was made by it; and the world knew it not. That as many as received it, to them gave it power to become the sons of God, even to them that believe on its name. That this power became flesh, and dwelt among us (and we beheld its glory, the glory as of the only begotten of the Father,) full of grace and truth. John bare witness of it, and cried, saying, This was it of which I spake. It that cometh after me is preferred before me, for it was before me." No plain man would ever have thought of reading, " In the beginning was God, and God was with God, and God was God."

Should it be said, in opposition to the observations which I have made concerning the intelligibleness of the Scriptures, that my antagonists will grant that the Scriptures are thus plain, in points of essential importance to our duty and salvation ; but need not be supposed to be so in mere speculative opinions : I answer, that no doctrine is of *more importance*, whether speculative or practical, than *that* which teaches the *character of Christ;* except that which teaches the existence and perfections of God. If Christ be a *creature*, all the worship, and all other regard rendered to him as the Creator, is unquestionably mere idolatry; the sin, which of all sins is the most strongly threatened and reproved in the Scriptures. If Christ is God, then a denial that he is God is all that is meant by impiety. It is a denial of his primary and essential character; of the attributes which in this character belong to him; of the Relations which he sustains to the universe, and will for ever sustain; of the actions which he has performed, and will perform throughout eternity; and of the essential ' glory, which he had with the Father before ever the world was.' • Man is a being, made up of an animal body and a rational mind. Should I deny that a particular person possessed a rational mind, would it not be justly said that I denied him to be a man, and refused to acknowledge his primary and most essential character? If Christ is God-man, and I deny him to be God, do I not at least as entirely deny his primary and most essential character? In other words, do I not plainly ' deny the Lord that bought me?' It is evidently impossible for him who makes this denial to render to Christ those regards, that confidence, love, reverence, and obedience which a man, who believed Christ to be God, would feel himself indispensably bound to render. Indeed, were it possible, he would necessarily, and in the very act of rendering them, condemn himself as guilty of idolatry. On the other hand he who believes Christ to be God, cannot refuse to render them, without condemning himself as guilty, and without being actually guilty, of the plainest and grossest impiety, because he withholds from the true God the homage and obedience due to his character. The Unitarians censure the system of the Trinitarians as being idolatrous, and them as being idolaters. If the Unitarian scheme is true, the censure is just. *We*, on the other hand, and with equal justice, if our scheme is true, declare them to be guilty of direct and gross impiety; because they worship not ' the Father, the Son, and the Holy Ghost;' the Jehovah of the Scriptures; the Jehovah Aleim, ' who is one Jehovah;' but another and very different God.

The admission of the Deity of Christ, therefore, if he be really God, is a fundamental doctrine of Christianity, mistakes about which are altogether dangerous and dreadful. This is plainly felt to be the case by the plain people even among the Socinians. For Mrs. Barbauld informs us, that although the errors of the Trinitarians '' are losing ground among thinking people, yet there is in that class (among the Socinians,) who are called serious Christians, a sort of leaning towards them ; an idea that they are, if not true, at least good to be believed ; and that a salutary error is better than a dangerous truth."

Can it then be believed, that God can have directed the Scriptures to be so written that the true meaning of them in a case of this fundamental importance, a case in which mankind are in so imminent danger of becoming either impious, or idolatrous, is so obscure as to make plain men utterly unable to find it out, however honestly disposed ; and that the great body of religious men should, in all ages of the Church, have totally and infinitely mistaken their real intention ?   Can that mode of interpretation which leads of course to this conclusion, be the true one ?

II. *The Unitarians reject the doctrine, that Christ is God, and the obvious meaning of all those passages which teach it, because the doctrine is mysterious.*

This I object to as a totally irrational ground of such rejection.   There are two reasons which will effectually prove this irrationality.

1. *All mankind readily admit, and, if they believe any thing, must every moment admit, mysteries, as the objects of their faith.* This world is made up of atoms. What are they ?   Dr. Priestley informs us, that they are " centres of attraction and repulsion."   This definition, translated out of Latin English into Saxon English, is, that " atoms are centres of drawing to, and driving from :" a definition which I believe it would puzzle Dr. Priestley himself to unriddle, and at least as applicable to points of space as to atoms.   They are also defined to be " solid extended somethings."   What is the *something* thus solid and extended ?   Here our inquiries are stopped, and an atom is found to be an absolute mystery. The world is made up of atoms.   What binds them together, so as to constitute a world ?   *Attraction*, it is answered. What is attraction ?   To this there is no answer.   The world, then, on which we tread, in which we live, and about which we think we have extensive knowledge, is wholly formed out of particles absolutely mysterious, bound together by a power equally mysterious.

These atoms constitute *vegetables*.   What is a vegetable ?

" An organized body," it is answered ; " the subject of vegetable life." What is vegetable life ? To this question there is no satisfactory answer. In the same manner are we conducted to a speedy end in all our inquiries concerning the mineral, vegetable, and rational worlds.

Mystery meets us at every step, and lies at the bottom of the whole. The power, by which this Discourse was thought, or written, or spoken, defies all human investigation.

If mysteries, then, are found everywhere in the *works* of God ; can it be supposed, that they are not found in the *character* and *being* of the same God ? There is nothing more mysterious, more absolutely inexplicable, in the doctrine of the Trinity, than in the power by which, and the manner in which, mind acts upon matter.

2. *The Unitarians themselves, though professedly rejecting mysteries, admit them into their creed without number.* That a creature created all things, upholds all things, possesses all thi.s, rules all things, and is the final cause of their existence ; that a creature should be ' the same yesterday, to-day, and for ever ;' that he should be the final judge and rewarder of the just and the unjust ; that he should sit on the throne of the heavens, and receive the prayers of inspired men in this world, and the everlasting praises of the heavenly host in the world to come ; or that God, if these things are not so, should have caused or permitted them to be written in his word ; are, to say the least, mysteries as entire and as inexplicable as any which have ever entered the thoughts of man. It ill becomes those, who admit these things, therefore, to reject any thing merely on account of its being mysterious.

III. *The Unitarians take an unwarrantable license, with the language of the Scriptures.*

I know not that I can express my own views of this subject, within the same compass, better than in the following words of a respectable writer, which are a part of some Observations concerning Dr. Priestley's Notes on the Scriptures. " It is a leading and determined purpose of Dr. Priestley's Notes to serve the cause of what is arrogantly termed Unitarianism ; and he has certainly kept this purpose in view. To say the least, he is a zealous and resolute advocate. His maxim seems to have been, to maintain his cause at all events.

Seldom is he at a loss for a gloss or an evasion, in aiming at the accomplishment of his object.   If he meets with a passage whose indubitable reading, and whose obvious plain meaning are such as every unbiassed man would pronounce favourable to the diety and atonement of Christ, the Doctor is ready with ample stores of metaphorical, enigmatical, and idiomatical forms of interpretation.; and stubborn must be that text which will not bend under one or other of his modes of treatment. In some cases *a various reading*, though none of the best, is called in to his assistance.   Should this aid fail, some learned critic, or other is at hand with *a conjectural alteration*.   Or, if none of these means appear advisable, the philosophical commentator has in reserve a kind of *logical alkali*, which will at least neutralize a pungent passage ; for example, the sage observation, ' *About the interpretation of it critics differ much.*'

" And lastly, in very desperate instances, a method is resorted to, the most simple and compendious imaginable ; and that is, *to say nothing at all about them !* " .

One of the modes in which the Unitarians take unwarrantable license with the language of the Scriptures, is to pronounce passages to be *interpolated*, which are abundantly evidenced by Manuscripts, ancient versions, and quotations in writings of the fathers, to be *genuine* parts of the Scriptures.

Another is, to declare, without warrant, *words* and *phrases* to be *wanting* ; and *then to supply them* ; where they are supplied by *no* authority but *their own*.   Thus Grotius and Dr. Clark supply the word ιστω in that remarkable text, Romans ix. 5 ; and then translate it, ' Of whom, as concerning the flesh, Christ came, who is over all, God' BE ' blessed for evermore.'

This, it will be observed, does not aid them at all, because he ' who is over all things,' is of course *God*.

Another mode is, to *annex a meaning* to some particular *word*, or *phrase*, which *suits their own purpose*, but which is entirely aside from all customary use.   Thus Pierce interprets ουκ αρπαγμον ηγησατο το ειναι ισα Θεω ; ' He thought it no robbery to be equal with God ;' to mean, *He was not eager, or tenacious, to retain that likeness to God :* a translation, which no criticism can justify, or satisfactorily explain.

Another mode of the same nature is, to *suggest the conjectural opinion* of some other *critic*, or some *learned friend*; which is introduced with so much gravity, as to give a kind of weight and speciousness to the peculiar interpretation proposed. Thus Dr. Priestley,* commenting on John xiv. 2, ' In my Father's house are many mansions;' says, " Perhaps, with a learned friend of mine, we may understand *the mansions in his Father's-house*, of which Jesus here speaks, to signify, not places of rest and happiness in heaven, but *stations of trust and usefulness upon earth*; such as he was then about to quit," &c. Here *the house of God* is made to mean *earth*, and *mansions, stations*; and Christ, of course, was *going away* to prepare a place for his Apostles *here*, where he and they then were; and was to come again, to receive them in the place whither he himself was going, that ' they might be with him' *there*, by continuing *here*.

Another mode of the same nature is, *an unbounded licence in making the scriptural language figurative.*

That the language of the Scriptures is to a great extent and in a high degree figurative, is unquestionably true. But certainly there are limits to this character, not only in scriptural, but all other language. It must I think be admitted, that we are to consider the language of the Scriptures especially, and of all other good writings generally, as figurative, only in accordance with the following rules.

(1.) That the figure be agreeable to the state of the mind of him who uses it; that is, to his views and feelings.

2.) That it be founded on some analogy or relation to the subject.

(3.) That it accord with the discourse, so far as to make sense.

(4.) That in the Scriptures it violate no doctrine declared, at least by the writer.

(5.) That it be so obvious, as not to demand invention or contrivance in the reader.

(6.) That it be explicable according to the opinions, or other circumstances of those for whom it was written, so as to be capable of being understood by them.

(7.) That it suit the occasion and other circumstances of the discourse.

* Eclectic Review, No. ii, Vol. ii.

But how, according to these or any other rules of construing language, are we to interpret the declaration, ' For by him were created all things, that are in heaven and that are in earth, visible and invisible, whether they be thrones, or dominions, or principalities, or powers,' to mean, that *Christ published the Gospel and constituted the Christian church?* Is it the same thing to *publish the Gospel,* as to *create?* Is it the same thing to *constitute the church,* as to *create?* Are the Gospel and the church ' *all things* that are in heaven and that are in earth?' Are they ' all things *visible and invisible?*' Who are the ' thrones,' the ' dominions,' the ' principalities,' and the ' powers?' Are they bishops, elders, and deacons: the only officers ever supposed to belong to the church?

The Holy Ghost is by Unitarians denied to be a person, and is commonly asserted to be no other than *the power of God :* the name *Spirit* being, in their view, always figurative. According to what rules of construction are we, on this plan, to interpret the following passages; in which I shall substitute the word *power* for *Ghost,* or *Spirit* ; always intending by it, however, the *divine* power.

- ' All manner of sin and blasphemy shall be forgiven unto men ; but the blasphemy against the Holy' *Power* ' shall not be forgiven unto men.   Matt. xii. 13. ' Baptizing them in the name of the Father, and of the Son, and of the Holy' *Power.* Matt. xxviii. 19.   ' Why has Satan filled the heart, to lie unto the Holy' *Power?* Acts v. 3.   ' God anointed Jesus with the Holy *Power* ' and with power.' Acts x. 33.   Romans xv. 13, ' That ye may abound in hope through the power of the Holy' *Power.*   Romans xv. 19, ' Through mighty signs, and wonders, by the power of the' *Power* ' of God.' ' In demonstration of the   *Power,* ' and of power.'   John xvi. 13, ' Howbeit, when he, the' *Power* ' of truth has come, he will guide you into all truth ; for he shall not speak of himself ; but whatsoever he shall hear, that shall he speak,' &c. &c.

More instances cannot I think be necessary to elucidate this part of the subject.

The last mode which I shall mention, a mode adopted when a passage is to stubborn to bend to any of the preceding, is, to leave it with such an observation as this : " Critics are very much divided about the meaning of this passage ;" insinuating to the reader, that the passage is so obscure and perplexed, that he is to despair of any explanation.

In this manner, it seems to me, the Scriptures must soon become such as the Prophet Isaiah declared they would become to the Jews, at a certain future period. ' The vision of all,' says that Prophet, chapter xxix. 11, ' is become unto you as the words of a book that is sealed ; which men deliver to one that is learned, saying, Read this, I pray thee ; And he saith, I cannot, for it is sealed ;' and the book is delivered ' to him that is not learned, saying, Read this, I pray thee; and he saith, I am not learned.'

IV. *I object to the Unitarians direct unfairness in their conduct towards Trinitarians.*

The unfairness here intended respects two particulars.

1. *They treat the Trinitarians as if they were Tritheists, or held the existence of three Gods.*

This they do in several methods, particularly, *the name Unitarian*, as I formerly observed, is designed to denote that they, among Christians, *exclusively* hold the existence of one God. The very name itself, therefore, is intended to declare, that Trinitarians hold the existence of *more Gods than one.* An imputation which, they well know, every Trinitarian rejects with abhorrence.

Again: in arguing with Trinitarians, they customarily undertake to prove that the Scriptures, in a great variety of passages, *assert that there is but one God·;* as if this were the *very point,* or at least *one* point, in debate between *them* and *Trinitarians.* Accordingly, when they have proved this point, which a child can easily do, they commonly triumph, and appear to consider the dispute as ended, and their antagonists overthrown. In this way they insinuate to their readers that Trinitarians hold the existence of more Gods than one ; and that all their arguments are intended to support this doctrine. Whereas every Unitarian perfectly well knows that the unity of God is as entirely and as professedly holden by Trinitarians as himself; that none of their arguments are directed against it ; and that this point has never been, and never can be, in debate between him and them. That the doctrine of the Trinity involves or infers the existence of more Gods than one, every Unitarian has a right to prove, and may with perfect fairness prove, if he can. But to insinuate, that Trinitarians believe the existence of more Gods than one, and to treat them as if they thus believed, when it is perfectly well known that every Trinitarian disclaims such belief with indignation, is conduct which, in my view, admits of no justification.

2. *The Unitarians customarily undertake to prove that Christ is a man ; and thence triumph also, as if they had refuted the doctrine of their opposers.* Now it is well known to every Unitarian, that the *Trinitarians* with one voice *acknowledge Christ to be a man ;* and that this point, therefore, is not in controversy between him and them.

It is wholly disingenuous, therefore, to insinuate that it is in debate, or to attempt to make it a part of the controversy, when they know that Trinitarians as uniformly hold it as themselves. Of these facts, however, they usually take not the least notice, but appear to consider both points as the principal topics in debate. Such conduct in their antagonists the Unitarians would censure with severity.

I shall conclude this discussion with two observations.

The first is, *that the Unitarians are extensively disagreed concerning the person of Christ.* The Arians consider him as a super-angelic being : The Socinians partly as a man, ' in whom dwelt all the fulness of the Godhead bodily ;' and partly as a man, differing from other men only by being wiser and better : The Sabellians, as God manifested in one manner. The Patripassians, as the Father living and suffering in the man Jesus Christ. Some of the Unitarians hold, that he created the universe ; some that he made an atonement for sin ; some that he ought to be worshipped ; and some deny all these doctrines. This difference is derived from two sources ; one is, that their reason or philosophy dictates nothing concerning Christ in which they can harmonize. The other is, that the Scriptures in no very satisfactory manner support either of their opinions. But it ought to be observed, that this very difference is of such a nature as strongly to indicate that the Scriptures exhibit Christ as God.

The second observation is, *that Unitarianism has an evident tendency to infidelity.*

This is strongly evident in the manner in which the Unitarians speak of the Scriptures, the insufficiency which they attribute to them for settling religious doctrines, and the superior sufficiency which they attribute to reason.   It is evident, also, in the laxity of their ideas concerning what genuine religion is, their want of veneration for the sabbath, their want of attendance on the public worship of God, and their devotion to the pleasures and amusements of life.

Dr. Priestley acknowledges, that " the Unitarian societies do not flourish : that their members have but a slight attachment to them, and easily desert them."

Voltaire also says, " that down to his own time only a very small number of those called Unitarians had held any religious meetings."

Dr. Priestley also say, that " many Unitarians have become more indifferent to religion in general, than they were before ; and to all the modes and doctrines of religion."   Concerning himself, he says, " that he was once a Calvinist, and that of the straitest sect ; then a high Arian ; next a low Arian ; then a Socinian ; and in a little time a Socinian of the lowest kind, in which Jesus Christ is considered as a mere man, the son of Joseph and Mary, and naturally as fallible and peccable as Moses, or any other Prophet."   He also says, " he does not know when his creed will be fixed."   This I consider as the true progress, nature, and tendency of Unitarianism.   The end of this progress in most men is easily foreseen.   Let him, therefore, who finds himself inclined to think favourably of these opinions, consider well before he embraces them, what will probably be the final termination of his religious system.

SERMON XLII.

INCARNATION OF CHRIST.

GOD SENDING HIS OWN SON IN THE LIKENESS OF SINFUL FLESH.
ROMANS VIII. 3.

I HAVE, in several preceding Discourses, endeavoured to settle the meaning of the phrase, ' God's own Son,' used in this passage of the Scriptures. This was indispensably necessary at the opening of all the observations intended to be made concerning the doctrines of the Christian system. As these doctrines are truths, partly unfolding to us the character and conduct of this wonderful Person, and partly disclosing to us the consequences of his interference in the behalf of mankind ; as his character, in a greater or less degree, affects every doctrine of what is appropriately called the Christian religion ; and as those who set out with different views of his character, proceed farther and farther asunder, so as to form in the end entirely different systems of religious doctrine ; it became indispensable that this great point should, as far as possible, be fixed at the beginning. If the attempt to do this has been successful, in the degree which I have hoped, it will contribute not a little to settle on a firm foundation most of the doctrines which remain to be investigated. My own views concerning them it will, at least, contribute to explain.

In this passage we are informed, that ' God sent his Son in the likeness of sinful flesh.' The meaning of this phrase (' the likeness of sinful flesh,') will be obvious from similar phrases in Philippians ii. 7, 8, ' He was made,' or, as it is in the Original, ' He existed in the likeness of men ; and being found in fashion as a man.' In the first of these phrases, the original word, ὁμοιώματι, is the same with that translated ' likeness,' in the text. In the second, it is σχήματι, a term of a kindred signification, denoting *form* or *fashion*. In the passage in Philippians, the phrases, ' He existed in the likeness of men,' and, ' He was found in fashion as a man,' denote, that he was a real man. In the text, the phrase, ' the likeness of sinful flesh,' denotes, that *he was sent in real flesh* ; here figuratively called *sinful*, because it is in all other instances, except that of Christ, *the flesh*, or body, *of sinful beings*.

The Doctrine contained in this passage, is, therefore, the following :——

THAT CHRIST, WHEN HE APPEARED IN THIS WORLD, WAS A REAL MAN.

This doctrine, like that of the Deity of Christ, has been extensively disputed.

The Heretics generally, who embraced the Gnostic philosophy, denied Christ to have been a man. Some individuals and some classes held, that he was clothed in a body of air ; that he suffered only in appearance ; and that Judas Iscariot suffered in his stead.

To all these and the like doctrines, they were led by philosophizing on this subject. It is a just observation of Lardner, that " Heretics were, in the general, men of a curious and inquisitive turn of mind, and greatly indulged this disposition, which led them to speculate on many points of doctrine concerning which the Scriptures had afforded little or no light. When the Scriptures were in some cases inconsistent with their notions, they were for making them yield to their philosophical opinions. Thus the simplicity of truth was banished, and endless divisions arose." Tertullian also says, that " heresies are derived from philosophy ; and that secular wisdom is a rash (or fool-hardy) interpreter of the divine nature and disposition."

These observations are, with equal force and justice, applicable to heresies of modern days, and those of the ancients ; and few of either will be found to have arisen from any other source, beside a philosophy too proud or too knowing to submit implicitly to the testimony of God.

There are two modes of conduct with respect to religion, in which the mind may be justly said to act rationally. One is, *to determine, antecedently to our knowledge of revelation, as well as we can, what is religious truth, by our reason ;* the other, *to find out and embrace when we have become acquainted with Revelation, what it declares to be religious truth.* In the former of these situations *Reason* is our only guide. In the latter, its only business is to discover whether the professed revelation is a real one ; and, after this point is settled affirmatively, to discover and receive whatever it declares. *God* has now become our guide ; and as he can neither deceive nor be deceived, our duty is to receive his testimony implicitly. Had this plain and equitable rule been uniformly followed, Christianity would never have been thus distorted, nor the Church rent asunder by such lamentable divisions.

The reason why the Docetæ, one class of the ancient Unitarians, denied Christ to be a man, was the general principle of the Gnostics ; *that moral evil has its seat in matter.* Hence they held, that the human soul, which they believed to have been originally pure, derived its contamination solely from its union with the body. It was no unnatural consequence for those who embraced this doctrine to adopt the impossibility of an union between God and the human body ; since such an union was, of course, supposed to be capable of contaminating even the divine purity.

Their philosophy, therefore, seems necessarily to have led them into the conclusion, *that Christ, whom they believed to be God, was never united to a human body.* In the same manner has the philosophy of other sects led them also to embrace doctrines directly opposed to the express declarations of the Scriptures.

That Christ was a man, in the absolute sense, is easily made evident by many kinds of proof, and by almost numberless passages of Scripture.

1. *He is called a man, and the Son of Man, in a very great multitude of instances.*

The number of instances in which he has this latter appellation is no less than *seventy-one.* In sixty-seven of these instances it is given to him by *himself,* once by Daniel, once by St. Stephen, and twice by St. John in the Revelation. In giving this appellation to himself, it will I suppose be acknowledged, that he disclosed his real character, and was what he calls himself, *the Son of Man.*

When he is styled a man, also, he is described with just such characteristics, those excepted which involve error or sin, as belong to other men.   He is exhibited as meek, lowly, and dutiful to his parents ; as hungry, thirsty, and weary ; as sustained and refreshed by food, drink, and sleep ; as the subject of natural affection ; as weeping with tenderness and sorrow ; as the subject of temptations, infirmities, and afflictions ; and, generally, as having all the innocent characteristics which belong to our nature.

2. *The history of his birth, life, and death is unanswerable proof that Christ was a man.*

Christ was born, lived, and died essentially in the same manner as other men.   He ' increased in wisdom ' as well as ' in stature ;' wrought with his hands, ate, drank, slept, suffered on the cross, gave up the ghost, and was buried, in the same manner as other men.

3, *This point is argued at large and proved by St. Paul, in the second chapter of the Epistle to the Hebrews.*

In the passage containing this argument are the following declarations : ' For as much, then, as the children are partakers of flesh and blood, he also himself took part of the same :' and ' Wherefore in all things it behoved him to be made like unto his brethren.'

The proofs, which I have alleged will, it is presumed, be considered as abundantly sufficient.   That Christ had a human body cannot be questioned.   It is equally unquestionable, that to increase in wisdom, to be tempted, to be sorrowful, to be dutiful to human parents, together with other things of a similar nature, are attributed neither to *God* nor to *the human body,* but are appropriate characteristics of *the human soul.*   Christ, therefore, had a human soul as well as a human body, and was in the absolute sense, a man.

But he was not a man only.

This also is evident from numerous scriptural declarations. St. Paul says, Philippians ii. 5, ' He who was in the form of God, and thought it no robbery to be equal with God, nevertheless made himself of no reputation (εκενωσε, *emptied himself,* or *divested himself,* of this *form of God,* the glory and greatness which he before possessed ;) and, ' taking upon himself the form of a servant, was born (or existed,) in the likeness of men.' It is not my intention, in quoting this passage, to insist on the Deity of Christ, so unequivocally declared in it; but only to observe, that he who was thus a man was, antecedently to his appearance in this human character, a person entirely distinct from what he was as a man.

Antecedently to his ' being born in the likeness of men,' he existed, and existed in ' the form of God, and thought it no robbery to be equal with God. Nevertheless, (*ἰαυτὸν ἐκένωσε,*) he emptied himself.' He existed, therefore, previously to his appearance as a man, and ' emptied himself' voluntarily, when he (voluntarily, also) ' took upon himself the form of a servant, and was born in the likeness of men.' In other words, the person, here spoken of as ' being in the form of God,' became incarnate. This person, I have attempted to show, was divine; and no other than *the Word, or Son of God.*

The great objection to the doctrine of the incarnation of Christ is an objection of philosophy only, and in my view a very unphilosophical objection. " It is a doctrine," say the objectors, " wholly *mysterious* and *inexplicable.*"

After what was urged in the preceding Discourse on the subject of mysteries, very little can be thought necessary to be added here. Let it however be observed, that the truth of the objection is cheerfully acknowledged by me; and, so far as I know, by all who hold this doctrine. At the same time, it is an objection without force; and is *idly* urged, to say the least, by *Unitarians.* When the Arians will explain how their super-angelic being became the infant, and ultimately the man, Jesus Christ, and did, and suffered, and accomplished the things asserted of Christ; when the Socinians will explain how he who was created by the Holy Ghost, was born of Joseph and Mary; how organized matter thinks; how he who began to exist at his birth, existed antecedently in the form of God;' ' emptied himself;' and was then ' born in the likeness of men;' and when both, or either, of them will explain how the things, said in the Scriptures concerning Christ, are true, and at the same time consistent with their respective schemes; or how God could say them, if they were not true; I think I may venture upon an attempt to explain the mystery of the incarnation. Until we know the nature of the divine existence, and the nature of the human soul, we shall never be able to determine how far God may unite himself with such a soul, or whether such an union is impossible.

On this and every other question concerning the nature of the divine existence, and of the existence of finite minds, we cannot even begin to form ideas, but must be indebted for whatever facts we either know or believe to the testimony of God.

For aught that we are able to determine, a finite mind may be so far united to the infinite mind, as that all the views, affections, purposes, ends, and agency of both, which are not discordant in their very nature, may exactly coincide; and, independently of their character as finite or infinite, constitute but a single character and a single agency. But, as I have before said, for all our just conceptions on this subject, we are and must be indebted to the testimony of God only; and beyond this testimony, as well as without it, we literally know nothing.

This testimony, as it relates to the doctrine under consideration, is in my view complete. That Christ is truly and essentially *God* has, if I mistake not, been sufficiently evinced; and also that he appeared in this world a *man* in the absolute and perfect sense. This account of his character will be advantageously elucidated by a summary comparison of the representations made of him in both these characters.

As GOD it is said:

That he is God, the true God, the mighty God, the great God, Jehovah, I am, and Emmanuel, &c. That his goings forth were from of old, from everlasting; that he was in the beginning; set up from everlasting, or ever the earth was, &c. That he was in the beginning with God; rejoicing alway before him; present, when he prepared the heavens, and laid the foundations of the earth; and possessed of glory with him before ever the world

As MAN it is said:

That he was an infant, a child, a man, a carpenter, the son of Joseph and Mary, and the brother, or cousin german, of James and Joses. That he was born in the reign of Herod the Great, and of the Roman emperor Augustus Cæsar. That he was born in Judea; in Bethlehem, the city of David; in the stable of an inn; and was cradled in a manger. That he was refused a place in the inn, forgotten in the stable, and unfurnished even was. With reference to his greatness *as God* united to man, it is said, that Gabriel predicted his birth, an angel declared to the shepherds of Bethlehem that he was born, and a choir of the heavenly host sung together his natal hymn.

That he is the same yesterday, to day, and for ever.

That all things are his; that he upholds them by the word of his power, and that they were made for him, and by him.

That he is Lord of all things, of angels, principalities, and powers; and will subdue, and is able to subdue, all things unto himself, and put all opposition under his feet; and that his throne and dominion are for ever and ever.

That he was originally rich in the possession of all things; and the continual delight of his Father in the heavens: where the angels unceasingly worshipped him.

That at the close of this world, he will come in the clouds of heaven with power, and great glory, and with all his holy angels; will summon the dead from their graves; will gather all nations before

with the ordinary comforts, provided for the children of peasants.

That he grew while a child really and perceptibly, in wisdom and stature, and in favour with God and man, and therefore changed day by day, and that through his life.

That he had not where to lay his head, and was sustained, without any property of his own, by the bounty of his disciples, and, at times, of others.

That he was subject to the Jewish and Roman governments paid tribute, and performed all the usual duties of a child to his parents, and of a subject to his ruler; and was exposed to the direct assaults and temptations of the devil.

That, for our sakes, he became poor, afflicted, despised, and rejected of men; a man of sorrows and acquainted with grief; lightly esteemed, hated, and persecuted.

That he was betrayed by Judas; seized by the Roman soldiers; brought before the Sanhedrim; judged, condemned to death; again brought before Pilate, judged and condemned; buffeted, crowned the throne of his glory; will judge both angels and men according to their works; will punish the wicked with an everlasting destruction from the glory of his power; will conduct the righteous into heaven; and will cause them to live, and reign, with him for ever and ever.

Finally, in his *divine character*, it is said, that he was in the form of God, and thought it no robbery to be equal with God.

with thorns, mocked, spit upon, scourged, nailed to the cross, and carried to the tomb.

But that having emptied himself, and taken upon him the form of a servant, he was born in the likeness of men; and being found in fashion as a man, he became obedient unto death, even the death of the cross.

At the close of this wonderful career he was raised from the dead. He himself informs us, that ' he laid down his own life' voluntarily, and that no one was ' able to take it out of his hands.' He also informs us, that ' he himself took it up again.' Accordingly, he rose from the grave on the third day, and after conversing familiarly with his disciples ' concerning the things pertaining to the kingdom of God,' forty days, he ascended to heaven in a cloud of glory, attended by the heavenly host; entered the world of glory in triumph, and ' sat down on the right hand of the majesty on high;' or as it is elsewhere expressed, ' This man, after he had offered one sacrifice for sins, sat down for ever on the right hand of God.' ' At his name,' henceforth, ' every knee' is required to ' bow, of things in heaven, and things in earth, and things under the earth; and every tongue to confess, that he is the Lord,' or sovereign of all things, ' to the glory of God the Father.' The throne of infinite dominion is accordingly, and appropriately, styled ' the throne of God and the Lamb.' Before this throne, ' the four living ones cry, Holy, holy, holy, Lord God Almighty. who wast, and who art, and who art to come. The four-and-twenty elders cast their crowns at his feet, and say, Thou art worthy, O Lord! to receive glory, and honour, and power, for thou hast created all things, and for thy pleasure they are, and were created.   And the multitude of angels round about the throne, and the living ones, and the elders, say with a loud voice, Worthy is the Lamb that was slain to receive power, and riches, and wisdom, and strength, and honour, and glory, and blessing : and every creature, which is in heaven, on the earth, under the earth, and in the sea, is heard, saying, Blessing, and honour, and glory, and power, be unto him that sitteth on the throne, and unto the Lamb, for ever and ever.' To this divine ascription, the four Living Ones subjoin their solemn ' Amen.'

On this comparative view of the wonderful subject under consideration, I make the following remarks :

1. *It is evident to the least consideration, that the things which are here said of Christ are exceedingly unlike each other.*

So unlike are they that, if we suppose two beings to be the subjects of holiness, their characters cannot be more different from each other, than the things are which are here declared concerning Christ.

Let any man attempt to describe two, the most distant characters of two, the most distant holy beings, and he will find himself unable to place them farther asunder than these two characters of Christ are placed.   Therefore,

2. *These two characters cannot be given to any being possessed of a simple nature.*

That they are all truly said will not be here called in question.   If we suppose the person of whom they are said to be *only God*, we shall be obliged either to say, with the Sabellians, that Christ was no other than God manifesting himself in one particular form ; or, with the Patripassians, that the Father lived here, suffered, and died, as a man ; or, with the Docetæ, that Christ was God only ; that his appearance as a man was an illusion ; that he had a visionary body ; and suffered only in appearance and pretence ; while Judas Iscariot, or some other culprit, was crucified in his stead.

It is plainly impossible, that the same simple being should be ' set up from everlasting,' be the ' Alpha and Omega, the beginning and the ending ;' and yet ' be born in Judea in the reign of Herod the Great :' be ' the same yesterday, to-day, and for ever ;' and yet ' increase in wisdom, and in favour with God and man :' ' create all things visible and invisible ;' and yet ' be made of a woman :' be the lawgiver to the universe, and yet ' be made under the law :' ' uphold all things by the word of his power ;' and yet be a petitioner for the daily supplies of his wants, and the protection of his person : possess all things, and yet ' have not where to lay his head :' ' know all things ;' and yet not know, as, if we adopt the common interpretation, we must suppose he did not know the time of the destruction of Jerusalem : Be the final judge and rewarder of the quick and the dead ; and yet be tried, condemned, and executed by men : and be ' in the form of God,' and justly ' think it no robbery to be equal with God ;' and yet ' be a servant,' a man, and a frail and dying man.

But all these things, and innumerable others, substantially of the same nature in both respects are declared concerning Christ. All also are declared by God himself. They are therefore true, and true in the natural, obvious sense. Of course, they are ' worthy of all acceptation.'

It follows then *that Christ is*, notwithstanding the sneers of Unitarians, *God and man*. In the language of the Scriptures, ' The Word became flesh, and dwelt among us.' Yet, humble as were the station and circumstances in which he appeared, ' we' are able still to ' behold his glory, the glory as of the only begotten of the Father.'

3. *There are three important facts recorded concerning Christ, in which he differs wholly from all created beings, and which merit the attentive consideration of every serious man.*

(1.) *He always taught in his own name, even when altering and annulling the acknowledged word of God.*

Christ came to change the Mosaic system into the Christian ; and accordingly substituted the latter for the former. In every part of this employment he taught in his own name. The preceding prophets had uniformly introduced their instructions with ' Thus saith the Lord ;'——' Thus saith Jehovah.' Christ, immediately after addressing his consolations to his disciples by way of preface, introduces his sermon on the mount in the following manner : ' Think not that I am come to destroy the law or the prophets;' that is, the system of religion in the Old Testament: ' I am not come. to destroy but to fulfil. For verily I say unto you,' &c. This phraseology he repeats everywhere throughout this sermon, and throughout the Gospel. Not once does he say, ' Thus saith the Lord,' during his ministry, nor teach with any authority except his own. Now it is evident, that the authority which he actually assumed was equal in his view, and in the view of the Scriptures, to that which sanctioned the declaration of the Old Testament, because he changes and annuls both the doctrines and the precepts of the Old Testament at his pleasure.

In the same manner, when he appeared unto St. Paul in the way to Damascus, after informing Paul that he was ' Jesus, whom he persecuted,' he commissioned him to preach the Gospel to the gentiles, and sent him as his apostle to them, by his own authority, without appealing to any other.

As, therefore, the authority assumed in these cases is equivalent to that by which the Old Testament was revealed, he who rightfully assumed it was God.

The same authority, also Christ assumed and exhibited, generally, when he wrought *miracles;* and he never makes mention of any other.

(2.) *The apostles uniformly appeal to the authority of Christ in their preaching and miracles.*

' In the name of Jesus Christ,' says St. Peter to the impotent man, ' rise up, and walk.'

' By what power,' said the Sanhedrim to Peter and his companions, ' or by what name, have you done this?' that is, healed the impotent man. ' Be it known unto you all,' answered the apostle, ' and to all the people of Israel, that by the name of Jesus Christ of Nazareth, whom ye crucified, whom God raised from the dead, even by him doth this man stand here before you whole.' ' Æneas,' said Peter, ' Jesus Christ maketh thee whole.' ' All authority,' says our Saviour, ' is delivered to me in heaven and in earth. As my Father hath sent me, so send I you.'

Under this commission the apostles preached and acted, and in multiplied instances have declared to us that it was the authority of God.

A single declaration of this sort will suffice for them all. Mark xvi. 20, ' And they went forth, and preached every-

where, the Lord working with them, and confirming the word
with signs following.   Amen.'

(3.) *In the Revelation of St. John, it is to be observed,
Christ receives the praises of the heavenly host, both singly
and in conjunction with the Father, but never unites in them.*

Neither Christ nor the Holy Spirit is ever called upon to
perform the great duty of all creatures to praise God, or to
pray to him.   Both these duties Christ performed as a man,
when here on earth, but he is never exhibited as performing
the duty of praise in heaven.   All other virtuous beings are
exhibited as making this their constant worship, and a prime
part of their duty.   But amid all their ascriptions of praise to
God, Christ is nowhere exhibited as uniting with them in this
duty, in itself so delightful to a virtuous mind, and so naturally
and obviously obligatory on every rational being.   The whole
multitude of saints and angels, with the four living ones at
their head, join without exception in the heavenly song;
' Blessing, and honour, and glory, and power be unto him that
sitteth on the throne.'   But the only part ever attributed to
Christ, is to be united in receiving the ascription together
with ' him that sitteth on the throne:' for the ascription is
made ' to him that sitteth on the throne, and to the Lamb,
for ever and ever.' *

I have now finished the observations which I intended to
make concerning this interesting subject, and exhibited what
appears to me to be the true meaning of the remarkable
phraseology in the text, ' God sending his own Son in the
likeness of sinful flesh,' and of other similar passages found in
the Scriptures : such as, ' The word was made flesh ;' ' the
seed of David according to the flesh ;' ' of whom, as concerning the flesh, Christ came ;' ' Christ is come in the flesh,' &c.

I shall now conclude the Discourse with the following

REMARKS.

1. *This doctrine teaches us, in the strongest manner, the
condescension of Christ.*

* Rev. v. 13

In this light it is considered by St. Paul, in that memorable passage, Phil. ii. 5, &c. ' Let this mind be in you, which was also in Christ Jesus : who being in the form of God, thought it not robbery to be equal with God ; but made himself of no reputation, and took upon him the form of a servant, and was made in the likeness of men.'

No subject presents to us so wonderful an example of condescension as the incarnation of Christ ; nor could any fact fill our minds with the same astonishment, were it not that we have been accustomed to hear it repeated from the cradle, and, like the state of the weather, rendered an object of perpetual familiarity ; a thing almost of course, in the ordinary current of our thoughts, by unceasing inculcation.

From these causes we pass it without serious attention, and, even when we dwell upon it, scarcely realize its nature. The impressions which it makes on the mind resemble those made on the eye of such as have been long accustomed to them, by a delightful landscape, a stupendous cataract, or a mountain which loses its summit in the clouds. At the view of these a stranger is fixed in exquisite delight, and has all his thoughts engrossed and his emotions absorbed by the wonderful scene. No language will in his view serve to describe, and no picture to image, on the one hand the beauty, or on the other, the sublimity of these illustrious objects. To do them justice in his representations, and to spread fairly before others the views, formed of them by his own mind, he will labour in thought, select and refuse, alternately, the language which offers itself, and will at last sit down discouraged, without a hope of being able to render his conceptions visible to other eyes, or to do any thing like justice to what was so magnificent in the view of his own. Those, in the mean time, who have long lived in the neighbourhood of the same objects, will in many, though not indeed in all instances, survey them without emotion, and even without attention ; apparently as insensible to the beauty and grandeur as the horses which they ride, or the oxen which they drive.

Such seem but too commonly to be the views formed by most men concerning the incarnation of Christ, and such the insensibility with which it is but too generally regarded. Even Christians, like their predecessors mentioned in the Gospel, are, in innumerable instances, ' fools ' in this respect, ' and slow of heart to believe,' or even to realize.

But let us, for a moment at least, lay aside these obtuse views, these ' eyes ' which ' are dull of seeing,' these ' hearts ' too ' gross to understand.' Let us shake off the torpor which benumbs our frame, and rouse ourselves to perception and feeling. Let us regard this wonderful subject with common justice, and common candour.

The glorious Person, who in the Scriptures is designated by the appellation, ὁ Λογος τυ Θευ. or the Word of God, ' In the beginning created the heavens and the earth ;' and said, ' Let there be light, and there was light ;' ' Let there be a firmament, and there was a firmament.' His hand also lighted up the flame of the sun, and kindled the stars. He ' upholds ' the universe ' by the word of his power ;' and preserves order and regularity throughout all the parts of this amazing system.

In the heavens he shines with inexpressible splendour. On the earth he lives and works, provides and sustains, and satisfies the wants of every living thing. Throughout immensity he quickens into life, action, and enjoyment the innumerable multitudes of intelligent beings. The universe which he made, he also governs. The worlds of which it is composed, he rolls through the infinite expanse with an almighty and unwearied hand, and preserves them in their respective places and motions with unerring harmony. From the vast storehouse of his bounty he feeds and clothes the endless millions whom his hand has made, and from the riches of his own unchangeable mind informs the innumerable host of intelligent creatures with ever improving virtue, dignity, and glory. To all these he allots the respective parts which they are qualified to act in the boundless system of good which his wisdom contrived, and his power has begun to execute, furnishes them with the means of being useful in his eternal kingdom, and thus prepares them to be amiable and excellent in his sight, and instruments of perpetually increasing good to each other.

At the head of this great kingdom he ' sits upon a throne high and lifted up,' ' far exalted above all heavens ;' surveys, with an intuitive view and with divine complacency the amazing work which his voice has called into being, and beholds it increasing without intermission in happiness, wisdom, and virtue, and advancing, with a regular progress, towards consummate glory and perfection.

Although ' he is not worshipped, as though he needed any thing, seeing he giveth unto all life, and breath and all things ;' yet before him angels bow and veil their faces. ' The four living ones rest not day nor night, crying, Holy, holy, holy, Lord God Almighty, who wast, and who art, and who art to come.'   And the whole multitude of the heavenly host, ' the number of whom is ten thousand times ten thousand, and thousands of thousands,' unite in the everlasting song, ' Blessing, and honour, and glory, and power, be unto him that sitteth upon the throne, and unto the Lamb, for ever and ever.'

From this stupendous height of greatness and enjoyment, this divine Person, passing all the bounds between God and man, between the infinite mind, and lifeless matter, united himself to ' man, who is but a worm ;' assumed to himself a human soul and a human body, and in a manner incomprehensible by us, and not improbably by all other creatures, became thenceforth *God-man*, inseparably united in one most wonderful and mysterious Person.

Of this singular act the *end* was not less glorious, than the *act* itself was amazing.   It was to save a race of rebellious creatures, whom he needed not, from misery and ruin ; of creatures, whom with a word he could have returned to their original nothing, and whose places with another word he could have filled with equal or greater numbers, at his pleasure ; all obedient, faithful, and happy.   I shall not, however, dwell on this subject at the present time.   Occasions still more appropriate will hereafter bring it up to view.   The single point on which I would now insist, is the infinite condescension of Christ.

This glorious person ' humbles himself to behold the things which are done under the sun.'   How much more when he came from his ' high and holy place ' to dwell beneath that sun, and take up his residence on his footstool!   All this, however, he was pleased to do.   ' He emptied himself, took upon himself the form of a servant, and was born in the likeness of men.'

What were the views which angels formed of this new and astonishing event?   Easily may we imagine that all heaven was lost in wonder, and buried in silence, to behold this transition from infinite glory to supreme humiliation, from the throne of the universe to a tenement of clay.   How instinctively ought we, uniting with angels in the same views and the same emotions, to behold, wonder, and adore!

2. *What a pattern of condescension is here set before us for our imitation.*   St. Paul makes this practical use of the doctrine under consideration.   ' Let the same mind be in you,' says he to the Philippians, ' which was also in Christ.'

Condescension is here enforced on the race of man with an authority and example literally infinite.   The divine wisdom dictated the condescension of Christ, and the divine goodness carried it into execution.   In it we see the manner in which the infinite mind is pleased to act, and which boundless excellence approves and loves.   This, then, is a character and conduct to which we are urged by the highest of all considerations, the approbation and example of God.   Would we, then, be like God; would we be ' perfect as he is perfect;' would we obtain his approbation; would we inherit the blessings which he confers on those who are approved by him; would we become really excellent and lovely; we shall ' give all diligence,' that ' the same mind may be in us which was also in Christ.'   We shall ' condescend to men of low degree;' be ' meek and lowly of heart;' be satisfied with humble stations, offices, and employments; and feel that no human interest is beneath our notice, and no human business unfit for us to perform, when we are called to perform it, and when others by the performance can be relieved, disposed to virtue, or made happy.

But how different is the usual conduct and the prevailing character of man!   All men sigh to be rich, and none are contented with humble circumstances.   All men pant to be great, and none are satisfied with a lowly condition.   The rich despise the poor, the great trample on the small.   When we become rich, we sigh for additional riches.   When we become great, we toil, and watch, and weary ourselves through life, to become greater.   All beneath us in these mere accidents, we overlook, contemn, insult, and style the dirt and scum of the earth.

Christ, on the contrary, became, voluntarily, not only a

man, but a poor man, a lowly man, the son of a carpenter, humble in his station, without place, or power, or wealth, and perfectly satisfied to be without them all.   His friends, his disciples, his apostles, were selected from the poor and lowly; and he alleged it is one unanswerable proof of his Messiahship, that by him ' the poor had the Gospel preached unto them.' This was the character of him whom angels worship, and whom the universe obeys.

Christ descended to these lowly men, and to these humble circumstances, from the throne of the heavens.   Shall not we, then, be willing to let ourselves down from the side, or even the summit of our mole-hill, to visit our fellow-emmets at the bottom?   How small the descent at the utmost?   How silly, how base, how contradictory to common sense, the pride which refuses to make it !

Often, very often, the men whom we despise as greatly beneath us, are better, wiser, and more excellent in the sight of God than ourselves.   Always we are odious to him, and contemptible in the eye of reason, for this very pride.   Let every proud man then feel, that for this very character which he so fondly cherishes, he is hateful in the sight of God, and justly contemptible in that of men ; that the character which he despises is the very character in which Christ chose to appear, and that the men whom he treats with abuse and insolence, are of that very class out of which Christ selected his friends and apostles.

SERMON XLIII.

COVENANT OF REDEMPTION.

WHEN THOU SHALT MAKE HIS SOUL AN OFFERING FOR SIN, HE SHALL SEE HIS SEED; HE SHALL PROLONG HIS DAYS, AND THE PLEASURE OF THE LORD SHALL PROSPER IN HIS HAND. HE SHALL SEE OF THE TRAVAIL OF HIS SOUL, AND SHALL BE SATISFIED; BY HIS KNOWLEDGE SHALL MY RIGHTEOUS SERVANT JUSTIFY MANY; FOR HE SHALL BEAR THEIR INIQUITIES. THEREFORE WILL I DIVIDE HIM A PORTION WITH THE GREAT, AND HE SHALL DIVIDE THE SPOIL WITH THE STRONG; BECAUSE HE HATH POURED OUT HIS SOUL UNTO DEATH; AND HE WAS NUMBERED WITH THE TRANSGRESSORS; AND HE BARE THE SIN OF MANY, AND MADE INTERCESSION FOR THE TRANSGRESSORS.

ISAIAH LIII. 10—12.

" IF HIS SOUL SHALL MAKE A PROPITIATORY SACRIFICE, HE SHALL SEE A SEED, WHICH SHALL PROLONG THEIR DAYS; AND THE GRACIOUS PURPOSE OF JEHOVAH SHALL PROSPER IN HIS HANDS. OF THE TRAVAIL OF HIS SOUL HE SHALL SEE (THE FRUIT) AND BE SATISFIED: BY THE KNOWLEDGE OF HIM SHALL MY SERVANT JUSTIFY MANY; FOR THE PUNISHMENT OF THEIR INIQUITIES HE SHALL BEAR. THEREFORE WILL I DISTRIBUTE TO HIM THE MANY FOR HIS PORTION; AND THE MIGHTY PEOPLE SHALL HE SHARE FOR HIS SPOIL; BECAUSE HE POURED OUT HIS SOUL UNTO DEATH, AND WAS NUMBERED WITH THE TRANSGRESSORS; AND HE BARE THE SIN OF MANY; AND MADE INTERCESSION FOR THE TRANSGRESSORS."

LOWTH.

IN the first chapter of the Epistle to the Ephesians, St. Paul declares, that ' God hath chosen us in Christ, before the foundation of the world; having predestinated us to the adoption of children, by Jesus Christ, to himself; according to the good pleasure of his will ; to the praise of the glory of his grace, wherein he hath made us accepted in the Beloved.'

The manner in which this transaction took place, and in which the purposes of it were accomplished, is recorded in the text. The Person who speaks in the text is unquestionably God the Father ; as is evident from the fact, that he calls Christ in the 11th verse ' my Servant.' The context, as you well know, is an eminent and remarkable prophecy concerning the birth, life, and sufferings of Christ ; and has been acknowledged as such, so far as my information extends, by both the Jewish and Christian churches universally, in every age since it was written. Almost the whole of it is occupied by an account of his humiliation and sufferings, described with such a degree of minuteness and exactness, as to wear the appearance rather of a history than of a prophecy.

In the text, a covenant is made on the part of the speaker, with the Person of whom he speaks ; or, on the part of God the Father with the Son. In the tenth verse, the first of the text, it is proposed, conditionally, in the following terms : ' When thou shalt make his soul an offering for sin, he shall see his seed ; he shall prolong his days ; and the pleasure of the Lord shall prosper in his hand.' In the translation of Bishop Lowth, which differs from the common one only by being more correct and explicit, it is, " If his soul shall make a propitiatory sacrifice, he shall see a seed, which shall prolong their days ; and the gracious purpose of Jehovah shall prosper in his hands." The difference lies, principally, in the second cause, " He shall see *a seed* which shall prolong *their* days." It could not, I think, with propriety be promised, as a reward to Christ for his sufferings, that, in any sense, he should prolong his *own* days ; but with the most perfect propriety, that he should see *a seed* which, in a sense hereafter to be explained, should prolong *their days.* The days of him, who ' is the same yesterday, to day, and for ever ;' ' the Alpha and the Omega, the beginning and the ending,' could not in any sense be prolonged in consequence of his sufferings, or of any other possible event. The word *his*, supplied by the translators, is supplied erroneously : since in the present translation it presents a meaning which plainly cannot be admitted. The justice of these remarks will be farther evident from the repetition of the same covenant in the 11th verse : ' He shall see of the travail of his soul;' that is, as explained by Lowth, " Of the travail of his soul he shall see the fruit and be satisfied;" ' By his knowledge,' or, as Lowth more correctly renders it, " By the knowledge of him shall my Servant justify many." *The justification of the many,* here spoken of, *connected with its consequences,* is the very reward promised in the preceding verse, in the words, ' He shall see a seed, which shall prolong their days:' and here the reward promised is no other than *the justification, and consequent eternal life, of those who should become interested in his death.*

Still farther is this interpretation evinced to be just by the repetition of the promise in the twelfth verse, or third of the text; ' Therefore I will divide him a portion with the great, and he shall divide the spoil with the strong; because he hath poured out his soul unto death;' or, as more happily rendered by Bishop Lowth, " Therefore I will distribute to him the many for his portion; and the mighty people shall he share for his spoil, because he poured out his soul unto death." It is not true that Christ has a portion divided to him with the great, or a spoil divided to him with the strong. ' He trod the wine-press alone, and of the people there was none with him.' Nor is there any one to share with him the reward of his sufferings; but he was alone in the sufferings and the reward alike. Accordingly in the Septuagint this passage is rendered, " For this cause shall he receive many for his inheritance, and shall share spoils of the strong."

Finally: The same thing is abundantly evinced in Psalm lxxxix. where also the same covenant is recorded. ' Once have I sworn by my holiness, that I will not lie unto David. His seed shall endure for ever, and his throne as the sun before me.' And again: ' His seed also will I make to endure for ever, and his throne as the days of heaven.' It is to be observed, that in all these passages *the reward* promised to Christ consists in *giving persons to him,* as ' seed,' ' the many,' ' the mighty people.' These are undoubtedly no other than ' the general assembly and church of the first-born;' styled elsewhere ' the children of God;' ' little children;' ' sons and daughters.' They are his own people, those in whom he has a peculiar property; persons justified in this manner have become ' his portion,' ' his spoil,' ' his seed.' The reward of his sufferings here promised is to consist of these.

It is not, however, to consist in the *persons* only, but in their *circumstances* also. It is not promised, merely, that they shall be given to him as a possession, but that they shall be given to him in a peculiar manner; attended with one circumstance, at least, which in the eye of the Promiser was considered as materially important to the nature of the gift. ' He shall see a seed, which shall *prolong their days*;' or, as in the corresponding passage, ' shall endure *for ever*.' The meaning of this phraseology is to be sought in the use of it in parallel passages, found in the Scriptures. In Psalm xv. David inquires, ' Lord, who shall abide in thy tabernacle? who shall dwell in thy holy hill?' and immediately answers, ' He that walketh uprightly, and worketh righteousness.' In Psalm xlix. 12, he says of the wicked, that, ' being in honour, they abide not, but are like the beasts that perish.' In Psalm cxxv. 1, he says, ' They that trust in the Lord shall be as Mount Zion, which cannot be removed, but abideth for ever.' In John xv. 10, our Saviour saith to his disciples, ' If ye keep my commandments, ye shall abide in my love, even as I have kept my Father's commandments, and abide in his love.' In 1 John ii. 17, it is said, ' And the world passeth away, and the lust thereof; but he that doeth the will of God abideth for ever.' In Psalm cii. 28, it is said, ' The children of thy servants shall continue, and their seed shall be established before thee.'

We are now prepared to settle the meaning of the phrase under consideration. ' To prolong their days,' ' to endure for ever,' is to ' abide in the tabernacle of God,' ' in his holy hill,' ' in the Heavens;' ' to abide in the love of Christ, as he abides in his Father's love, for ever:' to abide, when ' the World has passed away, and the lust thereof:' ' to be established before God,' or in his presence. In a word, it is to dwell for ever in Heaven, amid the enjoyments of a happy immortality. This is what the Scriptures consider as, *abiding*, *enduring*, and being *established*, whenever this language is applied to men. In opposition to this, the wicked are said to be *cut off*, and to *perish*, to be as the *grass*, to be *destroyed*, to be *no more*; and ' their candle ' is said to *go out*. This part of the promise, then, is no other than *that the seed of Christ shall enjoy a blessed eternity.*

In the passages quoted from Psalm lxxxix. au additional

promise is made in the same covenant.   It is there said, that 'his seed shall endure for ever, and his throne,' that is, his dominion over *them* particularly, 'as the days of heaven.' The same thing is also covenanted, in different phraseology, in Isaiah ix. 6, 7. 'For unto us a child is born, unto us a son is given ; and the government shall be upon his shoulder : and his name shall be called Wonderful, Counsellor, the Mighty God, the Father of the everlasting age, and the Prince of peace.   And of the increase of his government and peace there shall be no end.'   Here we are taught, that ' of the increase of the government' of Christ, that is, of its splendour and glory, ' and of the peace,' or prosperity, of his subjects accomplished by it, ' there shall be no end :' in other words, *that the glory of his government, and the happiness of his church, shall increase for ever.*

The condition on his part, to which these rewards are promised, is that ' he shall make his soul an offering for sin :' or *a propitiatory sacrifice.*   Another condition is also specified, as the procuring cause of the reward, in the last verse ; and therefore was undoubtedly included, although not expressed, in the two former verses ; this is, that ' he made intercession for the transgressors.'

In this passage, then, we have the substance of the *Mediation of Christ* drawn out in the essential particulars : *his humiliation, atonement, and intercession.*   The *reward* also, that is, the great object which was his inducement to undertake this mediation, is distinctly expressed : *viz.* that ' he should see a seed, which should prolong their days,' and that ' the gracious purpose of Jehovah should prosper in his hands.' This in the Epistle to the Hebrews is by St. Paul styled ' the joy set before him ;' that is, set before him in this promise, or covenant ; for which, he informs us, ' Christ endured the cross, and despised the shame.'

In the text also we are taught *the means by which*, on their part, *mankind become his seed,* expressed in the following declaration : ' By the knowledge of him shall my Servant justify many.'   By the knowledge of Christ here we are unquestionably to understand, *that knowledge* of God the Father, and Jesus Christ, whom he hath sent, which in John xvii. 3, he declares to be *life eternal ;* and which in the 8th verse he speaks of as being the same with evangelical faith.   ' They have known surely, that I have come out from thee; and they have believed that thou didst send me.' By this faith, as you well know, we are abundantly declared in the Scriptures to be justified. The declaration of Paul to Peter, when, at Antioch, ' he separated himself from the Gentiles, through fear of them that were of the circumcision, and was *therefore* to be blamed,' may stand in the place of all other passages, on this point. ' We, who are Jews, and not sinners of the Gentiles, knowing that a man is not justified by the works of the Law, but by the faith of Jesus Christ, even We have believed in Jesus Christ, that we might be justified by the faith of Christ, and not by the works of the Law; for by the works of the law no flesh shall be justified.' *The faith of the Gospel* is, therefore, the *knowledge* by which, it is said in the text, Christ ' shall justify many.' The reason why it is called *knowledge* here and elsewhere is, that it involves views so just, extensive, and firmly established concerning this glorious Person; whereas, in the same mind no such views existed, antecedently to the exercise of this faith. For Christ, like every other spiritual object, can only be ' spiritually discerned.'

All these things, also, are exhibited to us in the form of a *covenant*. To this covenant, as to every other, there are two parties : God, who promises ; and his Servant, who was to justify many. A condition is specified, to which is annexed a promise of reward. The condition is, that Christ should ' make his soul an offering for sin,' and ' make intercession for the transgressors ;' or, in other words, execute the whole office of a Priest for mankind. The reward is, that he should ' receive the many for his portion,' and that they should ' prolong their days,' or endure for ever. It is remarkable, that this covenant on the part of God the Father, like that made with Noah, and that made with Abraham, and various others recorded in the Scriptures, is in Psalm lxxxix. exhibited as *a promissory oath.* ' Once have I sworn by my holiness, that I will not lie unto David : His seed shall endure for ever, and his throne as long as the sun.'

I have dwelt minutely on the explanation of this passage of Scripture, because I have not seen it discussed in this manner, or with a reference to what is the main subject of it ; and because I believed that a minute examination was necessary to a distinct and satisfactory knowledge of what is contained in it.

If this explanation be admitted, the text contains the following.

DOCTRINE:

THAT GOD THE FATHER ENTERED INTO A COVENANT WITH CHRIST, IN WHICH HE PROMISED HIM, ON CONDITION THAT HE SHOULD BECOME A PROPITIATION AND INTERCESSOR FOR SINNERS, AS A REWARD OF HIS LABOURS AND SUFFERINGS, THE FUTURE POSSESSION OF A CHURCH, WHICH UNDER HIS GOVERNMENT SHOULD BE GLORIOUS AND HAPPY FOR EVER.

Concerning this covenant, usually called *the covenant of redemption,* I make the following observations :—

I. *This covenant was made from eternity.*

In the first chapter of the Epistle to the Ephesians, St. Paul, speaking of himself and his fellow-Christians, says, ' Blessed be the God and Father of our Lord Jesus Christ, who hath blessed us with all spiritual blessings in heavenly places in (or through) Christ, according as he hath chosen us in him before the foundation of the world, that we should be holy and without blame before him in love ; having predestinated us unto the adoption of children, by Jesus Christ, to himself, according to the good pleasure of his will.' In this passage St. Paul teaches us, that God blesses his church, or Christians, with all spiritual blessings ; or, as in the Original, ' with every spiritual blessing ; through Christ, according as he hath chosen us in him before the foundation of the world :' and that he has ' predestinated us,' particularly, ' unto the adoption of children unto himself,' through Christ also.

This choice of his church, then, this ' predestination of it to the adoption of children through Christ,' existed ' before the foundation of the world.' But this choice, this ' predestination of the church to the adoption of children, unto himself through Christ,' is the very same thing which, in another form, is declared in the text. The covenant mentioned in the text was therefore a transaction existing before the foundation of the world ; or, as this phraseology uniformly means in the Scriptures, from *eternity.*

The text itself was written seven hundred years before Christ. It will not be supposed, that the transaction recorded in it was then first admitted into the counsels of God ; or that

he, ' with whom is no variableness, nor shadow of turning,'
changed his mind in the days of Isaiah concerning this mighty
object.   If any person should be at a loss concerning this fact,
let him remember that this covenant contains the very same
promises which were made to David, Abraham, and our first
parents ; to all of whom the same wonderful transaction was,
in terms less explicit, disclosed.   The transaction itself, and
the objects which it involved, were unquestionably the most
important parts of the providence of God towards this world.
It cannot, therefore, be believed, that it was left unprovided for
when the system was originally formed.   Undoubtedly it was
the object which was chiefly in view in the providence of God,
and was an original part of the system.   Accordingly, St.
Peter says concerning Christ, that ' he was foreordained before the foundation of the world ;' St. John calls him ' the
Lamb, slain from the foundation of the world ;' and Christ
himself, at the day of judgment, styles the state of glory and
happiness, destined for the righteous, ' the kingdom prepared from the foundation of the world.'   ' Come, ye blessed
of my Father, inherit the kingdom prepared for you from the
foundation of the world.'   But this kingdom, and the church
which inherits it, is the very subject of the covenant contained
in the text.

2. *This covenant was the basis, on which was founded
the whole system of providential dispensations towards the
Church.*

Out of this covenant arose the mediation of Christ; his
incarnation, life, preaching, miracles, humiliation, sufferings,
and glorification.   Out of this covenant arose the mission of
the Spirit of Grace, who came into the world to execute the
purposes of Christ's redemption.   Out of this covenant arose
the Gospel, or the Scriptures of the Old and New Testament,
which that Spirit taught to the Prophets and Apostles, and
which communicates to us all the knowledge which we possess
of the will of God concerning the salvation of mankind.   Out
of this covenant arise the renovation and purification of the
human soul ; the light, comfort, peace, hope, and joy which it
receives in the present world, and in the end, its admission
into the heavens.   Finally, out of this covenant will arise the
glory, peace, and happiness which will be found in that pure
and exalted world by the whole ' assembly of the first born.'

All these, and all things pertaining to them, result obviously from the wonderful transaction recorded in the text.

3. *The Church, thus promised to Christ as the reward of his mediation, is formed of a great multitude of mankind.*

It will not be necessary for me to inquire at the present time, either in what manner this multitude will be gathered, or of whom it will be composed. It is sufficient for the present purpose that the assertion which I have made is expressly contained in the text. ' By the knowledge of him shall my Servant justify *many.*' ' I will distribute *the Many* to him for his portion, and the *mighty people,*' that is, a great multitude, ' shall he share for his spoil.' Accordingly, St. John informs us, that he saw in the heavens a great multitude, which no man could number, of all nations, and kindreds, and people, and tongues, standing before the throne, and before the Lamb, clothed with white robes, and palms in their hands ; crying with a loud voice, and saying, Salvation to our God, who sitteth on the throne, and unto the Lamb.'

4. *In this covenant a reward was promised to Christ, sufficiently great to induce him to undergo all the humiliation and sufferings of his Mediatorial character.*

This we know by the fact. In accordance with this covenant he actually assumed this character, and voluntarily underwent all its sufferings. But, were we at a loss concerning this subject otherwise, we are directly assured by St. Paul, that Christ ' for the joy set before him, endured the cross, and despised the shame.' What the *joy* of Christ was, he himself has, I apprehend, expressly declared to us in the 8th chapter of Proverbs. His words are, ' When he appointed the foundations of the earth, then was I by him, as one brought up with him ; I was daily his delight, rejoicing alway before him ; rejoicing in the habitable part of his earth, and my delights were with the sons of men :' that is, with his church, the glorious reward, which was promised to him from the beginning.

From these summary observations, concerning the Covenant of Redemption, I derive, by way of inference, the following

REMARKS.

1. *The salvation of the church of God, that is, of all righ-*

*teous men, was an original part of the system of God's provi-
dence towards the inhabitants of this world.*

If the observations made in the progress of this Discourse
are just, then it follows, by irresistible consequence, that the
salvation of the righteous, or of all who will be ultimately
saved, was contemplated and resolved on by God from the
beginning, or from everlasting.   It was, also, made the subject of a solemn covenant between the Father and the Son.
It was not, therefore, in any sense, a thing which grew out of
a *contingency*, according to the scheme of Dr. Price and
others ; a remedy provided for *evils unforeseen* ; a thing
grafted upon the fall of man, which they consider as an accident, springing out of that liberty of contingency which they
suppose indispensable to the free volitions of a moral being.
St. Paul teaches us, that God the Father ' created all things
by Jesus Christ ; to the intent, that now unto principalities
and powers in heavenly places might be known *by* the church
the manifold wisdom of God : according to the eternal purpose, which he purposed in Christ Jesus our Lord.'   Here it
is declared to be a part of the *eternal purpose of God* in Jesus
Christ, to create all things by him, to the intent that principalities and powers might know, *by means of the church*, that is,
by means of his dispensations to the church, ' the manifold
wisdom of God.'   Of course, *the existence of the church* was
an essential part of this eternal purpose.   Of course, also, the
existence of the church was foreknown and resolved on, as a
part of this purpose.   Its existence, therefore, was in no sense
contingent, in no sense accidental, in no sense dependent on
any thing by which it could be prevented.   In accordance
with this declaration, St. Paul says, 2 Tim. i. 9, ' Who hath
saved us, and called us with an holy calling, not according to
our works, but according to his own purpose and grace, which
was given us before the world began.'   In this passage Christians are said to be ' saved according to the purpose and grace
of God, given to them,' in the strong figurative language of
the apostle, ' before the world began ;' that is, in simpler
language, resolved on, established for them, given in the
counsels of God, so as to be indefeasible by any subsequent
event.   Thus in this passage, explained in the corresponding
one of Titus i. 2, ' In hope of eternal life, which God, that
cannot lie, promised before the world began.'   Here the

grace and salvation, said in the passage last quoted to be given, is called ' eternal life,' and is declared to be ' promised before the world began.' The existence of the church, the eternal life of its members, and the grace by which that life is attained, were all ' promised before the world began;' promised, I apprehend, in the covenant which we have been contemplating; and, plainly, an essential part of the providential system relating immediately to the inhabitants of this world.

2. *The salvation of the righteous is certain.*

If the salvation of the righteous was an original and essential part of the providential system; if it was contemplated, purposed, and resolved on; if it was promised to Christ, as the reward of his labours and sufferings; if it was the condition on the part of the Father in a covenant with the Son; then it is perfectly evident, that it cannot fail; but will certainly be accomplished. The language of God on this subject is, ' My counsel shall stand, and I will do all my pleasure.'

As the salvation of the church is thus certain, the salvation of every righteous man is for the same reason equally certain. Every righteous man is a part of the church; one of *the many* thus promised to Christ in the covenant of redemption, and assured of the certain attainment of eternal life by the unchangeable promise of God. Let no such man indulge a moment's apprehension that he shall be forgotten of God, either in this life, or in death, or at the resurrection, or at the judgment, or at the final entrance of the church into heaven. He who has given ' a cup of cold water to a disciple, in the name of a *disciple;*' he who has consecrated ' two mites' to the service of God; he who has willingly befriended ' the least of Christ's brethren,' is absolutely certain of his reward.

3. *We are taught by this doctrine, that the mediation of Christ furnishes a complete foundation for our acceptance with God.*

The mediation of Christ was the condition of our acceptance which God himself proposed, and proceeding from his own good pleasure. It was therefore, originally and absolutely pleasing to him. He is ' the same yesterday, to-day and for ever.' It will, of course, be always and equally pleasing. We are not, therefore, left to the necessity of debating, or even inquiring, whether the satisfaction of Christ is sufficient for all men? that is, whether there is a quantum of merit, mathematically estimated, on which every man may rely, because it is so great, as to rise to any definite or supposed limit. Independently of all discussions of this nature, every man is assured that, if he is interested in this covenant by becoming one of ' the seed,' or followers, of Christ, by possessing that ' knowledge' or faith which is the condition of justification ; he will certainly also be accepted of God, as being one of those whom this promise included.

The number and the greatness of the sins committed by any man, and the degree of guilt which he has accumulated, however discouraging or overwhelming it may prove in the hour of deep contrition, ought in no wise to persuade the penitent to doubt, even for a moment, of the sufficiency of Christ as an expiation for him. One sin only is mentioned in the Scriptures as admitting of no atonement : *viz.* ' blasphemy against the Holy Ghost.' Others are indeed exhibited as peculiarly dangerous, because, acquiring peculiar strength by habit, they conduct men, with few exceptions, to final impenitence and immoveable hardness of heart. But none of these is declared to be in itself beyond the reach of forgiveness. For the sin against the Holy Ghost repentance never existed. He, therefore, who has good reason to believe that he is the subject of faith in the Redeemer, and repentance towards God, has equal reason to believe that his sins are blotted out, and his soul accepted through the atonement of Christ, sufficient for him, and for all others who are like him.

With the same confidence may the anxious, trembling sinner rely on the same righteousness as the ground of his own future acceptance with God. The language of God on this subject is, ' Him that cometh unto me,' that is, in this manner, ' will I in no wise cast out.' The sole concern of every sinner ought, therefore, to be the attainment of this evangelical character ; the very thing which is intended by coming to God ; and not curious inquiries, nor anxious doubts, concerning a point so easily settled in this manner, and so clearly decided by the Scriptures.

SERMON XLIV.

CHRIST A PROPHET.

HIS PERSONAL PREACHING.

AND HE SAID UNTO THEM, WHAT THINGS? AND THEY SAID UNTO HIM, CONCERNING JESUS OF NAZARETH, WHO WAS A PROPHET, MIGHTY IN DEED AND WORD, BEFORE GOD, AND ALL THE PEOPLE.

LUKE XXIV. 19.

IN the preceding Discourse I considered, at some length, the Covenant of Redemption. In the terms of this covenant, I observed, was contained the substance of Christ's employment, as the Mediator between God and man, and the reward which he was to receive in this character. By the substance of his employment, I intend the things which he did and suffered, alike, while in the execution of the mediatorial office. These things naturally follow the Covenant of Redemption, in a system of theology, and therefore naturally demand our next examination.

In the Scriptures, Christ is frequently spoken of as the *Prophet*, *Priest*, and *King* of mankind. This distribution of his mediatorial character into three great and distinguishing parts is, undoubtedly, the most proper which can be made; and is amply authorized by the Spirit of God. It will, therefore, be followed in these Discourses.

The first, and at the same time the most remarkable, designation of the Redeemer as a *Prophet*, is found in the 18th chapter of Deuteronomy. In the 15th verse, Moses says to the Israelites: ' The Lord thy God will raise up unto thee a Prophet from the midst of thee, of thy brethren, like unto me; unto him ye shall hearken.' This promise, we learn from the verses immediately following, was given to the Israelites, in answer to their petition, at the foot of Mount Horeb: ' Let us not hear again the voice of the Lord our God, neither let us see this great fire any more, that we die not.' In answer to this petition, the Lord said unto Moses: ' They have well spoken that which they have spoken. I will raise them up a Prophet from among their brethren, like unto thee; and will put my words in his mouth; and he shall speak unto them all that I shall command him. And it shall come to pass, that whosoever will not hearken unto my words, which he shall speak in my name, I will require it of him.'

In this very remarkable prediction we are taught,

(1.) That a Prophet *should, at some subsequent period, be raised up in the Jewish church, and of that nation, who should be like unto Moses;* that is, *one who, like Moses, introduced a new dispensation, to stand in the place of the Mosaic; as that, at the time of this prophecy, was introduced into the place of the patriarchal dispensation.* In the last chapter of Deuteronomy, written, not improbably, by several hands, and closed perhaps by Ezra, it is said, ' There arose not a prophet since in Israel, like unto Moses.' If this was really written by Ezra, it is a direct testimony, that *the Prophet* marked out in this prediction, did not arise until after the captivity. In John i. 19—21, we are informed, that the Jews, to wit, the Sanhedrim, to whom belonged the right of inquiring into the authority and commissions of prophets, sent a solemn delegation to John the Baptist, to demand of him an account of his character. They first asked him, particularly, ' Art thou Elias?' and, upon his answering in the negative, asked him again, ' Art thou that Prophet?'——ὁ προφητης; *The Prophet,* by way of eminence. In John vi. 14, the five thousand Jews whom Christ fed with five loaves and two fishes, under the strong impression of that wonderful miracle said concerning Christ, ' This is of a truth that Prophet, that should come into the world.' In John vii. 40, we are told, that the multitude of the Jews in the temple, after hearing the discourses of Christ recorded in this chapter, said, ' Of a truth, this is THE Prophet.'

The first of these passages assures us that, in the judgment of the Sanhedrim, the Prophet foretold by Moses, who was to be ' like unto him,' had not arisen when John the Baptist began to preach : and the two last assure us of the same fact, according to the judgment of the people at large.   Of course, it is fairly presumed to have been the belief of every preceding age.   The two last passages also teach us, that Christ appeared in a character so like that of the expected Prophet, as to be repeatedly acknowledged in this character by the Jewish people.

(2.) *This Prophet was to appear with a divine commission, as an inspired teacher from God:* ' I will put my words in his mouth, and he shall speak unto them all that I command him.'

(3.) *His appearance was to be such, as not to alarm or terrify the people of the Jews.*

This is evident from the fact, that he was promised in answer to a petition of that people, in which they requested that they might no more hear the awful voice of God, nor see the fire by which Mount Sinai was surrounded.   God, approving of the request, answers, that he will ' raise them up a Prophet from the midst of them ;' one who should be of ' their brethren ;' one, of course, who was to be like themselves ; a man, conversing with them, as friend with friend ; who should ' not cry, nor lift up, nor cause his voice to be heard in the streets ;'* but who should be ' anointed by the Spirit of the Lord to preach good tidings to the meek ; and to proclaim the acceptable year of the Lord,'† with the ' still, small voice' of wisdom, truth, and righteousness.

From these things it is evident, that no other prophet sustained all these characteristics but Christ, even his ' enemies themselves being the judges.'   That Christ sustains them all is unanswerably certain ; particularly, that he wrought ' mighty signs and wonders,' and that ' he was known of God face to face.'   St. Peter, in his sermon to the Jews, Acts, iii. has, by directly applying this prophecy to Christ, assured us, that he was the prophet intended, and therefore precluded the necessity of any farther inquiry.

In the text, the same character is attributed to him by Cleo-

---

* Isaiah xlii. 2.   † Isaiah lxi. 2.

phas, as he himself decisively informs us, by adding, in a following verse, ' We trusted, that it had been he who should have redeemed Israel.'   At the same time, the text furnishes us with a summary account of the manner in which the Redeemer discharged his prophetical office, by declaring, that he ' was a prophet mighty in deed and word, before God and all the people.'   To discuss this subject is the design of the following Discourse.

Prophecy may naturally be divided into two parts : *The communication of the will of God to mankind, concerning their duty and salvation ;* and *the prediction of future events.*

The power by which both these were done was no other than inspiration ; for man is as unable to divine the will of God, as to foresee future events.   Both these parts of the prophetical character Christ sustained in the most perfect degree : but the revelation of the will of God to mankind, the original, and far the most important part of the business of a Prophet, and that which is alike pointed out in the text, and in the prediction of Moses, is the characteristic of the Redeemer especially intended to be, at this time, the subject of consideration.

In Newton's Dissertations on the Prophecies may be found an ample illustration of the nature and extent of Christ's predictions.

The prophetical instruction or preaching of Christ, is in the Scriptures distributed into that which he communicated in *his own person,* and that which he communicated *by his apostles.*   The former of these shall be first considered.

In an examination of the *personal preaching* of Christ, the following things demand our attention.

I. *The necessity of his executing the office of a preacher ;*
II. *The things which he taught ;*
III. *The manner in which he taught ;* and,
IV. *The consequences of his preaching.*

I. *I shall consider the necessity of Christ's assuming the office of a Preacher.*

It is obvious to every man, that Christ might have appeared in the world in the humble character in which he actually appeared, have wrought the miracles recorded of him, suffered the death of the cross, and, generally, have done every thing recorded of him, either as an act, or a suffering, and then, instead of teaching mankind the way of life and salvation with his own mouth, might have taught it to his apostles by the inspiration of the Holy Ghost, and commissioned *them* to publish it to mankind.

This course, however, he did not pursue. On the contrary, he has chosen to teach it extensively in his own person. For this conduct of his there were, doubtless, very substantial reasons. Some of them were probably withholden from mankind. Others are discernible with sufficient clearness. Even these are not, indeed, very often called up to view, and by most men are probably unknown and unthought of. Yet, so far as they can be known, they are capable of being highly useful, and means of no small satisfaction to a serious mind. Among them the following may, I think, be mentioned, as possessing a real and sufficiently obvious importance.

1. *Christ may be fairly believed to have assumed the office of a Preacher* (or that branch of the prophetical office which I have specified as the subject of discourse,) *that the Gospel might appear plainly and undeniably to be his.*

Christ is, and from everlasting was designed to be, the great and visible agent in all things pertaining to the present world. In Col. i. 14, &c., we have the following account of his character : ' In whom we have redemption through his blood, even the forgiveness of sins. Who is the image of the invisible God ; the firstborn of every creature. For by him were all things created, that are in heaven, and that are in earth, visible and invisible, whether they be thrones, or dominions, or principalities, or powers : all things were created by him, and for him. And he is before all things : and by him all things consist. And he is the head of the body, the church : who is the beginning, the firstborn from the dead ; that in all things he might have the pre-eminence. For it pleased the Father, that in him should all fulness dwell.' In this passage Christ is declared to be the ' image,' or manifest representative, of the invisible God ; and the ' firstborn,' or head, of the whole creation ; the Creator of all things, existing before all things ; the Upholder of all things ; and the ' firstborn from the dead ;' a character which he is said to hold, ' that in all things he might have the pre-eminence ;' because, as the apostle adds, ' it was *well-pleasing* * to the Father, that in him all fulness should dwell.'   Now it is evident, that it was a necessary as well as proper part of this great design, not only that he should be the author of the Gospel, but that this fact should be completely proved, and perfectly known.   The publication of the Gospel to mankind is evidently one of the chief dispensations of divine providence in the present world.   As, therefore, it was the ' good pleasure of the Father, that in all things he should have the *pre-eminence*,' so it was peculiarly proper, that he should be pre-eminent in a thing so important and glorious as the publication of the Gospel.

St. James in the ivth chapter and 10th verse of his Epistle, informs us, that in the church of God ' there is one lawgiver, who is able to save and to destroy,' that is, Christ.   Christ then, being the only lawgiver in his church, it seems to be indispensable, that the Gospel, which contains his laws, should be seen to be his ; that all who read it may know his pleasure with certainty, and never be left to doubt whether any given doctrine or precept was given by him, or was derived from the comments of others.   The difference between these two cases cannot, I suppose, need any explanation.

But if Christ, instead of preaching the Gospel in person, had left it to be published by the apostles only, the question, *whether it was his Gospel*, would have been instantly raised up against its acceptance by mankind.   Infidels would have boldly denied it to be his ; and Christians would have been perplexed, not only concerning their proper answer to this denial, but also concerning their own faith and duty.   Even now, Unitarians, as well as Infidels, hold out a distinction between *the Gospel* ; that is, as they intend, the personal instructions of Christ ; and *the Epistles*, which they consider as the mere comments of Christ's followers.   Thus Lord Bolingbroke declares the system of religion, both natural and revealed, to be excellent, and plainly taught, as it was taught by Christ and recorded by his evangelists : " a complete system to all the purposes of religion."†   Nay, he speaks of it directly as revealed by *God himself.*‡   " Christianity, genuine Christianity," he says again, " is contained in the Gospel : it is the word of God."|| At the same time Lord

* Ευδοκησε.   † Leland, vol. ii, p. 163. 164.   ‡ Page 169. || Ibid.

Bolingbroke declares, that St. Paul has preached another Gospel; and that the New Testament contains two Gospels. In the same manner, Mr. Chubb declares, that St. Paul preached another Gospel, which was *contradictory* to that of *Christ*. Unitarians also are plainly unwilling to allow the same respect and confidence to be due to the apostolic writings, which they appear to consider as due to the words of Christ ; and, like the infidels above mentioned, admit that the Gospels possess a higher character than the Epistles.

To what a length this scheme of thought would have been carried, had Christ never preached at all, and how far the character of the New Testament, as an undoubted revelation, would have been acknowledged, if the doctrines and precepts which it contains had been declared by the apostles only, it is difficult to divine. From the nature of the subject, the facts just recited, and others like them, it may be easily believed that the character of the New Testament, as inspired, would have been seriously affected ; and with respect to multitudes, who now admit it unconditionally, overthrown ; and that the character of Christ, as the lawgiver of the church, would have been obscured. In some instances it would have been doubted, and in others denied ; and his pre-eminence in this important particular would, to a great extent, have been unseen and unregarded.

2. *It was necessary that Christ should preach the Gospel, that he might sanction its doctrines, precepts, and ordinances with his own authority.*

The doctrines, precepts and ordinances of the Gospel are rules of the faith, practice, and worship of all to whom it is made known. Whenever a rule of this nature is published to any man, the great question naturally asked by him is always, " By what authority am I required to conform to this rule ?" In matters of conscience, even an ignorant man knows that no being except God has any right to prescribe to him rules of obedience. When God prescribes to him, the prescription is a law ; when man prescribes to him, it is only advice : but between law and advice the difference, in this case, is infinite.

Christ, as has been remarked, is the only and the rightful lawgiver to his church. Had he not declared the Gospel in his own person, the question whether it was his Gospel, would have arisen, not only against its claims to be a revelation, but also against its authority, and consequent obligation. The authority of the apostles, as men, is certainly less than that of Christ, as a man; for he was a wiser and better man than they.

According to every scheme of Christianity, even according to that of the Socinians, the authority of the Gospel terminates in Christ, as the original publisher of it to mankind; and in this view is of more import, and higher obligation, than if it had terminated in the apostles. The apostles might, indeed, have been admitted as upright and unexceptionable witnesses of facts, and full credit might have been given to their testimony. But when they prescribed rules of faith and practice, their authority would easily have been questioned, for in this case they would have needed not only an unexceptionable character, but a divine commission. Had the apostles told us (as, if Christ had not personally preached the Gospel, they must have told us) only, that Christ was born, lived, and died at such a time, and in such a manner; it is not easy to conceive how they would have proved satisfactorily to mankind their reception of such a commission from him. The mind would instinctively, fondly, and anxiously have asked, " whether this distinguished person did not, while in the world, teach those around him the superior wisdom, which he possessed? If he did not, why he did not? If he did, why were not his instructions recorded?"

The absolute want of an answer to these questions would, I think, have left this subject in a state of obscurity, not only distressing, but perplexing and dangerous.

Of this obscurity infidels would not have failed to avail themselves, as they now do of every seeming difficulty and disadvantage under which they suppose Christianity to labour. They would have asked triumphantly, " How does it appear that these doctrines, precepts, or ordinances, are Christ's, and not merely the dictates of his followers? In many instances we acknowledge them to be true doctrines, sound and useful precepts, and harmless ordinances, such as may be believed, and obeyed, reasonably enough; but where is the proof, that they were intended to be laws of faith and conduct, binding the consciences of men? If this had been their character, would not Christ, the source of this system, have declared it,

Q 2

during his residence on earth? The fact, that he did not, to say the least, renders the point doubtful; and, of course, releases mankind from any obligation to obey."

What infidels would thus have boldly advanced, Socinians would probably have readily admitted; and multitudes of cold and timid believers would, as probably, have followed in their train. In this manner, the whole system might have assumed a new face, and the whole church a different character.

All these things would, also, have acquired peculiar strength and consistency, from the fact, that *the apostles attribute the Gospel wholly to Christ, as being originally and exclusively his.* " Where," it would be asked, " is the proof of this great fact? No record is left of the instructions of Christ himself, to indicate his pleasure. This certainly is strange, and, if it was really his will that we should obey these precepts and receive these doctrines, unaccountable. In a case of such importance, he cannot be believed to have left us in any doubt, much less in so serious a perplexity. His absolute silence, therefore, in a matter of this magnitude, furnishes no small reason to believe, that he intended and required no conformity or obedience, of this nature, on our part."

From these objections, and others like them, the church, and those individually and successively of whom in every period it was to be formed, would undoubtedly have experienced many difficulties and perplexities in the way of their faith and obedience. Nor would the powerful arguments, derived from the lives and the miracles of the apostles, be able to remove these difficulties. In spite of these arguments, difficulties even now exist, sufficiently perplexing to stumble the weak, and ensnare the unguarded. It is hardly necessary to add, that by the supposed silence of Christ all these would be mightily enhanced.

The Gospel is probably reverenced by those, who reverence it at all, in a degree generally proportioned to their views concerning its Author. Trinitarians regard it with the highest veneration; Arians with a less degree; and Socinians, particularly the followers of Doctor Priestley, with the least. Even these, however, regard Christ with more respect than they render to the apostles. Had the Gospel been preached by the apostles only, there is reason to fear that, by every one of these classes of men, it would have been regarded with a still lower degree of veneration. To believe its doctrines, to obey its precepts, and to celebrate its ordinances, would have been felt to be a duty less powerfully incumbent on mankind, less obligatory, and less necessary to the attainment of salvation.

It ought here to be remarked, that the Scriptures themselves furnish a solid foundation for the distinction. St. Paul, Heb. ii. 1—3, says, 'Therefore' (that is, on account of the exalted character of Christ, displayed in the preceding chapter,) ' we ought to give the more earnest heed to the things which we have heard, lest at any time we should let them slip.   For, if the word spoken by angels was stedfast, and every transgression and disobedience received a just recompence of reward ; how shall we escape, if we neglect so great salvation ; which at the first began to be spoken by the Lord, and was confirmed unto us by those that heard him ?'   In the preceding chapter, the apostle had proved the entire and infinite superiority of Christ to angels. From this character of the Saviour he derives the inference just read ; *viz.* the utter hopelessness of escape to such as neglect the salvation, which *He* published with his own mouth.   The justice of the inference he proves by the fact, that even those who disobeyed the word spoken by angels were uniformly and equitably punished.   Those therefore, he says, cannot possibly escape punishment, who neglect the word spoken by Christ, a person so much greater and better than angels.

Again, chap. x. 28, 29, he says, ' He that despised Moses' law died without mercy.   Of how much sorer punishment, suppose ye, shall he be thought worthy, who hath trodden underfoot the Son of God ?'   In both these instances the apostle evidently considers the guilt of disobeying Christ as greater than that of disobeying other publishers of the word of God ; and of course attributes to Christ, as a preacher of the Gospel, an authority superior to that of any other person.   These very passages, had they been written, as substantially they might have been, would perhaps have been quoted against the apostles themselves, if Christ had not preached the Gospel in person.

3. *It was necessary that Christ should preach the Gospel, that he might appear in the world as a preacher of truth, and righteousness.*

The importance of Christ's assumption of this character will be evident from the following particulars :—

(1.) *The importance of the character itself.*

No intellectual character is so great or so important as this. The highest wisdom and authority are here united, and exhibited with unrivalled lustre. The subjects unfolded are the most interesting in the universe : the character, pleasure, and works of God ; the nature and destiny of man ; the nature of holiness and sin ; the laws by which our duty is prescribed and regulated ; the means by which eternal life is obtained ; the termination of this earthly system ; and the introduction of another, wholly new, immortal and divine.

In the assumption of this character, Christ became the lawgiver and teacher of a world, and indeed of the universe ; unfolded all the wisdom and all the holiness attainable by mankind, throughout endless duration ; and disclosed the perfect attributes, and immeasurable glories of Jehovah. Angels, in his instructions, saw what all the splendours of the heavenly system had never illuminated ; and found a wisdom displayed on the footstool of the Creator, which their own exalted world, notwithstanding the perfection with which it is arrayed, had never ushered into light. In this character, then, it was suitable to the glory of Christ that he should have the *pre-eminence.*

(2.) *The lustre which it shed upon his life.*

Christ is the only teacher ever found in this world, whose life exactly and perfectly accorded with his instructions. No object is so edifying as this accordance. The perfect holiness of the Redeemer would have been less clearly seen, and less deeply felt, if we could not have compared his actions with the perfect rules of life uttered by his own mouth. This truth needs no other evidence, except the continual appeal to the fact, made by all Christians in their conversation and writings ; an appeal showing more forcibly than arguments can do, the strong impressions made by this fact on their minds. The peculiar excellence and dignity of Christ is here seen with the highest advantage, as being seen in the strongest light, and seen alone.

(3.) *The proof which it furnished, that all his precepts are capable of being obeyed, with a suitable disposition, by a human being.*

Christ was a man, as well as God ; differing from other men only in wisdom and excellence. In this character he perfectly observed every precept which he uttered, so far as it was applicable to himself.   In this manner he taught, unanswerably, that other teachers, and all other men, would do the same, if they possessed, and so far as they possessed, the same disposition.   The precepts, therefore, are reasonable in themselves, and all the difficulty found by us in obeying them, arises from our disinclination.   Had Christ left the Gospel to be preached by the apostles only, this trait in his character would, at the best, have been dimly seen, and feebly regarded.

(4.) *The example which he has furnished to all future preachers of the Gospel.*

The example of Christ in this respect is perfect. A particular display of its excellencies will, however, be more advantageously made hereafter.   Suffice it now to observe, that it was an example indispensably necessary for men in every period of time, and peculiarly at the time when it was furnished. The Gospel then *began* to be preached ; and the manner in which it ought to be preached, all future preachers needed to know for their direction ; the gentleness, meekness, candour, patience, clearness, simplicity, firmness, boldness, and unwavering integrity which every preacher ought to display, which Christ alone has perfectly displayed, but which thousands of preachers have exhibited in far higher degrees than they would ever have reached, if they had not been presented with this glorious example to direct and animate them in this great duty.

The examples of this nature, actually existing at that time in the world, were such as tended only to mislead and corrupt those who followed them. The pride of both Jewish and heathen teachers, the dissoluteness of their lives, their covetousness, their sickly love of human applause, the blind devotion of the former to the silly and immoral traditions of the elders, and the theoretical spirit, the sophistry, and the empty declamation of the latter, render a new example, free from all these deplorable defects, indispensable to all future teachers who wished to benefit their fellow-men,

4. *It was necessary that Christ should preach the Gospel, in order to the authoritative abolition of the peculiarities of the Mosaic system.*

These peculiarities are called by St. Peter, Acts xv. 10, ' a yoke, which neither our fathers, nor we' (that is, the Jews,) ' were able to bear.' For the Gentiles at large it would have been not only an insupportable yoke, but a system of rites and duties with which their accordance would, in many cases, have been impossible. Still all these were sanctioned by an authority confessedly divine. Equal authority was necessary to abrogate them. Yet this abrogation was absolutely necessary to the success of the Gospel. The authority of the apostles would not, I think, in this case, have been submitted to by the Jews, nor easily have been placed in their estimation above, nor in an even balance with that of Moses, but would probably have been classed with that of the prophets who succeeded Moses, and who were universally and justly considered as possessing an authority inferior to *his*.

The Jews were taught to expect the only material change which would ever exist in the Mosaic system from *that* *Prophet*, ' whom the Lord their God was to raise up unto them, like unto Moses.' This Prophet, not one of the apostles could claim to be. Not one of them, therefore, could arrogate to himself the authority by which that system was to be changed. This belonged exclusively to Christ, the Prophet thus foretold; the Prophet from whom the Scriptures themselves taught the Jews to expect material alterations in their religion.

Had Christ then been silent on this subject, it is not easy to conceive how the Jews could have been persuaded that the system was to be changed at all; nor, if *they* had not been persuaded, how the Gentiles could either have realized or maintained this important fact.

5. *It was necessary, that Christ should preach the Gospel, to furnish an opportunity of faith and conversion to the Jews, who lived at that time.*

Although Christ, as a preacher, was less successful than his apostles, yet we learn from the Scriptures, that several hundreds and, if I mistake not, that in all probability, thousands believed his word. The importance of this event needs no explanation, so far as the salvation of these believers only is considered. But there is another point of view in which this subject demands an explanation at the present time. The persons converted by the preaching of Christ, were themselves the only preachers of the Gospel whom at his ascension he left behind him in the world. From his preaching they derived their own conversion, and their qualifications for the business of converting others. The existence of these preachers, since all Christians become converts by means of the truths contained in the Gospel, was absolutely necessary to the conversion of their fellow-men ; and the preaching of Christ was equally necessary to the conversion of themselves.

When we remember, that in the number of the preachers of the Gospel the apostles are included, the importance of this article will appear in its proper light. To them the whole Christian world, throughout the past, present, and future ages of time, confessedly owes its redemption from spiritual darkness, and its introduction ' into the marvellous light ' of Christ's kingdom.

But it is only indebted to them in the immediate sense. Ultimately, this immense blessing is owing to the preaching of the Redeemer himself. The importance of his preaching, therefore, may be fairly estimated from the greatness of the blessing.

6. *It was necessary that Christ should preach the Gospel, for the purpose of furnishing important evidence of its divine origin.*

Interesting evidence of the divine origin of the Gospel is derived from the fact, that it was preached by Christ ; and *that* in two ways.

(1.) *It cannot be rationally supposed, that a mere man, educated as he was, without any advantages beside those enjoyed by the poor people of the Jewish nation, generally, could have devised the Gospel by the strength of his own mind.*

The Jews asked, with the utmost good sense, this question concerning our Saviour : ' How knoweth this man letters, having never learned ?' John vii. 15. The only rational answer to this inquiry is, that what they meant by *letters*, viz. *the wisdom which he taught*, he received immediately from God. It is plainly impossible, that he should have devised this wisdom, had he been ever so advantageously educated, either from the frivolous and superstitious doctrines of his countrymen, or from the vain, gross, erring, and self-contradictory philosophy of the heathen. Scarcely any thing can be imagined more unlike the Gospel of Christ, than the instructions given by both these classes of men. But Christ was not thus educated. On the contrary, he was in the proper sense an unlearned man. That which he taught sprang up, therefore, originally in his own mind. But no other such mind ever appeared in this world. Nor was such wisdom ever taught here by any man, whether learned or unlearned. That it should be taught by a man unlearned, as he was, from the mere force of his own mind, is a far more improbable counteraction of those laws, which regulate and limit the nature of man, than a Revelation from God can be, of any supposable laws of nature.

(2.) *Christ proved the Gospel to be from God by his life and miracles.*

Christ asserted his doctrine to be derived immediately from God. To prove the truth of this assertion he wrought a multitude of wonderful miracles, and appealed to *them,* as decisive evidence that it was true. A miracle can be wrought by none but God ; for no other being can suspend or counteract that infinite power, which is unceasingly employed in bringing events to pass, according to those which are called the laws of nature. But God cannot work a miracle to support a falsehood ; for this would be no other than a declaration that the falsehood was true. The miracles of Christ therefore, were an unquestionable proof that his Gospel is a Revelation from God.

The holiness of his life is another proof of the divine origin of the Gospel ; a proof not less solid, although, perhaps, less frequently allowed its full force. No miracle is a more palpable contradiction to the laws which respect the nature of man in this world, than the perfect holiness of Christ. At the same time, this character forbids, as absurd and contemptible, the supposition, that he was capable of uttering a known falsehood.

But Christ declared that his Gospel was from God. Coming from such a person, the assertion cannot, without perfect irrationality, be called into question.

Had not these proofs of the divine origin of the Gospel been furnished by Christ, the evidence on this subject would undoubtedly stand on very different ground, and want not a little of its present strength and completeness.

7. *It was necessary that Christ should preach the Gospel,*

in order to the fulfilment of numerous prophecies, which fore-
told this part of his character.

One of these, contained in Isaiah lxi. and applied by Christ
to himself, Luke iv. 18, 19, may stand in the place of all
others. ' The Spirit of the Lord is upon me, because he hath
anointed me to preach the Gospel to the poor ; he hath sent
me to heal the broken hearted, to preach deliverance to the
captives, and recovering of sight to the blind ; to set at liberty
them that are bruised ; to preach the acceptable year of the
Lord.'

The predictions of the Scriptures were not written merely
that they might be fulfilled ; but when they were written, it
became indispensablo that they should be fulfilled. The prophetical character of Christ was predicted, because it was
an event determined on by infinite wisdom, because of its own
intrinsic importance and utility to the universe, and because
the prediction itself also was in many respects useful and important. After it was once written, those who hear me will,
without the aid of an explanation, discern with a glance, that
its fulfilment became indispensable.

For all these reasons, and some others, which we can comprehend, and undoubtedly for others which lie beyond our
reach, it was necessary, that Christ should assume and execute
the office of a preacher of the Gospel. It is hoped that this
attempt to elucidate a subject, so interesting in itself, of such
magnitude in the scheme of redemption, and yet so rarely an
object of investigation, or even of attention, will not be unedi-
fying to those persons who regard the mediation of Christ with
reverence and complacency.

SERMON XLV.

CHRIST A PROPHET.

HIS PERSONAL PREACHING.

THE THINGS WHICH HE TAUGHT.

THE OFFICERS ANSWERED, NEVER MAN SPAKE LIKE THIS MAN.
JOHN VII. 46.

IN the last Discourse, I proposed to consider *the character of Christ as a Prophet,* or, as the great Preacher of truth and righteousness, under the following heads:——
    I. *The necessity of his preaching the Gospel:*
    II. *The things which he taught:*
    III. *The manner of his preaching:* and,
    IV. *The consequences of his preaching.*
    The first of these subjects I discussed at that time. I shall now proceed to an examination of

    II. *The things which he taught.*
    In the context we are informed, that the Sanhedrim sent officers to take Christ, as he was preaching in the temple, and bring him before them. When they returned without him, they were asked by the Sanhedrim, why they had not brought him. They answered in the words of the text, ' Never man spake like this man:' that is, The things which he said, and the manner in which he said them, were such as never before were exhibited by any human being.

These words were uttered by Jews, his enemies; by officers and dependants of the Sanhedrim, his most bitter enemies; by those officers when commissioned to seize him for trial, and punishment; by those officers, therefore, when under the strongest motives to take him, as being exposed to danger and punishment, if they did not take him; and, finally, are uttered, as containing the only reason why they did not take him. All these facts teach us, that the things which Christ spoke, and the manner in which he spoke them, were singularly excellent and impressive; so excellent and impressive, as to induce these Jews to allege it, as the only reason why they had not performed their official duty. It is not easy to conceive how a more convincing testimony could have been given to the unrivalled excellency of Christ's preaching. Particularly will this appear, if we remember, that the doctrines and precepts of Christ violated all the prejudices of the human heart, especially of Jews; and that there was nothing in his *manner* of the kind which is usually called *popular*, or calculated to catch, for the moment, the applause of his audience, and produce a favourable bias towards the speaker. In the consideration of this and the following heads, we shall have opportunity to examine, in some measure, how far the things recorded of Christ will warrant us to entertain the same opinion.

Among other things taught by Christ, I shall mention,

1. *The abolition of the peculiarities of the Mosaic system.*

The Mosaic system consisted of three great parts, the moral, the judicial or political, and the ceremonial. All the peculiarities of this system belong to the two last; the first being in its own nature applicable to mankind generally, in all circumstances. That these peculiarities were one day to be abolished was often indicated by the prophets of the Old Testament, from the days of Moses down to those of Malachi. This seems to be sufficiently indicated by our Saviour himself, in his discourse to the disciples, going to Emmaus. Luke xxiv. 25, &c., ' Then he said unto them, O fools, and slow of heart to believe all that the prophets have spoken. Ought not Christ to have suffered these things, and to enter into his glory? And, beginning at Moses and all the prophets, he expounded unto them, in all the Scriptures, the things concerning himself.' The things concerning Christ are here asserted to have been spoken by Moses and all the prophets: *viz.* his life,

death, and exaltation.   But with these, we know, was interwoven a change in the Mosaic system ; a change, therefore,
more or less exhibited by Moses, and by all the succeeding
prophets ; by some of them expressly, by others only in hint,
allusion, or inference.

St. Paul, who informs us, that Christ hath ' blotted out this
handwriting of ordinances, which was against us, and contrary to us ; taken it out of the way, and nailed it to his cross ;'
who declares, that Christ ' hath made both,' (Jews and Gentiles) ' one ; and broken down the middle wall of partition ;
abolished in his flesh the enmity between them, even the law
of commandments, contained in ordinances,' argues this fact
also at length, as declared by the Prophet Jeremiah.   ' For,'
saith he, ' if that first covenant had been faultless, then should
no place have been sought for the second.   But finding fault,
he saith, Behold the days come, saith the Lord, when I will
complete a new covenant with the house of Israel and the
house of Judah, &c. By saying, A new covenant, he hath
made the former old.   Now that which decayeth, and waxeth
old, is ready to vanish.*' See Jer. xxxi. 31, &c. ; Heb.
viii. 7, &c.

The Mosaic system, therefore, was originally designed in
part (viz. that part of it, which consisted of ' the commandments contained in ordinances') to be abolished at some
future period.   It was also to be abolished, when the ' new
covenant was to be *completed* ; the covenant originally published to Abraham, but completed under the Christian dispensation.

That it was to be abolished by Christ, is indicated in the
prophecy concerning him, dwelt on so largely in the preceding
Discourse.   ' I will raise up unto them a Prophet like unto
thee ;' that is, a Prophet who, like thee, shall bring into the
church a new dispensation, and change whatever needs alteration in the old, even as thou hast done with respect to the
patriarchal dispensation.

The same truth is also abundantly declared by preceding
prophets, especially Isaiah, who describes at large the very
changes actually made by Christ in this dispensation, almost as
distinctly as the apostles ; at least in several particulars.

* Macknight.

Christ published this abolition of the peculiarities of the Mosaic system,

(1.) *By teaching that the Gentiles, as well as the Jews, were henceforth to be the people of God.*

'And I,' saith he, 'if I be lifted up, will draw all men unto me.' John xii. 32.   Again: 'And other sheep I have, which are not of this fold; them also must I bring, and they shall hear my voice; and there shall be one fold, and one Shepherd.'

The Jews under the dispensation of Moses, were the only people of God.   All others who became members of the church, became such by being proselyted to the Jewish religion, and obeying the Jewish laws throughout; in other words, by becoming Jews, in every thing except blood.   But Christ here declares, that the Gentiles, as such, shall become members of his church, and belong to his fold; hear and follow him, and thus constitute a part of the people of God.

(2.) *By teaching the uselessness of external rites.*

Christ exhibited in many ways the emptiness of external rites; particularly by declaring, that 'meats and washings,' and other things of the like nature, neither purified on the one hand, nor, on the other, defiled the man; and universally by showing, that internal purity and integrity constituted the only object of the divine approbation, and the only title to the kingdom of God.

(3.) *By instituting a new ministry in the Church.*

This he did by commissioning the apostles, and all other ministers, Matt. xxviii. 18, &c., to 'go into all the world, preaching the Gospel, and discipling all nations, and baptizing them in (or into) the name of the Father, and of the Son, and of the Holy Ghost.'   In this commission he invested a new set of men, in the place of Jewish priests and Levites, with all the authority and offices of ministers in the future church of God.   The Jewish ministry was, therefore, henceforth done away.

(4.) *By substituting baptism and the Lord's Supper for the Jewish sacraments of circumcision and the passover.*

Christ made baptism the initiatory ordinance of the Christian church, and the Lord's Supper the confirmatory one. Circumcision, therefore, and the passover ceased of course. Besides, the death of Christ, the antitype of the passover, having taken place, the passover which typified it ceased of course.

(5.) *By substituting a new, simple, and spiritual worship for the ceremonial worship of the Jews.*   In his discourse with the Samaritan woman, Christ said, ' The hour cometh, and now is, when the true worshippers shall worship the Father, in spirit and in truth ; for the Father seeketh such to worship him.   God is a Spirit ; and they that worship him, must worship him in spirit and in truth.'

In the parable of *the sower* also, he declares, that they, who ' received the seed in good ground, are such as receive the word in an honest and good heart ;' and that these only are either fruitful or accepted.

(6.) *By teaching that God was to be worshipped acceptably, wherever he was sincerely worshipped, and not in the temple at Jerusalem only.*

In the above-mentioned conversation with the Samaritan woman, Christ said, ' Woman believe me, the hour cometh, when ye shall neither in this mountain, nor yet at Jerusalem, worship the Father.'   He also, as you well know, predicted the destruction of Jerusalem, the temple, and its services ; declaring that ' not one stone ' of the temple ' should be left upon another, which should not be thrown down ;' that ' Jerusalem should be trodden down of the Gentiles, until the times of the Gentiles should be fulfilled ;' and that ' all these things should come to pass ' during the continuance of the then existing generation.   In the mean time, he declared to his disciples, that ' wherever two or three of them should be met together in his name, there he would be in the midst of them.'

It needs no proof, that in these declarations he ' caused the sacrifice and the oblation to cease,' and put a final end to the peculiarities of the Mosaic system.

2. *Christ taught the same system of religion which was taught by Moses.*

The system of religion taught in the Old and New Testament is one and the same.   This Christ has himself sufficiently declared in his Sermon on the Mount.   One of the first declarations in it is this : ' Think not I am come to destroy the law and the prophets ; I am not come to destroy, but to fulfil.'

The system of *natural religion* taught in the Scriptures is one and unchangeable. ' Sooner shall heaven and earth pass away than one jot or one tittle of the law' on which it is founded, and by which the duties of it are required. As the law is unchangeable, so the duties which it requires are unchangeable also. The relations on which this law is founded, and whence these duties arise, are eternal and immutable. Of course the law itself, the duties which it requires, and the conditions of acceptance and rejection, together with all the truths or doctrines which in natural religion, or the religion founded on mere law, are the proper, obligatory objects of faith, must for ever be the same. Accordingly, our Saviour, when the lawyer asked him, ' Which is the first and great commandment of the law?' declared, after reciting the two great commands, that ' on these two hang all the law and the prophets,' or the system of religion contained in the Old Testament. At the same time he recited these commands, as being those on which was also suspended his own religion, which were still in full force, and the foundation of all virtue or moral excellence.

Nor is the *Christian system* substantially different in the New Testament from what it is in the Old. By the Christian system, I intend *the system of doctrines and duties, by means of which apostate creatures are restored to obedience and favour.* ' The Gospel,' says St. Paul, ' was preached to Abraham.' It was also disclosed to our first parents. ' Christ,' says St. Peter, ' preached' (that is, by the voice of Noah) ' to the spirits in prison:' *viz.* the rebellious world, imprisoned under the divine sentence, during one hundred and twenty years preceding the deluge. ' Your father Abraham,' says our Saviour to the Jews, ' rejoiced to see my day; he saw it, and was glad.' ' All these,' says St. Paul, speaking of the Old Testament witnesses, from Abel to Daniel and his companions, ' died in faith;' that is, the faith of the Gospel. ' Now, therefore,' says the same apostle again to the Ephesian Christians, ' ye are no more strangers and foreigners, but fellow-citizens with the saints, and of the household of God: And are built upon the foundation of the apostles and prophets; Jesus Christ himself being the chief corner-stone.' It would be useless to recite more passages to this purpose, although many more might easily be recited. These prove in the most deci-

sive manner, that there is one system of religion only taught
in the Old and New Testament; one law, on which the whole
is ultimately founded; one system of doctrines and duties of
what is called *natural religion;* one system of doctrines and
duties of the *Christian system,* appropriately so called: that
the Gospel was preached not only to Abraham, but to the
Jewish and patriarchal churches in every age: that good men
have always died in the faith of the Gospel; that the foundation of the prophets and apostles is the same; and that of both
Jesus Christ is the chief corner-stone.

3. *Christ taught all the fundamental doctrines of this
system.*

By the fundamental doctrines of the Christian system, I
intend those which are necessary to be believed and obeyed in
order to the attainment of salvation. Such, for example, are
the existence and perfections of the one God; the law of
God; its righteous and reasonable character; the rebellion,
apostasy, and corruption of man; the impossibility of justification by the works of the law: Christ's own divine character
as the Son of God, and the Saviour of men; justification by
faith in him; the nature and necessity of regeneration, faith,
repentance, and holiness of heart and life; a future state; a
judgment; and a recompence of reward to the righteous and
the wicked, beyond the grave.

I will not say, that the belief of every one of these is indispensable to salvation, but they are all essential parts of one
system; and within this list is found whatever is thus necessary
to be believed. That Christ taught all these things will not,
I suppose, be questioned by any man, who admits that they
are at all taught in the Scriptures.

4. *Christ taught the religion of the Scriptures more plainly
and perfectly than those who went before him.*

In a former Discourse, I considered the character of the
Redeemer *as the light of the world;* and observed, that he is
exhibited in the Scriptures as the source of all knowledge
natural, revealed, and spiritual, concerning moral subjects.
Agreeably to this general character, he appeared with peculiar
splendour as the great luminary of the world while executing
the office of a preacher of truth and righteousness. Every
subject which he discussed, he illustrated, and every duty
enjoined by him he inculcated, with a force, distinctness,

and impression, utterly unrivalled by any preceding instructor.

Particularly; he explained the nature and extent of *the divine law* far more perfectly than Moses and the prophets. Of this truth his Sermon on the Mount is the most illustrious instance of which we are able to form a conception. In this wonderful discourse he inverted some, and subverted others, of the Jewish opinions, established a long time before he commenced his ministry, concerning the substance of the Mosaic religious system; explained the extent and comprehensiveness of the law; and taught the wonderfully various, minute, and exact manner in which its precepts are applicable to the moral concerns of mankind. David had formerly said, while addressing himself to the Most High, ' Thy commandment is exceeding broad.' But Christ first unfolded the extension of the divine law to every thought and affection, as well as to every word and action, of mankind. At the same time, he exhibited the nature of genuine obedience in a light new and altogether nobler than had before been imagined; presenting to the eyes of mankind this obedience, otherwise termed holiness, or virtue, as more expanded, more dignified, more refined, and formed for a destination superior to what was found in the instructions given by the wisest men under the Mosaic dispensation. Whatever was limited, and merely Jewish, he took away; cleansing the intellect from every film which had bedimmed or narrowed its views; and releasing the heart from every clog which had checked the progress of its affections. The soul, therefore, freed in this manner from its former corporeal incumbrances, was prepared by his instructions to ' renew its strength, to mount up with wings as an eagle, to run' in the Christian course ' and not be weary, to walk and not faint.'

In the same perfect manner, and to a considerable extent in this very discourse, as well as more fully in his discourses at large, he explained *the Gospel* to mankind. The scheme of salvation to apostates through a Redeemer was very imperfectly taught by Moses, and was left in no small degree of obscurity even by David and Isaiah. It was reserved for Christ, by whom ' came grace and truth,' to make the ' way of holiness a highway, in which way-faring men, though fools,' were by no necessity compelled to ' err.' So fully, so distinctly, so com-

R 2

f

pletely has Christ pointed out the way to eternal life, that we often see heathens, savages, slaves, and even little children, as well as unlettered men in Christian countries, entering into it, and walking safely onward to the end.

Among the things which Christ has thus clearly explained to mankind, I have selected the following :——

(1.) *He taught mankind, that the heart is the seat of all virtue and vice, or, in scriptural language, of holiness and sin.*

Matt. xv. 16. ' Jesus said to his disciples : Are ye also yet without understanding? Do not ye yet understand, that whatsoever entereth in at the mouth goeth into the belly, and is cast out into the draught. But those things which proceed out of the mouth, come forth from the heart, and they defile the man. For out of the heart proceed evil thoughts, murder, adulteries, fornications, thefts, false witness, blasphemies. These are the things which defile a man ; but to eat with unwashen hands defileth not a man.' And again, Matthew xii. 34, ' He said to the Pharisees, O generation of vipers ! how can ye, being evil, speak good things ; for out of the abundance of the heart the mouth speaketh. A good man out of the good treasure of the heart bringeth forth good things ; and an evil man out of the evil treasure bringeth forth evil things.'

By declaring, that the heart was the only seat of good and evil, Christ taught us several lessons of great importance to our safety and well-being.

[1.] *He taught us particularly, how to distinguish with accuracy between moral good and evil.*

So long as men supposed moral good and evil to lie either wholly or partially in their external actions, it was impossible that they should make this distinction with any degree of accuracy ; for the very same external actions, so entirely the same as to be distinguished by no human eye, proceed from principles directly opposite, and are intended to promote directly opposite ends. In the actions themselves, therefore, there is no difference ; and, of course, no foundation for any distinction in their moral character. But, when the good and evil are referred to the heart, the intention, the accordance with different motives, we cannot fail, unless through an unnecessary and therefore criminal negligence, to discern whether we form good or bad intentions, and whether we accord with good or evil motives.   In this manner our duty, and our disobedience also, are in ordinary cases, to say the least, made plain and obvious ; and we are saved from that perplexity and suspense, whose only influence it is to delay, bewilder, and distress the mind.

[2.] *In this manner, also, Christ has taught us, where our principal safety lies ; viz. in carefully watching our thoughts.*

David in those golden precepts, recited by Solomon in the fourth chapter of Proverbs, had long before our Saviour's incarnation said, ' Keep thy heart with all diligence ; for out of it are the issues of life.'   But this precept seems to have been imperfectly understood, and little insisted on, and its importance imperfectly realized, by those who preceded the Redeemer.   He, on the contrary, by showing that the heart was the only seat of good and evil, and teaching that the nature of the streams was derived solely from the fountain, taught also, in a manner which could not be misapprehended, that the supreme duty and interest of man lay in guarding the fountain itself from every impurity.   As all good and all evil commence here, to watch the state of the thoughts and affections becomes a duty of immeasurable importance.   Proportionally important is the lesson by which this duty is taught and enjoined.

[3.] *In the same manner, also, Christ taught the emptiness of external and ceremonial performances.*

Many of the Jews, and all the heathen, placed the whole of their religion in such performances.   Christ struck at the root of this fruitful stem of falsehood ; a production not unnaturally cherished by the splendid ceremonies of the Mosaic ritual.

Although the religion of the heart was actually taught, and taught with great force and propriety, in the Mosaic system, yet the splendour of the worship which it enjoined, and the strong impressions made on the imagination by the nature and multitude of its rites, easily drew off the attention of gross and careless minds from the thing typified to the type, from spiritual worship and real duty to a mere external observance.

For several ages before Christ appeared, the Jews, and among them the teachers of their law, had leaned more and more towards an unqualified approbation of mere external rites, and a general substitution of mere external conduct for the duties enjoined by religion.   To the opinions of these men Christ, on many occasions, opposed himself in form, and with irresistible efficacy.   Whatever stress may be laid upon them by others, it is impossible for his disciples to regard them as being virtuous, even in the remotest sense; or as being of any moral use, except as occasional aids and means of virtue.

(2.) *Christ taught mankind, that virtue consists solely in loving God with all the heart, and our neighbour as ourselves.*

' On these two commands,' said he to the scribe, ' hang all the law and the prophets.'   Out of these commands arise all the precepts taught by Moses and the prophets; precepts, which have no other nature nor end but to explain and enjoin this universal law of God.   He who keeps these, therefore, keeps them all.   Of course, he is the subject of that obedience which God has required; of moral excellence, of real amiableness in the sight of his Maker.

The distinction between virtue and vice, exhibited under the first head, as so successfully made by the doctrine there specified, was here completed.   When virtue is made to consist wholly in love, and love itself is at the same time so exactly defined, all the facility is given which can be desired, for the purpose of discriminating between virtue and sin.

(3.) *Christ taught, that the meek and lowly virtues, as they are called, or in other words exercises of virtue, are superior in their excellency to any others.*

Mankind have universally admired magnanimity, active courage, contempt of danger and death, and other exercises of a bold and vigorous spirit.   Nay, so greatly have they admired them, not only as to regard with a forgiving eye those who have exhibited them, even in the midst of crimes and excesses, but to yield to them, when guilty of every enormity, their universal and unqualified applause.   I do not deny, that these may be indications and exercises of virtue.   There are undoubtedly occasions, on which we are required to be ' strong, and of a good courage;' and, when we assume this character from a sense of duty, and for just and benevolent purposes, we are really, and may be eminently virtuous.

On the other hand, the meek and lowly exercises of this

spirit; such as meekness, humility, patience, submission, gentleness, placability, moderation, and forgiveness, although perhaps by most persons allowed to be virtuous, are yet by almost all unadmired and unesteemed. Still, our Saviour has unquestionably exhibited these, both in his instructions and in his example, as wholly superior to the others. He descants on them oftener, he dwells on them more ; he presents them more frequently to us in his life ; or rather his whole life is an uninterrupted exhibition of them. He plainly attaches to them a higher importance, as they are in themselves ; and he makes them more essential to the character of a Christian, and to the attainment of salvation. This, it must be acknowledged, is a current of instruction running directly counter to that of poets, historians, and philosophers in all ages, and to the general course of human feelings relating to this subject. It cannot but be useful to examine, for a moment, how far this conduct of the Redeemer accords with the decisions of experience and common sense.

It is evident beyond a debate, that the meek and lowly virtues have in themselves no tendency to produce any part of those miseries with which mankind have afflicted each other. If we were humble, we should never become the authors of those evils which have regularly sprung from pride. If we were meek, we should not impatiently feel injuries, nor give pain in those numerous instances in which it is created by wrath. If we were gentle, we should not do injuries to others. If we were forgiving, we should not revenge them on others. If we were moderate, we should prevent the evil effects which alway spring from ungoverned passions, particularly from envy, wrath, and the passion for pleasure. If we were placable, we should cut off the mass of calamities which is found in alienation of heart, unrelenting aversion, and irreconcileable estrangement of affection, and instate in its place that serene and self-approved enjoyment which springs from the cordial reconcilement of minds, previously the seats of real though imperfect good-will. If we were patient, we should neither murmur at God, nor at each other, and should at the same time lessen half the evils which we felt, by a quiet submission to the hand of our Creator. Who does not see that, if these virtues had their full and proper influence on human hearts and human affairs, man would assume a new character, and the world a new face? Who does not see, that a great part of the guilt and misery now suffered would vanish, and that in its place would be found peace and happiness, transcending all easy estimation?

Equally evident is it also from experience, that those in whom these virtues presided, have never in fact produced these miseries. Often have they been among the principal sufferers, but never numbered among the actors of this tragedy. As this position cannot and will not be denied, to insist on it any farther would be useless.

On the other hand, to that characteristic of man, which is styled *heroism*, have been owing a great part, and that usually the most dreadful part, of human sufferings. Active courage has in every age filled the world with tumult, contention, and bloodshed; destroyed the labours and enjoyments, the peace and hopes of men: overturned temples, consumed cities with fire, and converted kingdoms into deserts. All these are causes of misery only. At the same time, it has rarely done good except by accident; and, however admired and applauded by the silly mind of man, has undoubtedly been one of the chief curses which God has permitted to visit this unhappy world.

I have already said, that I do not deny these exercises of heroism to be capable, in certain circumstances, of being virtuous, and even eminently virtuous. Still, it ought to be remarked, that if the *other class* of virtues were to have their proper influence on mankind, *these* would not exist, because there would be no occasion for them. Were no injuries done, there could be no occasion for resisting them, and of course no demand for active courage. The exercises of this spirit therefore are, at the most, of a secondary importance, and can be called forth only by preceding crimes. The meek and lowly virtues are, on the other hand, original and essential ingredients of happiness in every world, are indispensable to all private and public enjoyment, and are, therefore, of primary and inestimable value. The preference given by our Saviour to these virtues is, of course, a proof of real and divine wisdom.

(4.) *Christ in the same complete manner taught the way in which fallen beings may again become virtuous and happy.*

He explained his own character, as the propitiation for sin, and the Saviour of sinners ; the willingness of God to pardon, justify, and accept them on account of his righteousness, through faith in him, accompanied by repentance, and followed by holiness of heart and life.   He taught mankind, that their character by nature is sinful and odious to God, and that their own obedience can never be accepted as an expiation for their sin, or a ground of their justification ; that, unless they are born again of the Spirit of God, and possess a new and spiritual character, they cannot see the kingdom of God ; and that in acquiring this character they become his disciples indeed, and prove themselves to be such by ' doing whatsoever he hath commanded.'   All these things, united, constitute that character, which being assumed, those who before were apostates return to God, and to their obedience of his will ; and may evangelically claim, through his promise, a title to eternal life.

(5.) *Christ established his church in a new form, appointed in it new ministers, constituted a new discipline, and directed anew the peculiar duties of both its officers and members.*

The church under the Mosaic dispensation was properly a national one ; consisting, with the exception of such as became proselytes, and thus in a sense Israelites, of those only, and of all those, who were descended from Abraham, Isaac, and Jacob.   Christ constituted the church of the spiritual children of Abraham, who were ' Jews inwardly,' though not ' according to the flesh ;' and ' whose praise was not of man, but of God.'   Instead of the priests, who were ministers of the Jewish church, he appointed *ministers of the Gospel* to be officers in the Christian church.   Its discipline, also, ceased to be the severe and dreadful system of proceedings enjoined under the Mosaic dispensation, and became a course of advice, reproof, and, in cases of irreclaimable obstinacy, a solemn separation from the offender, all administered with the most prudent care, the tenderest good-will, and the most exemplary moderation.   The peculiar duties of Christians towards each other were summarily directed by the *new commandment ;* which, to the common *benevolence* required by the moral law towards all men, superadds *brotherly love,* or the exercise of *complacency* towards the evangelical character of their fellow Christians.   The peculiar duties of ministers, as enjoined by Christ, are generally to preside over the worship and discipline of the church, to preach the Gospel, to dispense, and, together with their fellow Christians whose duty it is also to receive, the sacraments of the New Testament.

(6.) *Christ taught also the great doctrines concerning a future state of being.*

These are the separate existence of the soul after death, the resurrection from the dead, the final judgment, the misery of the wicked, and the happiness of the righteous, throughout eternity. Concerning these great subjects, the heathen only formed conjectures, supported by very imperfect arguments. The Jewish Scriptures also, although really containing these doctrines in substance, exhibited them in dim and distant view. ' Life and immortality were brought to light,' that is, were clearly shown and fully proved, ' by Christ' alone. To him the world is indebted for its certain knowledge and extensive views of things beyond the grave ; things, in comparison with which all that exists in the present life is ' nothing, less than nothing, and vanity.'

From this summary view of the instructions of Christ, it is evident, that he has taught every thing necessary for the knowledge of our duty, the attainment of holiness, and the best conduct of a virtuous life ; has established his church on a new and happier foundation, instituted a simpler and purer worship, suited its whole economy to the circumstances of all nations, prepared it to extend easily and happily throughout the world, furnished mankind with the best means of obtaining salvation, and engaged them by the most cogent motives, placed before their eyes, to seek effectually a glorious and blessed immortality.

SERMON XLVI.

CHRIST A PROPHET:

THE MANNER OF HIS PREACHING.

NEVER MAN SPAKE LIKE THIS MAN.

JOHN VII. 46.

IN my last Discourse I considered the second division of the proposed examination of Christ's prophetical character, viz. *the things which he taught.* I shall now proceed to consider,

III. *The manner of his preaching.*

Concerning this subject I observe, that Christ preached,

1. *With perfect plainness and simplicity.*

By the plainness of Christ's preaching, I intend generally, that he preached in such a manner as to be easily understood by all who were willing to understand him.

Particularly, he used the *plain, common language of mankind ;* and, on no occasion, the *technical language,* customarily used by *men of science,* and extensively used at that period by all the votaries of the fashionable philosophy. That he has never used this language will undoubtedly be admitted by those who read his instructions, there being not even a solitary instance of it in all his discourses.

That Christ acted with entire wisdom in this particular, is manifest from many considerations. The common language of men is the only language which men, generally, can understand. If Christ had used any other language, particularly technical language, scarcely one of a hundred of those who

heard him, or of those who read his discourses, would have
been able to know what he meant.   To all these the book
containing his instructions would have been ' a sealed book ;'
and almost every man who read it would have been obliged to
say, I cannot understand it, for ' I am unlearned.'

Nor would technical language have been of much real use
to *learned* men.   In natural and mathematical science this
language has, I acknowledge, been employed with success,
and that to a considerable extent.   But in moral science,
which involves all the instructions of Christ, the same thing
cannot be said without many abatements.   The subjects of
moral science are, generally, less distinctly and definitely conceived of, than those of natural, particularly of mathematical
science ; and on this account, and because we have no sensible, exact standard, to which we may refer them, the terms of
moral science are, to a great extent, used at first indefinitely,
and are afterwards rendered still more indefinite by the loose-
ness and imperfection of thinking in succeeding writers.

At the same time, moral subjects are so important, so deeply
interest the feelings, and awaken so many biasses and prejudices, that where our discernment, left to itself, might enable us
to fasten on definite ideas, and to choose proper terms to express them, our biasses still lead us into error, and prevent us
partly from perceiving the true import of the language used by
others, and partly from an unwillingness to accord with it,
when perceived.

From these causes, and others like them, the technical language of moral science has generally been loose and indefinite,
to a greater degree than the common language of men ; and
such must have been the language used by our Saviour, if he
had adopted the technical language of his time. This language
also, originally difficult to be understood, would have been
rendered still more obscure by every attempt to translate it
into the languages of other nations.   Terms of this kind have
often no customary use which can be appealed to, to fix their
signification; and, being used only by some individual author,
or in a peculiar sense by that author, it must be left to criticism, and often to conjecture, to determine their meaning.
When used by several authors, they are commonly used with
some variation of sense, either light or serious.   In this case,
their signification becomes more doubtful, and the discourses

in which they are found more perplexed.   If I mistake not, no terms in ancient authors are so doubtful as those appropriated to philosophy, many of which seem to have their meaning scarcely settled even at the present time.   With these sources of doubt before them, translators would have been extremely perplexed, and would have perplexed their readers still more by their own terms, chosen, often erroneously, to express the doubtful meaning of their originals.   But the language used by our Saviour, was suited to all men; the best language for philosophers themselves, the only language for other men.   All men can understand it better than any other, most men can understand no other.

The plainness of our Saviour's manner is conspicuous, also, in *the obvious nature of his allusions and illustrations*.   These were all derived from objects familiar to the apprehension of mankind at large, according to the rule of eloquence in this respect laid down by Cicero.   Every reader of our Saviour's discourses must have observed this fact.   The ' city set on a hill;' ' the salt of the earth;' ' the candle, which is not to be set under a bushel, but on a candlestick;' ' the vine and the branches;' ' the shepherd and the sheep;' are instances which cannot be forgotten.   These, and others of the like nature, are the happiest of all allusions, and the best of all illustrations.   They are natural, but forcible; everywhere offering themselves, and everywhere beautiful; familiar, but possessed of sufficient dignity; and attended always with this high recommendation, that they are easily understood by men in every situation of life.

The plainness of our Saviour's manner is remarkably evident, also, *in his parables*.   Instruction appears to have been communicated in allegorical discourses generally resembling these, from the earliest ages.   But no instructor ever formed them so happily as Christ.   The subjects alluded to are chosen with supreme felicity, and the allusions are conducted with the utmost skill and success.   The allegorical part of the story is always just and impressive, commonly beautiful, not unfrequently sublime, and in several instances eminently pathetic.   The meaning which it is intended to convey is at the same time definite, clear, and obvious.   The parable, instead of shading the thought, illumines it, and instead of leaving the reader in doubt, contributes not a little to the satisfaction of his inquiries. When we consider the perplexed, enigmatical manner in which both Jewish and Gentile teachers, at that time, conveyed many of their most important instructions, we shall, on the one hand, see this characteristic of our Saviour's discourses in a stronger light, and, on the other, shall be led to admire suitably the wisdom with which in this respect he taught mankind.

Nearly allied to the plainness of our Saviour's instructions is their *simplicity*. By simplicity, in this case, I mean that general characteristic of discourse, in which both the thoughts and words appear to have been adopted without the effort of selecting, and merely because they offered themselves; and to follow each other in the order in which they offered themselves, without contrivance, and in the manner most remote from either study or affectation. Of this important characteristic, as critics universally agree, the ancient writers furnish more numerous and more perfect examples than the moderns. Among ancient writers, those who penned the Scriptures hold, by general acknowledgment, also, the first place. But amid these, as well as all other instructors of mankind, Christ as a pattern of perfect simplicity stands unrivalled. His discourses, though fraught with doctrines of the most profound and wonderful wisdom, and sentiments of the highest sublimity and beauty, appear still, as if neither the words nor the thoughts were the result of the least study, but sprang up spontaneously in his mind, and flowed from his tongue in a sense instinctively, in a manner strongly resembling that of children. The impression made by the manner in which they are delivered, is, that they are the result of mere unadulterated nature, prompting the speaker with an unresisted impulse, as if he knew how to speak in no other manner. The effect of this manner of discoursing is undoubtedly in an eminent degree happy, whatever may be the subject or the drift of the discourse. When this is didactic, simplicity gives the teacher the most desirable aspect of artlessness, candour, and sincerity. When it is historical, beside presenting the speaker as invested with these important characteristics, it lends the utmost beauty and impressiveness to his narration. When it is sublime or pathetic, it presents the objects which excite these emotions in the strongest light, and excites the emotions themselves in the highest degree which is possible. As examples, illustrating

in the most perfect manner the truth of all these observations,
I allege particularly, Christ's Sermon on the Mount; his Para-
bolic Sermon, recorded Matt. xiii. ; several of his discourses
with the Jews, recorded by St. John; those addressed to his
disciples, commencing with the xivth chapter; his intercessory
prayer in the xviith of that Evangelist; the Lord's Prayer;
the parables of the Prodigal Son, the Rich Man and Lazarus,
and the Good Samaritan; and the discourses concerning the
destruction of Jerusalem, and the final judgment, in the xxivth
and xxvth of Matthew.   The parable of the Prodigal Son,
particularly, may be alleged as the first example of beautiful
and pathetic simplicity which has been ever given to mankind;
as without a rival, and without a second.

2. *Christ exhibited in his manner of instructing the most
perfect modesty and delicacy.*

Both Jewish and heathen teachers, before the time of Christ,
were remarkable for pride, vanity, and of course for boasting.
Pharisaical and stoical pride have been proverbial for near two
thousand years.   The Grecian philosophers exhibited to the
world their true character, in this respect, by calling themselves
Σοφοι, or *wise men.*   Those of the East assumed denominations
equally arrogant and contemptible.   The pride and vanity
which they exhibited in this manner, they manifested also in
every other form, and on every convenient occasion.   Like a
disagreeable odour, this unbecoming character eludes every
attempt to conceal it, and forces itself upon the mind, where-
ever the writer becomes the subject of his own thoughts.

In direct and perfect opposition to them all, Christ, though
teaching with a wisdom and greatness of character altogether
unrivalled, has not suffered, I need not say a proud or vain
thought, but even the most distant appearance of such a
thought, to escape from his lips.   Though more frequently
than any other teacher compelled, by the nature of his mediatorial office, the tenour of his discourses, and the disputes
in which he was engaged with the Jews, to become the subject of his instructions to them; and although doing and saying that which, far more than any thing ever done or said,
must awaken the conviction of personal greatness and superiority, yet he has never even in the most remote hint or allusion intimated a single indulgence of either pride or vanity
in his own mind.   No resemblance of boasting can be found

in all his discourses.   Himself, as an object of admiration or
applause, is for ever out of sight and out of remembrance.

Delicacy is the kindred, the ally of modesty, and an attribute of instruction as well as an excellency of character which
appears to have been very imperfectly known to the teachers,
both Jewish and heathen, who lived at or before the time
of our Saviour.   From them all he is perfectly distinguished
by the most complete exhibition of this excellence.   Not a
sentiment, not a word, has fallen from his lips which can give
pain, in this respect, to a mind of the most finished refinement
and virtue ; not a word, not a sentiment, fitted to awaken one
improper thought, or to allure in the least degree to any unbecoming action.

3. *Christ taught with entire boldness and integrity.*

These highly honourable characterestics of our Saviour's
instruction are everywhere visible, and, so far as I know, universally acknowledged.   Particularly are they conspicuous in
his open, intrepid attacks on the Pharisees and Sadducees,
the men who at that time held the whole power of the Jewish
government, and the whole influence over the Jewish nation.
These sects also were the leaders of that nation in all their
bigotry, their miserable superstition, and their deplorable devotion to a mere outside morality and worship.   They corrupted them in their moral and religious principles, and introduced a sensual, loose, and nearly atheistical system of doctrine
and practice.   To these men Christ, with no defence but his
own wisdom, innocence, and purity, opposed himself with
uniformity, vigour, and immoveable firmness ; exposing the
unsoundness of their wretched doctrines, the futility of their
arguments, the hypocrisy of their professions, and the enormous
turpitude of their lives.   All this he did with such clearness of
evidence, and such pungency of reproof, that they themselves
often shrunk from the detection, and trembled for the very existence of their principles and their power.

At the same time, and in the same manner, he reproved and
exposed all the popular prejudices of his country.   Gentle,
modest, and humble beyond example, he united with this
character an unyielding fixedness of principle and deportment,
and a perfect destitution of that love of popularity, and that
desire of applause, which are such prominent traits in the
character of most of those who have attempted the instruction

of mankind.   There is not in his instructions a single instance
of the least concession to any religious, civil, or personal prejudice of his countrymen.   On the contrary, he treated them
all openly, uniformly, and alike.   Even their favourite doctrine, that they were, and were ever to be, the peculiar people
of God, together with all the mischievous consequences which
they derived from it, he resisted on many occasions, and in
many forms; declaring that they were not, in the true and
scriptural sense, the children of Abraham; and showing them,
that their natural descent from this patriarch would not, by
itself, be the least advantage to them, while the abuse of
their privileges would only increase their guilt, and enhance
their final condemnation.

Nor was Christ less direct and sincere in reproving his
friends.   In them, notwithstanding all the gentleness and tenderness with which he taught them, he allowed no variation
from truth or duty; and reproved them on every occasion for
their prejudices, bigotry, unbelief, contentions, faults and follies of every kind.   Exact truth and unwarping holiness appear evidently to have been the objects which he made the
standard of all his instructions, as well as of his life.   No
tenderness, friendship, or gentleness of disposition, no fear of
the populace or the powerful, prevented him from reaching
this standard on every occasion; no zeal transported him
beyond it.   He, and he alone, among those who have taught
mankind, knew how to make all the affections of man perfectly accordant with truth and duty, and perfectly subservi-
ent to   the establishment of them in the world.

4. *Christ taught mankind with an authority peculiar to
himself.*

This characteristic of Christ's teaching was twofold.

(1) *The authority derived from the weight of his precepts,
and the manner in which they were inculcated.*   This I take
to be especially what is intended by St. Matthew in the following passage; ' And it came to pass, when Jesus had ended
these sayings,' (that is, the sayings contained in his sermon
on the mount) ' the people were astonished at his doctrine;
for he taught them as one having authority, and not as the
scribes.'   In the authority of this kind, Christ far excelled
every other instructor.   No precepts are so important as his,
no manner of teaching is so dignified and so commanding.

When we remember, that he appeared as a poor man, without friends or influence, without power or splendour ; that he proposed a new system of religion and morals ; that he attacked, in many respects, the former system, the bigotry with which it was regarded, the prejudices of the multitude, and the enormous wickedness of the great ; when we farther remember, that in the minds of many, he overset them all, and in the minds of many more, shook them to their foundations : we cannot hesitate to acknowledge, with the Jewish officers, that, in this particular, ' Never man spake like this man.'

(2) *Christ taught mankind with a singular official authority.*

This is conspicuous in two things.

[1.] *He uttered neither opinions nor advice.* All the dictates of Christ's teaching are of the kind which the Greeks call *dogmas*, that is, positions peremptorily asserted, without any doubt expressed, any wavering, any uncertainty, any suggestion of the possibility of error. Every doctrine is exhibited as an absolute law of faith, and every precept as a positive rule of practice. Every thing which he uttered carries with it evidently the assurance, that his doctrines are true and certain, that his precepts are just and reasonable, and that himself is invested with full authority to prescribe both, as obligatory rules of faith and practice.

[2.] *Christ taught in his own name, and without appealing to any authority but his own.*

This fact was mentioned in a former discourse ; but it will be proper briefly to consider it, also, at the present time. All the prophets of the Old Testament prefaced their instructions with ' Thus saith the Lord.' Christ commenced his ministry with explaining, altering, and annulling many things said by *them* under this authority, and acknowledged by *him* to be thus said. His own instructions, however, he never prefaced in this manner, but merely said, ' I say unto you ;' or, on solemn occasions, ' Amen ; Verily, I say unto you.' The authority here assumed by him was such, as to warrant him in repealing that which had been spoken by prophets in the name and by the authority of God, and was, therefore, an authority equal to that under which these prophets had spoken.

In this exercise of authority Christ stands alone, being

wholly distinguished from all other teachers, both sacred and profane.   The apostles, it will be remembered, taught only in the name of Christ.

5. *Christ taught with uniform and singular patience, gentleness, and kindness.*

I have grouped these excellencies of our Saviour's manner of teaching, as I have several of those already mentioned, on account of the intimate relation which they bear to each other.

To dwell on this subject with minuteness cannot be necessary.   All readers of the Gospel know how often Christ bore with the dulness, prejudices, and unbelief of his disciples ; how often he reiterated the same instructions ; how patiently he removed their prejudices ; how frequently he had occasion to pronounce them ' of little faith ;' and how universally, and how often without reproving them, he bore with their numerous infirmities.   There is not an instance in his life of an impatient, petulant word ; not a single expression of the kind which we term passionate ; not an occasion on which he lost, in the least degree, that absolute self-controul, by which he was elevated above all the children of Adam.   When the ambitious sons of Zebedee, through their more ambitious mother, asked of him the privilege of ' sitting, the one on his right hand, and the other on his left ;' he calmly replied, ' It is not mine to give.' When the body of his disciples ' strove, which of them should be greatest, he took a little child and set him in the midst of them ; and when he had taken him in his arms, he said unto them, Whosoever shall receive one of such children, in my name, receiveth me ; and whosoever shall receive me, receiveth not me, but him that sent me.'   When Peter denied him in so shameful and bitter a manner, the only reproof which he gave him is recorded in these words, ' and the Lord turned, and looked upon Peter.'   Over Jerusalem, the seat of so much guilt, the scene of the messages and of the slaughter of so many prophets, and speedily about to be the scene of his own sufferings, he wept with inexpressible tenderness, and said, ' How often would I have gathered thy children, as a hen gathereth her chickens under her wings ; but ye would not ! '

6. *Christ taught by his example.*

It is a proverbial observation, that example is far more instructive than precept ; an observation verified by the experience of mankind every day and in every place. No precepts are, indeed, seriously influential on the mind of the pupil, unless they are believed to have some good degree of influence upon the life of his instructor. On the contrary, where the instructor is supposed to speak with sincerity, and from the heart, and to be himself governed in his conduct by the very principles which he recommends to others, very plain instructions have commonly very great power. Example, therefore, may be safely pronounced to be the best of all instructions, and the only mode of consummating the instruction of the voice.

In this kind of teaching Christ stands alone. The prophets and apostles are here left out of comparison, and out of sight. As for the heathen philosophers, their example was a mere contrast to their instruction, I mean, to such parts of it as were just and commendable. What they taught of this nature, they refuted in the daily conduct of their lives. But Christ's life was a perfect practical comment on all that he taught, and a perfect illustration of the nature and efficacy of his precepts. Hence his instructions have been unrivalled in their influence on mankind, and have produced effects to which there has been in the history of the world no parallel.

I have here mentioned several primary characteristics of the *manner* in which Christ taught mankind. To form a more complete estimate of its excellence, it will, however, be necessary to consider *what he did not do*, as well as *what he did*. The superlative wisdom of the Redeemer was manifested as truly in what he avoided, as in what he accomplished.

On this subject I observe,

1. *That he utterly declined to gratify the mere curiosity of men.*

Many questions were proposed to him by the Jews, of such a nature as to demand answers which could only gratify curiosity. Several more of the same kind, were addressed to him by his disciples. To all these he declined the answers which were solicited. There are, also, very many subjects concerning which curiosity has ever been awake, and which not only are intimately connected with the scriptural system of religion, but are mentioned by Christ in many forms, and in some particulars extensively discussed. But such parts of these subjects as excite mere curiosity, he has invariably left in silence; and never tempted nor satisfied at all this roving, restless propensity.   Over all subjects of this kind he has drawn the curtain of absolute concealment, and hidden them entirely from human eyes.

Among these subjects, it will be sufficient to mention one. The circumstances which attend a future state of happiness, awaken, perhaps, as extensively and as naturally the wishes of the mind to be minutely informed, as any thing belonging to the destiny of man.   On this immense subject Christ has, however, taught nothing except what we plainly needed to know, and has withheld every thing else from our investigation.   Others have often indulged a wandering fancy, and, in the wildest excursions concerning a future state, have attempted to explore the regions of future being, as travellers search distant countries in the present world.   But Christ has chosen barely to inform us of the existence and general nature of these regions; things which we are deeply interested to know, and left these outlines to be filled up by our own actual experience, when we shall have become possessed of that happy state of being.   When we remember how many uncertainties would have arisen out of such a disclosure, had it been made; how many questions of difficult solution, or incapable of being solved, and, in a word, how greatly and how often the mind would have been perplexed concerning subjects unconnected with its real good, we cannot hesitate to acknowledge the perfect wisdom manifested in this concealment.

2. Christ taught without sophistry.

The integrity displayed in the *reasonings of our Saviour*, is equally exact and perfect with that exhibited in his *declarations of facts*.   In the age in which he lived, both the Jewish and heathen teachers were distinguished for false reasoning, as a species of art.   The doctrines which they taught needed this defence.   Accordingly, we find it employed by them on almost every occasion.   Many specimens of the subtleties of the Sadducees and Pharisees are recited to us in the New Testament, particularly in the Gospels.   Quibbles, paradoxes, and fetches were the custom of the time, and were shamelessly employed to defend every favourite opinion, and attack every adversary.   But false reasoning is as real a violation of in-

tegrity as false declarations, is often as mischievous, and is
always a proof of gross depravity, or gross inattention to our
duty. Christ, therefore, the perfect pattern in this as in all
other conduct, has alleged no argument but a real one, has
given no argument any more force than it really possesses, and
has expressed no more confidence in any argument than he
really felt. The glorious contrast which he exhibited, in the
exact simplicity and sincerity with which he reasoned on every
occasion, to the subtlety and sophistry of all with whom he
reasoned, and of a vast multitude of other teachers, is a pattern for all succeeding reasoners, which, if universally followed, would free the world from a great part of its doubts
and errors, and the deplorable guilt and misery by which they
are followed.

3. *Christ has authorised no intolerance.*

It is well known, that the Jews, who were distinguished for
their spiritual pride and bigotry, and who regarded other
nations with an almost absolute intolerance, were never more
strongly marked by these characteristics than at the time when
our Saviour appeared. Even the apostles were not exempt
from a share of this character. 'Master,' said John, 'we
saw one casting out devils in thy name, and we forbade him,
because he followeth not with us. And Jesus said unto him,
Forbid him not; for he that is not against us is for us.' Again,
John and James, moved with indignation against the inhabitants of a Samaritan village, because they declined to receive
their Master, said to him, ' Lord, wilt thou that we command
fire to come down from heaven, and consume them, as Elias
did ? But he turned, and rebuked them, and said, Ye know
not what manner of spirit ye are of. For the Son of Man is
not come to destroy men's lives, but to save them.' So in-
tolerant was the spirit even of the beloved disciple, and so
benevolent, it ought to be added, was that of Christ.

In this nation, and at this period, was Christ born and educated. But instead of imbibing, countenancing, or warranting
intolerance and bigotry, he taught, in all instances, their odi-
ousness and guilt, and enjoined, with respect to every subject
and person, the most absolute moderation, liberality, and candour ; not, indeed, the fashionable liberality of licentious men
in modern times, a professed indifference to truth and holiness,
but a benevolent and catholic spirit towards every man, and a

candid and just one towards every argument and opinion. Distinctions of nations, sect, or party, as such, were to him nothing; distinctions of truth and falsehood, right and wrong, were to him every thing. According to this scheme he framed both his instructions and his life.

4. *Christ taught without enthusiasm.*

All the language and all the sentiments of our Saviour, were the language and sentiments of a person perfectly satisfied of the goodness of the cause which he had espoused, immoveably attached to it, and earnestly engaged to promote it among mankind. Still, this earnestness, this fixedness of character, differed greatly from that of most persons who have undertaken the reformation of their fellow-men. In our own, as in all preceding ages, those who have assumed the character of reformers almost of course make a parade of their piety, and a merit of their peculiar devotion to the cause in which they have embarked, and aim at gaining proselytes by a nice scrupulosity concerning things commonly esteemed innocent, animosity against those whose opinions they censure, and impassioned addresses to such as listen to their instructions. Christ was the opposite of all these. Little things always in his instructions appeared little. Harmless things he regarded as harmless. Great and important things only has he taught us to regard as great and important. In his life there was no ostentation of any thing. He ' came eating and drinking ' like other men, and in his human nature and appearance differed from them in nothing but superior wisdom and purity of character. In his discourses every thing is serious, solemn, and earnest; but every thing, at the same time, is uttered with moderation, without passion, without declamation.

No discourses in the world are more distant from fanatical declamation, and no character is more unlike that of an enthusiast, than the discourses and character of Christ. A spirit of serenity, of self-possession, of impassionate sweetness, of principled excellence, reigns throughout all his instructions and throughout all his life, of which elsewhere there is no example.

5. *Our Saviour sought in his instructions for no applause.*

In this characteristic also he was equally singular and perfect. The love of applause is the most universal; and probably the most seductive, of all human passions, particularly in minds raised by intelligence above the common level. So seductive is it, that Cicero pronounced it to be true virtue. But of this passion not a single trace appears in the whole history of Christ. The good or ill opinion, the applause or censure, of his fellow-men, whether friends or enemies, seem as if they had not been thought of by him, and as if no capacity of being influenced by them had been an original attribute of his mind. With a magnetic constancy, his thoughts and discourses were pointed alway to truth and rectitude; and the world had no power of producing in them a momentary variation.

Such was the manner in which Christ taught mankind: a manner all his own; copied from none who preceded him, and imperfectly imitated by the best and wisest of those who came after him; a manner perfectly suited to the supreme excellence of his character, to the divine commission which he bore, to the illustrious system of truth which he taught, to the glorious errand on which he was sent, and to the perfect nature of that Being whose representative he was to the children of men.

SERMON XLVII.

CHRIST A PROPHET:

CONSEQUENCES OF HIS PREACHING.

AND THE OFFICERS ANSWERED, SAYING, NEVER MAN SPAKE LIKE THIS MAN.

JOHN VII. 46.

IN the three preceding Discourses, I have considered the prophetical character of Christ, under these three heads : 1. The necessity of his assuming the office of a prophet ; 2. The things which he taught ; and 3. The manner in which he taught them.

I shall now proceed·to the consideration of the fourth head originally proposed concerning this subject, viz. *The consequences of his preaching* ; and, after a brief examination of these, shall conclude my observations on the personal preaching of Christ with a few remarks.

The preaching of Christ produced,

1. *A general astonishment in those who heard him.*

' And it came to pass,' says St. Matthew, that ' when Jesus had ended all these sayings, the people were astonished at his doctrine ; for he taught them, as one having authority, and not as the scribes.' Two things are here mentioned as causes of the astonishment occasioned by Christ's sermon on the mount : the things which he taught, and the manner of teaching. ' The people were astonished at his doctrine : for he taught them as one having *authority* and *not as the scribes.*'

It cannot be thought strange, that a scheme of doctrine so new, so solemn, so simple, so pure, so amply fraught with inherent evidence of its truth, and in all these respects so opposite to that which they were accustomed to hear from their own teachers, should produce an unusual degree of wonder in the minds of this people.   Nor is it any more strange, that such a manner of teaching as that employed by Christ should have its share in producing this effect, and enhance the surprise occasioned by his instructions. ' We, who hear these instructions from the cradle, to whom they are presented weekly from the desk, and daily by the Bible, cannot easily conceive the degree in which they could not fail to impress the minds of men when they were first published in the world. They were then new and strange, and, both in the matter and the manner, were in a great measure singular.   They were employed on the most important of all subjects, the sin and holiness, the ruin and recovery of mankind.   They professed to contain and communicate the will of God concerning these subjects, and of course to be a message from heaven.

At the same time, they censured, both implicitly and explicitly, most of the doctrines taught by the Pharisees and Sadducees, most of their precepts, and the general tenour of their lives.   The doctrines they showed to be false ; the precepts unsound, and immoral ; and the conduct of those who taught them, to be unworthy of the profession which they made, and contrary to the Scriptures which, in pretence at least, they believed.   These men, either alternately or conjointly, had for a long period held an entire and commanding influence over the Jewish nation.   Highly venerated for their wisdom, and in many instances for their apparent sanctity, their countrymen scarcely called in question their claims to this influence, or to the character on which it was founded.   But, when Christ entered on his ministry, he stripped off the mask by which they had been so long concealed, and left both their folly and their wickedness naked to every eye.   The system which they had so long taught without opposition he showed, irresistibly, to be a strange compound of truths derived from the Scriptures, of falsehood and weakness, of superstitious scrupulosity and fanatical zeal, professedly drawn from the traditions of the elders, and of gross immorality and glaring hypocrisy, generated by their own minds.   Their pretended sanctity both of doctrine and deportment, he proved to be a mere veil, assumed to conceal their enormous avarice and ambition, pride and cruelty.   As the means of future acceptance with God, he showed that they could never avail, and that, therefore, they could only delude and destroy their credulous disciples. That such instructions as these, delivered by a person whose whole life was a direct contrast to that of those whom he thus censured and refuted, who evidently appeared to be under the influence of no selfish passion and no sinister motive, whose precepts required and whose conduct exemplified piety and benevolence without a mixture; delivered too in a manner so clear, so direct, and solemn, so universally convincing and impressive, should astonish all who heard them, cannot be thought strange even by us.   Such was, indeed, their effect; and to such a degree as to induce those who heard them to pronounce the teacher on different occasions, ' a prophet,' a ' great prophet,' ' *the* Prophet foretold by Moses,' and ' the Messiah.'   When we remember, that this teacher appeared in the character and circumstances of a Jewish peasant, without a name, without education, without friends, we cannot but perceive that the effect of his teaching was, in this respect, very great.

2. *The preaching of Christ produced great opposition both to himself and to his doctrines.*

I have already recited many causes of this opposition. There were many more.   But all of them may with propriety be reduced under these general heads.   The novelty and excellency of his doctrines, the strictness and purity of his precepts, his birth, his character, the justice and pungency of his reproofs, the disappointment of the expectations of the Jews concerning the glory and splendour of his Messiahship, and the fears of the Pharisees and Sadducees that he would destroy their influence and power.   All these things thwarted some selfish passion of his hearers, and many of them thwarted every such passion.   It is not therefore to be wondered at, that they should oppose one who taught and lived so as uniformly to reprove them for their whole moral character and daily conduct.

This opposition commenced almost with his ministry, and was carried on to its termination.   It was however, carried on with different degrees of vehemence by the different classes of

Jews. The *great*, that is, the Pharisees and Sadducees, hated Christ with far more uniformity and rancour than the common people. The reasons are obvious. He exposed their systems of doctrine and modes of teaching, refuted their arguments, reproved their abominable conduct, displayed to the people at large their folly and wickedness, and threatened them with the total ruin of their reputation and authority. These were offences not to be forgiven by proud, bigotted, unprincipled, and malignant men. They were not in fact forgiven. Throughout his whole public life they exercised the most furious resentment against him, and hesitated not to adopt every measure to compass his destruction. All that sagacity could devise or art execute, was employed to ensnare and entrap the Redeemer in his words and actions. When these measures failed, as they always did, resort was had to violence and power. These at length succeeded; and the most perfect human malignity was finally gratified by seeing the Saviour nailed to the cross.

The *people, at large* regarded him with far less bitterness than their leaders. It is several times mentioned, that the efforts of the Sadducees and Pharisees to destroy Christ were prevented of success by their fear of the people. It is frequently testified, in substance, that ' the common people heard him gladly.' It is also evident, that, had not appeals been made to their doubts, fears, and prejudices, with great art and perseverance, and on many occasions, their attachment both to him and his doctrines would have risen still higher, and much more nearly accorded with their interest and duty. On a number of occasions, however, *they* indulge the most violent animosity against him. Almost at the commencement of his preaching, the inhabitants of Nazareth attempted to put him to a violent death, by forcing him down the precipice of the hill on which their city was built. Several times afterwards their countrymen endeavoured to stone him, and in the end united, at the instigation of their rulers, in accomplishing his death, with a fury approximating to madness.

3. *The preaching of Christ produced the conversion of a considerable number of his hearers.*

The number of those who were converted by the preaching of Christ cannot be estimated with any exactness. The eleven apostles, the seventy, the more than five hundred brethren, to whom at one time Christ appeared in Galilee after his resurrection, are numbers mentioned in the Scriptures.   The last not improbably included the two first.   To these we ought, I think, to add a considerable number more, since it is often said, that ' some of the people,' and ' many of the people, believed on him.'   No reason occurs to me why we should not, generally at least, consider the faith here spoken of as evangelical.   If this be admitted, the number of converts made by the preaching of Christ must have greatly exceeded the largest number specified in the Gospel.

Still it is, I suppose, generally believed, that the success with which Christ preached the Gospel was small, compared with that of the apostles, and compared with that which we should naturally expect to follow preaching of such singular excellence ; especially when the perfection of his life and the glory of his miracles are connected with the nature of his preaching.   The success, however, was upon the whole such as to enable the Gospel to take effectual root in this sinful world, and to provide the means of supplying preachers throughout all succeeding ages, and of spreading the Gospel, within a moderate period, over a great part of the earth.

I have now finished the observations which I proposed to make concerning the personal preaching of Christ ; and shall conclude this Discourse with a few REMARKS, naturally flowing from the considerations suggested on this subject.

1. *These considerations call up to our view, in an interesting manner, the glory and excellency of Christ as a teacher.*

From the things which have been said in these Discourses, it is, if I mistake not, clearly manifest, that both the matter and manner of Christ's preaching were singularly important and excellent.   The errand on which he came into the world was the greatest which ever entered into the conception of rational beings, or which was ever proposed in the providence of God.   Of this vast and sublime purpose the preaching of the Gospel was a primary and indispensable part.   To this part he appeared perfectly equal.   The will of God the Father concerning the duty and salvation of men, he entirely understood ; and, together with it, the character, the sins, errors, ignorance, and wants of those to whom he was sent ; their hatred of truth, their opposition to their duty, and their reluctance to be saved.   The same perfect acquaintance he also possessed with the nature and import of the preceding Revelation : its types, prophecies, and precepts, the false glosses made on its various contents by the teachers who went before him, and the miserable prejudices imbibed by those whom he taught. These errors he detected and exposed; these sins he powerfully reproved; and the truth and duty opposed to them he enjoined with a force and evidence wholly irresistible. In this manner he taught the way of life with such clearness, that ' he who ran might read,' and that ' way-faring men, though fools,' could ' not ' necessarily ' err therein.'

At the same time, he adorned these instructions with a candour, frankness, gentleness, and sweetness of demeanour, with a sincerity, boldness, and energy of character, immensely honourable to himself, and supremely great and lovely in the view of every just and discerning mind. Over all, his daily example as a moral being, cast a glorious lustre, at once transcendently beautiful in itself, and illuminating in the strongest manner the nature and excellence of all that he said.

If Christ had not come into the world, if he had not preached the Gospel, what would now have been the condition of mankind ? The Mosaic system, of necessity confined almost entirely to the Jewish nation, had, before the advent of our Saviour, degenerated chiefly into a mere mass of externals. The *moral* part of this system was in a great measure neglected or forgotten ; the *ceremonial* had almost wholly occupied its place.

Even this, also, had lost its proper designation, and influence. The *sacrifices*, instead of being regarded as mere symbols of that real and great atonement ' which taketh away the sins of the world,' and to typify which they were originally instituted, seem to have been at this time considered as expiations in themselves. The *ablutions*, which were intended only to direct the eye to the cleansing of the soul by the blood of Christ, and the affusion of the Spirit of grace, appear to have lost their typical character, and to have been exalted by a gross imagination into means of washing away the stains of the soul, and making it pure in the sight of God. The *oblation of incense* was apparently supposed by the suppliant to ascend with his prayers to the heavens, and to accompany them with a sweet odour to the throne of God. To ' wear long clothing,' to ' make broad their phylacteries,' to ' pray in the corners of the streets,' to ' fast twice a week,' to ' bow down the head like a bulrush,' to ' sit in sackcloth and ashes,' and to ' tithe mint, annise, and cummin,' were considered as the price paid for heaven ; the price with which salvation might assuredly be purchased.   In the mean time, piety to God, ' justice, judgment, and mercy' towards men, and that government of our passions and appetites, without which neither can exist, were kept out of sight, and out of remembrance.   Pride and avarice, cruelty and lust, reigned without controul and without opposition.   Scarce an effort seems to have been made, or even thought of, to check the tide of declension.   The progress was rapid and unimpeded, till the measure of iniquity became full.   About forty years after the crucifixion, the crimes of the Jewish nation . according to the testimony of Josephus, himself a Jew, rose to such a height, as to forbid the longer continuance of any civilized state or social union among this people.   Furious animosity, unexampled pollution, civil war raging with singular violence, unparalleled treachery, and murder without bounds, then became the prominent and almost the only features of the Jewish character.   The rest of the world was absolutely overspread with Polytheism, and all the debasement and all the miseries to which it so frequently gives birth.

Had not Christ, then, come into the world, and preached the Gospel to mankind, the Jews would, perhaps, have been, substantially, what, since the destruction of their nation, they have been in fact ; reprobates, outcasts from God, possessing hearts ' harder than the nether millstone ;' impervious to truth, impenetrable by argument, shorn from the side of virtue, vagabonds in the moral as well as in the natural world, roaming now in quest of gain or prey to satisfy immediate lust, now wandering in a benighted wilderness, through every bye-path, to find eternal life, and mistaking the glimmerings of every *ignis fatuus* by which they are misled for the light of heaven.

We, in the mean time, together with all the present offspring of the gentile world, should have been prostrating ourselves before calves and crocodiles, dogs and cats, an image of brass, or the stock of a tree.   Instead of the churches which, on a thousand hills, now stand open for the worship of Jehovah we should, with the heathen of the old world, have consecrated to a multitude of brutal gods the dark groves, and still darker caves of our mountains, or erected, with immense expense and suffering, splendid temples to the honour of thieves, strumpets, and murderers, or for the inhabitation of blocks and statues. Instead of the hymns which here daily ascend to heaven, perfumed with the incense of redemption, our ears would have been stunned with the outcries of the priests of Baal, or the yells of the priestesses of Bacchus. Instead of the communion table, which now holds out the bread of life, and invites us to eat and live, altars would here have smoked with the offerings of pollution, or streamed with the blood of human victims. Instead of listening to the invitations to renounce iniquity, to believe on the Lord Jesus Christ, and to lay hold on a glorious immortality given by God himself, and announced weekly from this desk, the youths who are before me might, in some instances at least, have been trembling beneath the frown of a Druid, prepared to plunge his knife into their bosoms, as an offering to the gods of superstition : no uncommon fate of bright and promising young men in ancient times, throughout that island from which our ancestors emigrated to this country.

From all these evils, and from that perfect dissolution of the moral character of which they are either the cause or the substance, Christ has delivered those, who receive and obey his instructions. The darkness, in which men ‘ groped, and stumbled, and fell,’ in the pursuit of eternal life, he has scattered by the sunshine of the Gospel. The objects of our faith and the rules of our duty he has written in living colours. To ignorant, sorrowful, and despairing man, despairing of future enjoyment and future being, he has proclaimed the ‘ glad tidings ’ of life eternal. To rebels and enemies he has ‘ published ’ everlasting ‘ peace.’ To Zion he has announced that the God who reigns over heaven and earth, is her God. ‘ How beautiful on the mountains are the feet ’ of this divine messenger, descended from the regions of immortality to proclaim ‘ grace, mercy, and peace ’ to this ruined world !

2. *Christ as a preacher is a perfect pattern to every minister of the Gospel.*

That he is such a pattern in the *substance of his preaching* is a truth, which can need no comment. Every minister, whatever may be his opinions in other respects, will admit, unconditionally, that what Christ has said is the guide and the substance of all which he is to say.   Nor are many words necessary to show that he is a pattern equally perfect, and equally obligatory, as to his *manner*.   It is not here intended, that the *characteristical* manner of Christ, by which he was distinguished from every other preacher, is *demanded* of any minister of the Gospel.   In this respect, Christ cannot be copied by any man.   The style in which the inhabitants of the East spoke their discourses, differs materially from that which has been adopted in Europe and this country, and each is suited to the taste of the respective inhabitants.   The characteristical style of each individual, also, differs usually from that of other individuals, and that of each will ever be the best for himself, and that which he will most advantageously employ in discoursing with his fellow-men.   The manner of Christ, in this respect, is not here intentionally required of any preacher. It is wholly peculiar to him, and inimitable by others.   At the same time, although every preacher may learn the best lessons from the *plainness and simplicity* with which the Redeemer taught, and is bound ever to keep him in view, as in this respect the proper object of a general imitation, yet it ought also to be observed, that no preacher is warranted to assume the *authority* with which Christ taught, enjoined, and reproved, or the *peremptoriness* with which he threatened and promised.   These are characteristics peculiar to himself, which nothing but direct inspiration will authorize any man seriously to imitate, and which, accordingly, no Christian, except the apostles, has ventured to assume.

The *spirit* discovered by the Redeemer in his manner of instruction is the object which it is designed here to urge upon preachers of the Gospel for their imitation; particularly the *candour, patience, gentleness,* and *tenderness* displayed by him on every proper occasion.   These are characteristics which cannot fail to adorn every discourse addressed by a preacher of the Gospel to his fellow-men.   If a preacher has any sense of his own guilt, dangers, wants, hopes, or blessings, he cannot fail to feel, in a corresponding manner, those of others.   If he have just views of the worth of his own soul and the importance of his own salvation, he cannot but tenderly regard the souls and the salvation of others.   If he comprehend at all his own infirmities, and the unceasing need which he has of tenderness and patience from his fellow-men, if he remember at all how persuasive and efficacious candour and gentleness have heretofore been in influencing his own mind, he cannot but discern the importance of exercising them towards his flock.

Nor is it less indispensable, that the Preacher should possess and exhibit the same *openness, boldness,* and *integrity.* The *possession* of these things is absolutely necessary, in order to the *appearance* of them in his discourses and in his life. All counterfeits will at the best be suspicious, and chiefly fail of their intended effect after a little period. But a full conviction of the Preacher's unmingled integrity, which, if it exist, can scarcely fail of being distinctly perceived, will more powerfully persuade his hearers than all the arts of reasoning and eloquence attainable by the human mind. At the same time, this characterestic will aim at doing them good in ten thousand ways unthought of by the insincere preacher. Beyond this, it will accomplish the good, where all skill and contrivance will fail. To an honest, open, undaunted preacher, thoroughly believed to be such, all men will listen who will listen at all. By such a preacher all men will be moved, who in the same circumstances will be moved at all. His discourses will, of course, appear to be delivered in earnest; not, perhaps, with animation or eloquence, properly so called : with respect to these, his constitutional character may be unfavourable, and his habits unhappy ; but with seriousness, solemnity, and the appearance of a realizing conviction that he is uttering the message of God. Such a message, so uttered, can scarcely fail of making some useful impression on the mind. If not, it will be because the mind is not in a state fitted to receive useful impressions.

3. *The Preaching of Christ is a forcible reproof to ministers.*

Ministers, if we may judge from the sermons which they publish, are, in some instances at least, guilty of *sophistry.* Every preacher, who indulges himself in this mode of reasoning, has failed to propose or to remember Christ as his pattern ; and, whenever he solemnly reviews this part of his conduct, must feel himself powerfully reproved by the open, sim-cere, and exact argumentation of his Redeemer, his fair and candid statements of the opinions of his adversaries, and his solid answers to their cavils.

Ministers, at times, are *petulant, angry, and contentious, not for truth, but for victory.* Let him who indulges any part of this spirit look to the example of his Saviour, and be ashamed of his neglect to ' walk as Christ also walked.' Let him lay aside the spirit of a disputant and a champion, and resume that of a disciple of his glorious Lord.

Not a small number of preachers, in one country and another, *affect a strongly impassioned, fervid, and enthusiastic manner of writing and uttering their discourses.* Their language is always intended to be vehement, bold, and highly figurative, their tones loud and violent, and their gestures accordant with both. No part of this character can be found in the preaching of Christ. Not the most distant resemblance to enthusiasm can be found in any thing which he said, or in the manner in which it was said; not an attempt to appear impassioned, not an effort to display what is customarily called eloquence. When the subjects which he canvassed inspired warmth, prompted imagination, and led to the adoption of figurative language, he indulged them, just as mere nature led. But he never summoned them to his assistance as a part of his scheme, nor, what is more to the present purpose, did he ever form the scheme with an intention to give himself opportunity of calling in these auxiliaries to his discourse. A temperate manner, solemn indeed, and plainly earnest, far distant from that cold and uninterested mode sometimes seen in the desk, but still temperate on all ordinary occasions, and raised only on extraordinary ones, was the characteristical manner of the Redeemer. His voice was pre-eminently the ' still, small voice' of truth and piety, and he did ' not strive, nor lift up, nor cause it to be heard in the streets.'

How different this pattern from the efforts of separatical preachers, and indeed of many others, in our own times! There is no small reason to fear that by many men of modern days Christ, if now on earth, would be thought a very imperfect example of the best mode of preaching.

Ministers, in some instances, employ their discourses in *minute, wire-drawn disquisitions.* Such disquisitions can rarely be necessary in the desk, and wherever they are not

necessary they are mischievous.   No example of this nature
can be found in the preaching of the Redeemer.   The minds
of hearers are lost in such disquisitions; their feelings
blunted; and the truth and duty recommended, are forgotten
in the labour of following the ingenious discussions of the
preacher.

The *timidity* of ministers is also forcibly reproved by that
undaunted firmness which Christ displayed in the midst of his
bitter enemies, men from whom he could expect nothing but
hatred and violence. It is to be always remembered, that there
are occasions on which some subjects cannot be urged with
any hope of success, and only with a prospect of disadvantage.
It will therefore not only be justifiable, but commendable, to
withhold the communication of certain truths and the injunc-
tion of certain duties in peculiar seasons, because those, who
should hear, ' cannot' (in the language of Christ) ' bear them
now.'   But the preacher is bound to withhold them only because he is fairly convinced, that the communication will do
evil and not good.   Even here, great caution is to be used,
lest the preacher's own timidity and not the performance of his
duty be the governing motive.   In all cases, where this duty
does not forbid (and these instances are, of course, few,) he
is bound to speak the truth boldly and plainly, whether ' they
will bear, or whether they will forbear.'   Let every timid
preacher, who ' shuns to declare the whole counsel of God'
under the influence of his timidity, fix his eyes on the example
of his Saviour, and he will see himself most affectingly reproved, and most solemnly reminded, that the ' fear of man'
only ' bringeth a snare.'

The *love of applause* may be said to be instinctive in the
mind of man, and has, of course, a seat in that of preachers,
as well as of other men.   Against this seductive passion,
always ready to operate, and operating almost of course with
an unhappy influence, every preacher will find the strongest
guard in the example of the Redeemer.   No instance can be
produced, in which this passion appeared in him.   To teach
truth, and enforce duty on his hearers, was plainly the whole
end proposed by him in all his instructions.   Such ought to
be the only end aimed at in the discourses of every minister
of the Gospel.

Finally : All persons who assemble to hear the Gospel are

here taught the manner in which they are bound to receive the truth.   They are bound to receive it in its purity and simplicity, just as it was taught by Christ.   They are bound to hear it with a reverential, ready, and obedient mind, as the law of life, and the only means of salvation.   The Jews, who would not thus receive it, perished.   Those who at the present time will not receive it in this manner will, unless they assume a new character, perish also ·

SERMON XLVIII.

CHRIST A PROPHET:

PREACHING OF THE APOSTLES.

AND HE SAITH UNTO THEM, GO YE INTO ALL THE WORLD, AND
PREACH THE GOSPEL UNTO EVERY CREATURE. HE THAT BELIEV-
ETH, AND IS BAPTIZED, SHALL BE SAVED; BUT HE THAT BE-
LIEVETH NOT SHALL BE DAMNED. AND THEY WENT FORTH,
AND PREACHED EVERYWHERE; THE LORD WORKING WITH
THEM, AND CONFIRMING THE WORD WITH SIGNS FOLLOWING.
AMEN.

MARK XVI. 15, 16, 20.

IN a former Discourse I proposed to consider the prophetical
character of Christ, as displayed, in his personal preaching,
and in his preaching by his apostles. The former of these subjects I have accordingly considered at large; the latter I shall
now examine with some attention. In the text we are presented, among other things, with *a commission* given to his
Apostles, and others, to ' go into all the world, and preach
the Gospel to every creature;' and with an account of the
fact, that under this commission ' they went forth, and
preached everywhere.' Their preaching, therefore, was a
business of mere delegation, and a mere performance of a
duty enjoined by Christ. In other words, *Christ preached
the Gospel by their instrumentality.*

In the consideration of this subject, it will be proper to
show,

I. *The fact, that the apostles actually preached the Gospel
of Christ; or were inspired:*

II. *The necessity of their preaching the Gospel :*
III. *The things which they preached :* and,
IV. *The consequences of their preaching.*

I. *I shall endeavour to show, that the apostles actually preached the Gospel of Christ ; or were inspired.*

Many Unitarians, who have admitted that Christ himself was inspired, have, nevertheless, both questioned and denied the inspiration of his apostles. As this is a subject of vast importance in the Christian scheme, it cannot but be necessary in a System of Theology to settle, as far as may be, just opinions concerning this subject. I shall, therefore, consider it at some length. It will be remembered, here, that we are not at issue with infidels. The persons with whom we contend, however unfavourable to the Scriptures their opinions on this or any other subject may seem, are yet professed believers in divine Revelation. We are, therefore, at full liberty to bring whatever arguments we please from the Scriptures themselves. Nay, the Scriptures are in the present case peculiarly proper sources of evidence, sources to which our antagonists can make no objection. When Dr. Priestley denies what he calls the *particular inspiration* of the several books of the Bible, he alleges, as his warrant for this denial, that *they do not pretend to any such inspiration.* Whether this doctrine is true, I shall now proceed to examine.

1. *The commission and the fact recorded in the text, prove that the apostles were inspired.*

In the text, the Apostles are commissioned to preach the Gospel, or ' good news' of salvation. In other words, they were commissioned to declare the *terms* on which God will forgive sin, and restore sinners to his favour and blessing. These terms it was impossible for them to know, except by means of immediate revelation to themselves, or information from a person to whom they were revealed. The Gospel, it is agreed by all who believe it, discloses the will of God concerning this subject. But this will cannot be known, except by direct communication from God. The knowledge of it, therefore, must terminate, of course, in ultimate revelation. If, then, it was not revealed immediately to the apostles, it was communicated to them verbally by Christ. But no power of human memory could enable them to retain such a mass of communications, for any length of time, much less for such a length of time as intervened between their reception of them, and the publication of those writings in which they were conveyed to the world. If we consider the numerous events in the life of Christ which they have recorded, and still more the numerous discourses which they have professed to recount, we must either admit, that these records are very imperfectly true, because necessarily not exact, or that the apostles had such supernatural assistance as to make them exact, and in this manner true. This assistance can be no other than inspiration. The Gospel of St. Matthew was written, according to the earliest calculation, *eight years* after the death of Christ; that of Mark, and that of Luke, about the year 64, more than twenty years after the death of Christ; and that of John, to say the least, at a much later period. Nothing can be more evident, than that these writers could not, for such a length of time, retain, by the mere natural force of memory, the things which they have recorded. Particularly is this impossibility manifest with respect to the numerous discourses recorded by St. John, of which in so great a proportion his Gospel consists; discourses, differing from all others ever known in the present world, strongly characteristical, and therefore fairly presumed to be genuine; discourses, raised up by events distinctly recorded, and perfectly suited to those events, composed of questions and answers, arguments and objections, so minutely specified as to wear the appearance of having been taken down on the spot and at the moment with uncommon skill and felicity. He who believes that St. John could have remembered these things in his old age, by the mere natural force of memory, certainly can find no difficulty in admitting any proposition because it asserts something miraculous; for no miracle involves a more absolute counteraction of the known laws of nature than that which is involved in this supposition. Instead of being thus tenaciously retained, at the end of so many years, it is scarcely credible that they could have been remembered in the same manner for one day.

But if the evangelists when professedly recording these discourses did not record them exactly, they did not record them truly. If Christ did not say the very things which they have asserted, their assertions are so far false, and they cannot sustain even the character which Dr. Priestley concedes to them, of deserving the confidence of mankind as witnesses, for their testimony plainly cannot be true.

Beyond this, we know *beforehand*, that it is untrue; for, according to this scheme, it is not possible that it should be true. The utmost that can be said of it, according to this scheme, is, that it may be a well meant, but must be a loose, general, and unsatisfactory account in many, and those often important, particulars. *Necessarily untrue*, and everywhere, unless in some few prominent particulars, *necessarily uncertain*.

But can it be supposed, that Christ directed the apostles to preach the Gospel in this manner? Can he be supposed to have directed them to preach it at all, if they were necessitated to preach it in this manner only? Can he, who came to publish the will of God to mankind concerning this immensely important subject, have left it to be chiefly published, under his authority, by the mere force of human memory, and mixed with human frailties and human opinions; and thus, necessarily, to have become a mass of truth and falsehood, so blended, that those who read their writings or heard their discourses could never be able to separate the falsehood from the truth? Does any human legislature suffer its own laws to be published in such a manner? Was Christ possessed of less wisdom, or less integrity, or less benevolence, than human legislators? Did God give him a commission thus to act? Or did he fail to discharge the duties of the commission which he really received?

Further: The evangelists have left all their declarations, in the form of *unqualified, peremptory assertions*. If, then, the assertions are not true, the authors of them are false witnesses concerning Christ. They have boldly and roundly declared *that* to have been said and done, which they did not know to have been said or done. This is no other than direct dishonesty, such as nothing can justify or palliate. He who directly asserts that for truth, which he does not know or believe himself to know to be true, is a liar. The apostles, therefore, instead of deserving credit as witnesses, must in this case be branded as liars, even with regard to the facts, in relating which, Dr. Priestley assures us, they are wholly to be trusted. To deserve credit in this, and to discharge the duties even of common honesty, they ought to have told us, originally, that the facts and conversations which they were about to relate, were recorded by them in as faithful and exact a manner as was in their power ; but that, as they wrote from mere memory, they could give only qualified assertions, of which, although as correct as they could make them, they could not, however, be certain. In this case, they would have discharged their duty, and deserved credit. Their writings would have then claimed the title of a revelation just as much as any other piece of honest biography, and no more. But the writers would have acted the part of honest men.

2. *This doctrine is evident from a part of the same commission recorded by St. John.*

' Then said Jesus unto them, Peace be unto you. As my Father has sent me, even so send I you. And when he had said this, he breathed on them, and saith unto them, Receive ye the Holy Ghost. Whose soever sins ye remit, they are remitted unto them ; and whose soever sins ye retain, they are retained.' John xx. 21——23. In this passage of Scripture, Christ tells his disciples, that he gives them generally the same mission which the Father had given him ; so that they were now to stand in his place, as ambassadors from God to this sinful world. That they might be qualified to discharge the duties of this mission, he gave, or as I conceive it ought to be understood, he promised, them the Holy Ghost ; even as he had been ' anointed with the Holy Ghost, and with power,' to qualify him for the duties of the same mission.

That the reception of the Holy Ghost was indispensable to their entrance on their mission is evident from Luke xxiv. 49, where Christ, referring to this mission, says, ' Behold I send the promise of my Father upon you. But tarry ye in Jerusalem, until ye be endued with power from on high.' And, again, from Acts i. 4, where St. Luke informs us, that ' being assembled together with them, he commanded them, that they should not depart from Jerusalem, but wait for the promise of the Father, which, saith he, ye have heard of me.' That the Holy Ghost was ' the promise of the Father,' or the object here promised, will not, I suppose, be questioned. If it should be, the point is unanswerably proved by the fact, that the apostles waited in Jerusalem, with scrupulous obedience to this command, and did not begin to preach the Gospel at all, till, on the day of Pentecost, they actually received the Holy Ghost in the wonderful manner described at the beginning of the following chapter.   On this occasion they became in the strict sense inspired ; as I shall have opportunity to evince in the sequel. ·

In the last verse of this quotation, Christ declares to them, ' Whose soever sins ye remit, they are remitted to them ; and whose soever sins ye retain, they are retained ;' that is, *Ye shall prescribe and publish the terms on which the sins of the whole human race shall be remitted or retained.*   Now let me ask any sober man, whether he can possibly believe that God placed this stupendous and amazing power in the hands of these men, and left them to exercise it, merely according to the dictates of their own discretion, and the strength of their own memory ?   Was *their* understanding, or the understanding of any created being, sufficient to enable them to prescribe and publish the terms, obedience to which should be followed by the forgiveness of sin, and disobedience to which should prevent sin from being forgiven ?   Our Saviour declares, expressly, in this passage, that whose soever sins they remitted God would remit ; and whose soever sins they retained, God would retain.   In other words, the very terms which they should prescribe, as the proper foundations for the remission or retention of sin, would be the terms according to which God would remit or retain them.   That this was intended in the most absolute, unqualified sense to be fulfilled, is rendered certain by the 2d verse of the text.   ' He that believeth, and is baptized, shall be saved ; but he that believeth not shall be damned.'   Here our Saviour declares, that he who cordially believes the Gospel preached by the apostles, shall have eternal life ; and that he who does not thus believe this Gospel, shall not have eternal life.   It will be remembered, that the apostles alone published the Gospel to mankind.   The Gospel, as published by them, therefore, is that which is the object of belief here referred to by Christ ; for by this Gospel only do we become acquainted with the character, mission, doctrines, precepts, or even the existence of a Saviour.   Of course, the only belief of which Christ can be supposed to speak in this passage, is the belief of the Gospel which *they* have published.

On the belief of this Gospel, then, Christ has made the salvation of the whole human race absolutely to depend ; that is, so far as it should be published to them.   Can it be supposed, that the infinitely wise and just God, who is perfectly acquainted with the weakness of the human mind, who perfectly knows that many, very many, errors exist of course in the best and wisest men, who perfectly knew that very many errors must in this very case be published by these men, if left to themselves, and that any number, even one, of those errors would prove fatal, not to one only, but to hundreds and thousands, and millions, nay, to the whole body of the human race, unless he himself should ultimately forgive sin on terms not his own, and not accordant with the dictates of his own wisdom and righteousness——can it be supposed, that the infinitely wise and just God committed to these frail, erring beings the incomprehensibly important business of publishing, from their own judgment and memory, the terms on which the sins of that and every succeeding age should be forgiven or retained ?   Can he have said, that after they had published such terms as to themselves appeared the proper ones, ‘ he who believed them should be saved, and he who believed them not should be damned ? ’

To this conclusion, however, the scheme of those with whom I am contending irresistibly conducts us ; for the only alternative is, that Christ has here uttered an untruth.   If those who believe the apostles in this case, will *not be saved*, and those who believe not, will *not be damned ;* if the sins which *they* remit, in the Gospel published by them, will *not* be remitted by God, and the sins which *they* retain, will *not* be retained by him ; then Christ has here declared an absolute falsehood, in the most solemn and important of all cases. Of course, he may be fairly presumed to deceive in every other case, and cannot deserve the confidence of mankind in any thing.   This conclusion, together with the doctrine on which it is founded, is, I suppose, too horrid to be admitted by any man who does not regard the Scriptures with absolute contempt.

3. *The same truth is evident from the promise given to the apostles by our Saviour in his last discourses, of the descent of the Holy Ghost upon them.*

The several parts of this promise, so far as they refer particularly to the point in question, are contained in the following passages :——

' But the Comforter, who is the Holy Ghost, whom the Father will send in my name, he shall teach you all things, and bring all things to your remembrance, whatsoever I have said unto you.' John xiv. 26.

' But when the Comforter is come, whom I will send unto you from the Father, even the Spirit of truth, who proceedeth from the Father, he shall testify of me.   And ye also shall bear witness, because ye have been with me from the beginning.' John xv. 26, 27.

' Howbeit, when he, the Spirit of truth, is come, he shall guide you into all *the* truth ; and he shall show you things to come.   He shall glorify me ; for he shall receive of mine, and shall show it unto you.' John xvi. 13, 14.

In this promise are included the following things :——

(1.) That the Spirit would certainly come to the apostles, after the ascension of Christ.

(2.) That he would testify to them concerning Christ: ' He shall testify of me.'

(3.) That this testimony would be accompanied by the coincident testimony of the apostles: ' and ye also shall bear witness,' &c.

(4.) That the Spirit of truth should receive from Christ that which was *his ; viz.* his truth, pleasure, or Gospel; and should declare it to the apostles : ' He shall receive of mine ' (of the things which are mine, Greek,) ' and shall declare it unto you.'

(5.) That he should glorify Christ in this communication.

(6.) That he should ' show ' to the apostles ' things to come,' or future things ; or, in other words, should endue them with the gift of prophecy.

(7.) That he should ' guide the *apostles* ' into all ' (*the*, Greek) ' truth :' that is, into all evangelical truth, *the truth*, by way of eminence.

(8.) That he should teach them all things ; that is, all things which they needed to be taught originally, or which Christ had not already taught them : ' he shall teach you all things.'

(9.) That he should bring up to the full view of their memory the things which Christ had taught them : ' And shall

bring all things to your remembrance, whatsoever I have said
unto you.'

It will be evident to the slightest attention, that the things,
here promised, contain whatever is involved in *the plenary
inspiration* of the Apostles.   The testimony given by them,
was a testimony concerning Christ.   It glorified Christ in the
highest manner conceivable.   All the parts of it were exhibited by them, as parts of Christ's own Gospel ; and, united
together, they are declared by them often to be the Gospel
of Christ.

This testimony contains, also, a wonderful exhibition of their
remembrance of the things which Christ said, and did ; such as
must plainly be impossible, unless they had been divinely
assisted.   Farther, it contains *all the truth :* that is, all evangelical truth, or the whole will of God concerning the salvation of men.   Finally, it contains many wonderful predictions
concerning future things, of which many have been already
fulfilled in a marvellous manner.

Concerning all these things, except one, there cannot be
even a debate ; and that one is, that the apostles were guided
by the Holy Spirit into *all* evangelical truth.   On this I shall
have occasion to say more hereafter.   At present I shall confine my remarks to the promise itself.   Concerning this I
observe, that it either was fulfilled, or it was not fulfilled.   If
it was fulfilled, then the Apostles wrote and preached the
Gospel under the plenary inspiration of the Holy Ghost ; because the promise assures them of such inspiration in the
amplest terms conceivable.   If it was not fulfilled, then Christ
was a false prophet ; because he promised that which he did
not fulfil.

4. *The same truth is evident from the testimony of the
apostles themselves.*

Dr. Priestley, in his Letters to the Philosophers and Politi-
cians of France, makes the following observation ; " That the
books of Scripture were written by particular divine inspiration, is a thing to which the writers themselves make no
pretensions."   I have often been astonished at this declaration, especially as coming from a minister of the Gospel.
Whether there be any foundation for it or not, will farther
appear.

(1.) *They testify, that the Holy Ghost descended on them,*

in the same manner and with the same effects which Christ had promised.

This testimony is thus summarily given: On the day of Pentecost, while the apostles and their companions were together, waiting for the promise of the Father, or the descent of the Holy Ghost; ' a sound came from Heaven, as of a rushing, mighty wind; and it filled the room, where they were sitting. And there appeared unto them cloven tongues, as of fire, and sat upon each of them: and they were all filled with the Holy Ghost, and they began to speak with other tongues, as the Spirit gave them utterance.' The things which they spoke are testified by those, who heard them, in these words: ' We do hear them speak in our tongues the wonderful works of God.' In this story we have a direct account of the descent of the Holy Ghost upon the apostles and their companions, exactly according to the promise of Christ. We are informed, that the Holy Ghost became to them the Spirit of inspiration, endowing them with the supernatural power of ' speaking with tongues,' or languages which they had never learned, and of ' speaking ' in those languages ' the wonderful works of God.' Accordingly we find St. Peter, on this very occasion, addressing the assembly, whom this wonderful miracle had called together, ' with a new spirit,' with views of the mission of Christ altogether new, and with an equally extraordinary knowledge of the Jewish Scriptures. Nothing was more unlike his former character in all respects, except that he was before, as well as now, a good man. Before, he had spoken and acted ' as a child :' he had now become ' a man, and put away childish things.'

Besides, we find him and the other apostles immediately afterwards employed, not only in preaching in the same manner, but also in performing wonderful miracles, to prove that what they preached was the truth of God.

(2.) *They testify directly, that the Gospel which they preached was revealed to them by God.*

A few proofs of this nature, out of a great multitude which can be directly alleged from the New Testament, are all which the time will allow me to recite. ' In the Gospel,' says St. Paul, ' the righteousness of God is revealed from faith to faith.' ' The Gospel is the power of God to salvation.' Romans i. 16, 17. Can either of these things be possibly said with truth concerning mere uninspired opinions? ' We speak the wisdom of God in a mystery, even the hidden wisdom, which God ordained before the world unto our glory. Eye hath not seen, nor ear heard, neither have entered into the heart of man, the things which God hath prepared for them that love him. But God hath revealed them unto us by his Spirit. Now we have received, not the spirit which is of the world, but the spirit which is of God, that we might know the things which are freely given us of God. Which things also we speak, not in the words which man's wisdom teacheth, but which the Holy Ghost teacheth; comparing spiritual things with spiritual.' Or, as the last phrase is rendered by Dr. Macknight, *explaining spiritual things in spiritual words.* In this passage, the things contained in the Gospel are directly asserted to be revealed to the apostles by the Spirit of God; to be ' the wisdom, even the hidden wisdom,' of God; and to be ' freely given unto them of God.' It is also asserted, that they had received the Spirit of God for this very end, *viz.* that they might ' know these things.' Finally, it is declared, that Paul and his companions spoke these things to others, not in the words devised by human wisdom, but in words directly taught by the Holy Ghost; and that they thus explained spiritual things in words which were also spiritual; or, if the common translation be preferred, ' comparing the spiritual things,' thus revealed, with other ' spiritual' things revealed in the Old Testament.

Again: ' Let a man so account of us, as of the ministers of Christ, and stewards of the mysteries of God.' 1 Cor. iii. 1. ' Ministers of Christ,' here denote those commissioned by Chris. to preach the Gospel of Christ; ' Stewards of the mysteries of God,' those who are intrusted by God with his own will revealed by him, and otherwise hidden from mankind.

Again; ' I certify you brethren, that the Gospel which was preached by me was not after man;' (that is, devised by human reason) ' For I neither received it of man, neither was I taught it, but by the revelation of Jesus Christ. It pleased God to reveal his Son in me, that I might preach him among the heathen,' or Gentiles. Gal. i. 11, 12, 15, 16.

Once more : ' If any man think himself to be spiritual (that is, a spiritual man, possessing the miraculous power of discerning spirits or doctrines,) ' or a prophet, let him acknowledge. that the things which I write unto you are the commandments of the Lord.' One would think, that such as now stand in the place of these spiritual men in the church, *viz.* Ministers of the Gospel, would feel themselves bound to make the same acknowledgment.

These may serve instead of near two hundred different passages, in which, in one manner and another, St. Paul asserts explicitly, the inspiration of himself and his companions in the Gospel : for these decide the point, if any declarations can.

I intended to have recited declarations to the same purpose from the other writers of the New Testament ; but, as the time is so far elapsed, I shall omit them.

(3.) *They declared the same thing by styling the Gospel which they preached, the Gospel of God, and of Christ.*

Quotations, to prove this fact cannot be necessary for such as read the New Testament. I shall therefore only observe, it proves directly, that this Gospel was revealed by God : otherwise, any other human production on the same subject might be called the Gospel of God.

(4.) *The importance attached by them to the Gospel, is a full declaration that it was revealed to them.*

They declare, that it is ' the power of God unto salvation to every one that believeth ;' ' a savour of life unto life ;' ' able to make men wise to salvation ;' ' quick (or living,) and powerful,' &c. ; ' piercing,' &c. ; ' a discerner,' &c.

They declare, that Christ ' will punish with an everlasting destruction them that obey not this Gospel.'

St. Paul says, ' Woe is me, if I preach not the Gospel.'

He farther says, ' If any man, or if any angel, preach another Gospel' (that is, another than *this* which he preached to mankind,) ' let him be accursed.'

He also says, ' God shall judge the secrets of men,' at the final day, ' according to this Gospel.'

He says also, ' that God shall send' upon a portion of mankind ' strong delusion, that they should believe a lie, that they might all be damned, because they believe not the truth,' (that is, this very Gospel,) ' but had pleasure in unrighteousness.'

St. Peter, also, styles it ' the word of God,' ' incorruptible seed ;' pronounces it the means of regeneration, and eternal life ; declares, that it ' lives and endures for ever ;' and asserts, that ' the angels,' stooping down, ' desire to look into it.'

Let me now ask, whether all or any one of these things can possibly be said concerning the mere opinions of men ?

(5.) *The apostles wrought innumerable miracles to prove the truth of the Gospel.*

God only can work a miracle, and therefore he wrought these miracles. If the Gospel was not revealed to the apostles, then it is a mere collection of human testimonies and opinions, and of course, to a considerable extent at least, is false.   According to this supposition, then, God wrought miracles to prove a mixture of false and true human opinions, incapable of being separated by man, to be true.   The supposition, that God wrought miracles to prove the truth of even just human opinions, is absurd.   The supposition, that he wrought miracles to support any falsehood, is blasphemy.

To this evidence the apostles appeal with full confidence. The third verse of the text is such an appeal : ' And they went forth, and preached everywhere ; the Lord working with them, and confirming the word with signs following.   Amen.' In the same manner St. Paul, Heb. ii. 3, 4, says, ' How shall we escape, if we neglect so great salvation ; which at the first began to be spoken by the Lord, and was confirmed unto us by those that heard him ?   God also bearing them witness, both with signs and wonders, and divers miracles, and gifts of the Holy Ghost, according to his own will.'   In these two passages, the sacred writers plainly consider the miracles wrought by the apostles as the testimony of the Father and the Son to the fact, that the Gospel preached by them was dictated by God, and communicated by inspiration.

(6.) *The Apostles spent their lives for the Gospel.*

It is not here my intention to dwell on what the apostles either did or suffered.   It is sufficient to observe, that they gave up voluntarily all earthly comforts and hopes, and underwent cheerfully all the evils which can betide human life, for the sake of the Gospel.   All these things they encountered, solely from confidence in Christ, his promises, doctrines, and precepts, as the source and the means of eternal life.   All these things they terminated, also, by quietly yielding their lives to a violent and untimely death · a death, which, together with their other sufferings, was foretold to them by their Master. Thus they ' esteemed all things but loss, for the excellency of the knowledge of Christ ; for whom they suffered the loss of all things :' ' Accounting not even their lives dear to them, so that they might finish their course with joy, and the ministry which they had received of the Lord Jesus, to testify the Gospel of the grace of God.'

Now the Apostles knew whether Christ was what he professed himself to be, so far as his character was an object of human observation.   Particularly they knew whether his promises to them concerning their life, their supernatural endowments, their inspiration, and the power of working miracles, were fulfilled, or not.   If they were not fulfilled, they could not but know that Christ was an impostor ; and could not have failed to give up a cause from which nothing but evil had sprung, or could ever spring.   Their perseverance is therefore complete proof, that these promises were all fulfilled ; that the Holy Ghost descended on them, ' guided them into all the truth ;' taught them all things,' pertaining to this subject ; or, in the language of St. Peter, ' pertaining to life and godliness ;' ' brought to their remembrance all things whatsoever Christ had said unto them ; and shewed them things to come.' They have, therefore, in this manner proved that they were inspired ; so inspired as to become authoritative teachers of the will of God concerning our salvation ; and as to assure us, that whatever they have taught is true, and even in so momentous a case is to be believed and obeyed with final safety to our well-being.

SERMON XLIX.

CHRIST A PROPHET:

PREACHING OF THE APOSTLES.

AND HE SAID UNTO THEM, GO YE INTO ALL THE WORLD, AND
PREACH THE GOSPEL UNTO EVERY CREATURE. HE THAT BELIEV-
ETH, AND IS BAPTIZED, SHALL BE SAVED; BUT HE THAT BE-
LIEVETH NOT SHALL BE DAMNED. AND THEY WENT FORTH,
AND PREACHED EVERYWHERE; THE LORD WORKING WITH
THEM, AND CONFIRMING THE WORD WITH SIGNS FOLLOWING.
AMEN.

MARK XVI. 15, 16, 20.

IN the preceding Discourse, I proposed from these words to consider the following subjects:——

I. *The fact, that the apostles actually preached the Gospel of Christ, or were inspired:*

II. *The necessity of their preaching the Gospel:*

III. *The things which they preached:* and,

IV. *The consequences of their preaching.*

The first of these heads I examined largely in that Discourse. I shall now proceed to the consideration of the three last.

On the second, *viz. The necessity of their preaching the Gospel*, I make the following observations:——

Christ, in his discourse to the Apostles, recorded John xvi. says, ' But when the Comforter is come, he shall testify of me. And ye also shall bear witness.' This testimony they accordingly gave to the Messiahship, and universal character of their

Master, in their *oral preaching, their writings, their miracles,* and *their lives.* All these they uniformly attributed to *him.* Their doctrines and precepts they declared to be derived from his instructions and the inspiration of his Spirit, their miracles from his power, and their holiness from his grace, all communicated by the same divine agent. In his name, and under the authority of a commission given by him, they preached, wrote, and acted, as the propagators of the Gospel and the builders of the church. Thus every thing which they said or did was a testimony borne to Christ.

That this testimony should be thus borne by the Apostles, was necessary in the divine economy of redemption,

1. *Because the apostles had been with Christ from the beginning.*

It has doubtless been observed by those who hear me, that I have all along mentioned the apostles as if *alone* concerned in this business. It is hardly necessary to remark, that under this name I mean here to include their inspired coadjutors also.

The reason which I have now alleged is given by Christ himself, and is recited in his own words, John xvi. 27, ' And ye shall bear witness also, because ye have been with me from the beginning.'

The importance of this reason will be manifest, if we consider the nature of a great part of the testimony which the Apostles have given concerning the Redeemer. This is composed partly of facts, and partly of discourses, at both of which they were present, and to which they were, of course, eye and ear witnesses. The only decisive human evidence concerning facts is the evidence of our senses, customarily called *experience.* This, wherever it exists in its perfection, is universally acknowleged to be decisive. In it all other human evidence concerning facts is supposed to terminate, and, whenever it is valid, actually terminates. If, then, human testimony were to be given to the mission, character, and doctrines of Christ, it must be indispensable that it should rest on this kind of evidence. No other persons could be valid witnesses of the life and miracles of Christ but those who saw them, nor of his discourses but those who heard them. Accordingly, St. Paul, though an incontrovertible witness to the divine origin of the Gospel in many respects, was not employed to write a history of the Redeemer; while Luke and Mark, though not apostles, were made his historians by the Spirit of God, because, as St. Luke says of himself, ' they had perfect understanding of all things from the very first.'

It is true that God could, if it had pleased him, have disclosed every one of the things recorded in his Gospels to any other person, by an original revelation. It is not, however, the way established in the Divine proceedings to furnish miraculous communications, where they are not plainly necessary, or miraculous evidence, where evidence derived from other sources is sufficient. Besides, there would have been a serious imperfection attending any such revelation, if the facts revealed had been unattested by those in whose presence they took place. The mind would instinctively have asked, why none of those who were present had testified their existence, and why no record, no valid trace of them, had been conveyed down from the beginning? It must, I think, have been impossible, or at least very difficult, to answer these questions in such a manner as to satisfy the mind by which they were proposed.

The importance of this evidence in the case before us cannot but be manifest to every one accustomed to investigations of this nature, and peculiarly to such as have been conversant with debates concerning the divine origin of the Gospel. Every such person knows that, among the arguments on this subject, that which is derived from the impossibility of the apostles being deceived with respect to the great facts which are the basis of the Gospel, as having been eye and ear witnesses, and witnesses competent and unexceptionable, has ever holden a primary place. Every man versed in this subject knows this to be an argument which infidels have never been able to obviate, and which, after the efforts of two centuries, as well as all those made in ancient times, remains immoveable, and beaten in vain by the billows of opposition.

2. *Because the apostles survived the ascension of Christ.*

From this circumstance many advantages were derived of very great importance. Had Christ written the whole Gospel, that is, all which he can be supposed to have written, and written it at the only time when he can reasonably be imagined to have written it, not a small, nor unimportant, part of the things pertaining to his own history and discourses, as we now find them in the Gospels properly so called, *must have been lost to the world.* The account must, I think, have been closed antecedently to the institution of the Lord's Supper; for, from the commencement of the celebration of the passover preceding it, he does not appear to have had any opportunity of writing at all. Of course, the celebration of this passover, the institution of the eucharist, his washing the disciples' feet, and his instructions on that occasion, his consolatory discourses, his intercessory prayer, his agony in the garden, the treachery of Judas, his trial, condemnation, death, and burial, his resurrection, his subsequent appearance to his disciples, and his final ascension to the heavens, together with all the things connected with them, could have found no place in the Gospel. But these constitute a large part of the objects of our faith, the means of our instruction, and the rules of our duty. I need not observe, that these also are objects of the utmost consequence to every man who reads the Gospel, essential parts of the dispensation, without which the system would be broken and lame, without which the most important inquiries of the mind could never be satisfied, and without which the chief wants of the probationer for eternal life could never be supplied.

Further: Christ uttered a number of *predictions*, which were not fulfilled during his life, nor intended to be; but which, according to the nature of his declarations, *were to be fulfilled soon after his ascension.* Among these, were his prophecies concerning the descent of the Holy Ghost at the day of Pentecost, the success of the apostles in preaching the Gospel, the miracles which they were to accomplish, the sufferings which they were to undergo, and the extensive establishment of the church by their preaching among the nations of men. All these prophecies are of such a nature, that the mind of every reader would unavoidably demand an account of their fulfilment. Had no such account been given, (as, if the Gospel had been finished by Christ, must have been the fact,) the omission would have been perceived by every reader to be an unhappy chasm in the history of the church, which nothing could successfully fill up, and about which there would have arisen many doubts, perplexities, and distresses.

The *Christian sabbath* was adopted as a commemoration of the *resurrection of Christ from the dead.* The only hint concerning it which we find given by Christ, is contained in his answer to the Pharisees, when they asked him, why his disciples did not fast, as did their own disciples, and those of John the Baptist ; ' The children of the bride-chamber cannot fast while the bridegroom is with them : but the days come, when the bridegroom shall be taken away ; then shall they fast.' Christ was taken away on the evening preceding the seventh day, or Jewish sabbath, and during the whole of that day lay buried in the tomb. On this day, then, he declares they should fast ; and in this declaration indicates that the Jewish sabbath should then come to an end, so far as the day was concerned on which it was celebrated. The sabbath is *a festival*, not *a fast* ; a day of joy only, and not of sorrow. When, therefore, Christ declared that the seventh day should be a day of fasting to his immediate disciples, he may fairly be considered as indicating that this day should no longer be a sabbath to *them*.

In conformity to this indication, the apostles introduced the first day to Christians for their future observance as the sabbath by their own adoption of it in their religious practice. In this manner, principally, is it announced to us in their writings, as the proper sabbath for all the followers of the Redeemer. On the wisdom displayed in this manner of introducing the Christian sabbath, I design to discourse more particularly hereafter. It is sufficient to observe at the present time, that, had Christ completed the Gospel, it is not easy to see how this manner of introducing the sabbath could have taken place, and it is evident that this account of it could not have been given.

Finally : The whole history of the church, contained in the Acts of the Apostles, would, in this case, have been lost to the Christian world. No part of the word of God is, in many respects, more filled with instruction or consolation than this book. The doctrines which it contains are of the highest importance for their wisdom, the precepts for their plainness and excellence, the examples for their number, their variety, and their adaption to the different circumstances and characters of Christians. The history of this book, also, is of the greatest value for its edifying and instructive nature, for the satisfaction which it furnishes concerning the state of the church at that interesting period, for the life, sufferings, and deliverances, the preaching and success of the apostles, the opposition which they met, and the causes which produced it; the sufferings, patience, and perseverance, the errors and faults, of the first converts; the progress of Christianity and the extension of the church; together with a multitude of other things interwoven with these.   How useful, how necessary these things are, to instruct, edify, and comfort every Christian, particularly every minister, I need not explain; nor need I observe, that in a Gospel written by our Saviour they could have had no place.

3. *Because it was necessary, that the immediate followers of Christ in the propagation of Christianity should be clearly seen to be commissioned of God.*

It will be readily acknowledged, that a body of men, so small, so uneducated, so humble, so unfriended as the apostles and their companions were, must have wholly failed of spreading the Gospel through the world by any efforts which they could have made, independently of peculiar assistance from heaven.   Let us inquire, then, what was the assistance, which they needed?   Was it the gift of *speaking with tongues?* What purpose would this have answered, if their minds had been ignorant concerning what they were to speak, or whether that which they were about to speak was the will of God, and justly demanded the faith and obedience of their hearers. Was it the power of *working miracles?*   For what purpose were their miracles to be wrought?   For what purpose could they be wrought?   Plainly for no other, but to prove that *that* which was spoken by those who wrought them was true.   But if they were not inspired, that which they uttered was, and could at the best be, no other than the opinions and the remembrance of honest men.   Of course, it must necessarily be partially false.   Their miracles, therefore, would be wrought to prove the truth of falsehood; and God, if they actually wrought miracles, would set his seal to this falsehood, and employ his power to deceive their hearers.   To refute this blasphemous opinion certainly cannot be necessary.

It is plain, then, that no assistance could be given to them, short of inspiration, which would at all qualify them for the diffusion of the Gospel, and the erection of Christ's kingdom in the world.   The sole end of all other miraculous powers, so far as their commission and their employment were con-

cerned, was evidently to prove them inspired with a knowledge of the divine will concerning the salvation of men, and
sent to declare it to their fellow-men. Independently of this
great purpose, their supernatural powers were of no other
use, except to amuse and astonish mankind.

In exact accordance with this scheme, St. Paul, in 1 Cor
xii. asserts directly the inspiration of himself and his companions in the ministry; and in the fourteenth chapter declares the superiority of it to all other supernatural endowments
for the edification of the church. ' To one,' he says, ' is given
by the Spirit the word of wisdom; to another, the word of
knowledge; by the same Spirit. To another, faith; to
another, gifts of healing; to another, to the working of
miracles; to another, the discerning of spirits,' or doctrines. In
the 31st verse he directs them to ' covet earnestly the best gifts.'
In the 39th verse of the xivth chapter, he says, ' Wherefore,
brethren, covet to prophesy,' that is, to declare the will of God
by inspiration, ' and forbid not to speak with tongues. Greater,'
he says, ' is he that prophesieth, than he that speaketh with
tongues.' And again, ' Now, brethren, if I come unto you
speaking with tongues, what shall I profit you, except I shall
speak to you either by revelation, or by knowledge, or by
prophesying, or by doctrine?' All these are only different
words to express that inspiration by which they either originally received, or unerringly understood, proposed, explained,
or enforced, divine truth. Without this, he declares expressly,
that he should not profit the church in its spiritual concerns
at all. Accordingly, after having directed them to ' covet
earnestly the best gifts,' he farther directs them to ' covet the
gift of prophesying, and not forbid speaking with tongues:'
as much as to say, covet to receive from God, by revelation,
divine truth, and the gifts of unerringly explaining, declaring,
and enforcing it to others, as being things of supreme importance and usefulness; at the same time, forbid not to speak
with tongues, as being an endowment really, though very
subordinately, useful.

From these passages I think it is unanswerably evident,
that a revelation, such as Dr. Priestley, without meaning, calls
particular, existed in a standing manner in the minds of the
apostles and their companions; in *the latter*, to direct them
in their preaching; in *the former*, for the same purpose, and

the still more important one of committing the word of God to writing, for the instruction of all succeeding generations. So extensive and common was this revelation, as to be made the proper subject of a system of directions from St. Paul to the Corinthian church; a thing wholly inexplicable, if this fact had not existed.

From these observations it is plain, that without inspiration all the other supernatural endowments of the apostles must, if given, have been given to no valuable end; that, on the contrary, they would only have served to establish falsehood and delusion; and that, unless they were inspired, it may certainly be concluded that they were in no other respect supernaturally endowed. Their inspiration, therefore, was absolutely necessary to prove their commission to be from God.

If it had not been made evident that the Apostles were commissioned from God, this fact must, I think, have been fatal to the cause of Christianity. In this case, although we might have acknowledged Christ to be a divine missionary; yet we should naturally and unanswerably have said, What authority did these men possess to transmit his instructions and precepts to us? What proof have we that they understood them, remembered them, or expressed them with correctness and certainty? Why are we bound to regard what *they* have said, any more than the numerous gospels written by others? Christ wrote nothing. Had he intended to require our faith and obedience to his precepts, he would undoubtedly have taken effectual care that we should receive them in such a manner, and from such persons, as would assure us that they were his, and only his.

To us, it ought to be observed, the inspiration of the apostles furnishes a proof that they were commissioned from God, which is additional to the proofs given to those who heard them preach. In their writings they have left on record a number of important prophecies. Several of these have been remarkably fulfilled, and others are daily receiving their fulfilment. In the fulfilment of these prophecies we have a direct proof of their inspiration, and consequently of their divine commission, which is immoveable, and which could not, in the same degree, be discerned by their contemporaries.

4. *Because many preachers were necessary for such an extensive establishment of the church as that which actually took place, the great body of whom needed, for a time, to sustain the same character.*

On this subject it will not be necessary to dwell. If the preceding arguments be allowed to prove the point for which they were alleged, it will undoubtedly be also conceded, that inspiration was as necessary for some, at least, of those who preached in one place, as for any who preached in another. It may, perhaps, be objected, that this is proving too much, and alleging inspiration in a wider extent than has hitherto been pretended.

To prevent any misconceptions on this point, I will state my own views of this subject a little more particularly than I have hitherto done. The inspiration of the apostles I suppose to have consisted in the following things :—

(1.) That they received immediately from God every part of the Christian dispensation which they did not know by other means.

(2.) That in the same manner they were furnished with a foreknowledge of future events.

(3.) That in things which they did otherwise know partially, the deficiences of their knowledge were in the same manner supplied.

(4.) That those things which they had once known, and which were parts of the Christian dispensation, were by divine power brought distinctly and fully to their remembrance.

(5.) That they were directed by the Holy Spirit to the selection of just such things, and such only, and to precisely such a manner of exhibiting them, as should be true, just, most useful to mankind, and most agreeable to the divine wisdom.

(6.) That each one was left so far to his own manner of writing or speaking, as that the style was strictly his own ; and yet that the phraseology used by him in this very style was so directed and controlled by the Holy Spirit, as to lead him to the most exact and useful exhibition of divine truth ; his own words being, in this important sense, words not devised by human wisdom, but taught by the Holy Ghost ; and,

(7.) That each inspired man was, as to his preaching or his writing, absolutely preserved from error.

All these particulars cannot be applied in the same degree, and some of them cannot be applied at all, to *all* the inspired preachers.   But, in my own view, every such preacher enjoyed the benefits of inspiration so far as he needed them to enable him to preach the Gospel truly and usefully to mankind ; so far as to preserve him from false narratives, erroneous doctrines, and unsound or useless precepts.   That this was equally necessary for every preacher before the written canon furnished mankind with an unerring standard, with which they might compare the things which were preached to them, so as to determine their soundness or unsoundness, will, I suppose, be granted by all those who acknowledge the necessity of inspiration to any preacher.

5. *Because it was necessary that Christ should appear to act and to controul the affairs of his church after his ascension.*

The apostles preached, wrought miracles, spoke with tongues, and executed all the parts of their ministry under the authority, in the name, and by the power of Christ.   ' In the name of Jesus Christ of Nazareth I command thee to arise and walk.'   ' Æneas, Jesus Christ maketh thee whole.'   ' Christ, having received the promise of the Father, hath shed forth this, which ye see, and hear.'   ' If Christ be not risen, then is our preaching vain, and your faith is also vain.'   ' I can do all things through Christ strengthening me.'   ' Paul, an apostle of Jesus Christ.'   This is the language which, in substance, the apostles use on every occasion when the subject comes into view.   At the same time, they inform us that their commission was given them by Christ ; and that in his name, and by his mission, and in no sense of themselves, they went forth to preach the Gospel, and to evince its divine origin by miracles.   The power by which they acted in all their wonderful works, the wisdom which they preached, and the grace by which they were sanctified and sustained, they ascribe wholly to him.   Beyond this, they declare, that while he resided in this world he promised them all these things, and that he continually and exactly fulfilled
sence with them on various occasio
manded by their circumstances, and

behalf, whenever it was necessary, they testify in the amplest and most decisive manner. Thus, in every thing which they taught or did, he is the fountain whence every stream proceeded. He, according to their own declarations, is the agent, and they are merely instruments in his hand.

But this agency of Christ on earth after he had ascended to the heavens, is a most important, indispensable, and glorious part of his character ; important and indispensable to mankind, and glorious to himself. Evidence is furnished by it to prove, that he is in all places, and beholds all things ; that he is faithful to perform every thing which he has promised, and able to do every thing which Christians need ; which no Unitarian, hitherto, has had sufficient ingenuity to answer, or avoid. We see him actually exemplifying in his conduct all these things to his early followers, and are therefore certainly assured that, so far as our necessities require, he will substantially exhibit them to us. Christians in all ages succeeding that of the apostles, are here furnished with the strongest proofs, that he possesses all those attributes on which their hope may most securely repose, and the most lively incitements to centre in him their evangelical confidence.

6. *Because the Gospel, in its present form, is far more useful to mankind than if it had been written by one person, on one occasion, and in one manner.*

By *the Gospel*, here, I mean *the whole New Testament.* Christ, I acknowledge, could have written it, if he had pleased, in the very form, nay, in the very words, in which it is now written. But it would have been a plain and gross absurdity for Christ to have written *a history*, such as the Acts of the Apostles, or such as that of the events immediately preceding and succeeding *his own death*, concerning facts which had not yet happened ; or epistles to churches not yet in being, concerning business, duties, and dangers of which no vestige had hitherto appeared to have existed. It is not, therefore, irreverent or improper to say, that Christ could not, so far as we can conceive, have written the New Testament in its present form, without palpable improprieties interwoven in the very nature of the work.

In its present form, the Gospel is far more useful, than it would have been, if written in the manner which I have supposed, in many respects. It is in a much greater degree composed of *facts* ; unless, indeed, the same facts had been communicated in predictions.   In the *historical form* in which they now appear, they are much more easily and strongly realized, more readily believed, more capable of being substantiated by evidence, and more powerfully felt, than if they had been only predicted.   *The Epistles* are also, in a great proportion of instances, written on subjects of real business, and for that reason are more easily proved to be genuine, are far more interesting and far more instructive than would otherwise have been possible.   Their different dates continue the indubitable history of the church through a considerable period, and furnish us with a number of very important facts which we could not otherwise obtain.   Their direction to churches in different countries presents to us, also, with the extension and state of the church in different parts of the world at that time. The business concerning which they were written, occasions a display of the difficulties, doubts, errors, temptations, controversies, and backslidings——the faith, comforts, hopes, repentance, brotherly love, piety, and general excellence of the Christians to whom they were addressed.   These are the peculiarly interesting circumstances of all other Christians.   The instructions, therefore, the exhortations, commands, reproofs, encouragements, and consolations addressed to these churches, are to all other Christians, as to them, the very best means of reformation, improvement, and comfort.

The examples of the Apostles, which in a Gospel completed by Christ could not have been recorded, are among the most edifying as well as most interesting parts of the sacred canon.

The variety of form and manner now introduced into the New Testament, is attended with peculiar advantages.   It renders the Scriptures far more *pleasing*.   A greater number of persons will read them.   All who read them will read them oftener, and will more deeply feel their contents.   It renders them far more *instructive*.   In consequence of the various application of the doctrines and precepts to so many different concerns of mankind, clearer views are given of their extent and comprehensiveness.   By a comparison also of the different passages thus written with each other, as they are thus written with a various reference and application, new truths are obviously as well as certainly inferred from them, almost without any limitation of their number.   The truths also which are

thus inferred are always important, and frequently of very
great importance.   By this variety of manner, application,
and inference, the Scriptures are always new, improving, and
delightful, and exhibit incontrovertible evidence of divine wisdom in the manner in which God has directed them to be
written, as well as in the wonderful and glorious things which
they contain.

I have now finished this interesting head of my Discourse,
and shall proceed to the consideration of the two remaining
ones, which, respecting subjects generally understood, will demand our attention but a few moments.

*The Third subject proposed was the Things which the
Apostles preached.*

On this I observe,

1. *The apostles have written the whole New Testament,
both the things which were said and done by Christ, and the
things which were said and done by themselves.*

2. *They have either originally communicated, or materially
explained, many doctrines and precepts which were either
omitted or partially communicated by Christ.*

Among these I select the following :——

The connection which runs through the whole system of
Redemption ; the Patriarchal, Mosaic, and Christian dispensations ; their mutual dependence ; the absolute dependence of
all on Christ ; and the sameness of the manner and principles
of salvation in all ; the extent of the curse, and the unhappy
efficacy of the apostasy of our first parents ; the parallelism
between the first and second Adam, and between the ruin and
recovery of mankind ; the imperfection of the Sinaitic covenant ; the superior glory and blessings of the covenant of
grace ; the priesthood of Christ, formed after the order of
Melchisedek ; his government of the world for the benefit of
the church ; his intercession in behalf of his followers before
the throne of God ; the preaching of the Gospel to Abraham
and to the Israelites ; justification by the grace of God through
faith in the righteousness of Christ, founded on that righteousness as its meritorious cause ; the sameness of Abraham's justification with that of all other saints, both before and after
the coming of Christ ; the sameness of the religion of the
Old and New Testament ; the extension of the mediation of

Christ, not only to the Jews but to all mankind ; the nature of evangelical faith ; the nature of evangelical love ; the progressive sanctification of Christians by the Holy Ghost ; the difficulties of the Christian warfare, and the struggle between sin and holiness in the sanctified mind ; the nature and circumstances of the resurrection ; the process of the final judgment ; the conflagration of the earth and visible heavens ; the worship rendered to Christ in the heavenly world ; and his peculiar agency in administering to his followers the happiness of a glorious immortality. These, together with a train of important prophecies concerning the affairs of the church throughout every age of the Christian dispensation, the apostles have added to the other contents of the Scriptures, or more perfectly explained them to mankind.

IV. *The consequences of their preaching.*

1. *The apostles and their converts were furiously persecuted soon after they had begun to preach the Gospel, particularly by the Jews, and not long after by the Gentiles also.*

.This subject is too well known to need a discussion from me. It is extensively recorded in the New Testament, and largely insisted on in ecclesiastical history.

2. *The apostles preached the Gospel with wonderful success.*

Beside the many thousand converts whom they made among the Jews, they spread the Gospel from Hindoostan to Gaul, and planted churches throughout a great part of the Roman empire, in Persia, Hindoostan, and several other countries. The number of their disciples in these extensive regions was immensely great, and this vast wilderness was made . to blossom as the garden of God.

Exclusively of the residence of Christ in the world, nothing has ever taken place among mankind so wonderful and glorious as this event ; nothing more unlike the ordinary progress of things, nothing more declarative of the presence and agency of God, nothing more evincive of the reality of Revelation. Whether we consider the religion to which mankind were converted, the difficulty of producing a real reformation in the human heart, the original character of the converts, the bigotry of the Jews, the ignorance and wickedness of the Gentiles, the vastness, uniformity, and enduring nature of the change, or the seeming insignificance of the instruments by which it was brought, fishermen, publicans, and tent-makers, few, feeble, friendless, despised, persecuted, and, in many instances, put to a violent death, we are astonished and lost. A thorough discussion of the importance of this fact, the success of the Gospel, might easily and usefully fill a volume, but cannot be pursued at the present time. It has been a theme of exultation and joy to all succeeding ages of the church, and, as we have the best reason to conclude, of peculiar wonder and transport in the world above.

The *evidence* which it furnishes to the divine origin of the Gospel is immoveable, and has accordingly been always insisted on by Christians with superiority and triumph. Infidels have laboured to diminish and obscure it with extreme earnestness and assiduity, but they have laboured in vain. Gibbon, particularly, with much art, a malignant hostility to the Christian cause, and the most strenuous exertion of his talents, has struggled hard to account for this event by assigning it to other causes than the true one. The real effect of his labours has, however, been to leave the evidence of the inspiration of the apostles more clear, more convincing, and more unexceptionable, than it was before.

SERMON L.

THE PRIESTHOOD OF CHRIST.

ORIGIN, OFFICE, AND CHARACTER OF THE PRIESTHOOD.

PROOFS OF THE PRIESTHOOD OF CHRIST.

THE LORD HATH SWORN, AND WILL NOT REPENT: THOU ART A PRIEST FOR EVER, AFTER THE ORDER OF MELCHISEDEK.

PSALM CX. 4.

IN a series of Discourses, I have considered the prophetical character of Christ. I shall now proceed, according to the plan originally proposed for the investigation of his office as Mediator between God and man, to consider his *priesthood*.

In order to a proper examination of this subject, it will be useful to examine summarily,

I. *The origin,*

II. *The office,*

III. *The character of a priest;* and,

IV. *Enquire in what manner the office and character of a priest may be said to belong to Christ?*

I. *The office of a priest* undoubtedly had its *origin* in the first ages of the world. The earliest mention made of this subject in form, is found in Genesis xiv. 18, ' And Melchisedek, king of Salem, brought forth bread and wine ; and he was the priest of the most High God.' The office was, however, in being long before this period. Cain and Abel performed the public duties of it for themselves; and there is no reason to doubt that it was regularly continued from their time, through every succeeding period, to the coming of Christ.

So soon as mankind became distributed into families, it appears highly probable that the Father of the family exercised this office in all instances, in behalf of himself and his household. Several instances of this nature are recorded: Noah was plainly the priest of his own family, and Abraham, Isaac, Jacob, and Job, of theirs'. It is probable that heads of families generally held the office in the same manner.

When mankind became settled in tribes and nations, the prince, or chief ruler, and at times some other ruler of great distinction, became the priest of the nation. Thus Melchisedeck was at the same time the king and priest of the people of Salem; and thus, as we know from profane history, many other princes held the same office among the people over whom they presided.

Under the Mosaic economy the office was, by divine institution, appropriated to a particular class of men. All these, except one, were originally ordinary priests, over whom that one presided, in the character of high priest. To this officer peculiar duties and privileges were attached. His weight and influence were almost invariably second only to those of the Prince, and not unfrequently paramount even to them. Similar establishments were early made among the gentiles. In the time of Joseph, we find the priests a separate class of men in the land of Egypt. An institution, essentially of the same nature, appears to have existed in many other nations at a very early date, and a priesthood, in one form or another, has been found in almost all the nations of men in every age of the world. This fact proves, unanswerably, that the priesthood has its origin either in a divine appointment, handed down by universal tradition, or in such a sense felt by the human mind of its utility and importance, as to persuade all nations, for this reason, not only to institute, but to maintain it with great expense and self-denial. As we find the office commencing with the very first age of the world, we are furnished by this fact with a strong presumptive argument, to prove that it was derived originally from a divine institution. This argument receives no small strength from the consideration that the office, however corrupted and mutilated, was in substance everywhere the same, and was professedly directed to the same objects.

II. *The office of a priest involved the following things.*
1. *Intercession.*

This is so universally acknowledged to have been always a part of the duties of a priest, as to need neither proof nor explanation. In conformity to it Aaron and his sons were commanded to bless the children of Israel, by praying for them in this remarkable language: ' Jehovah bless thee, and keep thee. Jehovah make his face to shine upon thee, and be gracious unto thee. Jehovah lift up his countenance upon thee, and give thee peace.' In the same manner also, in the days of the Prophet Joel, ' the priests, the ministers of the Lord,' were commanded to ' weep between the porch and the altar, and to say, Spare thy people, O Lord, and give not thine heritage to reproach, that the heathen should rule over them. Wherefore should they say among the people, Where is their God?'

Among the Gentiles also priests customarily prayed for the people.

2. *Another branch of the priest's office was the offering of sacrifices and other oblations.*

' Every high priest, taken from among men,' says St. Paul, ' is ordained for men in things pertaining to God, that he may offer both gifts and sacrifices for sin.' Intercession seems to be a duty of natural religion, and may be easily supposed to be a service properly performed by beings who have not fallen from their obedience. But, in such a state, the offering of sacrifices could evidently have no propriety, nor foundation. Sacrifices are, in my view beyond all doubt, of divine appointment, and have their foundation in the apostasy of man. Of this the proof seems to me complete, both from reason and Revelation. It cannot be supposed, as it cannot be proper, that on this occasion I should enter upon a detailed account of this proof. It will be sufficient to observe, that sacrifices existed among all the ancient nations, and that therefore they are derived from one common source; that no nation beside the Jews can give any account of the origin of this rite, or any reason for which it was founded ; nor show, unless loosely and unsatisfactorily any purpose which it could rationally be expected to answer ; that all nations still hoped by means of their sacrifices to become acceptable, though they could not tell how or why, to their gods, and accordingly made the offering of sacrifices the principal rite of their respective religions ; that, to a great extent, they offered the same sacrifices, and those chiefly such as are styled *clean*, in the Scriptures. These sacrifices were also esteemed in some sense or other, though none of the heathen could explain that sense, expiations for sin. At the same time it ought to be observed, that there is, to the eye of reason, no perceptible connection between sacrifices and r ligion ; and that there is nothing in this rite, particularly, which can lead the understanding to suppose it in any sense expiatory. The true dictate of reason on this subject is, that the causeless destruction of the life of an animal must be in itself an evil, an act of inhumanity, a provocation to God, only increasing the list of crimes in the suppliant ; while, on the contrary, the supposition that God can be appeased or reconciled by the death of an animal burnt upon an altar, is an obvious and monstrous absurdity. Well might Balak doubt, when he asked so anxiously under the strong influence of traditionary custom, ' Will the Lord be pleased with thousands of rams, or with ten thousands of rivers of oil ? Shall I give my first-born for my transgression, the fruit of my body for the sin of my soul ?' The only ' sacrifices of God,' that is the only sacrifices which God will accept, if he will accept any from man, are, in the eye of common sense, as well as in that of David, ' a broken spirit and a contrite heart ;' a disposition, as specified by Balaam in his answer to Balak, ' to do justly, to love mercy, and to walk humbly with our God.' From these observations, taken in their connection, it is, I think, fairly evident, that sacrifices were not, and cannot have been devised by mankind.

In the Scriptures the same doctrine is, I apprehend, rendered unquestionably certain. Abel offered a sacrifice to God, and was accepted. By St. Paul we are informed, that he offered this sacrifice in faith. While it is incredible, that he should have *devised* this rite as an act of religion, it is antiscriptural, and therefore incredible, that he should have been accepted in any act beside an act of obedience to God. But such an act his sacrifice could not have been, unless it had been commanded of God. Nor is it possible to conceive in what manner his faith could have been exerted, or to what object it could have been directed, unless it was directed to some divine promise. But no divine promise is, in the Scriptures, exhibited as made to mankind, except through the Redeemer. Abel, therefore, must have believed in the future existence and efficacious interference of that ' seed of the woman,' which was one day ' to bruise the head of the serpent.' With the eye of faith he saw that, through this glorious person, there was ' forgiveness with God,' and therefore ' feared,' or reverenced him. He ' hoped ' in the divine promise, that through him ' there was plenteous redemption ' for the children of men ; and in the exercise of this hope he performed such acts of worship as God had enjoined. Had he, on the contrary, like Nadab and Abihu, brought an offering which the Lord *had not commanded*, we are warranted from analogy to conclude that he would have been rejected, as *they* were.

After the deluge, Noah, as we are told, ' builded an altar unto the Lord ; and took of every clean beast, and of every clean fowl, and offered burnt-offerings on the altar.' On this occasion, also, the offering was accepted. To this fact the same reasoning is applicable with the same force. But it is farther evident from this story, that both *fowls* and *beasts* were, at *that* time known and designated as *clean*, and *unclean*. That this designation existed in the time of Noah, and was customary language, known to him and others at that time, is certain from the fact, that he selected only such as were clean : and is still farther illustrated by the fact, that God directed him ' to take of every clean beast, and every clean fowl, by sevens, into the ark ;' and that Noah exactly obeyed this command, and therefore perfectly knew what it imported. Beasts and fowls were, of course, distinguished as clean and unclean ; or, in other words, as those which might, and those which might not, be offered to God. But beasts, in themselves, are all equally clean and equally unclean ; nor can common sense discern a reason why one should be offered rather than another, any more than why any of them should be offered at all. The distinction of clean and unclean, or acceptable and unacceptable, cannot have been found in any thing but the divine appointment. · But this distinction we find thus early made ; and, as Abel offered clean beasts also, and the firstlings of his flock, the very sacrifice commanded afterwards to the Israelites, there is ample reason to conclude that the same distinction was made from the beginning.

The sacrifices of the Scriptures involve a plain, and at the same time a most important meaning. All of them were typical merely, and declared in the most striking manner the faith of the worshipper in the great propitiatory sacrifice of the Redeemer, and in the blessings promised by God through his mediation. Considered in this light, sacrifices are highly significant acts of worship, worthy of being divinely instituted, deeply affecting the heart of the suppliant, naturally and strongly edifying him in faith, hope, and obedience, and well deserving a place among the most important religious rites of all who lived before the oblation of the great sacrifice made for mankind.

From this view of the subject it is, I think, clearly evident, that sacrifices were divinely instituted ; and that this institution was founded in the future propitiatory sacrifice for sin made by the Redeemer. It is, of course, evident also that this part of the priest's office is derived from the apostasy of mankind, and can have a place only among beings who need an expiation.

3. *Another part of the priest's office was to deliver the oracles, or answers of God to the people.*

This was done, partly by the now inexplicable mode of Urim and Thummim, and partly by declarations made in the common manner.

The heathen priesthood, in imitation of that which was instituted by God, gave the pretended answers of their oracular divinities to such as came to consult them.

4. *Another part of the priest's office was deciding the legal controversies of individuals, or judging between man and man.*

For the institution of this duty of the priests, see Deuteronomy xvii. 9, 10. Accordingly, several of the priests are mentioned, in succeeding ages, as judges of the people.

5. *Another part of the priest's office was to instruct the people in the knowledge of the divine law.*

' The priest's lips,' says Malachi, ' should keep knowledge ; and they should seek the law at his mouth ; for he is the messenger of the Lord of Hosts.'

Of all the parts of this office the offering of sacrifices and other oblations is undoubtedly the most prominent and important. It was originally enjoined in the authoritative separation of Aaron and his sons to the priesthood. It is everywhere more insisted on as the great business of the priests, throughout the law of Moses, and throughout the whole history of the Jewish economy. It is accordingly mentioned *alone* by St. Paul, in his Epistle to the Hebrews, chapter v. verse 1, as the sum of the duty of the high priest. ' Every high priest— is ordained—that he may offer both gifts and sacrifices for sins.' This, then, is the peculiar office or duty of the priesthood, while the others are only appendages.

In the performance of this duty, the priest was everywhere considered in the law of Moses as making an atonement for the sins of the person or persons by whom the offerings were presented ; sometimes for individuals, sometimes for the whole nation. This great object, the only rational means of explaining the institution of sacrifices, is abundantly inculcated in the formal institution itself, and in all the precepts by which the duties of it are regulated, so abundantly, that I know not how it can be misconstrued. Accordingly, the Scriptures have been understood in this manner only by the great body of Christians from the beginning.

But nothing is more evident, than that ' it is impossible for the blood of bulls and of goats to take away sins.' These sacrifices, therefore, were never designed to purify those by whom they were offered. They were plainly and certainly mere types, holding forth to the suppliant the great and real sacrifice, by which the author of it ' hath perfected for ever them that are sanctified.' ' In burnt offerings and sacrifices for sin,' God said by David, Psalm xl. ' he had no pleasure.' They were not, therefore, ordained for their own sake, but to point the eyes of worshippers to the Son of God, who ' came to do his will ; for whom a body was prepared ;' and who, ' having offered,' in that body, ' one sacrifice for sins, sat down for ever at the right hand of God.'

The scheme of atonement, then, appears evidently to have

been a part, and a chief part, of the divine economy in the present world in all ages, or from the beginning.

Accordingly, when Christ had performed this great duty of his own priesthood, the priesthood of men ceased. The Jewish priesthood was terminated within a few years after his ascension. The office, except as holden by Christ, has no place in the Christian church, and, unless in a figurative sense, cannot be applied to Christian ministers without a solecism.

III. *The character of a priest, as disclosed in the Scriptures, consisted principally of the following things:*—

1. *A priest must be called of God.*

' No man,' says St. Paul, ' taketh this honour unto himself, but he that is called of God, as was Aaron. So also Christ glorified not himself to be made an high priest, but he that said unto him, Thou art my Son, this day have I begotten thee.' Nothing is more plain, than that he who ministers to God in divine things, ought to be approved of God; and it is clearly evident that he, who is not called, cannot expect to be approved. To thrust one's self into an office of this nature must be the result of mere impudence and impiety; a spirit which cannot meet the divine acceptance.

2. *A priest must be holy.*

Aaron and his sons were originally sanctified, externally, by a series of most solemn offerings and ceremonies. The *garments* of the High Priest were also pronounced holy, and styled holy garments. The *oil* with which he was anointed was styled holy, and was forbidden to all other persons, on a severe and dreadful penalty. ' HOLINESS TO THE LORD' was engraved on a plate which he was directed to wear upon his mitre.

' Such an high priest,' says St. Paul, ' became us, who is holy, harmless, undefiled, and separate from sinners.'

No absurdity can be more obvious or more gross than an unholy, polluted character in a man whose professional business it is to minister to God. The very heathen were so sensible of this, that their priests claimed generally, and laboured to preserve, that character which they esteemed sanctity.

3. *A priest must be learned in the Scriptures.*

As the Priests were to ' teach,' so they were to ' keep

knowledge.' Ezra, accordingly, is declared to have been ' a ready scribe in the law of Moses,' and to have ' prepared his heart to seek the law of the Lord, and to do it, and to teach in Israel statutes and judgments.' Artaxerxes, also, in his decree testifies, that ' the wisdom of God was in the hand of Ezra.' Every priest was implicitly required to possess these three great characteristics of the priesthood.

I have discussed the preceding subjects, viz. The *origin*, the *office*, and the *character* of the priesthood, that the various observations which I shall have occasion to make in the farther examination of the priesthood of Christ may be the more distinctly understood.

IV. *I shall now inquire in what manner the office and character of a priest may with propriety be said to belong to him.*

In the text, God the Father is exhibited as having sworn with a solemn and unchangeable decree to the Son, ' Thou art a priest for ever, after the order of Melchisedek.' As the person to whom this oath was addressed is expressly declared, both by Christ and St. Paul, to be Christ, there can be no debate concerning this part of the subject.

Farther: As Christ is here declared by God the Father to be a priest, it cannot be questioned that he sustained this office. It may, however, be proper to remind those who hear me, and who wish to examine the scriptural account of this subject, that the establishment and explanation of the priesthood of Christ occupies a great part of the Epistle to the Hebrews.

But, although this fact cannot be questioned, it cannot easily fail to be a useful employment in a Christian assembly to show, that Christ actually sustained the whole character and performed all the duties of a priest of God. This purpose I shall endeavour to accomplish in the remainder of the present Discourse.

1. *Christ sustained the whole character of a priest of God.*

(1.) *He was called of God to this office.* Of this the proof is complete in the passage already quoted, from Hebrews v. 4, 5. ' No man taketh this honour unto himself, but he that is called of God, as was Aaron. So also Christ glorified not

himself, to be made an high priest; but he that said unto him,
Thou art my Son, to-day have I begotten thee.' In the following verse the apostle, with unanswerable force, alleges the
text as complete proof of the same point. ' As he saith also
in another place, Thou art a Priest for ever, after the order
of Melchisedek.' In the 9th and 10th verses also he renews
the declaration in a different form, from the same words.
' And, being made perfect, he became the author of eternal
salvation unto all them that obey him; Called of God an high
priest after the order of Melchisedek.' In consequence of this
divine call to the priesthood, he was anointed to this office,
not with the holy anointing oil employed in the solemn consecration of the Aaronic priesthood, but with the antitype of that
oil, the Spirit of grace, poured upon him ' without measure'
by the hand of God.

(2.) *He was holy.* ' Such an high priest,' says St. Paul,
' became us, who was holy, harmless, undefiled, and separate
from sinners.' ' Who did no sin,' says St. Peter, ' neither was
guile found in his mouth.' ' The prince of this world cometh,'
says our Saviour, ' and has nothing in me:' that is, nothing
on which he can found an accusation against me.

(3.) *He was perfectly acquainted with the law of God.*
This is abundantly declared by Christ himself in many forms;
particularly, when he says, ' For the Father loveth the Son,
and showeth him all things, whatsoever he doeth.' And
again: No one knoweth the Father but the Son, and he to
whomsoever the Son will reveal him.'* And again ' I am
the light of the world.'† And again: ' Thy law is within my
heart.'‡ Of this acquaintance with the divine law he gave
the most abundant proofs while he resided in this world, in
his discourses generally. But in his Sermon on the Mount
he gave a more clear, minute, and comprehensive explanation
of its nature and extent than was ever furnished elsewhere to
the children of men.

2. *He performed all the duties of a priest of God, except
one, to wit, determining judicially the controversies between
men; a thing irreconcileable to his office as a priest.*

(1.) *He taught the Law, or will of God to his people, and
ultimately to mankind,* in a manner far more extensive, per-
spicuous, forcible, and every way perfect, than all the priests

* Matt. xi. 28.   † John ix. 5.   ‡ Psalm xl. 8.

and all the prophets who preceded him had been able to do. On this subject I have dwelt, while considering his character as a prophet, with so much minuteness as to preclude all necessity of farther discussion.

In this instruction he has included ' all things pertaining to life and to godliness,' necessary to be known by man ; and, therefore, has involved in them every *oracular answer*, or *answer of God*, to the inquiries of mankind after their interest and duty, which they can ever need on this side of the grave.

(2.) *He has performed, and still performs for this sinful world the great office of an intercessor.*

' But this man,' says St. Paul, ' because he continueth ever, hath an unchangeable priesthood. Wherefore he is able, also, to save them to the uttermost that come unto God by him ; seeing he ever liveth to make intercession for them.' ' If any man sin,' says St. John, ' we have an advocate with the Father, Jesus Christ the righteous.' Of this intercession his prayer in the xviith chapter of John has been considered as an example.

Finally : *He performed the great duty of offering sacrifice.* ' Who needeth not daily, as those high priests, to offer up sacrifice, first for his own sins, and then for the people's : for this he did once, when he offered up himself.' And again : ' Now, once in the end of the world hath he appeared to put away sin, by the sacrifice of himself. And, as it is appointed unto men once to die, but after this the judgment ; so Christ was once offered to bear the sins of many.' It will be unnecessary farther to multiply proofs of this point.

It may, however, be useful to obviate a difficulty which may, not very unnaturally, arise in the mind when contemplating this subject. It is this :——How can Christ be said to have *offered himself*, when he was apprehended, condemned, and crucified *by others ?* This difficulty will be easily removed, if we remember the following things :——

[1.] *That Christ could not, without incurring the guilt of suicide, have put himself to death : and therefore could not be virtuously offered, on his own part, unless put to death by the hand of others.*

[2.] *That he voluntarily came into the world to die for sinners.*

[3.] *That he predicted his own death, and therefore certainly foreknew it :* and,

[4.] *That he could, with perfect ease, have resisted and overcome his enemies ;* as he proved unanswerably by his miracles, and particularly by compelling, through the awe of his presence, those very enemies to fall backward to the ground, at the time when they first attempted to take him. From these things it is evident, beyond a debate, that he himself ' made his soul an offering for sin ;' and of himself, ' laid down his life, and took it up again, when none could take it out of his hand.'

From these considerations it is evident that Christ was in the most proper sense, a priest of God ; and that he sustained all the characteristics and performed all the duties belonging to the priesthood ; particularly, that he was called of God, consecrated, and anointed to this office ; and that he performed the great duty of offering sacrifice, for which the office was especially instituted.

Let me now ask, whether these things, so strongly and abundantly declared in the Scriptures, can be made, in any sense, to accord with the Unitarian doctrine, that Christ died *merely as a witness to the truth of his declarations.* Every Christian martyr, as his name sufficiently indicates, yielded his life as a testimony to the truth. But was every Christian martyr, therefore, a priest of God ? Did every martyr offer sacrifice ? Was St. Paul a priest ; or St. Peter ? They were both witnesses to the truth, and voluntarily gave up their lives as a testimony to the truth. But did they, therefore, offer sacrifice ? Were they, therefore, priests ? Did any man ever think of applying to them language of this nature.

But, further : Christ is expressly and often declared to have offered himself a *sacrifice for sins.*

For whose sins did he offer this sacrifice ? Not for his own ; for ' he did no sin, neither was guile found in his mouth.' For the sins of others, then, was this offering made. According to the declaration of St. Peter, ' He bore our sins in his own body on the tree.' His sacrifice of himself was, therefore, an atonement, an expiation of the sins of mankind.

Thus, from the nature, origin, and institution of the priest's office, it is evident that Christ, the great high priest of our profession, became, by the execution of his official duties (if I may call them such) ' a propitiation for the sins of the world.' So far is the Unitarian doctrine on this subject from being countenanced by the scriptural representations, that it is a direct contradiction of every thing said in the Scriptures concerning the priesthood, and particularly that of Christ.

On this subject I propose to insist more at large hereafter : but I thought it useful to show, at the introduction of it into a System of Theology, that it was essential to the very nature of the priest's office. Nor can I fail to wonder how any man, reading the accounts given of it in the Bible, should adopt any other opinion concerning this part of the mediation of the Redeemer.

SERMON LI.

THE PRIESTHOOD OF CHRIST:

HIS HOLINESS OF CHARACTER.

FOR SUCH AN HIGH·PRIEST BECAME US, WHO IS HOLY, HARMLESS, UNDEFILED, SEPARATE FROM SINNERS, AND MADE HIGHER THAN THE HEAVENS.

HEBREWS VII. 26.

IN the preceding Discourse, I considered the *origin, office, and character, of the priesthood;* and showed, that this office, in the strictest sense, *belonged to Christ;* and that the end of its establishment in the world was no other than to hold out--to the view of the ancients the priesthood of the Redeemer.

Among the characteristics of a priest, I mentioned it as an indispensable one, that he should be *holy.* This characteristic of the Redeemer I shall now make the subject of consideration; and in discussing it shall,

I. *Mention several particulars in which this attribute was exemplified.*

II. *Explain its importance.*

I. *I shall mention several particulars in which this attribute of Christ was exemplified.*

In the text the Apostle declares, that Christ was ' holy, harmless, undefiled, and separate from sinners.' The word ' holy,' in this passage, naturally denotes *the positive excellence of Christ's character;* the word ' harmless,' *an absolute free-*

dom *from the guilt of injuring and corrupting others;* the word ' undefiled,' *his freedom from all personal corruption;* and the phrase ' separate (or separated,) from sinners,' *the entire distinction between him and all beings who are, in any sense or degree, the subjects of sin.* The character here given of Christ by the apostle includes, therefore, all the perfection of which, as an intelligent being, the Saviour was capable. It ought to be remarked, that *this character* is given of him *as a priest;* and, of course, belongs especially to him as exercising this part of his mediatorial office.

It will be obvious to a person examining this subject with a very moderate degree of attention, that Christ, in order to sustain this character, must have fulfilled all the duties enjoined on him by the positive precepts of the divine law, and have abstained from every transgression of the negative ones · that in thought, word, and action alike he must have been uniformly obedient to the commands of God; that his obedience must have been rendered in that exact and perfect degree in which it was required by those commands; and that it must have included, in the same perfect manner, all the duties which he owed immediately to God, to mankind, and to himself: in other words, that his virtue, or moral excellence, must have been consummate.

That such was in fact the character of Christ we have the most abundant testimony.

The Scriptures declare every part of this character. St. Peter asserts directly, that ' he did no sin;' that ' guile was not found in his mouth;' and styles him ' a Lamb without blemish, and without spot.' He calls him ' the Holy One, and the Just;' and declares, that ' he went about doing good.' St. Paul declares, that ' he knew no sin.' St. John declares, that ' in him was no sin.' David styles him ' the Holy One of God.' Isaiah, or rather God speaking by Isaiah, calls him his own ' righteous servant;' ' his elect;' ' his beloved, in whom his soul delighted.' Jeremiah styles him, ' the Lord, our righteousness.' Christ himself declares, in his intercessory prayer to the Father, ' I have glorified thee on earth, I have finished the work which thou gavest me to do;' and asserts, that ' the Father' and himself ' are one;' and that he, ' who hath seen him, hath seen the Father.' He also says, ' The prince of this world cometh, and hath nothing in me.' At his baptism also, and during his transfiguration, God the Father himself declared his character in those memorable words, ' This is my beloved Son, in whom I am well pleased.' A similar testimony was given by the Spirit of truth, when he ' descended' upon Christ ' in a bodily shape, like a dove.'

To these and the like declarations, which might be easily multiplied to a great extent, various other kinds of testimony are added in the Scriptures.

The Jews who lived on the borders of the sea of Galilee, when assembled to behold the cure of the deaf man who had an impediment in his speech, exclaimed, amid their astonishment at the miracle, ' He hath done all things well.' During his life his enemies laboured hard to fix some imputation upon his character, but their efforts terminated in the groundless and senseless calumnies, ' that he cast out devils by Beelzebub, the prince of devils ;' and that he was ' a man gluttonous, and a wine-bibber ; a friend of publicans and sinners :' calumnies, daily and completely refuted by the testimony of those among whom he continually spent his time, and even by the demons which he cast out, and the maniacs whom they possessed. Even these felt themselves constrained to say, I know thee, who thou art, the Holy One of God.'

In his trial before the Sanhedrim, and afterwards before Pilate, every art which cunning could devise, fraud sanction, or malice execute, was practised, in order to fasten upon him at least some species of criminality. But, in spite of all the subornation and perjury to which they had recourse, they were unable to prove him guilty of a single fault. Pilate's repeated examinations of him terminated with this public declaration, ' I find no fault in this man.'

Judas, after he was called as a disciple, lived with him through all his public ministry, and was a witness of his most private conduct, a companion of his most retired hours, a partner in his most undisguised conversation. At these seasons, if ever, the man is brought out to view. At these seasons hypocrisy and imposture feel the burden of concealment too strongly not to throw off the mask, uncover themselves to obtain a necessary relief from the pressure of constraint, and cease awhile to force nature, that they may be refreshed for new imposition.

But Judas never saw a single act, and never heard a single

word which, even in his own biassed judgment, left the smallest stain upon the character of his Master. This he directly
declared to the chief-priests in that remarkable assertion, ' I
have sinned, in that I have betrayed innocent blood.' Far
beyond this, when the least fault in the conduct of Christ, could
he have recollected it, would have relieved the agonies of his
conscience, and justified, or at least palliated, his treason, he
put an end to his own life, because he could not endure the
misery springing from a sense of his guilt. In this gross and
dreadful act he gave, therefore, the strongest testimony which
is possible to the perfect innocence of the Redeemer.

Correspondent with this testimony is that of all antiquity.
Neither the Mishna nor the Talmud, which contain the whole
substance of the Jewish testimony on this subject; neither
Celsus, Porphyry, nor Julian, who may be fairly considered
as having given us the whole of *heathen* testimony, have fixed
upon Christ the minutest charge of either sin or folly. To the
time of Origen, we have his declaration (which is evidence of
the most satisfactory nature,) that within the vast compass of
his information nothing of this nature had ever appeared. In
modern times, the enemies of Christianity have laboured with
great industry and ingenuity to fasten upon him some species
of accusation : but they have laboured in vain. Unlike in this
respect, that glorious orb, to which he is compared in the
Scriptures, nothing has ever eclipsed his splendour, no spot
has ever been found on his aspect.

That we may form just and affecting views of this part of
our Saviour's character, it will be useful, without dwelling any
longer on a general survey of his holiness, to proceed to the
consideration of those *particulars in which it was* especially
exemplified.

1. *The piety of Christ was uniform and complete.*

His supreme *love* to God was divinely manifested in the
cheerfulness with which he undertook the most arduous, and
at the same time the most benevolent of all employments, and
of course that which was most pleasing to him, and most
honourable to his name. His *faith* was equally conspicuous
in the unshaken constancy with which he encountered the innumerable difficulties in his progress ; his *patience,* in the
quietness of spirit with which he bore every affliction ; and his
submission, in his ready acquiescence in his Father's will, while

requiring him to pass through the deepest humiliation, pain, and sorrow. However humbling, however distressing his allotments were, even in his agony in the garden, and in the succeeding agonies of the cross, he never uttered a complaint. But, though afflicted beyond example, he exhibited a more perfect submission than is manifested by the most pious men under small and ordinary trials. No inhabitant of this world ever showed such an entire reverence for God, on any occasion, as he discovered on all occasions. He gave his Father at all times the glory of his mission, his doctrines, and his miracles : seized every proper opportunity to set forth, in terms pre-eminently pure and sublime, the excellence of the divine character ; and spoke uniformly in the most reverential manner of the word, the law, and the ordinances of God.

At the same time, he was constant and fervent in the worship of God ; in prayer, in praise, and in a cheerful compliance with all the requisitions of the Mosaic system, civil, ceremonial, and moral ; celebrated the fasts, feasts, and sacrifices of his nation, and thus, according to his own language, ' fulfilled ' in this respect ' all righteousness.' Such, in a word, was his whole life ; so unspotted, so uniform, so exalted, that all persons who have succeeded him, both inspired and uninspired, have found themselves obliged, whenever they wished to exhibit a perfect pattern of piety, to appeal to the example of Christ.

2. *His performance of the duties which he owed to mankind was equally perfect.*

This part of our Saviour's character cannot be properly understood without descending to particulars. I observe, therefore,

(1.) *That his filial piety was of this remarkable nature.*

Notwithstanding he was so magnificently introduced into the world by a long train of types and predictions, and by illustrious instances of the immediate ministration of angels, he was entirely obedient throughout almost all his life to the commands of his parents. No person was ever so ushered into life, or marked out by Providence for so extraordinary purposes. No person so early engrossed the attention and admiration of the great and wise by his mental endowments. Whatever could awaken in his mind the loftiest views of ambition, enkindle a strong sense of personal superiority, or produce feelings of absolute independence, he could recount among the incidents which either attended him at his birth, or followed him in his childhood.

Still no child, no youth, no man of riper years, was ever so respectful and dutiful to his parents. ' To them' in the language of St. Luke, ' he was subject,' evidently, till he ' began to be about thirty years of age.' To this period he lived contentedly a humble, retired, and unobserved life, following quietly the occupation of his father with such industry and regularity, as to be known familiarly by the appellation of *the carpenter.*

Civilized men have united with a single voice to applaud and extol Peter the Great, Emperor of Russia, for his moderation and condescension, displayed in labouring at the employment of a ship-carpenter, in the Saardam. Unquestionably, this conduct was the result of sound wisdom and unusual self-government on the part of this great man, and fairly claimed the admiration which it received. What, then, shall be said,——when we behold him whose title was the *Son of God,* whose birth angels proclaimed, predicted, and sung, to whom angels ministered at his pleasure ; who commanded winds, and waves, and life, and death ; who triumphed over the grave, and ascended to heaven——working at an employment equally humble, not a few days only, but the principal part of his life ; and all this, not to subserve the purposes of ambition, but from a sense of duty, and in the exercise of filial piety !

The same character was gloriously manifested by Christ during his public ministry. Particularly while he hung upon the cross, suffered the agonies of that excruciating death, and ' bore the sins of mankind in his body on the accursed tree,' when he saw his unhappy mother pierced with anguish by his side, he forgot his own woes, commended her to the care of his beloved disciple John, as his future mother, and that disciple to her as her future son, and thus made provision for her maintenance and comfort through life. Thus he began, and thus he ended.

(2.) *Of the same perfect nature were his candour and liberality.*

The spirit which is denoted by these two names is substantially the same, and differs chiefly by being exercised toward different objects. That this spirit should exist at all in Christ will naturally seem strange, when we remember that he was born of a humble family, in the most bigoted nation in the world, and in the most bigoted age of that nation, and was educated in that humble manner which naturally leads the mind to imbibe with reverence the bigoted sentiments of the great, and to add to them the numerous and peculiar prejudices springing from ignorance. But from all this influence he escaped without the least contamination. There is not an instance recorded in his life in which he was more attached to any person or thing, or more opposed to either, than truth and wisdom must entirely justify. There is no instance, in which he ever censured or commended those of his own nation, or of any other, either more or less than plain justice demanded. On the contrary, he commended every thing approved by wisdom and piety, and reproved every thing bigoted, partial, prejudiced, and faulty in man.

A great part of the people of his nation were his enemies, and among the most bitter of these were the Pharisees. Yet he said to his disciples, ' The Scribes and Pharisees sit in Moses' seat : all, therefore, that they say unto you, do. But do ye not after their works ; for they say, and do not.' No commendation of the precepts of these men could easily have been conveyed in more expressive language than this. By directing his disciples to follow their precepts, he declared them in forcible terms to be true and right, that is, with such exceptions as he has elsewhere made, and as the same exact regard to truth demanded.

The same disposition he manifested in the case of the Syrophenician woman ; and in that of the Roman centurion. The Jews considered all the heathen nations as deserving nothing but contempt and detestation, and called them *dogs*. But Christ preferred the faith of the centurion, although a Roman, to that of all other persons with whom he conversed, even to that of his own apostles.

. In the same generous manner he treated the publicans, regarded by their countrymen as the vilest of sinners. In the same manner also he treated the Samaritans, against whom the Jews exercised the most furious hatred, and with whom they refused to have any ' dealings,' even those of the most indifferent and necessary kind.

The same disposition he showed with respect to doctrines, opinions, and customs. No specimen can be produced from the history of his life of bigoted attachment to his own doctrines, or those of his nation, or those of his friends; of prejudice against those of strangers or enemies; of favouritism or party spirit, of contracted regard to any custom because sanctioned by public usage or general respect; of reluctance to conform to any innocent practice, by whomsoever adopted, or of any narrowness of mind whatever.

When invited to a marriage, he cheerfully went; when bidden to a feast, he readily consented to become a guest. Nor did it make any difference, because the host was on the one hand, Matthew, or Zaccheus, a publican; or, on the other, Simon, a Pharisee. In a word, he adopted and commended nothing except what was true and right, and neither refused nor condemned any thing except that which was false and evil. Nor did it make the least difference with him whether that which was approved or censured was adopted by friends or enemies.

(3.) *His prudence was consummate on all occasions.*

Particularly was it manifested in avoiding the wiles and open assaults of the Jews. Notwithstanding the invincible firmness of mind universally displayed by our Saviour, notwithstanding he lost no opportunity of doing good, yet he never wantonly exposed himself to any suffering; discovering clearly, on every occasion, a total opposition to that vain and idle fool-hardiness which rushes into danger, merely to gain the reputation of being courageous.

The same prudence is strongly evinced in teaching his disciples and others, as their minds were able to receive his instructions; giving ' milk to babes,' and ' strong meat to men;' opening new doctrines and duties by degrees, and never ' pouring new wine into old bottles.' At the same time, he commended his precepts both to the heart and the understanding by *their form*. At one time he communicated them in short *aphorisms*, easily understood, deeply felt, long remembered, and readily applied to practice. At another, he conveyed them in *parables*, simple, beautiful, natural, and affecting, catching the imagination and feelings, as well as convincing the understanding. At another, he entered into plain, but profound, curious, and unanswerable *reasonings*, showing both from the works and the word of God, that his precepts were just, and his doctrines true. Thus he charmed by variety and novelty, as well as proved by argument and evidence; and ' became,' innocently, ' all things to all men, that' at least he ' might gain some.'

The same character he discovered in a manner not less remarkable, in answering the questions and resolving the cases proposed to him by the Pharisees and Sadducees. In every instance of this nature he refuted their arguments, exploded their opinions, defeated their crafty designs against him, and publicly put them to shame and to silence. Thus he beautifully illustrated the truth of that memorable declaration which he had anciently made concerning himself, ' I, Wisdom, dwell with Prudence.'

The same truth he still more strikingly illustrated by the uniform tenour of his life. This was such as to defeat all the malicious accusations of his numerous and bitter enemies, and to place his character beyond a doubt of its innocence and uprightness. To this end it was not sufficient that he was *really* innocent and upright. It was additionally necessary that he should be consummately prudent. In proportion to their want of prudence, all men are endangered in this respect, and most become sufferers. But Christ was regularly considered as an innocent man by all persons even of moderate candour, had a high reputation for worth in the eyes of the public, and, when tried on the accusation of enemies and villains before a malignant and unprincipled tribunal, was pronounced clear of every imputation. Equal proof of prudence as well as innocence was never furnished in the present world.

(4.) *His integrity was equally perfect.*

This dignified characteristic is strongly visible in several of the things already recited as proofs of his *candour ;* candour itself being no other than a particular mode of exercising integrity. Of this nature are his impartial censures and commendations of his friends and his enemies. The same spirit is conspicuous in his reproofs which, on the one hand, were bold, open, and sincere, and, on the other, were perfectly free from selfishness and ill nature. It is also strikingly evident in the perfect simplicity of his instructions and conversation. In them all there cannot be found a single instance of flattery, sarcasm, ambiguity, affectation, vanity, arrogance, or ill-will. Nay, nothing is enhanced beyond the strictest bounds of propriety. Nothing is so coloured as to deceive, nothing left so defective as to mislead. The strongest specimen ever given of integrity in the manner of communication is found in the instructions of Christ.

Many persons have been distinguished for their integrity, and so distinguished as to leave behind them in their history little or no stain upon their reputation in this respect. But Christ differs, evidently, from them all in the *degree* in which he manifested this attribute ; and so differs from them, as that simplicity and openness of communication forms a remarkable characteristic of the *style* in which he spoke ; and constitutes, eminently, what may be called *his own original manner.* As this runs through all his discourses, as recited by the several Evangelists, it is evident from this fact, that it was his own manner and not theirs.

The same illustrious attribute was, in the same manner, evinced in all his conduct. By applause he was never allured ; by obloquy he was never driven. Popular favour he never coveted ; popular odium he never dreaded. To friends and enemies, to the populace and the Sanhedrim, he declared truth, and proclaimed their duty, without favour or fear. When he stood before the Sanhedrim, and was on trial for his life, being adjured by the high priest to declare whether he was the Son of God, he boldly said, though he knew that death would be the consequence, ' I am.' And, to place the declaration beyond all reasonable doubt, subjoined, ' And ye shall see the Son of man sitting on the right hand of power, and coming in the clouds of heaven.' In a word, he treated all men while he was teaching, exhorting, and reproving them, as merely rational and immortal beings, and not as friends or enemies, nor as members of any sect, party, or nation. In this manner he left a noble example to every succeeding teacher of mankind.

(5.) *His benevolence also was without an example.*

Many of the observations already made strongly illustrate this glorious attribute of the Redeemer. It will, however, be useful to mention other things more particularly, as exemplifications of this disposition. Among the numerous miracles wrought by Christ, there is not one which was not performed for the direct purpose of lessening distress or danger, or producing safety, comfort, and happiness to mankind. Many of these miracles, also, were wrought for those whom he knew to be his enemies, with the full conviction on his part that they would continue to be his enemies. While his life was filled up with that peculiarly bitter provocation which arises from ingratitude daily repeated, never wearied, and even increased by the very kindness which should have melted the heart, even this provocation never slackened his hand, nor moved his resentment. When he came in sight of that ungrateful city, Jerusalem, where so many prophets had been killed, where so many of his benevolent offices and so many of his wonderful miracles had been performed in vain ; notwithstanding all the injuries which he had received from the inhabitants, notwithstanding they were now employed in devising means to take away his life, ' he wept over' the guilty, abandoned spot, and cried with inexpressible tenderness, ' O Jerusalem, Jerusalem ! that killest the prophets, and stonest them who are sent unto thee, how often would I have gathered thy children together, even as a hen gathereth her chickens under her wings, and ye would not.' On the cross he forgave, and prayed, and secured eternal life for murderers, while they were imbruing their hands in his blood, and rendering a most bitter death still more bitter by adding insult to agony. At the same time, he communicated faith, and peace, and hope, the forgiveness of sin, and an earnest of immortal glory, to the miserable malefactor who, by his side, hung over the burnings of devouring fire.

(6.) *Equally wonderful was his disinterestedness.*

This attribute, though often considered as the same with benevolence, is really a qualification of benevolence ; as is evident from the mere phraseology, so customarily adopted, of *disinterested benevolence.* But it is the crown, the glory, the finishing of this character.

There is not an instance in which Christ appears to have proposed his own private, separate good, as the end either of his actions or sufferings. He came to live and die for others, and *those* enemies, and sinners. From them he needed and could receive nothing. From him they needed every thing, and from him alone could they receive that which they needed. For such beings all his labours, instructions, and sorrows were planned and completed. The objects which he had in view were the most disinterested, public, and honourable which the universe has ever known ; the deliverance of mankind from sin and misery, their elevation to virtue and happiness, and the supreme glory of God in this divine and most wonderful work. These objects he accomplished with extreme difficulty and self-denial, and with immense expense on his own part. This arduous work he began with a fixed purpose, pursued with unshaken constancy, and triumphantly completed in spite of every discouragement, difficulty, and danger. On all his progress heaven looked with wonder and gratulation, and, at his return to that happy world, the ransomed of the Lord exclaimed, and will for ever exclaim, ' Worthy is the Lamb that was slain, to receive power, and riches, and wisdom, and strength, and honour, and glory, and blessing !'

SERMON LII.

THE PRIESTHOOD OF CHRIST.

HOLINESS OF CHARACTER

HIS SELF-GOVERNMENT.

FOR SUCH AN HIGH PRIEST BECAME US, WHO IS HOLY, HARMLESS, UNDEFILED, SEPARATE FROM SINNERS, AND MADE HIGHER THAN THE HEAVENS.

HEBREWS VII. 26.

In the preceding Discourse, I considered *the holiness of Christ as one great branch of his priestly character.* In the course of this consideration I stated, summarily, my views concerning the manner in which Christ performed the duties, owed by him immediately to God, and to mankind. I shall now make a few observations concerning those which he owed more immediately to *himself.* The two former classes are generally denoted by the names *piety* and *benevolence;* the latter is usually denominated *temperance,* or *self-government.*

It ought here to be observed, that our Saviour's life was regulated by the rules of perfect virtue in all those ordinary and less delicate cases, in which mankind so commonly transgress, and in which we usually look for the proofs of a gross and guilty character. The truth is, imputations of the kind here referred to are not made on the Redeemer even by the worst of men, and have ceased, notwithstanding the groundless and brutal calumnies of his contemporary enemies, who accused

him as ' a man gluttonous and a wine-bibber, a friend of publicans and sinners,' to have any place in the belief, or even
in the obloquy, of mankind.   To say, that our Saviour was
chaste and temperate, is so far from seeming like a commendation of his character, that it rather wears the aspect of that
cold approbation which is considered as grudged, and is
yielded merely because it cannot with decency be refused.
Nay, it may with strict propriety be said that the very approach to this subject savours in a degree rather of impropriety
and indelicacy, and wears more the appearance of an anxious
and sedulous disposition to shield a doubtful reputation, by
watchful efforts to say every thing which can be said in its
favour, than of a sober determination to utter the sincere approbation of the understanding, and the just applause of the
heart.

   With these observations premised, I observe,
   1. *That the industry of Christ was wonderful.*
   St. Peter describes the character of the Redeemer in these
memorable words, ' who went about doing good.'   Acts x. 38.
This emphatical description exhibits the active part or side of
his life just as it really was ; and, though extremely summary,
it is complete.   Doing good was his only proper, professional,
employment ; in this employment he did not, like other beneficent persons, stay at home, where he might meet with solitary
and casual objects of his kindness, but went unceasingly from
place to place to find the greatest number, and those on whom
his kindness might be most advantageously employed.
   The whole life of Christ was a perfect comment on this text.
He himself has often told us his own views concerning the
great duty of industry in the service of God.   When his
mother gently reproved him for the anxiety which he had
occasioned to his parents when, at twelve years of age, he staid
behind at Jerusalem, while they went forward three days'
journey towards Nazareth ; he replied, ' How is it that ye
have sought me ?   Wist ye not, that I must be about my
Father's business ?'   This honourable scheme of life, so early
adopted, and so forcibly expressed, was the uniform rule of his
conduct at every succeeding period, and is often mentioned by
him, as such, during the progress of his public ministry.   Thus,
in his reply to the disciples, asking him a question concerning

' the man, who was born blind,' he said, ' I must work the
works of him that sent me, while it is day. The night cometh,
when no man can work.' John ix. 4. Thus, when the Pharisees informed him, that ' Herod would kill him,' and urged
him, therefore, to ' get him out, and depart thence,' he said
unto them, ' Go ye, and tell that fox, Behold, I cast out devils,
and I do cures, to-day and to-morrow; and the third day I
shall be perfected. Nevertheless, I must work to-day, and
to-morrow, and the day following.' Thus, also, he declared,
universally, the character of his life, in those memorable
words, ' The Son of man came not to be ministered unto, but
to minister.' Who could claim, with so much propriety, to be
ministered unto as Christ? From whom ought not ministering
to be expected, rather than from him? Finally, when he was
conversing with the woman of Sychar, and his disciples solicited him to eat, he answered, ' My meat is to do the will of
him that sent me, and to finish his work.'

In exact accordance with the spirit of these declarations,
we find him, immediately after his baptism, going into the
wilderness to suffer and to overcome in his temptation. As
soon as this was ended, he journeyed unceasingly throughout
Judæa, Galilee, and Peræa, and occasionally in the neighbouring countries, instructing, healing, comforting, and be-
friending all whom he found willing to hear his words, or fitted
to receive his assistance. His early life was a life of industrious labour, literally so called. His public life was also an
uninterrupted course of laborious exertions, made in a different manner, a period filled up with duty and usefulness.
With an unwearied hand he scattered blessings wherever he
went. The manner in which, and the object to whom, the
good was to be done, were to him things indifferent, if it was
really done. Whether they were friends or enemies, Jews or
heathen, disciples or strangers; whether they were to be
taught, healed, restored to sight, hearing, or life; he was
always prepared to bestow the blessing, wherever there was
necessity to demand, or faith to receive it. So wonderfully
numerous were the labours of Christ, as to furnish a solid
foundation of propriety for that hyperbolical and singular declaration of St. John, with which he concludes his Gospel:
' And there are also many other things, which Jesus did;
the which, if they should be written every one, I suppose that

even the world itself could not contain the books that should be written.   Amen.'

A stronger instance of this disposition can hardly be given, than one of those, to which I have already alluded.   Hungry, weary, and faint in his journey through the country of Samaria, he came to the neighbourhood of the city Sychar, and seated himself ' on Jacob's well.' A woman, a miserable inhabitant of that city, came out to draw water, and presented him with an object to whom good might be done, and who infinitely needed it.   Forgetting all his own sufferings, our Saviour applied himself with the utmost diligence to accomplish the conversion of this sinful woman, and that of her countrymen.   After he had conversed a considerable time with her, she left him to call the people of the city.   His disciples ' then prayed him, saying, Master, eat.   But he said unto them, I have meat to eat, that ye know not of.   Therefore said the disciples one to another, Hath any man brought him aught to eat?   Jesus saith unto them, My meat is to do the will of him that sent me, and to finish his work.'   The sentiments here expressed, and on this occasion gloriously exemplified in the diligence with which he devoted himself to the business of converting this poor woman and her neighbours, were the rules by which he governed his whole life.

As he drew near to the close of his ministry he appears to have been even more industrious, if possible ; and to have taught and done more than during any former period of the same length, as if he thought the remaining time valuable in proportion to its shortness.

Thus he was able to say with perfect confidence and exact truth, after he had ended his ministry, ' Father, I have glorified thee on earth ; I have finished the work, which thou gavest me to do.'

2. *His fortitude was not less remarkable.*

This characteristic of Christ is everywhere discovered, and with the highest advantage. To form just views of it, we ought to remember that he was alone, poor, and friendless ; that he was more opposed than any other person ever was ; and that he was opposed by the government and nation of the Jews, especially by the learned, wise, and great.   We ought to remember that, wherever he was, he found enemies, enemies to his person and to his mission, subtle, watchful, persevering, base, and malignant. All his strength, in the mean time, was, under God, in himself, in his mind, in his wisdom and virtue. Yet he met every danger with unshaken firmness, and immoveable constancy. He bore, not only without despondency, without shrinking and without a murmur, but with serenity and triumph, all the evils of life, and, except the hiding of his Father's face, and the manifestations of his anger against sin, all the evils of death. At the same time, all this was done by him, while these evils were suffered by continual anticipation.

They were, in a sense, always in his view. He foretold them daily, and yet encountered them with invincible constancy. Other men, however boldly and firmly they encounter *actual* calamities, are yet prone to sink under such as are *expected*. The distresses of a foreboding heart who can bear?

When, during his agony in the garden, the 'sweat' flowed from him in the form ' of great drops of blood,' he coolly met the guard which approached to seize him, reproved Peter for his violence, healed the wounded ear of Malchus, secured the escape of his disciples, and delivered himself up to those very soldiers whom his presence had awed into statues.

With the same invincible spirit he endured the miseries and injuries of the crucifixion. All the insults which were mingled with his agonies on the cross were insufficient to remove his self-possession, or disturb his serenity for a moment. Amidst them all he was able to forget himself, to pity and admonish the daughters of Jerusalem, to provide for the future comfort of his mother, and to pray for the forgiveness and salvation of his murderers.

3. *Not less wonderful was his meekness.*

Meekness is a voluntary and serene quietness of mind under provocations perceived and felt, but of choice unresented.

No person was ever so abused or provoked as Christ, nor in circumstances which so greatly aggravated the provocation. He came from heaven, lived, and died only to do good to his enemies, and received all his abuses while occupied in this divine employment. Ingratitude, therefore, and that of the blackest kind, was mingled with every injury, and added keenness to its edge. At the same time, every abuse was causeless and wanton, without even an imaginary wrong done by him to excite ill-will in his persecutors.

But no person ever bore any provocation with such meekness as he exhibited in every instance of this nature. Neither revenge nor wrath, as this word is usually understood, ever found a place in his breast. His character was maligned, his actions were perverted by the worst misconstruction, himself was insulted often and alway, and all the amiableness and worth of his most benevolent conduct insolently denied; yet ' when reviled, he reviled not again; when he suffered, he threatened not; but committed himself to him that judgeth righteously.' In his trial particularly, and at his crucifixion, he was mocked and insulted beyond example. Yet though beaten, buffetted, pierced with thorns, spit upon, derided with mock-worship, and wounded with every other insult which the ingenuity of his enemies could devise, he quietly submitted to them all.

The *nature* of all these also he *perfectly understood*, and the sting which each conveyed he deeply felt. The tenderness of Christ's affections, the exquisiteness of his sensibility, are strongly evident, not only in the history of his life, but also in those remarkable predictions contained in Psalms xxii. xl. lxix. and lxxxviii. Here, in prophetical language, Christ utters the very feelings which he experienced both while he lived, and when he died. No picture of sorrow is drawn in stronger colours, or formed of more vivid images, or can more forcibly exhibit exquisite tenderness and sensibility. In this picture the injuries and insults which Christ received while on earth hold a distinguished place, particularly those which surrounded him at his trial and crucifixion.

The manner in which he felt them all he himself has explained to us in these Psalms, and has taught us to consider them as filling his heart with anguish and agony. Still, he quietly yielded himself to them all without a momentary resentment, without a single reproachful or unkind observation. No cloud of passion appears to have arisen in his breast, or obscured for a moment the steady sunshine of his soul. Calm, and clear, and bright, amid the rage of the tempest beneath, he pursued his celestial course with an undisturbed progress, with a divine serenity.

4. *Equally extraordinary was his humility.*

No person ever had the same reason to entertain a high opinion of himself, or would have been so naturally justified, or so far excusable in indulging lofty thoughts of his own character, and in wearing a deportment of superiority to his fellow-men. No person was ever so ushered into the world. Think, for a moment what it is for a person to be prophesied of during four thousand years before he was born; to be announced to the world repeatedly in the songs and predictions of angels; to be the antitype of a long train of august institutions, and a glorious succession of the most distinguished personages numbered among mankind. No person ever did so great and wonderful things. Think what a splendour of character is displayed in healing the sick, cleansing the leper, restoring soundness to the lame, hearing to the deaf, sight to the blind, and speech to the dumb, in calling the dead from the grave, silencing the winds and the waves, and casting out demons from the possession of man; and all this by a command. Think what it is to receive the homage and obedience of angels, to be proclaimed by a voice from heaven, ' the beloved Son of God,' to have the Spirit of God descend upon him in a visible form, and to see all nature, animated and unanimated, obey his voice and execute his pleasure, and thus to stand alone among the race of Adam, exempted from the common character of men by marks the most clear, certain, and glorious.

His situation, at the same time, was such as most to excite vain glory, and flatter ambition. To these wonderful things he rose from the most humble condition of life, a condition heightening by contrast the splendour of all the great things which he did and received. Persons rising from such a condition into the admiration of mankind, are usually much more strongly affected than those who have lived always in superior circumstances, and been from the beginning objects of distinguished applause.

Christ also possessed far more wisdom than any other person ever possessed; wisdom, respecting the most noble and sublime subjects, such as the character of God, the invisible world, divine providence, and the nature, duties, and everlasting concerns of man. On all these subjects the wisdom contained in his instructions totally excels all the wisdom of the greatest and wisest men of every age. This wisdom, also, he possessed without the aid of education. His precepts and doctrines were his own, and underived from any preceding instruction. But nothing inflates the pride of wise men than to be indebted for their wisdom to themselves alone, to native genius, to original thought, invention, and research, and thus to have become the authors of discoveries which have eluded the ingenuity and escaped the invention of all who went before them.

These things his countrymen saw, heard, and acknowledged, and that in a manner experienced by no other inhabitant of this world. They saw him often engaged in disputes with the greatest men of his age and country concerning subjects of the highest importance. They saw *him* uniformly and completely victorious, and *them* always put to silence and to flight. His triumph they not only beheld, but frequently enjoyed; and, on account of it, publicly gave glory to God. They declared him to be a prophet, the peculiar prophet promised by Moses, and the Messiah; rang his praises throughout Judea, and the surrounding countries; attempted to make him their king; and, spreading their garments where he was to pass, sung hosannas before him, to glorify his character.

But, fitted as these motives were to kindle every latent spark of pride in the human heart, and to blow up a flame of ambition which should reach to heaven, he was superior to them all, and that from the beginning. At twelve years of age he astonished the wise and great among his countrymen with his wisdom; yet he obeyed the first call of his parents, and returned with them from the scene of applause to their humble cottage. When his countrymen sought him that they might place him on a throne, he retired into the desert. When greeted with hosannas by the enraptured multitude, he changed neither his demeanor, nor his daily employments; but forgot the splendour, the applause, and himself, to weep over Jerusalem, and deplore the approaching ruin of that ungrateful city.

He chose the humblest life, the humblest associates, the humblest food, the humblest dress, and the humblest manners, and voluntarily yielded himself to the most humiliating death. Nor was his character more distinguished by greatness, wisdom, and moral dignity, than by his humility of mind and life. He himself has alleged it, as one proof of his Messiahship, that ' the poor had the Gospel preached to them' by his mouth.

REMARKS.

I have now finished the observations which I proposed to make under the first general head, mentioned in the preceding Discourse ; and have given an account, so far as I thought necessary, of several things in which the holiness of the Redeemer was exemplified. The second, viz. the importance of this attribute to his priesthood, I shall reserve for future discussion ; and shall proceed to make two or three Remarks, naturally arising from what has been already said.

1. We have here seen ample proof, that Christ was what he declared himself to be.

The precepts of Christ required mankind to be absolutely holy, or perfect, and allowed no defect of obedience, as well as no degree of transgression ; declaring this character to be the only one which, for its own sake, could be accepted of God. In what has been said, we have the fullest proof that he was exactly such as he taught others to be, a complete example of the character which he required. Of all the things attempted by man on this side of the grave none is more difficult, or more transcends human efforts, than the attainment of this perfection. The world has never seen a second specimen of this character. How remote then must it be, when the best of mankind have fallen so far short of it, from the possible attainment of hypocrites, impostors, and pretenders ? How distant from every counterfeit ? How absolutely unattainable, hitherto, by the least blemished integrity, and the most exalted piety which has been merely human. A single act, or a few actions may to the eye of spectators seem great, spotless, and exalted. A retired life, little seen and scarcely observed, may not disclose its defects. But a life spent in the midst of mankind, and daily exposed to the view of multitudes, and filled up with actions of every kind, cannot fail to discover, even in the best of men, continual and numerous imperfections. Perfect rectitude of heart, therefore, can alone have produced perfect rectitude of life in our Saviour. Of course, he was what he declared himself, and what he is everywhere declared to be, in the Scriptures. Of course, he was the Messiah, the Son of God, the Saviour of mankind. His doctrines and precepts were from God, and require, with divine authority, the faith and obedience of all men. His ' life ' was given as ' a ransom for many,' and his ' flesh for the life of the world.' He did not, therefore, die *to bear witness to the truth of his doctrines* ; but as ' *a propitiation for sin,' and* ' a ransom for sinners.' As such, therefore, we are required to believe on him, if we wish to be saved.

A strong additional proof of the truth, now under consideration, is furnished by *the circumstances* in which Christ was *born*, and *lived*. He was born, and educated, as has been observed before, in the humblest circumstances, and continued in them throughout his life. With plain and ignorant men only did he spend almost the whole of his days ; men whom he instructed, but from whom he could never receive instruction. At the same time, the learned men of his age and country had wandered in their doctrines far from truth and righteousness. Their opinions, grounded partly on a perverted Revelation, and partly on a wretched and debasing collection of traditions, were to a great extent false, foolish, and stupid beyond all easy conception. Their worship was a vain and miserable round of external rites. Their morals, also, were licentious, and polluted by all the dictates of lust, pride, and avarice ; and their whole character was a gross and dreadful mixture of bigotry, hypocrisy, oppression, violence, and impurity.

In such an age, in such circumstances, among such men, and in the midst of such errors and sins, Christ was born and educated, lived and died. Let every honest, every sober man now say, whence it arose that he was an exception to the character of all his countrymen, and to that of mankind ; that his wisdom transcended that of all other men, and that his life left that of every child of Adam out of comparison, and out of sight ; a ' sun of righteousness,' at whose presence every star disappears from the firmament.

2. *These observations strongly evince the inspiration of the apostles.*

This perfect character of Christ they have left on record. It is perfectly delineated, not by general description, or loose unmeaning panegyric, but by filling up a plain, simple, natural history with characteristical actions and discourses, and tracing features distinct in themselves, and yet harmonious, blending into one complete whole, totally distinguished from every other character hitherto drawn by man; as unlike, nay, much more unlike, any other person ever seen or heard of in this world, than that of Hamlet, Lear, Achilles, or Hector.

Attempts to form such a character as should be acknowledged to be perfect, have been often made, but they have invariably failed of success. The efforts of the heathen philosophers and poets to paint their wise and perfect men are well known to be miserably imperfect. The Æneas of Virgil is a picture of this kind, but, notwithstanding the genius of the writer, is so far from perfection, as not to be even amiable, but gross, vicious, and hateful. The *wise man of philosophy* is little better; for he is impious, proud, impure, false, and unfeeling. Infidels have succeeded no better; and even Christians have been compelled to derive all that is good and commendable in the characters drawn by them from the very record left by the apostles, the life, precepts, and doctrines of Christ.

Whence, then, were these men able to perform a task too hard for all the rest of their fellow-men? Plainly, not from learning, for they had none; not from genius, for in this most of them were evidently excelled by many others; not from the examples furnished to them in their own Scriptures: Abraham, the most perfect example of this nature exhibited at length, is wonderfully inferior to the character of Christ, although wonderfully superior to the best men of heathen antiquity. All the saints of the Old Testament could not, were their excellencies united, supply the most ingenious mind with materials out of which the life of Christ could be formed, even by such a mind. Nor could all the doctrines contained in that invaluable book enable such a mind to originate, by its own powers, the instructions of Christ. The character is not only superior but singular. The wisdom is not only greater, more various, and more satisfactory, but it is wrought into forms, communicated in discourses, and started by incidents, all of which are too particular, too natural, and too appropriate to admit, not the belief merely, but the possibility of their having been compiled. The character is perfectly new and original, like nothing which preceded and nothing which has succeeded it. At the same time it is all of a piece, every

part being suited exactly to every other part, and all the parts
to the whole.   As this character could not have been formed
by the apostles, without an actual example, it was equally
impossible that it should have been formed, *at the time* when
they wrote, with the aid of such an example.   The Gospel of
St. Matthew was, according to the earliest computation,
written, as I formerly observed, eight years after the death of
Christ.   How plainly impossible was it that he should have
remembered Christ's Sermon on the Mount, his Parabolical
Sermons, or his discourses concerning the destruction of
Jerusalem and the final judgment?   How evidently impossible is it, that he should have made them?   Who could make
them now?   Compare them with the noblest efforts of Socrates,
Plato, Aristotle, and Cicero.   Who now, what peasant, what
beggar, what child of twelve years of age, would take their
discourses as his creed, as the directory of his conscience, as
the law of his life?   But the discourses of Christ were the
creed, the wisdom, the boast, the glory of Bacon, Locke,
Newton, Butler, Boyle, Berkeley, Addison, and Johnson.
Can it be imagined that the Jewish publican possessed a mind
sufficiently sublime and capacious, sufficiently·discerning and
pure, to command the admiration, belief, and obedience of
these great men?   Can it be believed that, with all the wisdom
of the world before them, and their own superior understanding to direct their choice, they, and ten thousand other enlightened men, should bow with a single heart and voice to
precepts and instructions devised by the mere native abilities
of this uneducated inhabitant of Judea?

But if Matthew could not have devised nor remembered
the life and discourses of Christ, what shall be said of John?
His Gospel was written about fifty years after the death of the
Saviour, and contains more, and more wonderful discourses of
this glorious Person.   All these also are exhibited as springing out of appropriate occasions minutely specified, and are
exactly fitted to each occasion.   The writer, it is to be remembered, was a fisherman on the lake Gennesaret, and followed
this business some time after he arrived at manhood.   A mere
fisherman, therefore, wrote the Gospel of St. John.   Suppose
the experiment were now to be made.   Suppose an American
fisherman, who had read the Bible from his childhood, were to
be employed to form a new Gospel, and to delineate anew, as

particularly as John has done, the life and discourses of such a person as Christ, both of them to be drawn wholly from the stores of his own mind. What must we, what must all men be obliged to believe would be the result of his efforts? Undoubtedly, the same narrow-minded, gross, and contemptible compound which we now and then behold in a pamphlet, written by an ignorant man, which scarcely any person reads through, unless for the sake of seeing what such a man can write ; a production devoid of understanding, wisdom, incident, character, entertainment, and thought ; a trial of patience, a provocative of contempt and pity. Such, all analogy compels us to believe, must have been the Gospel of St. John, had it been devised by the mere force of his own mind.

That he could have remembered the incidents and discourses contained in it, after the lapse of fifty years, I need not attempt to disprove ; since it was never believed, and will never be believed by any man.

But the Gospel of John was written by a fisherman : the writer himself declares it, and the declaration is confirmed by the testimony of all antiquity. Read this book, consider the sublime and glorious wisdom which it contains, and the wonderful life which it records, and then tell me whether the supposition, that it was revealed, or that it was written without revelation, involves the greater miracle.

SERMON LIII.

THE PRIESTHOOD OF CHRIST.

HOLINESS OF HIS CHARACTER.

IMPORTANCE OF THIS ATTRIBUTE TO THE DISTINCTION OF HIS CHARACTER, &c.

FOR SUCH AN HIGH PRIEST BECAME US, WHO IS HOLY, HARMLESS, UNDEFILED, SEPARATE FROM SINNERS, AND MADE HIGHER THAN THE HEAVENS.

HEBREWS VII. 26.

In the two preceding Discourses I have considered *the personal holiness of Christ,* in its three great divisions of *piety, benevolence, and self-government.* I shall now proceed to a discussion of the second head of discourse, originally proposed concerning this subject, and endeavour to

Explain the importance of this attribute to Christ, as the high priest of mankind.

I wish it to be distinctly remembered, that I am not inquiring why personal holiness or inherent moral excellence, was necessary to Christ. Personal holiness is indispensable to every rational being in order to his acceptance with God, being no other than the performance of his duty in whatever situation he is placed. My inquiries respect solely the necessity of Christ's manifesting to the world his holiness of character in a life of perfect obedience, such as he actually exhibited.

Christ might have become incarnate, and died immediately, and yet have been a perfectly holy being.   I ask here why it was necessary for him, as the high priest of men, to exhibit such a life as he actually lived.

The pre-eminent holiness of Christ was, in this character, necessary to him.

I. *To give him that distinction which was indispensable.*

We are so accustomed to regard Christ as an extraordinary person, as hardly to ask for any reason why this peculiarity of character was necessary to him, or what influence it had, or was intended to have, on his priesthood.   I shall not be able to do justice to this subject, yet I will suggest a few considerations which have occurred to me at the present time.

It will be readily believed by all persons who admit the priesthood of Christ, that this office was the most important ever assumed in the present world.   He who has expiated the sins of mankind, and opened the way for their reconciliation to God, their restoration to holiness, and their introduction to heaven, has undoubtedly sustained the most important character, and performed the most important acts which have been ever known to the human race.   That a person of whom these things can be truly said must be rationally supposed to be separated from the rest of mankind, by many marks both of personal and official distinction, is an assertion which needs no proof.   All men are by the very nature of the case prepared to admit beforehand, that he who is destined to so extraordinary an office must also possess an extraordinary character.

The Jews, led by the several predictions given in their Scriptures concerning the Messiah, and perhaps in some degree, also, by the nature of the case, formed concerning him apprehensions generally of this nature.   They mistook, indeed, the things by which his personal character was to be distinguished, but were perfectly correct in their belief, that his character was to be singular, as well as his office.   His life, in their view, was to find its peculiar distinction in external splendour, conquest, and dominion over all nations, who were to be subjugated by his arm.   He was to reign with a glory utterly obscuring that of every preceding conqueror, and was to divide among them, his favourite people, the pomp, wealth, and power of this lower world.   To them as ' the people of the saints of the Most High,' was, in a literal sense, to be ' given the kingdom and dominion, and the greatness of the kingdom under the whole heaven.'   To a people, conquered as they were, impatient of their yoke, panting for liberty and independence, proud of their pre-eminence as the chosen people of God, gross in their conceptions of divine truth, and confining, with an animal relish, all real good to the gratifications of sense, it can scarcely seem strange, that this should appear a rational interpretation of the prophecies concerning the Redeemer, particularly of some, which are couched in terms highly figurative.   From such a people, in such a state, we could hardly expect just apprehensions concerning those sublimer glories of the Messiah which lay in excellence of mind, and excellence of life, obtained the unmingled complacency of the Father, and called forth the admiration, love, and homage of all the virtuous among mankind.   Still even the expectations of the Jews accord with the general truth, that he who sustains *such an office*, must also possess a *character* suited to that office.

The necessity of this character, to give distinction to Christ as the high priest of mankind, appears in a striking manner from several considerations.   Particularly, it was indispensable to the *accomplishment of the end of his priesthood*; and, therefore, *of his whole mediatorial office*, that he should *engage*, to a great extent, *the attention of mankind*.   On this, in a great measure, depended the importance and success of his public ministry, both among his contemporaries, and among men of all succeeding ages.   Had he not been an object of public curiosity and inquiry in his own time, his instructions, if uttered at all, must have been uttered to the rocks and the winds; and his character, unregarded in that age, would have been forgotten in the next.   Or, if we suppose a record to have been made of his instructions, they would have been the instructions of an individual, obscure, not only on account of his parentage, and the humble circumstances of his life, but on account of every thing else.   Whatever they were, however wise, pure, and unexceptionable, they would have failed to arrest the attention and command the regard of future times, because they were not enforced by a distinguished character in their author.   For extraordinary sentiments the mind instinctively looks to an extraordinary man. If Christ had not been separated from the rest of the children of Adam by singular characteristics, it would have been boldly questioned whether these instructions ever came from him ; and the record which asserted them to be his, could scarcely have been furnished with such proofs of authenticity as to place the question beyond rational doubt. If this point had been admitted, new and equally perplexing inquiries would have arisen concerning the authority of the teacher ; concerning the strangeness of the fact, that God had destined such a man to the office of giving such precepts to the world ; and concerning the irreconcilableness of so insignificant an appearance with a character distinguished by such wonderful wisdom.   Strong objections are even now made by infidels to the humble character in which Christ appeared. What would they not have objected, if he had been marked by nothing extraordinary ?

These observations respect Christ in all his offices.   Had he not possessed this distinction in some clear, acknowledged manner, and in a degree unquestioned, he would never, in any sense, have become the object of any peculiar regard ; and would, of course, have failed of the end of his mission.   The arguments already alleged are, therefore, applicable to every part of his character as Mediator.   But they are, in some respects, peculiarly applicable to his priesthood.   A great part of the truths which he taught respected himself, as the high priest of the human race.   These were truths indispensable to the salvation of mankind.   The atonement made by him in this office for the sins of men, is the only foundation even for the hope of eternal life.   The belief of men in this great fact is the basis of all our confidence in Christ as our Saviour ; and this confidence is the only mean of our justification.   But in this fact few men, to say the most, can be supposed to have believed, had not Christ been distinguished from other persons by peculiar and very honourable characteristics.   There is something so repugnant to all our most rational and satisfactory thoughts, in the supposition that a person, ranking in all things with such beings as we are, should sustain this glorious office, and accomplish this marvellous end, that it can hardly be imagined to have gained admission into the mind of any sober man.

Should it by answered, that *a distinction of some kind or*

other, in the degree specified, was indeed necessary to the character of Christ, in order to render him the object of the confidence or even the attention of mankind, but that *this distinction was sufficiently established by his power of working miracles,* so often and so illustriously exemplified while he was in the world ; I answer, that this power distinguished Christ from other inhabitants of the earth very honourably, but could not distinguish him sufficiently for the purpose in view.   For, to say nothing of the fact, that in this respect he was not sufficiently unlike Moses and Elijah, who also wrought many and great miracles, or his apostles, who ' did greater works than ' his own ; to say nothing of the contrariety to all rational thinking in the supposition that a man, invested with no other proofs of an extraordinary character, should work such stupendous miracles, or any miracles at all, it is perfectly evident, that he could never be the object of any *moral* regard, unless in his moral character he had appeared sufficiently important to claim it, much less of that *supreme* moral regard, *evangelical faith.*   In the exercise of this faith, the soul surrenders itself absolutely into the hands of Christ.   But such a surrender cannot be made, unless to a being of such consequence as to make the act rational and warrantable in the view of the understanding.   But the understanding can never be persuaded that a person undistinguished by pre-eminent holiness, however superior might be his natural or supernatural endowments, could be regarded by God as an acceptable propitiation for its sins.   Nor could it by any means of which I am able to conceive, feel itself warranted to exercise this confidence toward any being unpossessed of that consummate rectitude, particularly of that sincerity and good-will upon which it is ultimately founded.   If Christ had not in this respect been superior to other men, the faith placed in him would, I think, have been the same with that which is placed in other men, and have differed from that neither in kind nor degree.

Holiness is the supreme distinction of moral beings, and the supreme object of moral regard, especially, in all cases, where the approbation and acceptance of God, or the confidence of intelligent creatures, are concerned.   Is this the object on which our thoughts ultimately rest, in comparison with which all others are of little importance ?

II. *To enable him to magnify the law of God, and make it honourable.*

Christ performed this important office, an office predicted by the prophet Isaiah, and also by himself, many ages before his incarnation, in a manner absolutely perfect. The following particulars will, if I mistake not, illustrate this subject with advantange.

1. *Christ in his own obedience showed that the law was capable of being perfectly obeyed by mankind.*

By this I mean, that beings possessing exactly such natural powers as we possess are, if properly disposed, proved by the obedience of Christ to be capable of perfectly obeying the law of God.

There is no reason to believe that Christ possessed any other natural powers than those which are possessèd by mankind generally. The difference between him and them lay, radically, in the disposition ; *his* being that of a dutiful child, and *theirs* being froward and rebellious. With these powers Christ perfectly obeyed the law of God, and thus proved that it might be perfectly obeyed by any other person possessing the same powers. No difference of intellect can be pleaded here ; because Christ thus obeyed in every stage of his life ; with the intelligence of an infant, of a child, of a youth, and of a man. The least degree of intelligence which he possessed after he became a moral agent is, therefore, sufficient to enable any other moral agent thus to obey. The difficulty of obeying experienced by us does not, therefore, lie in the want of understanding.

The importance of this article will be easily realized, if we call to mind how prone we are to justify ourselves in sin, and to feel secure from the danger of punishment, from the consideration, that we have not, naturally sufficient power to obey ; and if, at the same time, we remember that, even to the present day, not only ordinary men and plain Christians, but even philosophers and divines, hold this doctrine, and insist on it as a part of their customary instruction. The proof here furnished, that the doctrine is wholly erroneous, is complete ; for it can never be said, that the mind of Christ at its entrance upon moral agency possessed more intelligence, and more natural ability to obey, than that of a mature man. Christ obeyed throughout his infancy and childhood.   Bacon, Newton, and Locke were sinful beings.   The reason why they were sinful beings was not a defect of intelligence.   The difference between them as moral beings, and Christ while an infant or a child, was a moral difference, involved moral turpitude on their part, and rendered them deserving of blame and punishment.

In this manner Christ proved the practicability of obedience, and the reasonableness of the law.   If he, with the same natural powers which we possess, could obey the law, obedience is naturally and certainly practicable to us.   If Christ obeyed while an infant, or a little child, the requisitions of the law cannot be unreasonable.   The *importance of his glorifying the law*, in this respect, needs no illustration.

2.   *Christ, in obeying, furnished mankind with an extensive and most useful comment on the law of God.*

A moment's recollection will show us, if we need to be shown, that the nature of all precepts is more perfectly seen in those *actions* which are *conformed to them*, than it can be in the *abstract contemplation* of the precepts themselves. The life of Christ was exactly conformed to the precepts of the divine law, and was, therefore, a more perfect exhibition of their true nature than any other of which they were capable. It was, particularly, a perfect exhibition of the *nature* and *extent* of every requirement, so far as it was applicable to *him*.   In seeing what *he did*, we learn exactly what *we* are required to *do ;* more exactly than we could possibly learn from the precept itself.

It exhibited, also, the *beauty* and *excellency* of obedience. This is discerned very imperfectly in the mere contemplation of the precept by which it is required.   That application of the precept, through which alone its proper influence can be discerned by mere contemplation, is made so imperfectly and seen so obscurely by the mind, that the proper efficacy of the precept cannot, in this way, be ever realized.   In *example*, in *actions*, on the contrary, the true nature, the beauty, the desirableness of the wise and good precepts by which such actions are governed, are distinctly perceived and comprehended. The example of Christ is, beyond debate, far the most amiable and glorious of all the moral objects ever exhibited to mankind.   At the same time, it is an exact display of the nature and influence of the precepts of the divine law, as being no other than a course of mere obedience to them.

Thus Christ has taught us what it is to obey the law of God ; what conduct is obedience, in every situation in which he was placed ; in what respects, within what limits, and to what degree, obedience is to be exhibited ; what words we are to use, what actions to perform, what affections to indulge, and to discover ; and when, or how far, we are to withhold, to restrain, and to deny them all. These several things, also, he has taught us with a distinctness and perfection of which all other instruction is incapable. At the same time, he has shown us the beauty and loveliness of obedience in the strongest colours, divinely fair, divinely amiable ; beheld by God the Father with infinite complacency, and admired. loved, and adored with supreme regard by angels and good men.

3. *Christ in his obedience has made the law honourable, because it was the obedience of a person possessed of infinite dignity.*

I have formerly, and, as I flatter myself, with success, attempted to show, that Christ was God as well as man. In these united natures he was one person ; and all his actions were the result, not only of human views and affections, but of a divine approbation and choice ; of a created mind voluntarily devoted to perfect rectitude and to perfect truth, and thus coinciding in the most exact manner with the will of God ; and of the divine wisdom, complacently regarding all the dictates and conduct of this mind, and concurring with it in every affection and effort. The obedience of Christ is the obedience of this glorious person.

As Christ is a person of *infinite knowledge,* it is impossible that he should not discern with entire exactness the propriety or impropriety of becoming *a subject* to the law of God, in the character of Mediator. In conformity to this perfect discernment he became such a subject. In this character he discerned with the same exactness the propriety or impropriety of all the conduct presented, by the circumstances in which he was placed, to his view ; and of course the propriety or impropriety of his absolute obedience to the divine law. But in this manner he actually obeyed.

The *infinite rectitude* of Christ prompted him to that conduct, and that only which in all respects was right. But, under the influence of this rectitude, he became subject to the law ; and, when he had become a subject, conformed his whole life, in every minute as well as every important particular, to the precepts of that law. In this manner he showed with the most decisive evidence, the evidence of life and conduct, that infinite knowledge and rectitude dictated to him to assume the office of Mediator, to become a subject of the divine law, and in that character to yield to its precepts an universal and perfect obedience.

Christ is a person of *infinite dignity*. By this I mean, not only the splendour of moral and intellectual greatness with which his character is invested, but the dignity also which is conferred by omnipotence, eternity, and immutability, and by supremacy of station and dominion. With this transcendent exaltation over all things in heaven and in earth, he still chose to become subject to the divine law ; and as a subject to obey every one of its precepts which at any time respected either his character or his conduct. Thus he taught, in a manner which cannot be questioned, and with a decisiveness allowing of no doubt, that infinite knowledge and rectitude regarded the divine law as possessing such infinite excellence and glory, that it was not unbecoming a divine person to conform his own actions to its dictates, even in the minutest particulars ; that it was not unsuitable to a divine person to become subject to its controul, and in this state of subjection to obey its precepts in an absolute manner.

These considerations exhibit my own views of that *active obedience or righteousness* of Christ, by which we are said in the Scriptures to be *justified*. Christ, as a *mere man*, was of necessity subject to the law of God equally with all other moral creatures. His obedience in this character, therefore, was necessary to his own justification, and could not be the means of ours. As a *divine person*, he was subject to no law, and needed and could need no justification. By the union of his divine and human natures he became *one person*, as Mediator between God and man ; in such a sense *one*, that all his actions and sufferings became the actions and sufferings of this one Mediator. The value which was inherent in his conduct as a divine person, was in consequence of this union extended to all the conduct of the Mediator, Jesus

Christ. When, therefore, this glorious person voluntarily yielded himself as a subject of the divine law, the act was the result of infinite knowledge and rectitude, and was in-stamped with the worth necessarily belonging to all the de-terminations and conduct to which these perfections give birth. The same moral excellence and glory are attached to all the acts of Christ's obedience, subsequent to his assumption of the character of a subject. Every one of them is an act of the Mediator; and derives its true worth and importance from the greatness and excellency of his personal character.

As Christ assumed the office of a Mediator and the condition of a subject voluntarily, as he was originally subject to no law, and could be required to yield no act of obedience, he could, if he pleased, become with propriety *a substitute for others*, and perform in their behalf vicarious services which, if possessing a nature and value suited to the case, might be reckoned to their benefit, and accepted in their stead. Had these services been due on his own account, and necessary to his own justification, as all the services of intelligent creatures are, throughout every moment of their existence, they could never have assumed a vicarious character, nor have availed to the benefit of any person, at his final trial, besides himself. Now, the services of the real Mediator were all gratuitous; demanded by no law, and in no sense necessary to the justification of himself. All, therefore, that could in this case be required, to render them the means of justification to others, must be these two things only; that they should be of such a kind as to suit the nature of the case, and that they should be of sufficient value.

That the actual services of the Mediator were suited to the real nature of the case, we know; because they were pre-scribed and accepted by the Father. We may also be satis-fied of this truth by the manner in which the subject is exhi-bited by the Scriptures. The law of God is there declared, as it is also by the nature of the fact itself, to be dishonoured by the transgressions of men. This dishonour, as is evident from both these sources of information, is equally done to the character and government of the lawgiver. To pardon the transgressors in this case would be to consent to the dishonour, and to acknowledge practically that the law which they had transgressed, the character of the lawgiver who prescribed it, and the government founded on it, were unreasonable and unjust.   It would be to declare, and that in the most solemn manner, that such obedience as was enjoined by the law could not be demanded nor expected by a righteous and benevolent lawgiver.   But this declaration would be false ; and could therefore never be made on the part of God.

But, when Christ offered himself as the substitute for sinners, he ' restored,' to use his own language, ' that which he took not away.'   He restored that honour to the divine law, character, and government which men had refused to render; and removed the dishonour done to them all by their disobedience.   Nay, he did much more.   In obeying the precepts of the law, he testified that they were such as infinite perfection was pleased to obey; that the government founded on them, and the character of him who published them to the universe, as the rule by which he intended to govern it for ever, were of the same glorious and perfect nature.   This testimony none but Christ could give.   A testimony of equal weight the universe could not furnish.   Thus, in a manner which nothing else could rival, ' he magnified the law, and made it honourable,' according to the prediction of God by the Prophet Isaiah, in the sight of angels and men.

The influence of this conduct of Christ upon the future obedience of virtuous beings could not fail to be supreme. What creature, however exalted, can refuse to be subject to that law to which the Son of God voluntarily became subject? Who can deny those precepts to be reasonable, all of which *he* exactly and cheerfully obeyed?   Who can hesitate to believe that law to be ' holy, just, and good ;' who can doubt that it is infinitely honourable to its Author, and supremely beneficial to the universe, when he knows and remembers that a person of infinite knowledge, rectitude, and dignity of his own accord submitted both his affections and his conduct to its absolute controul.   So far as I can see, higher glory was reflected on this great rule of righteousness by the obedience of Christ, than could have resulted from the united obedience of the whole intelligent creation.

It is hardly necessary to observe, that the obedience of Christ and his *holiness* are convertible terms, and that all the importance of the things mentioned under these three heads, is no other than the importance of this attribute to his priestly character.

III. *To give the necessary efficacy to his sufferings for mankind.*

The sufferings of Christ were of no value as mere sufferings. There is no worth or excellence in the mere endurance of evil. The real merit of the sufferings of Christ, as of all other meritorious sufferings, lay in these two things ; that they were undergone for a valuable end, and that they were borne by a good mind with the spirit of benevolence and piety. The end for which Christ endured the cross, and all the other evils of his humiliation, was the best of all ends, the glory of God, and the salvation of men. The mind of Christ is the best of all minds ; and the spirit with which he encountered and sustained his sufferings, was that of supreme benevolence and supreme piety.

In undertaking the office of a Mediator between God and man, he gave the most solemn and glorious testimony to the equity of the divine law in all its precepts and in all its penalties. In enduring the sufferings which he underwent as the substitute for sinners he completed this testimony, by cheerfully consenting in this character to obey and to suffer. If he had not been perfectly holy, he would, instead of becoming a substitute for others, have needed a substitute for himself, to expiate his sins. No supposition can be more absurd than that Christ should make an atonement for the sins of others, when he needed an atonement for his own sins ; or that God should accept him as a Mediator for sinners, when he himself was a sinner ; or that he should become the means of delivering mankind from the penalty of the law, when he himself deserved to suffer that penalty.

Thus it is evident, that without consummate holiness Christ would not only have utterly failed to execute to the divine acceptance the office of a priest, but that he could not have entered upon that office.

IV. *To qualify him for executing the office of intercessor.*

Absolute holiness seems entirely necessary to render the prayers of any being, even when offered up for himself, if offered in his own name, acceptable to God. The same holiness seems even more indispensable to render intercession for others accepted, and especially for a world of sinners. Such intercession, also, appears plainly to demand, as a previous and essential qualification on the part of the intercessor, that he should acknowledge in the amplest manner the perfect rectitude of the divine government in condemning sinners to that punishment, for their deliverance from which his intercession is undertaken. It cannot, I think, be supposed even for a moment, that God would accept of any person in this office who denied, doubted, or did not, in the most open and complete manner, acknowledge the equity and propriety of his administrations. It seems farther necessary, that he who made this acknowledgment should be a competent judge of the nature of the divine government so that the acknowledgment should be made with intelligence and certainty, and not be merely a profession of faith.

The holiness of Christ, manifested in his obedience both to the preceptive and penal parts of the divine law, was the most direct and complete acknowledgment of the rectitude of the divine law and the divine government which was possible ; because it was voluntarily undertaken, and perfectly accomplished. It was at the same time the obedience of a person who was a finished judge of the nature of both, from the entire rectitude of his disposition, and the unlimited greatness of his understanding. It was also the acknowledgment of a person possessed of infinite dignity in the nature of his attributes, in the supremacy of his station, and in the eternal and immeasurable extent of his dominion.

As an intercessor, therefore, Christ comes before his Father both in the most amiable and the most exalted character ; having confirmed, beyond all future debate, the rectitude of his law and government, and supremely glorified his name in the sight of the universe, and pleading with divine efficacy both his obedience and his sufferings on the behalf of those for whom he intercedes. What must not such an intercessor be able to obtain ? From such an intercession what may not penitent sinners hope ? How plain is it, that ' such an high priest became us ; was fitted to expiate all our sins, and to secure to us ' an inheritance undefiled and unfailing,' in the everlasting love of God ; an high priest ' who was holy, harmless, undefiled, separate from sinners, and made higher than the heavens ? '

SERMON LIV.

THE PRIESTHOOD OF CHRIST.

HOLINESS OF HIS CHARACTER.

IMPORTANCE OF THIS ATTRIBUTE.

HIS EXAMPLE.

HE THAT SAITH HE ABIDETH IN HIM, OUGHT HIMSELF ALSO SO TO WALK EVEN AS HE WALKED.

1 JOHN II. 5.

IN my last Discourse I considered the importance of *the holiness of Christ* in his character of *high priest*, as being necessary to give him *that distinction, without which the attention and confidence of men could not have been excited towards him*; as necessary to enable him *to magnify the law of God*; and to become a *propitiation* and an *intercessor* for the children of Adam.

The subject which naturally offers itself next for our consideration is, the importance of this attribute to Christ, *as an example to mankind.*

That Christ was intended to be an example of.righteousness to the human race, is completely evident from the passage of Scripture which I have chosen for the theme of this Discourse. ' He that saith he abideth in him ;' that is, he who professes himself a Christian, ' ought himself also so to walk even as he walked.' Every Christian is here required to follow the example of Christ. But every man is bound to become a Christian : therefore every man is required to follow the same example. ' I have given you an example,' said our Saviour, when he washed his disciples' feet, ' that ye should do as I have done to you,' John xiii. 15. And again: ' If any man will serve me, let him follow me,' John xii. 26. ' Be ye followers of me,' says St. Paul, ' even as I also am of Christ,' 1 Cor. xi. 1. ' Let this mind be in you which was also in Christ Jesus,' says the same apostle, urging upon the Philippians the duty of humility, and arguing at length their obligation to be humble from our Saviour's example, Phil. ii. 5, &c. In the like manner he urges upon the Romans the character of benevolence, from the same source of argument, Rom. xv. 1, &c.; and the Hebrews to patience and fortitude in the Christian race, Heb. xi. 1, &c. It will be useless to multiply passages any farther to this purpose. Even these will probably be thought to have been unnecessarily alleged.

The example of Christ is formed of his *holiness* directed by his *wisdom*, or more properly by his *understanding*. Of all its parts holiness is the substance and the soul. Without this attribute he would only have been a more sagacious sinner, and therefore a more malignant example, than other men. A proper exhibition of the example of Christ, in which its nature and usefulness are sufficiently displayed for the present purpose, will, of course, be a proper exhibition of the importance of this attribute to Christ in this character.

The excellence of Christ, as an *example to mankind*, I shall attempt to exhibit under the following heads :—

I. *He was an example of all virtue.*

By this I intend, that he was an example of piety, benevolence, and self-government, alike. This truth has been sufficiently illustrated in the two first sermons on this subject. To add any thing, therefore, to what has been so lately said must be unnecessary.

1. *By the example of Christ, considered in this light, we are decisively taught that virtue is no partial character.*

The apprehension, not unfrequently entertained, that a man may love God and not love his neighbour, and yet be a virtuous man, that is, in the evangelical sense ; the contrary upprehension, much more frequently entertained, that a man may love his neighbour and not love God; and the opinion, still more generally adopted, that a man may love both God and his neighbour, and thus be virtuous, while he yet does not confine his passions and appetites within scriptural bounds, are completely done away by the example of Christ. ' He that saith he abideth in him,' is in the text required to ' walk as he walked:' and in Rom. viii. 9, St. Paul declares, that ' if any man hath not the spirit of Christ, he is none of his.' But if any man *has* the spirit of Christ, it will dictate the same conduct which it dictated to Christ. If he is Christ's therefore, in other words, if he is a virtuous man, the subject of that holiness of which Christ was the subject, and beside which there is no virtue, he will ' walk as Christ also walked.' This is one of those commands of our Saviour which he himself has made the test of our discipleship, and of our love to him. If therefore we are his ' disciples indeed,' if we ' love him,' we shall ' keep' this ' command;' and be as he was, pious, benevolent, and self-governed, alike.

2. *Christ performed all the duties of life prompted by these three great divisions of virtue.*

This conduct of our Saviour teaches us irresistibly, that he who does not carry the virtue which he professes into practice, or who does not perform those acts, or external duties, which are the proper effusions of such a spirit as that of Christ, is not a disciple of Christ. Christ habitually prayed to God. He who does not thus pray is, therefore, not a disciple of Christ. Christ praised God, blessed and gave thanks for his food, worshipped God in his house, and celebrated all the institutions of the sanctuary. He, therefore, who does not these things, since he walks *not* ' as Christ also walked,' has *not* ' *the spirit of Christ,*' *and* ' is none of his.' Christ also universally befriended, in all the ways of justice and charity, his fellow men, by furnishing that relief to their wants and distresses which they needed. In vain will that man pretend to be his disciple who is unjust in his treatment of others, or who does not readily open his heart and his hand to relieve his fellow-creatures in their wants and distresses; or who does not, like the Redeemer also, administer to them advice, reproof, and consolation, as they need; and employ, with sincere and tender affection, all the proper means in his power to promote their salvation. Christ spoke the truth at all times with perfect exactness. No liar, no prevaricator, no sophist, can be his disciple. Christ abstained from every fraud, and from every hard bargain, from gaming, from reproaches, from obloquy, from obscenity, from jesting with sacred things, from loose and irreverent observations concerning God, his works, word, and institutions, from all ' idle words,' and from wrath, bitterness, and revenge. He who indulges himself in these, or any of these, is not Christ's disciple.

At the same time, the example of Christ in this respect teaches us in the most decisive manner, that he who performs one class of these external duties, and neglects the others, or who abstains from one class of sins, and commits another, is not a disciple of Christ. For example : a man may pay his debts, speak truth, and give alms to the poor ; yet, if he does not pray to God in his closet, his family, and the church, he is not a disciple of Christ.

Generally : the example of Christ teaches us, beyond· a debate, what may indeed be clearly proved from the nature of the subject, that virtue has not, and cannot have, a partial existence. No man can love God without loving his neighbour ; or his neighbour, without loving God ; or both, without restraining his passions and appetites. He who supposes himself to do one of these things when he does not the others, is guilty of a gross self-deception, and is employed in preventing his own attainment of eternal life.

II. *Christ was an example to all classes of men.*

It ought, I think, rationally to be expected, as plainly it ought to be most earnestly desired, that the person intended by God to be the great pattern of righteousness to mankind, should so appear, and live, and act in the world, *as to become such a pattern to men of every description.* Such a pattern Christ has in fact become ; a fact derived, in a great measure, from the *lowly circumstances* in which he was born, lived, and died.

Had our Saviour appeared, as the Jews expected him to appear, in the character of a prince and conqueror, reigning with unprecedented splendour, perpetual triumph, and universal dominion, he would, as an example, have been useful to but few of mankind, and to them in comparatively few respects. The great and splendid only would have been materially benefited, and even they in but a small part of the truly excellent human characteristics. In the seat of splendour and dominion certain exercises of virtue may be exhibited with peculiar advantage ; such, for instance, as are attendant on the just and wise administrations of government, and the honourable distributions of princely favour. But these are chiefly such as few of mankind have it in their power to imitate. Men in exalted stations, princes, nobles, and statesmen may, indeed, learn wisdom, worth, and dignity of character from these attributes, when displayed in a superior manner by persons occupying places of superior distinction. How *few* persons derive moral advantages from reading the actions of kings and conquerors recorded in general history, compared with the *multitudes* who are seriously profited by a single instance of well conducted biography ?

In the humble station which Christ actually occupied all his excellencies were and are plainly seen to have been merely *personal*, springing from nothing accidental, blended with nothing adventitious the inherent excellencies and the natural emanations of his own goodness of character, neither enhanced nor obscured by the dazzling glare of office, nor liable to any misapprehensions of ours from that prejudiced awe, that imposing veneration, with which we are prone to regard the great. The virtues of Christ were, in the strictest sense, all his own ; the excellencies of an intelligent being merely ; of a man, unincumbered with office, place, or power, or any other of those gaudy trappings, in our attention to which just views of the real character are apt to be perplexed or lost. These excellencies constitute an example for man *as such ;* and are, therefore, fitted to instruct and improve every child of Adam.

To the *great* he became a glorious pattern of that condescension, meekness, and humility which they ordinarily need, in a peculiar manner, to learn, and which, when learned, is their prime ornament and glory. When kings and nobles behold *him*, who was declared by a voice from heaven to be the beloved Son of God, and who on earth commanded the winds and the waves, and raised the dead to life, characterizing himself as ' meek and lowly of heart,' and retiring into a desert to avoid the offer of a throne, it is impossible that they should not feel, unless lost to rational sentiments, their own pride, haughtiness, and irritability strongly reproved. If they have hearts open to rational conviction, and not dead to virtuous impressions, it is impossible for them not to feel that the meekness and lowliness of mind which in the Redeemer were so excellent and exalted, must, of course, constitute the highest amiableness and exaltation of their own characters.

To men of *inferior classes*, down to the peasant and the beggar, the slave and the child, Christ is an universal example. In all the excellencies of which they are capable, or which are compatible with their circumstances, Christ has gone before them, as a glorious original, which they are required unceasingly to copy. The pattern is distinct; it can therefore be clearly seen. It is exactly suited to their circumstances; with a suitable disposition it can, therefore, be easily followed. It is faultless; and can, therefore, conduct them to no sin. It is sublime and lovely; and allures, therefore, irresistibly to virtue.

When we remember, that men of these classes constitute almost all the human race; when we remember, that among them are found almost all those who are willing to follow any virtuous example; when we remember, that Christ, by appearing and living in humble circumstances, has furnished a perfect pattern of righteousness to this part of mankind, and consulted in this efficacious manner their highest good; when we remember, that he has, at the same time, with equal efficacy, pursued the best interest of the remaining class, those in exalted stations, by recommending to them the virtues which they most need to be taught; we shall see, in the clearest manner, the perfect wisdom of the Redeemer in condescending to appear in so humble a character. ' To the Jews' this was ' a stumbling block,' to infidels it has been ' foolishness.' But the foolishness of God is,' in this as in all other respects, ' wiser than men.'

To *ministers of the Gospel* the example of Christ commends itself with peculiar energy. Christ himself was a minister of the Gospel; sent by his Father in the same manner in which he has sent them. As a ruler in his Church, as a preacher and pattern of righteousness, he is the great archetype, of which they are bound to be as exact copies as it shall be in their power to become. It ought here to be observed, that Christ, not improbably to render his example more useful to them by adapting it more to their circumstances and their capacity of imitation, has in this respect acted almost only in the character of a mere man, and not as the searcher of hearts, nor as the lawgiver of his church. Where he has acted otherwise, the distinction is so clearly and successfully made, that it may usually be understood without difficulty. His example in this, as in all his private conduct, is that of a mere though perfect man, is of course easily transferred to the practical concerns of every minister, and is both understood and followed without perplexity. Ministers, therefore, are peculiarly without excuse if they are not followers of Christ.

I shall only add on this part of the subject, that the example of Christ is to all men *authoritative*. It is not merely a bright and beautiful pattern which we are invited to copy, because this conduct will be pleasing, honourable, and useful to us ; but it is a law also ; requiring of us, with divine authority, to ' go, and do likewise.' Our obligation to obey is indispensable. Nor can any man be excused for a moment, who does not labour faithfully to resemble Christ in all the merely personal and moral parts of his character.

III. *The example of Christ was perfect.*

By this I intend, that in all cases he did exactly *that*, and that *only*, which was *right*. The truth of this observation I have sufficiently illustrated in a former Discourse. Nothing more, therefore, will be necessary on this subject at the present time than to show its application and usefulness to the concerns of mankind. Regarded in this light, Christ is to us a finished standard of moral excellence, and as such has taught us,

1. *What we ought to be*

In the progress of these Discourses, I have endeavoured to show the manner in which Christ walked, in which he glorified God, and did good to men. The two great commands of the moral law, which regulate, or should regulate, the conduct of all intelligent creatures, are, ' Thou shalt love the Lord thy God with all thy heart ; and thy neighbour as thyself.'

In conformity with the first of these commands, God held

the supreme place in his views and affections.   He came into the world to accomplish a work which his Father had appointed him.   This work, in all its parts, he steadily pursued while he was in the world ; and when he left the world his work was done ; so that he was able to say at the close of life, ' Father, I have glorified thee on earth ; I have finished the work which thou gavest me to do.'   But he did *nothing else*. When he left the world he left nothing unfinished, and nothing superadded.   The end of all which he did, or said, or thought, was the glory of his Father.   This end he accomplished, and in the pursuit left *himself* out of consideration ; cheerfully subordinating to it his own convenience, pleasure, and comfort, and cheerfully undergoing every trouble, difficulty, and danger. The whole language of his heart, on which the whole language of his life was a glorious comment, was, ' Not my will, but thine be done !'   This is the pattern which we should set always before us ; this the piety, at which we should unceasing aim.

To *mankind* also he yielded himself, to promote their comfort, relieve their distresses, and secure their salvation.   God is always glorified when good is voluntarily done to mankind, and was in this manner singularly glorified by Christ.   He taught men truth and righteousness.   He taught them all the doctrines which they needed to know, and all the duties which they were required to perform, for the attainment of eternal life.   At all times he prayed for them, even while he was agonizing on the cross ; and wrought for them, with extreme self-denial, many wonderful and beneficent miracles.   In a word, he lived in such a manner, that even his hard-hearted, unbelieving, and malignant countrymen were compelled to say, ' He hath done all things well.'

In the mean time, *he did nothing ill.*   He never omitted a duty nor committed a sin.   He was neither idle, nor vain. He neither flattered nor slandered, neither deceived nor defrauded, neither corrupted nor neglected his fellow-men.   By their favour he was not enticed, by their resentment he was not awed.   His mind indulged no wrath, his bosom harboured no revenge.   Boldly and uniformly, without fear and without fondness, he told the truth, and did that which was kind, just, and right.

To friends he was never partial, to enemies he was never

resentful. In his virtues he was not rigid, in his doctrines not severe, in his worship not superstitious; but in all was rational, gentle, meek, faithful, self-possessed, and sublimely excellent.

He was born in an age in which ' pure, undefiled religion' had wonderfully decayed, and given place to an almost absolute round of superstitious and vain externals. Whenever men rely on these observances for acceptance with God, they resign of course all ideas of internal purity. He who expects that *washing his hands* will give him a title to heaven, will never concern himself with *cleansing his heart*. In such a state of things, wickedness of every kind will triumph; all the doctrines of Religion will be modelled to the views and feelings of those who practise it; and the whole system of faith will become a complication of folly, falsehood, authoritative dogmas, and implicit submissions of credulity. But in an age and country distinguished by these evils more than, perhaps, any other, Christ uniformly and victoriously resisted them all. He received no doctrine, he required his hearers to receive none, except when known and proved by unanswerable evidence to be from heaven. All his own instructions he proved in this manner. Not an instance can be produced, in which he used the argument from *authority*. In his conduct there is not an example of superstition, enthusiasm, or bigotry. Harmless enjoyments he never refused, sinful ones he never indulged. No man was the better or the worse treated by him, on account of the sect, party, or nation to which he belonged.

In his beneficence he was a glorious example to all men. His affections were literally universal, and his beneficence was an exact expression of his affections. As it was dictated by no idle dreams of philosophy, by no cobweb system of abstraction, but by plain, practical truth, it was real, useful, uniformly honourable to himself, and invariably profitable to mankind. He never spent his time in sending his thoughts abroad to distant countries, to inquire what errors, abuses, or sufferings existed there, which demanded correction, reformation, or relief. He did not sit down in the exercise of vain philanthropy, to employ life in unavailing sighs and tears for the sufferings of distant countries and ages, nor give himself up to the useless despair of doing *any* good to mankind, because he could not do *all* which their circumstances required. He did not satisfy himself with lamenting the distresses of his fellow men, and teaching others to relieve them. In a manner directly opposed to this visionary, useless philosophy, he made his whole life a life of the most active beneficence. Instead of seeking for objects of charity in Persia or at Rome, he found them in his own country, on the spot where he was, among the sufferers daily presented to his eyes. During his private life he contributed by his daily efforts to support and befriend the family of his father. Throughout his ministry he took an effectual and daily charge of his own family of disciples, and travelled unceasingly from one place to another, to find new objects on whom his kindness might be successfully employed. Thus he ' loved' mankind, ' not in word, neither in tongue, but in deed, and in truth.' The weight of his example is, in this respect, singular ; because the great purposes of his mission were more extensive, more absolutely general, than any which ever entered into the human mind. Like his views, his benevolence also was in the absolute sense universal. Yet he spent his life in doing good within the sphere in which he lived, and to the objects within his reach. Thus he has taught us irresistibly that, instead of consuming our time in wishes to do good where we cannot, the true dictate of universal goodwill is to do it where we can.

At the same time, he ' denied all ungodliness and worldly lusts.' No avaricious, ambitious, proud, or sensual desire found a place in his mind. Every selfish aim was excluded from his heart, every unworthy act from his life. Omniscience itself, looking into his soul with a perfect survey, saw nothing but pure excellence, supreme beauty, and divine loveliness ; a sun without a spot ; a splendour formed of mere diversities of light and glory.

The perfection of this wonderful example we cannot expect nor hope to attain ; but a character of the same nature we may and, if we would be interested in the favour of God, we must acquire. Like him, we must consecrate ourselves absolutely to the glorification of God. Like him, we must willingly and always do good. Like him, we must steadily resist temptation and overcome iniquity.

Obedience, and not pleasure, must be the commanding object of our purposes. The pleasure at which we supremely aim must be, not the pleasure of sense, but ' the peace which passeth all understanding;' ' the joy which no stranger meddles withal;' a self-approving mind, the consciousness of personal worth, the enjoyment of virtuous excellence, accompanied and cherished by a glorious hope of the final approbation of God, and an eternal residence in his house in the heavens.

2. *The example of Christ teaches us how far the character of mankind is from what it ought to be.*

We are often told very flattering things concerning the dignity and worth of man, the number and splendour of his virtues, and the high moral elevation to which he has attained. The errors into which we fall in forming this estimate of the human character are, together with many others respecting our own character, the consequence of referring the conduct of ourselves and our fellow-men to a false standard of moral excellence. No man ever intends to rise above the standard which he prescribes for himself; all men expect to fall below it. If the standard, then, be too low, their character will be lower still. If it be imperfect, their life will be more imperfect. If it be erroneous, their conduct, under its influence, will err still more extensively. The true aim of every man ought to be pointed at perfection. Of perfection he will indeed fall short; but his life will be more excellent than if he aimed at any inferior mark. For this reason probably, among others, the Scriptures have directed us to make the attainment of perfection our daily as well as ultimate aim.

The formation of a defective standard of excellence was one of the predominant errors and mischiefs of the ancient philosophy. The wise man of the Stoics, Platonists, and Peripatetics felt himself to be all that he ought to be, because he so grossly misconceived of what he ought to be. Proud, vain, impious to the gods, a liar, and adulterer, and even a Sodomite, he still boasted of his morality and piety, just as the Stoic boasted of his happiness while writhing under the pangs of the cholic, or the gout. The reason plainly was,, he believed all these enormities to be consistent with the character of a wise man. Cicero thought *war* (that is, the butchery of mankind, and the devastation of human happiness,) when undertaken for the love of glory, and unstained with peculiar cruelty, *justifiable.* Why? Because he had previously de-

termined *the love of glory* to be *virtue*, or the real excellence
of man, and therefore concluded that the means of indulging
and gratifying this passion must be, at least, consistent with
virtue.   In the same manner, men of all descriptions, when
they have formed to themselves a false standard of excellence,
are satisfied, if they only embrace the errors and commit the
sins which that standard allows ; and will in fact embrace more
errors, and commit more sins.

He who will compare himself with the perfect standard of
virtue furnished by the life of Christ, will see at once and
without a doubt, how far his character falls below what God
has required.   The best man living will in this case cordially
unite with Paul in exclaiming, ' O wretched man that I am !
Who shall deliver me from the body of this death ?' and with
Job, humbled by the immediate presence of God, in the
kindred exclamation, ' Wherefore I abhor myself, and repent
in dust and ashes.'   How different, will he say, is my life
from that of the Redeemer !   How different the heart from
which it has been derived !   ' To me belongeth shame and
confusion of face, because I have sinned, and done this
great wickedness.'   But to thee, O divine Saviour of men,
be *blessing, and honour, and glory, for ever and ever.
Amen.'

If such be the state of the best, in the light of this comparison, what must be the state of others ?   What of men who
feel themselves to be, not only decent, but in a good degree
virtuous, and safe ?   What shall be said of him who neglects
the worship of God in his family, or closet, who attends in the
sanctuary occasionally only, and is inattentive to the worship
when present, who neglects the relief of the poor and distressed, who justifies lying in certain circumstances, who uses
sophistry, who makes hard bargains, who preaches moral
essays, effusions of genius, and metaphysical disquisitions,
instead of. the Gospel, and himself, his resentments or his
flattery, instead of Christ, who wastes his time in light and
fanciful reading, or devotes life to amusement, instead of duty ?
All these, and all other similar persons, are contrasts to the
character of Christ, and not resemblances.   They ' walk ' not
' as Christ walked.'   ' The same mind ' is not in *them*, ' which
was in Christ.'

The meek and lowly virtues were peculiarly the virtues of

the Redeemer.　By this I mean, that he exhibited them most frequently, urged them most extensively and forcibly, and described his own character as being formed of them in a peculiar degree.　The proud, therefore, the vain, the insolent, the wrathful, and the revengeful are irresistibly compelled, when they read his character, to know that they are ' none of his.'

IV. *The example of Christ was highly edifying.*
By this I intend, that it was of such a nature as strongly to induce and persuade mankind to follow him.　On this part of the subject, interesting as it is, I can make but a few observations.

1. *The example of Christ was singular.*　No other corresponding with it has ever appeared in the present world. The best of men are only faint and distant copies of his excellence.　When exhibited by him it was a novelty, and has since been always new, as well as always delightful.　In this view, it is formed to engage attention, and command a peculiar regard.

2. *It was the example of an extraordinary person;* who taught wonderful wisdom, lived a wonderful life, and wrought wonderful miracles.　Such a person naturally compels, beyond any other, our admiration and respect; an admiration mightily enhanced by a consideration of the circumstances in which he was born and lived, the humble education which he received, the lowly condition and character of those with whom he consorted, the superiority of his precepts and life to those of all who went before him, and their total opposition to those of his own contemporaries.　All these considerations lead us to a full and affecting conviction, that his wisdom was self-derived, and his life the mere result of his own unrivalled virtue. Accordingly, all these facts astonished those who lived around him, and have filled with wonder men of every succeeding age.

3. *The example of Christ was an example of benevolence only.*　All his employments were directed to no other earthly end than the promotion of human happiness.　His miracles were directed only to such objects as feeding the hungry, healing the sick, giving sight to the blind, and restoring life to the dead.　His precepts and his life terminated in illuminating the

soul, diminishing the power of sin, invigorating virtue, and securing the salvation of men.

4. *It was the example also of a person struggling with suffering and sorrow, unceasing obloquy and bitter persecution.* The heathen could say, " The Gods themselves behold not a nobler spectacle than a good man firmly enduring adversity." Christ was supremely good, and encountered extreme adversity. The patience with which he submitted, and the firmness with which he endured, invest his character with a greatness to which there is no parallel. The fire of persecution, instead of consuming him, merely lent its gloomy lustre to show the splendour of the object which it surrounded.

5. *It was the example of a person employed in accomplishing the greatest work, which was ever done, and introducing into the universe the most extensive good which it ever beheld.* There is a moral grandeur, a divine sublimity in this employment of Christ, at which the mind gazes with wonder, and is lost ; which angels behold with amazement and rapture, and which eternity itself will hardly be able to unfold to a created understanding.

6. *It was the example of a person devoting all his labours, and undergoing all his sufferings, for the benefit of others, and proffering with an open hand the immense good, which he procured at an immense price, to strangers, sinners, apostates, enemies to himself, and children of perdition.* Not for himself, but for guilty, ruined men, he was born, lived, laboured, suffered through life, and expired on the cross. To every one who is willing to be like him he shut the prison of woe, and opened the gates of heaven.

7. *It is an example in itself pre-eminently beautiful and lovely.* His meekness, gentleness, humility, compassion, and universal sweetness of disposition, are not less distinguished than his greatness and glory. Solomon, beholding his character in distant vision, exclaimed, ' He is the chief among ten thousand, and altogether lovely !' David, in prophetic view of the excellence of his life, exclaimed, ' Thou art fairer than the sons of men.' God the Father, beholding him with infinite complacency, announced his character to the world with a voice from heaven, ' This is my beloved Son, in whom I am well pleased.' To these divine declarations all virtuous beings have subjoined their Amen.

Finally: *It is an example in which divine wisdom and excellence united with the most perfect human mind, coinciding with all its designs, and guiding it to unmingled excellence.* To the amiableness and beauty of the most finished created virtue, were superadded and united the authority and greatness of the Divinity, by which that mind was inhabited.

The combination, therefore, was a combination of all that is lovely with all that is awful, exalted, and divine. What mind that can be persuaded from sin must not this example persuade? What mind that can be allured to holiness must not this example allure?

SERMON LV.

THE PRIESTHOOD OF CHRIST.

HIS ATONEMENT.

BEING JUSTIFIED FREELY BY HIS GRACE THROUGH THE REDEMP-
TION THAT IS IN JESUS CHRIST. WHOM GOD HATH SET FORTH
TO BE A PROPITIATION, THROUGH FAITH IN HIS BLOOD, TO DE-
CLARE HIS RIGHTEOUSNESS FOR THE REMISSION OF SINS THAT
ARE PAST, THROUGH THE FORBEARANCE OF GOD. TO DECLARE,
I SAY, AT THIS TIME, HIS RIGHTEOUSNESS; THAT HE MIGHT BE
JUST, AND THE JUSTIFIER OF HIM WHICH BELIEVETH IN JESUS.
ROMANS III. 24—26.

IN a former Discourse I proposed to consider, as parts of the Priesthood of Christ, the *holiness* of his character;——the *sacrifice* which he offered for sin;——and, the *intercession* which he makes for sinners.

The first of these subjects has been examined at length. The present Discourse shall be occupied by the second, *viz.*

THE SACRIFICE OF CHRIST FOR THE SINS OF MEN.

In considering this subject I shall endeavour to show,
I. *The nature,*
II. *The necessity,*
III. *The existence of an atonement for sin,*
IV. *The manner in which it was performed,*
V. *Its extent.*

I. *I shall attempt to show the nature of an atonement.*
The word *atonement*, in its original sense, always denotes

some amends or satisfaction for the neglect of some duty, or the commission of some fault ; a satisfaction with which, when supposed to be complete, the person injured ought reasonably to be contented, and to demand of the offender nothing more on account of his transgression. This satisfaction may, in certain cases, be made by the offender himself. Whenever he has owed some piece of service, and this was all he has owed, he may, if he have failed to perform this duty, atone for the fault by a future service, which he did not owe, and which is equivalent to that which he neglected, and to the damage occasioned by his neglect. A servant, who owes an estimated day's work to his master every day, may, if he have neglected to work half a day, atone thus for his fault, by such future labour as shall be equivalent to the extent of his neglect, and to the injury occasioned by it to his master. In this case it will be seen, that the atonement respects only the fault which has been committed. The servant owed his master so much labour : the payment of so much labour would be a discharge therefore of the debt. But we do not say, that the debt in this case is atoned. The fault only which has been committed, in neglecting or refusing to pay in the proper season and manner, demands or admits of an atonement. In every other case where an atonement exists, it is in the same manner a satisfaction for an injury or fault.

In some cases, the party offending cannot atone for his offence, but the atonement, if made at all, must be made vicariously, that is, by the intervention of a third person between the offender and the offended. Of this nature is every case, of which the offender owes as absolutely every duty which he could afterwards perform, as he owed that, the non-performance of which constituted his fault. In this case, all his future efforts are necessarily due for the time being, and can, therefore, never become a satisfaction for faults which are past. Amends for any injury can never be made by services which are due to the injured person on other grounds, and the refusal of which would constitute a new injury. In other words, they must be services rendered only on account of the injury already received. He, therefore, who owes to another all his services for himself, can never become the means of atoning to him for the faults of another. In all cases of vicarious atonement, the substitute must be under no personal obligation to render the services which are to be accepted as a satisfaction of the *principal,* or in other words the *offender.* Nothing is more plain, than that which is due to *himself,* cannot be transferred to the account of *another.*

In every case of personal or vicarious atonement, *the services rendered must be of such value as to become a reasonable and full satisfaction for the injury done;* all that justice can fairly demand or render ; such as will place the person injured in as good a situation as that which preceded the injury. Where the injury has been great, therefore, or multiplied, the services must also be proportionally great.

An *atonement for a crime,* committed against a government of any kind, *supposes the offender,* if he is to receive the benefit of it, *to be pardoned.* In this case, it must be such as to leave the government in as good a state, as firm, as honourable, as easily and certainly efficacious in its future operations, after the offender is pardoned, as it would have been, if he had been punished with exact justice. In no other manner can it become a satisfaction for the injury. If all the services of the offender, in this case, were due to the government after his crime was committed, it would be impossible for the atonement to be made, unless by another person.

Sin is a crime committed against the government of God. All the services of sinners are owed to God for the time being. No future services of any sinner, therefore, can be any satisfaction for his past sins. If an atonement be made in this case, then, it must be made by a substitute ; and this substitute must be able to render services of sufficient value to repair the injury done. In the performance of these services he must leave the divine government as firm, as honourable, as efficacious in its operations, after the atonement is made, as it was before the crime was committed.

It will perhaps be objected here, that the divine government cannot become less firm, or less honourable than it originally was, because it is supported in its full strength by infinite power and wisdom. To this objection I answer, that the government of God over his moral creatures, is *a moral government ;* that is, a government of rules and motives ; or of laws, rewards, and punishments. Such a government, even in the hand of omnipotence, may become weak and inefficacious, in the view of its subjects. A law which, after it has been violated, is

not vindicated by punishing the violator, loses of course a part
its authority. A moral governor will cease to be regarded
with veneration, if, when he is insulted by his subjects, he does
not inflict on them the proper punishment. A government of
mere power may be upheld in its full strength by the exercise
of power only. But a moral government cannot be thus preserved, unless the motives to obedience are continued to the
view of its subjects in their full force. An atonement for
sin, therefore, that is, a complete atonement, must be such as
to leave these motives wholly unimpaired. It must consist of
such services as, whatever else may be their nature, will, after
the sinners are pardoned, leave the government of God in no
degree less venerable, less efficacious, or less likely to be punc-
tually obeyed, than before the sins were committed. As these
sins have been numerous, and very great ; it is farther evident, that the services rendered as a satisfaction for them must
be of great value.

II. *I shall endeavour to show the necessity of an atonement.*

In order to understand this part of the subject, and I fore-
warn my hearers that it is a part of high importance to the subject itself, and to all just views of the Christian system, it will
be necessary to bring up to view the state of man, as a transgressor of the divine law.

The language of this law, and its only language, was,
' He that doeth these things shall live by them.'——' This do,
and thou shalt live.'——' Cursed is every one, that continueth
not in all things written in the book of the law, to do them.'
This law God published, as the rule by which his own infinite
wisdom and rectitude determined to govern the world. Of
course it is a right and just rule. Of course, also, it is a rule
which the same wisdom and rectitude are pledged to maintain
in its full force. The very reasons for which it was enacted
require, with their full strength, that it should be also maintained. If it was wise and right to enact it, it was equally
wise and right to maintain it. If to enact it was the dictate
of infinite wisdom and rectitude, to maintain it must equally
be the dictate of the same attributes.

If these observations be admitted, and it is believed that
they cannot be refused an admission, it follows of necessity,

that no sinner can be forgiven, consistently with this law, or the honour of the lawgiver, unless on the ground of an atonement. In the law he had declared, that ' the soul which sinneth shall die.' To pardon the sinner, without any change from that state of things which existed when the law was published, would be to declare, by declining to carry the sentence of the law into execution, that infinite wisdom and rectitude had formed new views concerning the sentence of the law, and the demerit of the sinner; views, contrary to those with which the law was published. When the law was published, God declared that the sinner should die. Now he must declare, by pardoning the sinner, that he should not die. Yet no change in the state of things had taken place, nor is any supposed to have taken place, to occasion this change in the divine conduct. No reason is even supposed why the conduct of God should be thus changed. The change itself must, of course, be wanton, causeless, and disgraceful to the divine character. If the law was *originally* just, it was *now* just. Justice, therefore, required the execution of its penalty upon every transgressor. In pardoning the transgressor, God would declare that the law was not just, in direct contradiction to the declaration which he made of its justice, when he published it, as the rule by which he intended to govern the world. If the law was originally *wise*, it must now be wise to execute it. But in pardoning the sinner, God must declare that the execution of the law was not consistent with wisdom. If the Law was originally *good*, that is, formed by a benevolent mind, so as to promote benevolent purposes, it was now equally good. But in pardoning the sinner, God must declare that the execution of the law was inconsistent with the dictates of benevolence. The change, therefore, manifested in the divine character and conduct, by pardoning the sinner, where no change of circumstances existed to justify it, would, on the one hand, be great and essential; no less than God's denying himself; and, on the other, would be causeless, weak, and contemptible. Can such a change be attributed, even in thought, to the immutable and perfect Jehovah?

In the law, God had manifested an infinite love to holiness, and an infinite hatred to sin; or, if the language should be preferred, a supreme love to the one, and a supreme hatred to the other. But, to pardon the sinner without any change in the state of things, would be to treat the sinner and the faithful subject exactly in the same manner, or to treat the sinner in the same manner as if he had faithfully obeyed. . Declarations made by conduct are altogether the most solemn and efficacious of all declarations. In this conduct, therefore, God would, in the most solemn manner, declare that he regarded holiness and sin alike, because he treated the sinner and the saint alike; and that neither of them was an object of his serious regard. The views of a lawgiver are always expressed in the whole of his government, taken together, and from this cannot but be distinctly understood. If his laws are unwise, *he* will be pronounced to be unwise. If his administration be unwise, he will be considered as sustaining the same character. If *either* of them be unjust, he will be pronounced to be unjust. If they be inconsistent, inconsistency will necessarily be attributed to his character. How perfect a violation would this conduct be of the attributes of justice, wisdom, and immutability!

At the same time, all subjects of the divine government would be encouraged to disobedience by these proofs of a changeable, weak, and inconsistent character. Angels, we know, *can* disobey. This is complete proof that all inferior creatures are capable of the same disobedience. Angels *have* disobeyed, when, at least, they supposed the law to mean exactly what it threatens; and without the least hope, founded on any declaration of God, of any possible exemption from the penalty actually denounced. Man also disobeyed in the same circumstances. Both also revolted when, antecedently, they had been only and perfectly holy. In these facts we have complete evidence that no class of holy beings is secure from disobedience, even under a law which gives not a single encouragement of escape to those who disobey. Should such encouragement then be holden out by the actual forgiveness, much more by the universal forgiveness, of the penitent, without an atonement, who might not be expected to rebel? Who, when temptation powerfully assailed, and the wish to sin was strongly excited, would not feel assured of his own future repentance, and his consequent safety from future punishment?

Of such beings, as men now are, it ought to be observed, that they themselves furnish ample proof of what might be rationally expected under such a dispensation. This will appear, if we consider,

1. That the atonement of Christ has completely opened the door for the exemption of all penitents from the punishment threatened by the law ; and yet, that the number of those who really repent is ordinarily very small, compared with the number of those who transgress.

2. That not even one of these becomes a penitent of his own accord, as the Scriptures abundantly assure us ; but assumes this character only in consequence of the immediate influence of the Divine Spirit upon his heart.

3. That of this number, few, very few, are ever awakened or convinced by the encouragements and promises of the Gospel ; but almost all by the denunciations of the law. The blessings of immortality, the glories of heaven, are usually, to say the least, preached with little efficacy to an assembly of sinners. I have been surprised to see how dull, inattentive, and sleepy such an assembly has been, amidst the strongest representations of these divine subjects, combining the most vivid images with a vigorous style, and an impressive elocution.

4. That those persons who disbelieve a future punishment are distinguished by a licentiousness of character, even beyond other licentious men. Repentance and religion are certainly never seen by the common eye among infidels, or universalists ; and no revival of religion, no considerable prevalence of religion, has, so far as I know, been the consequence of preaching Unitarian doctrines.

All these are direct proofs, that men who now sin so extensively and perseveringly, would, if the denunciations of the law were proved to be false, by the extension of forgiveness to sinners without an atonement, sin with a harder heart, with a bolder hand, and throughout a more uniformly guilty life.

Restraint is a necessary part of every law and every government : ' Hitherto shalt thou come, but no farther,' being invariably the language of both. All restraint is a hindrance of inclination ; a prohibition of the indulgence of desire. In itself, it is always regarded as an evil ; and is really such, whenever it does not prevent some other evil, or accomplish some good. Adam, in a state of innocence, in the end considered the prohibition of the forbidden tree as an evil. We, with sinful propensities only, should undoubtedly regard, and naturally do in fact regard, every restraint in the same manner. If, then, God were *not* to execute the sentence of the law upon us for our transgressions, but were to forgive the sinner without an atonement, we should undoubtedly sin, not only invariably, but with a boldness, constancy, and extent, not often seen even in this guilty world.

If any person should think this conclusion harsh and severe, let him remember how soon after the apostasy mankind, in the possession of long life and abundant enjoyments, forgot the loss of their immortality ; and corrupted themselves to such a degree, that the infinitely benevolent Author of their being thought it necessary to sweep away the whole human race, except one family, with the besom of destruction. Let him remember, how little reformation followed the overthrow of Sodom and Gomorrah, or the terrible plagues of Egypt. Let him remember, that the Israelites worshipped a calf at the foot of Mount Sinai ; and sunk into all the abominations of the Canaanites, as soon as the generation which destroyed them had gone to the grave. Let him remember that, amid all the judgments and mercies which they received, they apostatized from God at the end of every little period, and were finally given up, as hopeless, to captivity and ruin. Let him remember, that their descendants crucified Christ ; and that, after the sufferings of eighteen hundred years, and those extreme, they are still unbelieving, impenitent, and harder than the nether millstone. Let him remember, finally, how soon the Christian world itself degenerated into idolatry, impurity, persecution, forgetfulness of God, a general corruption of Christianity, and a general dissolution of morals. With these things in his view, it will be impossible for him to think the conclusion which I have drawn, either unwarrantable, or unkind.

But it may be said, that *although all these evils might indeed take place, if God should pardon sinners without repentance ; still the forgiveness of penitents involves no such consequence.* To this allegation, which I believe to be made by almost every human heart, I answer,

1. *The threatening of the law against transgression is absolute.* ' The soul that sinneth shall die.' In this threaten-

ing there is no mention, and plainly no admission, of repentance, as the foundation of escape to the transgressor.   If an
exception was intended to be made in favour of the penitent,
why was it not expressed, or at least hinted, by the law?
There is not, that I know, a single intimation of this nature in
any of the expressions which it contains.   Should it be said,
that, although the exception is not made in the words of the
law itself, yet it is sufficiently declared in the *comments on
the law*, given us by Moses and the succeeding prophets; I
answer, that, wherever these commentators speak of repentance, as connected with our escape from the curse of the law,
they speak of it, either as connected with the atonement of
Christ, or not.   If they mention it as connected with this
atonement, then the objector will be obliged to admit that the
atonement itself is the foundation of the penitent's escape.
If they do *not* speak of it as connected with the atonement,
then it follows, that the penitent is pardoned, under the *law*,
or legal dispensation.   An act of pardon is an act of grace;
and no act is more eminently gracious, or free.   To this grace
the Gospel can add, and does in fact add, nothing material.
' Grace,' therefore, ' came,' according to this supposition,
originally by Moses, and not by Christ; and the Gospel is
not the ' good news,' or the ' glad tidings of the grace of
God,' as it is often styled by the writers of it; because the
tidings which it professes to bring, were long before published
by the law.

Farther: It will not be in this case true, that ' Heaven and
earth shall sooner pass away, than one jot or one tittle of the
law shall pass, until all be fulfilled.'   Not only one jot or one
tittle, but the whole penal sentence of the law is, according to
this scheme, left, and will for ever be left unfulfilled; without
any other reason to forbid its fulfilment, beside what existed,
and was known to exist, at the time when it was published to
the world.

2. *The absolute threatening of the law was denounced by
God in the exercise of his infinite perfections.*   When he
denounced it therefore in this manner, that is, unconditionally,
he acted wisely and justly.   The denunciation he intended
either to execute, or not.   If he did not intend to execute it,
he acted, so far as I am able to discern, insincerely; because
in publishing it he declared, that he *would do* what he intended

not to do. If he intended to execute it, he will certainly execute it ; because no reason exists, in the case supposed, to forbid the execution, which did not exist, in this view, when he published the threatening. It will not be denied, that he foresaw every instance of repentance which would afterwards be exhibited by mankind. As God is immutable, it must, at the least, be conceded, that he cannot be supposed to change his determinations in any case, especially a case of such importance, where no reason whatever exists for the change, beside those which existed when the determination was made.

3. *The repentance of the sinner cannot be an atonement for his crime.* Repentance consists in sorrow for sin, confession of it, an acknowledgment of the justice of God in punishing it, resolutions of future obedience, and actual reformation. These things undoubtedly constitute an important change in the character of the sinner ; but they alter not the nature or degree of the guilt which has already incurred. For *this* he is condemned ; and for this, even according to his own penitential views, he has merited punishment. In what manner does his present penitence affect this guilt ? Certainly in no such sense as to lessen its degree, or desert of punishment. In what manner then can it prevent him from being punished ? Plainly in none, except that which will make amends for the evils which he has committed ; the dishonour which he has done to the law and government of God. But what is there in his repentance which can make these amends ? In what manner will it discover that the character of God, in threatening punishment to his sins, and declining, on account of a repentance originally foreseen, to inflict that punishment, was the same character ; or that God, when he threatened the punishment, and when he refused to execute it, regarded holiness and sin in one unchangeable manner ? Will his sorrow for sin make it cease to be sin ? Will the confession of his guilt make him cease to be guilty ? Will his acknowledgment of the justice of the punishment which he has deserved, make it cease to be just ? Will his resolutions of amendment, or his actual reformation, efface or lessen the guilt of his past life ? None of these things will, I suppose, be pretended. How, then, can the repentance of a sinner become a proper ground for his forgiveness and acceptance ? If he is actually forgiven

on this ground, it cannot but be seen, and will with truth be said, that God in the formation and the administration of his law has acted inconsistently ; and that either the law was unjust and unreasonable, or that his failure to execute it was unwise and dishonourable to himself. For this evil, which, for aught that appears, may be great beyond any assignable limit, this scheme furnishes, so far as I can see, no remedy.

But it may be farther asked, *Would it not be more honourable to God, or at least equally honourable to forgive the penitent without an atonement ? Whence is it, that suffering or punishment becomes necessary to the establishment of his glory in the government of the universe ?*

To these questions I answer, that it ill becomes a creature of yesterday to employ himself in contriving a government for the universe ; or a system of regulations by which the Author of the universe may direct his immense and eternal administration. Even to understand that state of things which really exists, is, in a few instances only, possible for us ; and in almost all, utterly transcends the extent of our faculties. A little child would be very absurdly employed in contriving a system of government for a kingdom, or in forming decisions concerning the wisdom or folly, the justice or injustice, by which it was governed. The universe is more disproportioned to the powers of a man, than a kingdom to those of a child ; and the government of God as absolutely transcends the comprehension of an angel, as that of a prince exceeds the understanding of a child. An attempt to answer these questions, therefore, must be, and from the nature of the case be seen to be, lame, imperfect, and in many respects unsatisfactory. Nothing more can be expected on this subject by a sober man, than a removal or diminution of some of the most obvious doubts ; and even this, perhaps, may be attempted in vain. Let it be remembered, however, that the difficulties attendant upon our inquiries in the present case arise, not from any perceptible absurdity of what we know, but from the mere inexplicableness of what we do not know ; from *the nature of the subject*, in itself free from all absurdity, but incomprehensible by such minds as ours.

With these things premised, I will suggest, as a direct but partial answer to these inquiries, the following observations :—

1. *We are prejudiced judges of this subject.* Our own

case, and that a case immensely interesting to us, is concerned. Where we have interests depending of very moderate importance, our judgments usually are partial. Here they must of course be extremely partial.

2. *No government of the universe can become the character of the Creator, except a moral government.* A government of *force* would be obviously destitute of any moral excellence, or any intellectual glory. The ruler, so far as he was obeyed, would be obeyed only from fear, and never from confidence or love. This is the obedience of a slave; as the government would be that of a tyrant. It is unnecessary to multiply words, to prove that in this case the ruler could never be reverenced nor loved by his subjects; or that his subjects could never be virtuous and amiable in themselves, or loved and approved by him.

3. *The law of God is, and must of necessity be, a rule of action for an immense multitude of beings, that is, for the whole intelligent universe, throughout eternity.* The wise and perfect regulation of this vast kingdom cannot but require a course of administration in many respects different from that by which a little part of this kingdom might, perhaps, be effectually governed. Regulations, also, which are to extend their influence through eternity, must of course differ from those whose influence is confined to a little period of time. Particularly,

4. *The motives to obedience must be great, uniform, always present, and always operative.* We well know, by familiar experience, that a little state can be kept in order by what is commonly called a very gentle administration: that is, the government may consist of mild laws, holding out motives to obedience of moderate efficacy, and an administration of those laws, presenting by its gentleness similar motives. Whereas a great empire, containing vast multitudes of people, can be successfully controlled only by what is called a more vigorous or energetic government; inducing obedience by more powerful motives, addressed unceasingly to every subject, both in the laws and in the administration. The degree, to which these motives need to be extended in the government of the universe, can be comprehended only by an unlimited understanding.

5. *All motives to obedience are comprised in natural good*

and natural evil ; that is, *in enjoyment and suffering.* As a moral government influences only by motives, and only in this way preserves the peace and ensures the happiness of those who obey ; it is plain, that these motives, found in enjoyment and suffering, must, in such a kingdom as this, possess, if its peace and happiness are to be secured, very great power; power, sufficient to accomplish the end. How great the suffering or enjoyment proposed by the law, and produced by the administration, as motives to obedience and disobedience, must be, God only can determine.

6. *A great part of all the motives to obedience in such a government is presented by the uniformity and exactness of the administration.* No state in the present world is ever well governed, is ever orderly, peaceful, and happy, under an administration inconsistent with itself ; an administration at one time rigid, at another lax ; at one time severe, at another indulgent. This is proverbially acknowledged. Such a government of the universe would, not improbably within a little time, throw its affairs into confusion; and involve its inhabitants in very extensive evil, if not in absolute ruin. If the law of God, then, were not to be executed, unless occasionally ; if its penalties were not inflicted on penitents ; this inconsistency would be seen in all its extent, and be productive of all its evil consequences. But this could not be honourable to God, nor, as it would seem, useful to his intelligent kingdom.

7. *The law of God is formed in such a manner, as to ensure, if obeyed, the supreme glory of his character, and the highest happiness of his subjects.* Nothing can be so honourable to God as to sit at the head of an immense and an eternal kingdom, composed of subjects who ' love him with all the heart, and each other as themselves ;' a kingdom therefore, of perfect order, harmony, and rectitude. But these immense blessings are secured as well as generated by this law. A law of such importance can neither be given up, nor changed in any manner, consistently with the honour of God.

8. *The advent of Christ is everywhere exhibited as fraught with peculiar blessings to mankind.* It was published by the angel to the Bethlehem shepherds, as an event the news of which were ' good tidings of great joy.' It was sung by his heavenly companions as the foundation and source of ' glory

to God in the highest, peace on earth, and good-will towards men.' But if Christ did not make an atonement for sin, it will be difficult, I presume it will be impossible, to point out or to conceive in what respect his advent was of such importance, either to the glory of God, or to the good of mankind. On this ground, he certainly was not *the means* of pardon to men; because they are pardoned without his interference. He was not the means even of *publishing* this pardon; for it had been published long before, and amply, by the prophets of the Old Testament. ' A broken heart, and a contrite spirit,' says David, ' thou wilt not despise.' ' Let the wicked forsake his way,' says Isaiah, ' and the unrighteous man his thoughts; and let him turn to the Lord, for he will have mercy on him, and to our God, for he will abundantly pardon.'

If Christ made an atonement for the sins of mankind, all the magnificent expressions concerning his mission and character, the declarations, that he is the only Saviour of mankind, and that ' there is salvation in no other,' are easily understood; if not, I am unable to see how they can be explained. Particularly, I am unable to discern how God is so solemnly said to be peculiarly glorified by the mission of Christ; for, according to this scheme, he was sent for no purpose which had not been accomplished before; and which might not, for aught that appears, have been accomplished afterwards, without his appearance in the world.

SERMON LVI.

THE PRIESTHOOD OF CHRIST.

HIS ATONEMENT.

ITS EXISTENCE:

THE MANNER IN WHICH IT IS PERFORMED:

ITS EXTENT.

BEING JUSTIFIED FREELY BY HIS GRACE THROUGH THE REDEMP-
TION THAT IS IN CHRIST JESUS. WHOM GOD HATH SET FORTH
TO BE A PROPITIATION, THROUGH FAITH IN HIS BLOOD, TO DE-
CLARE HIS RIGHTEOUSNESS FOR THE REMISSION OF SINS THAT
ARE PAST, THROUGH THE FORBEARANCE OF GOD. TO DECLARE,
I SAY, AT THIS TIME, HIS RIGHTEOUSNESS; THAT HE MIGHT BE
JUST, AND THE JUSTIFIER OF HIM WHICH BELIEVETH IN JESUS.
ROMANS III. 24—26.

IN the last Sermon I proposed to discourse on *the atonement of Christ*, under the following heads :——
I. *The nature*,
II. *The necessity*,
III. *The existence of an atonement for sin* :
IV. *The manner in which it was performed* :
V. *Its extent*.
The two first of these I considered sufficiently in that Discourse. The three last I propose to examine at the present

time; and shall proceed, without any preliminary remarks, to show,

III. *The existence of an atonement for sin.*

It is hardly necessary to observe here, that, as all our knowledge of this subject is revealed, all proofs of the fact in question must be derived from Revelation. The proofs which I shall allege, I shall arrange under the follow heads:——

1. *Those passages of Scripture which speak of Christ as a propitiation for sin.*

These are the text; 1 John ii. 2; and 1 John iv. 10. Of these, the text first claims our consideration. In the text it is declared, that God hath set forth Christ ' to be a propitiation.'

The word, here rendered *propitiation,* is ιλασηριον. This word is used only twice in the Greek Testament; *viz.* in the text, and Hebrews ix. 5. Its proper meaning is *the propitiatory,* or *mercy-seat;* as it is rendered in the latter passage. The mercy-seat in the tabernacle and temple, was the place where God manifested himself peculiarly by the Shechinah, or visible symbol of his presence; heard the prayers and accepted the offerings of his people; and dispensed to them his mercy, in answer to their supplications. The mercy-seat, we are taught in the text, was a type, of which Christ, the true ιλασηριον, was the antitype. In *him* God hears our prayers, and dispenses his own mercy to us. The mercy-seat, the place where God exhibited himself as thus propitious to mankind, was itself a mere shadow or symbol, denoting Christ; the means by which he is rendered propitious. Although the word differs, therefore, from that used in the other passages mentioned, the meaning is the same. It is accordingly rendered in the same manner by the translators.

A propitiation for sin is the means by which God is rendered merciful to sinners. Christ is here declared to be the propitiation. But the only possible sense in which Christ can have become the means of rendering God merciful to sinners, is by making an atonement for them. This atonement I have explained to consist in making sufficient amends for the faults which they have committed, and placing the law and government of God in such a situation, that when sinners are pardoned, *both* shall be equally honourable and efficacious, as before. The motives to obedience, also, must in no degree

2 c 3

be lessened.   Farther: the character of God, when pardoning sinners, must appear perfectly consistent with itself, and exactly expressed by the law.   Finally: God must be seen to be no less opposed to sin, and no less delighted with holiness, than when the law was formed.

The doctrine is completely established by the text.   God is here said to have set forth Christ ' to declare his righteousness,' or, as it is better rendered by Macknight, ' for a proof of his own righteousness in passing by the sins which were before committed, through the forbearance of God ; for a proof, also, of his righteousness at the present time, in order that he may be just, when justifying him who believeth in Jesus.'   In this passage, the end for which Christ was set forth to be a propitiation, is asserted to be, *that Christ might declare, or be a proof of the righteousness of God, in passing by, or remitting, sins which were past ; and of his righteousness, also, at the present time, when justifying believers.*   In these assertions we are taught in the most unambiguous manner, that unless Christ had been set forth as a propitiation, the righteousness of God, in remitting past and present sins, would not have been manifested.   It is also declared in the same decisive manner, that if Christ had not been set forth as a propitiation, God would not have been just, when justifying believers. Christ, therefore, in the character of a propitiation, and only in this character, has made the pardoning, or justification, of sinners consistent with the justice of God.   To pardon sinners, therefore, without a propitiation, would have been inconsistent with divine justice, and of course impossible.

The same doctrine is farther confirmed by St. John, who, in his first epistle ii. 2, and iv. 10, declares, that Christ ' is a propitiation for our sins.'   The word, used in both these passages, is *ιλασμος*; the proper English of which is ' a propitiation,' a propitiatory sacrifice, or sin-offering.   This word is often used by the Seventy ; and appropriately signifies, in their use of it, *a sacrifice of atonement.*   Thus Κριος *ιλασμου* * is a ' ram for a sin-offering ;' and *προσφιρειν ιλασμος* † is ' to offer a sin-offering.' The same signification it has, and can only have, as used by St. John.

---

* Lev. vi. 6, 7 ;—Numb. v. 8.
† Ezek. xliv. 27 -Parkhurst ;—Macknight.

2. *Those passages of Scripture, which speak of Christ as a ransom for mankind.* These are Matthew xx. 28; the corresponding passage in Mark x. 45; and 1st of Timothy ii. 6. The passage in Matthew is, ' Even as the Son of Man came not to be ministered unto, but to minister, and to give his life a ransom for many.' That in Mark is a repetition of this. That in Timothy is, ' Who gave himself a ransom for all, to be testified in due time.' The word translated *ransom* in the two first of these passages, is λυτρον; which signifies *the price paid for the deliverance of a captive from the slavery or death, to which among the ancients a captive was or might be regularly condemned.* The word in Timothy is αντιλυτρον; which, according to Estius, denoted *the ransom paid for the life of a captive, by giving up the life of another person.* The λυτρον might be *a sum of money.* But the signification in all these passages is unquestionably the same in substance; because exactly the same thing is referred to in them all. This, in the passage from Timothy, is declared to be giving up his own life for the life of sinners;' or, in other words, ' dying, that sinners might live.' I know not how the fact, that Christ made an atonement, could have been declared in more explicit, or more forcible language.

Of the same nature are all those passages, which declare, that we are *redeemed by Christ.* The Greek word, which signifies to redeem, is λυτρον; as that which signifies redemption is απολυτρωσις: both derivatives from λυτρον, *ransom.* Every one, who has read his Bible, knows, that Christ is there appropriately styled our Redeemer; and that we are often said to be ' redeemed,' and to ' have redemption,' by him. For example, Ephesians i. 7, ' In whom we have redemption through his blood.' Rev. v. 9, ' Thou hast redeemed us to God by thy blood.' Gal. iii. 13, ' Christ redeemed us from the curse of the law, being made a curse for us.' In all these, and various other passages of the New Testament, it is declared, that ' Christ redeemed us:' that is, he brought us out from the bondage and condemnation of sin ' by his blood,' and by ' being made a curse for us,' in that he died upon the accursed tree. It will be unnecessary to multiply words, to show that exactly the same thing is here taught, as in those passages, where Christ is declared to have ' given himself as a ransom.'

8. *Those passages, in which Christ is spoken of as a sub-stitute for mankind.*

These are very numerous, and of many forms. A few of them only can be recited at the present time. 'Surely,' says Isaiah, he has borne our griefs, and carried our sorrows.' 'But he was wounded for our transgressions, he was bruised for our iniquities: the chastisement of our peace was upon him; and with his stripes we are healed.' 'The Lord has laid upon him the iniquity of us all.' For the transgression of my people was he stricken.' 'By his knowledge shall my righteous servant justify many.' 'When thou shalt make his soul an offering for sin.' 'For he shall bear their iniquities.' 'And he bare the sin of many.'* These passages can need no explanation. Language cannot more clearly or more strongly assert, that Christ was a substitute for sinners; that he bore their sins, and suffered for their iniquities; or, in other words, that he became an atonement for them.

Daniel, in his ix. chapter, recites, from the mouth of Gabriel, the following words: 'Seventy weeks are determined upon thy people;—to finish the transgression, and to make an end of sins, and to make reconciliation for iniquity, and to bring in everlasting righteousness,—and to anoint the Most Holy.' In the following verse he farther informs us, that at the end of the 'seventy weeks,' the 'Messiah should be cut off, but not for himself.' Accordingly, at the end of seventy weeks, or four hundred and ninety years, 'from the going forth of the commandment to rebuild Jerusalem,' published by Artaxerxes Longimanus, the 'Messiah *was* cut off, but not for himself;' that is, within four years after he had been anointed by the Holy Ghost, according to the same prediction. The effect of his being cut off, was to make an end of sin, and to make reconciliation for iniquity.

1 Cor. xv. 3, 'Christ died for our sins, according to the Scriptures.' Here it is not only asserted, that 'Christ died for our sins;' but this fact is said to have taken place 'according to the' general tenour of the 'Scriptures.' The same doctrine is taught by Christ himself, first to Cleophas and his companion, and next to the eleven; Luke xxiv. 25, 26, 45, 46. Then he said unto them, 'O fools, and slow of heart to

* Isaiah liii.

believe all that the prophets have spoken? Ought not Christ to have suffered these things, and to have entered into his glory? Then opened he their understanding, that they might understand the Scriptures; and said unto them, Thus it is written; and thus it behoved Christ to suffer, and to rise from the dead the third day.' In both these passages our Saviour asserts his death to have been *due,* or *necessary;* because it had been before declared by the prophets, and in the Scriptures; reproves the two disciples for not thus understanding and believing the prophets; and teaches them, that this is the substance of all which the prophets had spoken; and the eleven, that to understand this great fact in a proper manner, is to understand the Scriptures themselves at large.

Gal. i. 4, ' Who gave himself for our sins, that he might deliver us from this evil world.' Hebrews i. 3, ' When he had by himself purged our sins.' 1 Peter ii. 24, ' Who his own self bare our sins in his own body on the tree; that we, being dead to sins, should live unto righteousness : by whose stripes ye were healed.' 1 John iii. 5, ' He was manifested to take away our sins.' Rev. i. 5, ' Unto him that loved us, and washed us from our sins in his own blood, and hath made us kings and priests unto God.'

In every one of these passages, as well as many others, it is evident beyond all debate, that Christ stood in the place of mankind,——bore their sins and healed them by the stripes which he suffered——that our iniquities were laid on him——that he washed our sins away——became a curse for us——was wounded for our transgressions——made reconciliation for iniquity——and was cut off, not for himself, but for mankind. The same doctrine is taught with equal precision in many other forms of expression; but, I presume, it is unnecessary to add any thing farther on this part of the subject.

4. *I argue the same doctrine from those passages, in which we are said to be ' forgiven, or ' saved,' for his sake, or in his name.*

Acts iv. 12, ' Neither is there salvation in any other; for there is none other name under heaven, given among men, whereby we must be saved.' Acts xiii. 38, ' Be it known unto you, therefore, men and brethren, that through this man is preached unto you the forgiveness of sins.' 1 John ii. 12, ' I write unto you, little children, because your sins are forgiven

you for his name's sake.'   1 Cor. vi. 11, ' But ye are washed,
but ye are sanctified, but ye are justified, in the name of the
Lord Jesus.'   Eph. iv. 32, ' Even as God for Christ's sake
hath forgiven you.

Now it is plain, that we cannot be forgiven, washed, justified, or saved, *for the sake of Christ*, unless Christ was, in
some sense or other, a substitute for us——stood in our place——
did something which we had failed to do——made amends for
faults which we had committed——or in other words, made that
atonement for sin which God was pleased to accept.   Of the
very same import are those passages of the Old Testament, in
which sin is said to be forgiven, and blessings to be bestowed,
upon mankind by God, ' for his name's sake,' or ' for his own
sake.'   In Exod. xxiii. 21, God, speaking of his own Angel,
says, ' Beware of him, and obey his voice ;' and ' provoke
him not ; for he will not pardon your transgressions : for my
name is in him.'   The Jews of ancient times considered ' the
name of God,' mentioned in a great number of passages in the
Old Testament, as being no other than one appellation of the
Messiah ; and construed those passages in which the forgiveness of sin was promised for the sake of the name of God, in
some, and probably in all instances, as intending, and really
though figuratively expressing, *forgiveness for the sake of the
Messiah*.   Thus, when in Isaiah xlviii. 9, God says, ' For my
name's sake will I defer mine anger ;' and in the 11th verse,
' For mine own sake will I do it :' when the Psalmist says,
Psalm xxv. 11, ' For thy name's sake pardon mine iniquity ;'
and Psalm cix. 21, ' Do thou for me, O God, the Lord, for
thy name's sake ;' and Psalm cxliii. 11, ' Quicken me for thy
name's sake ;' and when the church says, Psalm lxxix. 9,
' Help us, O God of our salvation, for the glory of thy name;
and deliver us, and purge away our sins for thy name's sake ;'
the phraseology is exactly equivalent to what it would be, if
for the sake of Christ, had been substituted in each of these
cases.   This, however, is not mentioned as being necessary to
the proof of the doctrine in hand ; but as evidence that the
same views of it are given us in both Testaments.

On the same ground we are required to *offer up our prayers
to God in the name of Christ*.   In John xvi. 23, our Saviour
says, ' Verily, verily, I say unto you, whatsoever ye shall ask
the Father in my name, he will give it you.   Hitherto have

ye asked nothing in my name; ask, and ye shall receive, that your joy may be full:' And again: ' At that day ye shall ask in my name:' and in John xiv. 13, 14. ' And whatsoever ye shall ask in my name, that will I do, that the Father may be glorified in the Son. If ye shall ask any thing in my name, I will do it.' See also John xv. 16. St. Paul also (Colossians iii. 17,) ' And whatsoever ye do in word or deed, do all in the name of the Lord Jesus, giving thanks to God and the Father by him.' The direction given to ·us, to offer up our prayers and thanksgivings in the name of Christ; and the promise, that in this case, and in this only, we shall be heard; teaches us in the strongest manner, that our prayers are acceptable to God for *his sake*, and not our own; and that in offering them we are to rely wholly for acceptance, and for blessings of every kind, on what he has done, and not on what we have ourselves done. Of course, the audience and acceptance which are granted, and the blessings which are given to us, are granted and given for the sake of Christ, and not for our own sakes. But no reason can be alleged, why blessings should be given to us for the sake of Christ, unless he has interfered in some manner or other in our behalf, and done something for us, which has made it pleasing and proper in the sight of God to give us blessings on this account, which otherwise he would not have thought it proper to give. If God will not give us blessings on our own account, it is undoubtedly because we have done something which renders it improper for him thus to give them. Otherwise, the same benevolence which feeds the ' sparrow' and the ' raven,' would certainly be ready to bless us. We, therefore, by our sins have forfeited our title to all blessings, and even to the privilege of asking for them. If God will give us blessings on account of Christ, it is certain that Christ has done something for us which has removed this impropriety, and which God accepts on our behalf, notwithstanding the forfeiture. In other words, he has made it consistent with the honour of the divine character and government, that the benevolence which we had forfeited, should be renewedly exercised towards us.

5. *I argue the same doctrine from the sacrifices under the law of Moses.*

St. Paul tells us, that the ancient ' tabernacle was a *figure* for the time present.' In the service performed in it, victims were continually offered, under the name of ' sin-offerings ;' and by them an atonement was made for the sins and for the souls of the people.　On this subject, the passages which declare the doctrine here specified, are found almost everywhere in Exodus, Leviticus, and Numbers, and cannot need to be repeated at this time.　But we know from the same apostle, that ' it is not possible for the blood of bulls and of goats to take away sin.'　Yet *this blood* is said, in thirty or forty passages, to be the means of making an ' atonement' for those who offered it.　In what manner was this true?　St. Paul himself has taught us that it was true in the typical, or figurative, sense only.　All these sacrifices, as he has taught us expressly in the 9th and 10th chapters of the Epistle to the Hebrews, were only types of the sacrifice of Christ; and the atonement *professedly* made by them, was only a type of the *real* atonement made by him.　Particularly, the ceremonial of the sacrifice on the great day of expiation, when the high priest made an atonement for himself, his family, the priests, and the whole congregation of Israel, was a remarkable and most lively type of the death and resurrection of Christ.　On this day, the tenth day of the seventh month annually, two goats were selected for an offering to God.　One of these was killed, and his blood sprinkled upon the mercy-seat, and before the mercy-seat, and upon the horns of the altar.　This was called making an atonement for the holy place, and reconciling the holy place, the tabernacle, and the altar unto God, as having been polluted during the preceding year, by the imperfect and impure services of sinful beings.　On the head of the living goat ' the high priest laid both his hands, and confessed over him all the iniquities of the children of Israel; and sent him away by a fit man into the wilderness.' Of this goat it was said, that ' he should bear upon him all their iniquities unto a land not inhabited.'　This religious service cannot, I think, need any explanation.

I shall now proceed to consider,

IV. *The manner in which the atonement was performed.*
On this subject I observe,

1. *That, in my own view, all the sufferings of Christ were included in the atonement which he made for sin.*

Christ was perfectly holy.　No part of his sufferings, th

fore, can have been inflicted or undergone for his own sake. He was always ' beloved' of God ; and whatever he thought, spoke, or did, was ever ' well-pleasing' in his sight.   When, therefore, we are told, that ' it pleased Jehovah to bruise him,' it was not as a punishment ; for he never merited punishment : not a wanton, causeless infliction ; for God cannot be the author of such an infliction.   It was only as a substitute for mankind that he was afflicted in any case, or in any degree ; or because he had ' laid on him the iniquities of us all.'   I understand all such general expressions as these, ' Ought not Christ to have suffered?'——' it behoved Christ to suffer'—— ' Christ must needs have suffered'——' Christ suffered for us' ——' who being rich, became poor, that ye through him might become rich'——as directly indicating, that all his sufferings were parts of his atonement.

2. *The death of Christ, together with its preceding and attendant agonies, especially constituted his atonement.*

This must, I think, have been already made evident from many passages quoted under the third head of discourse, as proofs of the existence of an atonement for sin.   I shall, however, add to these several others, which must, it would seem, place the point now in question beyond a doubt.

In the text it is said, that ' Christ is set forth as a propitiation, through faith in his blood.'   But if the blood of Christ was not the means of his becoming a propitiation, it is difficult to conceive in what sense *his* blood can be the object of our faith, any more than the blood of Jeremiah, Peter, Paul, or any other martyr to the truth of God.   ' But if we walk in the light,' says St. John, ' the blood of his Son Jesus Christ cleanseth us from all sin.'   Ephesians i. 7, ' In whom we have redemption through his blood, the forgiveness of sins ; according to the riches of his grace.'   Ephesians ii. 13, ' But now in Christ Jesus, ye who sometimes were afar off, are made nigh by the blood of Christ.'   1 Peter i. 18, 19, ' Ye were not redeemed with corruptible things, but with the precious blood of Christ, as of a lamb without blemish, and without spot.' Rev. i. 5, ' Who washed us from our sins in his blood.'   Rev. v. 9, ' Thou hast redeemed us to God by thy blood.'   Rom. v. 9, ' Being justified by his blood.'   In these passages it is directly asserted, that mankind are washed, cleansed, justified, forgiven, redeemed, and made nigh unto God, by the blood of

Christ.   He who admits the existence of an atonement, cannot, with these declarations in view, hesitate to admit also, that it was accomplished by his *blood*, that is, by his death and its connected sufferings.   The views of Christ himself concerning this subject cannot easily be mistaken, if we remember that he said, ' he came to give his life a ransom for many;' that ' the good shepherd giveth his life for the sheep.'   ' I am the living bread, which came down from heaven ; if any man eat of this bread, he shall live for ever.   And the bread that I will give is my flesh, which I will give for the life of the world.' John vi. 51.

3. *The peculiar agonies, which preceded and attended the death of Christ, and in which the atonement made by him for sin   peculiarly consisted, were chiefly distresses of mind, and not of body.*   This I think evident from many considerations.

(1.) *There is no reason so far as I can see, to suppose that the bodily sufferings of Christ were more severe, or even so severe, as those which have been experienced by many others.*

The death of the cross was undoubtedly a very distressing death.   But it was probably less distressing than that experienced by many of the martyrs.   Some of these were roasted by a slow fire.   Some were dislocated on the rack, and suffered to expire under long continued tortures.   Some had their flesh taken off piece by piece, in a very gradual manner, with red hot pincers.   Others expired under various other kinds of exquisite sufferings, devised by the utmost ingenuity of man, and protracted with the utmost cruelty.   Multitudes of these martyrs, however, have sustained all their distresses without a complaint, and expired without a groan.

Multitudes also, both of martyrs and others, have died on the cross itself ; and, for aught that appears, with bodily anguish not inferior to that which Christ endured.   Yet of these, it would seem, numbers have died in the same peaceful manner.   Even the thieves who were crucified together with our Saviour, seem to have died without any complaint.

Yet Christ uttered a very bitter complaint on the cross ; and complained also in a similar manner in the garden of Gethsemane.   Whence arose these complaints ?   Not from his want of resignation to the will of God ; for no other person was ever so resigned : not from the want of fortitude ; for no other person evor possessed it in an equal degree. The very complaints which he utters do not appear to have any respect to his bodily sufferings, but to have originated entirely from a different cause, and that cause purely mental ; as I shall have occasion farther onward to explain.

(2.) *Christ is expressly said to have made his soul an offering for sin.*

Isaiah liii. 19, ' When thou shalt make his soul an offering for sin.' In the margin, ' When his soul shall make an offering for sin.' In Lowth, ' If his soul shall make a propitiatory sacrifice.' But if his soul was indeed the sin-offering, then the sufferings which he underwent as an atonement for sin, were peculiarly the sufferings of his soul, or mental sufferings. Accordingly, they are called ' the travail of his soul.'*

(3.) *The complaints of Christ,* in Psalms xxii. xl. lxix and lxxxviii. *appear to indicate that his sufferings were chiefly sufferings of mind.*

Such, at least, is the impression made on my mind by reading these passages of Scripture ; an impression, resulting not so much from detached parts, as from the whole strain of the composition. To this mode of examining the subject I shall refer those who hear me, for their own satisfaction.

4. *The agony which Christ underwent in the garden of Gethsemane exhibits the same truth.*

Christ in this garden had his sufferings in full view. The prospect was so terrible, that it forced from him ' sweat, as it were great drops of blood falling to the ground.' At the same time he prayed earnestly thrice, that ' if it were possible, this cup might pass from him.' It cannot, I think, be imagined even with decency, and certainly not in any consistency with the character of Christ as manifested elsewhere, that the mere prospect of death, even of a most cruel and bitter death, was so overwhelming to his mind, as to convulse his constitution in this manner, or to force from him such a prayer. Perhaps no person, under the mere apprehension of death, was ever agitated in an equal degree. Had it not ' pleased Jehovah to bruise him,' there is no reason to believe that he would have been anxiously solicitous concerning the utmost evils

---

*He shall see of the travail of his soul, and, be satisfied. Ibid.

which he could suffer from the hands of men. He had directed even his disciples, notwithstanding their frailty, ' not to fear them who could kill the body, and after that could do no more.' It cannot be supposed that his own conduct was not exactly conformed to this precept.

5. *Christ himself appears to have decided this point in the manner already specified.*

In his exclamation on the cross, he said, ' My God, my God, why hast thou forsaken me ?' As this was his only complaint, it must, I think, be believed to refer to his principal suffering. But the evil here complained of, is being *forsaken by God.* In the language of the Psalmist, ' God hid his face from him ;' that is, if I mistake not, withdrew from him wholly those manifestations of supreme complacency in his character and conduct, which he had always before made. As this was in itself a most distressing testimony of the divine anger against sin, so it is naturally imagined, and, I think, when we are informed that ' it pleased Jehovah to bruise him,' directly declared in the Scriptures, that this manifestation was accompanied by other disclosures of the anger of God against sin, and against him as the substitute for sinners.

The views and feelings of one mind towards another can produce the highest sense of suffering, of which we are capable. The esteem and love of intelligent beings are, when united, the most exquisite of all enjoyment ; and are naturally, and in all probability necessarily, coveted more than any other, except the approbation of our own minds. Their mere indifference towards us, when they have opportunity of being so far acquainted with us as to give room for being esteemed and loved by them, is ordinarily the source of severe mortification. In proportion as they are more intelligent and worthy, their love and esteem are more important to us, and more coveted by us ; and the refusal of it creates in us more intense distress.

The complacency of God, whose mind is infinite, and whose disposition is perfect, is undoubtedly the first of all possible enjoyments. The loss of it, therefore, and the consequent suffering of his hatred and contempt, are undoubtedly the greatest evils which a created mind can suffer ; evils, which will in all probability constitute the primary anguish experienced in the world of woe. Omniscience and omnipotence are certainly able to communicate, during even a short time, to a finite mind such views of the hatred and contempt of God towards sin and sinners, and of course towards a substitute for sinners, as would not only fill its capacity of suffering, but probably put an end to its existence. In this manner, I apprehend, the chief distresses of Christ were produced. In this manner, principally, was that testimony of God against disobedience exhibited to the Redeemer, and ultimately to the universe, which so solemnly supported the sanctions of the divine law, and so illustriously honoured the divine government, as to prevent the pardon of sinners from being regarded *by* intelligent creatures as the mere indulgence of a weak and changeable disposition in the infinite ruler.

6. *The active obedience of Christ was, in my apprehension, essentially concerned in his atonement.*

This position I shall illustrate under the following particulars.

(1.) *If Christ had not obeyed the law perfectly, he could not have atoned for the sins of mankind at all.*

It was as ' a lamb without blemish, and without spot,' that he became a proper, acceptable offering; and in this character only. Had he been stained with iniquity, his sufferings would have been, and would have been regarded as the mere punishment of his own sins, and not as an expiation for the sins of others. Had he been of a neutral character, his sufferings would have been of no apparent value. On the contrary, they would have been considered as strange, inexplicable, and resembling those accidents which, being unconnected with any thing preceding or succeeding, are fitted only to excite a momentary attention and wonder. The *excellency* of Christ gave all the real value and efficacy to his sufferings. But, can it be said, that *that* which gave all the real value to his sufferings, constituted no part of the atonement which he made by them? The atonement of Christ certainly did not consist in mere suffering, but in such sufferings of such a person. But Christ could not have been such a person without his active obedience; nor could his sufferings have been of such a nature, if he had not been such a person. If he had not suffered, he could not have atoned for sin at all. If he had not obeyed, his sufferings would have been of no value.

(2.) *It was indispensable to the existence of the atonement of Christ, that he should magnify the law and make it honourable.*

This I consider as having been done by his obedience in the first instance, and in the second by his sufferings. The former was as truly indispensable as the latter; and was indispensable to the existence of the latter. In the predictions of the Old Testament, and the declarations of the New, similar stress is laid on both these great articles. As I have expressed my views of this subject in a late Discourse, I will not repeat them here; but will only add, that the obedience of Christ as truly honoured the preceptive part of the law, as his sufferings the penal. The doctrine which has been taught by some wise and good men, that if the law is not discerned in itself to be ' holy, just, and good,' the obedience of Christ cannot make it appear so, but only show, that it was a law which he was so desirous to support as to be willing to obey it, is, I am bound to say, contrary to my own conviction. The character of Christ, as *excellent*, is certainly capable of being seen and realized, independently of the divine law. Christ, as all those with whom I am now contending will acknowledge, is a divine person. Surely we are not obliged to have recourse to the law of God, as the only means of proving the excellency of his character. Independently of this, we are able to prove, that the infinite mind is possessed of infinite excellence; and of course cannot but discern, that a law which this excellence is disposed to obey, as well as to promulgate, must be of the most glorious kind possible. The mere promulgation of the law consists in *declarations* only. But who does not know, that *actions* carry with them an evidence far more convincing, and especially far more impressive, than any declarations whatever? At the same time, the transcendent *dignity* of the Son of God lends the same lustre to his obedience as to his sufferings; and renders the former of the same influence in recommending the *precepts* of the law, which the latter possess in vindicating its *penalty*. Besides, the same objection may be made against the proof derived from the sufferings of Christ, that the penalty of the law is just. For it may with the same propriety be alleged, that if the penalty of the law does not appear just in itself, the sufferings of Christ can never make it appear so; since they prove no more, than that Christ was so desirous to support the law, as to be willing for this end to undergo such sufferings. Should it be said, that the sufferings of Christ involved *self-denial*; and that thus they exhibited the sincerity of his regard for the law, because self-denial is the strongest proof of sincerity : I answer, that his consent to become a subject, and all the parts of his obedience, involved self-denial also ; less, apparently at least, in degree ; but the same in kind.   Should it be said, that the sufferings of Christ were a testimony of *God's displeasure against sin*, and of the righteousness of the penalty denounced against it : I answer, so is his obedience equally a testimony of God's complacency in the precepts of the law, and the righteousness of requiring his intelligent creatures to obey them.   Should it be said, that his sufferings were *inflictions from the hand of God:* I answer, that his obedience was required by God, and was therefore equally a testimony of his pleasure.   Finally, should it be said, that Christ's obedience was *voluntary ;* I answer, that his sufferings were equally voluntary ; otherwise, they would never have existed ; or, if we suppose them to have existed, would have had no efficacy.

Upon the whole, the attempts made to discriminate between these parts of Christ's mediation, and to assign to each its exact proportion of influence in the economy of redemption, seem to me to have been very partially successful.

V. *I shall now in a few words, consider the extent of Christ's atonement.*

On this subject I observe,

1. *The atonement of Christ was complete.*

By this I mean, that it was such as to vindicate the law, government, and character of God.   This we know, because Christ repeatedly declared, that his work was finished ; because it was appointed and accepted of God, as we are assured by the many testimonies of his approbation given to Christ ; and because the Spirit of grace descended in a glorious manner on the day of Pentecost, to carry the design of it into execution.

2. *The degree of suffering which Christ underwent in making this atonement, was far inferior to that which will be experienced by an individual sufferer beyond the grave.*

It will not be supposed, as plainly it cannot, that Christ suffered in his divine nature.   Nor will it be believed that any created nature could, in that short space of time, suffer

2 D 2

what would be equivalent to even a slight distress extended through eternity.

3. *The atonement of Christ was still of infinite value.*

The atonement of Christ, great as his distresses were, did not derive its value principally from the degree in which he experienced them, but from the infinite greatness and excellency of his character. Although the divine nature is necessarily unsuffering ; yet, in this case, it exactly coincided in its dictates with all the conduct of the created mind of Christ and lent to that conduct its own infinite weight and worth.

4. *The atonement of Christ was sufficient in its extent to open the door for the pardon of all human sinners.*

This doctrine is so often and so plainly declared in the Scriptures, that I am supprised to find a doubt concerning it entertained by any man. ' Who gave himself,' says St. Paul, ' a ransom for all, to be testified in due time :' and again, ' Who is the Saviour of all men, especially of them that believe.' ' He is the propitiation for our sins,' says St. John, ' and not for ours only, but also for the sins of the whole world.' It is needless any farther to multiply passages to this effect.

When this Discourse was first written, disputes concerning the *extent* of the atonement had not openly appeared in this country ; and I did not suppose it to be necessary to canvass the question with any particularity. The length of the present Discourse forbids me to dwell upon the subject now ; yet I will very briefly suggest two or three arguments for the consideration of my audience.

1. If the atonement of Christ consisted in making such amends for the disobedience of man as should place the law, government, and character of God in such a light, that he could forgive sinners of the human race, without any inconsistency ; then these amends, or this atonement, were all absolutely necessary, in order to render such forgiveness proper, or consistent with the law and character of God in a single instance. The forgiveness of one sinner without these amends, would be just as much a contradiction to the declarations of the law, as the forgiveness of a million. If, then, the amends actually made were such that God could consistently forgive

one sinner, he might with equal consistency and propriety forgive any number, unless prevented by some other reason. The atonement, in other words, which was necessary for a world, was equally necessary, and in just the same manner and degree, for an individual sinner.

2. The atonement was by the infinite dignity and excellence of the Redeemer rendered infinitely meritorious. But it cannot be denied, that an infinitely meritorious atonement is sufficient for all the apostate children of Adam.

3. If the atonement of Christ consisted in suffering what those for whose sins he atoned deserved to suffer, his mediation did not lessen the evils of the apostasy. All the difference which it made in the state of things was, that he suffered in the stead of those whom he came to redeem, and suffered the same miseries which they were condemned to suffer. In other words, an innocent being suffered the very misery which the guilty should have suffered. Of course there is in the divine kingdom just as much misery, *with* the mediation of Christ, as there would have been *without* it ; and nothing is gained by this wonderful work, but the transfer of this misery from the guilty to the innocent.

4. If Christ has not made a sufficient atonement for others beside the elect, then his Salvation is not offered to them at all, and they are not guilty for not receiving it. But this is contrary to the whole tenour of the Gospel, which everywhere exhibits sinners as greatly guilty for rejecting Christ. Yet if Christ be not offered to them, they cannot be guilty of rejecting him.

5. The Gospel, or glad tidings published by Christ, is said to be good tidings unto all people. But, if there be no atonement made for the sins of all people, the Gospel, instead of being good news to them, is not addressed to them at all.

6. Ministers are required to preach faith, as well as repentance, to all sinners as their duty. But if no atonement has been made for their sins, they cannot believe ; for to them Christ is in no sense a Saviour, and therefore not even a possible object of their faith.

Should it be asked, Why, then, are not all men pardoned ? I answer, Because all mankind do not evangelically believe in this atonement, and its author. No man is pardoned merely because of the atonement made by Christ ; but because of his own acceptance also of that atonement, by faith. The way is open, and equally open, to all; although all may not be equally inclined to walk in it.

The proffers of pardon on the very same conditions are made, with equal sincerity and kindness, to every man. He who does not accept them, therefore ought to remember that nothing stands in his way, but his own impenitence and unbelief.

SERMON LVII.

THE PRIESTHOOD OF CHRIST:

HIS ATONEMENT.

OBJECTIONS ANSWERED.

APPLICATION.

BEING JUSTIFIED FREELY BY HIS GRACE THROUGH THE REDEMP_
TION THAT IS IN CHRIST JESUS. WHOM GOD HATH SET FORTH
TO BE A PROPITIATION, THROUGH FAITH IN HIS BLOOD, TO DE-
CLARE HIS RIGHTEOUSNESS FOR THE REMISSION OF SINS THAT
ARE PAST, THROUGH THE FORBEARANCE OF GOD. TO DECLARE,
I SAY, AT THIS TIME, HIS RIGHTEOUSNESS; THAT HE MIGHT BE
JUST, AND THE JUSTIFIER OF HIM WHICH BELIEVETH IN JESUS.
ROMANS III. 24—26.

HAVING finished the observations which I intended concerning the atonement of Christ, as proofs of its existence, and
explanations of its nature; I shall now proceed to consider
some *objections* to this doctrine; and to suggest several practical *remarks* to which it naturally gives birth.

Among the objections alleged against this doctrine, I select
the following, as particularly deserving attention.

1. It is objected, *that a vicarious atonement for sin is not
consistent with the dictates of reason.*

" The sin," it is observed, " is ours; and cannot belong to
another. Whatever atonement is to be made ought, therefore,
to be made by *us :* particularly such an atonement, as is here

insisted on ; *viz.* such an one, as is to be made by suffering. The sufferings which are necessary to expiate our guilt, are due from the sinner only, and cannot be justly inflicted on any other person."

I cheerfully agree with the objector, that the sinner cannot *claim* such an interference on his behalf, as is made by the atonement of Christ. Strict justice demands the punishment of the sinner only : and can, in nowise, require the punishment of another in his stead. But I still deny the consequence which the objector derives from these premises.

No person who has observed the affairs of the present world with attention, can hesitate to admit that vicarious interference, to a great extent, producing in great numbers both good and evil consequences, is a prominent feature of the providential system by which the affairs of this world are regulated. Children thus become rich, well educated, intelligent, religious, and everlastingly happy, by the agency of their parents ; while other children owe, in a great measure, to the same agency the contrary evils of poverty, ignorance, vice, and final ruin. Friends by their interference become the means of wealth, reputation, advancement, holiness, and everlasting life, to their friends ; and rescue them from poverty, bondage, disgrace, profligacy, and perdition. Enemies accomplish all the contrary evils for their enemies ; and by temptation, slander, fraud, and treachery, effectuate for those whom they hate every kind of destruction. A great part of the business of human life, both public and private, is in the strict sense vicarious ; the benefits or the injuries rarely terminating in the personal good of the agent only, but almost of course extending to others. The agency of Washington has beneficially affected every inhabitant of the United States. That of Moses extended blessings to the Israelitish nation through fifteen hundred years. That of St. Paul and his companions has spread holiness through the Christian world for seventeen centuries ; and added many millions to the general assembly of the first-born. Nay, this very agency will hereafter become the means of converting the whole human race to Christianity, people heaven with ' a great multitude which no man can number, of all nations, kindreds, and tongues,' and diffuse glory, honour, and immortal life, throughout never-ending ages.

From these observations it is evident, that vicarious agency is so far from being an unreasonable thing in itself, as in one form and another to constitute an important part of the present system of things, and to have a very extensive and very efficacious influence on the most interesting concerns of mankind. The whole analogy of human affairs in the present world furnishes us, therefore, with every reason to expect that vicarious agency would be adopted, more or less, in every part of the providential system.

What the state of the world thus naturally teaches us to look for, Revelation countenances in the strongest manner. A single instance will be sufficient to place this truth in the clearest light. Every one who is at all acquainted with the Scriptures, perfectly well knows that they require of all men intercession for their fellow men, and that to this intercession blessings are both promised and declared to be given. ' Is any sick among you?' says St. James, ' Let him call for the elders of the church, and let them pray over him—and the prayer of faith shall save the sick, and the Lord shall raise him up ; and, if he have committed sins, they shall be forgiven him.' If restoration from disease, and the forgiveness of sins, blessings of the greatest temporal and spiritual magnitude, are promised and given in consequence of the intercession of others, our minds can set no limits to the propriety or the efficacy of vicarious interference, exhibited in other forms.

In the present case (the case objected to,) the propriety of admitting vicarious interference is complete. Mankind were all sinners, were all condemned by the unalterable law of God ; and were all, therefore, destined to final ruin. In themselves there was no power to expiate their sins, or to prevent their destruction. When it is remembered, that their number was incalculable, and that each of them was immortal, the case must be admitted to have been great and interesting beyond any finite comprehension. Both the magnitude of the case, therefore, and its desperate nature, demanded of a benevolent being every effort capable of being demanded. Whatever could with propriety be done was plainly and loudly called for by circumstances so deplorable, a wretchedness so vast, a doom extending to a collection of intelligent creatures so plainly incomprehensible. But vicarious efforts could here be made, and made with propriety and success. The law and government here dishonoured could, and I hope it has been proved that they could, be supported in their full strength and efficacy; the sin could be expiated; the sinners restored to holiness, the favour of God, and immortal life; and the character of God appear, not only with the same, but increased glory. Thus, from the nature of the case, as well as from the analogy of things, a vicarious interference is so far from being, in the present instance, improbable or improper, that it is strongly recommended to our belief by the very best presumptive evidence.

2. It is objected, *that the punishment of an innocent person, such as Christ was, is inconsistent with the plain dictates of justice.*

To punish an innocent person for a fault not his own will not be denied to be unjust. Nor will an inquiry now be instituted concerning the question, whether it would be consistent with justice to require, in any possible case, a being perfectly holy to suffer for the sake of other beings of a different character, in order to relieve them from greater sufferings. Neither of these will be necessary at the present time. The objection may be completely answered in another manner. For,

(1.) *That Christ actually suffered, while yet he was perfectly holy, the objector cannot deny.* He, therefore, suffered for himself, or for mankind. If he suffered for mankind, the existence of an atonement is admitted. If he suffered for himself, then the objector must admit that he was punished, while yet he was perfectly holy; and, of course, that God can inflict suffering, not only on holy beings, but for their own sake; or in other words, can retribute punishment to obedience. I leave the objector to choose which part of this alternative he pleases.

(2.) *Christ was not required to suffer.* This is taught in the Scriptures, in a great multitude of passages, and in many forms, too well known to be specified here. Christ *voluntarily assumed* the office of a Redeemer; voluntarily became a substitute for man; and of his own accord ' gave his life as a ransom for many.' It is true, that in all this he obeyed the will of his Father; but it is not true, that he did not voluntarily enter upon every part of this course of obedience. ' When he was in the form of God, and thought it no robbery to be equal with God; he took upon himself the form of a servant;' and 'laid down his own life,' when 'none could take it out of his hand.'   But it is evident, that there can be no injustice in requiring a being perfectly holy to fulfil his own engagements, and to do what he has covenanted to do; although by this covenant he has engaged to yield himself to personal suffering.   To consent to suffer may be on his part right, when by his suffering he can redeem others from greater suffering, or accomplish in any way what will, on the whole, be superior good.   On the part of God also, it may, and if nothing extraneous prevent, must be right to accept of his sufferings in such a case, if voluntarily proffered.   The objection, therefore, is destitute of weight.

3. It is farther objected, that *if Christ expiated the sins of mankind, God is obliged by justice to bestow on them salvation.*

This objection is derived from misapprehensions concerning the nature of the atonement.   The Scriptures in speaking on this subject, very frequently as well as very naturally speak in figurative language.   Particularly, they exhibit us as ' bought with a price;' as ' purchased;' as ' redeemed;' that is, literally understood, as bought from a state of bondage and condemnation by the blood of Christ; as ransomed by the λυτρον, or price of redemption.   This language, derived from that fact in human affairs which, among the customary actions of men approaches nearest in resemblance to the atonement of Christ, seems unwarily to have been considered as describing literally this atonement.   But this mode of considering it is plainly erroneous.   We are not, in the literal sense, *bought*, or *purchased*, at all.   Nor has Christ, in the literal sense, paid any price to purchase mankind from slavery and death.

The error into which the objector has fallen has, I acknowledge, been countenanced by many Christians who have held the doctrine of the atonement.   These have supposed the satisfaction for sin made by the Redeemer, essentially to resemble the satisfaction made for a debtor by paying the debt which he owed.   In this case it is evident that, if the creditor accept the payment from a third person, he is bound in justice to release the debtor.   As the two cases have been supposed to be similar, it has been concluded that, since Christ has made such a satisfaction for sinners, God is in justice also bound to release them.

This, however, is an unfounded and unscriptural view of the subject. There is no substantial resemblance between the payment of a debt for an insolvent debtor, and the satisfaction rendered to distributive justice for a criminal. The debtor owes money ; and this is all he owes. If, then, all the money which he owes is paid and accepted, justice is completely satisfied, and the creditor can demand nothing more. To demand more, either from the debtor or from any other person, would be plainly unjust. When, therefore, the debt is paid by a third person, the debtor is discharged by justice merely. But when a criminal has failed of doing his duty, as a subject to lawful government and violated laws which he was bound to obey, he has committed a fault, for which he has merited punishment. In this case, justice, not in the *commutative*, but the *distributive* sense, the only sense in which it can be concerned with this subject, demands, not the future obedience, nor an equivalent for the omitted obedience, but merely the punishment of the offender. The only reparation for the wrong which he has done, required by strict justice, is this punishment ; a reparation necessarily and always required. There are cases, however, in which an atonement, such as was described in the first of these Discourses, may be accepted ; an atonement by which the honour and efficacy of the government may be preserved, and yet the offender pardoned. In such a case, however, the personal character of the offender is unaltered. Before the atonement was made, he was a criminal. After the atonement is made, he is not less a criminal. As a criminal, he before merited punishment. As a criminal, he no less merits it now. The turpitude of his character remains the same ; and while it remains he cannot fail to deserve exactly the same punishment. After the atonement is made it cannot be truly said, therefore, any more than before, that he does not deserve punishment. But if the atonement be accepted, it may be truly said that, consistently with the honour of the government and the public good, he may be pardoned. This act of grace is all that he can hope for ; and this he cannot *claim* on account of any thing in himself, or any thing to which he is entitled, but only may *hope*, from the mere grace or free gift of the ruler. Before the atonement was made, the ruler. however benevolently inclined, could not pardon him consistently with his own character, the honour of his government, or the public good. After it is made, he can pardon him, in consistency with them all ; and, if the offender discover a penitent and becoming disposition, undoubtedly will, if he be a benevolent ruler.

From these observations it is manifest, that the atonement of Christ in no sense makes it necessary that God should accept the sinner on the ground of justice, but only renders his forgiveness not inconsistent with the divine character. Before the atonement, he could not have been forgiven ; after the atonement, this impossibility ceases. The sinner can now be forgiven, notwithstanding the turpitude of his character, and the greatness of his offences. But forgiveness is an act of grace only ; and to the same grace must the penitent be indebted for all the future blessings connected with forgiveness.

I have now considered all the objections against the doctrine of the atonement, which I consider as claiming an answer ; and shall therefore proceed, as I proposed at the commencement of this Discourse, to make some practical remarks, arising from the preceding observations, on this important subject.

REMARKS.

From these observations it is evident,

1. *That those who trust in the expiation of Christ will certainly inherit the favour of God.*

In the text it is said, that God ' set forth Christ as a propitiation for sin, through faith in his blood, to declare his righteousness ; that he may be just, when justifying him that believeth in Jesus.' The end for which Christ was set forth as a propitiation, is, that God, consistently with justice, may justify those who believe in Christ. The peculiar and essential nature of the faith of such as believe in Jesus is, in one important particular. exactly defined also in the text, when it is styled ' faith in his *blood :*' the faith through which alone he is exhibited in the text as becoming a propitiation to men. This faith, or as I shall take the liberty to call it, *trust* or *confi-*

dence, (for such I hope hereafter to show it to be) is not, indeed, nor is it here asserted to be, faith in the atonement *only;* but it is faith in the atonement *pre-eminently.* We are required to believe in the whole character and in all the offices of Christ; but we are required, peculiarly, to believe in him as the great propitiatory sacrifice for sin. Every one who is the subject of this faith, the real and only means by which we become interested in this propitiation, is amply exhibited in the text as entitled to justification.

That every such believer will certainly inherit the favour of God cannot be rationally doubted. While he was yet a sinner, condemned and ruined, God, moved by his infinite benevolence, sent into this world his beloved Son, to become incarnate, to become a subject of his law and a substitute for mankind, to lead a life of humiliation, and to die the accursed death of the cross, that he might redeem such sinners from the curse of the law, from a guilty character and the endless miseries of devouring fire. The condition proposed by himself, on which we become entitled to the blessings of this redemption, are all summed up in this single phrase, ' faith in Christ,' and pre-eminently in his *atonement.* This condition the believer has performed ; and is, therefore, entitled to these blessings. His title is secured to him by the covenant of redemption, by the immutable promise of God to him, by the glory and excellency of Christ's mediation, and by that amazing and immense purpose of infinite love, which proposed and accomplished all the parts of this wonderful work. Who can doubt for a moment, that he who proposed, he who accomplished, this astonishing design, will go on to accomplish every thing which it draws in its train? ' He that spared not his own Son, but delivered him up for us all, how shall he not, with him also, freely give us all things?' Can any thing be too dear to be given to those for whom Christ was given? Can any thing be too great to be expected by those who are united to the Son of God, as ' members of his body, of his flesh, and of his bones ;' who are become ' his seed' in the everlasting covenant ; and to whom, unasked, he has from his own overflowing goodness given ' the glory, which he had with the Father before ever the world was ?'

Let every believer, then, be completely assured that his cause is safe in the hands of God. He has ' chosen the good part,' and it ' shall never be taken from him.' He who has begun to befriend him in this infinite concern, will ' never leave him nor forsake him.' ' All the steps of a good man are ordered by the Lord. Though he fall, yet shall he rise again; and his mercy God will not utterly take from him.' In the seed sown in his heart ' there is a blessing,' the beginning of immortal life. Cold and wintry as is the climate beneath which it has sprung, unkind and barren as is the soil in which it grows, doubtful and fading as we often see its progress, it cannot die. The hand that planted it will cultivate it with unceasing care, and will speedily remove it to a happier region, where it will flourish, and blossom, and bear fruit for ever. ' I am persuaded,' says St. Paul, ' that neither death, nor life, nor angels, nor principalities, nor powers, nor things present, nor things to come, nor height, nor depth, nor any other creature, shall be able to separate us from the love of God, which is in Christ Jesus our Lord.'

2. *It is equally evident, that those who reject the atonement of Christ are without any hope of the divine favour.*

The favour of God is proffered to the inhabitants of this world through Christ alone ; and those only are promised an interest in it who cordially believe in him, as the expiation of sin. Had there been any other condition upon which this glorious blessing could be communicated, the same benevolence which planned and accomplished our redemption would undoubtedly have communicated it to us. No such communication has, however been made. On the contrary, it is often declared in the most explicit language, that ' he who believeth not shall be damned.'

Even if the Scriptures had been silent, and no such awful declarations had been found in them, the nature of the subject holds out the strongest discouragement to every presumption of this kind. After such amazing efforts made on the part of God to bring mankind back from a state of rebellion, and to restore them to virtue and happiness, it cannot but be believed, that their obstinate continuance in sin must be regarded by him with supreme abhorrence. His law condemned them for their original apostasy to final ruin. To the guilt of this apostasy, unatoned, unrepented of, and therefore remaining in all its enormity, they in this case add the peculiar guilt of reject-

ing the singular, the eminently divine goodness of God manifested in this wonderful provision for their recovery.   In what
manner they could more contemptuously despise the divine
character, in what manner they could more insolently affront
the divine mercy, it is beyond my power to conceive.   No
other offer can be so kind, no other blessing so great, no other
display of the divine character of which we can form a conception, so lovely.   The ingratitude, therefore, is wonderful, the
insolence amazing, the guilt incomprehensible !   ' If,' then,
' the righteous scarcely be saved, where shall these unbelieving, ungodly sinners appear ? '   If it be ' a fearful thing ' for
all men, for heathen and for Mohammedans, ' to fall into the
hands of the living God,' what must it be for these men, to
whom Christ is offered freely, daily, and alway ; who sit, from
the cradle to the grave, under the noon-day light of the Gospel,
and bask through life in the beams of the Sun of righteousness?

Whence do these persons derive their hope ?   From their
character ?   That could not save them under the law.   It is
the very guilt for which they are condemned.   From their
repentance ?   They exercise none.   Even if they did, it could
never be accepted.   A perfect repentance, as has been heretofore proved, cannot become an expiation for sin.   But such
repentance was never exhibited by men.   Their repentance is
not even a sorrow for sin.   On the contrary, it is the mere
dread of danger, a mere terrified expectation of punishment.
Who, however abandoned, does not at times experience such
repentance as this ?   Whoever dreamed that the dread of
death ought to excuse the felon from the gibbet ?

Let every unbeliever, then, tremble at the approach of the
judgment.   Let him no longer say to himself, ' Peace, peace ;
when sudden destruction is coming upon him.'   Let him ' turn
to the strong hold,' while he is yet a ' prisoner of hope.'   ' Let
him turn to the Lord with all the heart, with fasting, with
weeping, and with mourning : for he is gracious and merciful,
slow to anger, and of great kindness, and repenteth him of the
evil.   Who knoweth, if he will turn, and repent, and leave a
blessing behind him ? '

3. *It is evident from the observations made in these Discourses that mankind are infinitely indebted to Christ for
expiating their sins.*

Christ by his atonement has redeemed mankind from under the curse of the law. The sufferings to which they were doomed by this curse were endless sufferings. Without an expiation, a deliverance from these sufferings was impossible. Equally impossible was it for any other person beside Christ to make an expiation. From mere compassion to our ruined world he undertook the arduous labour of delivering us from these stupendous sufferings, and accomplished it at the expense of his own blood. Infinitely ' rich, for our sakes he became poor, that we through him might become rich.' For him we had done nothing, and were disposed to do nothing. For us, influenced by his own overflowing goodness, he did all things. He taught us as our prophet, ' all things pertaining to life and godliness.' He lived before us as our example ; he died for us, as our propitiation ; he rose from the dead, as the earnest of our resurrection to endless life. He entered heaven, as our forerunner ; he assumed the throne of the universe, as our ruler, protector, and benefactor   At the end of the world he will appear as our judge and rewarder ; and will conduct to the mansions of eternal life 'all those who have cordially accepted of his mediation ; and will there, throughout interminable ages, ' feed them with living bread, and lead them to fountains of living waters.' To the obligations conferred by such a benefactor what limits can be set ? Our deliverance from sin and sorrow is a boundless good ; our introduction to endless virtue and happiness is a boundless good. But of all this good the atonement of Christ is the foundation, the procuring cause, the commencement, and the security. ' Worthy is the Lamb, that was slain, to receive power, and riches, and wisdom, and strength, and honour, and glory, and blessing.' Such is the everlasting song, to which the ' four living creatures' in the Heavens subjoin their unceasing ' Amen.'

With this glorious subject in our view, can we fail to be astonished at the manner in which the Saviour of the world is treated by multitudes of those whom he came to redeem ? By what multitudes is he regarded with cold-hearted unbelief, and stupid indifference ! By what multitudes, with open opposition and avowed hostility ! By what multitudes, with shameless contempt, insolent sneers, and impudent ridicule ! How often is his glorious name profaned and blasphemed by those whom he died to save from endless perdition ! How many miserable wretches tottering on the brink of eternal ruin, while in the house of God, while in this house, and while his agonies endured for them, are resounding in their ears, quietly compose themselves to sleep, or busily employ themselves in whispering, amusement, and mirth ; forgetful that they have souls to be saved or lost, and destitute of a wish to be interested in the Saviour !   Had Christ been as regardless of these miserable beings as they are of him, nay, as they are of themselves, what would have become of them in ' the day of wrath ?' What will become of them in that dreadful day, if they continue to treat Christ as they have treated him hitherto ?

4. *It is evident from these observations, that the Gospel alone furnishes a consistent scheme of salvation to mankind.*

The Gospel takes man where it finds him, in a state of sin and ruin, condemned by the law of God to final perdition, and incapable of justification, by his own righteousness.   In this situation it announces to him a Saviour, divinely great and glorious, divinely excellent and lovely ; assuming his nature to become an expiation for his sins ; revealing to him the way of reconciliation to God ; and inviting him to enter it, and be saved.   The acceptance of this expiation it announces from the mouth of God himself.   The terms in which we may be reconciled it discloses with exact precision and perfect clearness ; so that ' he who runs may read ;' so that beggars and children may understand and accept them.   Faith in the Redeemer, repentance towards God, and holiness of character, involve them all.   They are terms reasonable in themselves, easy to us, and productive of incomprehensible good to all who embrace them.   To overcome the stubbornness of our hearts, Christ has commissioned the Spirit of grace to sanctify us for himself, to draw us with the cords of his love, to guide us with his wisdom, to uphold us with his power, and to conduct us under his kind providence to the heavens.   In this scheme is contained all that we need, and all that we can rationally desire.   The way of salvation is here become ' a highway, and way-faring men, though fools, need not err therein.'

The religion of the Gospel is a religion designed for *sinners.*   By the expiation of Christ it opens the brazen door which was for ever barred against their return.   Here the supreme and otherwise immoveable obstacle to the acceptance of sinners is taken away. If sinners were to be accepted, it was not ' possible that this cup should pass from' Christ. The next great obstacle in the way of their acceptance is found in their unholy, disobedient hearts, propense ' to evil only and continually ;' and the next, their perpetual exposure to back-sliding, and to falling finally away. These obstacles, immoveable also by any means on this side of heaven, the Spirit of grace, by his most merciful interference in our behalf, entirely removes. Man, therefore, in the Gospel finds his return from apostasy made possible, made easy, made certain ; actually begun, steadily carried on in the present world, and finally completed in the world to come.

But no other scheme of religion presents to us even plausible means of removing these difficulties. Natural religion, to which infidels persuade us to betake ourselves for safety, does not even promise us a return to God. Natural religion is the religion of *law* ; of that law, which in the only legal language declares to us, ' Do these things, and thou shalt live ; but the soul that sinneth shall die.' These things, the things specified in the requisitions of the law, we have not done ; and therefore cannot live. We have sinned, and therefore must die. It has been formerly shown, that the law knows no condition of acceptance or justification, but obedience. Concerning repentance, faith, forgiveness, and reconciliation, concerning the sinner's return to God, and his admission to immortal life, the law is silent. Its only sentence pronounced on those who disobey is a sentence of final condemnation.

Whatever we may suppose the law to be, we have disobeyed its precepts. Nothing has been ever devised or received by man, as a law of God, which all men have not disobeyed. Infidels cannot devise such a law as they will dare to call a law of God, and publish to men under this title, which they themselves, and all other men, have not often disobeyed. From the very nature of law, a nature inseparable from its existence as a law, disobedience to its precepts must be condemned ; and if nothing interfere to preserve the offender from punishment, he must of necessity suffer. To what degree, in what modes, through what extent, these sufferings will reach, the infidel cannot conjecture. To his anguish no end appears. Of such an end no arguments can be furnished by his mind, no tidings have reached his ear, and no hopes can rationally arise in his heart.   Death, with all the gloomy scenes attendant upon a dying bed, is to him merely the commencement of doubt, fear, and sorrow.   The grave to him is the entrance into a world of absolute and eternal darkness.   That world, hung round with fear, amazement, and despair, overcast with midnight, melancholy with solitude, desolate of every hope of real good, opens to him through the dreary passage of the grave.   Beyond this entrance he sees nothing, he knows nothing, he can conjecture nothing, but what must fill his heart with alarm, and make his death-bed a couch of thorns.   With a suspense scarcely less terrible than the miseries of damnation itself, his soul lingers over the vast and desolate abyss ; when, compelled by an unseen and irresistible hand, it plunges into this uncertain and irreversible doom, to learn by experience what is the measure of woe destined to reward those, ' who obey not God,' and reject the salvation proffered by his Son.

In such a situation what man not yet lost to sense and thought, not yet convinced that he has committed the sin which cannot be forgiven, would not hail with transport the dawn of the Gospel ; the clear rising of the Sun of righteousness, to illumine his path through this melancholy world, to dispel the darkness of the grave, to shed a benevolent light upon the entrance into eternity, and brighten his passage to the heavens.

SERMON LVIII.

THE PRIESTHOOD OF CHRIST:

HIS INTERCESSION.

BUT THIS MAN, BECAUSE HE CONTINUETH EVER, HATH AN UN-CHANGEABLE PRIESTHOOD. WHEREFORE HE IS ABLE ALSO TO SAVE THEM TO THE UTTERMOST, THAT COME UNTO GOD BY HIM ; SEEING HE EVER LIVETH TO MAKE INTERCESSION FOR THEM.

HEBREWS VII. 24, 25.

HAVING in a series of Discourses examined, as far as I thought it necessary, the personal holiness of Christ, and his atonement for sin; I shall now proceed in the order originally proposed, to consider *his intercession.*

In the first verse of the text, St. Paul declares, that Christ, in contradistinction to earthly high priests, ' has an unchangeable priesthood;' or, as the Original more exactly signifies, ' a priesthood which passeth not from one hand to another.' In the last verse he infers from this fact, that ' he is able to save ' his followers ' to the uttermost; because he ever lives to make intercession for them.' The intercession of Christ, therefore, is here declared to be *real*—to be *made for his followers*—and to be *effectual* to *their salvation.* Of course, it claims, in a high degree, our serious attention.

To intercede denotes, originally, *to go between one person and another.* In its secondary or figurative sense, the only one in which it seems now to be used, it denotes *offering petitions in behalf of another ;* and, in the Scriptures, *offering such petitions to God.* On this subject we have St. John as a commentator, to direct us. 'If any man sin,' says the apostle, 'we have an advocate with the Father, Jesus Christ the righteous.' The original word here translated 'advocate' is παρακλητος. It denotes either a person who in the Roman courts, under the appellation of *patronus,* attended a client, and in countenancing, advising, and interceding for him, took an efficacious care of his interest : or an agent of one of the states, either allied or tributary to Rome, who took a similar care of the interests of that state before the Roman Government, and interceded, from time to time, with the emperor on its behalf, as those interests demanded. Such is one of the offices assumed by Christ in the Heavens.

It will be seen at a glance, that this subject is merely a scriptural one. All our knowledge concerning it is derived from Revelation only. Reason can add nothing but conjecture to what the Scriptures have taught ; and you are not now to learn that additions of this nature are of very little value. The observations which I propose to make concerning it, I shall arrange under the following heads :——

I. *The character and circumstances of those for whom Christ intercedes :*

II. *The manner in which his intercession is performed.*

Under the former of these heads I observe,

1. *That they are the children of God.*

In proof of this position I cite the following passages :——

(1.) The text. ' Wherefore he is able to save to the uttermost them that come unto God by him : seeing he ever liveth to make intercession for them.' It cannot but be seen, that St. Paul speaks here of no other intercession than that which is made for such as come unto God by Christ.

(2.) The passage already quoted from 1 John ii. 1. ' My little children, these things write I unto you, that ye sin not. And if any man sin, we have an advocate with the Father, Jesus Christ the righteous.' The persons who are here said to have an advocate with the Father, are the persons denoted by the word ' we :' that is, St. John, and those to whom he writes ; or whom he here styles ' little children :' in other words, the children of God.

(3.) Romans viii. 34, ' Who is he that condemneth? It is Christ that died : yea rather, that is risen again : who is even at the right hand of God; who also maketh intercession for us.' The persons for whom Christ is here said to intercede, are those included in the word ' us ;' those who in the preceding verse are called ' God's elect ;' and of whom it is said, that none shall hereafter be able to lay any thing to their charge ;' and of whom in the verses following it is declared, that nothing, whether present or future, ' shall be able to separate them from the love of God, which is in Christ Jesus our Lord.'

I know of no passage in the Scriptures which even seems to teach any other doctrine, except Isaiah liii. 12, ' And he made intercession for the transgressors.' Of this passage, I observe, [1.] that *saints* may be, and with the utmost propriety are, considered as designed by the word ' transgressors,' in this place. Saints both before and after their regeneration, are transgressors ; and in this character only need the intercession of Christ.

[2.] The *murderers of Christ* are very naturally designated in this place, by ' transgressors :' and the passage may be considered as a prophecy of the intercession which he made for them on the cross.

In the same verse it is said, ' He was numbered with the transgressors ;' that is, with the thieves between whom he was crucified ; and with all the other capital criminals condemned to the same death. All these were eminently transgressors ; and with them he was numbered or reckoned when he was pronounced to have the same character, and sentenced to the same infamy and sufferings. As the word ' transgressors ' denotes malefactors or murderers in the former of these clauses, it is very naturally understood to denote persons of the same character in the latter. In the former clause, also, the prophet speaks *one* fact which took place on the day of Christ's crucifixion ; it is very naturally supposed, therefore, that he pursues the same subject through the verse, and that the intercession mentioned by him, was made on the same day. If these remarks are just, the prophet may be fairly considered as predicting, in this passage, the prayer of Christ for his murderers, ' Father, forgive them ; for they know not what they do !' This was a real and wonderful instance of intercession, and was gloriously answered in the conversion of several thousands of these persons to the faith and obedience of the Gospel.

2. *The Children of God are still the subjects of backsliding and sin, in greater or less degrees, while they live.*

In every child of God there still exists ' a law in his members,' which wars ' against the law in his mind,' and often brings him ' into captivity to the law of sin, which is in his members.' It is to be remembered, that all such sins are committed not only against the law, but against the grace of God, and are aggravated by this high consideration. Originally, they were apostates; but afterwards they were·reconciled to God by faith in the blood of his Son. For this unspeakable blessing their obligations to obedience are increased beyond measure. Against these obligations, and against their own solemn covenant, recognizing and enhancing them, they still have sinned. Their ingratitude, therefore, is peculiar, and all their transgressions are heightened by the amazing consideration that they have been redeemed, sanctified, and forgiven.

3. ·*Notwithstanding their backslidings, they are not utterly cast off.*

' My mercy,' saith God, ' will I keep for him for evermore; and my covenant shall stand fast with him. His seed also will I make to endure for ever, and his throne as the days of heaven. If his children forsake my law, and walk not in my judgments; if they break my statutes, and keep not my commandments: Then will I visit their transgression with the rod, and their iniquity with stripes. Nevertheless, my loving kindness I will not utterly take from him, nor suffer my faithfulness to fail.' Psalm lxxxix. 28—33. This is the universal language of the Scriptures concerning this subject. ' Persecuted, but not forsaken; cast down, but not destroyed; perplexed, but not in despair; chastened, but not killed.' Such is the language of the apostles, and such was their condition. ·Such also, in various respects, is that of all their followers.

For the obliteration of the sins of persons so circumstanced, it cannot be irrational to suppose, that some provision would be made by him, who sent his Son to die for them; and who had promised in the covenant of redemption that they should endure for ever.

II. *I shall consider the manner in which the intercession of Christ is performed.*

On this subject I observe,

1. Some of the ancients were of opinion, that Christ executes this office *by presenting, continually, his human nature before the throne of his Father.* Aquinas also, a more modern writer, says, " Christ intercedes for us by exhibiting, with a desire of our salvation, to the view of the Father the human nature, assumed for us, and the mysteries celebrated or accomplished in it."

It will be admitted on all hands, that Christ *does* thus exhibit his *human* nature in the heavens ; nor can it be denied, that this is a continual exhibition of what he has done and suffered for the glory of his Father, and the salvation of his Church. All this was done by him in the human nature ; which is, therefore, an unceasing and affecting symbol of his wonderful labours for these great ends. The same exhibition is, also, a strong and constant memorial of his own love to his followers, and his earnest desires that they may be forgiven and saved. These desires, therefore, together with these labours and sufferings, being all forcibly exhibited in this presentation of his human nature before ' the throne. of the Majesty in the heavens,' it is, I think, a well founded opinion, that in this manner the intercession of Christ is, partially at least, performed. In support of this opinion we are to remember, that the high priest, whose intercession was a type of that of Christ, made this intercession, not by offering prayers for the people in the most holy place, but by sprinkling the blood of sacrifices on the mercy-seat. As the blood of the sacrifice was here presented before God by way of intercession, so Christ is considered as presenting the memorials of his sacrifice before God in the heavens ; and as the high priest by this act opened to the Israelites the earthly holy places, so Christ is considered as in the like manner opening the heavenly holy places to his own followers for ever.

2. *Christ pleads, substantially, for the forgiveness of the sins of his followers, their preservation in holiness, and their final acceptance into Heaven.*

Intercession in its very nature involves petition. The manner in which it is performed may vary, but the substance is always the same. In whatever manner, therefore, Christ may be supposed to intercede for his children, he must, substantially, offer up petitions on their behalf. That they need this intercession cannot be rationally doubted. The blessings to which they are conducted are the greatest of all blessings : their final forgiveness, acceptance, purification, and eternal life. Of these and all other blessings they are wholly unworthy. That much is necessary to be done for such persons, in order to save them from punishment and secure to them immortal happiness, is a doctrine accordant with the dictates of common sense. In this world great evils are remitted and great blessings procured to the undeserving, by the intercession of the worthy and honourable. Analogy, therefore, leads us to look to similar means for the accomplishment of similar purposes, in the universal providence of God. Especially will this seem natural and necessary, where the greatest blessings are to be obtained for those who are *unworthy of the least of all blessings.*

3. In John xvii. we have, if I mistake not, *an example of this very intercession.*

This chapter is the last communication of Christ to his apostles before his death. In it he recites, briefly, his wonderful labours for the glory of his Father, and for the good of his children ; declares, that he had finished the work allotted to him ; and announces, that he was bidding adieu to the scene of his humiliation, and preparing to enter into his glory.

On these grounds, he prays his Father to sanctify and perfect his children ; to keep them while they were in the world, from the evil ; to make them one in their spirit, their character, and their pursuits ; and to cause the love which he exercised towards Christ, to rest upon them. At the same time he declares, that he had given to them his own glory ; and that it was his will that they should be where he was, and behold his glory for ever. All these illustrious things also he solicits on the ground of his Father's love to him, and his own labours and sufferings in obedience to his will.

In this prayer of Christ we have probably a fair specimen of his intercession in the heavens. The same things are recited, and the same things requested here, which we are taught to expect there ; and all is asked of God which can contribute to their safety or their happiness.

If these observations be allowed to be just, it will be seen that the great ends of Christ's intercession are to preserve his followers from final backsliding ; an evil to which, if left to themselves, they would certainly be exposed, notwithstanding all the virtuous principles which they possess; to obtain the forgiveness of those sins which they commit after their regeneration; and to secure their reception into the world of glory. These ends are of the highest importance to them, and in the highest degree declarative of the goodness of God.

This method of proceeding on the part of God, is wholly accordant with the common dictates of the human mind. Similar means, as I have observed, are used, and efficaciously used, to procure the remission of punishment and the enjoyment of good for unworthy men in the present world. That which is done here, therefore, and has ever been done with the plainest propriety and the most decisive efficacy, strongly illustrates the reasonableness and propriety of what is thus done in the heavens.

From these observations I infer,

1. *The perfect safety of the children of God.*

Christ, the Son of God, and the infinitely meritorious Redeemer of men, intercedes for their preservation in holiness, the forgiveness of their backslidings, and their final acceptance into Heaven. ' The Father always heareth' the Son. It is impossible that his intercession should fail, or that the purposes of it should not be accomplished. His followers, therefore, though exposed to ten thousand dangers, and to numberless temptations, enemies, and backslidings, though always in a state of peril, and living only a doubtful and scarcely perceptible life, will pass safely through all these hazards, and finally arrive at the possession of perfect holiness and everlasting joy.

In the preceding Discourse I evinced the truth of this doctrine by arguments drawn from the *atonement* of Christ. It is equally evident from his *intercession.* Christ, in his prayer at the tomb of Lazarus, says to the Father, ' I knew that thou hearest me always.' In his intercessory prayer, in the xviith of John, he declares, that he intercedes not only for his apostles and their fellow-disciples then existing, but also ' for them, who should believe on him through their word;' that is, the Gospel. Those then who believe on him through the Gospel, are universally interested in that intercession of Christ, which ' the Father heareth always.' Of course, their safety is complete, their interest in the divine favour indefeasible, and their title to endless life unalterably secure.

2. *We have here a strong proof, that Christ is unchangeable.*

In Proverbs viii. after giving a variety of testimonies of his compassion for sinners, he informs us, that ' before the mountains were settled, or the earth was made, he rejoiced in the habitable parts of the earth,' in a glorious foresight of the good which he intended to accomplish ; and that ' his delights were ' from eternity ' with the sons of men.' In the indulgence of this divine benignity, though infinitely ' rich ' in the possession of all good, ' yet for our sakes he became poor, that we through him might become rich.'   ' The Word, who was in the beginning with God, and by whom all things were made, became flesh, and dwelt among us ; and we beheld his glory (the glory as of the only begotten of the Father,) full of grace and truth.'   While he dwelt in this apostate world, he underwent a course of extreme humiliation, labours, and sufferings for the sake of mankind ; and in the end purchased for them the regeneration of the soul and a title to everlasting life, with the agonies of the cross.

To the heavens he has gone before, ' to prepare a place for them, and to receive them to himself.' In that glorious world, amid all the splendours of his exaltation, he forgets not for a moment those worms of the dust whom he came to redeem ; those backsliding, frail, sinning apostates, for whom he poured out his blood on the accursed tree ; but, in the strong language of the apostle, ever lives to make intercession for them.' By his intercession, as well as by his government, he secures their continuance in holiness ; ' cleanses them from secret faults ; restrains them from presumptuous sins :' and thus keeps them ' innocent of the great transgression.' Thus his love is, from everlasting to everlasting, the same boundless love ; to himself divinely glorious, to them great beyond example, beneficial beyond degree.

3. *The intercession of Christ most affectingly teaches us the grace of God in the salvation of sinners.*

Sinners are originally redeemed, forgiven, and sanctified by the mere sovereign goodness of God. After all these mighty works are accomplished, they are still guilty and undeserving;

they need the intercession as well as the atonement of Christ; and without it could not, so far as we are informed, be with propriety blessed in the heavens. In consequence of this intercession they are preserved from fatal declension, their sins committed after their regeneration are forgiven, and themselves admitted to the presence of God.

In heaven this intercession is continued for ever. Throughout eternity the children of God are thus furnished with the strongest evidence, that their everlasting happiness is the result of mere sovereign goodness and mercy; and that all the glory devising, accomplishing, and bestowing this happiness is to be ascribed to him. The praises of the heavenly world, and the gratitude whence they spring, will from this source derive a more exquisite rapture; their sense of dependence on God be more humble, intense, and lovely; and their perseverance in holiness find the most delightful, as well as the most powerful motives.

4. *How wonderful is the love of Christ to sinners!*

It is beyond measure wonderful that he should love them at all. What are they? Guilty, rebellious, odious creatures, opposed to his will, designs, and character; requiting his love with ingratitude, hatred, and contempt; ' crucifying him afresh' by *their unbelief;* ' and accounting the blood of the covenant, wherewith he was sanctified, an unholy thing.' Why did he love them? Not because they were rational beings. With a word he could have created millions of such beings for one of them; and all more rational and more exalted than themselves. Not because of their moral excellence; for they had none. None because he needed them; for he cannot need any thing, and they possessed nothing which they did not receive from him.

On the contrary, all his conduct towards them sprang from his own boundless good-will; his disinterested love. They were not deserving, but he was pitiful; they were not valuable, but he was bountiful; they were not necessary to him, but he was infinitely necessary to them. ' Herein is love; not that we loved God, but that he loved us, and gave his Son to die for us.' It was because Christ was superlatively good; and because we were ' poor, and wretched, and miserable, and blind, and naked, and in want of all things,' that this glorious person had compassion on us in our apostasy and ruin. He lived and died, he reigns and intercedes, that we might live, and not die. This great work he began to execute here, and he carries it on in the heavens throughout eternity.

In that world of glory, although elevated to the throne of the universe, and beholding all things beneath his feet, although loved, obeyed, and worshipped with supreme attachment and homage by the great kingdom of virtuous beings, he assumes and executes the office of an intercessor for the fallen children of Adam. In that world ' he is not ashamed to call them,' however degraded by their apostasy, and however odious by their guilt, by the endearing names of ' friends ' and ' brethren.' He is the universal ruler ; but he is not ashamed to appear as the ' elder brother, the first-born,' of this human assembly ; nay as a suppliant for those whom he rules. He is a person of infinite dignity and perfection, but he is not ashamed to appear as a companion to those who could originally ' say to corruption, Thou art our father, and to the worm, Thou art our mother and our sister.' Thus the character which he exhibited on earth, he sustains in heaven. He is still in the same manner ' meek and lowly of heart ;' and still ' feeds , his disciples and ' leads them to fountains of living waters.' To him they have been indebted for the atonement of their sins and the salvation of their souls, and to him they will be infinitely indebted for the communication of knowledge, holiness, and enjoyment throughout the endless ages of their being.

What character can be compared with this? Before it how does all other excellence fade! In it what exaltation and condescension are blended! What greatness and benignity united! What must be the mind in which these majestic and these sweet and lovely characteristics thus unchangeably and for ever harmonize ; a mind supremely great and glorious in the lowly station of a man, a child, a servant to a humble artisan, and divinely meek and condescending in the infinite splendour of universal dominion.

What dishonour is here reflected on the pride of men and fallen angels! Pride, unsatisfied with all present attainments, and making the greatest communications from God of distinction and glory the mere foundations of claiming more, and of murmuring because they are not elevated to higher honours, and replenished with more extensive enjoyments! How poor, how debased, how odious, how guilty is that pride! How contemptible does it appear, when compared with the Redeemer's condescension! In heaven there is no pride; on Earth and in Hell it is the prevailing character. Men are proud, fallen angels are proud. Christ is ' meek and lowly of heart.' What would become of the universe, were pride to find a place in the infinite mind?

5. *How differently are Christians regarded by Christ, and by evil men!*

Christ descended from heaven, and left ' the glory, which he had with the Father before ever the world was,' to befriend Christians. He became a man, he lived, he laboured through life, he hung upon the cross, and was buried in the tomb, to redeem them from sin and death. He arose from the dead, ascended to Heaven, ' sat down on the right hand of the Majesty on high,' became ' head over all things,' governs all things, and intercedes with his Father for ever, for the benefit of Christians. To save and bless them is, in a sense, his professional employment throughout eternity.

How different is the conduct of evil men towards the very same persons! In the eyes of these men, Christians are objects of contempt and hatred; and in their customary language are styled superstitious, enthusiasts, hypocrites, fanatics, and bigots. Men of the same character mocked and crucified Christ; their followers have ever since exhibited the same spirit; at times in the same, at other times in different manners; but in all its exhibitions the spirit has been the same.

Reason would naturally ask, when contemplating this subject, What evil have Christians done, to merit this treatment? Have they injured these enemies? Have they injured the public? Are they not as industrious, as peaceable, as just, as sincere, as kind, as useful, as other men? Do they not, as parents, children, friends, neighbours, magistrates, and citizens, perform the duties of life as faithfully, as those who are not Christians? Do they transgress the laws, oppose the government, or disturb the peace of society more than their enemies themselves? If they are guilty of such crimes, it can undoubtedly be proved; it ought to be proved; and they ought, accordingly, to be condemned and punished. To this no fair objection can be made even by Christians themselves.

But how far from these dictates of reason has been all the conduct of their adversaries! Have they even attempted any proof of this nature? Have not their accusations been general and indefinite, like the outcry raised against Paul and his companions, 'These, that have turned the world upside down, have come hither also:' the mere exclamations of undiscriminating malevolence, not the specific charges of sober conviction.

To this malevolence what an endless train of men, women, and children——of men covered with the hoary locks of age, of children, scarcely escaped from the cradle——have been offered up on the altar of persecution! What multitudes by the ancient heathen, what multitudes by the idolatrous apostates from Christianity, what multitudes by the infidels of modern times!

Where law and government have prevented these atrocities, how many private and personal injuries, how many sneers and taunts, how many stings of gall and bitterness, have christians been obliged to endure! How many aspersions have been cast on their doctrines, designs, and characters, merely to load them with shame! How frequently are their best intentions misconstrued, and their most benevolent labours perverted, in this very land, originally peopled by Christians, and consecrated to religion: this land converted by Christians from a wilderness into a habitation of industry, peace, civilization, and happiness: to change which from a howling wilderness into an asylum of persecuted piety, Christians encountered the perils of the ocean, and the sufferings of the desart; sustained all the horrors of savage war, and all the evils of famine, disease, and death. In this very land, how many enemies have risen up to the Church of God, among the descendants of these very Christians, and among the brethren of those who are persecuted! They know not, perhaps, that their curses are directed to the 'fathers who begat them,' or that 'their eye is evil towards the mothers who bore them,' nor mistrust, that their scorn is pointed against the source whence, under God, they have derived every enjoyment and every hope.

Against this source of blessings, the religion of Christians, they are more malignant than even against Christians themselves. The Bible is hated more than those who believe it; the doctrines and duties of Christianity more than its professors. What are those duties? They are all summed up

in those two great precepts, ' Thou shalt love the Lord thy
God with all thy heart, and thy neighbour as thyself; ' and in
the means of producing obedience to these precepts in the
soul of man.   What is there in these precepts which can be
the object of vindicable hatred? Who will stand up and say,
who will say in the recesses of his own heart, it is an odious
and contemptible thing to love God, to obey his voice, to
believe in his Son, to shun the anger of God, to escape from
endless sin and misery, and to attain everlasting virtue and
happiness?   Or is it, in the view of common sense, wise to
choose the anger of God rather than his favour, a depraved
character rather than a virtuous one, the company of apostates
and fiends rather than of saints and angels, and hell rather
than heaven?

Is it odious, is it contemptible, is it ridiculous, does it deserve obloquy and persecution, to ' love our neighbour as ourselves,' to exhibit universal kindness, to deal justly, to speak
truth, to fulfil promises, to relieve the distressed, to obey laws,
to reverence magistrates, to resist temptation, to be sober,
chaste, and temperate, and to follow all things which are
' honest, pure, lovely, and of good report? '

Is it, on the contrary, honourable, is it praiseworthy, does
it merit esteem and reward, to be impious, profane, and blasphemous; to be infidels; to have a seared conscience; to
possess a hard heart; to be unjust, unkind, and unfaithful;
to be false, perjured, and seditious; to be light-minded, lewd,
and gluttonous?

Is not the true reason of all this hostility to Christians, the
plain superiority of their character to that of their enemies?
Does not the hatred arise from their consciousness of this
superiority; from the impatience which they feel whenever
they behold it; from the wounds which neighbouring excellence always inflicts? Do they not feel that good men cast
a shade upon their character; reprove them, at least by the
silent and powerful voice of their own virtue; serve as a second
conscience, to hold out their sin before their eyes, and alarm
their hearts with a secret and irresistible sense of future danger? Do not wicked men say in their hearts, as they said at
the time when the Wisdom of Solomon was written, ' Therefore let us lie in wait for the righteous, because he is not for
our turn, and he is clean contrary to our doings. He upbraid-

eth us with our offending the law, and objecteth to our infamy the transgressings of our education. He professeth to have the knowledge of God, and calleth himself the child of the Lord. He was made to reprove our thoughts. He is grievous unto us, even to behold : for his life is not like other mens, his ways are of another fashion. We are esteemed of him as counterfeits ; he abstaineth from our ways as from filthiness ; he pronounceth the end of the just to be blessed ; and maketh his boast that God is his father. Let us see if his words be true, and let us prove what shall happen in the end of him. Let us examine him with despitefulness and torture, that we may know his meekness, and prove his patience. Let us condemn him with a shameful death ; for by his own saying he shall be respected.' Apply this description, and you will find it as exact and just, as if it had been written yesterday, and intended to mark out, in the most definite manner, the loose and profligate of our own land.

But let Christians remember.that these things will not always be. The time will come, it will soon come, when their enemies, however numerous, proud, and prosperous, ' will like sheep be laid in the grave. Death shall feed on them ; and the worm shall cover them. Their beauty shall consume away ; and the upright shall have dominion over them in the morning.' Then shall all the just ' be far from oppression, for they shall not fear : and from terror, for it shall not come near them.' God shall ' redeem them from the power of the grave,' and shall ' wipe away all tears from their eyes.' Then shall it be seen, that their ' light affliction ' in the present world was ' but for a moment,' and that its real and happy efficacy was no other than to ' work for them a far more exceeding and eternal weight of glory.'

SERMON LIX.

CHARACTER OF CHRIST,

AS A KING.

WHICH HE WROUGHT IN CHRIST, WHEN HE RAISED HIM FROM THE DEAD, AND SET HIM AT HIS OWN RIGHT HAND IN THE HEAVENLY PLACES; FAR ABOVE ALL PRINCIPALITY, AND POWER, AND MIGHT, AND DOMINION, AND EVERY NAME THAT IS NAMED, NOT ONLY IN THIS WORLD, BUT ALSO IN THAT WHICH IS TO COME. AND HATH PUT ALL THINGS UNDER HIS FEET; AND GAVE HIM TO BE THE HEAD OVER ALL THINGS TO THE CHURCH.

EPHESIANS I. 20—22.

I HAVE now in a series of Sermons examined the character of Christ, as the Prophet *and* High Priest of mankind. Under his prophetical character I have considered his preaching, by himself, and by his apostles——the things taught by both——the manner in which they were taught——and their consequences. Under his priesthood I have considered his personal holiness ——his atonement——and his intercession.

I shall now, according to the original scheme mentioned when I began to discuss the mediation of Christ, proceed to consider his character *as a King.*

That this character is given to Christ in the Scriptures, in instances almost literally innumerable, is perfectly well known to every reader of the Bible. In the second Psalm there is a solemn annunciation of the kingly office of Christ to the world. It is introduced with these words, ' I have set,' or, as in the Hebrew, have anointed, ' my king on my holy hill

2 F 2

of Zion.' ' Unto us,' says Isaiah, ' a Child is born; unto us a Son is given; and the government shall be upon his shoulder; and his name shall be called Wonderful, Counsellor, the mighty God, the Father of the everlasting age, the Prince of peace; and of the increase of his government and of his peace there shall be no end : Upon the throne of·David, and upon his kingdom, to order it, and to establish it with judgment, and with justice, from henceforth, even for ever.' ' The Lord hath sworn,' says David, ' and will not repent, Thou art a priest for ever, after the order of Melchisedek.' Melchisedek was both a king and a priest. The priesthood of Christ, therefore, was a ' royal priesthood ;' or the priesthood of a person who was at the same time *a king :* like Melchisedek, ' king of righteousness,' and a ' king of peace.' ' Thy throne, O God,' says David, ' is for ever and ever; and the sceptre of thy kingdom is a sceptre of righteousness.' ' He shall reign,' says Gabriel, when predicting his birth to Mary, ' He shall reign over the house of Jacob for ever, and of his kingdom there shall be no end.' ' His name,' says St. John, ' is called the Word of God ; and he hath on his vesture and on his thigh a name written, King of kings, and Lord of lords.'

In the text we are presented with several interesting particulars concerning the kingly office of Christ, which shall now be the subject of our consideration.

We are taught in this passage,

I. *That God hath exalted Christ to this dominion :*

II. *The extent of this dominion :*

III. *That this dominion was given and assumed for the benefit of the church.*

I. *We are taught, that God hath exalted Christ to this Dominion.*

This doctrine is repeatedly taught in the text, in the following expressions: ' He set him at his own right hand in the heavenly places.'——' *He hath put all things under his feet.*'—— ' He gave him to be head over all things.' In these expressions the exaltation of Christ to the dominion and dignity ascribed to him in the text, is as unequivocally attributed to the Father as it can be in human language. Of course, their plain import must be acknowledged by every Christian. I insist on this doctrine of the text; I have insisted on it; particularly because it has been made by Unitarians an argument against the divinity of Christ. " If," they say, " Christ is a divine person, whence is it that we hear so many things said in the Scriptures concerning his exaltation, and particularly of his exaltation by the Father? If Christ is God, how is it possible that he should be in any sense exalted? But should we, contrary to plain probability, suppose him to have undergone voluntarily an apparent humiliation, can he who is truly God be indebted to any other than himself for a restoration to his former dignity and greatness? To be exalted at all necessarily involves a preceding state of inferiority, particularly to the state to which he is exalted; and, certainly, of inferiority to the proper state and character of Jehovah. He who has all power, knowledge, wisdom, and greatness, cannot have more; and, therefore, can in no sense be exalted. To be exalted by *another* person, also, involves dependence on that person; and a dependent being cannot be God."

As this, in my view, is the most plausible argument against the divinity of Christ, and that which has had more weight in my own mind than any other, though, I believe, less relied on and less insisted on by Unitarians, than some others, I shall consider it with particular attention.

As a preface to the answer which I intend to this objection, I observe, that the argument contained in it is in my own view conclusive; and, if applied to the subject without any error, must be admitted in its full force. The error of those who use it, lies in the application made of it to Christ. That exaltation involves a state of preceding inferiority is, I apprehend, intuitively certain; and that he who is exalted by another must be a dependent being, dependent on him by whom he is exalted, cannot be denied. Let us see how far this argument is applicable to Christ, and how far it will conclude against his Deity.

It must be acknowledged by all Trinitarians, as well as others, that if Christ be God in the true and proper sense, it is impossible for him to be exalted above the dignity and greatness which he originally and always possessed. He cannot be more powerful, wise, or excellent. He originally possessed all things, and therefore can have nothing given to him. It cannot, of course, be in this sense that the scriptural writers speak of Christ as exalted.

But it is equally clear, and will be equally insisted on by every Trinitarian, that Christ is *man* as well as *God*. In this character it is evident that he can receive exaltation ; and that to any degree less than infinite. It is farther evident, according to the Trinitarian doctrine concerning Christ, that the Messiah, or Mediator, Jesus Christ, is distinguishable from Christ considered as God, and from Christ considered as man : being constituted by the union of the Eternal Word with the man Christ Jesus : " An union," as the Westminster Assembly expresses it, " of two distinct natures in one person for ever." This Mediator in his complete character began to exist at the birth of the man Jesus Christ, as being a person then new to the universe. Of this Mediator, then commencing his perfect existence, the predictions concerning the kingdom of Christ, and the accounts concerning his assumption of that kingdom, are, I apprehend, all or nearly all written. It is of the Mediator that it is said, ' I set my King on the holy hill of Zion.' It is of the ' Son ' who was ' born,' and whose ' name was called Wonderful, Counsellor, the mighty God ;' on whose ' shoulder the government was to be placed.' Of the Mediator Gabriel said, ' He shall reign over the house of Jacob for ever, and of his kingdom there shall be no end.' Of the Mediator St. Paul says, ' Wherefore God hath highly exalted him, and given him a name which is above every name ; that at the name of Jesus every knee should bow, of things in heaven, and things in earth.' It is of the Mediator that it is said in the text, ' God set him at his own right hand in the heavenly places, far above every name, that is named in this world, and in that which is to come :' and that it is farther said ' he hath put all things under his feet ; and given him to be head over all things to his church.'

As the Mediator Jesus Christ began to exist at the birth of the man Jesus Christ, so, until his resurrection, he existed in a state of humiliation only. The Word, though originally ' in the form of God, and' justly ' thinking it no robbery to be equal with God, yet' voluntarily ' took upon himself the form of a servant, and was made in the likeness of men.' In this form or character of a servant, he fulfilled all the several duties which he had engaged to perform, and in this humble character he acted till he arose from the dead.

It will not be denied, that this person, allowing him to have

existed, was capable of exaltation ; nor that, if he received it
at all, he must receive it from him under whose commission he
acted, and to whom he had voluntarily become a servant when
' he was made in the likeness of men.'

This person, it is plain, had received no kingdom until his
ascension to heaven ; had not before been ' head over all
things to the church ;' nor been ' exalted above every name
that is named in this world, and that to come.' This kingdom
is frequently spoken of as the reward of the labours and sufferings of Christ, in the character of Mediator. These labours
and sufferings had never before existed, and therefore could
not have been rewarded at an earlier period.

From these views of the subject it is clear that although
Christ, as God, was incapable of exaltation equally as of suffering ; yet as Mediator he was capable of both ; and that exaltation was with perfect propriety given him by the glorious
person under whose authority he placed himself, by voluntarily assuming the form of a servant. In this view of the subject the Trinitarians are so far from being inconsistent with
themselves, that they merely accord with the necessary consequences of their own doctrine.

II. *We are taught in the text the extent of this Kingdom.*
The word ' Kingdom ' sometimes denotes the rule which is
exercised by a king ; and sometimes the persons and regions
which he rules. According to the former of these senses,
David says, ' Thou hast prepared thy throne in the heavens ;
and thy kingdom is over all.' Of the latter sense, ' it shall be
given thee, to the half of the kingdom,' is an example.

1. *The kingdom of Christ is the universe.*
In the text, the extent of Christ's kingdom is repeatedly
denoted by the phrase ' all things.' The absolute universality
of this phrase is sufficiently manifest from the text itself, when
it is said, that ' he is set at the right hand of God, far above
all principality, and power, and might, and dominion, and
every name, that is named in this world, and that which is to
come.' But it is placed beyond all doubt in the corresponding
passage in Philippians ii. 10, where it is said, that ' every knee
should bow, of things in heaven, and things in earth, and
things under the earth, and that every tongue should confess,
'hat Jesus Christ is Lord.' ' Heaven and earth ' is the phrase

by which the Jews denoted the universe. When they meant to express this idea with emphasis, they sometimes added the phrase, ' under the Earth.' Here we have the most emphatical language ever used by a Jew to denote the Universe, and all things which it contains. ' Every knee ' in this vast dominion we are assured will one day bow to Christ ; and ' every tongue ' found in it will confess, at a future period, that ' Christ is Lord.' In the same manner, in Colossians i. 16. ' All things ' are said to be ' created by him, and for him ;' whether they be ' visible or invisible,' whether in ' heaven or in earth.' As in this absolutely universal sense they were made by and for himself, so from this passage we cannot doubt, that in the same sense they will be his absolute possession, and that *after* as well as *before* he became Mediator. This world, therefore, the planetary system, the stellary systems, the highest heavens above, and hell beneath, are all included, and alike included in the immense empire of which he is the head. Men are his subjects. Angels, both fallen and virtuous, are his subjects ; and the inhabitants of the innumerable worlds which compose the universe, ' confess that he is Lord, to the glory of God the Father.'

2. *His authority over this great kingdom is supreme.*

The whole course of providence is under his immediate control. ' He upholds all things by the word of his power,' and directs them with an universal and irresistible agency to their proper ends. The affairs of this world and all its inhabitants are directed by his hand. He has the ' keys of hell and of death,' or of the world of departed spirits. ' He openeth, and no one shutteth ; and shutteth, and no one openeth.' Into that world none enter without his bidding, and out of it none can come but by his permission. The world of misery beneath, is in the same manner under his absolute dominion ; and the glorious system of happiness in the heavens above, is the mere result of his wisdom, goodness, and power.

In the exercise of this dominion he will, at the close of this providential system, summon the dead from the grave, consume the world with fire, and judge both the righteous and the wicked, both angels and men. In the exercise of the same authority also, he will send the wicked down to the regions of darkness, and ' punish them with an everlasting destruction, from his presence, and from the glory of his power.'

III. We are taught in the text, that *this kingdom was given and assumed for the benefit of the church.*

This doctrine is directly asserted in the text; and will, therefore, not be questioned. In the exercise of his government over all things for the benefit of his church, he,

1. *Defends it from all enemies.*

The enemies of Christians are their temptations, internal and external; their sins, death, evil men, and evil angels.

Against their *temptations* he furnishes them with defence by all the instructions, precepts, warnings, reproofs, threatenings, and promises which are contained in his word. These constitute a continual and efficacious protection from the influence of lusts within, and enemies without, by rectifying the views of the soul concerning its interest and duty, awakening in it solemn consideration, alarming it with affecting apprehensions, encouraging it with hope, alluring it with love and gratitude, stimulating it with the prospect of a glorious reward, and thus prompting it to suspend the dangerous purpose, to watch against the rising sin, to oppose with vigour the intruding temptation, and to pray unceasingly for that divine assistance which ' every one that asketh shall receive.'

To the means of defence furnished by his word he adds continually the peculiar influences of his Spirit. This glorious agent commissioned by Christ for this divine purpose, diffuses through the soul the spirit of resistance, the hope of victory, the strength necessary to obtain it, and the peace and joy which are its happy as well as unfailing consequences.

From their *sins* he began to deliver them by his atonement. This work he carries on by his intercession, and completes by his providence. In the present world, where all things are imperfect, this deliverance partakes, it must be acknowledged, of the common nature; yet it is such, as to secure them from every fatal evil, and such as we know to be one of those things, which ' work together for their good.' Their progress towards perfect holiness is slow, irregular, and interrupted; yet it is real and important; producing hope, comfort, and perseverance unto the end.

At the *judgment* this deliverance will be complete. There the glorious effects of his atonement and intercession will be all realized. Every one of his followers will find himself entirely interested in them both; and will see, at that trying period, all his sins washed away, and nothing left to be ' laid to his charge.' These dreadful enemies, at this dreadful season, will be powerless, and overthrown ; and Christians will ' be more than conquerors through him that hath loved them.'

From *death* he has taken away its sting, and from the grave its victory. Death, so terrible to the impenitent, will be found by them to be no other than a rough, gloomy, unwelcome messenger, sent to summon them to the house of their Father. Over all its dangerous power they will triumph in a glorious manner, and be enabled to sing with everlasting exultation, ' O Death ! where is thy sting ? O Grave ! where is thy victory?' All the preceding diseases, sorrows, and trials through which they have passed in this vale of tears, they will distinctly perceive to have been scarcely enemies at all. On the contrary, they will appear to have been sent with infinite kindness, to check them in the career of iniquity, to warn them of approaching danger or existing sin, and to recal them effectually to the path of life.

Against *evil men* and *evil angels* he furnishes them throughout their pilgrimage with a continual and sufficient protection : not a protection, indeed, which will prevent them from suffering and sorrow ; but this is because suffering and sorrow are necessary to their safety and improvement. Hence they are maligned, calumniated, despised, persecuted, and at times brought to a violent death. They are also at times perplexed, ensnared, allured, and tempted to wander from their duty by art, sophistry, and falsehood. By the former class of evils they are gradually weaned from that love of the world, that desire of human favour, and that lust for human applause, which so naturally charm the eyes and fascinate the hearts even of Christians, and which are wholly inconsistent with the love of God. By the latter they are made sensible of their own weakness, taught their dependence on God, driven to their closets and their knees, and induced to ' walk humbly with God ' all their days, in the intimate and most profitable communion of faith and prayer.

' The triumphing of the wicked is short ;' and ' the upright shall have dominion over them in the morning.' When Christians are ' redeemed from the power of the grave,' they shall see all these enemies retiring behind them, and speedily vanishing, with the flight of ages, to a distance immeasurable by the power of the imagination. All around them will then be friends. God will then be their Father, angels their brethren, happiness their portion, and heaven their everlasting home.

2. *In the exercise of this authority he bestows on them all good, temporal and eternal.*

Of temporal good he gives them all that is necessary or useful for such beings in such a state. The world may be, and often is, a vale of tears; and life a solitary pilgrimage through ' a weary land.' Poverty may betide, afflictions befal, diseases arrest, and death, at what they may think an untimely period, summon them away. By enemies they may be surrounded, and by friends forsaken. They may be exposed to hatred, contumely, and persecution. Their days may be overcast with gloom, and their nights with sorrow. But he has assured them, and they will find the assurance verified, that these are ' light afflictions,' which only ' work for them an eternal weight of glory;' and that these as truly as all other things ' work together for their good.' Even these, therefore, however forbidding their aspect, will be found to be good for *them*; good upon the whole; good in such a sense as to render their whole destiny brighter, better, and more happy.

In the mean time, he furnishes them also, and furnishes them abundantly, with spiritual good. He furnishes them with the sanctification of the soul. He gives them light to discover their own duty, and his glory and excellency. He gives them strength to resist temptations; sorrow for their sins; patience, resignation, and fortitude, under afflictions; faith, to confide in him, and to ' overcome the world;' hope, to encourage their efforts, and to fix them firmly in their obedience; peace, to hush the tumults of the mind, and to shed a cheerful serenity over all its affections; and joy, to assure them of his glorious presence, and to anticipate in their thoughts the everlasting joy of his immortal kingdom.

In the future world, when death shall have been ' swallowed up in victory,' and ' all tears shall be wiped away from their eyes,' he will begin to bestow upon them eternal good. In this ' fulness of joy,' every thing will be only delightful. Their bodies, raised from the grave ' in incorruption, power, and glory,' will be ' spiritual, immortal,' ever vigorous, and ever young; their souls, purified from every stain, and luminous with knowledge and virtue, will be images of his own amiableness and consummate beauty; their stations, allotments, and employments will be such as become those who are ' kings and priests in the heavenly world; their companions will be cherubim and seraphim, and their home will be the house of their Father and their God.

At the same time, in bestowing all this good he himself is the dispenser, and the good dispensed. ' I,' says Christ, ' am the light of the world.' ' The city,' says St. John, ' had no need of the sun, neither of the moon, to shine in it; for the glory of God did lighten it, and the Lamb is the light thereof.' In other words, Christ is the medium through which all the knowledge of God is conveyed to the intelligent universe, his character discovered, and his pleasure made known. Of the heavenly world, particularly, he is here expressly declared to be ' the light:' ' The glory of God did lighten it, and the Lamb is the light thereof.' The Lamb is this ' glory of God,' which is said to be ' the light of Heaven.' Christ is not only the dispenser of the good enjoyed in heaven, but the very good which is dispensed; not only the dispenser of knowledge, but the thing known; not only the communication of enjoyment, but the thing enjoyed: the person divinely seen, loved, worshipped, and praised for ever. In his presence all his followers and all their happy companions ' with open face beholding' in him, ' as in a glass, the glory of the Lord, will be changed into the same image from glory to glory, as by the Spirit of the Lord.'

REMARKS.

From these observations may be, conclusively argued,

1. *The Divinity of Christ.*

From the text, and the comments here given on it, it is evident that Christ holds the sceptre of the universe, and rules the great kingdom of Jehovah. Let me ask, Who but the infinitely perfect one, can possibly hold such a sceptre, or control successfully, or even at all, such an empire? Unless he be *everywhere present,* how can he everywhere act, rule, and bring to pass such events as he chooses; such as are necessary to the divine glory, and the universal good? Unless thus

present, acting and ruling, how can he prevent the existence
of such things as will be injurious to this good; or fail to be
disappointed of his own purposes, and ultimately of the supreme end of all his labour? How evident is it, even to our
view, that inanimate things must cease to operate and to move
in their destined course, that animated beings must wander
out of it, and that rational beings must, if virtuous, go astray,
from the defectiveness of their imperfect nature; and, if sinful,
from malignity and design. The evil designs of the latter,
particularly, must, if he be not present, multiply in their numbers, and increase in their strength, until various parts of this
immense kingdom become disordered, and perhaps destroyed.
What an impression would it make on the feelings, what a
change in the affairs of this world, if mankind, if evil spirits,
were to know that the ruler of all things would be absent from
it even a single year! What courage would sinners gather!
With what strength, and to what a multitude, would sins ac-
cumulate! What a tempest of violence would ravage this
globe! To what a mountainous height would be heaped up
the mass of human misery!

Nor is *his absolute knowledge of all things* less indispensable than his universal presence. This knowledge is completely
necessary to enable him to discern the *ends* deserving of his
pursuit, and the proper *means* of their accomplishment.
When all these are resolved on, the same knowledge only can
direct the operations of these means, prevent their disorder
or their failure, preclude successful opposition, and avoid the
consequent confusion, disturbance, and disappointment. Especially is this knowledge indispensable to the efficacious government of rational or moral agents. The powers of these
agents are *thought, volition*, and *motivity*: all invisible to
every eye, except the omniscient; and, if discovered at all
before their operations exist, discovered by that eye only. But
these agents are beyond measure the most important instruments of the divine designs in this great kingdom; and, if not
prevented, the most able to disturb its order and happiness.
It is plain, therefore, that he who rules the universe must, in
order to prevent the disturbance of this kingdom, ' understand
the thoughts afar off;' or, as in the translation formerly in use,
' long before' they are formed.

By the same knowledge only is the same exalted person

qualified to be the final judge and rewarder of the universe. A great part of tho sin and holiness of such beings, and of the enhancements and dimunitions of both, lies altogether in their thoughts and volitions. To judge his creatures justly, then, it is absolutely necessary that he should ' search the heart and try the reins ' of every rational being.

With the same knowledge only can he determine, apportion, and execute the unnumbered allotments of intelligent creatures. These united form an immense and eternal system of providence ; compared with which the providence exercised in this world is but a point ; and this vast system must, indispensably, be contrived aright, and without any defect, from the beginning. The parts of which it will be composed will be literally infinite, and can be devised only by an infinite mind.

Nor is *omnipotence* less necessary for all these vast and innumerable purposes than *omniscience* and *omnipresence*. No power inferior to omnipotence could produce or hold together so many beings, or carry on to completion so many and so various purposes. To the power actually exerted for these ends every being must be completely subjected, and all created power entirely subordinate. An absolute and irresistible dominion must be exercised unceasingly over every part of his kingdom, or the great designs of creation and providence must be in continual danger of being finally frustrated.

Equally necessary is *infinite rectitude* for the just, benevolent, and perfect administration of such a government. The least defect, the least wrong, would here be fatal. From the decision there can be no appeal, from the arm of execution there can be no escape. A creature, if wronged here, is wronged hopelessly, and for ever. The ruling mind must, therefore, be subject to no weakness, passion, or partiality. Without perfect rectitude there can be no ultimate confidence ; and without such confidence, voluntary or virtuous obedience cannot exist.

Thus, when Christ is ' exalted to be head over all things,' and constituted the ruler, judge, and rewarder of the universe; he is plainly exalted to a station and character demanding infinite attributes, perfections literally divine. Either then be possesses these attributes, or he has been exalted to a station which, so far as reason can discern, he is unqualified to fill. But he was exalted to this station by unerring and boundless wisdom. Of course, he certainly possesses all the qualifications which it can demand. In other words, he is a person literally divine.

2. *From the same observations we may discern how greatly we need such a friend as Christ.*

That we are creatures wholly dependent, frail, ignorant, exposed, and unable to protect ourselves or provide for our interests, needs neither proof nor illustration. To us futurity is all blank. Between our present existence and the approaching vast of being, hangs a dark and impenetrable cloud. What is beyond it no human eye is able to discern, and no human foresight to conjecture. There, however, all our great concerns lie, and are every moment increasing in their number and importance. There we shall enjoy the exquisite emotions and the high dignity of immortal virtue, the pure pleasures of a serene, self-approving mind, the eternal interchange of esteem and affection with the ' general assembly of the first-born,' and the uninterrupted favour of God in the world of joy ; or we shall suffer the unceasing anguish of a guilty, self-ruined soul, the malignity of evil men and evil angels, and the wrath of our offended Creator, in the regions of woe. Between these infinitely distant allotments there is no medium, no intervening state, to which those who fail of final approbation can betake themselves for refuge. When, therefore, we bid adieu to this world, we shall meet with events whose importance nothing but omniscience can estimate, to us utterly uncertain, and utterly beyond our power.

Nay, the present moment, and every moment when present, is fraught with consequences incapable of being estimated by any finite understanding. On time eternity hangs. As we live here we shall live hereafter. If our time be well employed, and our talents well used, it will be well with us in the end. But if we abuse both here, it will be ill with us hereafter. The present moment is important, chiefly as it affects those which are future ; begins or strengthens an evil or virtuous habit, depraves or amends the soul, hardens or softens the heart, and contributes in this way to advance us towards heaven, or towards hell. There is no man who is not better or worse to day, by means of what he thought, designed, or did yesterday. The present day, therefore, is not only important in itself, as a season for which we must give an account, but because of the influence which it will have on the events of the morrow. Thus circumstanced, frail, irresolute, wandering, wicked, exposed to immense dangers, and yet capable of immense enjoyments, how infinitely desirable is it that we should have such a friend as Christ. In his mind are treasured up all the means of happiness, which we need, the immense power, knowledge, and goodness, the unchangeable truth, faithfulness, and mercy which, and which only, can provide and secure for us immortal blessings, or preserve us from evils which know no end. In all places he is present, over all things he rules with an irresistible dominion. No being, no event, can be hidden from his eye. No enemy, however insidious, or however powerful, can escape from his hand. His disposition is written in letters of blood on the cross. He who died that sinners might live, he who prayed for his murderers, while imbruing their hands in his blood, can need, can add no proofs of his compassion for men. This glorious Redeemer is also ' the same yesterday, to-day, and for ever.' Such a friend to man as he was when he hung on the cross, he will be throughout eternity ; and to every one, who sincerely desires an interest in his good-will, he will manifest his friendship in an endless succession of blessings.

While we wander through the wilderness of life, amid so many wants, how desirable must it be to find a friend able and willing to furnish the needed supplies ! Amid so many enemies and dangers, how desirable must it be to find a friend, able and willing to furnish the necessary protection ! Amid so many temptations to watch over us ! Amid so many sorrows, to relieve us ; in solitude, to be our companion ; in difficulties, our helper ; in despondence, our support ; in disease, our physician ; in death, our hope, resurrection, and life ! In a word, how desirable must it be to find a friend who, throughout all the strange, discouraging state of the present life, will give us peace, consolation, and joy, and cause all things, even the most untoward and perplexing, to ' work together for our good !'

On a dying bed especially, when our flesh and our hearts must fail of course, our earthly friends yield us little consolation, and no hope, and the world itself retires from our view, how delightful will such a friend be! Then the soul, uncertain, alone, hovering over the form which it has so long inhabited, and stretching its wings for its flight into the unknown vast, will sigh and pant for an arm on which it may lean, and a bosom on which it may safely recline. But there Christ is present, with all his tenderness and all his power. With one hand he holds the anchor of hope, and with the other he points the way to heaven.

In the final resurrection, when the universe shall rend asunder, and the elements of this great world shall rush together with immense confusion and ruin, how supporting, how ravishing will it be, when we awake from our final sleep, and ascend from the dust in which our bodies have been so long buried, to find this glorious Redeemer ' re-fashioning our vile bodies like unto his glorious body,' and re-uniting them to our minds, purified and immortal! With what emotions shall we arise, and stand, and behold the Judge descend ' in the glory of his Father, with all his holy angels!' With what emotions shall we see the same unchangeable and everlasting friend placing us on his right hand in glory and honour, which kings will covet in vain, and before which all earthly grandeur shall be forgotten! With what melody will the voice of the Redeemer burst on our ears, when he proclaims, ' Come ye blessed of my Father, inherit the kingdom prepared for you from the foundation of the world!' How will the soul distend with transport, when, accompanied by ' the church of the first-born,' and surrounded by ' thrones, principalities, and powers,' it shall begin its flight towards the highest heavens, to meet ' his Father and our Father, his God and our God!' What an internal heaven will dawn in the mind, when we shall be presented before the throne of Jehovah; and, settled amid our own brethren in our immortal inheritance and our final home, behold all our sins washed away, our trials ended, our dangers escaped, our sorrows left behind us, and our reward begun, in that world where all things are ever new, delightful, and divine!

At these solemn and amazing seasons, how differently will those unhappy beings feel, who on a death bed find no such friend; who rise to the resurrection of damnation; who are

left behind, when the righteous ascend to meet their Redeemer; who are placed on the left hand at the final trial; and to
whom in the most awful language which was ever heard in the
universe, he will say, ' Depart, ye cursed, into everlasting fire,
prepared for the devil and his angels.'

SERMON LX.

MIRACLES OF CHRIST.

JESUS OF NAZARETH, A MAN APPROVED OF GOD AMONG YOU, BY
MIRACLES, AND WONDERS, AND SIGNS, WHICH GOD DID BY HIM
IN THE MIDST OF YOU, AS YE YOURSELVES ALSO KNOW.

ACTS II. 22.

IN a series of Discourses, I have considered at length the
character of Christ as a Prophet, Priest, and King. I shall
now proceed to investigate his character as a *worker of
Miracles.*

In the text, Christ is styled, 'Jesus of Nazareth, a man
approved of God among' the Jews. This approbation is declared to have been testified ' by miracles, and wonders, and
signs, which God did by him in the midst' of that people :
and of all this it is asserted the Jews themselves had been
witnesses. These subjects I propose to consider in the following Discourse, so far as I shall judge necessary to my general design. I shall however, neglect the order of the text ;
and adopt one more suited to the present purpose. I shall

I. *Define a miracle :*
II. *Show that Christ wrought miracles :*
III. *Point out their importance.*

I. *I shall define a miracle.*

A miracle is a suspension or counteraction of what are
called the laws of nature. By the laws of nature I intend
those regular courses of divine agency which we discern in
the world around us. God, to enable us to understand his

works, and his character as displayed in them, and to enable us also to direct with success our own conduct in the various duties of life, and probably for other purposes, has been pleased to conform his own agency to certain rules formed by his wisdom; called by philosophers, laws of nature, and in the Scriptures, ' ordinances of heaven.'   To these laws all things with which we are acquainted by experience are usually conformed.   A miracle is either a *suspension* or *counteraction* of these laws; or, more definitely, of the progress of things according to these laws.   I have chosen both these words, because I would include all possible miracles, and because some events of this kind may more obviously seem to be suspensions, and others counteractions, of these laws.

II. *I shall show that Christ wrought miracles.*

In this case I shall, for the present, assume the story as true which is told us by the evangelists concerning the works of Christ, and refer my observations on this subject to another part of the discussion.   Taking it then for granted that Christ really did the things ascribed to him in the Gospel, I assert, that a considerable number of these things were real miracles. I say a considerable number, because it would be idle to extend the debate on the present occasion to any thing supposed to be of a dubious nature, and because, after every deduction which can be asked, a sufficient number will remain to satisfy every wish of a Christian, and to overthrow every cavil of an infidel.   Among other examples of this nature, I select the following :—

The case of the man, who was born blind; who observed justly concerning it, ' Since the world began it was not heard that any man opened the eyes of one that was born blind.' No arguments are necessary to prove this to have been a miracle in the perfect sense; for every individual knows, that it is a total counteraction of the laws of nature, that clay, made of spittle and earth, and smeared upon the eyes, should restore sight to a person born blind.   I select this case the rather, because it was formally examined by the Jewish Sanhedrim, and evinced to have been real beyond every doubt.

The case of *Christ's walking upon the water in the lake of Gennaseret*, is another equally unexceptionable.

The cures which he wrought on lepers by his mere word

and pleasure——cures which no other person has been able to perform by any means whatever, are instances of the same nature.   Of the same nature also, are those cases in which *he raised the dead to life : viz.* the daughter of Jairus, the son of the widow of Nain, and Lazarus.   That these persons were all really dead, there is not the least room to doubt ; that they were all raised to life is certain.

I shall only add two instances more——*one in which he fed four, and the other in which he fed five thousand men, besides women and children, with a few loaves of barley-bread and a few little fishes.*   In this miracle *creating power* was immediately exerted, with a degree of evidence which nothing could resist, or rationally question.

That all these were miracles, according to the definition given above, must I think be acknowledged without hesitation.   Arguments to prove this point, therefore, would be superfluous.

That these facts really took place, and that the narration which conveys the knowledge of them to us is true, has been so often, so clearly, and so unanswerably proved, that to attempt to argue this point here would seem a supererogatory labour.   All of you have, or easily can have, access to a numerous train of books containing this proof, elucidated with high advantage.   I shall, therefore, consider this subject in a manner extremely summary, and calculated to exhibit little more than a mere synopsis of evidence pertaining to the subject.   For this end I observe,

1. *The facts were of such a nature as to be obvious, in the plainest manner, to the senses and understanding of all men possessed of common sense.*

2. *The narrators were eye and ear-witnesses of them.*

3. *They were performed in the most public manner ;* in the presence of multitudes, the greater part of whom were opposers of Christ.

4. *They were generally believed ;* so generally, as to induce, customarily, the friends of the sick and distressed wherever Christ came to apply to him, with absolute confidence in his ability to relieve them : a fact which proves the universal conviction of the Jewish people at that time, that Christ certainly and continually wrought miracles.   But this conviction could

not have existed to any considerable extent, unless he had actually wrought miracles.

5. *The apostles had no possible interest to deceive their fellowmen.* They neither gained, could gain, nor attempted to gain, any advantage in the present world by publishing this story. On the contrary, they suffered through life the loss of all things while declaring it, and the religion of which it was the foundation, to mankind. In the future world, as Jews, believing the Old Testament to be the word of God, they could expect nothing but perdition, as the reward of their useless imposture.

6. *They were men whose integrity has not only been unimpeached, but is singular.* This is evinced by the fact, that innumerable multitudes of their countrymen, and of many other nations, embraced the religion which they taught ; committed to their guidance their souls, and their everlasting interests ; hazarded and yielded all that they held dear in this world for the sake of this religion ; and still esteemed these very men, through whose instrumentality they had been brought into these distresses, the very best of mankind. It is also proved by the farther fact, that in the ages immediately succeeding, as well as in those which have followed, their character has in this respect stood higher than that of any other men whatever.

7. *Their narratives wear more marks of veracity than any other which the world can furnish.*

8. *The existence of these miracles is acknowledged by Jews and heathen, as well as Christians, and was wholly uncontradicted by either for fifteen hundred years.*

9. *These narratives were the genuine productions of those to whom they are ascribed.* That they were written by these persons is unanswerably proved by the testimony of their contemporaries, and very early followers. That they have come down to us uncorrupted and unmutilated is certain, from the age and coincidence of numerous Manuscripts, from the versions early made of them into various languages, from the almost innumerable quotations from them found in other books still extant, from the joint consent of orthodox Christians and heretics, from the impossibility of corrupting them with success, because of the frequency and constancy with which they

were read in public and in private, because of the numerous copies very early diffused throughout all Christian countries, because of the profound religious veneration with which they were regarded, and because of the eagle-eyed watchfulness with which contending sects guarded every passage which furnished any inducement to corruption or mutilation.

No other history can boast of these, or one half of these powerful proofs of its genuineness and authenticity. If, then, we do not admit these narratives to be true, we must bid a final farewell to the admission of all historical testimony.

Mr. Hume has written an Essay to disprove the existence of the miracles recorded in the Gospel. In the introduction to this Essay he says, " he flatters himself he has discovered an argument which will prove an everlasting check to all kinds of superstitious delusion." When this Essay first appeared, it was received with universal triumph by Infidels, and with no small degree of alarm by timorous Christians. Since that time, however, it has been repeatedly answered ; it was most triumphantly refuted by Dr. Campbell, and completely exposed as a mere mass of sophistry, ingenious indeed, but shamefully disingenuous, and utterly destitute of solid argument, and real evidence.

After such ample refutation, it would be a useless employment for me to enter upon a formal examination of the scheme contained in this Essay. I shall, therefore, dismiss it with a few observations.

The great doctrine of Mr. Hume is this : " That according to the experience of man, all things uniformly exist agreeably to the laws of nature ; that every instance of our experience is not only an evidence that the thing experienced exists in the manner which we perceive, but that all the following events of the same kind will also exist in the same manner." This evidence he considers, also, as increased by every succeeding instance of the same experience. According to his scheme, therefore, the evidence that any thing which we perceive by our senses now exists, is made up of the present testimony of our senses, united with all former testimonies of the same nature to facts of the same kind. The existence of any fact, therefore, instead of being completely proved, is only partially proved by the present testimony of our senses to its existence. According to this scheme, therefore, we who are present in this house know that ourselves and others are present, partly by seeing each other present at this time, and partly by remembering that we have been present heretofore. Of course, the first time we were thus present we had not the same assurance of this fact, as the second time. This assurance became still greater the third time; greater still the fourth; and thus has gone on accumulating strength in every succeeding instance. Every person, therefore, who has been here one hundred times, has an hundred times the evidence that he is now here, which he had when he was here the first time that he was then present; and I, who during twenty-four years have been present many thousand times, know that I am now here with a thousand degrees of evidence more than is possessed concerning the like fact by any other person who is present. A scheme of reasoning which conducts to such a manifest and gross absurdity must, one would think, have been seen to be false by a man much less sagacious than Mr. Hume.

Every man of common sense knows, and cannot avoid knowing even at a glance, that all the evidence which we possess, or can possess, of the existence of any fact, is furnished by *the present testimony* of our senses to that fact. Of course, every such man knows equally well, that no testimony of the senses to any preceding fact can affect a present fact in any manner whatever. The person who is now present in this house for the first time, has all the evidence that he is here, which is possessed by him who has been here a thousand times before. The evidence of the senses to any single fact is all the evidence of which that fact is ever capable. Nor can it be increased, even in the minutest degree, by the same evidence repeated concerning similar facts existing afterwards, in any supposable number of instances. He who has crossed a ferry safely, never thought of crossing it a second time in order to know whether he was safe or not.

The influence which experience is intended by Mr. Hume to have on our belief of the existence of future events, is of the same nature. Past experience is, by his scheme, the great criterion for determining on all that which is to come. An event which has already been witnessed a thousand times is, in his view, to be expected again with a confidence exactly proportioned to this number. If an event, on the contrary, has not taken place, it is not to be at all expected; but regarded as incredible. Thus, if a ferry-boat has crossed the ferry a thousand times without sinking, the probability is, as one thousand to nothing, that it will never sink hereafter.

The analogy here referred to is founded on the general maxim, that " the same causes produce in the same circumstances the same effects." The instances in which causes and circumstances *apparently* the same, are *really* such, are so few, that, in the actual state of things, it can answer Mr. Hume's purpose in a very small number of cases only. Almost always the causes themselves, or the circumstances in which they operate, are in this mutable world so continually changed, that analogies founded on this maxim are rarely exact, and are, therefore, rarely safe rules for forming conclusions. All men are so sensible of this truth, that they easily and uniformly admit testimony as a sufficient proof of the fallacy of such conclusions. The smallest credible testimony will induce any man to believe that a ferry-boat has sunk, although it may before have crossed safely and regularly for many years. Much more do we always admit beforehand, that almost all events may come to pass, contrary in their nature and appearance to those which have already happened.

Mr. Hume exhibits to me a full conviction in his own mind that his scheme was unsound, by the recourse which he was obliged to have to the disingenuous arts of controversy. Thus he at first uses the word *experience*, which is all-important to this controversy, to denote, what alone it truly denotes, *the actual evidence of a man's own senses.* In the progress of his Essay, he soon diverts it into a sense entirely different; and means by it *the experience of all who have preceded us.* But of their experience we know nothing, except by *testimony;* the very thing to which Mr. Hume professedly opposes what he calls *experience.* On this testimony, styled by him *experience,* he founds an argument upon which he places great reliance, to overthrow the evidence of the same testimony. Thus he declares miracles to be contrary to all experience, meaning by it the experience of all mankind, when he knew that a part of mankind had testified that they in their own experience had been witnesses of miracles; for this testimony was the very thing against which he wrote his Essay.

Miracles he defines to be " violations and transgressions of the laws of nature." These words being regularly used to denote oppositions of moral beings to moral laws, and involving naturally the idea of turpitude, or wrong, were, I presume, used to attach to miracles an idea of some variation from that perfect moral conduct which we attribute to God.

" Miracles," he also says, " are contrary to our experience." In this declaration he is unhappy. They may be truly said to be *aside* from our experience ; but are in no sense contrary to it. All that can be said is, that we have not *witnessed* miracles. No man can say, that he has experienced any thing contrary to them.

Having made these observations, I proceed to examine Mr. Hume's capital doctrine, that *testimony cannot evince the reality of a miracle.* His argument is this : The evidence that any thing exists in any given case, is exactly proportioned to the number of instances in which it is known to have happened before. If then an event have happened a thousand times, and the contrary event should afterwards happen once ; then there are one thousand degrees of evidence against the existence of this contrary event, and but one in its favour. We are, therefore, compelled, by a balance of nine hundred and ninety-nine degrees of evidence against nothing to believe that this event has not taken place. We are here, as Mr. Hume teaches, to weigh experience against experience, and to be governed in our decision by the preponderating weight. In this manner he determines that our experience has in the number of instances furnished such a vast preponderation of evidence against the existence of a miracle, that if we were to witness it, we could not rationally believe it to have existed, until it had taken place as many times, and some more, than what he calls the contrary event. For example : if we have known a thousand deceased persons to have been buried, and none of them to have been raised from the grave ; we cannot rationally believe a man to have been raised from the grave, although we saw him rise, conversed with him, and lived with him ever so many years afterwards. Before we begin to believe that a person was raised from the dead, we must have seen, at least, one more person thus raised than the whole number who have been buried, and have not risen. Then, and not till then, we shall become possessed of one degree of evidence, that a person has been raised from the dead:

the whole influence of all the preceding resurrections being to diminish, successively, the previously existing evidence against the fact, that a person has been raised from the dead.   Our own experience of the existence of a miracle is thus not to be admitted as a proof of its existence.   But as testimony is founded on experience, and is evidence of a less certain nature, it is clear, that what experience cannot prove can never be evinced by testimony.

This reasoning has a grave and specious appearance, but is plainly destitute of all solidity.   Every man knows by his own experience, that the repetition of an event contributes nothing to the proof or certainty of its existence.   The proof of the existence of any event lies wholly in the testimony of our senses.   When the event is, as we customarily say, repeated, that is, when another similiar event takes place, our senses in the same manner prove to us the existence of this event.   But the evidence which they give us of the second has no retrospective influence on the first, as the evidence given of the first has no influence on the second.   In each instance the evidence is complete ; nor can it be affected by any thing which may precede it, or succeed it.   What is once seen and known, is as perfectly seen and known as it can be, and in the only manner in which it can be ever seen and known.   If we were to see a man raised from the grave, we should know that he was thus raised, as perfectly as it could be known by us ; nor would it make the least difference in the evidence or certainly of this fact, whether thousands, or none, were raised afterwards.

In perfect accordance with these observations has been the conduct of mankind in every age and country.   No tribunal of justice ever asked the question, whether a crime had been *twice* committed, in order to determine with the more certainty and better evidence, that it had been committed *once*.   No evidence of this nature before any such tribunal was ever adduced, or considered as proper to be adduced, to evince the existence of any fact, or to disprove its existence.   No individual ever thought of recurring to the testimony of his senses on a former occasion, to strengthen their evidence on a present occasion.

The man born blind (to apply this scheme directly to miracles) could not possibly feel the necessity or advantage of inquiring whether he had been restored to sight before, in order to determine that he had received it from the hands of Christ ; or of asking the question, whether he saw at any time before, to prove that he saw now.   The leper who acquired his health by the command of Christ, was as perfectly conscious of his restoration, as if he had been restored on twenty former occasions.   All around him also, when they saw the scales fall off with which he had been incrusted, and the bloom of health return ; when they beheld his activity renewed, and all the proofs of soundness exhibited to their eyes, perceived the cure as perfectly, as if they had been witnesses of one hundred preceding cures of the same nature.

What is true of these is equally true of all similar cases. Experience, therefore, is capable of completely proving the existence of a miracle.

What we experience we can declare, and declare exactly as it has happened.   Were this always done, testimony would have exactly the same strength of evidence which experience is admitted to possess.   It is not, however, always done.   Errors, both intentional and unintentional, and those very numerous, accompany the declarations of men.   Still the weight of testimony is very great ; so great, that the conduct of almost all the important concerns of mankind is regulated entirely, as well as rationally, by the evidence which it contains.   Should twelve men, known and proved to possess the uniform character of unimpeachable veracity, declare to one of us, independently (no one of them being acquainted with the fact that any other had made the same declaration,) that they had seen in the midst of a public assembly a leper cleansed, and the white, loathsome crust of the leprosy fall off, and the bloom and vigour of health return at the command of a person publicly believed to have wrought hundreds of such miracles, and to be distinguished from all men by unexampled wisdom and holiness, every one of us would believe the testimony to be true.   Especially should we receive their testimony, if we saw these very men endued with new and wonderful wisdom and holiness, professedly derived from the same person ; forsaking a religion for which they had felt a bigoted attachment, embracing and teaching a religion wholly new ; and in confirmation of this new religion professedly taught by God himself, working many miracles, forsaking all earthly enjoyments, voluntarily undergoing all earthly distresses, and finally yielding their lives to a violent death. A miracle, therefore, can be proved by testimony.

I have already pursued this subject farther than I intended in this Discourse. Some other considerations relative to it I shall probably mention hereafter. At the present time I will only remark farther, that Mr. Hume confidently but erroneously supposes a presumption to lie strongly against the existence of miracles. The presumption is wholly in favour of their existence. We know that innumerable miracles have taken place. The creation of the world is one immense complication of miraculous works, and the *first* beings of every sort were miraculous existences. As miracles were wrought here, so the analogy of the divine works, as well as the uniformity of the divine character, irresistibly compels us to believe that they will be wrought, wherever a sufficient occasion is presented. The illumination and reformation of mankind is a cause of this nature, existing in the highest degree. That God should work miracles to prove the truth and spread the influence of Christianity is, therefore, with the highest reason to be expected, especially as miracles are the most proper as well as most forcible of all proofs that a religion is derived from him.

III. *I shall now attempt to point out the importance of miracles.*

1. *The importance of the miracles of Christ is manifest in the immediate benefit of those for whom they were wrought.*

All the miracles of Christ were glorious acts of *beneficence*. In his own words, 'The blind received their sight, and the lame walked ; the lepers were cleansed, and the deaf heard ; the dead were raised up, and the poor had the Gospel preached to them.' That acts of this general nature were of high importance to those for whom they were done ; and that, multiplied as we are told they were, particularly by St. John, they constituted a mass of beneficence incalculably interesting to the age and country in which they existed, will not admit of a doubt.

2. *The miracles of Christ were of great importance to his character.*

They were important, first, as proofs of *power*. Christ, for the wisest and best reasons, appeared as the son of a carpenter, and lived alway in a state of general humiliation. But it was necessary also that his character, even in this world, should be distinguished by personal greatness. The distinction nothing could so effectually produce, as the power of controlling in this manner the laws of nature, and suspending or counteracting in this manner the agency by which the affairs of this world are carried on. As Christ wrought miracles in his own name, he was thus proved to possess this power in himself, as an inherent energy. But how superior is this power to all that can be boasted by the greatest men who have ever lived! What conqueror would not cheerfully barter all the power in which he glories, for the control of wounds and diseases, of winds and waves, of life and death? This power exhibited Christ in the midst of all his humiliation as greater than any and than all the children of Adam, and surrounded his character with a splendour becoming his mission. How important, how necessary, this greatness was to Christ, as the Mediator between God and man, I need not illustrate.

3. *The miracles of Christ were necessary as proofs of his benevolence.*

Benevolence is proved by action. But no actions were ever equally proofs of benevolence with the miraculous actions of Christ, except his condescension, atonement, and intercession. It would not have been possible for Christ in any other manner to exhibit the same character with the same strength. No actions could have been equally beneficent. The good done was the most necessary and the most useful to those for whom it was done. Those for whom it was done were persons to whom it is usually least done, who most need it, to whom it is of the highest consequence, and who, therefore, as objects of Christ's beneficence, illustrate more clearly than any others could do this excellence of his character. At the same time, it was beneficence accomplished by a person possessed of stupendous power and greatness, manifested in the very communication of the good. Those who possess great power very rarely manifest, and therefore are justly believed very rarely to possess, an eminent degree of good will. Intoxicated with their greatness, they are generally employed in displaying it to mankind, and in thus engrossing admiration and applause. From such persons Christ is gloriously distinguished, by employing his own unexampled power solely in communicating kindness to those around him.

In both these great particulars the miracles of Christ invest him with greatness and glory, to which there has been nothing parallel in the present world.

4. *The miracles of Christ are of vast importance, as proofs of the divinity of his mission.*

A miracle is an act of infinite power only, and is, therefore, a proof of the immediate agency of God. None but he can withhold, suspend, or counteract his agency exerted according to the laws of nature.

A miracle becomes a proof of the character or doctrine of him by whom it was wrought, by being professedly wrought for *the confirmation of either*. A miracle is the testimony of God. From the perfect veracity of God it irresistibly results, that he can never give, nor rationally be supposed to give, his testimony to any thing but truth. When, therefore, a miracle is wrought in confirmation of any thing, or as evidence of any thing, we know that that thing is true, because God has given to it his testimony. The miracles of Christ were wrought to prove that the mission and doctrine of Christ were from God. They were, therefore, certainly from God.

To this it may be objected, that miracles are asserted by the Scriptures themselves to have been wrought in confirmation of *falsehood* ; as, for example, by the magicians—the witch of Endor—*and by Satan in the time of Christ's temptation.*

If the magicians of Egypt wrought miracles, God wrought them, with a view to make the final triumph of his own cause in the hands of Moses more the object of public attention, and more striking to the view of mankind. This was done when the magicians themselves were put to silence, and forced to confess, that the works of Moses were accomplished by ' the finger of God.' But the truth is, the magicians wrought no miracles. All that they did was to busy themselves with ' their enchantments,' by which every man now knows that, although the weak and credulous may be deceived, miracles cannot possibly be accomplished. That this is the real amount of the history given by Moses, any sober man may, I think, be completely satisfied by reading Farmer's Treatise on Miracles.

The witch of Endor neither wrought, nor expected to work, any miracle. This is clearly evident from her astonishment and alarm at the appearance of Samuel. Saul, who expected a miracle, beheld Samuel without any peculiar surprise; she, who expected none, with amazement and terror.

Satan is said by the Evangelists to have taken our Saviour up into ' a very high mountain, and to have shown him all the kingdoms of the world in a moment of time.' The Greek word οικουμινς, here translated ' world,' very frequently signifies *land*, or *country*, and ought to have been thus rendered here; the meaning being no other, than that Satan showed our Saviour the four tetrarchies, or kingdoms, comprised in the land of Judea. In this transaction it will not be pretended that there was any thing miraculous.

The doctrine, that miracles have been, or may be wrought in support of falsehood, has been incautiously adopted by several respectable divines, and they have taught us, that we are to try the evidence furnished by the miracle, by the *nature of the doctrine* which it was wrought to prove. This, I apprehend, is infinitely dishonourable to the character of Jehovah; for it supposes, that he may not only countenance but establish falsehood. At the same time, it is arguing in a circle. It is employing the *doctrine* to prove the *miracle*, and, then, the *miracle* to prove the *doctrine*. That the miracles of Christ were complete proof of his doctrine, is clearly evident from the words of Christ himself, when he declares concerning the Jews, that ' if he had not done among them such works, as no other man did, they had not had sin: but that now they had no cloak for their sin.'

SERMON LXI.

RESURRECTION OF CHRIST.

———AND KILLED THE PRINCE OF LIFE, WHOM GOD HATH RAISED
FROM THE DEAD: WHEREOF WE ARE WITNESSES.

ACTS III. 15.

In the preceding Discourse, I made a number of general
observations concerning the miracles of Christ. The subject
which next offers itself to our view concerning this glorious
person, is *his resurrection*. This interesting subject I propose now to examine with particular attention. Its importance in a System of Theology can scarcely need to be illustrated.

If Christ was raised from the dead, he was certainly the
Messiah; or, in other words, whatever he declared himself to
be. His doctrines, precepts, and life were all approved by
God, possess divine authority, and demand, with the obligation of that authority, the faith and obedience of mankind.
To prove this fact, therefore, is to prove beyond a reasonable
debate the truth of the Christian system.

At the same time, the arguments which prove the reality of
this miracle, lend their whole force to the *other* miracles recorded in the Gospel. For this reason, I have reserved most
of the direct arguments in behalf of miracles for the present
occasion.

In the context we are informed, that ' a certain man, lame
from his mother's womb, who was now more than forty years
old, and who had been carried and laid daily at the gate of
the temple, called Beautiful, to receive alms of them that en-

tered into the temple,' was cured of his lameness by the command of St. Peter. So extraordinary an event astonished the Jews assembled to worship in the temple, and collected them in great numbers around Peter and John. Peter, observing their astonishment, addressed to them a pertinent and very pungent discourse, in which he informed them, that the Lord Jesus Christ, whom they had killed, and whom God had raised to life, had restored this lame man to soundness and strength. This proof of Christ's Messiahship he made the foundation of an earnest and persuasive exhortation to them to repent of their sins, and turn to God. The efficacy of this discourse on those who heard it was wonderful. About five thousand men received it with the faith of the Gospel, and were added unto the Lord.

In the text (the hinge, on which all this discourse of St. Peter turns,) he declares to the Jews the three following things :——

1. *That they had killed the Prince of life :*
2. *That God had raised him from the dead :* and,
3. *That the apostle himself and his companions were witnesses of this wonderful event.*

The first of these assertions has very rarely been doubted. I know of but a single instance in which it has been denied in form. Volney has made a number of silly observations, intended to persuade the world that Christ never existed ; and that the history of him contained in the Gospel is a fiction, compiled, with some variations and improvements, from the Hindoo tales concerning the god Creshnoo. I will not attempt a serious answer to such nonsense. Infidelity must be pitied, when it is driven to such fetches as this in order to support itself, and maintain its contest with Christianity.

The second assertion has been often disputed ; as, indeed, it must always be by every man who denies the revelation of the Scriptures, or the mission of Christ. It is the design of this Discourse to state the evidence concerning the great fact here declared with candour and fairness. It demands no other manner of statement ; as will, I trust be sufficiently evinced in the prosecution of this design. As the proof of this fact is almost all furnished by the apostles and their companions, the witnesses appointed by Christ himself, the evidence alleged here will of course be principally derived from them.

It will be unnecessary, therefore, to make the two last assertions of St. Peter the subject of distinct heads of discourse.

If the apostles have not given us a true account concerning the resurrection of Christ, it must be,

I. *Because they were themselves deceived :* or,

II. *Because they intended to deceive others.*

For if they were not themselves deceived, but knew the truth, and have faithfully declared it in their writings, the plainest and most ignorant man cannot fail to discern that Christ was certainly raised from the dead. That neither of these suppositions is just, I shall now attempt to prove.

I. *The apostles were not themselves deceived with regard to this fact.*

In support of this assertion I observe,

1. *The fact is of such a nature, that they were competent judges whether it existed or not.*

In the nature of the case, it is just as easy to determine whether a person once dead is afterwards alive, as to determine whether any man is living who has not been dead. A familiar instance will prove the justice of this assertion. Suppose a person, who was an entire stranger to us, should come into the family in which we live. Suppose he should reside in this family, eat and drink, sleep and wake, converse and act, with them exactly in the manner in which these things are done by us, and the rest of mankind. Suppose him, farther, to enter into business in the manner of other men ; to cultivate a farm, or manage causes at the bar, or practise medicine, or assume the office of a minister, and preach, visit, advise, and comfort, as is usually done in discharging the duties of this function. Every one of us who witnessed these things would, beyond a doubt, know this stranger to be a living man, in the same manner and with the same certainty with which we know each other to be alive.

The proofs of life in this and every other case are the colour, the motions, the actions, and the speech of a living man. These we discern perfectly by our senses, under the general regulation of common sense. The proofs thus furnished are *complete ;* and when united, as in a living man they always are, they have never deceived, they can never deceive, any man who has the customary use of his senses.

As these are complete proofs of the facts in question, so they are always *equally* complete. The evidence which they contain admits of no gradations, but is always entire, always the same, and in every supposable case perfectly satisfactory. Nor is there an instance within our experience, nor an instance in the records of history, which has impaired this evidence at all, or rendered it capable of being even remotely suspected.

Were this evidence not entire in every instance, considered by itself, were it capable of being suspected in the smallest degree, we should be obliged when we met, conversed, or bargained with each other, to settle the question whether we were mutually living beings. The farmer would be obliged, before he bought a piece of land of his neighbour, to settle by a formal investigation the question whether he was about to buy it of a real man,-or a phantom of the imagination. The judge, when called upon to try a prisoner, would in the same manner be compelled, before he began the trial, to decide, whether he had brought to him for adjudication a living being, or a spectre. The religious assembly would be equally necessitated to examine whether such an assembly was really gathered, and whether a real and living preacher was in the desk, or whether what seemed to be a preacher and a congregation were only the phantasms of a waking dream.

As these proofs are in every instance complete, so they are the *only* evidence of the fact in question. If then they can deceive us, we are left wholly without a remedy: for we have no other possible mode of coming to the knowledge of the fact.

To the case of the *stranger*, whom I have supposed, all these proofs have obviously a perfect application. We know as well as we can possibly know, we know beyond any possible doubt, that he is a living man. But we do not and cannot know, that he has never been dead, and afterward raised to life. To prove this, we must be supplied with totally new evidence, derived from totally other sources, than any hitherto supposed to be furnished by him. The evidence, therefore, that he is a living man, is wholly independent of the fact that he has, or has not, been raised from the dead; and is, by itself, absolutely complete. If, then, we should be afterwards informed, with evidence which could not be questioned, that this stranger had been actually dead, and buried, and had been afterwards raised to life, the evidence which we had before received, that he was a living man, from the time when we first became acquainted with him, could not in the least degree be affected by the fact, that he had before been dead. The story of his death and resurrection we should undoubtedly admit, if we acted rationally, only with extreme slowness and caution, and upon decisive evidence. But no one of us would or could hesitate to believe the man, circumstanced as above, to be alive. Otherwise, it is plain we could not know that any man is alive; for all the proofs which can attend this subject actually attend it in the case supposed. If, therefore, the evidence can be justly doubted in one case, it can with equal propriety be doubted in all.

That the apostles possessed all the means of judging accurately concerning the existence and the nature of these proofs, cannot be denied. They were possessed of the common sense, and had the usual senses of man. No judges could be better qualified for this purpose. Had Newton, Bacon, or Aristotle been employed in examining these proofs, they must have used exactly the same means of examination which were used by Peter and John. Had they summoned philosophy to their assistance, it could only have told them that it had no concern with cases of this nature.

2. *The apostles were unprejudiced judges.*

In proof of this assertion I observe,

1. *That the apostles were not enthusiasts.*

Enthusiasm is a persuasion that certain religious doctrines are true, derived from a peculiar strength of imagination and feeling, relying on internal suggestions supposed to come from God, and not relying on facts or arguments. In the whole history, preaching, and writings of the apostles there is not the least appearance of this character. According to their own accounts of themselves (which in this case we readily believe, because in their view they were accounts of their defects,) they were slow of belief, even to weakness and criminality. For this conduct they were often and justly reproved by their Master; and, as we see in their writings, received his declarations with difficulty when their evidence was complete. Nor were they finally convinced, even when uninfluenced by this sceptical spirit, except by evidence of the best kind, to wit, that of facts. These also existed before their eyes and ears, in the presence of multitudes and enemies, who were equally convinced with themselves. Nor were they witnesses of such facts once, twice, or a few times only ; but beheld them in an uninterrupted succession for several years. Had they not yielded to them in such circumstances, they must have been either idiots, or madmen.

Enthusiasts also appeal to their internal suggestions, as proof which plainly ought, in their view, to satisfy others. The apostles have never made such an appeal ; nor demanded belief on any other considerations, except those which reason in the highest exercise perfectly approves.

Enthusiasts always boast of the leaders whom they professedly follow. The apostles, although following the most extraordinary leader ever seen in the world, have written the history of his life without a single panegyric, and recorded the unparalleled injustice, abuse, and cruelty which he suffered from his enemies, both in his life and death, with only a single direct censure of those enemies, contained in these words, ' For they loved the praise of men more than the praise of God.'

Enthusiasts always boast of their own excellencies, and attainments. The apostles had higher reason for such boasting than ever fell to the lot of men. They set up a new religion, and to the belief and profession of it converted a great part of mankind. They wrought, or were certainly believed to work, miracles of the most stupendous nature, rose to an influence which kings never possessed, and ruled more human beings than most monarchs have been able to claim as their subjects. To this height of influence they ascended also from the humble employments of fishing, collecting taxes, and making tents. How few of the human race, nay, who beside these very men, would not have become giddy in the ascent from such a lowly condition to such distinguished eminence. Yet Matthew records nothing of himself, except that he was a publican, that he followed Christ, and that he once entertained him at his table. Mark and Luke do not even mention their own names. John says nothing of himself by way of commendation, unless that he was ' the disciple, whom Jesus loved,' and this he expresses obscurely, in the most modest manner conceivable.

Indeed, the subject of self-commendation seems never to have entered their thoughts.

There is, I acknowledge, one apparent exception to this remark in the writings of the apostles. I mean St. Paul's commendation of himself to the Corinthian church. This, however, is prefaced with a quotation from the Old Testament as the word of God, in which it is declared, that ' not he who commendeth himself is approved, but he whom the Lord commendeth.' He then pronounces boasting to be folly ; and declares himself to be compelled to this folly by the Corinthian church, because some of its members had denied his apostleship ; a denial fraught with the utmost mischief to the Christian cause, and particularly in that city. The things which he recites are calculated in the most perfect manner to establish his character as an apostle, and to refute the unworthy calumnies which they had uttered against him. At the same time they are accompanied with such proofs of ingenuousness, truth and modesty, as leave irresistibly on the mind a stronger impression of these attributes in St. Paul, than we could have felt, if he had not written this passage. Let it be remembered, that this is the conduct of a person who had converted half the civilized world.

In the mean time the apostles, in the most frank, artless, and faithful manner possible, do that, which enthusiasts never do at all ; that is, they record their own mistakes, follies, and faults, and those of very serious magnitude, acknowledged to be such by themselves, and severely censured as such by their Master. No example of this nature can be found in the whole history of enthusiasm, and no other such example in the whole history of man. Enthusiasm is always a proud, vain, boasting spirit, founded in the belief that the enthusiast is the subject of immediate and extraordinary communications from heaven, and, therefore, designated by God as his peculiar favourite ; raised of course above the human level ; and irresistibly prompted to publish on every occasion this peculiar testimony of heaven to its pre-eminent worth, and to unfold to the view of all around it a distinction too flattering to be concealed.

Enthusiasts also, in all their preaching and conversation on religious subjects, pour out with eagerness the dictates of passion and imagination, and never attempt to avail themselves of the facts or arguments on which reason delights to rest. Strong pictures, vehement effusions of passion, violent exclamations, loudly vociferated, and imperiously enjoined as objects of implicit faith and obedience, constitute the substance and the sum of their addresses to mankind. They themselves believe because they believe, and know because they know. Their conviction, instead of being, as it ought to be, the result of evidence, is the result of feeling merely. If you attempt to persuade them that they are in an error by reasoning, facts, and proofs, they regard you with a mixture of pity and contempt, for weakly opposing your twilight probabilities to their noon-day certainty, and for preposterously labouring to illumine the sun with a taper.

How contrary is all this to the conduct of the apostles! When a proof of their mission or doctrine was demanded of them, they appealed instantly and invariably to arguments, facts, and miracles. These convinced mankind then, and produce the same conviction now. The lapse of seventeen centuries has detected in them no error, and in no degree enfeebled their strength. Their discourses were then and are now the most rational, noble, and satisfactory discourses on moral and religious subjects ever witnessed by mankind. There is not an instance in them all in which belief is demanded on any other grounds than these, and on these grounds it is always rightfully demanded. But on these grounds it is never demanded by enthusiasts. There is not in the world a stronger contrast to the preaching of enthusiasts, than that of Christ and his apostles.

2. *The apostles were unprejudiced judges of this fact, because every thing respecting it contradicted their favourite prejudices.*

In common with their countrymen, they expected a conquering, reigning, glorious Messiah, who was to subdue and control all the nations of men. With him, also, they themselves expected to conquer and reign, together with the rest of the Jews, as princes and nobles in the splendid earthly court of this temporal Messiah. No expectation ever flattered the predominant passions of man so powerfully as this. It was the source of almost all their follies and faults, and, in spite of Christ's instructions and their piety, it broke out on every occasion, and clung to them with immoveable adherence till the day of Pentecost. For just at the moment of Christ's ascension, ten days only before that festival, they asked him, ' Lord, wilt thou at this time restore the kingdom to Israel?'

They did not and could not believe that he would die. After he had predicted his death at five or six different times in as plain language as can be used, St. John informs us, that ' they understood not that saying,' and that ' it was hidden from them.' Peter also, when Christ had uttered a prediction of this nature, understanding the meaning of the prediction, took upon himself the office of rebuking his Master, and said; ' Be it far from thee, Lord; this shall not be unto thee.'

Nor do they appear to have believed that he would live again. They plainly disbelieved all the testimonies of his resurrection, except that of their own eyes and ears; and regarded the accounts of their companions, whom on all other occasions they esteemed persons of unstained veracity, ' as idle tales.' It may seem strange that, believing as they did implicitly the declarations and messiahship of their Master, they should not believe that he would rise again, after his various prophecies concerning that event. But we are to remember that his death had violated all their prejudices, blasted all their fond hopes, and buried them in gloom and despondency. The Jews customarily, whenever passages of Scripture admitted of no interpretation accordant with their established opinions, resolved the difficulty, or rather removed it, by pronouncing the passage to be *mysterious.* The apostles in all probability had recourse to the same expedient to reconcile the predictions of Christ with that train of facts whose future existence they believed, and chose rather not to understand the true import of his predictions, plain as it was, than to admit an interpretation of them, which opposed all their riveted opinions. At the same time, melancholy as were their circumstances and their feelings, they were ill fitted for the business of commenting on the predictions of Christ, and seem not to have made even an attempt to gain the conviction which would so effectually have relieved their distresses. When, therefore they had evidence of his resurrection sufficient to convince any reasonable person, they still disbelieved, and were hardly brought to admit the testimony of their own eyes and ears. After various reports of his resurrection from those who had seen

him, reports so satisfactory, that Christ himself afterward ' up-
braided them with their unbelief, and hardness of heart,' because they had not believed them who had seen him after he
was risen ; ' Jesus himself stood in the midst of them, and
said, Peace be unto you. But they were terrified and af-
frighted, and supposed that they had seen a spirit. He then
said unto them, Why are ye troubled, and why do thoughts
arise in your hearts? Behold my hands and my feet ; that it
is I myself. Handle me, and see : for a spirit hath not flesh
and bones, as ye see me have. And when he had thus spoken,
he showed them his hands and his feet.' You are to remember,
that ' the print of the nails,' by which he was fastened to the
cross, was still perfectly visible both in his hands and feet.
These were, therefore, appealed to by Christ, because they
thus furnished evidence ' that it was he himself,' which no man
would counterfeit. Still ' they believed not for joy, and wondered.' To remove this doubt, which, like most that preceded
it, was the result of feeling, and not of judgment, he farther
said to them, ' Have ye here any meat?' In answer to this
inquiry, ' they gave him a piece of a broiled fish, and of an
honeycomb. And he took it, and did eat before them.' At
the end of this process only did they entirely believe that he
was risen from the dead.

From this story, written after they had all in the fullest
manner realized his resurrection, and therefore intended
severely to censure their own unbelief; from this story, written in a manner so perfectly artless and natural, and with
circumstances of such nice discrimination as the writer could
not have invented, and on both these accounts carrying with
it the clearest evidence of its truth, we have the strongest
proof that the apostles were ' slow of heart to believe' the
resurrection of Christ. Their assent was reluctant, and
gradual; such as is always yielded to evidence which con-
tradicts prejudices strongly imbibed.

I have observed, that the story of St. Luke is written in a
manner perfectly artless and natural, and with circumstances
of such nice discrimination as the writer could not have
devised. It is extremely natural to the human mind in a
state of despondency, either not to believe at all, or to believe with extreme difficulty, those things which would remove
its despondency. The good in question seems too great to

be realized, and therefore too improbable even to be hoped. The apostles for this reason disbelieved at first; and for the same reason continued their disbelief after Christ stood in the midst of them, and discovered himself to their eyes and ears. A strong and mixed emotion of pleasure and surprise partially overwhelmed their reason, and prolonged their doubts, in spite of the clearest evidence.   Never was the nature of man exhibited with more exactness, or with nicer discrimination, than in this remarkable declaration, 'They believed not for joy, and wondered.'

From these observations it is, if I mistake not, unanswerably evident, that the prejudices of the apostles were all directed against the resurrection of Christ, and that they were not inclined to admit this fact by any bias in its favour.

3. *The apostles had sufficient means and opportunities of judging whether Christ was raised from the dead.*

He appeared to some or other of them, or their companions, *eleven times*, distinctly recorded in the Scriptures.   He appeared to Mary Magdalene; to her companions with her; to Peter; to the disciples going to Emmaus; to James; to the ten apostles, Thomas not being present; to the eleven, Thomas being present; to the apostles again at the sea of Tiberias; to above five hundred brethren at once; to the apostles before, and during, his ascension; and finally to St. Paul in his way to Damascus.   Beside these instances, he appeared several times afterwards to St. Paul; and, as St. Luke informs us, 'showed himself alive after his passion by many infallible proofs; being seen of them forty days, and speaking of the things pertaining to the kingdom of God.' It ought to be particularly remembered, that in nine of the instances mentioned above, he appeared to the apostles themselves; in several instances to many, or all, of them; and once to more than five hundred disciples together.   Should we then admit such an illusion of the senses as infidels sometimes contend for to be possible, and mankind to be capable of being deceived by it in such degrees as *they* urge; still the improbability must, even according to their own principles, be very great, that two persons should, at the same time, experience exactly the same illusion concerning the same object, and concerning so many circumstances attending it.   Of a fact of this kind history furnishes no record, and conversation no testimony. All the extraordinary and inexplicable things actually testified, in which such illusions may be supposed to have taken place, have invariably existed, if they existed at all, to the view of *one person only.* No instance can be mentioned in which *two* unexceptionable witnesses have testified to the same illusion, at the same time, concerning the same thing. Far more improbable is it that *three* persons should thus experience the same illusion. When we raise this number to *eleven,* the improbability becomes incalculable ; and when to *five hundred,* it transcends all limit.

The improbability is also enhanced without measure, by *the repetition of this fact* in so.many instances, to so many persons, together with all the circumstances by which it was attended. But when we remember, that Christ not only appeared, but ate, drank, walked, and conversed with them, at so many different times, through forty days, and declared to them a great number of divine truths concerning the kingdom of God, the improbability ceases, and is changed into an impossibility. The apostles and their companions had here all the evidence that Christ was living, which they had of the life of each other ; all the evidence which we have, that those around us with whom we have daily intercourse are alive. If, then, the apostles could be deceived with respect to the fact that Christ was living, they could, with the same ease, be equally deceived with respect to the life of each other. With the same ease can we be equally deceived in our belief, that men whom we see daily, with whom we converse, and with whom we act, are living men. A stranger who has visited us, continued with us forty days, conversed with us, and united with us in eating, drinking, and the serious business of life, must, on the same grounds, be denied or doubted to be a living man ; and supposed to be a spectre, a phantom of the imagination, an illusion of the senses, or an inhabitant of a dream. To this length the principles carry us, on which alone we can deny that the apostles had perfect evidence that Christ was alive after his death. He who can admit these principles, has renounced the evidence of his senses ; and ought from motives of consistency, to believe a man to be a post, as readily as to believe him to be a man.

SERMON LXII.

RESURRECTION OF CHRIST.

———

——AND KILLED THE PRINCE OF LIFE, WHOM GOD HATH RAISED
FROM THE DEAD: WHEREOF WE ARE WITNESSES.

ACTS III. 15.

In the preceding Discourse I observed, that in this passage
St. Peter declares to the Jews the three following things :——

I. *That they had killed the Prince of Life:*

II. *That God had raised him from the dead :* and,

III. *That the apostle himself, and his companions, were
witnesses of these facts.*

The first of these assertions, I observed, had been scarcely
controverted, and therefore needed no discussion from me.
To establish the second, I remarked, was indispensable to a
System of Christian Theology, as being the great point on
which such a system must depend ; and therefore proposed it
as the immediate object of that Discourse. The evidence of
its truth, I further observed, was chiefly furnished by the apostles and their companions. This evidence, therefore, I proposed to state, and to show, that it was a proper and unexceptionable object of reliance for the truth of the important fact
declared in the text.

In pursuance of this design I observed, that if Christ was
not raised from the dead, the apostles were either *themselves
deceived,* or have of design *deceived others.* That they themselves were *not* deceived, I endeavoured to prove in that Discourse, and shall now attempt to show,

II. *That they have not deceived others.*

By this you will understand, that they have not deceived others *of design :* all other deceptions having been considered under the former head.

In support of this assertion I observe,

1. *That the known probity of the apostles places them beyond every reasonable suspicion of intentional deception.*

The probity of the apostles stands on higher ground, and has been regarded with higher confidence by mankind, than that of any other men whatever. This has been so often evinced, and with arguments so plainly unanswerable, that it would be probably thought tedious to expatiate on the subject at the present time. Suffice it then to say, that the histories which they have given us of our Saviour's life, contain more internal and decisive proofs of sincerity than any other human writings ; that they recite facts, and utter doctrines, with a simplicity and artlessness unequalled ; that their story, both as to the subject, and as to the manner, is such, as no impostor could or would tell ; that the character of Christ is drawn with excellencies so great, combined with features so distinctive, as to prove it beyond the power of human invention, and much more beyond the invention of such humble, uneducated men ; that, greatly as they respected.him, horrible as were the injuries which he received from his enemies, gross and abominable as was the character of those enemies, and intensely as the apostles abhorred both them and their conduct, they have recited his whole story without a single panegyrical remark concerning *him,* and without a single testimony of resentment, unkindness, or prejudice against *them.* Let it be remembered, also, that no impostor would have ever thought of terminating his account concerning a favourite and splendid character with the history of his trial and crucifixion as a malefactor ; that no impostor, if we were to suppose him to have done this, would have prefaced this history with a recital of his own disbelief that this favourite was to die ; especially after he had predicted his death many times, in the plainest language ; that no impostor would have recorded his own ignorance and disbelief of the true character, mission, and doctrines of the hero of his story ; or his severe and stinging reproofs of his follies and faults, and all this without disguise or palliation ; that the doctrines and precepts contained in the Gospel are beyond the discovery of *any* men, particularly of *such* men ; that, if an impostor could discover them, he could never have enjoined them on mankind, because of their spotless purity and perfect excellence ; that every impostor must, of course, have blended with the better doctrines and precepts which he thought proper to deliver, others sufficiently licentious to countenance, or at least to palliate, his own crimes ; that the end, uniformly proposed and intensely pursued in the Gospel, *viz.* the amendment of the human character, is such as no impostor would be willing to promote ; that four impostors, writing independently, or without concert, could not possibly have exhibited the same accordance of facts, nor the same perfect harmony of doctrines ; and that the character of the apostles was, in their own age, not only unimpeached, but considered as superior to that of all other virtuous men. To these proofs of integrity ought to be added that decisive one, their cheerful relinquishment of all the pleasures of this life, and their voluntary endurance of all its distresses, and, in the end, their voluntary surrender of life itself, for the sake of the religion which they professed, and of the Master whom they served.

That men who gave so many efficacious and uniform proofs of integrity, should conspire to palm upon mankind this gross imposition, is too replete with absurdity to be admitted by any sober man.

2. *The apostles had no interest in attempting to deceive mankind with respect to this event.*

In order to render the imposition profitable to its authors, it was necessary that it should be believed ; and, to gain credit elsewhere, it must first gain credit where it was originally published. The story was first declared to the Jewish nation ; and without a single hope or thought of spreading it among other nations. It was for twelve years confined to Jews only. Now, let me ask, what inducement had the apostles to believe that a tale, so incredible in itself, would be received by this people ? a tale concerning the resurrection of a crucified malefactor ; for such, if false, must the story have been ; and such, although true, it was believed to be by the Jews. By them Christ was regarded as an impostor, as a blasphemer of God, as an impious pretender to the Messiahship, and an impious opposer of a religion unquestionably derived from Heaven. Yet with Jews this publication was to begin, and, so far as they knew, to end; Jews beyond example bigoted to their own religion, and furious in their hostility to every other; the bitter persecutors of Christ, while he lived, and the accusers and witnesses who caused his death. What hope could any but a madman entertain that among such people such a story could gain even a solitary admission? To give credit to this story was in a Jew no other than to yield up his religion, his bigotry, his connection with the Jewish church, his interest in the public opinion of his countrymen, and in the protection of its government. It was to expose his possessions, his family, and his life, to become excommunicated, outlawed, and an outcast from society, and to place himself within the reach of all the dreadful threatenings contained in the law of Moses. At the same time, it was to acknowledge himself a murderer, a murderer of the Messiah, a murderer of the Son of God; to confess, that he had found this glorious person in the son of a carpenter; in a man, emphatically styled by him and his countrymen, 'a friend of publicans and sinners; a gluttonous man, and a wine-bibber?' It was, also, to renounce all his bright and dawning hopes of the deliverance of himself and his nation from Roman servitude, by that mighty Prince, with whom they were all in hourly expectation of triumphing and reigning over every nation on earth. All this, also, was to be done without any good to balance these mighty evils, either in hand or in reversion. Never was there a field so unpromising to the talents or the efforts of an impostor.

At the same time, this tale was to be told by the followers of the person professedly raised, and the enemies of those to whom it was told; by men, poor, ignorant, and despised, without friends, and without influence; abhorred by their countrymen, and regarded as apostates from their religion. Never were persons so ill qualified for successful efforts at imposition. Suppose such a story were now to be told. None of these embarrassments, it is evident, would attend the recital, except those which arise out of the story itself. The narrators would lie originally under no public odium. The subject would be obnoxious to no peculiar prejudice. The reception of it would be followed by no peculiar sacrifices; by no civil or religious disqualifications; by no loss of property, reputation, safety, or even quiet.   How plain is it, that such a story, if false, could not even here produce any other effect but pity, contempt, and ridicule?   To persuade others to believe it, is in the nature of the case a thing so hopeless and desperate, that no impostor has been found weak, rash, or impudent enough to think of making the attempt.   But, of all persons on earth, none were ever more disadvantageously situated to propagate such a story, than the apostles.   The Jews were certainly less inclined to believe this story than the apostles themselves.   *They* refused to believe it, long after very sufficient evidence had been furnished them of its truth. The Jews would certainly require evidence still more ample.   This the apostles could not but know, and therefore must have been hopeless of persuading them to believe it, unless themselves were able to support it by such evidence.   But this evidence could never be produced in support of a falsehood.

If the story did not gain belief, the attempt to spread it could be of no possible use to the apostles.   As, then, they could not entertain a single hope of inducing the Jews to believe it, they could have no possible inducement to attempt to palm it upon the Jews.   But if the Jews did not believe it, it could never be received by any other people.   Jews, in great numbers, were scattered over all the countries in which the apostles could ever hope or wish to spread the story.   These Jews carried on a continual correspondence with those at Jerusalem, and in immense numbers visited that city every year.   If, then, the story were not believed at Jerusalem, this fact would be perfectly well known wherever Jews resided.   But the knowledge that the story gained no credit at Jerusalem, the place where the event had professedly existed, would effectually prevent it from gaining the least credit in any other place.   To the spot, where the event was said to exist, all thinking men would have recourse, to learn the true state of the evidence concerning it.   If it were there found insufficient, it would at once be pronounced to be insufficient by all men.   The Gospel was, probably, directed by Christ to be preached *first* at Jerusalem and in Judea, for this as one great reason, that the story of his resurrection, on which his whole scheme depended, being established there in the immoveable belief of multitudes, might be successfully and irresistibly published in other countries.

But, whatever advantages the apostles could derive, or expect to derive from their imposture (if it were one,) must be wholly derived from persuading mankind to believe this story. They themselves perfectly understood, and frankly declared to mankind, that their whole system turned on this single hinge. ' If Christ be not *risen*, then is our preaching vain, and your faith is also vain,' is the constant language of all which they said. For proof of this you need only examine the sermons of St. Peter and St. Paul, recorded in the Acts of the Apostles. Unless this fact were established, therefore, they could not hope for a single follower, nor for the smallest reward. But of the establishment of this fact among either Jews or Gentiles, I flatter myself I have shown they could not, in the existing circumstances, form even the remotest hope. They had not, therefore, the smallest interest in making the attempt.

3. *They were assured, with absolute certainty, of suffering every imaginable disadvantage.*

All the losses and injuries mentioned under the preceding head, must have stared them in the face at the beginning. At every step of their progress new evils could not fail to arise, and those of the most distressing kind. Had they been blind enough not to have perceived their miserable destiny, before they commenced this wretched work of deception, the first attempt could not fail to produce the most ample conviction ; and to this every new attempt would add fresh proof. The scourge, the prison, and the cross have always proved effectual antidotes to imposition. All other dishonest men, are, equally with Voltaire, no friends to martyrdom. Had the apostles possessed the same character, they would have soon been wearied of the sufferings which they everywhere underwent. Everywhere they were hated, calumniated, despised, hunted from city to city, thrust into prison, scourged, stoned, and crucified. For what were all these excruciating sufferings endured ? Gain, honour, and pleasure are the only gods to which impostors bow. But of these the apostles acquired, and plainly laboured to acquire, neither. What, then, was the end for which they suffered ? Let the infidel answer this question.

As they gained nothing, and lost every thing in the present world, so it is certain that they must expect to gain nothing, and suffer every thing, in the world to come. That the Old Testament was the word of God, they certainly believed without a single doubt. But, in this book, lying is exhibited as a supreme object of the divine abhorrence, and the scriptural threatenings. From the invention and propagation of this falsehood, therefore, they could expect nothing hereafter but the severest effusions of the anger of God.

For what, then, was all this loss, danger, and suffering incurred? For the privilege of telling an extravagant and incredible story to mankind, and of founding on it a series of exhortations to repentance, faith, and holiness; to the renunciation of sin and the universal exercise of piety, justice, truth, and kindness; to the practice of all that conduct which common sense has ever pronounced to be the duty, honour, and happiness of man, and the avoidance of all that which it has ever declared to be his guilt, debasement, and misery. Such an end was never even wished, much less seriously proposed, by an impostor.

At the same time, they lived as no impostors ever lived, and were able to say to their converts, with a full assurance of finding a cordial belief of the declaration, ' Ye are witnesses, and God also, how holily, and justly, and unblameably, we behaved ourselves among you that believe.' That this was their true character is certain, from the concurrent testimony of all antiquity. Had they not nobly recorded their own faults, there is not the least reason to believe that a single stain would have ever rested on their character.

If, then, the apostles invented this story, they invented it without the remotest hope or prospect of making it believed; a thing which was never done by an impostor: propagated it without any interest, without any hope of gain, honour, power, or pleasure; the only object by which impostors were ever allured; and with losses and sufferings, which no impostors ever voluntarily underwent; proposed as their only end, or at least only end which has ever been discovered to mankind, an object which no impostor ever pursued, or even wished; and, during their whole progress through life, lived so as no impostor ever lived, and so as to be the most perfect contrast ever exhibited by men to the whole character of imposition.

III. *The Apostles were not deceived, and did not deceive others with regard to this fact ; but the fact was real.*

In support of this declaration I observe,

1. *That if Christ was not raised from the dead, it could certainly have been proved.*

Christ was put to death by the Roman governor, at the instigation of the government and nation of the Jews. His body was in their hands, and entirely under their control. They knew that he had predicted his resurrection. They knew that, if he should rise, or should be believed to have risen, his cause would gain more by this fact, or by this belief, than by every thing which he had taught or done during his life. All this they declared to Pilate in form, for the express purpose of guarding against this dreaded evil. ' Now the next day that followed the day of the preparation,' says St. Matthew, ' the chief priests and Pharisees came together unto Pilate, saying, Sir, we remember that that deceiver said, while he was yet alive, After three days I will rise again. Command therefore, that the sepulchre be made fast, until the third day ; lest his disciples come by night, and steal him away ; and say unto the people, He is risen from the dead. So the last error shall be worse than the first. Pilate said unto them, Ye have a watch : go your way ; make it as sure as you can. So they went, and made the sepulchre sure, sealing the stone and setting a watch.' In this remarkable passage we have a distinct account of their knowledge of Christ's prediction, that he should rise on the third day ; of their dread of the prevalence of a future belief that he had risen ; of their conviction that this belief would advance his cause more than all his preaching, life, and miracles ; and their earnest request to the governor, that effectual measures might be taken to prevent this peculiar evil. We are farther informed, that the governor, in compliance with their fears and their wishes, after reminding them that they had a watch or guard under their control, directed them, with a communication of unlimited authority, ' to make the sepulchre as sure as they could.' Finally, we are informed that, with this power in their hands, ' They went their way, and made the sepulchre sure ;' that is, according to their own judgment ; and we are completely assured that such eagle-eyed and bitter enemies, under the influence of such apprehensions, left no precaution untried, to secure themselves against the danger which they dreaded. Accordingly, the evangelist informs us, that they not only set a guard at the sepulchre, which we may be certain was more than sufficient, but also ' set a seal upon the stone which was rolled to it for a door ;' in order to produce complete and universal conviction that Christ was not raised, because the seal was unbroken.

But, notwithstanding all these precautions, thus carefully taken, the body was missing. In this great fact the sanhedrim and the apostles perfectly agree : it cannot therefore be questioned. The sanhedrim would, otherwise, have certainly produced it ; and thus detected the falsehood of the apostles' declaration that he was risen from the dead, and prevented it from gaining credit among the Jews.

There are but two ways in which it could be missing. It was taken away, or it was raised. If it was taken away, it was undoubtedly taken by the apostles. But this was not true ; because,

(1.) *They had no interest in taking it away.*

Christ had declared that he should *rise from the dead.* The mere taking away of his body, instead of evincing the truth of this prediction to the apostles themselves, would have been an unanswerable proof of its falsehood ; and, by consequence, of the falsehood of him who uttered it. If the prediction were unfulfilled, of which the presence of his dead body would have been the proper and complete proof, Christ was a false prophet, an impostor. Of course, the apostles could expect no possible advantage from following him, and plainly saw themselves exposed to every disadvantage. They had, therefore, no conceivable inducement to take away his body, nor even to accept it, if it had been offered to them freely. This, it is believed, has been sufficiently evinced under a former head.

To others they could never produce the body of Christ as evidence, either of *his* sincerity, or *their own ;* for it would nave completely destroyed the character of both. The only end, therefore, which the theft could answer, would have been to gain some credit to the story of his resurrection, from the fact that his body was missing. When we consider that the body was perfectly in the power of their enemies, the Jewish sanhedrim, it must be acknowledged, that an argument of some

force might be drawn form this fact in favour of Christ's resurrection.   At the same time, it is evident that this single fact
would have been wholly insufficient to establish the point ; and
the apostles, in attempting to palm the story on the world,
would have engaged in a cause wholly desperate.   We demand very important additional proof, derived from other
sources, to establish this point in our own minds.   The necessity of such proof the apostles could not but have seen with,
at least, as much certainty as ourselves ; they could, therefore,
never have been willing to take it away for this purpose.

(2.) *The apostles durst not take away the body of Christ.*
They knew that a guard was placed at the sepulchre, a
numerous and amply sufficient band of Roman soldiers.   They
themselves were few, friendless, and discouraged ; in hourly
expectation of being arrested and put to death, as followers of
Christ ; and voluntarily confined to a solitary chamber, for
fear of being either crucified or stoned.   The time was that
of the passover, when Jerusalem customarily contained more
than a million of people.   It was the time of the *full moon*.
The sepulchre was just without the walls of the city, and exposed therefore to continual inspection.   How could a body
of men, who had just before fled from a similar guard, notwithstanding their Master was present with them, venture to
attack this band of armed soldiers, for the purpose of removing the body of Christ from the sepulchre?   How, especially,
could they make this attempt, when they had nothing to gain ;
and when they must become guilty of rebelling against the
Roman government ; and, if they escaped death from the
hands of the soldiers, were exposed to this evil in a much
more terrible form ?

(3.) *The apostles, with respect to this subject, had formed
no plan ; and entertained no expectations and no hopes.*
They disbelieved the story of his resurrection, when asserted by the most unsuspicious witnesses ; his female disciples, and their own companions.   Nay, they disbelieved it
after he had appeared several times ; when they had seen and
known that his body was gone from the sepulchre, and even
when he had appeared to themselves.   The truth is, they were
completely discouraged and broken-hearted.   The death of
Christ had violated all their prejudices, destroyed their fondest
hopes, and sunk their spirits in the dust.   Nor was any ex-

pedient less fitted to revive their hopes, than the wretched cheat imputed to them by their enemies.

(4.) *The story told concerning this subject by the sanhedrim, and thoughtlessly believed by the great body of the Jews even to the present time, is itself strong evidence of the truth of the assertion which I am maintaining.*

This story, as you well know, is, that *the disciples stole the body of Christ, while the guards were asleep.* I will not here insist on the ridiculousness of this story, but will only consider it as the real account given by the sanhedrim concerning the disappearing of the body from the sepulchre. This sagacious collection of men, sharpened into extreme cunning by the constant management of human affairs in very difficult times, thought it proper to tell the world this story, as the best account which they could give of the subject. To what straits must their ingenuity have been driven, when they were compelled to such a resort? Every man knows that the guards would, of their own accord, have never ventured upon such a narration ; for it would have been the infallible cause of their condemnation to death. It is scarcely possible, that a Roman sentinel should acknowledge himself to have slept upon his post : nor is it much more possible, that a Jewish senate should, unless under extreme pressure of circumstances, publicly accord with so contemptible a tale. Had that senate been possessed of any truth which would at all have favoured their designs, they would have never disgraced their character by acknowledging their reliance, and persuading their countrymen to rely, on the testimony of a heathen guard, nor of any other men, concerning what was done when they were asleep. Had truth favoured their wishes in any manner, neither the senate nor the people of the Jews would have rested themselves, in a case of this consequence, nor indeed in any case, upon a story, which carried with it its own refutation.

2. *The Jews in great numbers believed the resurrection of Christ.*

The Jews most ardently hated Christ and his apostles. Him they persecuted throughout his public ministry, and at the end of it nailed him to the cross. The apostles directly charged them with these enormous crimes, particularly in this very sermon of St. Peter, from which I have taken my text.

On this ground they urged them to repentance ; asserting always before them, that he had risen from the dead. Clear and unanswerable evidence, as I have already remarked, is necessary to convince the most candid man of so wonderful an event. But to convince Jews, that the man whom they had hated and crucified, was risen from the dead—Jews, so opposed to his character, mission, and doctrines—Jews, who in admitting his resurrection, acknowledged themselves to have sinned in a manner unparalleled—demanded singular evidence. Yet three thousand of these Jews believed the apostles' declaration of this fact on the day of Pentecost, fifty days only after the crucifixion. Within a few days more, five thousand others adopted the same belief, and soon afterward very great multitudes.

The evidence of their faith is complete. All these men publicly professed it, and, in spite of their former prejudices and their furious hatred, submitted themselves to Christ, as the Messiah. This crucified man they acknowledged in that glorious character, and yielded themselves to him as the Son of God. Judaism, to which they had been attached with such bigotry, they now publicly renounced ; and gave up their ceremonious worship, their sabbath, temple, priests, and sacraments ; adopting in their stead the Christian worship, sabbath, and sacraments ; submitting themselves to the ministers of the Gospel ; and embracing a new life, a life of real holiness, to them in the highest degree self-denying and difficult. A great number of them also sold their possessions, and distributed the avails of them in mere charity to their Christian brethren. Beyond this, these converts voluntarily forsook their friends, their interests, and their hopes, and underwent a series of dreadful sufferings, terminating not unfrequently in a violent death.

To persuade men to renounce their religion, especially bigoted men, and to exchange a sinful life for a virtuous one, is undoubtedly as hard a task as was ever assigned to the human mind ; especially when that religion contravenes all the selfishness of man. Jews now exist in great numbers, and have existed ever since the crucifixion of Christ. They hold the same character, and the same religion. Christianity, the religion to which they are to be converted, is also the same. But more Jews were made converts to the religion of Christ by these two sermons of St. Peter, than have embraced it within the last sixteen hundred years. It is therefore certain, that the apostles possessed advantages for this end, which their followers have not possessed ; and these advantages independently of miracles, consisted, in a great measure at least, in the peculiar circumstances of their hearers. They knew and remembered the life, preaching, and miracles of Christ, and the wonderful events which attended his death. These, as is obvious from the declaration of St. Luke, greatly affected their minds. ' And all the people,' says the Evangelist, ' that came together to that sight, beholding the things that were done, smote their breasts, and returned.' The guards, also, went into the city, and told the story of the descent of the ' angel,' who ' rolled away the stone from the sepulchre,' the awful circumstances by which he was attended, and the resurrection of Christ. * When to these things were added the miraculous events of the day of Pentecost, and the marvellous cure of the lame man at the beautiful gate of the temple, these Jews yielded up their prejudices, and submitted to truths which they could no longer resist. The facts here specified were, in the hands of the Spirit of grace, the means by which such multitudes of enemies were converted to the faith of the Gospel.

3. *The sanhedrim believed the resurrection of Christ.*

In the Acts iv. we are informed, that the sanhedrim had the apostles brought before them for preaching in the name of Christ the doctrines of Christianity, and for affirming that Christ was risen from the dead. Had they believed that the apostles *stole away* the body of Christ, they would now certainly have charged them with this gross fraud, this direct rebellion against the Roman and Jewish government ; and, unless they could have cleared themselves of the crime, would have punished them for it with at least due severity. Such punishment would not only have been just, but it had now become necessary for the sanhedrim to inflict it, in order to save their own reputation. They had originated the story, and were now under the strongest inducements to support it. Yet they did not even mention the subject ; but contented themselves with commanding them to preach no more in the name of Christ.

* Matthew xxviii. 11.

In Acts v. we are told, that the whole body of the apostles were brought before them again, for continuing to preach in opposition to this command. On this occasion also they kept a profound silence concerning the theft, which they had originally attributed to the apostles; but charged them with disobedience to their former injunctions. In this charge are contained the following remarkable words : ' Did we not straitly command you, that ye should not teach in his name? and behold, ye have filled Jerusalem with your doctrine, and intend to bring this man's blood upon us.' *To bring the blood* of one person upon another, is phraseology frequently used in the Bible. In fifteen* different instances in which we find it there, it has but a single meaning; viz. *to bring the guilt of contributing to the death of a person, or the guilt of murder, upon another person.* When it is said, ' His blood shall be upon his own head;' it is clearly intended, that the guilt of his death shall be upon himself. When, therefore, the sanhedrim accuse the apostles of attempting to bring the blood of Christ upon *them,* they accuse them of an intention to bring upon them the guilt of shedding his blood ; this being the only meaning of such phraseology in the Scriptures.

Should any doubt remain in the mind of any man concerning this interpretation, it may be settled, I think, beyond all question, by recurring to another passage, to which hitherto I have not alluded. In Matthew xxvii. 24, 25, we are told, that when ' Pilate saw that he could prevail nothing' towards releasing Christ, ' he took water, and washed his hands before the multitude, saying, I am innocent of the blood of this just person ; see ye to it :' and that then ' all the people answered, and said, His blood be on us, and on our children.' The meaning of the phraseology in this passage cannot be mistaken ; and it is altogether probable that the declaration of the sanhedrim being made so soon after this imprecation, to the apostles, so deeply interested in the subject, and on an occasion which so naturally called it up to view, the sanhedrim referred to it directly.

But if Christ was not raised from the dead, he was a false

* Lev. xx. 9, 11, 13, 16, 27 ; Deut. xix. 10 ; xxii. 8 : 2 Sam. i. 16 ; xvi. 8 : 1 Kings ii. 37 : Jer. li. 35 : Ezek. xviii. 13 : xxxiii. 5 : Matt. xxiii. 35 ; Acts xviii. 6.

prophet, an impostor, and, of course, a blasphemer; because he asserted himself to be the Messiah, the Son of God. Such a blasphemer the law of God condemned to death. The sanhedrim were the very persons to whom the business of trying and condemning him was committed by that law, and whose duty it was to accomplish his death. If, therefore, his body was not raised from the dead, there was no guilt in shedding his blood, but the mere performance of a plain duty. His blood, that is, the guilt of shedding it, could not possibly rest on the sanhedrim, nor, to use their language, be brought upon them by the apostles, nor by any others. All this the sanhedrim perfectly knew; and therefore, had they not believed him to have risen from the dead, they could never have used this phraseology.

It is farther to be observed, that on both these occasions the apostles boldly declared to the sanhedrim, in the most explicit terms, that Christ was raised from the dead; yet the sanhedrim not only did not charge them with the crime of having stolen his body, but did not contradict, nor even comment on, the declaration. This could not possibly have happened through inattention. Both the sanhedrim and the apostles completely knew, that the resurrection of Christ was the point on which his cause, and their opposition to it, entirely turned. It was the great and serious controversy between the contending parties; and yet, though directly asserted to their faces by the apostles, the sanhedrim did not even utter a syllable on the subject.

Had they believed their own story, they would either have punished the apostles with death, as rebels against the Jewish and Roman governments, or confined them as lunatics in a bedlam.

IV. *Christ was raised from the dead, because the apostles converted mankind to his religion.*

The Apostles, from the beginning to the end, published the story of Christ's resurrection as the proof of his mission, and doctrines; and as the foundation on which rested their own commission, and the truth of the religion which they taught. To prove the reality of his resurrection, they publicly declared that he had invested them with the power of working miracles on all occasions, and openly asserted that they were possessed of this power. Here, then, the cause was fairly at issue between them and mankind. If they wrought miracles in proof of this story, the story was true of course; because, as I observed in a preceding Discourse, none but God can work a miracle; and God cannot support a falsehood.

That this was the real profession of the apostles is unitedly testified, without one dissenting voice, by all antiquity; heathen, Jewish, and Christian. It is, therefore, certainly true.

If the apostles, after having made this profession, did not work miracles, they were convicted of falsehood in a moment. Their cause fell at once; for they had rested it wholly on this single fact. The weakest man would see, at a glance, that they were cheats and liars, and could never place the least confidence in any of their declarations. They could not, therefore, have made a single convert.

But they did convert a great part of the civilized, and not a small part of the savage world. They, therefore, certainly wrought miracles in the manner which they professed, as proof of the reality of Christ's resurrection. The resurrection of Christ was of course real. God set to it his own seal, and placed it beyond every reasonable doubt.

That the apostles wrought miracles in great numbers, is completely proved also by the united testimony of heathen, Jews, and Christians. All these classes of men were deeply interested to deny this fact, if it could with any pretence be denied. The heathen and Jews would certainly have denied it; because they wished to prevent, as far as possible, other heathen and other Jews from embracing Christianity; and because, if they could have supported the denial, they would have stopped the growth of that religion in its infancy. Christians would have denied it; that is, such as became Christians in consequence of a belief in these miracles under any illusion which could have been practised on them, because they would certainly have detected the cheat, and must have strongly resented the villany, by which it had been played off upon themselves. I say these things, admitting the supposition that the imposture might succeed for a time; but, to my own view, such success must plainly have been impossible.

All these persons have, however, agreed in asserting that the apostles wrought miracles. The Jews and heathen attributed them to magic. Christians, under the influence of their conviction that miracles were thus wrought, hazarded and yielded every enjoyment of life, and very often life itself.

We have now, if I do not mistake, come to the clear and certain conclusion, that Christ was raised from the dead by the power of God.   But, if Christ was raised from the dead, it follows, by irresistible consequence, that he was approved of God ; and, of course, that he was the Son of God, and the promised Messiah, sent from heaven to communicate the divine will to mankind concerning their duty and salvation. The religion which he taught is in all its parts divine truth, the will of our Maker, and the sum and substance of all our interest and duty.   Of course, it cannot be rejected without infinite hazard ; it cannot be embraced without complete assurance of infinite gain, the favour of God in this world, and eternal life in the world to come.

SERMON LXIII.

AMIABLENESS OF CHRIST

IN

PUBLISHING THE GOSPEL TO MANKIND.

HOW BEAUTIFUL ON THE MOUNTAINS ARE THE FEET OF HIM THAT BRINGETH GOOD TIDINGS ; THAT PUBLISHETH PEACE ; THAT BRINGETH GOOD TIDINGS OF GOOD ; THAT PUBLISHETH SALVATION ; THAT SAITH UNTO ZION, THY GOD REIGNETH.

ISAIAH LII. 7.

IN a long series of Discourses I have investigated minutely the character and mediation of Christ ; and have considered his divine and human nature ; his offices as a Prophet, Priest, and King ; his miracles ; and his resurrection. I shall now close this great and interesting subject of theology by attempting to exhibit, summarily, *the excellency and amiableness of Christ,* as manifested in his interference on the behalf of mankind.

In the text, the prophet Isaiah presents to us the advent of a messenger of good tidings to mankind. This messenger is represented as announcing to the world ' good,' or happiness at large ; as ' publishing peace '——' salvation '——and the glorious news, that the God, who reigns universally, is the God of Zion. His appearance is exhibited by the prophet as filling his own mind with astonishment and extasy. Nothing could more forcibly convey to us the prophet's rapturous sense of the importance of these tidings, or his exalted views of the messenger who brought them, than the manner in which he dwells on these subjects, in the repeated and fervid exclamations of the text.   When the soul becomes the seat of strong emotions, and especially when it is agitated by strong alternations of wonder and joy, it usually finds language, in every form of phraseology, too feeble to give full vent to its feelings, or to convey them to others with such force, as to satisfy the demands either of the imagination or the passions.   When we ourselves feel, we wish others to feel ; and when our emotions become peculiarly ardent, we are prone to fear that the corresponding emotions of others will be less vivid than we desire. The mind in this case seizes the most forcible language within its reach, and, conscious that even this language halts behind its own fervours, naturally seeks to increase the impressions, by reiterating them in new and more animated phraseology. From this source were derived the exclamations of the text, peculiarly suited to the mind of Isaiah, whose imagination was not only more sublime, but on all occasions more ready to glow, than that of any other writer.

St. Paul applies this text to the ministers of the Gospel generally, and perhaps more especially to the first ministers. This application teaches us decisively, that the Gospel, the meaning of which word you know is merely ' good tidings,' is the subject of the annunciation in the text ; and that ministers of the Gospel at large are, in a loose and general sense, included in the purport of these exclamations.   The prophet, however, speaks of one messenger only ; and this messenger is the person who publishes the Gospel to mankind.   The Lord Jesus Christ is undoubtedly the messenger here intended, by whose voice the Gospel was originally communicated to the world.   The prophet, who beyond any other writer embodies all his thoughts, and holds them out to the view of the eye, exhibits this divine herald as advancing over the mountains surrounding the city of Jerusalem, and as proclaiming joyful news to its inhabitants.   The reader is transported to the spot ; sees this illustrious person approach, hears him proclaim the tidings which he comes to announce, and unites with the prophet and his exulting countrymen in their joyful exclamations.

The only characteristical circumstance on which the prophet rests in the text, is the *beauty* which adorned the person of this glorious messenger. ' How *beautiful* on the mountains are the feet of him that bringeth good tidings !' To the consideration of this subject I propose to devote the following Discourse.

In the discussion of it I shall consider,

I. *The persons, to whom these tidings were published :*
II. *The tidings themselves :* and
III. *The messenger who published them.*

I. *The persons to whom these tidings were published, were the children of apostate Adam.*

It will be useful to the design which I have proposed, to consider both *their character* and *their circumstances.*

Their character, like that of their progenitor, was formed of apostasy. Every man who searches his own bosom, or examines the conduct of his own life, is presented with irresistible evidence that he is a sinner. Let him form whatever rule of life he is pleased to prescribe, by which his duty to himself, to his fellow men, and to God, ought even in his own view to be regulated, and he will find himself, in innumerable instances, a transgressor of that rule. The heathen philosophers anciently, and the infidels of modern times, have formed such rules. Weigh them in their own balances, and they will invariably be ' found wanting.' Lax, licentious, and even monstrous as the laws are which they have proposed for the regulation of their own moral conduct, they still have not obeyed them, and will, if tried by them, be certainly condemned. How much more defective do they appear, when examined by the dictates of a sober and enlightened conscience ! How far more defective, when tried by the perfect law of God ! Searched by this law, it will be uniformly found, and every man faithfully employed in the search will be obliged to confess, that ' in our flesh dwelleth no good thing.'

Among the most affecting specimens of this evil character, a conscientious investigator will be deeply afflicted with those which constitute his own *personal debasement.* If he open his eye on what he has been, and on what he has done, he will find the most abundant reason to exclaim, with Job, ' I abhor myself, and repent in dust and ashes.' He will find that he has, in the true and evangelical sense, neither loved God, nor man ; that he has neither accepted of his Saviour, nor repented of his sins; that he has neither laboured to be a blessing, nor even endeavoured not to be a nuisance, to the divine kingdom. Instead of worshipping God ' in spirit and in truth,' according to the first dictates of his conscience and of Revelation, he will find that he has in truth prostrated himself to gold, to office, to fame, and to pleasure. Instead of the exact justice, unwavering truth, and expansive benevolence of the Gospel, he will see, written in the volume of his life with a pen of iron, a succession of melancholy scenes and acts of unkindness, insincerity, and injustice; all contrived and finished by a mind shrunk with selfishness, swollen with pride, heated with anger, debased with avarice, and steeled with insensibility. Page after page he will see stained with the licentious wanderings of an impure imagination, and deformed by the malignant purposes of an envious, angry, and revengeful spirit. In vain will his eye, pained with these narratives of shame and sin, wander from one leaf to another with an anxious, inquisitive search, to find the delightful records of filial confidence, submission, and gratitude to the Creator, or the sweet and cheering remembrances of evangelical charity towards those around him, or a portrait of himself, which shall be a fair counterpart to that of the good Samaritan. In vain will he watch and explore the humiliating story, to glean from it refreshing recollections of self-purification, the refinement of his mind, the amendment of his heart, or the cleansing of his life. Over himself he will find the most distressing reasons to mourn, as over a graceless and ruined child; ruined, on the one hand, by the gratification of pernicious appetites and passions, and on the other, by a senseless, thoughtless indulgence, doting with a mixture of idiocy and madness.

The public exhibitions of the human character are still more striking displays of human guilt. Almost the only government of mankind has been tyranny. Almost all the conduct of nations may be summed up in the rage of plunder, the fury of war, and the phrenzy of civil discord. Men seem to have thought their blessings too numerous and too great, and the duration of their life too long. Accordingly they have robbed each other of the former, shortened the latter, and struggled hard to reduce both to nothing. At what time has human blood ceased to flow? In what country have rage and revenge ceased to desolate? When and where have the cries of mourning and misery ceased to resound? The groans of suffering have echoed from California to Japan. The stream of sorrow has flowed without interruption for six thousand years. On all the public concerns of man, on every nation, on every age, have been labelled, ' Lamentation, mourning, and woe.'

Such has been the conduct of man towards man. Not less shameful, not less guilty, has been the conduct of man towards his Maker. Instead of rendering to this glorious Being, whose we are, and whom we are bound to serve, the direct, instinctive homage of the heart, and the cheerful obedience of the hands; instead of acknowledging his rightful government, rejoicing in his divine perfections, and voluntarily labouring to accomplish his exalted purposes; we have said to him with one united voice, ' Depart from us; for we desire not the knowledge of thy ways.' For Jehovah, the only living and true God, mankind have subtituted deities, formed by the imagination, graven by art, and molten in the furnace. The forest has been scoured, the ocean swept, and the sky ransacked, for objects of worship. The world has prostrated itself before men deformed with villany, and putrid with pollution. The knee has bent to the ox, the snake, the frog, and the fly. Nay, the heart has yielded its homage, prayers, and oblations to the stock of a tree; and parents have sacrificed their children to the great enemy of God and man. Look over the long page of history, and you will be astonished to see how rarely a country is mentioned, and how rarely a period occurs, in which you would be willing to have lived.

But guilt is not the only ingredient of the human character. It is scarcely less humble and insignificant, than it is guilty. We are born of the dust, allied to worms, and victims to corruption. Weak, ignorant, frail, perishing, and possessed only of an ephemeral existence, we still are proud; proud of our reason with all its errors, and of our temper with all its sins. We claim a kindred to angels; but, by a voluntary slavery to passion and appetite, assimilate ourselves to ' the beasts which perish.' We boast loudly of the dignity of our nature; and prostitute that nature daily, on objects of shame and remorse, and to purposes which we would not, for a world, have known even to our nearest friends. What a dreadful display of our character would our thoughts, wishes and designs make to mankind, if they were all printed in a volume, and read even by such eyes as ours! How few thoughts do we form, which we should be willing to have an angel know! How few purposes, over which an angel would not weep!

In this character, at the same time, we are immoveably fixed and perverse. No event, in the immense providence of God, has contributed to prove that there is in a sinful mind a tendency to renovation. Arguments plead, reason testifies, judgments warn, and mercies allure, in vain! 'The sinful heart is incased in adamant, and is proof even to the arrows of the Almighty. God 'calls' earnestly, and continually; but we 'refuse. He stretches out his hand,' both to smite and to heal, 'but we disregard.'

In consequence of our character, our circumstances have become deplorable. The law of God, with an unalterable sentence, has declared that 'the soul which sinneth shall die.' As a prelude to the execution of this penalty, thorns and briers have overspread this melancholy world. Toil and care, sorrow and suffering, disease and death, entered Paradise the moment it was polluted by sin; withered all its bloom, and blasted its immortality. Death, the dreadful offspring of this dreadful parent, has claimed the earth as his empire, and mankind as his prey. All nations have perished under his iron sceptre; 'the young man and maiden, old men and children.' Half mankind has he compelled to the grave in the dawn of childhood, and converted the world into one vast burying ground. We walk on human dust; and the remains of men once living are turned up by the plough, and blown about by the wind.

From this deplorable lot, and the guilty character of which it is the reward, there was, independently of Christ's mediation, no escape; and to both there was no end. With heaven our communication was cut off. No messenger ever came from that delightful world, to soothe the fears or awaken the hopes of mankind, concerning a future existence. If in the vast of being, or the boundless extent of divine benevolence, good was laid up in store for them, it was unknown. No tidings of relief or hope, no intimations of forgiveness or reconciliation, had ever reached this desolate region. Eternity, solemn and awful in itself, and more solemn and awful from its obscurity, became intensely dreadful to beings who could make no claims to acceptance, and find no solid ground of hope.

To such beings how delightful must be any tidings of good! How much more delightful, tidings of extensive good! How transporting, tidings of such good, which by their certainty banished distrust and doubt from the soul!

II. *The nature of these tidings next demands our consideration.*

This is exhibited in five forms of phraseology: ' That bringeth good tidings;—that publisheth peace;—that bringeth good tidings of good;—that publisheth salvation;—that saith unto Zion, Thy God reigneth.' The first and third of these forms indicate, generally, that the tidings are good, or joyful; and tidings concerning good of great value. The remaining forms teach us the nature of that good.

In the two first-mentioned forms of expression, we are assured, that the subject of these tidings is real good, attainable by us, reserved by God for our enjoyment, certain, future, and immortal. Good, fitted for the enjoyment of such minds as ours, such as God himself esteems real good, and such as it becomes his character to proffer and to bestow. The tidings concerning this glorious allotment are also in themselves pronounced to be good; because they are sincere and certain, and because they communicate easy and effectual means of making it ours.

It is styled in the second phrase, ' Peace.' Peace is the cessation of war, or contention; and in the present case, the cessation of our hostility with *God, ourselves* and *our fellow-men.* The soul of man is at war with *his Maker.* The great subject of controversy here, is our obedience to his will. This *he* requires, and *we* refuse. Nothing can terminate the contest but our submission; for it cannot be supposed, that the Creator will bend his own pleasure to the rebellious spirit of his creatures. In announcing these tidings to mankind, Christ first proclaims to them, that God is willing to be reconciled. This is intelligence which, before the mediation of Christ commenced, could never have gained credit, even in the world of benevolence itself. Angels knew no reward for revolt from their Creator, but final rejection: the reward to which their own companions had been irrevocably condemned. With wonder and amazement they saw a new system of dispensations commencing in this apostate world, and heard forgiveness and reconciliation proclaimed to man. Humble as was our origin, guilty and little as was our character, we were commanded, invited, and entreated to lay down the weapons of our warfare; to return to God, our duty, and our happiness; and to receive from his hands peace, commencing in this world, and extending its benign and delightful influence throughout eternity.

The soul reconciled to its God, becomes at once *reconciled to itself*. With himself man is as truly at war, as with his Maker. A contention, real, unceasing, and violent, is carried on between the conscience and the passions. Conscience claims to controul the man, as her original and rightful province. Against this claim a mob of furious passions revolt, and demand, and wrest out of her hands the controverted dominion. As in all cases where the order established by God becomes inverted, so here every real interest is sacrificed. The soul is debased with guilt, harassed by fear, tossed by a tempest of conflicting desires, wounded with remorse, and hastened onward to final destruction. Conscience, in the mean time, infixes all her stings into the heart of this miserable subject of domestic discord, and holds up her awful mirror before his eyes, presenting him with an exact and terrible portrait of himself; pale, languid, sickly with mental diseases, his spiritual life already gone, and himself, both soul and body, destined speedily to an eternal grave. But when the soul submits to its Maker, and bows its own will to his, the man becomes reconciled to himself. The controul of conscience is not only permitted, but chosen. The froward passions, like stubborn children who have renounced their filial impiety, bend with a gentleness and serenity before unknown, to a dominion now first discovered not only to be safe, but easy, reasonable, and delightful. No longer a seat of confusion and discord, the soul becomes henceforth a mansion of peace and harmony, where sweet affections rise and operate, under the controul and the approbation of conscience. The man is reconciled to himself; and, turning his eyes inward, beholds henceforth a prospect beautiful and lovely, an image of heaven, a resemblance, faint and distant indeed, but still a real resemblance, to the character of his Maker.

Peace with our *fellow-men* is the natural consequence of peace with ourselves; not indeed necessarily, nor uniformly; but always, so far as they are possessed of the same blessing, and under the influence of the same disposition. While the same internal hostility predominates in them, they are unfitted to be at peace with God or man. But the period is hastening when this happy state of mind shall be the state of all men, and peace shall prevail on earth, according to the full import of the hymn sung by angels at the birth of the Saviour. The tidings of the text will then be illustriously realized; and man, at peace with his Maker and himself, will be at peace also with all his fellow-men. The ' confused noise of the battle of the warrior' will then be heard no more; and ' garments ' be seen no more ' rolled in blood.' ' Violence shall ' then ' be no more heard in the' world ; ' wasting nor destruction within its borders.' The earth no longer convulsed by human passions, no longer gloomy and desolate with the miseries of human conflicts, will assume the aspect of a delightful morning in the spring, were all is verdant and blooming beneath, and all is bright and glorious above.

In the fourth of these forms of expression, this good is styled ' Salvation.'

Salvation denotes a deliverance from evil, and an introduction to the enjoyment of good. In the present case, both the evil and the good are immeasurable.

The *evil* is *two-fold*; a compound of *sin* and *misery*; both imperfect. in this world, and both finished in the world to come. From both in this world the deliverance announced is partial; beginning from nothing, and enlarging, and ascending, with a constant though unequal progress, towards perfection. The soul, before a mass of deformity and corruption, begins to be adorned with life, and grace, and beauty. With it angels love to commune, on it God is pleased to look with complacency.

From future sin and future misery the deliverance is complete. With death our last sins terminate, and our last misery is undergone. Cast your eyes forward through the vast of duration, and think what it would be to sin and suffer for ever. How amazing the evil! How astonishing the deliverance!

The *good* announced is *two-fold* also ; a glorious union of *virtue* and *enjoyment :* like the evil, imperfect here, and consummate hereafter.   The virtue of man in his present state is infantine ; tottering with an unsettled step, and lisping with half-formed accents.   In the future state, the mind, advanced to perfect manhood, is completely sanctified, and cannot fail of being completely blessed.   To enjoyment and virtue that state is wholly destined.   Every thing found in it, as once in the earthly Paradise, blossoms with life and happiness, and, like Adam, all its inhabitants are formed for immortality.

In the last phrase of the text, this good is disclosed to us in the declaration, ' that saith unto Zion, Thy God reigneth.'

God, the author of all things, is the source of all good. ' Every good gift,' in this and all other worlds, ' and every perfect gift, is from above ; and cometh down from the Father of lights, with whom is no variableness, neither shadow of turning.'   From him , the ocean, flow all those streams of holiness which water, enrich, and beautify his immeasurable kingdom.   His character, his moral essence, is ' love ;' and, wherever happiness is found, it may justly be said, that the name of every blessing is like that of the city seen in vision by Ezekiel, ' The Lord is there.'

With these tidings resounding in their ears, the children of Zion may joyfully say, ' This God is our God for ever and ever.'   To their present and everlasting good his boundless power, wisdom, and goodness are by himself graciously consecrated.   To renew, purify, preserve, protect, enlighten, guide, quicken, and save them in this world, and to form them in his own perfect image, and exalt them to his own perfect felicity in the world to come, is declared to be his constant and favourite employment.   In that glorious and happy world he will unveil his face to them, and give them to ' see as they are seen,' and to ' know as they are known.'   In the smiles of forgiving, redeeming, and sanctifying love, they will there rove, and bask, and brighten for ever.

III. *I shall consider the messenger who published these tidings.*

In the investigation of this subject I shall inquire.

Who he was ?

What he became ?

What he did? and,
What he suffered?

1. I shall inquire *who he was.*

(1.) *He was a person of supreme glory and dignity.*

This divine person was from everlasting, underived, independent, all-sufficient, and unchangeable in his being, wisdom, goodness, and power. All things were the work of his hand, and lay beneath his feet. At the head of a kingdom filling immensity and eternity, ' he was ;' and in comparison with him ' there was none else.' ' All nations before him were as nothing, and were counted unto him as less than nothing and vanity.' Angels in his presence veiled their faces, and archangels durst not attempt to penetrate the unapproachable light with which he clothed himself as with a garment. To obey him was their highest honour ; to please him was their greatest happiness. In his service they employed all their powers, and found all their transports. Suns lighted up their fires at his bidding ; systems rolled, to fulfil his pleasure ; and to accomplish his designs, immensity was stored with worlds and their inhabitants.

(2.) *He was rich in all good.*

' All things were' not only ' made by him,' but ' for him.' They were his property ; they were destined to fulfil his pleasure. When he looked on all the beauty, greatness, and glory, conspicuous in the beings which compose and which inhabit the universe, he beheld nothing but the works of his own hands, reflecting the boundless beauty, greatness, and glory which, in forms and varieties infinite, were treasured up from everlasting in his own incomprehensible mind. If he chose to bring into existence any additional number of creatures, to display new forms and varieties of power, wisdom, and goodness, pre-existent in his own perfect intellect, his choice would instantaneously give them being. To the universe which he had made, he could with infinite ease add another, and another ; and fill with worlds, and suns, and systems, those desolate wilds of immensity, where the wing of angels never ventured to rove, and whither no created mind ever sent out a solitary thought. Thus the universe of possible things was his own.

He was rich in the veneration and good will, the complacency and gratitude, of all virtuous beings. Heaven, throughout her vast regions, had from the beginning echoed to his praise. ' The morning stars' had ' sung' his perfections from their birth, ' and the sons of God shouted' his name ' for joy.' The everlasting hymn of that exalted and delightful world had ever been, ' Blessing, and honour, and glory, and power, be unto our God that sitteth on the throne, and unto the Lamb for ever and ever:' and to this divine ascription every virtuous world had continually as well as solemnly answered, ' Amen.'

He was rich in himself. His own mind was the mansion of all things great, excellent, and delightful. Pure from every stain, free from every error, serene without a cloud, secure beyond a fear, and conscious of wisdom and holiness only, himself was an ocean of eternal and overflowing good.

He was rich in the complacency of his Father. He was from everlasting his ' beloved Son, in whom he was ever well pleased.' ' From everlasting was he by him, as one brought up with him. He was daily his delight, rejoicing alway before him.' In the transcendent communion of the ever blessed Trinity, he experienced enjoyment which ' no' created ' eye hath seen, or can see,' and which no mind less than infinite can conceive. On this subject beings ' of yesterday' must not presume to expatiate. With the deepest reverence they can only exclaim, ' It is higher than heaven, what can we know?'

2. *This glorious person, to accomplish the good announced in these tidings, became man.*

Although ' he was' originally ' in the form of God, and thought it no robbery to be equal with God, yet he made himself of no reputation, took upon him the form of a servant, and was made in the likeness of men.' In this character of immense humiliation, he lived in this sinful, melancholy world. To man, ' who is a worm, and the son of man, who is but a worm,' he allied himself by birth, kindred, and character. All the infirmities of our nature, except sin, he voluntarily assumed ; sprang from a humble lineage, lived in a humble employment, was united to humble companions, and was invariably in humble circumstances. So depressed was he in all things, that he himself has thought proper to say, ' I am a worm, and no man.'

3. *In this situation he did all things well.*

His life was filled up with usefulness and duty; was laborious beyond example, and was wholly consecrated to the glory of God, and the good of mankind. In conformity to this great purpose, he spent all the former part of his life in an illustrious discharge of the duties of filial piety. In his public ministry he taught, with unceasing diligence, the law of God, the ruin of man by his disobedience, and the tidings of his recovery by his own mediation. The way of life he marked·out with an unerring hand; the means of life he disclosed with a benevolent voice. The duties to which man is summoned, he exemplified in his own perfect conduct.. The hopes which man was invited to cherish, he pourtrayed in colours of light. The door of heaven, shut before to this apostate world, he unbarred with his own power; and love invited ' labouring and heavy laden' sinners to enter in, and find ' rest.' Wandering prodigals, perishing with want and nakedness, and lost to the universe of God, he sought, and found, and brought home to his Father's house rejoicing. Wretches, ' dead in trespasses and sins,' he raised to spiritual and immortal life. This vast earthly catacomb he entered; and summoned together by his voice the bones of the immense congregation in its gloomy recesses, ' bone to his bone.' The host of skeletons he covered with flesh; and, breathing upon them the breath of life, bade them ' stand upon their feet, as an exceeding great army for multitude.'

4. *To accomplish this divine purpose, he underwent every humiliation, and every suffering.*

He was born in a stable, and cradled in a manger. The greatest part of his life he spent in the humble and laborious business of a mechanic, and literally earned his bread ' with the sweat of his brow.' Poor beyond the common lot of poverty, ' he had not,' while ministering immortal blessings to a world, a place ' where to lay his head.' For all the suffering he wrought miraculous works of beneficence; but the power with which they were wrought, ready at the call of others, was rarely exerted for himself. At the same time he was hated and persecuted day by day. Wickedness employed all its hostility against him; its pride and cunning, its malice and wrath; calumniated his name, invaded his peace, and hunted his life. By his friends he was betrayed and forsaken. By his enemies he was accused of drunkenness and gluttony, of impiety and blasphemy, of being the friend of sinners, and the coadjutor of Satan. From the agonies of Gethsemane he was conveyed successively to the iniquitous tribunal of the sanhedrim, to the bloody hall of Pilate, to the cross, and to the tomb. At the close of a life spent in bitterness and sorrow, he consummated all his sufferings by undergoing that last and greatest of all evils, the wrath of God, poured out upon him as the substitute for sinners.

All these things he *foresaw*, when he brought these tidings to mankind. They were always before him; and were indispensable parts of that mediation which he voluntarily assumed. They were undergone, therefore, in a continual anticipation. Every day ' he was' literally ' a man of sorrows, and acquainted with grief.' In the full view of them all, he came to this world, to proclaim ' peace and salvation' to those who despised, rejected, and persecuted him; who nailed him to the cross, and compelled him to the grave. To these very men he announced all good; himself, his favour, his kingdom, his house, his presence, his everlasting joy. Think what tidings these are! Think to whom they are published!

Thus, from a summary view of this subject, Christ, in publishing these tidings to mankind, appears invested with supreme amiableness and beauty. No attribute which forms, no action which becomes, the perfect character, is wanting in him. With all things in his hands, with all excellence and enjoyment in his mind, he pitied *us*, miserable worms of the dust; descended from heaven, became man, lived, and died, and rose again, that we might live for ever. With his own voice he proclaimed, in the tidings of the text, the very things which he has done, and suffered, and the infinite blessings which in this manner he has purchased for mankind. ' There is now, (he cries,) ' glory to God in the highest,' while there is ' peace on earth, and good-will towards men.' In this ruined world, so long enveloped in darkness, so long deformed by sin, so long wasted by misery, where guilt, and sorrow, and suffering have spread distress without control, and mourning without hope; where war and oppression have ravaged without, and remorse and despair consumed within; where Satan has ' exalted his throne above the stars of God,' while its sottish millions have bent before him in religious worship; in this ruined world, where, since the apostasy, real good was never found, and where tidings of such good were never proclaimed; even here, I announce the tidings of expiated sin, a pardoning God, a renewing Spirit, an opening heaven and a dawning immortality. Here peace anew shall lift her olive branch over mankind. Here salvation from sin and woe shall anew be found; and here God shall dwell and reign, the God of Zion. ' Come unto me, all ye that labour, and are heavy laden; and I will give you rest.' ' Incline your ear, and hear, and your souls shall live; and I will make an everlasting covenant with you, even the sure mercies of David.' ' The spirit of Jehovah is upon me, because he hath anointed me to preach good tidings unto the meek; he hath sent me to bind up the broken hearted, to proclaim liberty to the captives, and the opening of the prison to them that are bound.' ' I will greatly rejoice in the Lord; my soul shall be joyful in my God; for he hath clothed me with garments of salvation; he hath covered me with the robe of righteousness; as a Bridegroom decketh himself with ornaments; as a Bride adorneth herself with jewels.'

Every messenger of good news is, of course, desirable and lovely in the eyes of those who are deeply interested; and a part of that lustre, belonging to the tidings themselves, is by a natural association diffused around him by whom they are borne; especially because he is regarded as voluntarily announcing good to us, and as rejoicing in our joy. How glorious, how lovely then, does Christ appear, when coming with all the inherent splendour and beauty of his character, and the transcendent dignity of his station, to proclaim to us tidings infinitely desirable, of good infinitely necessary and infinitely great! Men to him were wholly unnecessary. Had all their millions been blotted out of the kingdom of God, they would not even have left a blank in the creation. With a word he could have formed, of the stones of the street, other millions, wiser, better, and happier; more dutiful, and more desirable. How divinely amiable does he appear, when the tidings which he brings, are tidings of his own arduous labours on our behalf, and of his own unexampled sufferings; labours and sufferings, without which, good tidings could never have reached us, and real good never been found in this miserable world! How divinely amiable does he appear, when, notwithstanding the apostasy and guilt of the race of Adam, he came, of his own accord, to publish these tidings of immortal good to rebels and enemies ; and, while proclaiming them, ' rejoiced in the habitable parts of the earth,' and found ' his delights with the sons of men.'

What, then, must be the guilt, what the debasement, of those who are regardless of the glorious declarations, hostile to the benevolent designs, and insensible to the perfect character of this divine herald !   How blind, and deaf, and stupid must they be to all that is beautiful, engaging, and lovely !   How grovelling must be their moral taste !   How wonderful their neglect of their own well being !   How evidently is their ingratitude ' as the sin of witchcraft, and their stubbornness as iniquity and idolatry !'   Were these tidings to be proclaimed in hell itself, one can scarcely fail to imagine that all the malice, impiety, and blasphemy in that dreary world would be suspended, that fiends would cease to conflict with fiends, that sorrow would dry the stream of never-ending tears, that remorse would reverse and blunt his stings, that despair would lift up his pale front with a commencing smile, that the prisoners of wrath (then ' prisoners of hope') would shake their chains with transport, and that all the gloomy caverns would echo to the sounds of gratitude and joy.   In our own world, once equally hopeless, these tidings are actually proclaimed. What must be the spirit of those who refuse to hear !

But, O ye followers of the divine and compassionate Saviour, infinitely different is the wisdom displayed by you !   When this divine messenger proclaims to you peace and salvation ; when he informs you that he has died, that you may live ; when he demands of you cordially to embrace his atonement, and accept his intercession ; you cheerfully hear, believe, and obey.   Conscious of your own guilty character, and ruined condition, you have yielded yourselves to him with all the heart, in the humble, amiable, penitent exercise of faith and love, and finally chosen him as your own Saviour.   On your minds his image is instamped ; in your life his beauty shines with real, though feeble, radiance ; in your character his loveliness is begun ; in your souls his immortality is formed.   On you his Father smiles, a forgiving God.   On you his Spirit descends, with his sanctifying and dove-like influence.   To you his word unfolds all his promises, his daily favour, his everlasting love.   To you hell is barred, and all its seducing and destroying inhabitants confined in chains. Heaven for you has already opened its ' everlasting doors ;' and ' the King of glory' has ' entered in,' to ' prepare a place for you.' The joy of that happy world has been already renewed over your repentance.   The Spirit of truth conducts you daily onward in your journey through life, and in your way towards your final home.   Death, your last enemy, is to you deprived of his strength and sting, and the grave despoiled of its victory.   Your bodies will soon be ' sown' in the ' corruption, weakness, and dishonour' of your present perishable nature, to be ' raised' in the ' incorruption, power, and glory' of immortality.   Your souls, cleansed from every sin, and stain, and weakness, this divine messenger will present before the throne of his Father ' without spot, or wrinkle, or any such thing,' to be acquitted, approved, and blessed.   In the world of light, and peace, and joy, enlarged with knowledge, and refined with evangelical virtue, he will unite you to ' the general assembly of the first-born,' and ' to the innumerable company of angels;' will make you ' sons, and priests, and kings to God,' and cause you to ' live and reign with him for ever and ever.'   ' All things' will then be ' yours ;' you will be ' Christ's ; and Christ' will be ' God's.'   Anticipate, and by anticipation enjoy to the full, this divine assemblage of blessings ; they are your birth-right.   But, while you enjoy them, deeply pity and fervently pray for your foolish, guilty, and miserable companions.

SERMON LXIV.

CONSEQUENCES OF CHRIST'S MEDIATION.

JUSTIFICATION.

JUSTIFICATION BY THE FREE GRACE OF GOD.

BEING JUSTIFIED FREELY BY HIS GRACE, THROUGH THE REDEMP-
TION WHICH IS IN CHRIST JESUS.

ROMANS III. 24.

IN the series of Sermons which I have preached hitherto, as
part of a System of Theology, I have considered the existence
and perfections of God ; the disobedience and apostasy of
man ; and the impossibility of his justification by his own
righteousness : the covenant of redemption made between the
Father and the Son ; the character, mediation, and offices of
Christ. The former class of subjects constitutes what is frequently called the religion of nature ; the latter, the first
branches of the Christian, or remedial system, grafted upon
that religion. Perfect beings are justified by their own obedience, since they fulfil all the demands of the divine law. To
them, therefore, the religion of nature is amply sufficient to
secure their duty, their acceptance with God, and their final
happiness. Sinful beings cannot thus be justified ; because
they have not rendered that obedience which is the only possible ground of justification by law. Of course, some other
ground of justification is absolutely necessary for them, if they
are ever to be accepted, or rewarded. For this the religion
of Christ professes to have made ample provision. In my ex-

amination of the character and offices of Christ, I have attempted to show that he has taught all which is necessary to be known, believed, or done by us, in order to our acceptance with God ; and has accomplished the expiation of our sins in such a manner, that God, in justifying us, may be just to himself, and to the universe. Thus far it is hoped, the way to our return from our apostasy has been made clear and satisfactory.

The next great question to be asked, and a question of infinite moment to every one of us, is, In what manner do we become interested in the mediation of Christ, and entitled to the glorious blessings which he has purchased for man? This question is partially answered in the text. Here we are said to be ' justified freely by the grace of God, through the redemption of Christ Jesus.' In this declaration our justification is immediately connected with ' the redemption of Christ,' as its meritorious or procuring cause. The source of it, also, on the part of God, is directly asserted ; as is also the manner in which it was accomplished. We are said to be ' justified freely ;' and ' justified by his grace.' All this is also said to be done ' through' by means of, or on account of, ' the redemption of Christ.' These subjects are intended to occupy the following Discourse.

In the course of my investigation I shall consider,

I. *In what sense mankind are justified under the Gospel.*

II. *In what sense we are freely justified by the grace of God.*

I. *I shall consider in what sense mankind are justified under the Gospel.*

The word ' justified,' as I observed in a former Discourse, is taken from the business of judicial courts ; and denotes the *acquittal* of a person tried by such a court, upon an accusation of a crime. The person accused, being upon trial found innocent of the charge, is declared to be just, in the view of the law ; and, by an easy and natural figure, is said to be *justified*; that is, made just. In this original, forensic sense of the term, it is obvious, from what has been said in a former Discourse, that no human being can be justified by the law, or before the bar of God. As all mankind have disobeyed this law, it is clear, that he ' whose judgment is' invariably ' according to truth,' must declare them guilty.

Still the Scriptures abundantly teach us, that ' what the law could not do, in that it was weak through the flesh, God, sending his own Son in the likeness of sinful flesh, and for a sin-offering,' has, by thus ' condemning sin in the flesh,' accomplished for multitudes of our sinful race.   It is however certain, that justification, when extended to returning sinners, must, in some respects, be of course a thing widely different from justification under the law.   A subject of law is justified only when he is in the full and strict sense just ; that is, when he has completely obeyed all the requisitions of the law.   In this case, his obedience is the only ground of his justification, and is all that is necessary to it ; because he has done every thing which was required of him, and no act of disobedience can be truly laid to his charge.   From this case, that of the penitent under the Gospel differs entirely.   He has been guilty of innumerable acts of disobedience, and has not fulfilled the demands of the law even in a single instance.   All these acts of disobedience are truly chargeable to him, when he comes before the bar of God at the final trial ; nor can he ever be truly said not to have been guilty of them.   If, therefore, he be ever justified, it must be in a widely different sense from that which has been already explained.   The term is, therefore, not used in the Gospel because its original meaning is intended here, but because this term, figuratively used, better expresses the thing intended than any other. The act of God, denoted by this term as used in the Gospel, so much resembles a forensic justification, or justification by law, that the word is naturally, and by an easy translation, adopted to express this act.

The justification of a sinner under the Gospel consists in the three following things : *pardoning his sins ; acquitting him from the punishment which they have deserved ; and entitling him to the rewards or blessings due by law to perfect obedience only.*

In order to form clear and satisfactory views of this subject, it will be useful to examine the situation of man, in his progress from apostasy to acceptance, as it is exhibited in the Scriptures.

In the covenant of redemption, the Father promised Christ, that, ' if he should make his soul a propitiatory sacrifice for sin, he should see a seed which should prolong their days;'* or, as it is expressed by God in the lxxxixth Psalm, ' His seed should endure for ever, and his throne,' that is, his dominion over them, as the days of heaven.' In this covenant, three things are promised to Christ, in consequence of his assumption and execution of the mediatorial office; (1.) That a seed shall be given him; (2.) That they shall endure and be happy for ever; and, (3.) That his dominion over them shall be co-extended with their eternal being. It was then certain, antecedently to Christ's entrance upon the office of Mediator, that he should not assume nor execute it in vain; but should receive a reward for all his labours and sufferings, such as he thought a sufficient one; such as induced him to undertake this office, and to accomplish all the arduous duties which it involved. This reward was to be formed of rational and immortal beings originally apostate, but redeemed by him from their apostasy, through the atonement made for their sins by his sufferings, particularly his death; and the honour which he rendered to the divine law by his personal obedience. All these redeemed apostates were to ' endure for ever' in a state of perfect holiness and happiness; and both this holiness and happiness were to be for ever progressive, under his perfectly wise and benevolent administration.

In this covenant, then, it is promised, that the persons here spoken of, and elsewhere declared to be ' a great multitude, which no man can number, of all nations, kindreds, and tongues,' should be ' the seed,' the children of Christ; his property: and that not only in a peculiar, but in a singular sense; not only created by him, as all other intelligent beings were, but redeemed by him also, and that at the expense of his own life.

The least consideration, however, will clearly show us, that sinners can never become Christ's in any such sense as to be accepted by him, unless they are delivered from the sentence of condemnation pronounced against them by the law of God. This law, I have formerly had occasion to observe, is unalterable. It is in itself perfect, and cannot be made better. God, the perfect and unchangeable being, cannot, without denying his perfection, consent to make it worse. Besides,

---

* Isaiah liii. 10.   Lowth

he has declared, that the universe ' shall sooner pass away, than one jot or one tittle of the law shall pass, until all shall be fulfilled.' Yet if this sentence be universally executed, the reward promised to Christ in the covenant of redemption, *viz.* the immortal holiness and happiness of those who in that covenant were promised to him as his seed, must of necessity fail. This sentence therefore, will not be universally executed ; because such an execution would ' render the promise of God of none effect.'

Farther : All who are involved in the execution of this sentence will not only suffer, but also sin for ever. But no words are necessary to prove, that a collection of sinners continuing to sin for ever, could in no sense constitute a reward to Christ, for his labours and sufferings in the work of redemption. From them he could receive neither love, gratitude, nor praise. In their character he could see nothing amiable, nothing to excite his complacency. In his government of them, his goodness and mercy would find no employment, and achieve no glory. Nor could they ever be *his*, in the sense of the covenant of redemption.

Thus it is beyond a doubt evident that, with regard to all those who are thus promised to Christ, the sentence of the divine law will not, and cannot be executed ; and that when they appear at their final trial, they will be acquitted from the punishment due to their sins, and delivered from the moral turpitude of their character. All this is plainly indispensable to the fulfilment of the covenant of redemption. Accordingly, we find it all promised in the most definite manner, wherever the subject is mentioned in the Gospel.

The first step, in the final fulfilment of the promises contained in this covenant, towards those who are the seed of Christ, is *the pardon of their sins.* Sin, until it is pardoned, is still charged to the sinner's account. Hence, he is in this situation exposed to the punishment which it has deserved. The pardon of sin is, of course, attended by the exemption of the sinner from punishment ; so much of course, that these things are usually considered as but one. They are, however, separable, not only in thought, but in fact. We do not always nor necessarily punish offenders, whom we still do not forgive. The offender may have merited, and may continue to merit punishment, and yet sufficient reasons may exist, why he should not be punished, although they are not derived from his moral character.   Forgiveness, in the full sense, supposes the offender penitent, and includes an approbation of his character as such, and a reconciliation to him of the person who forgives. But these things are not involved in a mere determination to exempt an offender from punishment.   On the part of God, however, in his conduct towards returning sinners, these things are not, I confess, separable in fact.

But the sinner might be forgiven, and acquitted from the punishment due to his sins, and yet not be rendered the subject of future blessings, much less of the blessings promised in the covenant of redemption.   He might be annihilated.   He might be placed in a state of happiness imperfect and mixed, like that of the present world ; or he might be placed in a state of happiness unmixed and perfect, and yet greatly inferior to that which will be actually enjoyed by the penitent children of Adam.   Another step, therefore, indispensable to the complete fulfilment of the covenant of redemption, is entitling them to the very blessings which are here promised ; viz. *the blessings of heaven* ; the first blessings, as I may hereafter have occasioned to show, in the kingdom of God.

These three things, which I have specified as being involved in the justification of mankind, are all clearly included and promised in the covenant of redemption ; and the connection of them, or of our justification with that work, as the only foundation on which our justification can rest, is I think too manifest, from what has been said, to be doubted.

Having thus stated what I intend by *justification*, under the *Gospel*, I shall inquire,

II. *In what sense we are said to be justified freely by the grace of God.*

From what has been said in a former Discourse, concerning the impossibility of justification by our own obedience, it is, I trust, evident that our justification can in no sense nor degree be said, with truth, to be merited by ourselves.   In this respect therefore, if it exist at all, it must of necessity be communicated freely.   It will, however, be necessary to a satisfactory explanation of this subject, to examine it particularly, so as to prevent any misconception concerning its nature and so as to obviate any objections which may arise in the minds of those who hear me.   To this examination it will be indispensable that I settle, in the beginning, the *meaning* which I annex to the term, ' grace,' on which the import of the proposition depends.

The word ' *grace* ' is used by the inspired writers in various senses.   It denotes :

(1.) *A free gift* ; which was, perhaps, its original meaning.

(2.) *The free, sovereign love of the Father, Son, and Holy Ghost*, the source of every such gift from God.

(3.) *The efficacious power of the Holy Ghost on the hearts of mankind ;* 2 Corinthians xii. 9.

(4.) *That state of reconciliation with God, which is enjoyed by Christians ;* Romans v. 2.

(5.) *Any virtue of the Christian character.*

(6.) *Any particular favour communicated by God ;* Eph. iii. 8.

Beside these, in common use it denotes *gracefulness of person, deportment, or character.*

In the text, it is manifestly used in the second sense ; and denotes *the free, sovereign love of God ;* the source of all our benefits.

That we are ' justified freely by the grace of God,' thus understood, I will now attempt to show by the following considerations :——

1. *Under the influence, or in the indulgence of this love, God formed the original design of saving mankind.*

The law of God is a perfectly just law.   But by this law man was condemned, and finally cast off.   Justice, therefore, in no sense demanded the deliverance of mankind from condemnation.   Of course, this deliverance was proposed and planned by the mere sovereign mercy of God.

2. *The covenant of redemption was the result of the same mercy.*

In this covenant, God promised to Christ the eternal happiness of all his seed ; that is, his followers.   Now it is certain, that no one of these obeyed the law of God.   This was certainly foreknown by God ; and, with this foreknowledge, he was pleased to promise this glorious blessing concerning creatures who were only rebels and apostates, and who merited nothing but wrath and indignation.   Sovereign love only could operate in favour of such beings as these.

3. *The same divine disposition executed the work of redemption.*

When Christ ' came to his own, his own received him not.' On the contrary, they hated, opposed, and persecuted him through his life, and, with a spirit still more malignant and furious, put him to death.

The very same spirit is inherent in the nature of all men. We ourselves, who condemn the Jews as murderers, still with the same pertinacity reject the Saviour. We neither believe, nor obey; we neither repent of our sins, nor forsake them; we neither receive his instructions, nor walk in his ordinances. Opposed to him in our hearts, we are opposed to him also in our lives.

The same opposition prevails in the whole race of Adam. Nor is there recorded on the page of history a single known instance in which it may be believed, even with remote probability, that man, from mere native propensity, or an original goodness of heart, has cordially accepted Christ. Certainly, nothing but the sovereign love of God could accomplish such a work as that of redemption, for beings of this character.

4. *The mission and agency of the Divine Spirit were the result of this love only.*

In the human character there is nothing to merit the interference of this glorious person on the behalf of mankind. Christ ' came to seek, and to ' redeem man, because he ' was lost.' The Divine Spirit came to sanctify him, because without sanctification he was undone. This the very fact of his regeneration unanswerably proves. Regeneration is the commencement of virtue in the soul. ' Without ' evangelical ' love,' says St. Paul, ' I am nothing:' that is, I am nothing in the kingdom of God; I have no spiritual or virtuous existence. From the necessity of regeneration then to man, and the fact, that he is regenerated, it is certain, that there is nothing in his nature, except his miserable condition, which could be an inducement to the Spirit of grace to interfere in human concerns.

What is true of *this* act of the Divine Spirit is equally true of his agency in enlightening, quickening, purifying, and strengthening man in the Christian course, and conducting him finally to heaven.

5. As all these steps, so plainly necessary to the justifica-

tion of man, are the result of the unmerited love of God; so *his justification itself flows entirely from the same love.*

Christ in his sufferings and death made a complete atonement for the sins of mankind. In other words, he rendered to the law, character, and government of God such peculiar honour, as to make it consistent with their unchangeable nature and glory, that sinners should, on the proper conditions, be forgiven. But the atonement inferred no obligation of justice on the part of God to forgive them. They were still sinners after the atonement, in the same sense and in the same degree as before. In no degree were they less guilty, or less deserving of punishment.

The supposition, incautiously admitted by some divines, that Christ satisfied the demands of the law by his active and passive obedience, in the same manner as the payment of a debt satisfies the demands of a creditor, has, if I mistake not, been heretofore proved to be unfounded in the Scriptures. We owed God our obedience, and not our property; and obedience in its own nature is due from the subject himself, and can never be rendered by another. In refusing to render it, we are criminal; and for this criminality merit punishment. The guilt thus incurred is inherent in the criminal himself, and cannot in the nature of things be transferred to another. All that in this case can be done by a substitute, of whatever character, is to render it not improper for the lawgiver to pardon the transgressor. No substitute can by any possible effort make him cease to be guilty, or to deserve punishment. This (and I intend to say it with becoming reverence) is beyond the ability of omnipotence itself. The fact, that he is guilty, is past, and can never be recalled.

Thus it is evident, that the sinner, when he comes before God, comes in the character of a sinner only; and must, if strict justice be done, be therefore condemned. If he escape condemnation, then, he can derive these blessings from mercy only, and in no degree from justice. In other words, every blessing which he receives is a free gift. The pardon of his sins, his acquittal from condemnation, and his admission to the enjoyments of heaven, are all given to him freely and graciously, because God regards him with infinite compassion, and is therefore pleased to communicate to him these unspeakable favours.

Should it be said, that God has promised these blessings to the penitent, in the covenant of redemption made with Christ, and in the covenant of grace made with the penitent; and has thus brought himself under *obligation* to bestow them: I answer, that this is indeed true, but that it affects not the doctrine. The promise made in these covenants, is a *gracious* promise, originated by the divine compassion. Certainly, this procedure on the part of God is not the less free or gracious, because he was pleased to publish his own merciful design of accepting penitent sinners, and to confirm it to them by a voluntary promise. As I have already remarked, every part of the divine conduct towards the sinner, every spiritual blessing which the sinner receives antecedently to his justification, is the result of grace only, or sovereign love. These preceding acts, therefore, being themselves absolutely gracious, can never render the act of justifying the sinner the less gracious, or render him the meritorious object of that justification, to which he could never have been entitled but by means of these preceding acts of grace. The promise of justification was made, not to a meritorious being, but to a sinner; a guilty, miserable rebel, exposed by his rebellion to final perdition. The fulfilment of this promise is an act equally gracious with that of making the promise itself.

Should it be said, that the sinner is renewed *antecedently to his justification;* and, having thus become a holy or virtuous being, has also become, either wholly or partially, a *meritorious* object of justification; I answer, that the law of God condemns the sinner to death for the first transgression. Now it will not be said, that the sanctified sinner is not chargeable with many transgressions, the guilt of which still lies at his door, and for which he may *now* be justly condemned, notwithstanding his repentance. This, it is believed, was made abundantly evident in a former Discourse, concerning the impossibility of justification by our own obedience. The sinner therefore, although sanctified, still deserves the wrath of God for all his transgressions; and according to the sentence of the law must, if considered only as he is in himself, be finally punished.

That the penitent is not *partially justified* on account of his *own merit* after he is *sanctified,* must I think, be acknowledged, if we attend to the following consideration :—

(1.) *It will be admitted, that all those who are sanctified, are also justified.*

' Whom he called, them he also justified ;' that is, he justified all those whom he ' called' effectually, or ' sanctified.' But it will not be denied, that some persons are sanctified on a dying bed, when they have no opportunity to perform any works of righteousness which might be the ground of their justification. The case of the penitent thief will, I suppose, be generally acknowledged to be substantially of this nature. It will not be denied, that some persons are ' sanctified from the womb,' as were Jeremiah and John the Baptist ; nor that of these some die, antecedently to that period of life when they become capable of direct acts of moral good and evil. The children of believing parents, dedicated to God, and dying in their infancy, will, I suppose, be allowed to be universally, instances of this kind. Concerning all the instances which exist of both these classes, it must be acknowledged, that without exception they are the subjects of justification ; and that they are in no sense justified on account of their own righteousness, but solely by the free grace of God, on account of the righteousness of Christ. If, then, others are justified partially, on account of their own righteousness, justification is given to some of mankind on one ground, or procuring cause, and to others on another, and very different ground. But no such doctrine is any where taught, or even hinted at, in the Scriptures ; and I presume, that no intelligent man acquainted with them, will pretend that any such diversity exists in the justification of mankind.

(2.) *The Scripture nowhere teaches us, that we are justified partly on account of our own righteousness, and partly on account of the righteousness of Christ.*

St. Paul, in the 27th verse of the context, pursuing the subject of justification by the free grace of God, says, ' Where is boasting, then ? It is excluded. By what Law ? Of works ? Nay ; but by the law of faith.' Here we are taught, that all boasting is absolutely excluded ; and that it is excluded, not by the law of works, but by the law of faith. But the same apostle says, that ' to him that worketh the reward is reckoned, not of grace, but of debt :' that is, the reward of justification and its consequences would be *due* to him who received it on account of his works. He then certainly *might* boast : that is, he might truly say that he had merited justification by his own works. If he had merited justification *partly* by his own works, he can truly boast of having merited that part of his justification. 'Boasting,' therefore, *cannot*, on this plan of justification, 'be excluded.' Yet the apostle elsewhere teaches us, that it was one end of the system of redemption, as established by God, ' that no flesh should glory in his presence,' but that ' he who glorieth,' should ' glory only in Christ,' 1 Cor. i. 29—31.

Besides, it is incredible, if this doctrine be true, that no mention of it should be made in the Scriptures. I know of no passage in the Scriptures so much relied on by its abettors, as the discourse of St. James, in the second chapter of his Epistle. In a future Discourse I design to examine the account given of this subject by St. James, and expect to show that he furnishes no support to it. Should I succeed in this expectation, it will probably be admitted by those who hear me, that the doctrine finds no countenance in the Scriptures, and must therefore be given up.

(3.) *The works of the best men never fulfil the demands of the law; and therefore cannot be the ground, either wholly or partially, of their justification.*

In the conclusion of the seventh chapter of the Epistle to the Romans, St. Paul describes his *own state*, as it was when he wrote this Epistle; or generally *after* his conversion. As this assertion has been doubted; and as respectable divines have supposed this discourse to be an account of St. Paul's state *before* he was converted, I shall attempt to prove the truth of my assertion. This I shall do very summarily, in the three following remarks :——

[1.] St. Paul observes, verse 22d, ' I delight in the law of God, after the inward man.' This assertion was never true of any man, antecedently to his regeneration. St. Paul does not say, that he *approves* of the law of God. This would have been a declaration concerning his *reason*, or his *conscience*. But he says, ' I *delight* in the law of God.' This is a declaration concerning his *feelings*, his *heart*. The *heart* of an unregenerate man never yet delighted in the divine law.

[2.] In the 24th verse, he exclaims, ' O wretched man, that I am! Who shall deliver me from the body of this death?'

From this exclamation it is certain, that the evil from which St. Paul so passionately wished a deliverance, was existing *at the time* when the passage was written. But at the time when the passage was written, St. Paul had been a convert many years. The evil existed, therefore, after his conversion.

[3.] In the 25th verse he says, ' So then, with the mind I myself serve the law of God.'

This assertion could never be truly made concerning any unregenerate man. The *mind* of every such man, we know from the mouth of the same apostle, ' is enmity against God ; not subject to his law, neither indeed can be.'

The account given by St. Paul of himself in this chapter, is then an account of his *moral state*, at the time when *the chapter was written*. As St. Paul, in all probability, was inferior to no other mere man in moral excellence ; he may be justly considered as having given us here a description of Christians in their very best state.

But, if in this state there is ' a law in their members, warring against the law of their minds, and bringing them into captivity to the law of sin, which is in their members ;' if, ' when they would do good, evil is present with them ;' so that ' the good which they would they do not ; and the evil which they would not, they do ;' how plain is it that, instead of meriting justification by their works, they daily violate the law of God, provoke his anger, expose themselves to condemnation, and stand in infinite need of the intercession of Christ, and the pardon of their sins, in order to their salvation !

Besides, the very best actions of regenerated men are imperfect, and fall short of the demands of the law. This position is so rarely contested, that I need not here allege arguments to evince its truth. But it cannot be pretended, that an obedience, which does not even answer the demands of the law in any case, but is invariably defective, and therefore in some degree sinful, can be the ground of justification to any man.

I have now finished the observations which I intended concerning this subject. If I mistake not, they furnish ample proof, that *we are* ' justified freely by the grace of God, through the redemption which is in Christ Jesus.' A few remarks shall conclude the Discourse.

REMARKS.

1. *From what has been said, it is evident that the salvation of mankind is a glorious exhibition of the character, and particularly of the benevolence of God.*

On this subject I cannot dwell ; and shall only observe summarily, that the work of our salvation was contrived and accomplished by God alone ; that the means by which it was accomplished, *viz.* the mediation of Christ, and the mission and agency of the Holy Ghost, far from lessening, only enhance our conceptions of the divine benevolence displayed in this work ; that the good-will manifested in doing any thing, is ever proportioned to the efforts which are made ; that, in the present case, the efforts actually made are the most wonderful which have been disclosed to the universe ; and that they, therefore, discover the good-will of the Creator to mankind, in a manner and in a degree wholly unexampled.

All this, at the same time, was done for beings entirely unnecessary to God. In himself therefore, in his own compassion, must have existed the originating, powerful, and productive cause of this wonderful event. What must have been the good-will of him, who sent his Son ' to seek and to save that which was lost ;' and to ' become obedient unto death, even the death of the cross,' that sinners and rebels might live !

2. *The Socinian objection against the doctrine of the atonement, that it is opposed to the scriptural account of the exercise of grace in our justification, is here seen to be groundless.*

If the observations made in this Discourse are true, the doctrine of the atonement, instead of lessening or destroying the exercise of grace in our justification, only renders this act of God more eminently gracious. If all these things which have been mentioned, particularly the atonement of Christ, were necessary to be done .in order to the salvation of mankind, the mercy which resolved on them all is far more strongly displayed, than if nothing more had been necessary than barely to forgive the sinner.

3. *If God be thus merciful, all the declarations of his mercy ought to be believed by us.*

The disposition, which could contrive and execute these things of its own mere choice, without any reward, without any expectation of any reward, for beings equally undeserving and unnecessary, can do all things which are kind and proper to be done. Especially can this disposition carry the things which it has contrived and begun into complete execution. To do this is its own natural bent, the mere progress of its inherent propensities. The declarations, therefore, which manifest the determination of him in whom this disposition resides, to accomplish all things pertaining to this work, ought cordially as well as entirely to be believed. To distrust them is equally absurd and guilty; absurd, because they are supported by the most abundant evidence; guilty, because the distrust springs from the heart, and not from the understanding.

Why should God be disbelieved, when he declares, that ‘ he has no pleasure in the death of the sinner?’ or when he proclaims, ‘ Whosoever will, let him come, and take the water of life freely?’ If he had wished to punish mankind for the gratification of his own views or pleasure, could he not have done it with infinite ease? To him it was certainly unnecessary to announce the forgiveness of sin, to send his Son to die, or to give his Spirit and his word to sanctify and save. This immense preparation depended solely on his own mere pleasure. He might have suffered the law to take its course. He might have annihilated or punished for ever the whole race of Adam; and with a command have raised up a new and better world of beings in their stead. Men are in no sense necessary to God. He might have filled the universe with angels at once; perfect, obedient, excellent, and glorious beings; and been loved, praised, and obeyed by them for ever. Why then, but because he was desirous to save poor, guilty, perishing men, did he enter upon the work of their salvation? Why did he give his Son to redeem them? Why did he send his Spirit to sanctify them? Why did he proclaim ‘ glad tidings of great joy unto all people?’ Why does he wait with infinite patience; why has he always waited to be gracious, amid all the provocations and sins of this polluted world? Why are the calls of mercy, after being so long and so extensively rejected with scorn and insult, repeated through one age after another? Why, after all *our* unbelief, are they repeated to us? Why are we, after all our transgressions, assembled this day to hear them? The true, the only answer is, God is infinitely kind, merciful, and willing ' to save to the uttermost.'

Let, then, this glorious Being be believed without distrust, without delay. Let every sinner boldly come to the throne of grace, to the door of life ; and be assured that, if he desires sincerely to enter, he will not be shut out.

SERMON LXV.

JUSTIFICATION.

THE DUTY OF BELIEVING.

THEREFORE WE CONCLUDE, THAT A MAN IS JUSTIFIED BY FAITH
WITHOUT THE DEEDS OF THE LAW.
More correctly rendered:
THEREFORE WE CONCLUDE, THAT MAN IS JUSTIFIED BY FAITH,
WITHOUT WORKS OF LAW.

ROMANS III. **28.**

IN the last Discourse I attempted to show, that in consequence of the redemption of Christ, man is justified freely by
the grace of God. The grace of God is the source, the mov-
ing cause, of this blessing to mankind. The next subject of
consideration before us, is *the means* by which man, in the
economy of redemption, becomes entitled to this blessing.
These in the text are summed up in the single article, *faith*.
which is here declared to be the instrument of justification.
To elucidate this truth is the design with which I have selected the present theme of discourse.

But before I enter upon the doctrine in form, it will be
necessary to remind you, that an objection is raised against it
at the threshold, which, if founded in truth, would seem to
overthrow it at once. It is this: that *faith* is so far from
being of a *moral* nature, as to be *necessary*, and *unavoidable*;
man being absolutely *passive* in believing, and under a physical impossibility of doing otherwise than he actually does;
whether in believing, or disbelieving. Of course, it is further

urged, an attribute, governed wholly by physical necessity, can never *recommend us to God* ; much less become the ground of so important a blessing, as justification.

It will be easily seen that, so long as this objection has its hold on the mind, and is allowed its full import, the doctrine of justification by faith can never be received, unless in a very imperfect and unsatisfactory manner. If faith is a thing over which we have no control ; if we believe only under the influence of a physical necessity, and, whether we believe or disbelieve, it is physically impossible for us to do otherwise ; then it is plain, that faith is so far from being praiseworthy, amiable, and capable of recommending us to God, as to merit and sustain no moral character at all. According to this scheme, therefore, faith and unbelief being equally and absolutely involuntary and avoidable, can never constitute a moral distinction between men. Faith can never be an object of the approbation nor unbelief of the disapprobation of God. Much less can we be praiseworthy in believing, or blameable in disbelieving. Still less can we on one of these grounds be rewarded, and on the other punished. Least of all can we, in consequence of our faith, be accepted, and blessed *for ever* ; and, in consequence of our unbelief, be rejected, and punished with *endless* misery.

All these things, however, are directly and palpably contradictory to the whole tenour of the Gospel. In *this*, faith is approved, commanded, and promised an eternal reward. Unbelief, on the contrary, is censured, forbidden, and threatened with an everlasting punishment. Faith, therefore, is the hinge on which the whole evangelical system turns. ' If ye believe not that I am he, ye shall die in your sins.' ' He that believeth on the Son hath everlasting life ; and he that believeth not, shall not see life ;' are declarations which, while they cannot be mistaken, teach us that all the future interests of man are suspended on this faith ; and are, at the same time, declarations to which the whole evangelical system is exactly conformed. If, then, our faith and disbelief are altogether involuntary, and the effect of mere physical necessity, God has annexed everlasting life and everlasting death, not to any moral character in man, but to the mere result of physical causes. A consequence so monstrous ought certainly not to be admitted. The Scriptures, therefore, must be given up, if this scheme is true.

I have now, I presume, shown it to be necessary that, before I enter upon the discussion of the doctrine contained in the text, *this objection should be thoroughly examined, and removed.* To do this, will be the business of the present Discourse.

In opposition to this objection, then, I assert, that *faith, and its opposite, disbelief, are, in all moral cases, voluntary exercises of the mind ; are proper objects of commands and prohibitions ; and proper foundations of praise and blame, reward and punishment.* This doctrine I shall endeavour to prove by the following arguments, derived both from reason and Revelation ; because the objection which I have been opposing has been incautiously admitted, at times, by Christians, as well as openly and triumphantly alleged by infidels.

1. *Faith is everywhere commanded in the Scriptures.*

' This is his commandment, that we believe on the name of his Son Jesus Christ,' 1 John iii. 23. ' Now after that John was put in prison, Jesus came into Galilee, preaching the Gospel of the kingdom of God, and saying, The time is fulfilled ; and the kingdom of God is at hand. Repent ye and believe the Gospel,' Mark i. 14. 15. In these two passages, we have the *command* to *believe the Gospel,* delivered by Christ in form ; and the declaration of the Evangelist, that it is ' the commandment of God, that we believe on the name of his Son Jesus Christ.' Whatever, then, we understand by faith, it is the object of a command, or law, which God has given to mankind ; a thing which may be justly required, and, of course, a thing which they are able to render, as an act of obedience, at least in some circumstances. God cannot require what man is not physically able to perform. But all obedience to God is voluntary. Nothing is or can be demanded by him, which is not in its nature voluntary, nor can any thing but the will of intelligent beings be the object of moral law. No man will say, that a brute, a stone, or a stream, can be the object of such law. Faith therefore, being in the most express terms required by a law or command of God, must of course be a voluntary exercise of the mind, in such a sense, that it can be rightfully required.

Farther : The language of the first of these passages most

evidently denotes, that *the command to* ' believe on the name of Jesus Christ,' is one' of *peculiar* and *pre-eminent importance.* ' *This* is his commandment:' as if there were no other; or no other which in its importance may be compared with this. Here St. John teaches us, that faith is pre-eminently required by God, in a manner distinct from that in which he requires other acts of obedience generally. Of course, faith is not only justly required of mankind by God, but is required in a manner more solemn than many other acts universally acknowledged to be voluntary.

Accordingly, a peculiar sanction is annexed to the law requiring our faith; ' He that believeth shall be saved; and he that believeth not shall be damned.'

The reward and the penalty here announced, are the highest which exist in the universe; and, therefore, directly indicate the obedience and the disobedience to be of supreme import. Nothing can be a stronger proof, that in the eye of God, faith and unbelief are voluntary, or moral exercises of man.

But it may be alleged, that the *faith* enjoined in these commands, is not a mere *speculative belief;* and, therefore, not the faith which, in the general objection opposed by me, is asserted to be physically necessary and involuntary. I readily agree, that the faith here enjoined is saving faith; and that this is not mere speculative belief. But such belief is an indispensable part of saving faith; and so absolutely inseparable from it, that without such belief saving faith cannot exist. Saving faith is always a speculative belief, joined with a cordial consent to the truth, and a cordial approbation of the *object* which that truth respects. When, therefore, saving faith is commanded, speculative belief, which is an inseparable part of it, is also commanded. It is not, indeed, required to exist *by itself;* or to be rendered without the accordance of the heart. But, whenever saving faith is required, speculative belief is absolutely required. Of course speculative belief is, at least in some degree, in our power; and may be rendered as an act of obedience to God.

To him, who believes in the inspiration of the Scriptures, these passages, and many others like them, furnish complete proof, that faith, whether saving or speculative, is an act of the mind, which is in such a sense voluntary, as to be the proper object of a command or law; that it may be justly required of mankind; and that it cannot be either refused or neglected, without guilt.

2. *The universal consent of mankind furnishes ample proof, that faith is, in many instances, a voluntary or moral exercise.*

The evidence which I propose to derive from this source, lies in the following general truth; *That in all cases, where mankind have sufficient opportunity thoroughly to understand any subject, and are under no inducement to judge with partiality, their universal judgment is right.* As I presume this truth will not be doubted, I shall not attempt to illustrate it by any arguments. That the present case is included within this general truth is certain. Every man who thinks at all, knows by his own personal experience, and by his daily intercourse with other men, whether his own faith and theirs be voluntary in many instances, or not; I say, *in many instances;* because, if the assertion be admitted with this limitation, it will be sufficient for my purpose. If, then, mankind have determined, that faith is sometimes voluntary, the doctrine against which I contend must be given up.

The language of mankind very frequently expresses their real views in a manner much more exactly accordant with truth, than their philosophical discussions. Men make words, only when they have ideas to be expressed by those words, and just such ideas as the words are formed to express. If, then, we find words in any language denoting any ideas whatever, we know with certainty that such ideas have existed in the minds of those by whom the words were used. Whenever these ideas have been derived from experience and observation, we also know that they were real, and not fantastical; and are founded, not in imagination, but in fact. In all languages are found words, denoting the same things with the English terms, *candour, fairness, reasonableness, impartiality,* and others, generally of the like import. The meaning of all these terms is clearly of this nature; that the persons to whom they are justly applied, use their faculties in collecting, weighing and admitting evidence, in a manner equitable and praiseworthy. Accordingly, all persons who do this are highly esteemed and greatly commended, as exhibiting no small excellence of moral character.

In all languages, also, there are words answering to the English words, *prejudice, partiality, unreasonableness,* and *unfairness.* By these terms, when applied to this subject, we uniformly denote a voluntary employment of our faculties in collecting, weighing, and admitting, evidence, conducted in a manner inequitable and blameworthy. Accordingly, persons, to whom these terms are justly applied, that is, the very persons who employ their faculties in this manner, are universally disesteemed and condemned, as guilty and odious.

All these words were formed to express ideas really existing in the human mind, and ideas derived from experience and observation. Of course, these ideas have a real foundation in nature and fact, and the words express that which is real.

As the terms which I have mentioned are parts of the customary language of a great nation, and as other nations have, universally, corresponding terms, it is certain, that these are the ideas of all men, everywhere presented by experience and observation, derived from facts, and grounded in reality. The common voice of mankind has, therefore, decided the question in a manner which, I apprehend, is incapable of error, and can never be impeached.

In perfect, accordance with these observations, we know, that *voluntary blindness to evidence, argument, and truth,* is customary phraseology in the daily conversation of all men. In accordance with these observations also, the declaration, that " none are so blind, as they who will not see," is proverbial, and regarded as a maxim.

3. *The mind is perfectly voluntary in the employment of collecting evidence, on every question which it discusses.*

All questions are attended by more or less arguments, capable of being alleged on both sides. These arguments do not present themselves of course ; but must be sought for, and assembled by the activity of the mind. In this case, the mind can either resolve or refuse to collect arguments, and in this conduct is wholly voluntary, and capable, therefore, of being either virtuous or sinful, praiseworthy or blameworthy, rewardable or punishable. Wherever its duty and interest, wherever the commands of God, or lawful human authority, or the well-being of ourselves, or our fellow-men, demand that we collect such arguments, we are virtuous in obeying, and sinful in refusing.

Sometimes we obey, often we refuse. Most frequently, when we perform this duty at all, we perform it *partially*. Concerning almost every question which is before us, we assemble some arguments, and refuse or neglect to gather others. In this employment the mind usually leans to one side of the question; and labours not to find out truth, or the means of illustrating it, but to possess itself of the arguments which will support the side to which it inclines, and weaken or overthrow that which it dislikes. Thus we collect all the arguments in our power, favourable to our own chosen doctrines, and oppose the contrary ones; and of design, or through negligence, avoid searching for those which will weaken our own doctrines, or strengthen such as oppose them. In all this our inclinations are solely and supremely active, and govern the whole process. For this conduct, therefore, we are deserving of blame; and, as the case may be, of punishment.

4. *The mind is equally voluntary in weighing, admitting, or rejecting evidence, after it is collected.*

It is as easy, and as common, for the mind to turn its eye from the *power* of evidence, as from the evidence itself. I have already shown that we can, at pleasure, either collect arguments, or refuse to collect them. With equal ease we can examine them after they are collected, or decline this examination; and after such examination as we choose to make is completed, we can with the same ease either admit, or reject them. The grounds on which we can render the admission or rejection satisfactory to ourselves, are numerous, and are always at hand. The arguments in question may oppose or coincide with some unquestioned maxim, principle, or doctrine, pre-conceived by us, and regarded as fundamental; and for these reasons may be at once admitted, or rejected. They may accord with the opinions of those whom we may think it pleasing, honourable, safe or useful to follow. We may hastily conclude that they are all the arguments which favour the doctrine opposed to ours, and deem them wholly insufficient to evince its truth. We may suppose, whenever they seem to conclude against us, that there is some latent error in them, discernible by others, if not by ourselves; which, if discerned would destroy the force. We may determine, whenever the arguments in our possession are apprehended to be inconclusive in favour of our own opinions, that there are others which, although not now in our possession, would, if discovered by us, determine the question in our favour. We may believe, that the arguments before us will, if admitted, infer some remote consequence, in our apprehension grossly absurd, and on the ground of this distant consequence reject their immediate influence. Or the doctrine to be proved may be so odious to us, as to induce us to believe that no arguments whatever can evince its truth. For these and the like reasons, we can weigh or not weigh, admit or reject, any arguments whatever; and conclude in favour of either side of perhaps every moral question.

A judge, in any cause which comes before him, can admit, or refuse to admit, witnesses on either side. After they have testified, he can consider or neglect their testimony, and can give it what degree of credit he pleases, or no credit at all. In all this he acts voluntarily; so perfectly so, that another judge, of a different disposition, could and would, with the same means in his possession, draw up a directly opposite judgment concerning the cause. Facts of this nature are so frequent, as to be well known to mankind, acknowledged universally, and accounted a part of the ordinary course of things. The *mind*, in considering doctrines, is usually this *partial* judge; and conducts itself towards its arguments, as the judge towards his witnesses. In this conduct it is altogether voluntary, and altogether sinful.

In the contrary conduct of collecting arguments with a design to know the truth, in weighing them fairly, and in admitting readily their real import, it is equally voluntary; and possesses and exhibits the contrary character of virtue, as really as in any case whatever. Accordingly, all men, when employed in observing these two modes of acting in their fellow-men, have pronounced the latter to be excellent and praiseworthy, and the former to be unjust, base, and deserving alike of their contempt and abhorrence.

5. *The doctrine which I am opposing, if true, renders both virtue and vice, at least in a great proportion of instances, impossible.*

All virtue is nothing else but voluntary obedience to truth; and all sin is nothing else but voluntary disobedience to truth, or voluntary obedience to error. Accordingly, God has required nothing of mankind, but that they ' should obey truth ;' particularly, *the truth* ; or evangelical truth.   Voluntary conformity to truth is, therefore, virtue in every possible instance. But we cannot voluntarily conform to truth, unless we believe it.   If our faith, then, is wholly involuntary, and necessary, it follows, of course, that we are never faulty nor punishable for not believing ; since our faith, in every case where we do not believe, is physically impossible.   For not believing, therefore, we are not, and cannot be, blameable ; and as we cannot conform to truth, when we do not believe it to be truth, it follows that, whenever we do not believe, we are innocent in not obeying.

For the same reason, whenever we believe error to be truth, our belief, according to this scheme, is compelled by the same phisical necessity ; and we are guiltless in every such instance of faith.   All our future conformity to such error is of course guiltless also.   Thus he who believes in the existence and perfections of Jehovah, in the rectitude of his law and government, and in the duty of obeying him, and he who believes in the deity of Beelzebub, or a calf, or a stock, or a stone, while they respectively worship and serve these infinitely different gods, are in the same degree virtuous, or in the same degree sinful.   In other words, they are neither sinful nor virtuous. The faith of both is alike physically necessary ; and the conformity of both to their respective tenets follows their faith, of course.

Should it be said that, *although faith is thus necessary, our conformity or nonconformity to what we believe is still voluntary, and therefore is virtuous* ; I answer, that were I to allow this, as I am not very unwilling to do, to be true ; still, the objector must acknowledge that a vast proportion of those human actions which have universally been esteemed the most horrid crimes, are, according to his own plan, completely justified.   He cannot deny, that the heathen have almost universally believed their idols to be gods, and their idolatry the true religion.   He cannot deny, that a great part of the wars which have existed in the world, have by those who have carried them on, been believed to be just ; that the persecutions of the Christians were by the heathen, who were the authors of them, thought highly meritorious ; that the horrid cruelties of the Popish inquisition were, to a great extent, considered by the Catholics as ' doing God service ;' and that all the Mohammedan butcheries were regarded by the disciples of the Koran as directly required by God himself. Nay, it cannot be denied by the objector, nor by any man who has considered the subject, that the Jews in very great numbers believed themselves warranted in rejecting, persecuting, and crucifying Christ. This is undoubtedly indicated by that terrible prediction of the Saviour, ' If ye believe not, that I am he, ye shall die in your sins.' Let the objector then, and all who hold his opinions on this subject, henceforth be for ever silent concerning the guilt usually attributed to these several classes of men, and acknowledge them to have been compelled by a physical necessity to all these actions, lamentable indeed, but wholly unstained with any criminality.

At the same time, let it be observed, that the determination of the will is always as the dictate of the understanding which precedes it. If, then, this dictate of the understanding is produced by a physical necessity, how can the decision of the will, which follows it of course, be in any sense free? If faith be necessary in the physical sense, every other dictate of the understanding must be equally necessary, and, of course, that which precedes every determination of the will. In what manner, then, can the determination of the will fail of being the mere result of the same necessity?

But if the determinations of the will are physically necessary, they cannot be either virtuous or sinful. If, therefore, these things are true, there can be, according to this scheme, neither virtue nor vice in man.

6. *This doctrine charges God with a great part, if not with all, the evil conduct of mankind.*

Whatever the system of things in this world is, it was contrived and created, and is continually ordered, by God. If mankind believe only under the coercion of physical necessity, then God has so constituted them, as to render their faith, in this sense, necessary and ' unavoidable. Whenever they err, therefore, they err thus necessarily by the ordinance and irresistible power of God. Of course, as the state of things in this, as well as all other respects, is the result of his choice, he has chosen that they should err, and compelled them to err by the irresistible impulse of almighty power. In this case, we will suppose them to design faithfully to do their duty, or, in other words, to conform their conduct to the doctrines which they actually believe, and suppose to be truth. In thus acting, they either sin, or they do not. If they sin, God compels them to sin: if they do not, still all their conduct is productive of evil only: for conformity to error is, of course, productive only of evil. By this scheme, therefore, this mass of evil, immensely great and dreadful, is charged to God alone.

At the same time, if in the same manner they embrace truth, their reception of it is equally compelled. Their conformity to it is, of course, no more commendable, than their conformity to error; and God has so constituted things, that they cannot conform to it of choice, or from love to truth, as such; but only from physical necessity. Or, if this should be questioned, they cannot conform to it from the apprehension that it is truth, because they have embraced it under the force of this necessity; and must conform to every thing which they have embraced in one manner only.

There are many other modes of disproving this doctrine, on which I cannot now dwell; and which cannot be necessary for the present purpose, if the arguments already advanced have the decisive influence which they appear to me to possess. I will only observe further, that the scheme which I am opposing is directly at war with all the commands and exhortations given us to ' search the Scriptures,' to ' receive the truth,' to ' seek for wisdom,' to ' know God,' to ' believe in Christ,' and to ' believe his word;' and with the commendations and promises given to those who do, and the censures and threatenings denounced against those who do not, these things. Equally inconsistent are they with all our own mutual exhortations to candour, to investigation, to impartial decision, and to all other conduct of the like nature; our commendation of those who pursue it, and our condemnation of those who do not. Both the Scriptures and common sense ought, if this scheme is well founded, to assume totally new language, if they would accord with truth.

Should any person suppose that I have annexed too much importance to truth, in asserting, that virtue in all instances is nothing else but a *voluntary conformity to truth;* and imagine, that it ought to be defined, *a voluntary conformity to the divine precepts:* he may gain complete satisfaction on this point, by merely changing a precept into a proposition.

For example: the precepts, 'Thou shalt have no other Gods before me,' and 'Thou shalt honour thy father and thy mother,' become truths, when written in this manner. It is right, or it is thy duty, to have no other Gods before me; or to honour thy father and thy mother.

I have now, if I mistake not, clearly evinced the falsehood of the doctrine which I have opposed, and shown it to be equally contrary to the Scriptures, and to the common sense of mankind.

Whenever this doctrine has been *honestly* imbibed, it has, I presume, been imbibed from a misapprehension of the influence of that acknowledged principle of philosophy, that in receiving impressions from all objects, the mind is *passive only*; and, therefore, is necessitated to receive just such impressions as the objects presented to its view are fitted to make. No man, acquainted with the state of the human mind, will call this principle in question. But no man of this character can rationally imagine that it can at all affect the subject of this Discourse, so as to furnish any support to the scheme which I am opposing.

The amount of this principle is exactly this; that God has so constituted the mind, and has formed objects in such a manner, that they uniformly present to the mind their *real state and nature*, and not another. Were this not the structure of the mind, and the proper efficacy of the objects with which it is conversant, it would either be never able to see truly, or would never know when it saw in this manner. This constitution of things, then, is indispensable to our discernment of their true nature; and without it we could never be able, satisfactorily, to distinguish truth from falsehood.

But nothing is more evident than that this constitution of things in no degree affects the subject in debate. In no sense is it true that, because we have such optics, and the things with which we are conversant such a nature, we are, therefore, obliged to turn our eyes to any given object, to view it on any given side, to examine it in any given manner; or to connect it in our investigation with any other particular set of objects. Truth is the real agreement or disagreement of ideas asserted in propositions. The relations of these ideas are its basis. Now we can compare and connect what ideas we please, in what manner we please, and by the aid of any other intervening ideas which we choose.   In this manner we can unite and separate them at pleasure ; and thus either come to the knowledge of truth, or the admission of falsehood, according to our inclinations.   All these things, also, we can refuse to do ; and in both cases we act in a manner perfectly voluntary.   Were we not *passive* in the mere reception of ideas, we should see to no purpose.   Were we not active in comparing and connecting them, we should see only under the influence of physical necessity.

From these considerations it is evident, unless I am deceived, that this principle, so much relied on by those with whom I am contending, has not the least influence towards the support of their scheme.

REMARKS.

From these observations we learn,

1. *Why men in exactly the same circumstances, judge and believe very differently concerning the same objects.*

When a question or doctrine is proposed to the consideration of several men, in the same terms, with the same arguments, and at the same time ; we, almost of course, find them judging and deciding concerning it in different manners. Were our judgment, or, what is here the same thing, our faith, the result of mere physical necessity , this fact could never take place.   But it is easily explained, as the natural course of things, where such judges as men are concerned. When a question is thus proposed, one declines or neglects to inquire altogether.   Another listens only to the evidence on one side.   A third, partially to that on both sides.   A fourth, partially to that on one side, and wholly to that on the other. And a fifth, to all the evidence which he can find.   One cares nothing about the question ; another is predetermined to give his decision on one side ; and another resolves to decide according to truth.   One is too lazy, another too indifferent, another too biassed, and another too self-sufficient, to discover truth at all.   In all these, except the candid, thorough examiner, the conduct which they adopt on this subject is sin. Inclination, choice, bias of mind, prevents them from ' coming to the knowledge of the truth.'   If they loved truth, as their duty demands, they would easily and certainly find it. Their indifference to it, or their hatred of it, is the true reason why they find it not ; and the real explanation of the strange manner in which they judge, and of their otherwise inexplicable faith in doctrines, not only absurd, but unsupported even by specious evidence.

2. *From these observations also it is evident, that faith may be a virtuous, and unbelief a sinful, affection of the mind.*
Truth is the foundation of all good. On this, as their basis, rests the character, designs, government, and glory of the Creator, and all the happiness and virtue of the intelligent universe. But the only way in which truth can be useful to intelligent creatures, or the means of the divine glory, is by being *believed.* Every degree of happy influence which truth has, or can have, on the intelligent kingdom, is, therefore, derived entirely from faith ; so far as absolute knowledge is not attainable. On faith, then, all these amazing interests wholly rest. That which is not believed cannot be obeyed. The influence of truth cannot commence in our minds, until our faith in it has commenced. Universal unbelief, therefore, would completely destroy the divine kingdom and the general happiness at once. Of course partial unbelief, the unbelief of many, a few, or one, aims directly at the same destruction.

Since, then, faith is a voluntary exercise of the mind, it follows that, whenever it is exercised towards moral objects, it is virtuous ; is an effort of the mind directed to the promotion of this immense good which I have specified. To the degree in which it may be thus virtuous, no limits can be affixed ; but it may rise to such a height as to occupy all the supposable powers of any intelligent creature.

On the contrary, unbelief, when directed towards moral objects, being always voluntary, is always sinful. Its efficacy, as opposed to the glory of God and the good of the universe, has been already mentioned. Its insolence towards the divine character is exhibited in the strongest terms by St. John, in this memorable declaration, ' He that believeth not God, hath made him a liar.' What a reproach is this to the Creator ! What an impious expression of contempt to the infinitely blessed Jehovah ! The very insult offered to him by the old serpent, in his seduction of our first parents! Them this unbelief destroyed ; and, from that melancholy day, it has been the great instrument of perdition to their posterity. Faith is the only medium of our access to God. 'To come to him' we 'must believe that he is ;' for without such belief he would be to us a mere nihility. *Atheism,* therefore, cuts a man off from all access to God ; and consequently from all love, and all obedience. Were the universe atheistical, it would cease from all moral connection with its Creator. *Deism,* though a humbler degree of the same spirit, produces exactly the same effects. 'He that believeth not the Son, hath not life ; but the wrath of God abideth on him.' *Practical unbelief,* the same spirit in a degree still inferior, is, however, followed by the same miserable consequences. A mere speculative belief leaves the heart and the life as it found them, opposed to God, and the objects of his indignation. The speculative believer, therefore, although advanced a step beyond the Deist, and two beyond the Atheist, is still disobedient and rebellious, 'without hope, and without God in the world.'

SERMON LXVI.

JUSTIFICATION.

THE NATURE OF FAITH.

THEREFORE WE CONCLUDE, THAT MAN IS JUSTIFIED BY FAITH, WITHOUT WORKS OF LAW.

ROMANS III. 28.

IN my last Discourse I attempted to show, that faith and unbelief are voluntary exercises of the mind, and may, therefore, be virtuous or sinful; and to refute the objections against this doctrine. This I did, without critically examining the *nature of faith*, which I purposely reserved for a separate discussion. This is evidently the next object of inquiry. I shall, therefore, endeavour in this Discourse to *explain the faith of the Gospel*; or the faith by which we are *justified*.

I. *Faith in this sense respects God as its object.*

'Abraham believed God, and it was counted to him for righteousness,' Gen. xv. 6; Rom. iv. 3; Gal. iii. 6; James ii. 23. 'Without faith it is impossible to please him: for he that cometh to God must believe that he is, and that he is the rewarder of them that diligently seek him,' Heb. xi. 6. 'Believe in the Lord your God; so shall ye be established,' 2 Chron. ii. 20. 'Who by him,' says St. Peter to the Christians to whom he wrote, 'do believe in God, that raised him up from the dead and gave him glory, that your faith and hope might be in God,' 1 Peter i. 21. 'The jailer rejoiced, believing in God with all his house,' Acts xvi. 34. 'That they who have believed in God might be careful to maintain good works,' Tit. iii. 8. 'Jesus answering saith unto them, Believe in God,' Mark xi. 27. 'He that believeth on him that sent me hath everlasting life,' John v. 24.

It will be unnecessary to multiply proofs any farther. I have made these numerous quotations, to show that, in the common language of the Scriptures, faith in God is commanded ; is the universal characteristic of Christians ; is declared to be the object of Divine approbation ; is 'counted to them for righteousness ;' and is entitled to an everlasting reward.

II. *The faith of the Gospel especially respects Christ as its object.*

'Ye believe in God,' says our Saviour to his apostles, 'believe also in me,' John xiv. 1. 'If ye believe not that I am he, ye shall die in your sins,' John viii. 24. 'He that believeth on the Son hath everlasting life :' 'He that believeth not is condemned already,' John iii. 36; John iii. 18; and John vi. 40. 'But to him that worketh not, but believeth on him that justifieth the ungodly, his faith is counted for righteousness,' Rom. iv. 5. In these passages it is evident, that to all such as are acquainted with the Gospel, it is indispensable that their faith respect Christ as its especial object ; that wherever this is the fact, they are assured of 'everlasting life ;' and wherever it is not, they will not 'see life, but the wrath of God abideth on them.'

III. *The faith of the Gospel respects Christ particularly as the Son of God.*

'He that believeth on *the* Son hath life, John vi. 40; John iii. 36. 'And he that believeth not *the* Son shall not see life.' Whosoever denieth *the* Son, the same hath not the Father.' 1 John ii. 23. 'He that believeth not is condemned already, because he believeth not on the name of the only begotten *Son of God.* John iii. 26.

IV. *The faith of the Gospel respects Christ as its object, in all his offices, but especially in his priestly office.*

1. *As a prophet, or the preacher of the Gospel.*

' Then said Jesus to those Jews who believed on him, If ye continue in my word, ye are my disciples indeed. And ye shall know the truth ; and the truth shall make you free. He that receiveth not my words hath one that judgeth him,' John xii..48. ' The words that I speak unto you, they are spirit, and they are life,' John vi. 63. ' That they might all be damned, who believed not the truth,' 2 Thess. ii. 12. ' The Gospel is the power of God unto salvation,' Rom. i. 16. ' In Christ Jesus I have begotten you through the Gospel,' 1 Cor. iv. 15.

2. *As a priest.*

' Whom God hath set forth to be a propitiation, through faith in his blood,' Rom. iii. 25. ' My blood is drink indeed,' John vi. 55. ' Whoso eateth my flesh and drinketh my blood, hath eternal life,' John vi. 54 ; see also 53, 56, and 57. ' So many of us, as were baptized into Jesus Christ, were baptized into his death,' Rom. vi. 3. Generally, all those passages, which speak of mankind as justified and saved by the blood and by the death of Christ, indicate, in an unequivocal manner, that our faith especially respects this as its object; because his death is especially the means of our salvation; since by this he became ' a propitiation for the sins of the world.'

3. *As a King.*

' Believe on the Lord Jesus Christ, and thou shalt be saved, thou and thy house,' Acts xvi. 31. ' No man can say, that Jesus is the Lord, but by the Holy Ghost,' 1 Cor. xii. 3. ' And they stoned Stephen, invocating, and saying, Lord Jesus, receive my spirit ; and he cried with a loud voice, Lord, lay not this sin to their charge,' Acts vii. 59 60. ' For I know in whom I have believed ; and am persuaded, that he is able to keep that which I have committed unto him against that day.' In all these instances the faith referred to is evidently faith in Christ, as the Lord, or ' King in Zion.' The two last passages exhibit very strong examples of faith in Christ, as the sovereign disposer of all things. To ' deny the Lord, who bought us,' St. Peter declares to be the means of ' bringing upon ourselves swift destruction,' 2 Peter ii. 1.

V. *The faith of the Gospel is an affection of the heart.*

' With the heart,' says St. Paul, ' man believeth unto righteousness,' Rom. x. 10.   This passage would be more literally translated, ' With the heart *faith exists* unto righteousness ;' that is, the faith which ' is accounted to man for righteousness,' or which is productive of righteousness in the life, hath its seat in the heart ; and the heart in this exercise co-operates with the understanding.   In the former of these senses, the faith itself is called, Rom. iv. 13, ' the righteousness of faith ;' the faith itself being a righteous or virtuous exercise.   ' For the promise, that he should be heir of the world, was not to Abraham, or to his seed, through law, but through the righteousness of faith,' Rom. iv. 13.   ' If thou believest with all thine heart,' said Philip to the eunuch, ' thou mayest be baptized,' Acts viii. 37.   The faith of the heart, therefore, was indispensable to the eunuch, as the proper subject of baptism.

VI. *The Faith of the Gospel is the faith of Abraham.*
    Both St. Paul and St. James have taught this doctrine so clearly and so abundantly, that I suppose no proof of this truth will be demanded.   I shall only observe, therefore, that by St. Paul the believing Gentiles are said to ' walk in the steps of the faith of Abraham ;' and to be ' the seed, which is of the faith of Abraham ;' and that on this account Abraham is called ' the father of all them that believe,' in reference to the promise, that he should be the ' father of many nations.' Rom. iv. 11, 12, 16.
    Having established, as I hope, these several points by clear, unequivocal, scriptural decisions, I proceed to the main object of this Discourse, to which all that has been said will be found to be intimately related and highly important, by every person who wishes to understand this supremely interesting subject ; viz. *the nature of that exercise* which thus respects *God as its object ;* which peculiarly respects *Christ as its object ;* which is *an affection of the heart ;* and which is of the very same nature with that faith, which ' was counted to Abraham for *righteousness.*'   I assert, then,

VII. *That the faith of the Gospel is that emotion of the mind, which is called trust, or confidence, exercised towards the moral character of God, and particularly of the Saviour.*
    All those of my audience who have been accustomed to

read theological writings must know, that few moral subjects have been so much debated as faith. The controversy concerning it began in the days of the apostles, and has continued to the present time. Many writers have undoubtedly adopted views concerning this subject which are not warranted by the Scriptures. Many others, who have been sufficiently orthodox, have yet appeared to me to leave the subject less clear and distinct than I have wished. Few of their readers have, I suspect, left the perusal of what they have written with such satisfactory views concerning the nature of faith, as to leave their minds free from perplexity and doubt. Most of them would, I apprehend, wish to ask the writers a few questions at least, the answers to which would, in their view, probably remove several difficulties, and place the whole subject in a more distinct and obvious light. The difficulty which in my own researches has appeared to attend many orthodox writings concerning it, has been this: it has been connected with various other things, which, although contributing perhaps to the writer's particular purpose, have yet distracted my attention, and prevented me from obtaining that clear and distinct view of faith which I wished. Like a man seen in a crowd, its appearance, although in many respects real and true, was yet obscure, indistinct, and unsatisfactory. I wished to see and survey it alone.

It will not, I suppose, be doubted, that evangelical faith, whatever is its object, is in all instances *one single exercise of the mind.* This being admitted, I proceed to show, that this exercise is the confidence mentioned above, by the following arguments :——

1. *This confidence was the faith of Abraham.*

This position I shall illustrate from two passages of Scripture.

The first is Heb. xi. 8, ' By faith Abraham, when he was called to go out into a place, which he should after receive for an inheritance, obeyed ; and he went out, not knowing whither he went.' In this passage of Scripture it is declared, that Abraham was called to go into a distant land ; and that, in obedience to this call, ' he went out, not knowing whither he went.' It is farther declared, that ' he went by faith,' that is, the faith so often mentioned in this chapter. That this was evangelical or justifying faith is certain ; because, at the close of the preceding chapter, it is mentioned as the ' faith by which the just shall live' (see verse 88;) because it is styled the faith, ' without which it is impossible to please God:' the faith, with which ' Abraham offered up Isaac;' * with which ' Moses esteemed the reproach of Christ greater riches than the treasures in Egypt;' with which believers are said ' to desire a better country, that is, an heavenly;' and on account of which, ' God is not ashamed to be called their God;' and to reward which he is said to have ' prepared for them a city;' or in other. words, heaven.† The faith, then, with which Abraham went out to the land of Canaan, was the faith of the Gospel.

The whole of the chapter is employed in unfolding the nature of this virtue. The manner in which this is done will, I am persuaded, be found upon a thorough examination to be singularly wise and happy. Faith is here described by its *effects ;* and by effects which it has actually produced. These are chosen with great felicity and success. The persons selected, are persons who lived long before the appearance of Christ. Of course they know very little concerning this glorious person, in the strict sense of the term, *knowing.* Their faith was, therefore, not at all confused and obscured by any real or apprehended mixture of knowledge. It existed simply, and by itself; and for that reason is seen apart from all other objects. In each of these persons it is seen in a new situation, and therefore, in some respects, in a new light. It appears in strong and efficacious exercise; and is therefore seen indubitably. It is exhibited as producing obedience in very many forms; and is thus exhibited as the source of obedience in every form. It is seen in many situations, and those highly interesting and difficult; and is therefore proved to be capable of producing obedience in every situation, and of enabling us to overcome every difficulty. In a word, it is here proved beyond debate, that faith is, in all instances, ' the victory which overcometh the world.'

The faith of Abraham exercised on this occasion was, then, the faith of the GospeL To understand its nature, as exhibited in this passage, it will be useful to consider the whole situation and conduct of Abraham, at the time specified.

* See James ii. 21—23.   † See Heb. xi. 6, 16, 17, 26.

When Abraham was called to go out of his own land, he knew not whither he was going; to what country, or to what kind of residence. He knew not whether the people would prove friends or enemies, kind or cruel, comfortable or uncomfortable neighbours to him; nor whether his own situation, and that of his family, would be happy or unhappy. Wholly uninfluenced by these considerations, and all others, by which men are usually governed in their enterprises, he still adventured upon an undertaking in which his own temporal interests and those of his family were finally embarked. Why did he thus adventure? The only answer to this question is, he was induced to go by a regard to the character of the person who called him. This regard was of a peculiar kind. It was not reverence, love, nor admiration. Neither of these is assigned by the apostle as the cause of his conduct. They might, they undoubtedly did, exist in his mind; but they did not govern his determination.

The emotion, by which he was compelled to leave his home, was *confidence*. God summoned him to this hazardous and important expedition, and he readily obeyed the summons. The true and only reason was, he confided entirely in the character and directions of God. God, in his view, was a being of such a character, that it was safe, and in all respects desirable, for Abraham to trust himself implicitly to his guidance. Such were his views of this glorious being, that to commit himself, and all his concerns, to the direction of God was, in his estimation, the best thing in his power; best for him, and best for his family. He considered God as knowing better than he knew, and as choosing better than he could choose for himself. At the same time he experienced an exquisite pleasure in yielding himself to the direction of God. The divine character was, to his eye, beautiful, glorious, and lovely; and the emotion of confiding in it was delightful. Sweet in itself, it was approved by his conscience, approved by his Creator, and on both accounts doubly delightful.

The prime object of this confidence was the moral character of God; his goodness, mercy, faithfulness, and truth. Unpossessed of these attributes, he could never be trusted by us. His knowledge and power would, in this case, be merely objects of terror, and foundations of that dreadful suspense, which is finished misery. The confidence of Abraham therefore was, evidently, confidence in the moral character of God.

It ought here to be observed, that the person, to whom Abraham's confidence was immediately directed, was the Lord Jesus Christ. ' No man hath seen God,' the Father, ' at any time.' The person appearing under the name of God to the patriarchs, was the Lord Jesus Christ. This is decisively proved in many ways ; and, particularly, by the direct declaration of St. Paul, 1 Cor. x. 9, ' Neither let us tempt Christ, as some of them also tempted, aud were destroyed of serpents.' The passage here referred to, and the only one in which this event is recorded by Moses, is Numb. xxi. 5, 6 : ' And the people spake against God, and against Moses ; Wherefore have ye brought us up out of Egypt, to die in the wilderness ? for there is no bread, neither is there any water ; and our soul loatheth this light bread. And Jehovah sent fiery serpents among the people, and they bit the people, and much people of Israel died.' The God, the Jehovah, here mentioned, is unequivocally declared by St. Paul to be Christ ; and that it was the same God who destroyed the Israelites on this occasion, that appeared throughout the Old Testament to the patriarchs and their descendants, will not be questioned. Christ, therefore, was the immediate object of confidence to Abraham.

Let me endeavour to exhibit this subject with greater clearness by a familiar example. A parent sets out upon a journey, and takes with him one of his little children, always accustomed to receive benefits from his parental tenderness. The child plainly knows nothing of the destined journey ; of the place to which he is going, of the people whom he will find, the entertainment which he will receive, the sufferings which he must undergo, or the pleasures which he may enjoy. Yet the child goes willingly, and with delight. Why? not because he is ignorant ; for ignorance by itself is a source to him of nothing but doubt and fear. Were a stranger to propose to him the same journey in the same terms, he would decline it at once, and could not be induced to enter upon it without compulsion. Yet his ignorance here would be at least equally great. He is wholly governed, as a rational being ought to be, by rational considerations. Confidence in his parent, whom he knows by experience to be only a benefactor to him, and in whose affection and tenderness he has always found safety and pleasure, is the sole ground of his cheerful acceptance of the proposed journey, and of all his subsequent conduct. In his parent's company he feels delighted, in his care, safe. Separated from him, he is at once alarmed, anxious, and miserable. Nothing can easily restore him to peace, or comfort, or hope, but the return of his parent. In his own obedience and filial affection, and in his father's approbation and tenderness, care and guidance, he finds sufficient enjoyment, and feels satisfied and secure. He looks for no other motive, than his father's choice, and his own confidence. The way which his father points out, although perfectly unknown to him, the entertainment which he provides, the places at which he chooses to stop, and the measures, universally, which he is pleased to take, are, in the view of the child, all proper, right, and good. For his parent's pleasure, and for that only, he inquires; and to this single object are confined all his views, and all his affections.

No characteristic is by common sense esteemed more amiable or more useful in little children, more suited to their circumstances, their wants, and their character, than confidence. Nor is any parent ever better pleased with his own little children, than when they exhibit this characteristic. The pleasure of receiving it, and that of exercising it, are substantially the same.

In adult years, men of every description reciprocate the same pleasure in mutual confidence, whenever it is exercised. Friends, husbands and wives, rulers and subjects, demand, experience, and enjoy this affection in a manner generally corresponding with that I have described.

The second passage, from which I propose to show that this confidence was the faith of Abraham, is Rom. iv. 20—22. ' He staggered not at the promise of God through unbelief, but was strong in faith, giving glory to God, and being fully persuaded, that what he had promised he was able also to perform; and therefore it was imputed to him for righteousness.' The faith of Abraham here described, in which he was ' strong, giving glory to God,' and ' which was imputed to him for righteousness,' was faith in the promise of God concerning the future birth of Isaac, through whom he was to become the progenitor of Christ, and the father of many nations, especially of believers of all ages. This faith was built on the moral character of the promiser. But faith in a promise, when it is directed to the disposition of the promiser, as is plainly the case here, because the fulfilment of the promise must depend entirely on this disposition, is the very confidence of which I have been speaking.

2. *This is the faith of the Old Testament.*

'Though he slay me, yet will I trust in him,' says Job, chapter xiii. 15.——' I will trust in the mercy of God for ever and ever,' Psalm lii. 8.——' I will trust in the covert of thy wings,' Psalm lxi. 4.——' The righteous shall be glad in the Lord, and shall trust in him,' Psalm lxiv. 10.——' They that trust in the Lord shall be as Mount Zion, which cannot be removed, but abideth for ever.' Psalm cxxv. 1.——' Who is among you that feareth the Lord?——let him trust in the name of the Lord, and stay upon his God, Isaiah l. 10.——' Cursed be the man that trusteth in man, and maketh flesh his arm, and whose heart departeth from the Lord. Blessed is the man that trusteth in the Lord, and whose hope the Lord is.' Jer. xvii. 5, 6.

No person acquainted with the Scriptures can, I think, hesitate to admit, that the exercise of mind mentioned in these passages under the name *trust*, is the same with that which in the New Testament is called *faith*. It is the character of the same persons, *viz.* the righteous, and their peculiar and pre-eminent character. The importance and the obligations assigned to it are the same ; and the blessings promised to it are the same. All who possess and exercise it are pronounced ' blessed ;' and all who do not possess it are declared ' cursed.'

In the verse following that last quoted from Jeremiah, the peculiar blessings of faith are declared to be the blessings of ' the man, who trusteth in the Lord. For he shall be as a tree planted by the waters, and that spreadeth out her roots by the river, and shall not see when heat cometh ; but her leaf shall be green ; and shall not be careful, in the year of drought, neither shall cease from yielding fruit.' The peculiar character as well as peculiar blessing of faith, is, that he who is the subject of it, shall ' abound in the work of the Lord.'

Such, precisely, is the glorious blessing here annexed to him who trusteth in the Lord ; a blessing which is evidently the greatest of all blessings ; for our Saviour informs us, that ' it is more blessed to give, than to receive ;' to communicate good, than to gain it at the hands of others : a declaration, which St. Paul appears to make the sum of all that Christ taught concerning this interesting subject.

3. *It is I apprehend, the faith of the New Testament, also.*

In various places in the New Testament this exercise of the mind is directly called by the names *trust* and *confidence.*

' In his name shall the Gentiles trust ;' quoted from Isaiah xlii. 4, where it is rendered, ' the isles shall wait for his law ;' in Matthew xii. 21, and Rom. xv. 12. That the word ' trust,' used here, denotes the faith of the Gentiles in the name of Christ, will not be questioned.

Ephesians i. 12, St. Paul says, ' that we,' (that is, himself and his fellow-christians,) ' should be to the praise of his glory, who first trusted in Christ.'

1 Tim. iv. 10, ' For therefore we both labour and suffer reproach, because we trust in the living God, who is the Saviour of all men, especially of those that believe.'

2 Tim. i. 12, ' For I know whom I have believed.' The word πεπιστευκα is, by the translators, rendered ' trusted,' in the margin. It is rendered also in the same manner by Croden, and, I think, correctly.

Heb. iii. 14, ' If we hold the beginning of our confidence stedfast unto the end ;' that is, our faith already begun.

Heb. xi. 1, ' Faith is the confidence of things hoped for.' This may, perhaps, be regarded as a general definition. The word πιστευω, of which one of the meanings is *trust*, ought, I think, to be extensively rendered by this English term, in order to express the true sense of the original. The same thing may also be observed concerning its derivatives.

But the proof which I especially mean to allege at the present time, is contained in the following things :—

(1.) The faith of Abraham is *the faith of the New Testament ;* and this has, I flatter myself, been already proved to be the *confidence* above mentioned.

(2.) In that extensive account of faith which is given us in the eleventh chapter of Hebrews, we are taught, that *the faith, exercised by the saints of the Old Testament, is the same with the faith of the Gospel;* and this is not only generally called *trust* in the Old Testament itself; but, as has been already proved in several instances, and, were there time or necessity, might be proved in all, is *no other* than the *confidence* which I have specified. All these persons confided in the promise of God, and in the moral character of him by whom they were given.

4. *The nature of the case, and the situation of the penitent, when he exercises faith in Christ, clearly evince the truth of the doctrine.*

The sinner is condemned and ruined. By the Law of God all hope of his recovery and salvation is precluded. Left to himself therefore, in his present situation, he cannot be saved. While he is in this miserable condition, Christ declares that *he* is able, willing, and faithful to save him; and that to this end the sinner must, indispensably, surrender himself into his hands, or give himself up to him, and consent to be saved by him in his own way. Now what can induce the sinner, in a case of this infinite magnitude, thus to give himself into the hands of Christ? Nothing but an entire confidence in his character, as thus able, willing, and faithful to save. But how shall the sinner know this? Or if he cannot know it, how shall he be persuaded of it? Know it in the proper sense of knowledge, he cannot; for it is plainly not an object of science. The *word* of Christ is the only ultimate evidence by which he must be governed; and this word depends, for all its veracity and convincing influence, on the moral character of Christ; on his goodness, faithfulness, and truth. Whenever the sinner, therefore, gives himself to Christ, according to his proposal, and in obedience to his commands, he does it merely because he places an entire confidence in his moral character, and in the declarations which he has made. In these he confides, because they are the declarations of just such a person, possessing just such a moral character. On this he trusts himself, his soul, his eternal well-being.

If he trusts in the instructions, precepts, and ordinances of Christ (for our faith is not unfrequently said to be exercised towards these,) it is only because they are the instructions, precepts, and ordinances of such a person. Some of them, indeed, he may discern to be true and right in themselves;

but for the truth of others, and the wisdom and safety of obeying them all, he relies, and must rely, only on Christ's character as their author.   If he believes in the righteousness of Christ, and the acceptableness of it to God, as the foundation of pardon and peace to sinners, he believes or trusts in it only because it is the righteousness of just such a person.

The same things are true of his faith in the invitations, promises, resurrection, ascension, exaltation, government, intercession, presence, protection, and universal blessings of the Redeemer.   The faith of the Christian is exercised towards all these things.   But all of them, separated from his moral character, are nothing to the believer.

From these considerations it is, I think, sufficiently evident, that the faith of the Gospel, whatever may be its immediate object, is no other than confidence in the moral character of God, especially of the Redeemer.

If I am asked, " What is confidence in moral character ?" I answer, look into your own bosoms, and examine what is that exercise of mind in which you trust a man for the sake of what he is ; a parent, for example, or a friend.   In this exercise you will find a strong illustration of the faith of the Gospel.

Confidence, or trust, is a complex emotion of the mind, and involves *good will to its object.*   We cannot thus confide in any person, whom we do not love.

It involves also, *complacency in the object,* or approbation of his character.   We cannot thus trust any person whom we do not esteem.

It involves a conviction, that the attributes which awaken our confidence, *really exist* in the person whom we trust.

It involves a persuasion, that, in the case, and on the terms proposed, the person in whom we confide is *ready to befriend us.*   Until this is admitted by us, there will be nothing about which our confidence can be exercised.

It involves *a sincere delight* in every exercise of it.   No emotion yields higher enjoyment than confidence.

It involves *a cheerful devotion to the interests and pleasure of the object trusted ; a disposition to promote those interests, and to conform to that pleasure.*   Towards a superior, it is thus the foundation of constant and ready obedience.

Generally: It is *the true and supreme attachment of a*

creature to his Creator ; in which he surrenders himself entirely into his hands, to be disposed of by him at his pleasure, and to be made the instrument of his glory.

REMARKS.

1. *This account of evangelical faith, if admitted, puts an end to all disputes concerning the question, Whether faith is a moral virtue.*

So long as the nature of faith is unsettled, every question depending on it must be unsettled also. If we do not determine what the faith of the Gospel is, we are ill prepared to decide whether it is of a moral nature, or not. If the faith of the Gospel be *a mere speculative assent to probable evidence,* although we may indeed be virtuous in the disposition with which we at times exercise it, as was, I trust, proved in the preceding Discourse ; yet, clearly, it is not necessarily virtuous, nor, if the mind stop here, can it be virtuous at all. In mere speculative belief, existing by itself, that is, in merely yielding our assent to probable evidence, we are, as I observed in the same Discourse, entirely passive, and in no sense virtuous. But if faith is confidence in God, of the nature here exhibited, it is beyond dispute virtue ; virtue of pre-eminent importance, and capable of existing in every possible degree. So far as I know, confidence, in this sense, has ever been esteemed voluntary, and acknowledged, therefore, to be of a moral nature. Plainly this is its true character. Accordingly, it is approved, loved, and commended by all mankind ; and undoubtedly merits all the encomiums given to it, both in profane writings, and in Revelation.

One of the principal reasons why the faith of the Gospel has been supposed to be a mere speculative belief, is probably this : *speculative belief* is the thing intended by the term, *faith,* in its *original sense.* It is not very unnatural, therefore, when we begin to read the Scriptures, to consider this as the meaning of the word in these writings ; nor is it very unnatural for men of a sanguine cast, men who have a system to defend, or men who change their opinions with reluctance, to retain an interpretation which they have once imbibed. We are not, therefore, to wonder that this opinion has been extensively spread, or pertinaciously retained.

But the Scriptures give no countenance to this doctrine. 'With the *heart* man believeth unto righteousness,' is the sum of their instructions concerning this subject.   He who can believe that a speculative assent to probable evidence, such as that which we yield to ordinary historical testimony, produced the effects ascribed to faith in the eleventh chapter of the Epistle to the Hebrews, can certainly believe any thing.

2. *This doctrine explains to us the manner in which faith is spoken of in the Scriptures.*

Particularly, we see abundant reasons why it is spoken of as a virtue; and is accordingly commanded in many forms, on many occasions, and to all persons; and why it is promised a glorious and endless reward.   At the same time we have explained to us, in the same satisfactory manner, the various scriptural accounts of its opposite, *distrust,* or *unbelief;* and the reasons why it is pronounced to be sinful, is everywhere forbidden, and is threatened with endless punishment.   This exhibition of faith also explains to us, in the most satisfactory manner, why faith is strongly and universally commended in the Scriptures, and why unbelief is reprobated in a similar manner; why saints are called believers and faithful, these names being considered as equivalent to the names holy and virtuous; and why unbelievers and infidels are terms used in the Scriptures as equivalent to sinful, wicked, and ungodly. We learn, further, why faith, directed to the word, ordinances, and providence of God, to the example, atonement, death, resurrection, and exaltation of Christ, or directly to the character of God and the Redeemer, is considered in the Scriptures as substantially of the same nature and as the same thing: the faith exercised being always the same moral act, springing from the same spirit, terminating in the same object, and producing the same effects.   If, therefore, it exists with reference to one of these objects, it exists also in successive acts, invariably towards them all.   Finally we see the reason why faith in God, in Christ, or in divine truth, is exhibited as being, in a sense, the sum of all duty, and the foundation of all present and future spiritual good; and why unbelief is presented to us as, in a sense, the sum of all disobedience, and the source of all spiritual evil both here and hereafter.

These and the like representations are easily explained, if by *faith* we intend *confidence* in the *moral character* of God and the Redeemer. This confidence is plainly the beginning and the continuance of union and attachment to our Creator; while, on the other hand, distrust is a complete separation of the soul from the author of its being. It is plainly impossible for him who distrusts God, to have any moral union to him, or any devotion to his pleasure.

Confidence is also the highest honour which an intelligent creature can render to his Creator. No act of such a creature can so clearly or so strongly declare his approbation of the divine character, or his devotion to the divine will, as committing ourselves entirely to him in this manner. In this act we declare, in the most decisive manner, the character of God to be formed of such attributes, as will secure our whole well being, and fulfil all our vindicable desires. Whatever can be hoped for from supreme and infinite excellence, we declare ourselves to expect from the character of God; and pronounce his pleasure to be, in our view, the sum of all that is excellent and desirable. In distrusting God, we declare in the same forcible manner precisely the opposite things; and thus, so far as is in our power, dishonour his character and impeach his designs.

3. *This account of faith strongly evinces the divinity of Christ.*

The faith which we are required to exercise in Christ, is as unqualified, as entire, and as extensive as that which we are required to exercise towards God. The blessings promised to it are the same, and the evils threatened to our refusal of it are also the same. No mark of difference with respect to these particulars is even hinted at in the Scriptures. This must, I think, be inexplicable, unless the attributes to which alone the faith is directed, and which alone render it our duty to exercise it, are in each case the same.

Besides, it is incredible that an intelligent being, rationally employed, should confide himself, his everlasting interests, his all, to any hands but those of infinite perfection. Stephen, 'full of the Holy Ghost,' could not, I think, as he was leaving the world, have said to any creature, 'Lord Jesus, into thy hands I commend my spirit.' No man in the possession of a sound mind, could, as it seems to me, say this even to Gabriel himself.

4. We learn from these observations, that the faith of the Gospel will exist for ever.

We often speak of faith, as hereafter to be swallowed up in *vision*, and intend by this, that it will cease to exist in the future world. In a qualified sense it is undoubtedly true; for many things which we now believe only, we shall hereafter know with certainty. But confidence in God, the Father, the Son, and the Holy Ghost, will exist for ever. Moral character seems not in its nature to be an object of science, properly so called. Spirits by every eye, except the omniscient, are discerned only through the medium of their actions, which are proofs of their natural attributes, and expressions of their moral character. Moral character is the amount of all the volitions of a moral agent. As these are free and independent, they are incapable of being known, but by the voluntary manifestations of the agent himself. United, they form and exhibit the whole moral character. In parts, though they denote it truly, they denote it imperfectly.

In every age of eternity it will be true that, in the physical sense, it is possible for God to oppress or destroy even his obedient creatures. The proofs that he will not, are found only in the disclosure of his moral character; and on these disclosures his virtuous creatures will for ever rely with undoubting confidence, and with the utmost propriety and wisdom. Knowledge, or science, in the strict sense, they will not I think be ever able to obtain of this immensely important subject, nor would they be benefited, were they able. Science is in no degree of a moral nature, nor of course attended by virtuous affections, nor followed by virtuous conduct. But confidence is in itself moral and virtuous, and capable of being the highest virtue of a rational creature. Amiable and excellent in itself, it is approved and loved by God; the foundation of delight in his character, the source of uninterrupted obedience to his will, an endearing and immovable union to him, a similar union to the virtuous universe, and the basis of all friendship and beneficence, in all their mutual

It will therefore revive beyond their vigour and perfection. With every new cellence and created worth, it will rise higher and higher without end. The mind in which it exists will in every stage of its progress become wiser, nobler, better, and happier. Heaven in all its concerns, its inhabitants, and dispensations, will from its influence assume without intermission a brighter aspect, and the immense, eternal kingdom of Jehovah continually become a more and more perfect mirror, reflecting with increasing splendour his supreme excellence and glory.

SERMON LXVII.

JUSTIFICATION.

THE INFLUENCE OF FAITH IN OUR JUSTIFICATION.

THEREFORE WE CONCLUDE, THAT MAN IS JUSTIFIED BY FAITH, WITHOUT WORKS OF LAW.

ROMANS III. 28.

HAVING shown, that we are justified freely by the grace of God, proved the duty of believing, and explained the nature of evangelical faith, in the three preceding Discourses; I shall now proceed to examine *the connection of faith with our justification.* The first of these Discourses was employed in discussing that which is done in our justification on the part of *God:* in this Discourse I shall examine the nature and influence of that which is done on the part of *man,* towards the accomplishment of this important event. We are justified freely, or gratuitously. Yet we are justified conditionally; not in our natural, corrupt, and universal state; but in consequence of a new and peculiar state, denoted by the word *faith.*

In discussing this subject, I shall include the observations which I think it necessary to make under the following heads :——

I. *The manner, in which faith becomes;* and,

II. *The propriety with which it is constituted, the means of our justification.*

I. *I shall attempt to describe the manner in which faith becomes the means of our justification.*

To exhibit this subject in the clearest light, it will be useful to return again to the covenant of redemption, in which the justification of mankind was originally promised. You will perhaps remember, that there are, as was formerly stated, three distinct promises contained in this covenant, beside the general one, which involves them all : that ' Christ shall see (or possess) a seed ;' that ' this seed shall prolong their days ;' (or endure, or be happy, for ever ;) and that ' *the throne (or dominion)* of Christ' over them ' shall be as the days of heaven :' (or, in other words, eternal.) The first of these promises, on which the other two are founded, is, ' that Christ shall see (or possess) a seed :' that is, he shall have a number, elsewhere said to be very great, of children, disciples or followers, *in consequence of* ' making his soul an offering for sin ;' or ' a propitiatory sacrifice.'

The great question naturally arising in this place is, In what manner do apostate men, of whom his followers were to consist, become his seed ? To this question I answer, *By faith.* In explaining the true and full import of this answer, every thing may be said which is necessary to the object under consideration. To this end, it will be proper to observe,

1. *That mankind do not become the children of Christ by creation.*

By creation all men are equally his children. But all men are not his children in the sense of this covenant. In this sense, those only are his seed, who are his disciples. But we know from innumerable passages of Scripture, that all men are not his disciples.

2. *Men do not become the children of Christ by their obedience to the law.*

No man has obeyed the law : and, therefore, ' by works of law no flesh can be justified.'

3. *Men do not become the children of Christ merely by his atonement.*

Christ was ' a propitiation for the sins of the whole world,' as well as for his disciples. But, the whole world is not included in the number of his disciples.

4. *Mankind do not become the children of Christ by their obedience wrought after they believe in him.*

No man ever obeys, in the scriptural sense, until after he has believed. But men are children of Christ whenever they believe, and *that*, whether they live to perform acts of obedience, or not.   Multitudes, there is every reason to suppose, die so soon after believing, as to render it impossible for them to perform any acts of obedience whatever.   All these are disciples of Christ.   Men, therefore, ' are justified by faith, without works of law.'

As these are all the modes in which mankind have ever been supposed to become disciples of Christ, beside that which is the main subject of this Discourse, the necessary conclusion from these observations will be, that *men become his children by faith, according to the meaning of this covenant.*

At the same time, the nature of the case furnishes the most conclusive evidence to this position.   Men in their original state are ruined and helpless.   In this state Christ offers himself to them as a Saviour, on the condition that they will become his ; or that they will ' come to him ;' or that they will give themselves up to him ; or in other words, voluntarily become his.   In the seventeenth chapter of John, verse 2d, Christ says, in his intercessory prayer to God, ' As thou hast given him,' (that is, Christ,) ' power over all flesh ; that he should give eternal life to as many as thou hast given him.' In the ninth verse he says, ' I pray not for the world, but for them which thou hast given me ; for they are thine.   And all mine are thine, and thine are mine ; and I am glorified in them.'   In these passages we learn that the Father gave to Christ, originally, some of the human race ; that all these are Christ's ; that he is glorified in them ; and that he gives them eternal life.

The covenant of grace made between God and mankind, is contained in these words, ' I will be your God, and ye shall be my people.'   In this covenant God is pleased to engage, on his part, to be the God of all who will be his ; and man, on his part, gives himself up to God, engaging to be his. Accordingly mankind are commanded to yield themselves to God.   ' Yield yourselves,' says St. Paul to the Romans, ' unto God, as those that are alive from the dead,' Rom. vi. 13.   ' Be ye not stiff-necked,' said Hezekiah to the Israelites, ' as your fathers were ; but yield yourselves unto the Lord ; and serve the Lord, that the fierceness of his wrath may turn away from you.'

According to this scheme, which is everywhere the scheme

of the Scriptures, those who are children of Christ, become such, first, by being given to him of the Father; next by giving themselves to him; and then by being received by him. ' Him that cometh unto me I will in nowise cast out;' John vi. 37. Thus it is evident, that that, which on the part of mankind, makes them Christ's children is their own voluntary gift of themselves to him. Accordingly St. Paul, speaking in the Second Epistle to the Corinthians, of the Macedonian Christians, says, that ' they first gave their own-selves to the Lord,' chapter viii. 5.

The act by which this voluntary surrender of ourselves to Christ is accomplished, is *the faith* or *confidence* of *the Gos-pel*. When Christ proposes himself to us as a Saviour, it is plain that we have no other security of the salvation which he promises, beside the promise itself, and this furnishes no security beside what is contained in his character. Confi-dence, then, in his character, and in his promise as founded on it, is that act of the mind by which alone it renders itself to Christ, and becomes his; one of his children, his disciple, his follower. Unless the soul confide in him, it is plainly impossible that it should confide or yield itself to him; and, unless it yield itself to him, it cannot become his. But the act of confiding in him is, in the case specified, the act also of confiding *itself* to him.

When the soul thus renders itself into the hands of Christ, it does it *on his own terms.* It casts off all former dependence on its own righteousness, whether apprehended or real, for acceptance with God, for forgiveness and justification. Con-scious of its entire unworthiness, and desert of the divine anger, the reality and greatness of its guilt, the justice of its condemnation, and the impossibility of expiating its own sins, it casts itself at the footstool of his mercy, as a suppliant for mere pardon, and welcomes him as the glorious, efficacious, and all-sufficient atonement for sin, and intercessor for sin-ners. With these views and affections, it yields itself up to him as a free will offering, with an entire confidence in all that he hath taught, and done, and suffered in the divine cha-racter of Mediator between God and man. In this manner it becomes his, here and for ever.

As his it is acknowledged, in accordance with that glorious promise, ' Him that cometh unto me I will in nowise cast out.' As his, its ' name is written in the Lamb's book of life ;' and it is invested with a sure, indefeasible title to all the promises of the Gospel ; particularly to those recorded in the second and third chapters of the Apocalypse ; and to ' the inheritance which is undefiled, and fadeth not away.'

It has been often debated, whether mankind are justified, in the full and proper sense, in this world, or in that which is to come. To the great question, concerning the manner of our justification, this point appears to me to be of little importance. Whenever a man thus gives himself into the hands of Christ, he becomes his, in the sense of the covenant of redemption ; and his title to justification in this character is complete. Whenever, therefore, he enters into the future world, and appears before the Judge of the quick and the dead, he comes in a character acknowledged in the covenant of redemption, with a title to acceptance founded on the promise of the Father contained in that covenant ; and pleads, with certain prevalence, his own performance of the condition on his part ; *viz.* faith in the Redeemer, as having brought him within the limits of that promise. As Christ's then, and as Christ's alone, as one of his seed, he is acknowledged, forgiven, acquitted, and received to the heavenly inheritance.

It is here to be observed, and always to be remembered, that the believer is not thus accepted *on account of his faith,* considered as *merit ;* or as furnishing a *claim,* in the nature of a work of righteousness sufficiently excellent to *deserve* justification, either wholly, or partially. Considered in every other light, except that of being one of Christ's children, or, in other words, considered merely as a moral being, he merits nothing at the hand of God but anger and punishment. If he were to be ' judged according to his works,' in this sense, he would be ruined. For although many of his actions are, in a greater or less degree, really virtuous, yet his sins also are many and very great ; enhanced by all the light which he has enjoyed, the grace which he has received, and the covenant which he has made. In this case, he would come before God as a mere subject of law ; no ' jot or tittle ' of which has ceased to bind him with its original obligatory force, or to demand from him, with all its original authority, exact obedience. Such obedience can here be the only possible ground of justification; and this obedience was never rendered by any child of Adam.

II. *I will endeavour to show the propriety with which faith is constituted the means of our justification.*

It has been already shown, that we are not justified by faith because it renders us deserving of this favour at the hand of God.   Still there is, I apprehend, an evident propriety in constituting faith the means of our justification.   If returning sinners are to be justified at all, It will, I suppose, be acknowledged, that it must be proper for God to justify them, in such a manner as shall most contribute *to his glory*, and *their good*.   This I shall endeavour to prove to be the real consequence of the manner in which they are actually justified.

It contributes peculiarly to the *glory of God*, in the following, among other particulars.

1. *It is a dispensation of grace merely.*

Every thing pertaining to this dispensation on the part of God, is the result of mere sovereign, unmerited love.   This attribute, thus considered, is by the divine writers everywhere spoken of as the peculiar glory of the divine character. Whenever they have occasion to mention it, they rise above themselves, utter their sentiments with a kind of rapture, and adopt the style of exclamation, rather than that of sober description.   'Who art thou,' says Zechariah, 'O great mountain? Before Zerubbabel thou shalt become a plain; and he shall bring forth the head stone thereof with shoutings; crying, Grace, grace unto it.'——' Behold, what manner of love,' says St. John, ' the Father hath bestowed on us, that we should be called the sons of God !'——' For this cause,' says St. Paul, ' I bow my knees unto the Father of our Lord Jesus Christ——that ye, being rooted and grounded in love, may be able to comprehend, with all saints, what is the breadth, and length, and depth, and height; and to know the love of Christ, which passeth knowledge.'——' Having predestinated us,' says the same apostle, ' unto the adoption of children by Jesus Christ to himself, according to the good pleasure of his will, to the praise of the glory of his grace; wherein he hath made us accepted in the Beloved : in whom we have redemption, through his blood, the forgiveness of sins, according to the riches of his grace.'——' Praise the Lord, says David, for he is good, for his mercy endureth for ever!" In this manner the subject is always considered, and always spoken of by the divine writers. I shall only add, that the angels themselves appear to entertain similar thoughts concerning it ; as was abundantly manifested when, at the birth of the Saviour, they sung, ' Glory to.God in the highest ; and on earth peace : good-will towards men.'

All men will probably agree, that love exercised towards enemies is the fairest and most illustrious specimen of goodwill, of which we have any knowledge. Exercised by God towards sinners, not only his enemies, not only lost and ruined, but eminently vile and guilty enemies, it is certainly seen in its consummation. In justifying mankind through faith in the Redeemer, this manifestation of love is seen in its fairest and most finished form. All the previous steps indispensable to its accomplishment, and beyond measure wonderful, were dictated and carried into execution by mere grace. By mere grace, when all these things are done, is the sinner accepted, without any merit of his own, and only in the character of one who has confidentially given himself to Christ. In this dispensation, then, this most glorious attribute of God is seen in the fairest light.

2. *It is fitted to produce the greatest degree of gratitude in man.*

In Luke vii. 40, we are told that Simon the Pharisee, at whose house our Saviour was sitting at meat, censured him for suffering a poor, sinful woman to anoint him with precious ointment ; and that Christ said unto him, ' Simon, I have somewhat to say unto thee. And he saith, Master, say on. There was a certain creditor, who had two debtors ; the one owed five hundred pence, and the other fifty. And when they had nothing to pay, he frankly forgave them both. Tell me, therefore, which of them will love him most. Simon answered, and said, I suppose, that he to whom he forgave most. And he said unto him, Thou hast rightly judged.'

From this passage of Scripture it is evident, that forgiveness confers a peculiar obligation, and inspires peculiar gratitude ; and that this obligation and gratitude are great, in proportion to the number and guilt of the sins which are forgiven. But the scheme of justification by faith, being a scheme of mere forgiveness, without any consideration of merit on the part of those who are justified, and the number and guilt of the sins forgiven being very great, the fairest foundation is laid here for the highest possible gratitude. This emotion, and its effects, will extend through eternity; and constitute no small part of the character, usefulness, and felicity, of the Redeemed; and no small part of their loveliness in the sight of their Creator. Had mankind been justified by works, either wholly or partially, this affection, and its consequences, could not have existed in the same manner, nor in the same degree.

3. *This dispensation is eminently honourable to Christ.*

St. Paul, in 1 Corinthians, chap. i. quoting from Jeremiah ix. delivers it as a precept intended universally to regulate the conduct of mankind, that ' he who glorieth should glory only in the Lord;' because ' he is made unto us wisdom, righteousness, sanctification, and redemption.' In conformity to this rule of conduct, we find it asserted, in the fifth of the Revelation, that the four living ones, and the four and twenty elders, fell down before the Lamb, and sang a new song; saying, Thou art worthy to take the book, and to open the seals thereof; for thou wast slain; and hast redeemed us to God by thy blood, out of every kindred, and tongue, and people, and nation: And hast made us unto our God kings and priests: and we shall reign on the earth.' Immediately upon this, the whole host of heaven exclaimed with a loud voice, ' Worthy is the Lamb that was slain, to receive power, and riches, and wisdom, and strength, and honour, and glory, and blessing.' Finally, both heaven and earth are exhibited as uniting with one voice in this sublime ascription, ' Blessing, and honour, and glory, and power, be unto him that sitteth on the throne, and unto the Lamb, for ever and ever.' At the close of this act of celestial worship, the four living ones subjoin their solemn ' Amen!' This passage needs no comment.

In the scheme of justification by faith it is evident that all the glory of saving sinners from endless guilt and misery, and of raising them to immortal happiness and virtue, centres in the Redeemer; and that, according to his own declaration, he is eminently glorified in this manner, in those who are given to him by the Father as his children. John xvii. 10.

4. *It is honourable to God that he should annex jus-*

out.'   As his, its ' name is written in the Lamb's book of life ;' and it is invested with a sure, indefeasible title to all the promises of the Gospel ; particularly to those recorded in the second and third chapters of the Apocalypse ; and to ' the inheritance which is undefiled, and fadeth not away.'

It has been often debated, whether mankind are justified, in the full and proper sense, in this world, or in that which is to come.   To the great question, concerning the manner of our justification, this point appears to me to be of little importance.   Whenever a man thus gives himself into the hands of Christ, he becomes his, in the sense of the covenant of redemption ; and his title to justification in this character is complete.   Whenever, therefore, he enters into the future world, and appears before the Judge of the quick and the dead, he comes in a character acknowledged in the covenant of redemption, with a title to acceptance founded on the promise of the Father contained in that covenant ; and pleads, with certain prevalence, his own performance of the condition on his part ; *viz.* faith in the Redeemer, as having brought him within the limits of that promise.   As Christ's then, and as Christ's alone, as one of his seed, he is acknowledged, forgiven, acquitted, and received to the heavenly inheritance.

It is here to be observed, and always to be remembered, that the believer is not thus accepted *on account of his faith*, considered as *merit* ; or as furnishing a *claim*, in the nature of a work of righteousness sufficiently excellent to *deserve* justification, either wholly, or partially.   Considered in every other light, except that of being one of Christ's children, or, in other words, considered merely as a moral being, he merits nothing at the hand of God but anger and punishment.   If he were to be ' judged according to his works,' in this sense, he would be ruined.   For although many of his actions are, in a greater or less degree, really virtuous, yet his sins also are many and very great ; enhanced by all the light which he has enjoyed, the grace which he has received, and the covenant which he has made.   In this case, he would come before God as a mere subject of law ; no ' jot or tittle' of which has ceased to bind him with its original obligatory force, or to demand from him, with all its original authority, exact obedience. Such obedience can here be the only possible ground of justification ; and this obedience was never rendered by any child of Adam.

II. *I will endeavour to show the propriety with which faith is constituted the means of our justification.*

It has been already shown, that we are not justified by faith because it renders us deserving of this favour at the hand of God. Still there is, I apprehend, an evident propriety in constituting faith the means of our justification. If returning sinners are to be justified at all, It will, I suppose, be acknowledged, that it must be proper for God to justify them, in such a manner as shall most contribute *to his glory*, and *their good*. This I shall endeavour to prove to be the real consequence of the manner in which they are actually justified.

It contributes peculiarly to the *glory of God*, in the following, among other particulars.

1. *It is a dispensation of grace merely.*

Every thing pertaining to this dispensation on the part of God, is the result of mere sovereign, unmerited love. This attribute, thus considered, is by the divine writers everywhere spoken of as the peculiar glory of the divine character. Whenever they have occasion to mention it, they rise above themselves, utter their sentiments with a kind of rapture, and adopt the style of exclamation, rather than that of sober description. ' Who art thou,' says Zechariah, ' O great mountain ? Before Zerubbabel thou shalt become a plain ; and he shall bring forth the head stone thereof with shoutings ; crying, Grace, grace unto it.'——' Behold, what manner of love,' says St. John, ' the Father hath bestowed on us, that we should be called the sons of God !'——' For this cause,' says St. Paul, ' I bow my knees unto the Father of our Lord Jesus Christ——that ye, being rooted and grounded in love, may be able to comprehend, with all saints, what is the breadth, and length, and depth, and height ; and to know the love of Christ, which passeth knowledge.' — ' Having predestinated us,' says the same apostle, ' unto the adoption of children by Jesus Christ to himself, according to the good pleasure of his will, to the praise of the glory of his grace ; wherein he hath made us accepted in the Beloved : in whom we have redemption, through his blood, the forgiveness of sins, according to the riches of his grace.' ' Praise the Lord,

*tification to virtue, and not to any thing of a different
nature.*

Faith is *virtue*. But the works of mankind, wrought before
the existence of faith in the soul, are in no sense virtuous.
Faith also is the *commencement* of virtue in man. It is highly
honourable to God that he should annex justification to the
first appearance of virtue in the human character. In this
manner he exhibits, in the strongest degree, his readiness to
forgive, accept, and save the returning sinner ; the greatness
of his mercy which, at the sight of the returning prodigal,
hastens to meet and welcome him, guilty as he has been, in
all his rags, and dirt, and shame, merely because he has set
his face in earnest towards his father's house ; and the sublime
and glorious pleasure which he enjoys in ' finding ' a son who
' was lost ' to all good, and in seeing him, once ' dead, alive
again ' to useful and divine purposes.

5. *It is honourable to God, that he should annex our justification to that attribute which is the true source of virtuous
obedience.*

That faith is the true source of such obedience, in all its
forms and degrees, is so completely proved by St. Paul in the
eleventh chapter of the Epistle to the Hebrews, as to admit
of no debate, and to demand no farther illustration. He declares directly and universally, that ' without faith it is impossible to please God' in any act whatever ; and that ' by faith
Enoch' in his obedience ' pleased God.' By necessary consequence, all the other worthies mentioned in that chapter
pleased him also, for the same reason. On account of their
faith he teaches us, that ' God is not ashamed to be called
their God ;' and ' has prepared them a city,' an everlasting
residence, a final home in the heavenly world. Finally, he
shows that faith is the real and only source of that obedience
which is the most arduous, self-denying, honourable to the
human character, and eminently pleasing to God. In a word,
every thing truly glorious which can be achieved by man, he
declares, in the latter part of the chapter, to be achieved by
faith alone.

St. John also assures us, that ' faith is the victory, which
overcometh the world ; the real power by which, on our part,
temptations are effectually resisted, snares escaped, enemies
overthrown, and heaven with all its blessings finally won.

While this scheme of justification therefore strips man of all pretensions to merit, and gives the whole glory of his salvation to his Maker, it furnishes the most efficacious means and the most absolute assurance of his future obedience, his perpetual improvement in holiness, and his certain advancement towards the best character which he will ever be capable of sustaining. The obedience springing from faith is voluntary, filial, and lovely. All other obedience is mercenary, and of no moral worth. It will not be denied, that a dispensation of which these are the consequences, is highly honourable to the character of its author.

Every person who has attended to these observations must clearly see that they illustrate, in various particulars, the *usefulness* of this dispensation to man : all of them plainly involving personal advantages, and those very great, to the justified ; as well as peculiar glory to the justifier. Two additional observations will contain all that is necessary to the farther illustration of this part of the subject.

(1.) *This dispensation is profitable to mankind, as it renders their justification easy and certain.*

Had our justification been made to depend on a course of obedience, it is not difficult to see that we should have been involved in many perplexities and dangers. Repentance at late periods of life would, particularly, have been exceedingly discouraged. It will not be denied that such repentance exists, nor, however rare we may suppose it, that it exists upon the whole in many instances. Nor can any man of common humanity avoid wishing that the number of these instances may be greatly increased. Such instances exist even on a dying bed, and, as there is good reason to believe, in considerable numbers. But how discouraging to such persons would it be, to know that their justification was dependent on their own obedience ! Is there not every reason to believe that most, if not all, persons in these circumstances would be discouraged from every effort, and lay aside the attempt as hopeless ? What, in this case also, would become of children dying in their infancy ? and what of persons perishing by shipwreck, the sword, and innumerable other cases, which terminate life by a sudden, unexpected dissolution ?

Farther : If justification were annexed to our obedience, how should the nature and degree of obedience be estimated ?

How pure must it be? What degree of contamination might it admit, and still answer the end? With what degree of uniformity must it be continued? With what proportion of lapses, and in what degree existing, might it be intermixed? These questions seem not to have been answered in the Scriptures. Who is able to answer them?

Again: From what principle in man shall this obedience spring? From the mere wish to gain heaven by it? or from a virtuous principle? From a virtuous principle, it will probably be answered. In reply, it may be asked, From what virtuous principle? I presume it will be said, From love to God. But it ought to be remembered that, where there is no confidence, there is no love, and therefore no virtue. Consequently, there is in this case nothing from which virtuous obedience can spring. How then can man be justified by his obedience?

But by annexing justification to faith, God has removed all these difficulties and dangers. It is rendered as easy as possible to our attainment. For the *first act* of virtuous regard to God which is exercised, or can be exercised, by a returning sinner, is *faith*. If, then, he can do any thing which is praise-worthy or virtuous, he can exercise faith. As his justification is inseparably annexed to this exercise by the promise of God, it is as certain as that promise is sure.

(2.) *This scheme provides most effectually for the happiness of man.*

Evangelical faith is an emotion of the mind, delightful in itself, and delightful in all its consequences. Faith is a ' wellspring of water' flowing out ' unto everlasting life.' All the streams which proceed from it in the soul of the believer are sweet, refreshing, and life-giving. Faith, fixing its eye on the unmerited and boundless goodness of God, sees in the great act of justification, faithfulness, truth, and mercy displayed, to which it neither finds nor wishes to find limits. The soul, in the contemplation of what itself has been, and what it has received, becomes fitted through this confidence for every thing excellent, and every thing desirable. Peace, and hope, and love, and joy rise up spontaneously under its happy influence; and flourish, unfavourable as the climate and soil are, with a vendure and strength unwithering and unfading. All the gratitude which can exist in such a soul is awakened by the strong consciousness of immense and undeserved blessings, and all the obedience prompted which can be found in such a life. Good of a celestial kind, and superior to every thing which this world can give, is really and at times delightfully enjoyed, and supporting anticipations are acquired of more perfect good beyond the grave.

This extensive and all-important subject is the principal theme of St. Paul's discourse in the seven first chapters of the Epistle to the Romans. In the eighth chapter he derives from it a train of more sublime and interesting reflections than can be found in any other passage of Scripture of equal extent. He commences them with this triumphant conclusion from what he had before said : ' There is, therefore, now no condemnation to them who are in Christ Jesus, who walk not after the flesh, but after the spirit.' He then goes on to display, in a series of delightful consequences, the remedial influence of the Gospel upon a world ruined by sin, and condemned by the law of God ; marks the immense difference between the native character of man, as a disobedient subject of law, and his renewed character, as an immediate subject of grace ; and discloses particularly the agency of the Spirit of truth in regenerating, quickening, purifying, and guiding the soul in its progress towards heaven. The consequences of this agency he then describes with unrivalled felicity and splendour ; and animates the universe with anxious expectation to see the day in which these blessed consequences shall be completely discovered. On the consequences themselves he expatiates in language wonderfully lofty, and with images superlatively magnificent. ' What shall we then say to these things ?' he exclaims ; ' If God be for us, who can be against us ? He that spared not his own Son, but delivered him up for us all, how shall he not with him also freely give us all things ? Who shall lay any thing to the charge of God's elect ? It is God that justifieth. Who is he that condemneth ? It is Christ that died ; yea, rather, that is risen again ; who is even at the right hand of God ; who also maketh intercession for us. Who shall separate us from the love of Christ ? Shall tribulation, or distress, or persecution, or famine, or nakedness, or peril, or sword ? Nay, in all these things we are more than conquerors, through him that hath loved us. For I am persuaded, that neither death, nor life, nor angels, nor principalities, nor powers, nor things present, nor things to come, nor height, nor depth, nor any other creature, shall be able to separate us from the love of God, which is in Christ Jesus our Lord.'

Such ought to be the thoughts of all who read, and peculiarly of all who have embraced, the Gospel. Here we find the true application of this doctrine, the proper inferences to which it conducts us. We could not have originated them, but we can imbibe and apply them. A scene is here opened without limits, and without end. On all the blessings here disclosed, eternity is inscribed by the divine hand. We are here assured an eternal residence, of immortal virtue, immortal happiness, and immortal glory; of intelligence for ever enlarging, of affections for ever rising, and of conduct for ever refining towards perfection. Whatever the thoughts can comprehend, whatever the heart can wish, nay, abundantly ' more than we can ask or think,' is here by the voice of God promised to every man who possesses the faith of the Gospel. When we remember that all these blessings were purchased by the humiliation, life, and death of the Son of God, can we fail to exclaim in the language of Heaven; ' Worthy is the Lamb that was slain to receive power, and riches, and wisdom, and strength, and honour, and glory, and blessing ! Amen.'

SERMON LXVIII.

JUSTIFICATION.

RECONCILIATION OF PAUL AND JAMES.

IN WHAT SENSE MANKIND ARE JUSTIFIED BY WORKS.

YE SEE THEN HOW THAT A MAN IS JUSTIFIED BY WORKS, AND NOT
BY FAITH ONLY.

JAMES II. 24.

THIS passage of Scripture, together with a part of the context, is directly opposed, in terms, to the doctrine which has been derived, in several preceding Discourses, from St. Paul's Epistle to the Romans. Infidels, and particularly Voltaire, have seized the occasion which they have supposed themselves to find here, to sneer against the Scriptures; and have triumphantly asserted that St. James and St. Paul contradict each other in their doctrine, as well as their phraseology. Nor are infidels the only persons to whom this passage has been a stumbling block. Divines, in a multitude of instances, have found in it difficulties which they have plainly felt, and have differed not a little concerning the manner in which it is to be interpreted.

Some divines, among whom was the first President Edwards, have taught, that St. James speaks of justification *in the sight of men* only; while St. Paul speaks of justification in the *sight of God*. This, I think, cannot be a just opinion. It is plain from the 21—23d verses, that St. James speaks of the same justification which Abraham received, and in which 'his faith was counted unto him for righteousuess.' It is also evident from the 14th verse, in the question, ' Can faith save him ?' From this it is plain that St. James had his eye upon the justification to which salvation is annexed.

Another class of divines have supposed, that St. James teaches here, *a legal* or *meritorious justification ;* and that *this* is the true doctrine of the Gospel concerning this subject. St. Paul, they therefore conclude, is to be so understood as to be reconcilable with St. James in this doctrine.

Others, among whom are the late Bishop Horne and Dr. Macknight, suppose, that St. James speaks of our justification, as accomplished *in part* by those *good works which are produced by faith ;* and this they maintain also to be the doctrine of St. Paul. It is believed that this scheme has been already proved to be unsound ; but as it is true that St. James really speaks of such works, it will be necessary to consider the manner in which he speaks of them more particularly hereafter.

Others, and among them Poole (whose comment on this chapter is excellent,) suppose, that St. Paul speaks of justification *properly so called ;* and St. James of the *manifestation,* or *proof,* of that justification. That in this sense the apostles are perfectly reconcilable, I am ready to admit ; but am inclined to doubt whether this is the sense in which St. James is really to be understood.

By this time it must be evident to those who hear me, that there is some real difficulty in a comparison of this passage of St. James with the writings of St. Paul. By a real difficulty I do not intend that there is any inconsistency between these two apostles ; for, I apprehend, there is none : but I intend, that there is so much obscurity in this discourse of St. James, as to have led divines of great respectability and worth to understand his words in very different manners ; and prevented them from agreeing, even when harmonious enough as to their general systems, in any one interpretation of the apostle's expressions. Even this is not all. Luther went so far as, on account of this very chapter, to deny the inspiration of St. James ; and one of Luther's followers was so displeased with it, as to charge this apostle with wilful falsehood.

St. James has been called, with more boldness than accu

xacy, a writer of paradoxes. This character was, I presume, given of him from the pithy, sententious, and figurative manner in which he delivers his thoughts. This manner of writing, very common among the Asiatics, seems to have been originally derived from their poetry. The most perfect example of it, in the poetical form, found in the Scriptures, is a part of the Book of Proverbs, commencing with the tenth chapter, and ending with the twenty-ninth. Here, except in a few instances, there is no connection intended nor formed between the successive sentences. The nine first chapters, the Book of Job, and Ecclesiastes, are examples of the nearest approximation to this unconnected manner of writing in continued discourses, which the Scriptures exhibit. In all these, although a particular subject is pursued through a considerable length, yet the connection will be found, almost invariably, to lie in the thought only. The transitions are, accordingly, bold and abrupt; and frequently demand no small degree of attention, in order to understand them. Probably, they are more obscure to us than they were to the Asiatic nations, to whom this mode of writing was familiar; since we have learned from the Greeks to exhibit the connections and transitions of thought, universally, in words; and to indicate them clearly in the forms of expression. The Wisdom of the Son of Sirach is another example of the same nature, which may be fairly classed with those already mentioned; as may also the prophecy of Hosea. Every person, in reading these writings, must perceive a degree of obscurity, arising not only from the concise and figurative language, but from the abruptness of the transitions also, which at times renders it extremely difficult to trace the connection of the thoughts.

St. James approaches nearer to this manner of writing, than any other prosaic writer in the Old or New Testament. He is bolder, more figurative, more concise, and more abrupt. That there should be some difficulty in understanding him satisfactorily, ought to be expected as a thing of course. We cannot wonder then, that different meanings should be annexed to the writings of this apostle; and from this source only, as I believe, are these different interpretations derived.

Having premised these observations, of which the use may easily be perceived, I now assert, that *both apostles* speak of the *same justification*, that which is *before God; and that they are* perfectly harmonious *in* holding the doctrine of justification by faith *without* works.

To elucidate the truth of this assertion, it will be necessary to remark, that there are two totally different kinds of faith spoken of in the Scriptures; one, a speculative belief or mere assent to probable evidence; the other, the confidence which has been already described in these Discourses. From the former of these obedience to God never sprang, and cannot spring. The latter is the source of all obedience. As both, however, are called by the same name, each has, in its turn, been declared to be the faith to which justification is annexed. To both this character was challenged in the days of the apostles. That doctrine of *antinomianism*, from which the name is derived, began in the days of the apostles; viz. that we are *released by the Gospel from obedience to the law.* Of course, whoever embraced this doctrine believed his faith to be sufficient for his justification, without any works of righteousness. Against this error, I believe with Doddridge and others, the apostle James directed this discourse. The question which he discusses, was not whether we were justified *by evangelical faith only;* or, partially by *that faith*, and partially by the *works which it produces;* but whether we are justified by a faith in its nature *unproductive of works;* viz. mere *speculative* belief; or whether we are justified by the faith of the Gospel, *from which all works of righteousness flow of course.* That this account of this subject is true, I shall now attempt to prove.

St. James introduces his discussion of this subject with these questions: ' What doth it profit, my brethren, though a man say he hath faith, and have not works? Can faith save him?' In the Original it is ѧ ʍιστις; *the* faith, which the man declares himself to have; or, as it is correctly rendered by Macknight, and various other commentators, *this faith* ' Can *this* faith save him?' Undoubtedly it *can*, if it can *justify* him; but this is nowhere asserted in the Scriptures. The justifying faith of St. Paul is ' the faith which worketh by love;' the faith of ' the heart,' with which alone ' man believeth unto righteousness.'

The uselessness of this faith St. James then elucidates by an allusion to that inactive and worthless benevolence so cele-

brated, in modern times by Godwin and other philosophers.
' If a brother or sister be naked, and destitute of daily food,
and one of you say unto them, Depart in peace ; be ye warmed
and be ye filled : notwithstanding, ye give them not those
things which are needful to the body ; what doth it profit ?'
As this philanthropy is not only of no use, and therefore of no
value, but a reproach to him who professes it, because his conduct gives the lie to his professions ; so the faith of him who
believes the Gospel, and whose life is not governed by the all-
important doctrines and precepts which it contains, is equally
destitute of worth, and equally reproachful to his character.
In the words of the apostle in the following verse, ' it is dead,
being alone ;' or, as in the Greek, ' by itself.'

In the eighteenth verse, he proves in the strongest manner,
that such a faith is not the faith of Christians. ' Yea a man,
(that is, a Christian,) ' may say, Thou hast faith, and I have
works : show me thy faith without thy works, and I will show
thee my faith by my works.'   Christ taught the great doctrine,
that Christians were to ' be known by their fruits ' only ; and
that these were the true, regular, and invariable proofs of that
faith by which they were constituted Christians. But the faith
which is without works is incapable of having its existence
proved at all.   This, therefore, cannot be the faith of Christians.

In the twentieth verse he exhibits this subject in a manner
which puts the account here given beyond all reasonable controversy. ' Thou believest that there is one God ; thou doest
well : the devils also believe, and tremble.'   The devils ($\tau\alpha$
$\delta\alpha\iota\mu o\nu\iota\alpha$, the dæmons) are, and by St. James are declared to
be, the subjects of speculative belief ; but it will not be pre-
tended that they can be the subjects of justifying faith. But
St. James teaches us, that the faith of which he is speaking
is the same with that of the devils.

With the same precision he exhibits the same thing, under
a different form, in the twentieth verse. ' But wilt thou know,
O vain man ! that faith without works is dead ?'   The Greek
words for ' vain man' are $\alpha\nu\theta\rho\omega\pi\epsilon$ $\kappa\epsilon\nu\epsilon$, properly rendered, *false
man*, or hypocrite.   But surely the faith of a hypocrite is not
the faith of the Gospel.   The last part of this verse would
be better translated, ' a faith without works is dead,' that is,
a faith which is without works.

In the four following verses, St. James illustrates this subject by a comparison of this faith of the hypocrite with that of Abraham. ' Was not Abraham our father justified by works, when he had offered Isaac his son upon the altar! Seest thou how faith wrought with his works, and by works was made perfect? And the Scripture was fulfilled, which saith, Abraham believed God; and it was imputed unto him for righteousness. And he was called the friend of God. Ye see, then, how that by works a man is justified, and not by faith only.'

In this part of the chapter all the real difficulty lies. To explain the true import of it, let St. James be his own commentator. After having given us the declaration, that Abraham was justified by works, when he ' offered,' or, as in the Original, *lifted up*, ' Isaac upon the altar,' and taught us, that ' faith co-operated with his works;' and *that* ' by works his faith was perfected;' he says, in the twenty-third verse, that ' the Scripture was fulfilled,' that is, *confirmed*, ' which saith, Abraham believed God, and it was counted to him for righteousness: and he was called the friend of God.' This passage of Scripture is found in Genesis xv. 6. That which he believed, was these two declarations. ' This shall not be thine heir;' viz. Eliezer of Damascus; ' but he who shall come forth out of thine own bowels, shall be thine heir.' And again: ' Look now toward heaven, and tell the stars, if thou be able to number them: and he said unto him, So shall thy seed be.' Confiding in these promises was that act of Abraham concerning which it is said in the, following verse, ' He believed in Jehovah, and he counted it to him for righteousness.' The act of lifting up Isaac upon the altar, by which, St. James says, ' this Scripture was fulfilled,' that is, confirmed, existed more than twenty years afterwards. In what sense, then, did that act confirm this declaration of Scripture? Plainly in this: it showed that the faith of Abraham was the genuine faith of the Gospel; a real, operative confidence in the promises of God. This it showed in a very forcible light, because the obedience was singularly great and self-denying. Exclusively of this, it will be difficult to find any sense in which the declaration can be true. That Abraham was justified by faith, and by that very act of faith here recited, is expressly declared by St. Paul, Romans iv. and Galatians iii.; and therefore cannot be disputed.   It is of no significance, here, to say, that Abraham's justification was *not completed in this world*, but will be completed at the *final trial;* or that it was completed, *when he entered the future world*.   It is sufficient for the present purpose, that his title to justification was complete and certain, when ' his faith was counted to him for righteousness.'   Had he then died, he would have been accepted of God, his sins would have been forgiven, and his soul made happy for ever.   He to whom all things are present, makes no new determinations concerning this subject.   It is plain, then, that an act of obedience existing a long time afterwards, could not alter that which was past; nor affect in any manner the justification of Abraham, which was already made certain.

From these observations it is I trust sufficiently evident, that this very case put by St. James is a clear proof, unless we are willing to deny an express declaration of Scripture as quoted by him, and written by Moses, that we are not justified, either partially or wholly, by works, in the common meaning of that phraseology; and that the true doctrine of St. James is no other, than that we are not justified by a speculative belief which is without works, but by the faith of the Gospel ' which worketh by love.'

This is further evident from the last clause of the 23d verse : ' And he was called the friend of God.'   That which made him the friend of God, was his faith, his confidence in God. The act of offering Isaac could in no sense make him the friend of God; but was merely a signal and glorious proof of this confidence, and the friendship which it involved and produced.

If these observations be admitted as just, it will be unnecessary to dwell on the two remaining verses.   The case of Rahab, in the following verse, is perfectly explained by that of Abraham.   In the concluding verse St. James solemnly repeats the great doctrine of this passage, which, by repeating it in three different instances, he clearly proves to be the main thing on which he meant to insist in these concise and emphatical words : ' For as the body without the spirit is dead, so faith without works is dead also :' or, as I should render it, ' *a* faith without works;' that is, such a faith as is without works.   The meaning of St. James is, not that evangelical faith when it is without works is dead, for it cannot exist without producing good works; but that such a faith as is unproductive of good works, viz. a mere speculative belief, is dead; and, like a corpse from which the soul has fled, is absolutely useless and loathsome to every beholder.

Having finished the remarks, which I proposed to make on this passage of St. James, I shall now proceed to show *the real influence of good works on the justification of mankind.*

1. *When we confide ourselves to Christ, we do it according to his own terms.*

Among these he has required us to ' do all things whatsoever he hath commanded us;' and ' to walk as he also walked.' But his commands involve every good work, and his example has presented to us an universal system of good works actually done by himself. To obey him, and to be like him, is therefore to perform every good work.

All this also he has required us to do voluntarily, faithfully, and alway. When, therefore, we confide in Christ, we surrender ourselves into his hands with a fixed intention, a cordial choice of universal obedience, as our whole future conduct.

2. *The faith of the Gospel cannot exist without good works.*

To the eleventh chapter of the Epistle to the Hebrews I appeal as complete proof of this position. That principle in the soul which produced the many, various, difficult, and exalted acts of obedience recorded in this chapter, is beyond a debate the well-spring of all obedience. The connection between these things is inseparable; and where the one does not exist, the other cannot. In this sense, then, a man is truly said to be justified by works; that he who has the good works which spring from the faith of the Gospel will be justified, and he, who has them not will not be justified. The title of the believer to justification is certain and complete so soon as he believes, because he will never cease to believe, and his faith will never cease to operate in universal obedience. But were we to suppose a case which never existed, and cannot exist, viz. that a man should believe with the faith of the

Gospel, and should afterwards cease to perform good works, that man, undoubtedly, would never obtain justification. On the contrary, he would become a final apostate, and an outcast from the kingdom of God. Thus have I expressed my own' views of the doctrine contained in this discourse of St. James, and shall only add, that this is equally the doctrine of St. Paul, of Christ, and of the whole Bible.

The observations made in this Discourse naturally suggest the following

REMARKS.

1. *It is evident, from this discourse of St. James, that no attribute or principle is of any value, except as it produces good works.*

By good works I intend here, and throughout this Sermon, all acts of piety, benevolence, and self-government. Two of these, faith and benevolence, or things which claim to be faith and benevolence, are examined in form by St. James; *viz.* the faith of Antinomians, and the philanthrophy of modern infidels; and both are proved, irresistibly, to be useless, and worthless. What is true of these is true of all other principles and opinions sustaining the same general character. The end of all thinking and feeling is action. Whatever terminates not in this is a mere cheat, a mass of rubbish, a nuisance to ourselves, and to mankind. All the good done in the universe is done by action. The most perfect and glorious principles which belong to the intelligent character, those which constituted the bliss of paradise, those which constitute the superior bliss of heaven, would be shorn of almost all their radiance were they to cease from their activity. There is, I acknowledge, in the reception of truth, and the indulgence of virtuous affections, an inherent value, a delightfulness inwoven in their own nature. The subject of them, if he were prevented by accidental circumstances from doing good, would, I acknowledge, still find real delight in the things themselves. But, were he to cease from doing good when it was in his power, he would be stripped of all his virtue and glory, and of almost all his enjoyment. ' To him,' says St. James, ' that

2 P 3

knoweth to do good, and doeth it not, to him it is sin.' Good actions only are blessings to the kingdom of God, and the only proofs of excellence of character.

In this great particular the Scriptures differ boundlessly from the favourite philosophy of modern times. Philosophy is satisfied with good words, and good wishes. The Scriptures, while they require those, demand with infinite authority, as indispensably to our acceptance with God, what is inestimably more valuable, good actions. Philosophy is satisfied to say, with coolness and composure, to the naked, starving wretch, ' Depart in peace : be thou warmed ; and be thou filled.' The Scriptures, with a divine compassion for the sufferer, and with an equal concern for the true interest of him who possesses the means of relief, compel us by infinite authority and an infinite example, to clothe, to feed, and to bless, so far as is within our power, all the children of want and woe. Beyond this, they require all useful conduct, whether it immediately respects God, our fellow-creatures, or ourselves ; and in this manner provide effectually for the happiness of mankind in the present world, and for their immortal good in the world to come.

2. *We here see that the Scriptures, and the Scriptures only, furnish us with an effectual source of good works.*

No obedience is of any worth in the sight of God or man, except that which is voluntary. ' God loveth the cheerful giver ;' and with his views those of mankind perfectly coincide. No obedience of our children or servants, no offices of our friends or neighbours, are of any value in our estimation, besides those which spring from the heart.

Of this obedience the Scriptures inform us, evangelical faith is the genuine spring, and the only spring in the present world. The faith of the Gospel, as I have frequently had occasion to observe, is an affectionate confidence in the character of Christ, in which it surrenders itself to him on his own conditions, to be his, and to be employed wholly and for ever in his service. To the mind, under the influence of this spirit, Christ, together with all his pleasure, commands, ordinances, and instructions, becomes supremely delightful. Obedience to his commands is to such a mind, of course, voluntary,

cheerful, and perpetual.   Its faith is the commencement, and
in a fallen creature the only commencement, as well as the
future support and soul of the virtuous character.

In the experience of mankind this great truth has been
abundantly proved.   The faith of the Gospel, and that alone,
transformed the first Christians from idolaters into saints;
beautified their minds with every grace, and adorned their
lives with every amiable action.   Faith alone induced them
boldly to renounce idols, and to worship the only living and
eternal God.   Faith withdrew them from impiety, deceit, fraud,
cruelty, revenge, intemperance, and impurity, and rendered
them pious, sincere, just, kind, forgiving, temperate, and chaste.
Faith, finally, enabled them to overcome all worldly considerations and affections, and to meet the rack, the faggot, and the
cross, in the lively hope, the supporting assurance, of being
approved by their Maker, and receiving from his hand a crown
of immortal glory.   In faith and its effects all real goodness of
character in the race of man, all that is pleasing in the sight of
God, has from that time, nay, from the beginning of the world
to the present hour, been found.   Nor is there any other entrance upon a life of virtue, nor any other foundation of persevering in real excellence.

In this all-important particular the Scriptures differ infinitely from the efforts of philosophy.   Philosophy never made
a single man really virtuous, or really amiable in the sight of
God.   Cicero, who was himself one of the greatest and most
learned of the heathen philosophers, declares in an unqualified
manner that they, so far as he knew, had never, even in a
single instance, reformed either themselves or their disciples.
Those who are extensively acquainted with modern infidels,
perfectly know that their principles have been equally unproductive of any proofs of a virtuous character.

But the Scriptures in the hands of the Spirit of God have,
in an endless multitude of instances, effectuated this glorious
reformation of man.   Long before the canon was begun by
Moses, a vast number of the human race, by embracing the
doctrines and precepts now published in the Scriptures, and
then communicated by occasional revelations, became the subjects of holiness, and the heirs of endless life.   In all these,
through every age and every country, the same faith was the
sole source of all their excellent and honourable conduct to-

wards God, and towards mankind. ' By faith,' says St. Paul,
' Abel offered a more acceptable sacrifice than Cain. By
faith Enoch was translated, that he should not see death. By
faith Noah, moved with fear, prepared an ark. By faith
Abraham, being called of God to go out into a place, which
he should after receive as an inheritance, went out, not knowing whither he went.' This is a testimony of God himself
concerning these worthies ; and they in this respect are repre-
sentatives of all the good men whom the world has ever seen.
Their faith was the faith of all such men ; and all the virtuous
conduct of such men sprang from the same source, whence
theirs was derived.

3. *From these things it is evident, that no religion except
Christianity is of any value.*

The end of all doctrines and systems which profess to be
useful, is no other than to make men virtuous. This end
Christianity accomplishes ; but it has been accomplished by no
religion beside. While the religion of the Old Testament
continued to be the only religion established by God, it was in
substance and, as understood by the saints of that period, the
same with the religion of the New. The chief difference was,
that they believed in a Messiah then future, and Christians
believe in a Messiah who has actually appeared. To them
' the Gospel was preached, as well as to ' Abraham ; and they
all believed in the Lord, who appeared unto Abraham ; ' and
it was counted to ' them ' for righteousness.' With Abraham,
they ' rejoiced to see the day of Christ afar off ;' and ' saw it,
and were glad.' With Job, they knew, that their ' Redeemer
lived, and that he would stand at the latter day upon the
earth : and that though after their skin, worms would destroy
their bodies, yet in their flesh they should see God.'

But there is not the least reason to believe, that any other
religion has contributed at all to make men virtuous. Some
truths have been found in every religion ; but they have universally so abounded in falsehoods, and those falsehoods have
been so absolutely believed and obeyed, that no moral good
appears to have been produced by them. On the contrary,
they have warranted and effectuated evils which cannot be
measured, sins without bounds, and miseries without number.
Those who believed them most sincerely, and obeyed them

with the greatest zeal, were among the most profligate of their votaries.

4. *It is evident from this discourse of St. James, that the religious character of all men is to be estimated by their works.*

'Shew me thy faith without thy works,' that is, if thou canst; and 'I will shew thee my faith by my works.' A faith without works is nothing in the Christian scheme, and can be shown neither to ourselves nor to others. Let us, then, be just to ourselves, and try ourselves as God will try us hereafter. Let us place no confidence, no hope, in a faith which is without works, nor ever dream that it is the faith of the Gospel. By our *fruits*, he ' who searcheth the hearts and trieth the reins' has declared, our characters are to be known. By this great rule of decision then ought every one to examine himself. If our ' faith worketh by love ;' if it ' hath its fruit unto holiness, its end will be everlasting life :' if not, it will only become ' the way to hell, going down to the chambers of death.' In what a dreadful manner will the speculative believer be disappointed, to find that the foundation on which he built was nothing but sand ; and how will he feel when he sees that building swept away by the final tempest! How will it embitter even perdition itself, to have been in this world secure of eternal life, to have gone to the grave with peace and hope, believing ourselves to be true disciples of Christ, children of the covenant, and heirs of a blessed immortality; and to be first awakened out of this pleasing, flattering, delusive dream by the condemning voice of the Judge! Oh that we were wise, that we understood these things, that we would consider our latter end !

SERMON LXIX.

JUSTIFICATION.

JUSTIFICATION BY FAITH DOES NOT LESSEN THE OBLIGATIONS OR THE MOTIVES TO OBEDIENCE.

DO WE THEN MAKE VOID THE LAW THROUGH FAITH? GOD FORBID: YEA, WE ESTABLISH THE LAW.

ROMANS III. 31.

IN a series of Discourses I have endeavoured to explain and prove the doctrine of Justification by faith without works.

Beside the direct opposition made to this doctrine, it has been opposed on account of its apprehended consequences, particularly, on account of this important consequence, that it renders the law of God useless, as a *rule of obedience.* This objection St. Paul foresaw, and thought proper to anticipate in this passage of Scripture ; ' Do we then make void the law through faith? God forbid : yea, we establish the law.' As if he had said, from the doctrine of justification by faith without works, which I have here asserted to be the true doctrine of the Gospel, I foresee it will be objected, that I render the law of God, as a rule of obedience, useless. This, however, is so far from being true, that the doctrine which I have taught in reality establishes the law.

So peremptory a declaration of the apostle might, one would think, have been amply sufficient to silence the objectors, and to have persuaded them that this opinion of theirs was totally unfounded, and precluded the necessity of any future effort to establish the doctrine. The fact, however, has been otherwise. The objection has been maintained ever since the apostle wrote. Even at the present time, it is a favourite and popular objection in the mouths of multitudes, and is alleged with triumphant confidence, in defiance, as I apprehend, of both reason and revelation..

It is remarkable, that the doctrine contained in the objection, has been strenuously holden by men of totally opposite principles ; those who assert, and those who deny, justification by faith. The former class are called Antinomians, the latter Arminians ; with whom are united in this particular, Arians, Socinians, Pelagians, and many others. It ought, however, to be observed, that Arminius himself, and many of his followers, have agreed in admitting without hesitation the doctrine of justification by faith.

As the scheme opposed in the text has been adopted by these two opposite classes of men, so it has been adopted with precisely contrary views. The former *admit* the doctrine that the law is made void by faith, as true ; and yet hold that we are justified by faith. Of course, they consider it as a part of the design of God to make the law void, and hold themselves to be under no obligations to obey its precepts. In their view the fact, that the doctrine of justification by faith *makes void* the law, is so far from being an objection to it, that it is an original part of the evangelical system ; a thing in itself proper, right, and good. The latter class bring this consequence as a direct and formidable *objection* against the doctrine of justification by faith, from which they suppose the consequence certainly and necessarily flows. Were they right in this supposition, I cannot, I confess, answer the objection ; nor should I know how, consistently with the Scriptures, to admit any doctrine which renders the law of God useless, or in the least degree impairs its authority.

These two different modes of considering this subject demand different answers. These I shall give under the following scheme ; viz. *that the doctrine of justification by faith lessens not in any degree, but establishes in the most effectual manner,*

I. *The obligations,* and

II. *The motives to obedience.*

Under the first of these heads I shall direct my arguments against the Antinomian, and under the second against the Arminian scheme concerning this subject.

I. *This doctrine does not lessen, but establishes the obligations which mankind are under to obey the law of God.*

In proof of this position I observe,

1. *The law is a transcript of the divine character.*

By this I intend, that to ' love God with all the heart, and
our neighbour as ourselves,' is to love God and our neighbour
in the very manner in which he loves both ; that is, so far as
creatures are capable of resembling their Creator. In other
words, it is to be perfectly benevolent. ' Beloved,' says the
Apostle John, ' let us love one another: for love is of God:
and every one that loveth is born of God, and knoweth God.
He that loveth not knoweth not God: for God is love.' In
this passage St. John refers, as he does also in the 12th and
13th verses of the first chapter of his Gospel, to two observations of Christ : ' Except a man be born of water, and of the
Spirit, he cannot enter into the kingdom of God.' ' And this
is life eternal ; that they might know thee, the only true God,
and Jesus Christ, whom thou hast sent.' ' Every one that
loveth,' he here informs us, is thus ' born of God, and knows
God,' in such a sense as is ' life eternal.' On the other hand,
he farther declares, that ' he who loveth not knows not God,'
in this sense. Hence it is plain that he who is not the subject
of this love, is not a child of God, nor an heir of eternal life.
Of course, he is not the subject of justification, nor of the faith
to which it is annexed. Finally, St. John asserts that ' God
is love ;' or that love is his whole moral character, and essence.
He, therefore, who is not the subject of this love, is not like
God, has not the same moral character, or, in other words, is
not ' renewed after the image of God.'

Again, the apostle observes in the 16th verse, ' He who
dwelleth,' or continueth, ' in love, dwelleth in God, and God
in him.' Of course, he who does not dwell or continue in
love, does not dwell in God, nor God in him.

But ' love is the fulfilling of the law.' To fulfil the law,
then, is *to be* ' born of God,' *to* ' know God,' to ' dwell in
God,' and to *have* ' God dwell in us.' Not to fulfil the law
is, of course, to be destitute of all these characteristics and
blessings. Thus the law expresses to us, and requires in us
the very same moral character which is the essence and glory
of God. That such a law should cease from any part of its
obligatory force is plainly impossible.

2. *The law is a perfect rule of righteousness.*

It is perfect, as *it requires nothing but righteousness.* To love God with all the heart, and our neighbour as ourselves, can never be in any degree or manner wrong. This will not be disputed.

It is perfect, as *it requires all possible acts of righteousness.* However high, however low, any moral being is, the law of God reaches and controuls all his possible moral conduct. Angels on the one hand, and little children on the other, can do nothing which is good, which at the same time is not required by this boundless rule of rectitude.

It is perfect, as *it prohibits every thing sinful;* that is, every thing of the nature of moral evil. ' Sin,' says the apostle, ' is a transgression of the law.' In this declaration is involved, not only that every transgression of the law is sin, but that the ' commandment is so exceedingly broad,' as to prohibit every thing which is of the nature of moral evil. But we need no testimonies on this subject. A little consideration will make it evident, that *to* ' love God with all the heart, and our neighbour as ourselves,' is necessarily incompatible with the existence of sin in the heart or life of him in whom this love is found ; and that, as ' love worketh no ill to his neighbour,' so it works no ill towards God.

If, then, we are released by the doctrine of justification by faith from our obligations to obey the law, we are released from our obligations to conform to a perfect rule of righteousness, to a law, a ' commandment,' which is absolutely ' holy, just, and good.' Can God be supposed to consent to this release ? Can it be rationally wished by man ? Must it not be regarded as a dreadful calamity by every good man ? To what would it amount ? To nothing more nor less than being released from all obligations to be virtuous.

3. *This doctrine is completely disproved by Christ.*

He denied it to be any part of the end of his mission. ' Think not, that I am come to destroy the law, or the prophets. I am not come to destroy but to fulfil.' That there may be no doubt concerning the connection between the phrase, ' the law and the prophets,, and the object here in view, let it be observed, that Christ, having recited the two great commands which I have mentioned, says, ' On these two hang all the law and the prophets.' If, then, he came not to destroy the law and the prophets, but to fulfil them, it was certainly no part of the end of his mission to destroy in any degree the two commands on which they are entirely suspended. He has declared the thing to be impossible. ' Sooner,' saith he, ' shall heaven and earth pass away, than one jot or one tittle of the law shall pass, until all be fulfilled.' This is no other than a declaration that God will sooner annihilate the whole creation, than consent to give up his law. Nor is this doctrine at all unbecoming the divine character. To create new heavens and a new earth is a thing easy to him, and can be accomplished by a command. But were he to give up his law in any instance, and with respect to any being, he must recede from governing the universe by a perfect rule and in a perfect manner. This would be to deny himself; for it would be no other then declaring, by a most solemn act, that he was willing that the universe should no longer be governed by a perfect rule ; and that he would henceforth, either not govern it at all, or govern it by an imperfect rule. The injury thus done to his character would be infinite ; nor can any bounds be set to the mischiefs which in such a case would accrue to the universe.

4. *This doctrine is everywhere denied by St. Paul.*

In the sixth chapter of the Epistle to the Romans, St. Paul declares that Christians ' are not under law, but under grace.' The Antinomians, totally mistaking in the meaning of this declaration, have supposed, that Christians are not under the law as a *rule of obedience ;* whereas the apostle meant only that they are not under the law as a *sentence of condemnation.* In the very next verse he says, ' What then ? shall we sin, because we are not under the law, but under the grace ? God forbid.' But not to obey the law is to sin. Again, in the first verse of the same chapter, he asks, ' What shall we say then ? shall we continue in sin, that grace may abound ? God forbid. How shall we that are dead to sin live any longer therein ? Let not sin, therefore, reign in your mortal body.' Of himself he says, ' I delight in the law of God after the inward man ; and with the mind I myself serve the law of God.' He also declares it to be the great end for which ' God sent his own Son in the likeness of sinful flesh and as a sin-offering, to condemn sin in the flesh, that the righteousness of the law might be fulfilled in' Christians, who ' walk not after the flesh, but after the Spirit.' If, then, Christians do not fulfil the righteousness of the law, that is, obey it, this great end of Christ's mediation must be frustrated. The same apostle declares, that ' circumcision is nothing, and uncircumcision is nothing; but keeping the commandments of God:' and that ' circumcision is nothing, and uncircumcison is nothing; but faith which worketh by love:' and that ' circumcision is nothing, and uncircumcision is nothing; but a new creature.' From these three passages it is evident, among other things, that he who ' keepeth the commandments of God,' is the same person in all instances with him who is possessed of the ' faith which worketh by love,' and who is ' a new creature.' So far, then, is faith from making void the law, that it is exhibited by the apostle as the very spirit with which its commandments are kept, and which thus becomes the means of establishing the law.

Finally : The same apostle says, ' Without holiness no man shall see the Lord.' Holiness, every person at all acquainted with the Scriptures knows, is nothing but obedience to the law. Without this obedience, then, a person who is the subject of faith, and of consequent justification, if we were to suppose such a case, would never ' see the Lord.' These passages, which I have selected without any labour, are ample proof of the falsity of this doctrine. Without any labour also many more might be easily added, which are equally explicit and unambiguous, from every part of the New Testament. The decision of St. James has been heretofore recited, as it exists in one passage ; but his whole Epistle, and the whole united voice of the Scriptures, is against this scheme. In truth, I am astonished that it should have been adopted by any sober man, who has read his Bible.

Let me ask the Antinomian, from which part of the law he considers himself as released ; or whether from the whole. Is he released from his obligation to love God? or to love mankind? or from restraining those passions which, if indulged, will prevent him from loving either? Or is he released from them all? In the former case he is released from being virtuous in part. In the latter he is released from all virtue. In other words, the doctrine of justification by faith has become to him a license. to hate or forget the God that made him, to hate or disregard his neighbour, and to give the reins to those passions which thus indulged will conduct him to absolute profligacy.

II. *The doctrine of justification by faith does not destroy or lessen the motives to obedience.*

Those with whom we have hitherto contended, it will be remembered, hold the doctrine of justification by faith, and admit this objection in its full force ; while they believe that, instead of lessening the evidence of the doctrine, the objection as well as the doctrine is an original part of the evangelical system. Those with whom we are now to contend, on the contrary, deny the doctrine of justification by faith ; and allege this objection as primary evidence of its falsehood. The argumentation, therefore, must now take a different course from that which has been already adopted, and in most respects proceed on different principles. The chief design hitherto has been, to take the doctrine of justification by faith as granted, because it is in fact granted by our antagonists ; and with this admission to show that the law remains in full force, as an obligatory rule of obedience. The design will now be to show that the objection against the doctrine, that it *lessens the motives to obedience,* is destitute of validity, because it is destitute of truth. For this purpose, I observe,

1. *That the obedience which precedes the existence of faith is destitute of any virtuous character.*

' Without faith it is impossible to please God.' The external acts of conformity to the law of God are frequently called by the name of obedience ; and for this reason only have I given them that name. But, in my own view, the Gospel considers them as utterly undeserving of such a title. They are there always exhibited as proceeding from ' an evil heart of unbelief ;' and we are decisively taught, that ' out of the evil treasure' of such a heart ' evil things only proceed.'

It is undoubtedly our duty ' to lay hold on eternal life,' and a gross sin to be negligent of this duty. But it cannot be pretended that the mere pursuit of this good, without any relish for its moral nature, and without any voluntary conformity to the will of God concerning it, is virtuous. In this case, it is pursued with the same spirit and the same views with which we labour to obtain property, office, or reputation ; and the mind is no less selfish in the one case, than in the other. No man is more scrupulous or more exact in external religious observances, than the superstitious man. Yet no other person beside himself dreams that his observances are virtuous. The Pharisees with great care ' tithed mint, anise, and cummin ;' and this they did with an intention to procure immortal life by what they esteemed obedience. For the same end they washed their hands, cups, pots, and other vessels ; ' made long prayers, gave alms, fasted often, and did many other things of an external nature with great care and exactness. So exact, so scrupulous were they in their outward religious conduct, that they were highly respected by the people at large, as good men. Still, they are pronounced by our Lord to be ' a generation of vipers,' and ' children of hell.' All their external offices of religion then, though directed, generally at least, to the attainment of eternal life, and performed with a strong expectation of securing it to themselves, were utterly destitute of virtue, and failed altogether of rendering them acceptable to God.

The young man who came to Christ to know ' what good thing he should do to inherit eternal life,' appears, in his original character, to have been more than usually amiable : for ' Jesus, beholding him, loved him.' The account which he gave of his own external obedience, appears to me to have been sincerely given. There is good reason to believe that he really and with uncommon care had, in the external sense, obeyed the commands of the decalogue. Still, he ' lacked one thing ;' and that was ' the one thing needful ;' viz. real or evangelical virtue.

From these examples, thus considered, it is evident that men may proceed far (it is difficult to say how far,) in external obedience, and yet be destitute of the evangelical character, and of every recommendation to God. Hence it cannot but be seen that external religious observances, existing in the highest degree, and performed primarily for the purpose of obtaining eternal life, are not in themselves, nor for this reason, virtuous, nor recommendations to the divine favour. If, then, the doctrine of justification by faith should in fact lessen the motives to this kind of obedience, as performed merely with these views, it cannot therefore with any truth be said to ' make void the law ;' or to lessen the motives to evangelical obedience.

The dictates of reason perfectly accord with those of the Scriptures concerning this subject. That service, which is emphatically called *mercenary*, or which, in other words, is performed solely for the sake of a personal reward, is never considered by mankind as being virtuous, however exactly performed. Hence the very term *mercenary*, though originally indicating nothing immoral, has in the most common use acquired a bad signification, and is customarily used and regarded as a term of reproach. Voluntary service only, in which good-will is exercised about the employment and towards the object which it respects, is acknowledged by mankind to be virtuous. Those who love *us*, merely because we love *them*, and who do good to *us*, merely because we do good to *them*, are considered by common sense, as well as by Christ, as no better than ' publicans and sinners.' They may be, they usually are, convenient to us, and we may love them with the same spirit with which they love us; but it is impossible for us rationally to esteem them virtuous in this conduct.

2. *The obligations of the law are not lessened by this doctrine; and therefore, the motives to obedience derived from this source continue the same.*

The nature of the law, its rewards and penalties, and the character and authority of the lawgiver, the relations which we sustain towards him, as creatures, and as subjects of law, are certainly in no respect changed by the scheme of evangelical justification. If there is a hint of this nature contained in the Gospel, I have never been able to find it. Until such a hint shall be produced, I shall take it for granted that there is none.

I know of nothing of this nature which can be alleged, even with plausibility, unless it is this : that the believer, being justified by faith, and having his title to justification *secured*, from the commencement of faith in his mind, the *penalty of the law* becomes to him a nullity. As I suppose this to be the chief thing aimed at by those who make the objection under consideration, and that in which the real difficulty is supposed to lie, I shall examine it with some degree of attention.

1. *The penalty of the law exists as truly against the Christian, as against the sinner; although in a different sense.*

The law denounces its penalty against ' every soul of man

that doeth evil.'——' Without holiness no man shall see the Lord.'

But it will be said, that those who hold the doctrine of justification by faith, hold also that of the final perseverence of the saints ; and by consequence deny that the penalty of the law will ever be executed on any of those who become the subjects of faith.   As this is fairly said, because it is said with truth, particularly, so far as I am concerned, I feel myself bound to give it a fair consideration.

Let it be observed, then, that the security which those who are the subjects of faith possess of eternal life, is not, in my view, connected with the first act of faith in this manner ; that they are the subjects of this *single act of faith*, and will afterwards be the subjects of *habitual* and *characteristical disobedience :* but in this manner ; that, having *once* exercised faith, they will *continue henceforth* to practise an *habitual* and *characteristical obedience to the end of life*.   ' If a man abide not in me,' saith our Saviour, ' he is cast forth as a branch, and is withered ; and men gather them, and cast them into the fire ; and they are burned.   If ye keep my commandments, ye shall abide in my love ; even as I have kept my Father's commandments, and abide in his love.'——' He that endureth to the end, the same shall be saved.'——' For we are made partakers of Christ, if we hold the beginning of our confidence stedfast unto the end.'   In every one of these passages the doctrine which I have specified is declared in terms so plain and unequivocal as to need no comment.   I shall only add one more, although multitudes might be easily added.   ' But I keep under my body, and bring it into subjection ; lest that by any means, when I have preached to others, I myself should be a castaway.'   If St. Paul, whose words these are, felt himself in any manner exposed to be finally cast away, and considered it as absolutely necessary to make these efforts in order to avoid this dreadful evil, and the Spirit of Truth dictated to him this doctrine and this conduct, nothing can be necessary to prove that all other Christians are, at least in an equal degree, exposed to the same evil, and need the same means to insure their escape.

The perseverence of Christians is, in my own view, completely secured by the promise of God ; but it is not secured by any compulsory or coercive act of almighty power.   It is accomplished by means and motives employed for this purpose, and rendered effectual by their own efforts, and the sanctifying energy of the Divine Spirit. If *they* were not to act, means would be furnished and motives addressed to them in vain. If they were not aided by the energy of the Divine Spirit, their efforts would be ineffectual.

The providence, word, and ordinances of God, are these means. Among the motives addressed to them for this purpose, are the promises of the Gospel, and the threatenings of the law ; by which I intend every thing contained in the word of God, calculated either to encourage, or to alarm. The promises assure the Christian, that he shall persevere ; but they do not assure him of this blessing on the supposition, that he ceases to obey, and yields himself again ' a servant to corruption.' On the contrary, they make it secure to him conditionally in this sense, that he never turns back, and refuses or neglects to ' walk any more with Christ :' that, on the contrary, he ' yields himself a living sacrifice to God,' and thenceforth ' walks in newness of life,' not perfectly, but habitually and perseveringly unto the end. At the same time, they give him certain assurance that, by the grace of God, he will be enabled thus to persevere. The threatenings, on the other hand, continually hold out to him the most awful denunciations against apostasy ; the most solemn alarms concerning sloth, worldliness, and backsliding ; and the most terrifying assurance that, if he does not endure in his duty unto the end, in the manner specified, he cannot be saved. Thus, while the event is made certain on the one hand, the means are made indispensable to it on the other. A well known passage of Scripture will sufficiently illustrate this position. The angel of the Lord assured Paul that no one of his companions in the ship should perish. Yet Paul afterwards declared to the centurion, and to the soldiers, that ' except' the seamen ' abode in the ship, they could not be saved.' In this part of the subject thus explained it will, I think, be impossible to find any thing which lessens in the view of a Christian his motives to obedience.

In the mean time, it is to be remembered, the Christian is very rarely assured of his own salvation, because he is very rarely assured that he is a Christian. Did he know from the commencement of his Christianity that he was certainly a

Christian, I freely confess that, in my own view, he would in ordinary cases be in no small danger of the evils intended in this objection. In the infant state of Christianity in the mind, there is usually so little religious knowledge, so little strength of affection, so infirm a state of virtuous habits, and consequently so little stability of religious character, while there is also so much remaining sin, so rivetted a predominance of evil habits, and so imperfect a prevalence of divine grace over them, that this interesting discovery might, in my own view, prove in no small degree detrimental to him, by producing in his mind a dangerous quiet, and a mischievous if not a fatal security.

Such, however, is not the fact. The state of the Christian, either by the nature of things, or by the divine constitution, or by both, is such, that in ordinary cases, though I acknowledge not always, the evidence which he possesses of being a Christian is in a good measure proportioned to the degree of his Christianity. When religion is feeble in the mind, when it is interrupted, when it is intruded upon by passion, appetite, temptation, care, error, or perplexity, its proofs become of course few, scattered, dim, and doubtful, and not unfrequently disappear. In the contrary circumstances, luminous seasons are enjoyed, evidences of grace multiply, and the soul is refreshed with alternations of hope, and peace, and joy. In his ordinary state, the utmost of which the Christian can boast, if I may rely upon the testimony of such Christians as I have conversed with, is a prevailing hope, or a comfortable persuasion that he is a disciple of Christ. In this situation the hope which he enjoys allures and encourages him to obedience, while it also prevents him from despondency. Numerous fears at the same time intervene, alarm him concerning the uncertainty of his condition, and compel him to new and more vigorous exertions for the performance of his duty. Thus he is preserved alike from the dangers of both despondency and security; and is kept, so far as such a being can be supposed to be kept, in a progressive and improving course of obedience. His ' path is like the shining light,' which, however dim and dusky, still ' shines more and more unto the perfect day.'

Whenever a Christian becomes possessed of the faith or hope of assurance, he is also so far advanced in virtue, that he is prepared to feel the influence of virtuous motives, to realize the glory and excellency of his Creator and Redeemer, the loveliness of virtuous affections and conduct, and the hatefulness of sin, sufficiently to need little assistance from the influence of fear. 'Perfect love casteth out fear;' and in this state a moral being is perfectly safe, without the aid of fear; perfectly inclined to do his duty, and perfectly guarded against the danger of backsliding. The assured Christian approximates towards this state, and is proportionally safe from the moral dangers of the present life.

In the like manner the inhabitants of heaven are unalterably assured of their eternal perseverance in obedience, and in the same general manner are enabled to persevere. They love God too intensely, they delight too absolutely in virtuous conduct, they hate sin too cordially, and are too efficaciously influenced by the Spirit of grace, ever to forsake holiness and relapse into sin. The assured Christian is chiefly kept alive in his obedience in the same manner, and differs from them principally in the degree of his sanctification.

3. *The scheme of justification by faith in Christ furnishes new, peculiar, and very powerful motives to obedience.*

This position will not be questioned. The whole purpose for which man is redeemed is, so far as himself is concerned, that he should 'walk in newness of life;' or that he should obey anew the law of God. To this great end he is now urged by motives of which the law knew nothing. God, unasked and undesired, has sent his Son into the world to redeem him. That glorious person became incarnate, lived, died, rose again, and ascended to heaven, where he reigns and intercedes, to accomplish his salvation. The Spirit of grace has sanctified him; the Father of all mercies has forgiven his sins. He has become a child of mercy, an heir of the divine favour, a member of the family which is named after Christ, has his 'name written in the Lamb's book of life,' and is entitled to a glorious immortality. When he remembers what he was, and to what he was doomed, considers what he now is, and to what he is destined, and realizes these wonderful efforts by which the infinitely happy change made both in his character and in his destiny is accomplished, he cannot as a Christian, the subject of an ingenuous, virtuous, and grateful disposition, fail to feel that motives wholly new, entirely peculiar, and wonderfully great, demand of him the most constant and exact obedience to the law of God. In this great particular, ' the law,' instead of being ' made void,' is, according to the language of the apostle, ' established ' by the scheme of justification by faith.

4. *The faith of the Christian is the real source of evangelical obedience.*

The truth of this assertion has been already sufficiently proved, and can never be rationally questioned, while the eleventh chapter of the Epistle to the Hebrews remains a part of the word of God. There it is shown, that faith is the direct source of obedience in all its forms, and all its degrees; of great attainments in Christian excellence, and of all attainments of this nature; of working righteousness, and inheriting promises; of pleasing God, and securing a title to the heavenly country. It is exhibited as the energy by which we vigorously act in the service of God, patiently submit, and firmly endure. It is exhibited as ' the victory, by which we overcome the world;' and ' the shield,' with which we become able to ' quench all the fiery darts of the adversary.'

Faith, then, is the spirit, the disposition, with which the Christian feels, and without which he cannot feel, the various motives to obedience furnished by the law of God; motives presented by the excellence of the law itself, and of the government founded on it, the greatness of its sanction, and the glory of its Author. In an eminent degree, also, is it the spirit which feels the peculiar motives presented by the evangelical scheme of justification, and mentioned under the last head. These, it hardly needs to be observed, can be realized by no other disposition. The mind, under the expectation of meriting justification, either wholly or partially, by its own righteousness, proportionally recedes from just and affecting views of the excellency of Christ's righteousness, and its infinite importance to itself. Its sense of obligation, and its motives to gratitude, are proportionally lessened; and in the same proportion are diminished its inducements to obey, and its actual obedience. In this all-important sense also faith is the only real establishment of the law.

5. *Those who have holden this doctrine have been the most exact and exemplary observers of the law.*

If this be admitted, it must be allowed to put the question out of debate ; for it cannot be denied that the scheme of those who obey the law most faithfully in their lives, is the scheme which most influences and ensures obedience. It is my business, then, to prove this position. For this purpose I refer you generally to those discourses in which I impeached the doctrine and the conduct of the Unitarians, and to the Letters of the Rev. Andrew Fuller on the moral tendency of the Calvinistic and Socinian systems. Your attention, at the present time is requested particularly to the following arguments, which I shall only state, and leave to your consideration.

(1.) Their *antagonists* have extensively acknowledged this position to be *true*. The confession of an adversary, in a practical case, may be usually assumed as decisive evidence.

(2.) Those who have held this doctrine, have by the same adversaries been censured, despised, and ridiculed, *as* being *unnecessarily exact* and *rigidly scrupulous* in their *observance of the duties of a religious life :* while their adversaries have styled themselves, by way of distinction, *liberal* and *rational Christians*. This could not have existed, had not these people thus censured been really exact, so far as the human eye could judge, in obeying the commands of God.

(3.) The sermons of ministers holding this doctrine have, with scarcely any exception, urged *stricter morality* on their hearers, than those of their adversaries. This any man may know who will read both, even to a moderate extent. But this could not have taken place, had not the doctrine itself been peculiarly favourable to obedience.

(4.) Those who have holden this doctrine have much more generally and punctiliously frequented the *house of God*, and observed the *duties of the Sabbath*, than their adversaries. This fact is acknowledged by both parties ; and therefore cannot be mistaken.

(5.) Those who have holden this doctrine have, among Protestants, been almost the only persons who have originated, supported, and executed *missions*, for the purpose of *spreading the Gospel among mankind*. This fact cannot be questioned. I shall leave you to judge of the evidence which it contains; and shall only observe, that the Papists have, indeed, prosecuted missions with great zeal; but that any one who will read the histories of them, will readily discern the end of their efforts to have been the extension of power, and the accumulation of wealth: not the diffusion of religion.

(6.) The *Papists*, have very generally holden the doctrine of justification *by works*; while the *Reformers*, almost to a man, hold that of justification *by faith*. The comparative morality of these two classes of men cannot here need any illustration.

SERMON LXX.

REGENERATION.

THE AGENT IN EFFECTING IT.

THE HOLY GHOST: HIS CHARACTER.

NOT BY WORKS OF RIGHTEOUSNESS WHICH WE HAVE DONE, BUT ACCORDING TO HIS MERCY HE SAVED US, BY THE WASHING OF REGENERATION, AND THE RENEWING OF THE HOLY GHOST.

TITUS III. 5.

In the six preceding Sermons, I have considered the manner, in which we become interested in the redemption of Christ; through free grace on the part of God, and on our part by evangelical faith. *The manner in which we become possessed of this faith*, is the next great subject of investigation in a System of Theology.

The text, after denying that we are saved by works of righteousness, and declaring that our salvation is according to the mercy of God, or through his free grace, asserts, *that this salvation is accomplished by the washing of regeneration, and the renewing of the Holy Ghost.*

There has been no small dispute among divines about the meaning of the third phrase in this passage; ' the washing of regeneration.' Some have supposed it to denote *baptism;* and some to denote the same thing with the following phrase, ' the renewing of the Holy Ghost.' Others have interpreted it in other manners. The second interpretation which I have

mentioned is, in my apprehension, the true one.   If baptism
be intended, the passage is equivalent to the declaration of
our Saviour to Nicodemus, ' Except a man be born of water,
and of the Spirit, he cannot see the kingdom of God.   He is
' born of water,' or baptised, indispensably, in order to his
admission into the *visible* kingdom of God ; and ' of the Spirit,'
indispensably also, in order to his admission into the *invisible*
and *eternal* Kingdom of God.   As his admission into the
former is a symbol of his admission into the latter, so baptism,
the means of his admission into the former, is a symbol of
regeneration, the means of his admission into the latter.   The
difference between the two interpretations which I have specified ; will therefore be found ultimately to be immaterial ;
the one referring the phrase to the *type*, and the other to the
thing typified.   On either scheme it must be admitted, that
the apostle declares mankind to be saved by *regeneration*.
Regeneration is therefore that event in the gracious providence
of God, by which we become the subjects of faith, entitled to
justification, and consequently heirs of salvation.

In the consideration of this subject, two things are in the
text presented to our inquiry :——

I. *The agent in this work.*
II. *The work itself.*

The *agent* in the work of renewing the human mind, is declared in this passage to be the Holy Ghost.   Two things are
naturally presented to us by the mention of a person sustaining so important a part in the economy of salvation ; a part,
without which all that has preceded would be wholly defective,
and exist to no valuable purpose.

I. *His character.*
II. *His agency.*

The former of these shall now engage our attention ; and
my own views concerning it will be sufficiently expressed in
this position :——

THE HOLY GHOST IS A DIVINE PERSON.

It is well known to those who hear me, that various classes
of men, who profess to receive the Bible as the rule of their
faith, have denied this proposition ; *viz.* those who deny the

deity of our Saviour.   The scheme of denial, however, has in
this case been materially different from that in the other.   In
that, *deity* was the object denied ; in this, *personality*.   On
all hands it is agreed, that the Holy Ghost is acknowledged
by Trinitarians to be a divine person ; but by Unitarians only
a divine attribute, asserted sometimes to be the *wisdom*, but
usually the *power* of God.   The chief subject of debate,
therefore, between us and the Unitarians, that is, those with
whom *we* have the chief concern, *viz.* the Arians and Socinians, is whether the Holy Ghost be a person, or an attribute.
In support of the Trinitarian doctrine concerning this subject,
I observe,

1. *The supposition that the Spirit of God is an attribute,
renders the language of the Scriptures unintelligible and unmeaning.*

I have had occasion to take some notice of this fact formerly ; it will be proper, however, to bring it up to view at
this time.   For example, then, it is said in Acts x. 38, ' God
anointed Jesus with the Holy Ghost, and with power.'   This
passage, read according to its real meaning as interpreted by
the Unitarians, would stand thus : ' God anointed Jesus with
the holy power of God, and with power.'   Rom. xv. 13, ' Now
the God of peace fill you with all joy and peace, in believing ;
that ye may abound in hope through the power of the Holy
Ghost :' that is, that ye may abound in hope through the
power of the holy power of God !   Verse 19, ' Through mighty
signs and wonders, by the power of the Spirit of God ;' that
is, mighty signs and wonders, by the power of the power
of God !   1 Cor. ii. 4, ' In demonstration of the Spirit and
of power :' that is, in demonstration of power, and of power !

I will not intrude upon your patience by repeating similar
passages any farther, as these are abundantly sufficient for
my purpose.   It cannot be necessary to bring proofs that the
infinitely wise God can never have directed his own word to
be written in this manner.   No sober man ever wrote in this
manner.   Nay, it may be confidently asserted, that such a
mode of writing was never adopted by any man of any
character whatever.

2. *This scheme renders our Saviour's account of the
blasphemy against the Holy Ghost unmeaning and incredible.*

This account is given us in various places; particularly Matthew xii. 31, ' All manner of sin and blasphemy shall be forgiven unto men; but the blasphemy against the Holy Ghost shall not be forgiven unto men.' Concerning this I observe,

(1.) *That blasphemy cannot be directed against an attribute.* Evil speaking, or speaking in a manner derogatory to character, can be directed only against a *percipient being;* because such a being only is capable of perceiving, or being in any way affected by the evil intended. When mankind speak evil against the word, sabbaths, ordinances, works, names, or titles of God, the evil is nothing, except as it is directed against God himself; because he alone, and not the things immediately blasphemed, can perceive or be affected with the evil which is spoken. In this manner all men have understood the subject.

It cannot be therefore that the Unitarians, when they read this passage, suppose the blasphemy in question to be directed against the power of God. They undoubtedly consider it as directed against God himself, through the medium of this attribute. I observe, therefore,

(2.) *It is inconceivable that blasphemy against God, universally and in all other forms should be forgiven, while the blasphemy against his power can never be forgiven.*

In the attribute of power there is plainly nothing which is peculiarly sacred. It is shared alike by good and evil beings; and does not contribute at all to distinguish their character, as moral beings, or to render them either good or evil. It is in no sense the foundation, nor an ingredient, of worth or moral excellence. It is not, and cannot be, the object of love, nor praise. It is therefore incredible, and certainly inexplicable, that ' all manner of blasphemy' against the whole character of God, particularly against his moral character, should be forgiven; and yet that blasphemy against this single natural attribute should never be forgiven. So far as the human understanding can discern, blasphemy against the holiness, faithfulness, truth, goodness, and mercy of God would be more expressive of malignant opposition, and of guilt in the blasphemer, than blasphemy merely against his power. St. John has declared, that ' God is love.' That is, love is the essence, sum, and glory of his moral character, and of himself. Blasphemy against this perfection, we should I think irresistibly conclude to be more heinous than against any other attribute. But according to this scheme, blasphemy against the power of God, a natural attribute, is so much more heinous than that which is directed against all the other divine attributes, nay, than that which is directed against God himself, and his whole character, including this very attribute of power, together with all others, as to be absolutely unpardonable ; while all other blasphemy can and will be forgiven. This, to say the least, is incredible.

If the Holy Ghost be a divine person, it would seem probable that, if any sin is incapable of being forgiven, blasphemy against the Holy Ghost would be that sin. The Holy Ghost is God employed in his most benevolent and wonderful work, that of restoring holiness to the soul of man ; in his most glorious character, that of the sanctifier ; in a work, demanding the supreme gratitude of mankind ; in a character, demanding their supreme reverence and love.

3. *That the Holy Ghost is not an attribute, is evident from* Acts v. 3. ' But Peter said, Ananias, why hath Satan filled thy heart, *to lie unto the Holy Ghost ?*'

A lie is a wilful deception, and can be told only to intelligent beings ; because such beings only can perceive the meaning of the declaration with which the liar intends to deceive ; or, in other words, because such beings only can receive the lie at his mouth. A child perfectly knows that he cannot lie to a tree or an ox, because they must be unconscious of what he says. But an attribute is as unconscious as a tree, or an ox ; and although God perceives all things, yet his *power* perceives nothing. A lie therefore cannot, in the physical sense of possibility, be told to the power of God.

4. *All the attributes and actions of a person are ascribed to the Holy Spirit.*

These are so numerous, and the varieties in which they are mentioned are so numerous also, that I shall only specify them in the most summary manner.

The Spirit of God is said *to strive.* ' My Spirit shall not always strive with man,' Gen. vi. 3.

To be sent forth. ' Thou sendest forth thy Spirit, and they are created,' Psalm civ. 30. ' God hath sent forth his Spirit

of his Son,' Gal. iv. 6.   ' The Comforter, whom I will send
unto you from the Father,' John xv. 26.

To move.   ' The Spirit of God moved upon the face of
the waters,' Gen. i. 2.

To know.   ' The Spirit searcheth all things, even the deep
things of God.   For what man knoweth the things of a man,
save the Spirit of a man which is within him ?   Even so the
things of God knoweth no one, but the Spirit of God, 1 Cor
ii. 10, 11.

Here let me ask, whether any man can conceive, that *knowledge*, one essential attribute of God, can with any meaning be
said to be an attribute of *power*, which is another ?   Or whether power can, in any words that have meaning, be said to
know any thing ?

The Spirit of God is said *to speak.*   ' He shall not speak
of himself ; but whatsoever he shall hear, that shall he speak,
John xvi. 13.   ' Then the Spirit said to Peter,' Acts x. 19.
' The Spirit said to Philip,' Acts viii. 20.   ' Let him that hath
an ear hear what the Spirit saith unto the churches,' Rev. ii. 7.
' The Spirit and the bride say come,' Rev. xxii. 17.

To guide. ' He will guide you into all the truth,' John xvi. 13.

To lead.   ' For as many as are led by the Spirit of God,
they are the sons of God,' Rom. viii. 14.

To help. ' The Spirit helpeth our infirmities,' Rom. viii. 26.

To testify.   ' The Spirit itself beareth witness with our
spirit, that we are the children of God,' Rom. viii. 16.   ' But
when the Comforter is come, even the Spirit of truth, he shall
testify of me,' John xv. 26.

To reveal.   ' As it is now revealed unto his holy prophets
and apostles by the Spirit,' Eph. iii 5.   ' But the Comforter
shall teach you all things, and bring all things to your remembrance, whatsoever I have said unto you,' John xiv. 26.

To search.   ' The Spirit searcheth all things,' 1 Cor. ii. 10.

To have a mind, or pleasure.   ' He that searcheth the
hearts knoweth what is the mind of the Spirit,' Rom. viii. 27.

To prophecy.   ' He shall show you things to come,' John
xvi. 13.   ' Now the Spirit speaketh expressly, that in the latter times some shall depart from the faith,' 1 Tim. iv. 1.

To intercede.   ' The spirit maketh intercession for us with
groanings which cannot be uttered,' Rom. viii. 26.

To give gifts.   ' For to one is given by his Spirit the word of wisdom ; to another, the word of knowledge ; to another. faith ; to another, the gifts of healing ; to another, the working of miracles,' &c. 1 Cor. xii. 8—10.

To work in the soul of man. 'All these worketh one and the same Spirit, dividing to every man as he will,' 1 Cor. xii. 11.

To work miracles. 'Through mighty signs and wonders, by the power of the Spirit of God,' Rom. xv. 19.

To sanctify. 'Ye are sanctified by the Spirit of our God,' 1 Cor. vi. 11.

To quicken, or give life. 'It is the Spirit that quickeneth,' John vi. 63. 'Put to death in the flesh, but quickened by the Spirit,' This is spoken of Christ, 1 Pet. iii. 18.

To be pleased. 'It seemed good to the Holy Ghost, and to us,' Acts xv. 28.

To be vexed. 'They rebelled and vexed his Holy Spirit,' Is. lxiii. 10.

To be provoked, to be resisted, and to be grieved.

That all these things should be said of an attribute, particularly of the attribute of power, will I believe be acknowledged to be incredible. That they should be dictated by God himself, and be the common language in which this attribute, or any attribute, is described in his word, is I think impossible. The language of the Scriptures is in all other cases, except those in which it involves the deity of the Son and the Spirit, the language of common sense, the plain, artless language of nature. Why should it not be so here ? Why should these two cases be, uniformly and solely, exceptions to that law by which all the remaining language of Scripture is governed ? Why should the scriptural writers, whenever these subjects come before them, and then only, desert their native style, that which alone they use on all other occasions, and adopt one totally new and singular ? Why should this be done by any writer ? Such a case it is presumed cannot be found in the world, except in these two instances. Why should it be found in so many of these writers ? Why should it be found in every scriptural writer.? Why, above all, should it be found in the language of Christ himself ? Still more : whence could these writers be induced to depart from their customary style whenever they had occasion to speak of these two subjects, and adopt such language as renders their real meaning ob-

scure, and not only obscure, but unintelligible; and not only
unintelligible, but so utterly lost in the strangeness of their
phraseology, that almost all their readers, and among them
the great body of the wisest and best, have totally mistaken
the real meaning, and derived from this very phraseology a
meaning infinitely different? Can this be supposed to have
been accomplished by the immediate providence of God himself, when disclosing his will to mankind concerning subjects
of infinite importance? Yet the Unitarians must suppose all
this, or give up their scheme.

But, it is replied, "The language of the Scriptures is
highly figurative; and among the figures used, bold personifications hold a distinguished place. Among these we find
the attributes of God personified. For example, in the
Proverbs of Solomon, particularly in the eighth chapter, we
find the divine wisdom represented as a living agent, possessing a variety of other attributes, and performing such
actions as are elsewhere ascribed to the Spirit of God."

This answer is the only specious one which has been, or, it
is presumed, can be made to the arguments alleged above.
I shall therefore consider it particularly; and reply,

[1.] *This personification of wisdom is exhibited in animated and sublime poetry.*

In such poetry, and in the loftier strains of eloquence, we
are to look, if anywhere, for bold, figurative language. The
whole tenour of the discourse here proceeds from an enkindled
imagination and ardent feelings. In this state of mind nature
instinctively adopts figurative language and bold images, and
readily imparts life, thought, and action to those objects, the
contemplation of which has excited the peculiar elevation.
With the writer, the reader in all such cases readily coincides.
The dullest man in the dullest frame easily catches the inspiration, and not only admits without hesitation the propriety of
this language and these images, but regards them as the only
things which are proper, natural, and suited to the strain of
thought.

But on ordinary occasions, which furnish nothing to raise
the mind above its common cool level, such a mode of writing
is perfectly unnatural, is at war with the whole tenour of
thought, and can be the result of nothing but an inexplicable
determination to write extravagance, and produce wonder.

Not an example of this nature can be found in the Scriptures, unless it be this which is now in debate.

Here this language and these images are adopted, if they are in fact adopted at all, on the most ordinary occasions; inferring the most tranquil, even, uninterested, state of the writer; in the simplest narratives, and the most quiet discussions. Who would look for a personification in such instances as the following? ' The Spirit said unto Peter '—' The Spirit said unto Philip '—' The Spirit caught away Philip '— ' Now the Spirit speaketh expressly '—' It seemed good to the Holy Ghost, and to us;' together with a vast multitude of others, exactly resembling these in their nature? If personifications are to be used in such cases, in what cases are they not to be used? And in what cases are we to use simple language?

To complete the strangeness of this representation, the Greek masculine pronouns and relatives are, in a multitude of instances, made to agree with the neuter substantive, Πνευμα, spirit; a mode of personification in all other cases absurd, and here, to say the least, inexplicable.

[2.] *The wisdom spoken of in the Proverbs is also a real person, and not an attribute; viz. the Lord Jesus Christ.*

This has been the unwavering opinion of the great body of divines; of most I believe, if not all, who are not Unitarians. Christ, as I apprehend, challenges this character to himself, Matthew xi. 19, ' Wisdom is justified of her children.' St. Paul, in 1 Corinthians, chap. i. ver. 24, attributes it to him directly, when he says, ' Christ the wisdom of God;' and in verse 30, when he says, ' Who of God is become unto us wisdom;' and in Col. ii. 3, where he says of Christ, ' In whom are hid all the treasures of wisdom.'

That the attribute wisdom is not meant by Solomon in this chapter, is completely evident from the 14th verse; ' Counsel is mine, and sound wisdom. Now it is impossible that Wisdom should possess wisdom; the possessor, and the thing possessed, being, by physical necessity, two things distinct from each other. It is also evident from the whole tenour of this chapter, as well as from several other parts of the discourse in the beginning of this book, particularly chap. i. 20—33, on which, however, I can dwell no longer at the present time.

[3.] Should it be still supposed, that the attribute of wisdom, and not Christ, is intended by Solomon ; *the passage, even if it were not poetical, would not involve such absurdities and difficulties as are involved in the supposition that the Holy Ghost is an attribute personified.* An extensive comparison of these two subjects cannot be expected on the present occasion. Suffice it to say, that wisdom is not said to appear ' in a bodily shape ;' is not introduced in form, as an agent in the common concerns of life ; is not spoken of by one living being, when discoursing of another living being, as a third living being, united with the other two in the transaction of real business ; Is never introduced in the Scriptures, in plain prose, as *speaking, hearing, commanding, guiding, sanctifying,* and universally doing such things as can be attributed only to a living person. Yet it must strike every person that, as wisdom is an attribute, involving consciousness and perception, all these things, and others like them, might be attributed to it with much more propriety than to the attribute of power.

5. *The Holy Ghost is a Divine Person.*

There will probably be little dispute concerning this declaration among those who acknowledge that the Holy Ghost is a person. The things which are said concerning the Spirit of God are so plainly such as evince infinite perfection, that few persons, probably none, who admit the personality of the Spirit, will deny his deity. Still, it will be useful on this occasion to exhibit several proofs of this truth.

(1.) *The names of God are given to the Holy Ghost in the Scriptures.* ' Now the Lord is that Spirit,' 2 Cor. viii. 17. This is a direct affirmation of St. Paul, that the Spirit is God.

' For who hath known the mind of the Lord? and who has been his Counsellor?' Rom. xi. 34. ' For who hath known the mind of the Lord, that he may instruct him?' 1 Cor. ii. 16. Both these passages are quoted from Isaiah xl. 13, ' Who hath directed the Spirit of the Lord? or, being his Counsellor, hath taught him?'

' And the Lord direct your hearts into the love of God, and into the patient waiting for Christ,' 2 Thess. iii. 5. Hence the person addressed in prayer, is plainly a distinct person from those mentioned by the names God and Christ, and of course is the Spirit of God ; to whom throughout the Scriptures the office of directing the hearts of Christians to their duty, is everywhere ascribed.

Peter says to Ananias, Acts v. 3, 4, ' Why hath Satan filled thine heart to lie unto the Holy Ghost ? Why hast thou conceived this in thine heart ? Thou hast not lied unto men, but unto God.'   Here the Holy Ghost is called God by the apostle, in as direct terms as are conceivable.

Acts iv. 24, 25, ' They lift up their voice to God with one accord, and said, Lord, thou art God, who hast made heaven and earth, and the sea, and all that in them is. Who by the mouth of thy servant David hast said, Why did the heathen rage, and the people imagine a vain thing ?'

Acts i. 16, Peter says, ' This Scripture must needs have been fulfilled, which the Holy Ghost spake by the mouth of David.'   The Holy Ghost is, therefore, the Lord God who spoke by the mouth of David.

(2.) *The attributes of God are ascribed to the Holy Ghost.*

Eternity.——' Christ, who through the eternal Spirit once offered himself to God,' Heb. ix. 14.

Omnipresence.——' Whither shall I go from thy Spirit ? Whither shall I flee from thy presence ?' Psalm cxxxix. 7. ' Your body is the temple of the Holy Ghost ;' that is, the bodies of all Christians,' 1 Cor. vi. 9.

Omniscience.——' The Spirit searcheth all things, even the deep things of God,' 1 Cor. ii. 10. ' Even so, the things of God knoweth no one, but the Spirit of God,' 1 Cor. ii. 11.

Holiness.——' The Holy Ghost,' ' the Holy Spirit ;' ' the Spirit of Holiness.'   *Passim.*

Grace.——' Hath done despite to the Spirit of grace.'   Heb. x. 29 ; see also Zechariah xii. 10.

Truth.——' The Comforter, the Spirit of truth,' John xiv. 17.

Glory.——' The Spirit of Glory and of God resteth on you,' 1 Pet. iv. 14.

Goodness.——' Thy good Spirit,' Neh. ix. 20.   ' Thy Spirit is good,' Psalm cxliii. 10.

Power.——' The power of God,' as exerted in working signs

and wonders, is ascribed to the Holy Ghost throughout the New Testament.

(3.) *The actions of God are ascribed to the Holy Ghost.*

Creation.——' By his Spirit he garnished the heavens,' Job xxvi. 13.   ' The Spirit of God hath made me,' Job xxxiii. 4 : see also Acts i. 24, 25, compared with Acts i. 16.

Working miracles, which, as you know, is either a suspension or counteraction of the laws of nature, or of the divine agency operating conformably to those laws, and is therefore, with peculiar evidence, an act of God himself.   This, as I have already remarked concerning the power exerted in it, is throughout the New Testament ascribed to the Holy Ghost.

Inspiration.——' Holy men of God spake as they were moved by the Holy Ghost,' 2 Peter i. 21.

Giving life.——' It is the Spirit that quickeneth,' John vi. 63.   ' Put to death in the flesh, but quickened by the Spirit,' 1 Pet. iii. 18.   ' He that raised up Christ from the dead shall also quicken your mortal bodies, by his Spirit that dwelleth in you,' Rom. viii. 11.

Sanctification.——This also is ascribed to the Holy Ghost appropriately, throughout the New Testament.

Instances of the same general nature might be easily increased in numbers, and the proofs might be easily multiplied to a great extent ; but as discourses so extensively made up of detached passages of Scripture are apt to be less interesting than could be wished, I shall desist.

(4.) *The Holy Ghost is a divine person, because he is united with the Father and the Son in the baptismal service, and in the blessing pronounced upon Christians by St. Paul.*

I have mentioned these subjects together, because they have some things in common.   Yet there are also some things in which they differ.   ' Go and teach all nations,' said our Saviour to his apostles, ' baptizing them in the name of the Father, and of the Son, and of the Holy Ghost.'

' The grace of our Lord Jesus Christ,' says St. Paul to the Corinthian church, and through them to all Christians, ' and the love of God, and the communion of the Holy Ghost, be with you all.   Amen.'

In the commission here given by Christ to his apostles, it is impossible that an attribute should with propriety or meaning be joined with persons, or a creature with one or more divine persons.   No absurdity can strike the mind with more force, than that Christ should direct the apostles to baptize in the name of God the Father, and of the Son, and of the *divine* power ! Nothing but impiety can, so far as I see, be contained in a direction to baptize in the name of God and of a creature. What creature would dare to associate himself with God in such an act of authority, and thus presume to ascend the throne of his Maker ?   The same things are equally true concerning the form of blessing above recited.   Can St. Paul be supposed to have united either a creature or an attribute with the eternal God in this solemn service ?   What blessings could either of these bestow ?   Both the creature and the attribute, considered by themselves, are in this view nothing.

But this form of blessing is a prayer, and is addressed equally to the Father, the Son, and the Holy Ghost.   Can St. Paul have addressed a prayer either to an attribute or to a creature ?

Farther : The blessing prayed for from the Holy Ghost is communion, or fellowship.   The request for this blessing involves therefore the declaration, that the Holy Ghost will, if the prayer be granted, be present with all those for whom this communion is supplicated, and present with that influence which is the source of spiritual and immortal life.   In other words, the Holy Ghost is here exhibited as omnipresent ; and as everywhere possessing, and at his pleasure communicating, life here, as the commencement of life hereafter.

I shall conclude this Discourse with observing, that *the divinity of the Spirit of truth furnishes Christians with the most solid foundation for gratitude and joy.*   It will be seen, in the progress of these Discourses, that he is the sum of all the moral blessings introduced into this world by the mediation of Christ.   He sanctifies the soul ; ' brings it out of darkness into marvellous light ;' improves it in holiness ; conducts it through the temptations and dangers of this life ; furnishes it with every gift and grace ; prompts it to all virtue and excellence ; and fills it with all spiritual enjoyment.   For this great work he is abundantly qualified by the possession of infinite perfection ; of all that is great, and all that is good. In this world he commences and carries it on.   In the future world he advances it to absolute perfection.   Through the ages of eternity he will supply, enrich, and adorn the soul with endless virtue, as the means of endless happiness and glory.

END OF VOL. II.

J. Haddon, Printer, Finsbury.

Check Out More Titles From HardPress Classics Series In this collection we are offering thousands of classic and hard to find books. This series spans a vast array of subjects – so you are bound to find something of interest to enjoy reading and learning about.

Subjects:
Architecture
Art
Biography & Autobiography
Body, Mind &Spirit
Children & Young Adult
Dramas
Education
Fiction
History
Language Arts & Disciplines
Law
Literary Collections
Music
Poetry
Psychology
Science
…and many more.

Visit us at www.hardpress.net

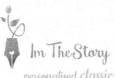